Second Edition

Sport
in the Sociocultural
Process

Marie Hart
Mills College

ωcb

Wm. C. Brown Company Publishers
Dubuque, Iowa

PHYSICAL EDUCATION

Consulting Editor
Aileene Lockhart
Texas Woman's University

PARKS AND RECREATION

Consulting Editor
David Gray
California State University, Long Beach

HEALTH

Consulting Editor
Robert Kaplan
The Ohio State University

Contents

Preface

What is the essence of sport in society—its meaning and function? How can the study of sport be approached in a complete and nonnormative way? It is imperative when studying any social or cultural phenomenon to examine it within its total cultural context. To gain the most complete understanding and knowledge of the why, who, and how of any group being studied calls for a careful look at all aspects of their living. If a folklorist were studying proverbs in a culture and only considered them in their literary form, devoid of contextual information, it would not assist her in understanding a specific culture or subculture. How the proverb is used, who is allowed to say it and to whom, and under what circumstances it is used are all significant. Only in recent years have we considered sport in this light. Sport as a sociocultural phenomenon must be studied in its contextual setting. How the sport is performed, under what circumstances, and who performs and who observes it, are all of prime importance in understanding the meaning of sport.

Often sport has been referred to as something operating outside of or separate from other cultural forms. It has been considered outside of ordinary life and responsibility, outside of the scrutiny that other values and norms receive. The ritual, costumes, and space especially set aside for the game have often given the environment and experience of sport a semisacred aura. "It is our sacred trust" has been a phrase used in the conversation of those working with athletes in games and sports.

This kind of romanticism has kept us from thoroughly investigating sport in its positive and negative aspects. We have believed and trusted, but not studied and researched. True, we have given scholarly consideration to aspects of improving the performance, but we have not studied the total sport expression as it occurs for the individual in his/her life experience. The situation within which each sport occasion—each specific one—occurs needs to be more fully explored. The people involved, the things said and done, before, during, and after the game, all need attention.

We have often stated generalizations regarding the positive functions and social rewards of sport while avoiding the study of its negative outcomes. It is because these generalizations are made without knowledge of the specific setting, identity of participants and spectators, and goings-on of the supporting and promoting groups that we continue to be vaguely positive about values in sport. When, for instance, do we ask and pursue the question: What is the relationship between one's acceptance in sport and acceptance in other social situations? That a second baseman is respected on the field for his skill but is rejected socially off the field is no longer justifiable in American society. That a woman runner is acclaimed and sent to the Olympics, but ignored on her return is inexcusable.

Throughout time, there appears to have been an intricate mutual interdependence between sport and culture. Sport may be differently structured in various cultures and probably in different time periods of the same culture. It is only by looking at the sport of a particular culture, at a particular place and time, that comparisons can be made and patterns can be established, and that vague, perhaps untrue, generalizations can be avoided. Is part of the present controversy in sport because the verbalized idealized goals and images of sport are not serving the social functions long attributed to them? Recent turmoil and questioning in sport may indicate that sport has become more socially relevant, that sport has more meaning in the everyday ordinary life of people and cannot be held apart in a sacrosanct vacuum.

It is possible that achievement, social status, social mobility (upward always inferred), and equality—the American values claimed as part of the sport experience—may not have been operable because sport has been set apart, separate from other social processes. It cannot function as a social system whereby a person enters into a full participation of American life, until the sports system is more open to various ethnic groups, all people of color, and to women. Until such a time it will continue to function effectively only for a few, embodying the disillusionment of a dream for the others.

A pay raise in professional sport does not necessarily mean a social raise. The experience of well-known, professional black athletes as they miss out on advertising revenue or try to buy homes in white suburbia provides ample proof of this. The negative social connotations often attached to the female athlete can isolate her socially, limiting her status and mobility. Accepted sports for females, such as tennis, are an exception not the rule. These examples and many more create an awareness that we need to study both the functions and dysfunctions of sport in American society, especially if we accept the principle that sport can function as a part of the social system, as a means of maintaining norms, serving goal attainment, and providing one way for individuals to adapt to society.

At this present time of questioning and redefinition of cultural values and norms, it seems crucial to be open to investigating and, in fact, energetically pursuing the place of sport in American society. It is important for the people in the center of studying, performing, and producing sport to be also in the middle of the reformulation of understandings of it. Formerly, because of the normative approach to the study of sport from those within it, many of the present criticisms were levied only by those outside of sport. Coaches and physical educators took these questions as antisport and did not feel obligated to seriously consider them.

Now, finally, the era of economic expansionism and the exclusively promotional approach to sport seem to be coming to an end. The era of self-criticism, research, and the examination of sport from within is happening. It is in support of this reformation that these articles by many of those asking the questions were collected. These are authors who have sought to understand sport in other than its performance aspects. Some of the authors included here present theoretical positions and constructs, while others have collected data on people in sport.

Part 1 of the book is organized to give the reader a cultural framework, a series of definitions, and some understanding of the cultural setting of sport in American society, as an orientation to the subsequent topics discussed. It is in the second part of the book that social systems and people in American sport are considered. What sports occur in the cities and in suburbia? Why? How are these games an extension of our social selves? "Coming of age" in America as a process of sport is a topic thoughtfully presented by several authors.

The second section also looks specifically at sport "American style." Does this really mean that the many faces of sport are expressed in a similar way by all people? "The American way of sport" may actually be the many ways of American sport, exemplifed by the various social and ethnic groups involved. Might it be that this means a use of sport to retain one's ethnic or social class identity rather than as a means for moving into the mainstream of American life? Several authors discuss this point.

How do social systems affect the people who operate within them? The religions, economics, education, and politics all seem to have direct and dynamic effect on the sports life of the American public. Many authors give the reader an inside view of these systems. Do they assist or trap the person in sport? How controlled by these powerful factors is the participating spectating public? What are the effects of the "system" on sport? Although there are many strong feelings about this, there is very little research and documented knowledge on the subject. Sport is presented as a fully functioning social system. How does sport as a well-regulated social system affect the individual engaged in it in American life?

This anthology does not include material relevant to the psychology of the sport experience. Recognizing the relationship of the psychological to the sociological aspects of consideration, the author omits this topic only because there is sufficient and significant material in this area to extend it into a full volume of materials on its own.

These presentations are only a starting place for thoughtful discussion, leading, it is hoped, toward active research. This book is intended for those who are somewhat new to the sociocultural study of sport, whether that be in physical education, sociology, anthropology, or any other study of human behavior in the social process. It is hoped that the reader will also concurrently be actively involved with courses in research procedures and seminars in specific aspects of sport in culture.

There has been a concerted effort in this second edition to increase the amount of information about a greater variety of ethnic groups. The number of authors who represent different ethnic groups and the number of women authors was consciously increased in this present volume.

As editor of this collection of articles I wish to personally and publically thank Genevieve Leighton and Sindi McGrath for their assistance in preparing the manuscript. And to those authors represented in this anthology I express my appreciation. Their response was encouraging. Recognition is also given to the many publishers, editors, and authors who granted permission to reprint the articles presented in this collection.

PART I

SPORT IN
CULTURAL
CONTEXT

SECTION

A

THEORIES AND DEFINITIONS

THEORIES AND
DEFINITIONS

It is imperative when studying any phenomenon to clarify definitions and examine theories. To do so helps to give focus and organization to the effort. Hopefully, Part I, Sport in Cultural Context, will be useful in that process and will help the reader to gain some perspective and insight into the relationship of sport to culture and particularly of sport to American culture.

McIntosh presents an overview of several theories and adds to these some of his own ideas about categorizing and analyzing sport. In considering the state of sport in the early 1960s, he did not see that concentration on technique or technical knowledge would necessarily obscure the play element in sport or corrupt those who play. It will be interesting to examine whether or not his assertion holds true for the past decade in the United States. Other authors present contrastingly different views. Has the concentration almost solely on technique and the athlete as a technical object been responsible for some of the storm of protest in American sport?

After gaining some background in the article by McIntosh it will be easier to focus in more depth on the writings of Huizinga. The author of *Homo Ludens* was one of the first theoreticians to take a serious look at "Man the Player" and to state that play was and is the ongoing resource of human cultural behavior. How a culture defines itself and its origins, as weapon maker, toolmaker, or player, may in fact have much to do with what it becomes. In the second article Huizinga considers play not only as precultural and pervading all of life, but also as the recreating and dynamic force which brings about new cultural forms. Stated in his own words:

> The spirit of playful competition is, as a social impulse, older than culture itself and pervades all life like a veritable ferment. Ritual grew up in sacred play; poetry was born in play and nourished on play; music and dancing were pure play. Wisdom and philosophy found expression in words

3

and forms derived from religious contests. The rules of warfare, the conventions of noble living were built up in play patterns. We have to conclude, therefore, that civilization is, in its earliest phases, played. It does not come from play like a babe detaching itself from the womb; it arises in and as play, and never leaves it.[1]

The slippery task of defining and differentiating among the concepts of play, game, and sport has tantalized many writers. Two authors, Schmitz and Loy, present their definitions and conclusions about these concepts in a straightforward and understandable manner.

In the article by Schmitz the focus is on sport. He states that it "manifests a distinctive mode of human life, combining creative freedom with disciplined order for the sake of skilled competition and earned victory." Schmitz emphasizes freedom within sport as the player or athlete is able to suspend ordinary obligations and rules.

Loy takes a more systematic and categorical approach to the definition of sport and describes the social structure in which sport resides. He takes sport from the game-occurrence level to that of an institutional pattern. The kind and degree of involvement of both producers and consumers of sport is analyzed by Loy in a section of his article called "Sport as a Social Situation."

In a penetrating essay on the stylization and modes of behavior in American sport, Felshin asserts that "sport functions as a repository for idealized values of the society." She creates optimism and hope in the future by stating, "without an all-male cast, the themes of sport promise a more creative and more humane psychodrama."

It is one thing to define sport, but how does sport help to define meaning in an individual's life? What does sport symbolize for individual athletes or for specific cultural groups? Metheny examines the question of man's conception of himself in the universe and his conception of himself among other men as he engages in sport.

1. Johan Huizinga, *Homo Ludens: A Study of the Play Element in Culture* (Boston, Mass.: Beacon Press, 1950), p. 173.

THEORIES OF HOW AND WHY

Peter C. McIntosh

Sport has always flourished in civilized societies even when the environment has not been favourable. Under the Roman Empire the professional athletes, tightly organized in their guilds and unions, converted the great stadia from Nîmes to Antioch into "closed shops," yet informal play and sport still persisted at a lower level. When monasticism thrust a repressive asceticism upon Christendom sport remained a solace and a joy to villagers and townsmen and even, on occasion, to monks. Calvinism and Puritanism in their extreme forms were unable to prevent ordinary people from committing the sin of indulging in sport. While the people played, philosophers and educationists examined the contribution that physical activities and training might make to the development of society and of the individual. Until the twentieth century, however, few attempts were made to examine why people played or how sportsmen achieved their results. Only recently has the phenomenon of sport and sporting performance been analysed by social scientists, physiologists, psychologists, physicists and mathematicians.

Some of the first investigations were concerned with play itself. The fact that animals, children and grown-ups all play excited the interest of researchers. Numerous and various attempts were made to define or describe the biological function of play. The discharge of superfluous vital energy, abreaction—an outlet for harmful impulses—wish-fulfillment, satisfaction of the imitative instinct, a form of training for the more serious side of life, satisfaction of an innate urge to dominate, these roles were ascribed to play as a feature of human existence.

5

In so far as sport is playful the roles could also be transferred to it as an individual and social phenomenon. All these psychological or biological theories of play made a fundamental assumption that play was a means to an end, that it had some biological purpose, and was ultimately determined by something that was not play. In the past, many, indeed most, philosophers and educationists had justified sport as a means to an end and few had seen it as self-justified, so now biologists and psychologists were making a similar assumption about play. J. Huizinga in the 1930s pointed to the fact that all such theories could only offer partial solutions to the problems which they set out to solve, because they left almost untouched the questions what play was in itself and what it meant for the player. In a book entitled *Homo Ludens* he set out to answer these questions and "to show that genuine, pure play is one of the main bases of civilization."[1]

Huizinga's concept of play was succinct. He recognized that not every language could have hit on the same concept and found a single word for it. He took, therefore, the concept corresponding to the English word *play* and defined it as follows—

> play is a voluntary activity or occupation executed within fixed limits of time and place according to rules freely accepted but absolutely binding, having its aim in itself and accompanied by a feeling of tension, joy and the consciousness that it is "different" from "ordinary life."

Huizinga claimed that this definition embraced play in animals, children and grown-ups, games of strength and skill, inventing-games, guessing-games, games of chance as well as exhibitions and performances of all kinds. It would also embrace dancing, even in its free forms and such non-competitive sports as hunting, and sports of adventure such as climbing, and crossing the Atlantic alone in a thirteen-ton yacht. When the etymology of the English word play is considered its relevance to adventure sports is even more obvious. *Play* comes from the Anglo-Saxon *plega*, or verb *plegan*. The oldest meaning of these words is "to vouch or stand guarantee for, to take a risk, to expose oneself to danger for someone or something." The words *pledge* and *plight* are both etymologically connected with *play*.

Huizinga did not identify play with sport nor did he say that play was an essential element in sport by definition. He did maintain that play was a valuable ingredient in sport, so valuable that when sport lost this particular element it became divorced from culture and had little dignity or worth for mankind. The precise relationship of play to sport is a matter for argument but a closer examination of Huizinga's definition of play shows how much is lost from sport if play is extinguished or obscured.

Huizinga's definition lays down three conditions which apply to play. First is freedom. The player cannot be forced to participate without the activity changing its nature. To run round a track by command of military or civil authority in order to prove a certain degree of attainment of fitness causes the act of running to be no longer play. Compulsory games at school are only play when the intrinsic interest and challenge so dominate the players that the original obligation is forgotten. For a number of boys and girls this never happens. The particular activity may then be valuable as a form of physical education, but it is not play. The contempt of some adults for sport has undoubtedly orginated in the extinction of the play element in their physical education in childhood and adolescence.

The second condition is separateness. According to Huizinga the activity must be circumscribed with boundaries of time and space that are precise and fixed in advance. Such circumscription certainly applies to all competitive games and sports. The running track, the cricket pitch, the fencing piste, the slalom course, the chess-board all prescribe the area of play. The time factor is known to the competitors in advance. But what of some of the non-competitive sports, angling, mountaineering, hunting? The prescription of time and space is very indefinite and may be changed by those who take part during the course of their activity. In these sports the physical environment itself, the river or loch, the peak, the habitat of the quarry provide the limitations which in other sports have to be imposed by definitions of time and space.

The third condition is regulation, and this is more fundamental than the other two conditions. Conventions and rules of a sport suspend the ordinary rules of life and for the duration of the sport the new law is the only one which counts. Even the play of animals appears to be regulated by certain self-imposed regulations eliminating serious injury or death. In the sports of human beings the degree and complexity of regulation varies. It might be thought to be least complex in the play and the sports of children and most complex in the sports of adults. This is not necessarily so. Hopscotch is much more carefully regulated than mob football, which has been played for centuries by adults. However, the purpose of the regulations is to define the sphere in which the ordinary rules of life are suspended, to define the unreality of the sport. They also help to define the nature of the skill to be employed or the way in which chance may operate. Limitation to provide scope for skill is very well exemplified in the off-side laws of team ball-games. There is no rule which has done more to transform violent and brutish sports into games of grace and skill. As recently as 1829 it was recorded that a Frenchman passing through Derby and seeing a game of football remarked that if Englishmen called this playing it would be impossible to say what they would call fighting. Football and other games have undergone some refinement since then and there is now hardly one team ball-game which does not work under an off-side regulation. Even basket-ball, which for many years was played without such a rule, now has the so-called "three-second" rule which prevents a player waiting under the opponents' basket to receive a pass and put the ball in. In games of skill the regulations strictly limit the areas for the operation of chance, strength and skill. They also provide artificial obstacles for the exercise of skill and thereby enable players to obtain an utterly useless but definite result. In a sport such as mountaineering the environment provides the regulation, yet artificial regulation is sometimes wanted in addition in order to preserve the play element. In the 1930s in Britain there were sharp differences of opinion on the justification for using pitons on English rock cliffs, and again in the 1950s disputes arose whether it would be legitimate to use mortars to dislodge snow and ice during an ascent of Mount Everest. Even in mountaineering, then, regulation or convention is necessary for the separation and differentiation of sport from ordinary life.

In amplification of his definition of play Huizinga notes that society is more lenient to the cheat than to the spoil-sports for the spoil-sport shatters the play world itself. He robs play of its illusion, i.e. *in-lusio*.

Modern pharmaceutical research has led to a problem of cheating which is only superficially scientific but in reality philosophical. In the Olympic Games of 1960 the Danish cyclist Knud Jensen collapsed during the one-hundred-kilometer race and died later. It was established that he had taken a drug, Ronicol, which has the general effect of stimulating the circulation by dilating the blood-vessels. The effect of the drug, the exertion of a big race and the heat of the day combined to kill him. In the next year Toni Hiebeler and his three companions made the first ascent of the North Face of the Eiger. Hiebeler and his companions also used Ronicol to stave off frost-bite. The use of the drug may well have saved their lives as well as enabled them to reach the summit. Death or glory has always been the ultimate alternative in mountaineering and in some other sports and is not incompatible with the fundamental concept of sport or with the play element in sport. Death, of course, immediately shatters the illusion of unreality and if death or glory is the inevitable as it was in many gladiatorial combats in ancient Rome then indeed the combat is neither play nor sport.

The use of drugs in sport can be questioned philosophically but not medically. It would only destroy the basis of sport if it broke the conventions or regulations defining the area of unreality, and to decide such an issue is difficult. Regulations are deliberately framed and specific; conventions, which are sometimes more important than the rules, are often unconsciously accepted and are non-specific. Malice, anger and loss of temper are generally thought to destroy sport, but where mechanical aids are concerned convention is capricious. In athletics starting-blocks and spiked shoes have been accepted, but built-up heels for high jumpers have been rejected. In lacrosse the use of body protection in Canada and the United States and the rejection of it in England have led to the development of two essentially different games, neither one being less nor more a sport than the other.

Drugs have hitherto been thought of as unsporting because their effect was to impair performance and the only way to use them was to administer them to an opponent. Poor Abraham Wood inadvertently drank liquid laudanum received from pretended friends while he was contesting a pedestrian contest with Captain Barclay Allardice in 1807 and shortly afterwards had to resign the match. More recent products have been found to have positive rather than negative effects on performance and a different situation has, therefore, arisen. No serious attempt has yet been made to regulate the use of drugs for positive assistance. Already caffeine is widely used by professional cyclists and Varidase was used by boxers in the Olympic Games in 1960 to minimize the effects of bruising. Other sportsmen take other drugs, some to stimulate, and some to relax or induce sleep between two strenuous efforts. Pharmaceutical research has been rapid and spectacular. The American Medical Association has estimated on the basis of research at Harvard that amphetamine alone could improve the performance of runners by one and a half per cent and swimmers by one per cent. As the use of drugs becomes more and more a part of daily life so the governing bodies of sport will need to decide how to regulate their use and still maintain a satisfactory and acceptable area of competition or play where the ordinary rules of life are suspended. Until that is done it is impossible to decide whether, in Huizinga's terminology, the taker of drugs is a cheat, a spoil-sport or neither.

The second part of Huizinga's book sheds light upon the manifestation of play in culture as a whole, in law, in literature, poetry and drama, in art and in war. This does not concern us here, but consideration of Huizinga's definition of play has already led us towards differentiating sports in order to understand their essence more fully. Three problems of relationship present themselves: the first lies between unorganized play and organized sport, the second between games of skill and games of chance, and the third between competitive and non-competitive sport. These problems arising from Huizinga's work have been tackled by Roger Caillois.[2] In order to clarify the problems and offer solutions to them he devised his own classification which is presented schematically in Table I.

The table shows a horizontal classification to deal with the problem of relationship between unorganized play and organized sport and a vertical classification to deal with the other two problems, that is to say the relationship between games of skill and games of chance and between competitive and non-competitive sport.

TABLE 1
Caillois' Classification of Play

	AGON *Competitions*	ALEA *Chance*	MIMICRY *Pretence*	ILINI *Vertigo*
PAIDIA Noise Agitation Laughter Dance Hoop Solitaire Games of patience Crossword puzzles LUDUS	Races ⎱ not reg- Combats ⎰ ulated Athletics Boxing Fencing Football Checkers Chess	Comptines Heads or tails Betting Roulette Lotteries	Childish imitation Masks Costumes Theatre	Children's swings Merry-go- round Tetter- totter Waltz Outdoor sports Skiing Mountain- climbing

The horizontal classification attempts to deal with a problem which was left unsolved by Huizinga, namely how to account for the variation of the play element in different games and sports, and its variation within a single sport performed at different levels of competence. Huizinga ended his book with a sweeping condemnation of sport which is difficult to support. He maintained that in modern sport the old play factor had undergone almost complete atrophy. Increasing systematization and regimentation had led to the loss of the play quality and the neglect of playing for fun. The division between professional and amateur had led to a situation where the professionals were marked off as inferior in standing to true players but superior in capacity, a situation which had produced an inferiority complex in amateurs. "Between them they push sport further and further away from the play sphere proper until it becomes a thing *sui generis*: neither play nor earnest. In modern social life sport occupies a place alongside and apart from cultural process." Huizinga even added that sport no longer had any organic cultural process.

It might have been easier to accept Huizinga's analysis in 1938 than it is in 1963. It is easy to see the encroachment of the principle of commercial entertainment upon the sphere of playing for fun in professional sport at the highest level and even in some so-called amateur sport at the same level. The price which the best performers pay for success is the sacrifice of almost all, but not quite all, the spontaneity and play element. The winner of the British Open Golf Championship in 1961 and 1962, Arnold Palmer, claimed that in the final days of preparation for a big competition he must have complete freedom from care; that he must be free to play a round or not, and even abandon a round if he felt a lack of enthusiasm for it. Part of his recipe for success was to maintain a vestige of the play element right into the big competition.

Whatever may be said of the divorce of professional and commercial sport as entertainment from the concept of sport as play, it would be difficult to maintain in the 1960s that the part-timers in sport suffer an inferiority complex because of the superiority of the professionals any more than amateur dramatic performers or amateur musicians suffer from a psychological complex because of the existence of professional actors and musicians performing in commercial theatres or municipal concert halls. In the public parks, on the commons and village greens, in halls, squash courts and swimming-baths the play element is very much a feature of sport. Systematization and organization by themselves do not appear to destroy or undermine sport.

Caillois' graduation from *paidia* to *ludus* is an attempt to show a progressive formalization of play from the spontaneous activities of children to the organized play of adults. He does not thereby answer Huizinga's strictures on modern sport but he does suggest that formalization is not incompatible with playing for fun.

In his vertical classification Caillois distinguishes competitive sport (*agon*) from games of chance (*alea*), from play which is dramatic (*mimicry*) and from activities which seek the sensations of falling or centrifugal force, games in which "people have deliberately sought out the confusion that a slight giddiness provokes."

The distinction between games of skill and of chance is illuminating. The former "implies discipline and perseverance. It makes the champion rely solely on his own resources, encourages him to make the best possible use of them, and forces him to utilize them fairly and within fixed limits which, being the same for everyone, result in rendering the superiority of the winner indisputable." The latter, on the contrary, is "based on an inequality external to the player, over which he has not the slightest control . . . fate is the sole agent of victory, and where rivalry exists, victory means only that the winner was luckier than the loser." In short, a game of skill is a vindication of personal responsibility in an artificially contrived situation, a game of chance is a resignation of the will, a surrender to destiny also in an artificially contrived situation. This is true only of the two types of game in their extreme form. In bridge or poker reason and psychological insight are allowed to the player as a means of defence against the lot assigned to him by fate.

A comparable distinction can be seen within that group of activities which seek satisfaction in speed, giddiness, vertigo, or the subjection of the being to the risk of loss of equilibrium or to its actual loss. In the fairground switchback the abandonment is complete, but in the downhill ski run the exhiliration of speed and hazard is heightened by the awareness of skill and of power to control the forces of nature to a safe and successful completion of the run. In such a sport there is acceptance rather than abandonment of responsibility. Caillois' category of vertigo is thus seen not to be fundamental but to subdivide within his classification of competition and chance depending on whether resourcefulness or resignation is the dominant factor.

The vertical classification is least satisfactory in dealing with non-competitive sport. The predatory sports, hunting, shooting and fishing, are not mentioned at all, nor is swimming in its non-competitive form. Mountaineering and other similar outdoor sports appear in the category of "vertigo" as if the climber derived his satisfaction from a feeling of giddiness rather than from the exercise of skill. But vertigo may never be experienced during a climb which may still be intensely satisfying to the climber. Dancing, too, is unhappily divided between vertigo, which includes the waltz, and mimicry, which presumably includes various forms of expressive dance.

Close consideration of Caillois' category of competition (agon) shows that it is not wide enough. The essential feature of sport, as distinct from other realms in which the element of play is to be found—games of chance and dramatic or mimetic play—is the striving for superiority and this may take a personal or an impersonal form. The playful element in this striving means that victory is never complete and for all time and that defeat is never irreparable. The effort to conquer an opponent, the self or an environment in play and only in play gives to sport its peculiar satisfaction and its especial virtue in human life.

The desire for superiority in play is itself subdivisible. To prove oneself or one's team better than an opponent or an opposing team within prescribed limits is the aim and object of all competitive sport. The areas for the exercise of skill for the sportsman to prove himself or herself "better than" are many and variable. The running-track, the cricket field, the tennis court, the billiard table, the football pitch, the swimming-bath, the river estuary and many other locations allow sportsmen with different aptitudes and abilities either singly or in pairs or in larger groups or teams to strive for superiority in their chosen sphere of useless contest. These activities comprise a broad category of sport.

A second category comprises combat sports. Here again the aim of the contestant is to prove himself "better than" an opponent. The special feature of personal contact with the opponent either directly through limb and body or indirectly through foil, blade or single stick deserves a special category.

A third category might be called conquest sports. In these the challenge is provided not by an individual or group of opponents but by an environment or a situation. Mountaineering is the purest example of a conquest sport although on occasion even here the environment may be personified. It was reported that the comment of one of the party which made the first successful ascent of Mount Everest was "we knocked the bastard off." A more sensitive reaction to a successful climb was that of Mallory many years earlier. He lost his life on Everest in 1924. "Have we vanquished an enemy? None but ourselves. Have we gained success? That word means nothing here . . . We have achieved an ultimate satisfaction." For most of those who take up conquest sports the appeal is just the impersonal nature of the challenge. Swimming, cycling, hiking, camping and many other activities offer opportunities for conquest sports. Much educational gymnastics, which is non-competitive, makes its appeal as a conquest sport.

There is a fourth category of physical activity which is not sport but which needs to be considered here because of affinity with it. In this type of activity the object is not to be "better than" but to express or communicate ideas and feelings using and enjoying the movements and sensations of the body in the process. Dance, dance drama, eurhythmics and some systems of gymnastics such as those developed by Medau or Idla fall into this category.

The classification of sport here given depends on the motive and the nature of the satisfaction which the sport gives, not upon the activity itself. Swimming when it is not competitive may well be a conquest nature of the satisfaction which the sport gives, not upon the activity sport. The environment of water has to be conquered by the would-be swimmer. It may even become an expressive activity when it takes the form of synchronized swimming and is done to a musical accompaniment. On the other hand mountaineering on occasions becomes competitive and the first ascent of the Matterhorn by Whymper and his party with its tragic ending became just that. Even dancing may become a competitive sport when prizes are given for the best troupe or group in a dance festival. Some sports, even while remaining competitive, may make their appeal to a particular individual for aesthetic rather than competitive reasons but such an individual is unlikely to be successful in the toughest contests. An American high jumper once said to his inferior English opponent: "Sure I like your style but I prefer my height." Many players feel in the midst of their vigorous activity that they are expressing their personality. Indeed, all sport is expressive in this sense, yet in competitive sport it is nevertheless true that the dominant object is to be "better than." In sport and in dance human motives are never simple but it seems justifiable to postulate dominant desires and corresponding satisfactions.

There may well be a sex link with the classification given above, with women being attracted more by the fourth category of expressive activities and men more often deriving satisfaction from sports in the first two categories. There are many good women games players and many men who are excellent dancers, yet the vast following of women for "keep fit" classes in Britain and for other similar systems of movement in other countries suggests that they find particular satisfaction in release of tensions and expression of feeling through rhythmical movement. Men on the other hand clearly dominate numerically the playing fields of the world, and more often derive satisfaction from proving their superiority in a chosen sport.

An "adolescent growth study" carried out in California in 1947 shows just such a sexually divergent pattern of interest. The study was carried out on adolescents by adolescents and was designed to find out what qualities were most admired in boys and girls of different ages. The most admired qualities among boys of eleven to thirteen years of age were skill in organized games, aggressiveness, boisterousness and unkemptness. At the age of sixteen admiration for physical skills, courage, strength and aggressiveness was retained, and even later at the age of nineteen skill in competitive sport still had prestige value.

On the other hand among girls success in games was tolerated but not imitated. At the age of sixteen good sportsmanship with the implication of active participation in sport was admired. At the age of nineteen athletic prowess carried little prestige by itself but skill in dancing and swimming was considered an advantage, so was skill in tennis, the competitive game above all others in which boys and girls can meet each other on common ground.[3]

Any society which is to provide a pattern of sport where all its members may satisfy their natural desires must afford opportunities in all categories. A feature of development in Europe and America and Australasia since the end of the war in 1945 has been the great increase of participation in conquest sports, such as camping, canoeing, sailing, skiing. For some the conquest sports become competitive after the basic skills have been mastered, but for very many the appeal of these sports remains impersonal for most of the time. The social significance of this growth of conquest sports is still obscure but some of its implications national and international will be examined in later chapters. There has also been a great increase in competitive sport both domestic and international at all levels from mediocre schoolboy football to first-class competition in the World Cup and the Olympic Games. This feature, too, will be examined in later chapters.

The "how" of sport has been investigated by so many researchers during the present century that it is only possible to notice in general terms two opposite approaches. In the first an interest in the problems of performance has shed light upon problems outside sport and has led to further investigations in other realms. The second approach, which is more common, has been from the opposite direction. Investigation of sport has been secondary to a primary interest in some other topic, such as disease or industrial techniques. An example of the first approach is the classical paper on "The Theory of Games of Strategy" presented by John von Neumann in 1928 to a mathematical congress. The paper was concerned with the following question—

n players S_1, S_2 . . . S_n are playing a given game of strategy G. How must one of the participants S_m play in order to achieve the most advantageous results?

A game of strategy, roulette, chess, baccarat, bridge, consists of a certain series of events each of which may have a finite number of distinct results. In some the outcome depends on chance, i.e., the probabilities with which each of the possible results will occur are known, but nobody can influence them. All other events depend on the free decision of the players. Von Neumann worked out a theorem on a system of constants which always satisfied three conditions expressed in the form of three equations. The theorem could only apply, however, to games of strategy where the free decisions of players could be implemented with precision as in draughts, bridge or chess. In games of strategy involving physical skill free decisions are but imperfectly implemented even by the most skillful players and the theorem is for them also imperfect.

In his final sentence von Neumann says: "In conclusion I would like to add that a later publication will contain numerical calculations of some well-known two-person games (poker, though with certain schematical simplifications and baccarat). The agreement of the results with the well-known rules of thumb of the games (e.g., proof of the necessity to bluff in poker) may be regarded as an empirical corroboration of the results of our theory." Von Neumann had at least satisfied himself that birds could fly.

Von Neumann's work stimulated a large number of mathematicians to analyse games of strategy. In 1959 the University of Princeton published four large volumes of such papers. The publication was sponsored by the Government's Office of Naval Research, not, presumably, because of the analysis of games of strategy was seen to have an important bearing upon the conduct of warfare.

The movement of investigators in the opposite direction, from military to sporting activities, is exemplified by the programme of the Division of Human Physiology within the Medical Research Council of Great Britain. The Division was set up in 1949 under Dr. Edholm and within two years was investigating two paramilitary problems—the physical development of cadets at the Royal Military College, Sandhurst, and survival at sea. The first problem led to an examination of the sporting activities of the cadets as well as their military training. The second problem led to experiments on channel swimmers. Experience during the war had suggested that maximum time for survival in water at the temperature of the English channel was five to six hours, yet channel swimmers were known to be in the water for any time from twelve to twenty hours.

The next investigations had less connexion with military problems although they were relevant to a parapolitical problem of national prestige. They concerned problems of climbing at high altitude first on Eric Shipton's expedition in 1951-2 to explore the Southern approaches to Everest, then on the expedition which went to Cho Oyu and finally on the ascent of Everest itself in 1953.

In 1955 the Division began work on the study of whole-body-training using brief daily training sessions. It became interested in peak performance in sport and has had research workers at the Olympic and Commonwealth Games. There have been other research teams from other countries investigating the physiological problems of sport and the general trend in the west is an increasing interest in the intrinsic problem and a fading interest in military, political, or other utilitarian considerations. At the same time in the communist countries research into sport is tightly harnessed to political purposes. Perusal of the research reports of, for instance, the High School for Physical Education at Leipzig in Eastern Germany shows that many, if not all, of the research projects are chosen with political considerations in mind. In the United States a proportion of the thousands of research projects on physical performance have had little purpose other than to secure a higher degree for the research worker. Undoubtedly, however, the sum of research has made coaching sport more intelligent and more systematic. There is a risk that concentration on techniques and technical knowledge may obscure the element of play in sport, but the majority of those who play are not noticebly corrupted by being informed why and how they do what they do.

BIBLIOGRAPHY

1. Huizinga, Johan. *Homo Ludens: A Study of the Play Element in Society.* 1938, p. 5. (English ed., London, 1949).
2. Caillois, Roger. "The Structure and Classification of Games," in *Diogenes,* No. 12 (Winter, 1955).
3. Fleming, C. M. *Adolescence.* London, 1948.

SEE ALSO

Cozens, F. W., and F. Stumpf. *Sports in American Life.* Chicago, 1953.
Henderson, R. *Bat, Ball and Bishop.* New York, 1947.
Neuman, J. von. *Theory of Games.* London, 1930.
Riesman, D., Glazier, N. and Denney, R. *The Lonely Crowd.* Princeton, 1950.
Stokes, A. "Psycho-Analytic Reflections on the Development of Ball Games." *International Journal of Psychoanalysis* 36, (1956).

THE PLAY-ELEMENT IN CONTEMPORARY CIVILIZATION

JOHAN HUIZINGA

Let us not waste time arguing about what is meant by "contemporary." It goes without saying that any time we speak of has already become an historical past, a past that seems to crumble away at the hinder end the further we recede from it. Phenomena which a younger generation is constantly relegating to "former days" are, for their elders, part of "our own day," not merely because their elders have a personal recollection of them but because their culture still participates in them. This different time-sense is not so much dependent on the generation to which one happens to belong as on the knowledge one has of things old and new. A mind historically focussed will embody in its idea of what is "modern" and "contemporary" a far larger section of the past than a mind living in the myopia of the moment. "Contemporary civilization" in our sense, therefore, goes deep into the nineteenth century.

The question to which we address ourselves is this: To what extent does the civilization we live in still develop in play-forms? How far does the play-spirit dominate the lives of those who share that civilization? The nineteenth century, we observed, had lost many of the play-elements so characteristic of former ages. Has this leeway been made up or has it increased?

It might seem at first sight that certain phenomena in modern social life have more than compensated for the loss of play-forms. Sport and athletics, as social functions, have steadily increased in scope and conquered ever fresh fields both nationally and internationally.

Johan Huizinga, *Homo Ludens: A Study of the Play Element in Culture* (Boston: The Beacon Press. Copyright 1950 by Roy Publishers. Reprinted by permission of Beacon Press.) Chapter 12. Reprinted by permission of Routledge and Kegan Paul, Ltd.

Contests in skill, strength and perseverance have, as we have shown, always occupied an important place in every culture either in connection with ritual or simply for fun and festivity. Feudal society was only really interested in the tournament; the rest was just popular recreation and nothing more. Now the tournament, with its highly dramatic staging and aristocratic embellishments, can hardly be called a sport. It fulfilled one of the functions of the theatre. Only a numerically small upper class took active part in it. This one-sidedness of mediaeval sporting life was due in large measure to the influence of the Church. The Christian ideal left but little room for the organized practice of sport and the cultivation of bodily exercise, except insofar as the latter contributed to gentle education. Similarly, the Renaissance affords fairly numerous examples of body-training cultivated for the sake of perfection, but only on the part of individuals, never groups or classes. If anything, the emphasis laid by the Humanists on learning and erudition tended to perpetuate the old under-estimation of the body, likewise the moral zeal and severe intellectuality of the Reformation and Counter-Reformation. The recognition of games and bodily exercises as important cultural values was withheld right up to the end of the eighteenth century.

The basic forms of sportive competition are, of course, constant through the ages. In some the trial of strength and speed is the whole essence of the contest, as in running and skating matches, chariot and horse races, weight-lifting, swimming, diving, marksmanship, etc.[1] Though human beings have indulged in such activities since the dawn of time, these only take on the character of organized games to a very slight degree. Yet nobody, bearing in mind the agonistic principle which animates them, would hesitate to call them games in the sense of play —which, as we have seen, can be very serious indeed. There are, however, other forms of contest which develop of their own accord into "sports." These are the ball-games.

What we are concerned with here is the transition from occasional amusement to the system of organized clubs and matches. Dutch pictures of the seventeenth century show us burghers and peasants intent upon their game of *kolf;* but, so far as I know, nothing is heard of games being organized in clubs or played as matches. It is obvious that a fixed organization of this kind will most readily occur when two groups play against one another. The great ball-games in particular require the existence of permanent teams, and herein lies the starting-point of modern sport. The process arises quite spontaneously in the meeting of vil-

1. A happy variation of the natatorial contest is found in *Beowulf,* where the aim is to hold your opponent under water until he is drowned.

lage against village, school against school, one part of a town against
the rest, etc. That the process started in nineteenth century England is
understandable up to a point, though how far the specifically Anglo-
Saxon bent of mind can be deemed an efficient cause is less certain. But
it cannot be doubted that the structure of English social life had much
to do with it. Local self-government encouraged the spirit of association
and solidarity. The absence of obligatory military training favoured the
occasion for, and the need of, physical exercise. The peculiar form of
education tended to work in the same direction, and finally the geography of the country and the nature of the terrain, on the whole flat and,
in the ubiquitous commons, offering the most perfect playing-fields that
could be desired, were of the greatest importance. Thus England became
the cradle and focus of modern sporting life.

Ever since the last quarter of the nineteenth century games, in the
guise of sport,[2] have been taken more and more seriously. The rules
have become increasingly strict and elaborate. Records are established
at a higher, or faster, or longer level than was ever conceivable before.
Everybody knows the delightful prints from the first half of the nineteenth century, showing the cricketers in tophats. This speaks for itself.

Now, with the increasing systematization and regimentation of
sport, something of the pure play-quality is inevitably lost. We see this
very clearly in the official distinction between amateurs and professionals (or "gentlemen and players" as used pointedly to be said). It
means that the play-group marks out those for whom playing is no longer
play, ranking them inferior to the true players in standing but superior
in capacity. The spirit of the professional is no longer the true play-
spirit; it is lacking in spontaneity and carelessness.[3] This affects the
amateur too, who begins to suffer from an inferiority complex. Between
them they push sport further and further away from the play-sphere
proper until it becomes a thing *sui generis*: neither play nor earnest.
In modern social life sport occupies a place alongside and apart from
the cultural process. The great competitions in archaic cultures had
always formed part of the sacred festivals and were indispensable as
health and happiness-bringing activities. This ritual tie has now been
completely severed; sport has become profane, "unholy" in every way
and has no organic connection whatever with the structure of society,

2. It is probably significant that we no longer speak of "games" but of "sport." Our
author may not have been sufficiently familiar with the development of "sport" in
the last ten or twenty years, here and in America, to stress the all-important point
that sport has become a business, or, to put it bluntly, a commercial racket. Trans.
3. Note G. K. Chesterton's dictum: If a thing is worth doing at all it is worth doing
badly! Trans.

least of all when prescribed by the government. The ability of modern social techniques to stage mass demonstrations with the maximum of outward show in the field of athletics does not alter the fact that neither the Olympiads nor the organized sports of American Universities nor the loudly trumpeted international contests have, in the smallest degree, raised sport to the level of a culture-creating activity. However important it may be for the players or spectators, it remains sterile. The old play-factor has undergone almost complete atrophy.

This view will probably run counter to the popular feeling of today, according to which sport is the apotheosis of the play-element in our civilization. Nevertheless popular feeling is wrong. By way of emphasizing the fatal shift towards over-seriousness we would point out that it has also infected the non-athletic games where calculation is everything, such as chess and some card-games.

A great many board-games have been known since the earliest times, some even in primitive society, which attached great importance to them largely on account of their chanceful character. Whether they are games of chance or skill they all contain an element of seriousness. The merry play-mood has little scope here, particularly where chance is at a minimum as in chess, draughts, backgammon, halma, etc. Even so all these games remain within the definition of play as given in our first chapter. Only recently has publicity seized on them and annexed them to athletics by means of public championships, world tournaments, registered records and press reportage in a literary style of its own, highly ridiculous to the innocent outsider.

Card-games differ from board-games in that they never succeed in eliminating chance completely. To the extent that chance predominates they fall into the category of gambling and, as such, are little suited to club life and public competition. The more intellectual card-games, on the other hand, leave plenty of room for associative tendencies. It is in this field that the shift towards seriousness and over-seriousness is so striking. From the days of *ombre* and *quadrille* to whist and bridge, card-games have undergone a process of increasing refinement, but only with bridge have the modern social techniques made themselves master of the game. The paraphernalia of handbooks and systems and professional training has made bridge a deadly earnest business. A recent newspaper article estimated the yearly winnings of the Culbertson couple at more than two hundred thousand dollars. An enormous amount of mental energy is expended in this universal craze for bridge with no more tangible result than the exchange of relatively unimportant sums of money. Society as a whole is neither benefited nor damaged by this futile activity. It seems difficult to speak of it as an elevating recreation in the sense of Aristotle's *diagoge*. Proficiency at bridge is a sterile excellence, sharpening the mental faculties very one-sidedly without enriching the soul in any way, fixing and consuming a quantity of intellectual energy that might have been better applied. The most we can say, I think, is that it might have been applied worse. The status of bridge in modern society would indicate, to all appearances, an immense increase in the play-element to-day. But appearances are deceptive. Really to play, a man must play like a child. Can we assert that this is so in the case of such an ingenious game as bridge? If not, the virtue has gone out of the game.

The attempt to assess the play-content in the confusion of modern life is bound to lead us to contradictory conclusions. In the case of sport we have an activity nominally known as play but raised to such a pitch of technical organization and scientific thoroughness that the real play-spirit is threatened with extinction. Over against this tendency to over-seriousness, however, there are other phenomena pointing in the opposite direction. Certain activities whose whole *raison d'être* lies in the field of material interest, and which had nothing of play about them in their initial stages, develop what we can only call play-forms as a secondary characteristic. Sport and athletics showed us play stiffening into seriousness but still being felt as play; now we come to serious business degenerating into play but still being called serious. The two phenomena are linked by the strong agonistic habit which still holds universal sway, though in other forms than before.

The impetus given to this agonistic principle which seems to be carrying the world back in the direction of play derives, in the main, from external factors independent of culture proper—in a word, communications, which have made intercourse of every sort so extraordinarily easy for mankind as a whole. Technology, publicity and propaganda everywhere promote the competitive spirit and afford means of satisfying it on an unprecedented scale. Commercial competition does not, of course, belong to the immemorial sacred play-forms. It only appears when trade begins to create fields of activity within which each must try to surpass and outwit his neighbour. Commercial rivalry soon makes limiting rules imperative, namely the trading customs. It remained primitive in essence until quite late, only becoming really intensive with the advent of modern communications, propaganda and statistics. Naturally a certain play-element had entered into business competition at an early stage. Statistics stimulated it with an idea that had originally arisen in sporting life, the idea, namely, of trading records. A record, as the word shows, was once simply a memorandum, a note which the inn-keeper scrawled on the walls of his inn to say that such and such

a rider or traveller had been the first to arrive after covering so and
so many miles. The statistics of trade and production could not fail to
introduce a sporting element into economic life. In consequence, there
is now a sporting side to almost every triumph of commerce or technology: the highest turnover, the biggest tonnage, the fastest crossing,
the greatest altitude, etc. Here a purely ludic element has, for once, got
the better of utilitarian considerations, since the experts inform us that
smaller units—less monstrous steamers and aircraft, etc.—are more efficient in the long run. Business becomes play. This process goes so far
that some of the great business concerns deliberately instil the play-
spirit into their workers so as to step up production. The trend is now
reversed: play becomes business. A captain of industry, on whom the
Rotterdam Academy of Commerce had conferred an honorary degree,
spoke as follows:

> "Ever since I first entered the business it has been a race between
> the technicians and the sales department. One tried to produce so much
> that the sales department would never be able to sell it, while the other
> tried to sell so much that the technicians would never be able to keep
> pace. This race has always continued: sometimes one is ahead, sometimes
> the other. Neither my brother nor myself has regarded the business as a
> task, but always as a game, the spirit of which it has been our constant
> endeavour to implant into the younger staff."

These words must, of course, be taken with a grain of salt. Nevertheless there are numerous instances of big concerns forming their own
Sports Societies and even engaging workers with a view not so much to
their professional capacities as to their fitness for the football eleven.
Once more the wheel turns.

It is less simple to fix the play-element in contemporary art than
in contemporary trade. As we tried to make clear in our tenth chapter,
a certain playfulness is by no means lacking in the process of creating
and "producing" a work of art. This was obvious enough in the arts of
the Muses or "music" arts, where a strong play-element may be called
fundamental, indeed, essential to them. In the plastic arts we found that
a play-sense was bound up with all forms of decoration; in other words,
that the play-function is especially operative where mind and hand move
most freely. Over and above this it asserted itself in the master-piece
or show-piece expressly commissioned, *the tour de force*, the wager in
skill or ability. The question that now arises is whether the play-element
in art has grown stronger or weaker since the end of the eighteenth
century.

A gradual process extending over many centuries has succeeded
in de-functionalizing art and making it more and more a free and

independent occupation for individuals called artists. One of the land-marks of this emancipation was the victory of framed canvases over panels and murals, likewise of prints over miniatures and illuminations. A similar shift from the social to the individual took place when the Renaissance saw the main task of the architect no longer in the build-ing of churches and palaces but of dwelling-houses; not in splendid galleries but in drawing-rooms and bed-rooms. Art became more inti-mate, but also more isolated; it became an affair of the individual and his taste. In the same way chamber music and songs expressly designed for the satisfaction of personal aestheticisms began to surpass the more public forms of art both in importance and often in intensity of expression.

Along with these changes in form there went another, even more profound, in the function and appreciation of art. More and more it was recognized as an independent and extremely high cultural value. Right into the eighteenth century art had occupied a subordinate place in the scale of such values. Art was a superior ornament in the lives of the privileged. Aesthetic enjoyment may have been as high as now, but it was interpreted in terms of religious exaltation or as a sort of curiosity whose purpose was to divert and distract. The artist was an artisan and in many cases a menial, whereas the scientist or scholar had the status at least of a member of the leisured classes.

The great shift began in the middle of the eighteenth century as a result of new aesthetic impulses which took both romantic and classical form, though the romantic current was the more powerful. Together they brought about an unparalleled rise in aesthetic enjoyment all the more fervent for having to act as a substitute for religion. This is one of the most important phases in the history of civilization. We must leap over the full story of this apotheosis of art and can only point out that the line of art-hierophants runs unbroken from Winckelmann to Ruskin and beyond. All the time, art-worship and connoisseurship remained the privilege of the few. Only towards the end of the nineteenth century did the appreciation of art, thanks largely to photographic reproduction, reach the broad mass of the simply educated. Art becomes public property, love of art *bon ton.* The idea of the artist as a superior species of being gains acceptance, and the public at large is washed by the mighty waves of snobbery. At the same time a convulsive craving for originality distorts the creative impulse. This constant striving after new and unheard-of forms impels art down the steep slope of Impressionism into the turgidities and excrescences of the twentieth century. Art is far more susceptible to the deleterious influences of modern techniques of production than is science. Mechanization, advertising, sensation-mongering have a much greater hold upon art because as a rule it works directly for a market and has a free choice of all the techniques available.

None of these conditions entitles us to speak of a play-element in contemporary art. Since the eighteenth century art, precisely because recognized as a cultural factor, has to all appearances lost rather than gained in playfulness. But is the net result a gain or loss? One is tempted to feel, as we felt about music, that it was a blessing for art to be largely unconscious of its high purport and the beauty it creates. When art becomes self-conscious, that is, conscious of its own grace, it is apt to lose something of its eternal child-like innocence.

From another angle, of course, we might say that the play-element in art has been fortified by the very fact that the artist is held to be above the common run of mortals. As a superior being he claims a certain amount of veneration for his due. In order to savour his superiority to the full he will require a reverential public or a circle of kindred spirits, who will pour forth the requisite veneration more understandingly than the public at large with its empty phrases. A certain esotericism is as necessary for art to-day as it was of old. Now all esoterics presuppose a convention: we, the initiates, agree to take such and such a thing thus and thus, so we will understand it, so admire it. In other words, esoterics requires a play-community which shall steep itself in its own mystery. Wherever there is a catch-word ending in -*ism* we are hot on the tracks of a play-community. The modern apparatus of publicity with its puffy art-criticism, exhibitions and lectures is calculated to heighten the play-character of art.

It is a very different thing to try to determine the play-content of modern science, for it brings us up against a fundamental difficulty. In the case of art we took play as a primary datum of experience, a generally accepted quantity; but when it comes to science we are constantly being driven back on our definition of that quantity and having to question it afresh. If we apply to science our definition of play as an activity occurring within certain limits of space, time and meaning, according to fixed rules, we might arrive at the amazing and horrifying conclusion that all the branches of science and learning are so many forms of play because each of them is isolated within its own field and bounded by the strict rules of its own methodology. But if we stick to the full terms of our definition we can see at once that, for an activity to be called play, more is needed than limitations and rules. A game is time-bound, we said; it has no contact with any reality outside itself, and its performance is its own end. Further, it is sustained by the consciousness of being a pleasurable, even mirthful, relaxation from the strains of ordinary life. None of this is applicable to science. Science is not only perpetually seeking contact with reality by its usefulness, i.e. in the sense that it is *applied*, it is perpetually trying to establish a universally valid pattern of reality, i.e. as *pure* science. Its rules, unlike those of play, are not unchallengeable for all time. They are constantly being belied by experience and undergoing modification, whereas the rules of a game cannot be altered without spoiling the game itself.

The conclusion, therefore, that all science is merely a game can be discarded as a piece of wisdom too easily come by. But it is legitimate to enquire whether a science is not liable to indulge in play within the closed precincts of its own method. Thus, for instance, the scientist's continued penchant for systems tends in the direction of play. Ancient science, lacking adequate foundation in empiricism, lost itself in a sterile systematization of all conceivable concepts and properties. Though observation and calculation act as a brake in this respect they do not altogether exclude a certain capriciousness in scientific activities. Even the most delicate experimental analysis can be, not indeed manipulated while actually in progress, but played in the interests of subsequent theory. True, the margin of play is always detected in the end, but this detection proves that it exists. Jurists have of old been reproached with similar manoeuvres. Philologists too are not altogether blameless in this respect, seeing that ever since the Old Testament and the Vedas they have delighted in perilous etymologies, a favourite game to this day for those whose curiosity outstrips their knowledge. And is it so certain that the new schools of psychology are not being led astray by the frivolous and facile use of Freudian terminology at the hands of competents and incompetents alike?

Apart from the possibility of the scientific worker or amateur juggling with his own method he may also be seduced into the paths of play by the competitive impulse proper. Though competition in science is less directly conditioned by economic factors than in art, the logical development of civilization which we call science is more inextricably bound up with dialectics than is the aesthetic. In an earlier chapter we discussed the origins of science and philosophy and found that they lay in the agonistic sphere. Science, as some one has not unjustly said, is polemical. But it is a bad sign when the urge to forestall the other fellow in discovery or to annihilate him with a demonstration, looms too large in the work done. The genuine seeker after truth sets little store by triumphing over a rival.

By way of tentative conclusion we might say that modern science, so long as it adheres to the strict demands of accuracy and veracity, is far less liable to fall into play as we have defined it, than was the case in earlier times and right up to the Renaissance, when scientific thought and method showed unmistakable play-characteristics.

These few observations on the play-factor in modern art and science must suffice here, though much has been left unsaid. We are hastening to an end, and it only remains to consider the play-element in contemporary social life at large and especially in politics. But let us be on our guard against two misunderstandings from the start. Firstly, certain play-forms may be used consciously or unconsciously to cover up some social or political design. In this case we are not dealing with the eternal play-element that has been the theme of this book, but with false play. Secondly, and quite independently of this, it is always possible to come upon phenomena which, to a superficial eye, have all the appearance of play and might be taken for permanent play-tendencies, but are, in point of fact, nothing of the sort. Modern social life is being dominated to an ever-increasing extent by a quality that has something in common with play and yields the illusion of a strongly developed play-factor. This quality I have ventured to call by the name of Puerilism,[4] as being the most appropriate appellation for that blend of adolescence and barbarity which has been rampant all over the world for the last two or three decades.

It would seem as if the mentality and conduct of the adolescent now reigned supreme over large areas of civilized life which had formerly been the province of responsible adults. The habits I have in mind are, in themselves, as old as the world; the difference lies in the place they now occupy in our civilization and the brutality with which they manifest themselves. Of these habits that of gregariousness is perhaps the strongest and most alarming. It results in puerilism of the lowest order: yells or other signs of greeting, the wearing of badges and sundry items of political haberdashery, walking in marching order or at a special pace and the whole rigmarole of collective voodoo and mumbo-jumbo. Closely akin to this, if at a slightly deeper psychological level, is the insatiable thirst for trivial recreation and crude sensationalism, the delight in mass-meetings, mass-demonstrations, parades, etc. The club is a very ancient institution, but it is a disaster when whole nations turn into clubs, for these, besides promoting the precious qualities of friendship and loyalty, are also hotbeds of sectarianism, intolerance, suspicion, superciliousness and quick to defend any illusion that flatters self-love or group-consciousness. We have seen great nations losing every shred of honour, all sense of humour, the very idea of decency and fair play.

4. Cf. *In the Shadow of To-morrow*, Heinemann, 1936, chapter 16.

This is not the place to investigate the causes, growth and extent of this world-wide bastardization of culture; the entry of half-educated masses into the international traffic of the mind, the relaxation of morals and the hypertrophy of technics undoubtedly play a large part.

One example of official puerilism must suffice here. It is, as we know from history, a sign of revolutionary enthusiasm when governments play at nine-pins with names, the venerable names of cities, persons, institutions, the calendar, etc. *Pravda*[5] reported that as a result of their arrears in grain deliveries three *kolkhozy* in the district of Kursk, already christened Budenny, Krupskaya and the equivalent of Red Cornfield, has been re-christened Sluggard, Saboteur and Do-Nothing by the local soviet. Though this *trop de zèle* received an official rebuff from the Central Committee and the offensive soubriquets were withdrawn, the puerilistic attitude could not have been more clearly expressed.

Very different is the great innovation of the late Lord Baden-Powell. His aim was to organize the social force of boyhood as such and turn it to good account. This is not puerilism, for it rests on a deep understanding of the mind and aptitudes of the immature; also the Scout Movement expressly styles itself a game. Here, if anywhere, we have an example of a game that comes as close to the culture-creating play of archaic times as our age allows. But when Boy-Scoutism in degraded form seeps through into politics we may well ask whether the puerilism that flourishes in present-day society is a play-function or not. At first sight the answer appears to be a definite yes, and such has been my interpretation of the phenomenon in other studies.[6] I have now come to a different conclusion. According to our definition of play, puerilism is to be distinguished from playfulness. A child playing is not puerile in the pejorative sense we mean here. And if our modern puerilism were genuine play we ought to see civilization returning to the great archaic forms of recreation where ritual, style and dignity are in perfect unison. The spectacle of a society rapidly goose-stepping into helotry is, for some, the dawn of the millennium. We believe them to be in error.

More and more the sad conclusion forces itself upon us that the play-element in culture has been on the wane ever since the eighteenth century, when it was in full flower. Civilization to-day is no longer played, and even where it still seems to play it is false play—I had almost said, it plays false, so that it becomes increasingly difficult to tell where play ends and non-play begins. This is particularly true of politics. Not very long ago political life in parliamentary democratic form was full

5. January 9th, 1935.
6. *Over de grenzen van spel en ernst in de cultuur*, p. 25, and *In the Shadow of To-morrow*, ch. 16.

of unmistakable play-features. One of my pupils has recently worked up my observations on this subject into a thesis on parliamentary eloquence in France and England, showing how, ever since the end of the eighteenth century, debates in the House of Commons have been conducted according to the rules of a game and in the true play-spirit. Personal rivalries are always at work, keeping up a continual match between the players whose object is to checkmate one another, but without prejudice to the interests of the country which they serve with all seriousness. The mood and manners of parliamentary democracy were, until recently, those of fair play both in England and in the countries that had adopted the English model with some felicity. The spirit of fellowship would allow the bitterest opponents a friendly chat even after the most virulent debate. It was in this style that the "Gentleman's Agreement" arose. Unhappily certain parties to it were not always aware of the duties implicit in the word gentleman. There can be no doubt that it is just this play-element that keeps parliamentary life healthy, at least in Great Britain, despite the abuse that has lately been heaped upon it. The elasticity of human relationships underlying the political machinery permits it to "play," thus easing tensions which would otherwise be unendurable or dangerous—for it is the decay of humour that kills. We need hardly add that this play-factor is present in the whole apparatus of elections.

In American politics it is even more evident. Long before the two-party system had reduced itself to two gigantic teams whose political differences were hardly discernible to an outsider, electioneering in America had developed into a kind of national sport. The presidential election of 1840 set the pace for all subsequent elections. The party then calling itself Whig had an excellent candidate, General Harrison of 1812 fame, but not platform. Fortune gave them something infinitely better, a symbol on which they rode to triumph: the log cabin which was the old warrior's modest abode during his retirement. Nomination by majority vote, i.e., by the loudest clamour, was inaugurated in the election of 1860 which brought Lincoln to power. The emotionality of American politics lies deep in the origins of the American nation itself: Americans have ever remained true to the rough and tumble of pioneer life. There is a great deal that is endearing in American politics, something naïve and spontaneous for which we look in vain in the dragoonings and drillings, or worse, of the contemporary European scene.

Though there may be abundant traces of play in domestic politics there would seem, at first sight, to be little opportunity for it in the field of international relationships. The fact, however, that these have touched the nadir of violence and precariousness does not in itself exclude the possibility of play. As we have seen from numerous examples, play can be cruel and bloody and, in addition, can often be false play. Any law-abiding community or community of States will have characteristics linking it in one way or another to a play-community. International law between States is maintained by the mutual recognition of certain principles which, in effect, operate like play-rules despite the fact that they may be founded in metaphysics. Were it otherwise there would be no need to lay down the *pacta sunt servanda* principle, which explicitly recognizes that the integrity of the system rests on a general willingness to keep to the rules. The moment that one or the other party withdraws from this tacit agreement the whole system of international law must, if only temporarily, collapse unless the remaining parties are strong enough to outlaw the "spoilsport."

The maintenance of international law has, at all stages, depended very largely on principles lying outside the strict domain of law, such as honour, decency, and good form. It is not altogether in vain that the European rules of warfare developed out of the code of honour proper to chivalry. International law tacitly assumed that a beaten Power would behave like a gentleman and a good loser, which unhappily it seldom did. It was a point of international decorum to declare your war officially before entering upon it, though the aggressor often neglected to comply with this awkward convention and began by seizing some outlying colony or the like. But it is true to say that until quite recently war was conceived as a noble game—the sport of kings—and that the absolutely binding character of its rules rested on, and still retained, some of the formal play-elements we found in full flower in archaic warfare.

A cant phrase in current German political literature speaks of the change from peace to war as "das Eintreten des Ernstfalles"—roughly, "the serious development of an emergency." In strictly military parlance, of course, the term is correct. Compared with the sham fighting of manoeuvres and drilling and training, real war is undoubtedly what seriousness is to play. But German political theorists mean something more. The term "Ernstfall" avows quite openly that foreign policy has not attained its full degree of seriousness, has not achieved its object or proved its efficiency, until the stage of actual hostilities is reached. The true relation betwen States is one of war. All diplomatic intercourse, insofar as it moves in the paths of negotation and agreement, is only a prelude to war or an interlude between two wars. This horrible creed is accepted and indeed professed by many. It is only logical that its adherents, who regard war and the preparations for it as the sole form of serious politics, should deny that war has any connection with the contest and hence with play. The agonistic factor, they tell us, may have been operative in the primitive stages of civilization, it was all very well then, but war nowadays is far above the competitiveness of mere savages. It is based on the "friend-foe principle." All "real" relationships between nations and States, so they say, are dominated by this ineluctable principle.[7] Any "other" group is always either your friend or your enemy. Enemy, of course, is not to be understood as *inimicus* or εχθρός, i.e., a person you hate, let alone a wicked person, but purely and simply as *hostis* or πολεμιος, i.e., the stranger or foreigner who is in your group's way. The theory refuses to regard the enemy even as a rival or adversary. He is merely in your way and is thus to be made away with. If ever anything in history has corresponded to this gross over-simplification of the idea of enmity, which reduces it to an almost mechanical relationship, it is precisely that primitive antagonism between phratries, clans or tribes where, as we saw, the play-element was hypertrophied and distorted. Civilization is supposed to have carried us beyond this stage. I know of no sadder or deeper fall from human reason than Schmitt's barbarous and pathetic delusion about the friend-foe principle. His inhuman cerebrations do not even hold water as a piece of formal logic. For it is not war that is serious, but peace. War and everything to do with it remains fast in the daemonic and magical bonds of play. Only by transcending that pitiable friend-foe relationship will mankind enter into the dignity of man's estate. Schmitt's brand of "seriousness" merely takes us back to the savage level.

Here the bewildering antithesis of play and seriousness presents itself once more. We have gradually become convinced that civilization is rooted in noble play and that, if it is to unfold in full dignity and style, it cannot afford to neglect the play-element. The observance of play-rules is nowhere more imperative than in the relations between countries and States. Once they are broken, society falls into barbarism and chaos. On the other hand we cannot deny that modern warfare has lapsed into the old agonistic attitude of playing at war for the sake of prestige and glory.

Now this is our difficulty: modern warfare has, on the face of it, lost all contact with play. States of the highest cultural pretensions withdraw from the comity of nations and shamelessly announce that "pacta non sunt servanda." By so doing they break the play-rules inherent in any system of international law. To that extent their playing at war, as we have called it, for the sake of prestige is not true play; it, so to speak, plays the play-concept of war false. In contemporary politics, based as they are on the utmost preparedness if not actual prepara-

7. Carl Schmitt, *Der Begriff des Politischen*, Hamburg, 1933.

tion for war, there would seem to be hardly any trace of the old play-attitude. The code of honour is flouted, the rules of the game are set aside, international law is broken, and all the ancient associations of war with ritual and religion are gone. Nevertheless the methods by which war-policies are conducted and war-preparations carried out still show abundant traces of the agonistic attitude as found in primitive society. Politics are and have always been something of a game of chance; we have only to think of the challenges, the provocations, the threats and denunciations to realize that war and the policies leading up to it are always, in the nature of things, a gamble, as Neville Chamberlain said in the first days of September 1939. Despite appearances to the contrary, therefore, war has not freed itself from the magic circle of play.

Does this mean that war is still a game, even for the aggressed, the persecuted, those who fight for their rights and their liberty? Here our gnawing doubt whether war is really play or earnest finds unequivocal answer. It is the *moral* content of an action that makes it serious. When the combat has an ethical value it ceases to be play. The way out of this vexing dilemma is only closed to those who deny the objective value and validity of ethical standards. Carl Schmitt's acceptance of the formula that war is the "serious development of an emergency" is therefore correct—but in a very different sense from that which he intended. His point of view is that of the aggressor who is not bound by ethical considerations. The fact remains that politics and war are deeply rooted in the primitive soil of culture played in and as contest. Only through an ethos that transcends the friend-foe relationship and recognizes a higher goal than the gratification of the self, the group or the nation will a political society pass beyond the "play" of war to true seriousness.

So that by a devious route we have reached the following conclusion: real civilization cannot exist in the absence of a certain play-element, for civilization presupposes limitation and mastery of the self, the ability not to confuse its own tendencies with the ultimate and highest goal, but to understand that it is enclosed within certain bounds freely accepted. Civilization will, in a sense, always be played according to certain rules, and true civilization will always demand fair play. Fair play is nothing less than good faith expressed in play terms. Hence the cheat or the spoil-sport shatters civilization itself. To be a sound culture-creating force this play-element must be pure. It must not consist in the darkening or debasing of standards set up by reason, faith or humanity. It must not be a false seeming, a masking of political purposes behind the illusion of genuine play-forms. True play knows no propaganda; its aim is in itself, and its familiar spirit is happy inspiration.

In treating of our theme so far we have tried to keep to a play-concept which starts from the positive and generally recognized characteristics of play. We took play in its immediate everyday sense and tried to avoid the philosophical short-circuit that would assert all human action to be play. Now, at the end of our argument, this point of view awaits us and demands to be taken into account.

"Child's play was what he called all human opinions," says late Greek tradition of Heraclitus.[8] As a pendant to this lapidary saying let us quote at greater length the profound words of Plato which we introduced into our first chapter: "Though human affairs are not worthy of great seriousness it is yet necessary to be serious; happiness is another thing. . . . I say that a man must be serious with the serious, and not the other way about. God alone is worthy of supreme seriousness, but man is made God's plaything, and that is the best part of him. Therefore every man and woman should live life accordingly, and play the noblest games, and be of another mind from what they are at present. For they deem war a serious thing, though in war there is neither play nor culture worthy the name, which are the things *we* deem most serious. Hence all must live in peace as well as they possibly can. What, then, is the right way of living? Life must be lived as play, playing certain games, making sacrifices, singing and dancing, and then a man will be able to propitiate the gods, and defend himself against his enemies, and win in the contest." Thus "men will live according to Nature since in most respects they are puppets, yet having a small part in truth." To which Plato's companion rejoins: "You make humanity wholly bad for us, friend, if you say that." And Plato answers: "Forgive me. It was with my eyes on God and moved by Him that I spoke so. If you like, then, humanity is not wholly bad, but worthy of some consideration."[9]

The human mind can only disengage itself from the magic circle of play by turning towards the ultimate. Logical thinking does not go far enough. Surveying all the treasures of the mind and all the splendours of its achievements we shall still find, at the bottom of every serious judgement, something problematical left. In our heart of hearts we know that none of our pronouncements is absolutely conclusive. At that point, where our judgement begins to waver, the feeling that the

8. *Fragments,* 70.
9. *Laws,* 803-4; cf. also 685. Plato's words echo sombrely in Luther's mouth when he says: "All creatures are God's masks and mummeries" (Erlanger Ausgabe, xi, p. 115).

world is serious after all wavers with it. Instead of the old saw: "All is vanity," the more positive conclusion forces itself upon us that "all is play." A cheap metaphor, no doubt, mere impotence of the mind; yet it is the wisdom Plato arrived at when he called man the plaything of the gods. In singular imagery the thought comes back again in the *Book of Proverbs,* where Wisdom says: "The Lord possessed me in the beginning of his ways, before he made any thing from the beginning. I was set up from eternity, and of old before the earth was made . . . I was with him forming all things: and was delighted every day, playing before him at all times; playing in the world. And my delights were to be with children of men."[10]

Whenever we are seized with vertigo at the ceaseless shuttlings and spinnings in our mind of the thought: What is play? What is serious? we shall find the fixed, unmoving point that logic denies us, once more in the sphere of ethics. Play, we began by saying, lies outside morals. In itself it is neither good nor bad. But if we have to decide whether an action to which our will impels us is a serious duty or is licit as play, our moral conscience will at once provide the touchstone. As soon as truth and justice, compassion and forgiveness have part in our resolve to act, our anxious question loses all meaning. One drop of pity is enough to lift our doing beyond intellectual distinctions. Springing as it does from a belief in justice and divine grace, conscience, which is moral awareness, will always whelm the question that eludes and deludes us to the end, in a lasting silence.

10. viii, 22-3, 30-1. This is the Douay translation, based on the Vulgate. The text of the English A.V. and R.V. does not bring out the idea of "play."

SPORT AND PLAY: SUSPENSION OF THE ORDINARY

KENNETH L. SCHMITZ

Sport and play are familiar, but their meaning is not obvious. Play is perhaps as old as man himself, and some will say older. Sport has undergone a remarkable development in some civilizations. It is pursued today by millions in the highly technological societies. Sport is sometimes firmly distinguished from play, and it certainly contains other factors. Nevertheless, the following reflection will suggest that sport is primarily an extension of play, and that it rests upon and derives its central values from play. On this basis it will be maintained that a generous acceptance of the play element in sport is essential for the full realization of this latter form of human behaviour.

The variety of play poses a grave difficulty in understanding it. Its very unity is problematic. Is there a single phenomenon of play which has sufficient unity to be called a special form of human behaviour? The present reflection moves within the context of certain uses not exclusive to English in which the word "play" occurs. Children play in the yard, waves play on the beach, lovers engage in erotic play, an actor plays a part, a musician plays an instrument, a footballer plays a game, a bettor plays the horses, and the gods play with men. The meanings are various; some are peripheral, extended or metaphorical uses. I think, however, that a central core of meaning remains which points towards an indeterminate yet coherent form of human behaviour. This complex structure I call the phenomenon of play.

Wittgenstein poses the difficulty when he lists a wide range of uses of the word "game." He thinks that the variety shows that there is no essence common to all games but only a family resemblance which permits a chain of different uses. I sympathize with much of what Wittgenstein says about the search for a common essence at all costs. Nevertheless, I think that he assumes too strong a doctrine of essence and too exacting a conception of language before he goes on to his refutation. He seems to tie the doctrine of essence to the doctrine of substance. Now this is an understandable conjunction in the light of much of traditional philosophy, but I do not think it is a necessary or a wise one. It might be said that I set out here to clarify the "essence" of play, but I certainly do not think that I will have established a "substance" of play. I have mentioned a "central core" and a "structure," but it may be more helpful to bear in mind more fluid and dynamic metaphors than the traditional figure of a static structure, idea or form. Gabriel Marcel often speaks of a phenomenon as present in varying degrees along a continuum. Or we might even picture an element as more or less present and more or less pure in a series of chemical solutions.[1] But these are only metaphors.

Nor should we be surprised if the same word is extended to activities which do not share an important central meaning. Ordinary usage is the usage of ordinary men, and not that of scientists or philosophers. Family resemblances suffice. It is enough in ordinary speech that one important similarity holds between a clear instance of play, such as children's frolic, and an extended usage, such as piano playing. Thus we speak of ball-players and easily transfer the vocabulary of play and sport to events such as war-games where the factor of contest so heavily weighs. Although the usage is clear enough, further thought may uncover reasons for the frequent association of contest with play but not its necessity for all forms of play. Then, too, the contest in war-games may prove alien in meaning and psychological tone to the contest which occurs in sporting games.

When reflective analysis seeks to isolate the phenomenon of play it must recognize still other hazards. The difficulty of bringing play to reflective clarity is a difficulty which all immediate and obvious phenomena share. Just as in emotion, for example, so too in play, we live under the spell of peculiar immediacy. We throw ourselves into the spirit of the frolic or game, and when reflection itself becomes an ingredient in playfulness it takes on the character of immediacy, serving the values and objectives of the game. Moreover, play compounds the difficulty by revealing itself in a way that is secretive and shy. It can dodge the determined attentions of reflection by encouraging an amused contempt for it, or by permitting itself to be banished to the years of growing-up. An adult and work-oriented thought finds it easy to neglect or to misrepre-

1. For example, G. Marcel, *The Mystery of Being* (Gifford Lectures, 1949-50), Regnery, Chicago, 2 vols, n.d.

sent it, as though it were not worthy of "serious" attention. It resists analysis and preserves its essential meaning by turning our accounts of it away from itself to some alien value. Of course, we must recognize the biological and psychological value of play, in relaxation and escape, in rest and exercise, in education and character-formation. But unless play is nothing but these functions, we cannot understand them fully without understanding *it*. The present intent, then, is to clarify the spirit of play, to determine its appropriate forms, and to characterize the element of play in sport.

There is a thicket of other difficulties, too. Play hides obscurely within a host of very complex phenomena and behaviours and is subtle enough to be easily confused with other forms. For a full analysis, it would be necessary to say what play is not. It seems easiest to see that play is not work, and yet it may call sometimes for very great effort. War may highlight the difference, for like work, war is serious, but like play it is non-productive. The words "conquest" and "victory" belong to the vocabulary of war. The first is said easily enough of work, and the second of play. Some forms of play also resemble war in having the element of contest in them; but the essence of war is deadly contest, it is heavy with death. The grave risk of life is not excluded from play, but if life is risked for some alien value, no matter how high, or if death is certain, the spirit of play is extinguished. There is a certain lightness about play which it shares with other forms of leisure. To be sure, play is not the same as good humor, for although it may be fun, it is not necessarily funny. G. K. Chesterton caught the mood when he remarked that certain affairs were too important to be taken seriously. Play consists in what we may call "non-serious" importance. Still, it cannot be equated simply with pleasure or amusement. Indeed, a full analysis of play would have to make room within it for ingredients of pain and discomfort. It would have to be asked, too, whether a high degree of cruelty, as in the ancient bear-baiting or the gladiatorial games, crushes, perverts or merely tempers the spirit of play.

Such an extended analysis of play is not appropriate here, and I turn instead to sketch out, briefly and tentatively, the positive character of this elusive blithe spirit.

THE VARIETIES OF PLAY

Play can be considered under four general varieties: frolic, make-believe, sporting skills and games. The least formal play is simple spontaneous frolic, and this is associated especially with the very young. It is that aspect of play which is found also in young animals, and its occasional appearance in adult humans seems to manifest the feature of neoteny so pronounced in man. Such play among kittens and puppies, or something very like play, may well be a kind of training along with a desire to satisfy curiosity and to express plain high spirits. It is usually intense and brief and tends to dissipate itself with the outburst of energy that makes it possible. It is an immediate and unreflecting expression of a kind of animal joy, a kicking off of the normal patterns of behaviour, purposeless and without constraint. "Horsing around" illustrates the manner in which the play-world can erupt for a brief moment. A practical joke can trigger a spontaneous display. Someone from the group splashes cold water upon the others lying at leisure in sun and sand, and an impromptu "battle" begins, with little or no declared object and with fluid changing of sides. It is a quicksilver form of play, dashing off now in one direction, now in another, fragmenting and rejoining forces in new combinations for new momentary objectives.

A second more or less informal variety of play is that of make-believe or "just pretending." This, too, is commonest with children but not exclusive to them. There is, of course, daydreaming, a sort of playing with images, roles and situations, though this tends to diminish with adult life or is translated into artistic creativity. Among adults the carnival such as the Mardi Gras, the parade such as the Santa or homecoming parade, and costume parties are examples of this variety of play, intermixed with elements of frolic. It is interesting that some form of the mask or costume is used as a means by which the adult can enter the play-world. In its secular shape as in its religious origin, the mask is a device for suspending the everyday world. The child, on the other hand, needs no such device and with nothing at all can create for himself the world which his playful imagination gives to him. There are usually no well-defined and explicit rules for pretending games, though the roles assumed determine a rough and approximate fittingness. One child is quick to tell another that she is out of character, and the adult who goes to a ball dressed as Bugs Bunny will find his part already somewhat defined for him. Such playfulness, however, is quite different from a theatrical role in which the part is already drawn *a priori* and the actor is expected to interpret and manifest it by using the words and situations provided beforehand by the playwright. What is uppermost in the play of the theatre is representation, whereas in play itself a rough approximation serves merely to suggest and maintain the illusion proper to it. On stage the play is for the sake of presentation, whereas in make-believe the representation is for the sake of play. More generally, it may be said that art and aesthetic experience centre upon the embodiment and expression of meaning, whereas play is for the sake of a certain form of action. In the ballet, for example, action is subordinated to gesture, but in genuine play, mimicry and expression are either incidental or for the sake of the action.

The more formal varieties of play take two styles: skills and games. The first style includes surfboarding, sailing, horse-riding, mountain-climbing, hiking and similar play activities. It calls for knowledge, skill and a certain endurance; so, at least in an elementary way, does the bouncing of a ball, jumping with a pogo stick, yawing a Yo-Yo and skipping rope. The final style of play is completely formal, such as the games of baseball, card-playing and the like. Both styles of play are contests. The former require the mastery of a skill in conformance with natural forces, such as the behaviour of wind and water or the motion of ball and rope. They may even have rudimentary rules. In the truly formal games, however, rules predominate, and although they are determined by agreement, they are held as absolutely binding. Even in solitaire one cannot actually *win* the game if he cheats. Cheating in play is the counterpart of sin in the moral order. It seeks the good of victory without conforming to the spirt of the game and the rules under which alone it is possible to possess it. In the flowery language of a bygone era; the crown of victory sits hollow upon the head of a cheat, who has excluded himself from the values of the game-world and can only enjoy the incidental fruits that sometimes attend a victory. This is quite apart from any moral do's or don'ts, and is written into the very texture of the game-world. In any case, the rules of play differ from those of morality. We can take up the game or leave it, but the rules of morality oblige without any conditionality. Moral rules apply within a context of human action and values that is not that of play and that may touch directly upon the issues of life and death.

In each of these four varieties of play different features predominate: in the frolic the aspect of spontaneous celebration, in imaginative pretense the aspect of creativity, in skill and game the aspect of contest. These aspects are met with in non-play situations too: celebration in worship, creativity in art and contest in work and war. It remains, therefore, to mark out their peculiar quality in the play-world and to indicate its ontological character.

PLAY AS SUSPENSION OF THE ORDINARY WORLD[2]

The spirit of play may be carried over into many activities and even subordinated to other purposes, but it is manifested and realized most

2. See Eugen Fink, *Spiel als Weltsymbol*, Kohlhammer, Stuttgart, 1960.

perfectly in the four varieties distinguished above. The essence of play comes into existence through the decision to play. Such a constitutive decision cannot be compelled and is essentially free. Through it arises the suspension of the ordinary concerns of the everyday world. Such a decision does not simply initiate the playing but rather constitutes it. That is, it does not stand before the playing as winding a mechanical toy stands before its unwinding performance, but rather it underlies and grounds the entire duration of play. This duration may be interrupted or ended at any time, and in this sense the play-world is fragile, ceasing to be either because of the intrusion of the natural world of ordinary concerns, the loss of interest on the part of the players, or the completion of the play-objective. Devices are sometimes used for entrance into and maintenance of the play-spirit, but they are subordinate to the essential demands of play. In a prevalent adult form of contemporary play, nightclubbing, which intends to resemble the frolic, alcohol is almost methodically used to make the transition from the ordinary world somewhat easier. The constant threat of the price tag at the end of the evening naturally makes the suspension of ordinary concerns rather more difficult. It goes without saying that too much alcohol brings about the demise of play, as do drugs, for play seems to demand a deliberate maintenance of itself in keeping with the voluntary character of its founding decision. Play may be a kind of madness, but it is self-engendered and self-maintained.

Inasmuch as the play-decision suspends ordinary concerns, it breaks open a new totality. The world of play with its own non-natural objectives and formalities may be said to transcend the natural world and the world of everyday concern. Of course, it must reckon with natural laws and cannot suspend their real effective impact. Players tire and drop out of the game or are injured; or there just isn't time for a last set of tennis or bridge; or the little girls playing house are called in for supper. Moreover, some forms of play, such as surfboarding or mountain-climbing, deliberately set for their objectives the conquest of natural forces. What is common to these and all forms of play is that natural processes do not determine the significance of the play. The player does not follow natural forces as such. Whereas the worker often follows them in order to redirect them as in cultivation, the player may resist them, ignore them as far as possible or create a new order of significance whose elements are non-natural, as in word-games. The surfer follows them in order to wrest from them a carefree moment of exhilarating joy; the archer takes them into account in order to hit a target of his own proposing; and the chess-player moves within a set of spatial possibilities that are ideal in themselves and only indicated by the board and chessmen.

Religion, art and play are rightly spoken of as ways of transcending the strictly natural world. Religion, however, does not suspend the world of nature. Quite the contrary, in its historical forms, it turns back from a sacred and alien distance towards nature in order to reawaken and restore it to its original freshness and creativity. Art and aesthetic experience transcend the natural world in the embodiment and expression of concrete, symbolic meaning. Art suspends the natural and puts it out of play when it gives ultimate value to transnatural objectives. Kant, of course, speaks of a certain detachment or disinterestedness. The sign of the transcendence of play over the natural world is manifest by a certain excess which characterizes its spirit. There is in it an uncalled-for exhilaration, a hilarity in the contest and in the mood of celebration. Like art and religion, play is not far from the feast, for art celebrates beauty and religion celebrates glory, but play celebrates the emergence of a finite world that lies outside and beyond the world of nature while at the same time resting upon it.

THE PLAY-WORLD AS A DISTINCTIVE ORDER

The space and time of play are not contiguous with natural space and time. The little child creates an area in the room in which battles are fought, seas sailed, continents discovered, in which animals roam and crops grow. Adults create the playing field which is a space directed according to the objectives and rules of the game. A ball driven to the right of a line is "foul," another landing beyond a certain point is "out of play." In chess the knight alone can jump and the bishop can only move diagonally. Play-space is not at all relative in most games and to the extent to which arbitrary rules are invented to that extent the space becomes more determinate and more absolute. Players hold willingly to the rules or those who do not have officials to encourage them in the most formal sports. This maintenance of the absolutely binding force of the rules is a free acceptance flowing out of and essentially one with the play-decision, and with the suspension of the natural ordinary world and the substitution of a new order. The laws of natural forces are put to use in an extraordinary way within an extraordinary world inspired by a motive that has suspended the ordinary interests of everyday life.

The structured order of play-space is especially evident in those games in which a single or double point in the play-space is the key to the contest, the privileged space of the goals, target or finishing-line. So, too, play-time is not contiguous with ordinary time, though it must frequently bow to it. In ice hockey sixty minutes of play-time are not sixty minutes of clock-time, and in baseball play-time is simply nine innings or more. Of course, natural space and time are the alien boundaries that ring about and mark the finitude of human play, but the play has its own internal boundaries set by the objectives and rules of the game. When a ball is out of bounds in many games the game-time stops also. Men set the objectives and rules of play and yet there is a certain sense in which the play-objective, freely chosen, sets its own basic rules. Play seems to begin by abandoning forms of everyday behaviour, but it maintains that abandonment in a positive and determinate way by creating a new space and time with new forms and rules of behaviour that are not determined by or functional within the everyday world but which nevertheless have a positive meaning of their own. Within its boundaries and objectives the play-world exhibits a totality of meaning and value that is strikingly complete and perfect. Play reveals itself as transnatural, fragile, limited perfection.

The suspension of the natural world and its subordination to the game or its sublimation into the play context can be described as the suppression of the real, where "reality" is restricted to the natural and ordinary world. Play then builds an illusion. Huizinga notes that the Latin word for play (*ludus*) is closely related to the word for illusion (*inlusio*).[3] The "inactuality" of play is most evident in the imaginative play of make-believe. This suspension of the "real" world by means of a play-decision releases a world of "unreality" which needs no justification from outside itself. It is a self-sealed world, delivering its own values in and for itself, the freedom and joy of play. As a piece of fine art needs no other defense than itself, and as the feast need exist for no other reason than its own values, so too play, though its claims must be balanced within the whole man against those of "reality," receives justification only through and in itself. As colour cannot validate its existence and meaning except to one who sees, so play cannot vindicate itself except to one who plays. To anyone else it appears superfluous. The stern Calvin Coolidge, it is said, once snorted that going fishing was childish, which only proved to fishermen that he was absurd. Play has its own built-in finality. It is in this sense objectless; it has no other object than itself.

Nevertheless, an adequate philosophy can free the mind from an exclusive preoccupation with the natural world and open it out onto all the modes of being. Each is seen to have its value. Like religion and art, play embodies a significance that is not fully grasped in clear concepts. As an analysis does not replace a poem or a painting, so a description of its rules is no substitute for play. But an analysis may open the mind to the gen-

3. *Homo Ludens: A Study of the Play Element in Culture*, (1944), Beacon, Boston, 1955, p. 36. See also Fink, *op. cit.*, pp. 66 ff.

uine reality of play. The proper vehicle of meaning in play is action and in this it is much closer to ritual and myth than to scientific concepts. Play is meaning embodied in action; it is "significant form"[4] precisely as human behaviour. The world which opens out through the play-decision is a world of possibilities closed off from the natural and ordinary world. Measured against the ordinary world the world of possibility opened up by play seems inactual and illusory; but measured in terms of being itself, it is a radical way of being human, a distinctive mode of being. It is a way of taking up the world of being, a manner of being present in the world in the mode of creative possibility whose existential presence is a careless joyful freedom.

I suggest, then, that there is a phenomenon of play which is an indeterminate yet coherent mode of human behaviour. It comes to be through a decision which does not simply initiate or occasion play, but which founds and underlies it. It is a decision which is freely taken and maintained, either spontaneously or deliberately. It is a decision which seeks to secure certain values for human consciousness and human existence, a certain meaning and a certain freedom. It may be called an activity of maintaining an illusion, if we speak in terms which still give primacy to the natural world. But it may also be called an activity of suspension, whereby the natural forces while not abrogated are dethroned from their primacy. More positively, it may be called an activity of constitution, which breaks open distinctive possibilities of meaning, freedom and value. It has no other essential objective than those implicit in the founding decision. It has its own time and space, boundaries and objectives, rewards and penalties. It is a distinctive way, voluntary and finite, of man's being-in-the-world. Playing in the world, man recovers himself as a free and transcendent being.

THE PLAY-ELEMENT IN SPORT

Two factors are especially prominent in sport: the first is the emphasis on good performance, and the second is the element of contest. If sport consisted simply of performance and contest, however, scholarship examinations would be reported in the sporting pages. Examinations are liable to be deadly serious and to be related directly to educational objectives which are part of the natural and social world.

Sport may be carried on at various levels of competence and preparedness, from the unplanned street game to the carefully planned amateur or professional sporting event. In the former, natural ability and past

4. Huizinga, *op. cit.*, p. 4.

experience determine the proficiency of the maneuvers. Planned events are usually preceded by exercises for general conditioning and precise training. These preparations are directed towards the performance of activities within a non-natural space and time and in accord with more or less formally specified rules. The excellence of the performance is judged within a matrix of values that flow from the decision to play this or that kind of game.

The performance, moreover, is for the sake of the contest, either against natural forces, such as in the high jump, or against other players, as in track meets. In some sports, there is only one contestant, as in hunting; but in most, as in team games, a contestant pits himself also against other players. The performance is tested by the contest of player against player, and the verdict is sealed by the victory.

It may seem that the play element is not essential to sport. Thus, for example, the sport of hunting lies very close to the natural needs of man. Moreover, it has little of formal rules. The various game laws are not to be confused with sporting rules, for they are meant to conserve the natural supply of game as a condition for further hunting. They are laws, not rules. Of course, if two huntsmen vie with each other for the largest or the quickest bag, we say that they have made a game out of it. Here again, they have imposed upon the natural value, namely, the food procured, a game-value, the prize of victory. Such a contest, however, is to be distinguished from the contest of bucks seeking a mate or tycoons seeking a fortune. It is imaginable that the latter might be taken up in a *spirit* of play, but it is not properly playful in its *form*. We see here a distinction between the forms of play and the spirit which inhabits them. This spirit can sometimes animate certain other forms of behaviour. Thus a man may bet in order to win and pay off the mortgage, or he may bet in order to risk something valuable to him. Only the latter is animated by a spirit of play. Even it is no longer play if it is compulsive, for it may then be the sublimation of the wish to totter between life and death.

In addition to good performance and contest, then, spontaneous creative freedom is inherent in play. This suggests that sport can be carried out without the spirit of play. Nevertheless, in the life of individuals and in the history of the race, sport emerges from play as from an original and founding existential posture. Sport is free, self-conscious, tested play which moves in a transnatural dimension of human life, built upon a certain basis of leisure. Sport is in its origin and intention a movement into transcendence which carries over from the founding decision to play and which builds upon that decision an intensified thrust towards the values of self-consciousness tested through performance, competition and victory. There is certainly a return to seriousness in the discipline of formal sport. There is training, performance and competition. But the objectives of sport and its founding decision lie within play and cause sport to share in certain of its features—the sense of immediacy, exhilaration, rule-directed behaviour, and the indeterminacy of a specified outcome.

Sport can be demanding, but its essence is as delicate as any perfume and can be as readily dissipated. There are three abuses which can kill the spirit of play within sport and reduce sport to something less than its fullest human possibilities.

The first abuse is the exaggeration of the importance of victory. I do not refer to the will to win, which must be strong in any highly competitive sport. Still, such a will must be situated within a more generous context—the desire to perform as well as it is humanly possible. Many factors not under the control of players or judges may determine the ultimate victor. Such an awareness does not tarnish the prize, but situates it properly within a limited and qualified texture. Victory in sports is not absolute, and it should not be allowed to behave like the absolute. The policy of winning at all costs is the surest way of snuffing out the spirit of play in sport. The fallout of such a policy is the dreary succession of firings in college and professional sport. Such an emphasis on victory detaches the last moment from the whole game and fixes the outcome apart from its proper context. It reduces the appreciation of the performance, threatens the proper disposition towards the rules and turns the contest into a naked power struggle. The upshot is a brutalization of the sport. And so, the sport which issued from the play-decision, promising freedom and exhilaration, ends dismally in lessening the humanity of players and spectators.

The second abuse stems from the rationalization of techniques within a sport when the rationalization is promoted by an exaggerated sense of the value of efficiency. Good performance is important and the best performance is a desirable ideal. A coach has always to deal with a definite group of individual players. He must assess their potential for the game, combining firmness with good judgment and enthusiasm with restraint. Hard coaching is to be expected, but under pressure of competition it is tempting to let moderation give way to an uninterrupted drive for limitless proficiency. An abstract tyranny of the possible may drive players beyond what they should be asked to give, compelling them to spend what they neither have nor can afford. Driven beyond their natural capacities, they lose the spirit of play, and the values which are supposed to be the initial and perhaps even the paramount reason for taking up the sport. There is a subtle and difficult difference between such tyrannic proficiency and the will to excel which every competitor must have and which leads him to pit his body and personality with and against others.

There is a difference between a tyrant and a coach who rightly demands the best his players can put forth. There is a difference, too, between a rationalization which sacrifices everything to technical competence and a reasonable improvement of techniques of training and performance which lift a sport to new accomplishments. Such a merely technical drive is more than likely in our age which tends to over-rationalize all life in the name of technical perfection. The deepest problems in our technological society centre about salvaging, promoting and developing truly human possibilities. Sport stands in a very sensitive position. It can be part of the drive to dehumanization, or in a very direct and privileged way, to the recapture of human values and human dignity. An ultimate and limitless demand for proficiency forced upon players and sport at the cost of all other values including those of play will diminish all who participate—players, staff and spectators.

The first and second abuses are internal threats which arise from detaching victory or performance from the context of play. The third abuse arrives from outside what is essential to sport. It arises with the presence of spectators and threatens to alienate the sport from its play-objectives and values. Such an alienation becomes even more likely when the commercial possibilities of a sport are exploited. The genuine essence of play cannot be present when it is play only for the spectators, as in the gladiatorial contests of the Roman circus in which contestants were often compelled against their wishes to face wild beasts or even one another. One of the requirements is that the participants also take up the activity in a spirit of play. In commercial sport, the spectators usually attend the game in a spirit of play, though some attend simply with friends or to be seen. The players, on the other hand, are under contract, though it is under contract precisely "to play." It seems an oversimplification, however, to discount professional sport as play merely because the players are paid. We do not call a work of fine art non-art simply because it is commissioned. Moreover, the distinction between amateur and professional is a social one, distinguishing those who pursue a vocation from those who pursue an avocation. Olympic sport claims to reflect the time when some games were part of the culture of a "gentleman." Amateurs today are of three kinds: the occasional players who are not very serious in their pursuit of the sport; those who, like many bowlers or curlers, are serious devotees of the sport but not under contract to play it; and those would-be pros who are not yet skilled enough to play the sport under contract. On the side of the professional player what threatens the purity of the spirit of play is the compulsion implied in the contractual obligation to render services at given times, to practice in order to maintain and improve skills, and to participate in games as required. But these demands are intrinsic to many games. The threat lies even more in the nature of the binding force. In professional sport it does not lie in interest in the game itself but rather is reinforced and ultimately enforced by values not intrinsic to the game. Perhaps the clearest distinction is between the wage the pro earns and the win or loss of the game. Win or lose, for a time at least he is paid a wage for services delivered; but he gets the victory only when "the gods of the game" smile upon him. Play ceases when the primary reasons for undertaking it are alien to the values of the play-world itself. Values intrinsic to the play-world include not letting down one's own teammates in team games, not begging off the contest because of personal discomfort, taking pleasure in performing activities within the rules of the game, prizing the victory and its symbols. Values that lie outside the play-world include agreement to deliver services for wages earned, abiding by a contract because of fear of being sued, playing out games in order not to be barred from further league participation, finishing out a sports career in order to achieve social and economic standing upon ceasing to play. These motives are not unworthy; they are simply not motives of play. A player may respect the values of play without directly experiencing them, as when he finishes out his sports' career as ably as possible in order to fulfill the possibilities of the game and thereby allow other participants and spectators to share in the values of the game. Heroism in sport often arises through the determination of a player to maintain the importance of the play-world even in the face of disturbances from the "real" world, such as painful injuries, private worries, physical exhaustion, or even fading interest, although the fan tends to look upon the latter as a betrayal. On the side of the spectator in professional and even in other organized sport, what threatens the purity of the spirit of play is the reduction of the players to hirelings, and the game to something which is expected to deliver to the spectator a period of pleasure for money paid. The commercialization of sport can, of course, be a way of seeing that the quality and abundance of playing is increased; but it can and often does simply pervert sport into just another profitable pleasure industry. Many things give pleasure. Some of them can be bought. The play-world is not one of them. Over-commercialization of sport disillusions the spectator and risks defeating the objectives of commercialization.

The play-world in general offers itself to anyone who wishes to enter it, either as participant or as spectator. But to receive the gift of play he must take up the values of the game as important in and for themselves. He may get angry with "his" team when it plays badly and boast of it when it plays well; but he will not view the players simply as objects employed to give him a pleasurable spectacle. This is a purely objectivist viewpoint and a form of reductionism. It is easy for a spectator to drift into this attitude, because his relation to the game is only partial. He bears no responsibility, and he lives the risks and thrills, defeats and victories in a moving but not a completely involved way. The player is committed with his body and plunges in as one participant; the spectator participates as the whole team, but indirectly. Nevertheless, play calls for and can achieve a vantage point which undercuts the distinction of the purely subjective and the purely objective, in which I am here and they are there. The fan enjoys a special complicity with his team and easily transfers the symbolic value of the victory to himself and his group. He feels himself in some sense one with the participants of the game. What unites them is the particular form of the play-world, and the importance of its objectives and values.

In sum, then, sport can nourish the spirit of objectivity, for it contains a native generosity with which it seeks excellence of form and action in obedience to conventional rules and submits freely to the award of victory or defeat according to those rules. In so doing, sport manifests a distinctive mode of human life, combining creative freedom with disciplined order for the sake of skilled competition and earned victory. In the engagement the player must encounter his opponent not as an enemy in war but as one whose excellence challenges him and makes possible his own best performance. Players and spectators discover in a new dimension the significance of competitors, team and fans. The sharp difference of subject and object is bridged by the common context and objectives. A fan may surprise himself applauding an exceptionally fine play against his own team, or at least unhappily admiring it. At a race-meet fans from several schools spontaneously urge on the front runner who seems able to beat the existing record, even though he will beat their own runners. It it a victory of man against time and space and himself. Of course, the spectator can be treated as one who needs bread and circuses, but wiser sports managers will try to transform an appetite for constantly renewed sensations into an experience of community. The radical breaking-down of more traditional ties has seen the rise of massive spectator sports. Is is not possible that the attraction of sport for non-players lies in the invitation to experience freedom, meaning and excellence in the context of a free community of individuals bound together by a common appreciation for the values of the game? In that experience of free community men discover new possibilities of human excellence and reach out to recover a fuller meaning of themselves.

THE NATURE OF SPORT:
A DEFINITIONAL EFFORT

JOHN W. LOY, JR.

Sport is a highly ambiguous term having different meanings for various people. Its ambiguity is attested to by the range of topics treated in the sport sections of daily newspapers. Here one can find accounts of various sport competitions, advertisements for the latest sport fashions, advice on how to improve one's skills in certain games, and essays on the state of given organized sports, including such matters as recruitment, financial success, and scandal. The broad yet loose encompass of sport reflected in the mass media suggests that sport can and perhaps should be dealt with on different planes of discourse if a better understanding of its nature is to be acquired. As a step in this direction we shall discuss sport as a game occurrence, as an institutional game, as a social institution, and as a social situation or social system.

I. SPORT AS A GAME OCCURRENCE

Perhaps most often when we think of the meaning of sport, we think of sports. In our perspective sports are considered as a specialized type of game. That is, a sport as one of the many "sports" is viewed as an actual game occurrence or event. Thus in succeeding paragraphs we shall briefly outline what we consider to be the basic characteristics of games in general. In describing these characteristics we shall continually make reference to sports in particular as a special type of game. A game we define as any form of playful competition whose outcome is deter-

From *Quest*, Monograph X (May, 1968): 1-15.

mined by physical skill, strategy, or chance employed singly or in combination.[1]

IA. "Playful." By "playful competition" we mean that any given contest has one or more elements of play. We purposely have not considered game as a subclass of play,[2] for if we had done so, sport would logically become a subset of play and thus preclude the subsumption of professional forms of sport under our definition of the term. However, we wish to recognize that one or more aspects of play constitute basic components of games and that even the most highly organized forms of sport are not completely devoid of play characteristics.

The Dutch historian Johan Huizinga has made probably the most thorough effort to delineate the fundamental qualities of play. He defines play as follows:

> Summing up the formal characteristics of play we might call it a free activity standing quite consciously outside "ordinary" life as being "not serious," but at the same time absorbing the player intensely and utterly. It is an activity connected with no material interest, and no profit can be gained by it. It proceeds within its own proper boundaries of time and space according to fixed rules and in an orderly manner. It promotes the formation of social groupings which tend to surround themselves with secrecy and to stress their differences from the common world by disguise or other means (Huizinga, 1955, p. 13).

Caillois has subjected Huizinga's definition to critical analysis (Caillois, 1961, pp. 3-10) and has redefined play as an activity which is free, separate, uncertain, unproductive, and governed by rules and make-believe (*Ibid.*, pp. 9-10). We shall briefly discuss these qualities ascribed to play by Huizinga and Caillois and suggest how they relate to games in general and to sports in particular.

IA1. "Free." By free is meant that play is a voluntary activity. That is, no one is ever strictly forced to play, playing is done in one's free time, and playing can be initiated and terminated at will. This characteristic of play is no doubt common to many games, including some forms of amateur sport. It is not, however, a distinguishing feature of all games, especially those classified as professional sport.

IA2. "Separate." By separate Huizinga and Caillois mean that play is spatially and temporally limited. This feature of play is certainly relevant to sports. For many, if not most, forms of sport are conducted in

---

1. This definition is based largely on the work of Caillois (1961) and Roberts and others (1959). Other definitions and classifications of games having social import are given in Berne (1964) and Piaget (1951).
2. As have done Huizinga (1955), Stone (1955), and Caillois (1961).

spatially circumscribed environments, examples being the bullring, football stadium, golf course, race track, and swimming pool. And with few exceptions every form of sport has rules which precisely determine the duration of a given contest.

IA3. "Uncertain." The course or end result of play cannot be determined beforehand. Similarly, a chief characteristic of all games is that they are marked by an uncertain outcome. Perhaps it is this factor more than any other which lends excitement and tension to any contest. Strikingly uneven competition is routine for the contestants and boring for the spectators; hence efforts to insure a semblance of equality between opposing sides are a notable feature of sport. These efforts typically focus on the matters of size, skill, and experience. Examples of attempts to establish equality based on size are the formation of athletic leagues and conferences composed of social organizations of similar size and the designation of weight class for boxers and wrestlers. Illustrations of efforts to insure equality among contestants on the basis of skill and experience are the establishment of handicaps for bowlers and golfers, the designation of various levels of competition within a given organization as evidenced by freshman, junior varsity, and varsity teams in scholastic athletics, and the drafting of players from established teams when adding a new team to a league as done in professional football and basketball.

IA4. "Unproductive." Playing does not in itself result in the creation of new material goods. It is true that in certain games such as poker there may occur an exchange of money or property among players. And it is a truism that in professional sports victory may result in substantial increases of wealth for given individuals. But the case can be made, nevertheless, that a game *per se* is non-utilitarian.[3] For what is produced during any sport competition is a game, and the production of the game is generally carried out in a prescribed setting and conducted according to specific rules.

IA5. "Governed by rules." All types of games have agreed-upon rules, be they formal or informal. It is suggested that sports can be distinguished from games in general by the fact that they usually have a greater variety of norms and a larger absolute number of formal norms (i.e., written prescribed and proscribed rules.[4] Similarly, there is a larger number of sanctions and more stringent ones in sports than in games.

3. Cf. Goffman's discussion of "rules of irrelevance" as applied to games and social encounters in general (1961), pp. 19-26).
4. E.g., compare the rules given for games in any edition of Hoyle's *Book of Games* with the NCAA rule books for various collegiate sports.

For example, a basketball player must leave the game after he has committed a fixed number of fouls; a hockey player must spend a certain amount of time in the penalty box after committing a foul; and a football player may be asked to leave the game if he shows unsportsmanlike conduct.

With respect to the normative order of games and sports, one explicit feature is that they usually have definite criteria for determining the winner. Although it is true that some end in a tie, most contests do not permit such an ambivalent termination by providing a means of breaking a deadlock and ascertaining the "final" victor. The various means of determining the winner in sportive endeavors are too numerous to enumerate. But it is relevant to observe that in many sport competitions were "stakes are high," a series of contests are held between opponents in an effort to rule out the element of chance and decide the winner on the basis of merit. A team may be called "lucky" if it beats an opponent once by a narrow margin; but if it does so repeatedly, then the appelations of "better" or "superior" are generally applied.

IA6. "Make-believe." By the term make-believe Huizinga and Caillois wish to signify that play stands outside "ordinary" or "real" life and is distinguished by an "only pretending quality." While some would deny this characteristic of play as being applicable to sport, it is interesting to note that Veblen at the turn of the century stated:

> Sports share this characteristic of make-believe with the games and exploits to which children, especially boys, are habitually inclined. Make-believe does not enter in the same proportion into all sports, but it is present in a very appreciable degree in all (Veblen, 1934, p. 256).

Huizinga observes that the "'only pretending' quality of play betrays a consciousness of the inferiority of play compared with 'seriousness'" (Huizinga, 1955, p. 8). We note here that occasionally one reads of a retiring professional athlete who remarks that he is "giving up the game to take a real job"[5] and that several writers have commented on the essential shallowness of sport.[6] Roger Kahn, for example, has written that:

> The most fascinating and least reported aspect of American sports is the silent and enduring search for a rationale. Stacked against the atomic bomb or even against a patrol in Algeria, the most exciting rally in history may not seem very important, and for the serious and semi-serious

5. There is, of course, the amateur who gives up the "game" to become a professional.
6. For an early discussion of the problem of legitimation in sport, see Veblen, 1934, pp. 268-270.

people who make their living through sports, triviality is a nagging, damnable thing. Their drive for self-justification has contributed much to the development of sports (Kahn, 1957, p. 10).

On the other hand, Huizinga is careful to point out that "the consciousness of play being 'only pretend' does not by any means prevent it from proceeding with the utmost seriousness" (Huizinga, 1955, p. 8). As examples, need we mention the seriousness with which duffers treat their game of golf, the seriousness which fans accord discussions of their home team, or the seriousness that national governments give to Olympic Games and university alumni to collegiate football?[7,8]

Accepting the fact that the make-believe quality of play has some relevance for sport, it nevertheless remains difficult to empirically ground the "not-ordinary-or-real-life" characteristic of play. However, the "outside-of-real-life" dimension of a game is perhaps best seen in its "as-if" quality, its artificial obstacles, and its potential resources for actualization or production.

IA6(a). In a game the contestants act as if all were equal, and numerous aspects of "external reality" such as race, education, occupation, and financial status are excluded as relevant attributes for the duration of a given contest.[9]

IA6(b). The obstacles individuals encounter in their workaday lives are not usually predetermined by them and are "real" in the sense that they must be adequately coped with if certain inherent and socially conditioned needs are to be met; on the other hand, in games obstacles are artificially created to be overcome. Although these predetermined obstacles set up to be conquered can sometimes attain "life-and-death" significance, as in a difficult Alpine climb, they are not usually essentially related to an individual's daily toil for existence.[10]

IA6(c). Similarly, it is observed that in many "real" life situations the structures and processes needed to cope with a given obstacle are often not at hand; however, in a play or game situation all the structures and processes necessary to deal with any deliberately created obstacle

7. An excellent philosophical account of play and seriousness is given by Kurt Riezler (1941, pp. 505-517).

8. A sociological treatment of how an individual engaged in an activity can become "caught up" in it is given by Goffman in his analysis of the concept of "spontaneous involvement" (1961, pp. 37-45).

9. For a discussion of how certain aspects of "reality" are excluded from a game situation, see Goffman's treatment of "rules of irrelevance." Contrawise see his treatment of "rules of transformation" for a discussion of how certain aspects of "reality" are permitted to enter a game situation (1961, pp. 29-34).

10. Professional sports provide an exception, of course, especially such a sport as professional bullfighting.

and to realize any possible alternative in course of action are potentially available.[11]

In sum, then, games are playful in that they typically have one or more elements of play: freedom, separateness, uncertainty, unproductiveness, order, and make-believe. In addition to having elements of play, games have components of competition.

IB. "Competition." Competition is defined as a struggle for supremacy between two or more opposing sides. We interpret the phrase "between two or more opposing sides" rather broadly to encompass the competitive relationships between man and other objects of nature, both animate and inanimate. Thus competitive relationships include:

1. competition between one individual and another, e.g., a boxing match or a 100-yard dash;

2. competition between one team and another, e.g., a hockey game or a yacht race;

3. competition between an individual or a team and an animate object of nature, e.g., a bullfight or a deer-hunting party;

4. competition between an individual or a team and an inanimate object of nature, e.g., a canoeist running a set of rapids or a mountain climbing expedition; and finally,

5. competition between an individual or team and an "ideal" standard, e.g., an individual attempting to establish a world land-speed record on the Bonneville salt flats or a basketball team trying to set an all-time scoring record. Competition against an "ideal" standard might also be conceptualized as man against time or space, or as man against himself.[12]

The preceding classification has been set forth to illustrate what we understand by the phrase "two or more opposing sides" and is not intended to be a classification of competition *per se*. While the scheme may have some relevance for such a purpose, its value is limited by the fact that its categories are neither mutually exclusive nor inclusive. For instance, an athlete competing in a cross-country race may be competitively involved in all of the following ways: as an individual against another individual; as a team member against members of an opposing

11. Our use of the term "structures and processes" at this point is similar to Goffman's concept of "realized resources" (1961, pp. 16-19).

12. Other possible categories of competition are, of course, animals against animals as seen in horse racing or animals against an artificial animal as seen in dog racing. As noted by Weiss: "When animals or machines race, the speed offers indirect testimony to men's excellence as trainers, coaches, riders, drivers and the like—and thus primarily to an excellence in human leadership, judgment, strategy, and tactics" (1967, p. 22).

team; and as an individual or team member against an "ideal" standard (e.g., an attempt to set an individual and/or team record for the course).[13]

IC. "Physical skill, strategy, and chance." Roberts and Sutton-Smith suggest that the various games of the world can be classified:

> . . . on the basis of outcome attributes: (1) games of *physical skill*, in which the outcome is determined by the players' motor activities; (2) games of *strategy*, in which the outcome is determined by rational choices among possible courses of action; and (3) games of *chance*, in which the outcome is determined by guesses or by some uncontrolled artifact such as a die or wheel (Roberts and Sutton-Smith, 1962, p. 166).

Examples of relatively pure forms of competitive activities in each of these categories are weight-lifting contests, chess matches, and crap games, respectively. Many, if not most, games are, however, of a mixed nature. Card and board games, for instance, generally illustrate a combination of strategy and chance. Whereas most sports reflect a combination of strategy and physical skill. Although chance is also associated with sport, its role in determining the outcome of a contest is generally held to a minimum in order that the winning side can attribute its victory to merit rather than to a fluke of nature. Rather interestingly it appears that a major role of chance in sport is to insure equality. For example, the official's flip of a coin before the start of a football game randomly determines what team will receive the kickoff and from what respective side of the field; and similarly the drawing of numbers by competitors in track and swimming is an attempt to assure them equal opportunity of getting assigned a given lane.

ID. "Physical prowess." Having discussed the characteristics which sports share in common with games in general, let us turn to an account of the major attribute which distinguishes sports in particular from games in general. We observe that sports can be distinguished from games by the fact that they demand the demonstration of physical prowess. By the phrase "the demonstration of physical prowess" we mean the employment of developed physical skills and abilities within the context of gross physical activity to conquer an opposing object of nature. Although many games require a minimum of physical skill, they do not usually demand the degree of physical skill required by sports. The idea of "developed physical skills" implies much practice and learning and suggests the attainment of a high level of proficiency in one or more

13. The interested reader can find examples of sport classifications in Schiffer (1965), McIntosh (1963), and Sapora and Mitchell (1961).

general physical abilities relevant to sport competition, e.g., strength, speed, endurance, or accuracy.

Although the concept of physical prowess permits sports to be generally differentiated from games, numerous borderline areas exist. For example, can a dart game among friends, a horseshoe pitching contest between husband and wife, or a fishing contest between father and son be considered sport? One way to arrive at an answer to these questions is to define a sport as any highly organized game requiring physical prowess. Thus a dart game with friends, a horseshoe pitching contest between spouses, or a fishing contest between a father and son would not be considered sport; but formally sponsored dart, horseshoe, or fishing tournaments would be legitimately labelled sport. An alternative approach to answering the aforementioned questions, however, is to define a sport as an institutionalized game demanding the demonstration of physical prowess. If one accepts the latter approach, then he will arrive at a different set of answers to the above questions. For this approach views a game as a unique event and sport as an institutional pattern. As Weiss has rather nicely put it:

> A game is an occurrence; a sport is a pattern. The one is in the present, the other primarily past, but instantiated in the present. A sport defines the conditions to which the participants must submit if there is to be a game; a game gives rootage to a set of rules and thereby enables a sport to be exhibited (1967, p. 82).

II. SPORT AS AN INSTITUTIONALIZED GAME

To treat sport as an institutionalized game is to consider sport as an abstract entity. For example, the organization of a football team as described in a rule book can be discussed without reference to the members of any particular team; and the relationships among team members can be characterized without reference to unique personalities or to particular times and places. In treating sport as an institutionalized game we conceive of it as distinctive, enduring patterns of culture and social structure combined into a single complex, the elements of which include values, norms, sanctions, knowledge, and social positions (i.e., roles and statuses).[14] A firm grasp of the meaning of "institutionalization" is necessary for understanding the idea of sport as an institutional pattern, or blueprint if you will, guiding the organization and conduct of given games and sportive endeavors.

---

14. This definition is patterned after one given by Smelser (1963, p. 28).

The formulation of a set of rules for a game or even their enactment on a particular occasion does not constitute a sport as we have conceptualized it here. The institutionalization of a game implies that it has a tradition of past exemplifications and definite guidelines for future realizations. Moreover, in a concrete game situation the form of a particular sport need not reflect all the characteristics represented in its institutional pattern. The more organized a sport contest in a concrete setting, however, the more likely it will illustrate the institutionalized nature of a given sport. A professional baseball game, for example, is a better illustration of the institutionalized nature of baseball than is a sandlot baseball game; but both games are based on the same institutional pattern and thus may both be considered forms of sport. In brief, a sport may be treated analytically in terms of its degree of institutionalization and dealt with empirically in terms of its degree of organization. The latter is an empirical instance of the former.

In order to illustrate the institutionalized nature of sport more adequately, we contrast the organizational, technological, symbolic, and educational spheres of sports with those of games. In doing so we consider both games and sports in their most formalized and organized state. We are aware that there are institutionalized games other than sports which possess characteristics similar to the ones we ascribe to sports, as for example chess and bridge; but we contend that such games are in the minority and in any case are excluded as sports because they do not demand the demonstration of physical prowess.

IIA. "Organizational sphere." For present purposes we rather arbitrarily discuss the organizational aspects of sports in terms of teams, sponsorship, and government.

IIAI. "Teams." Competing sides for most games are usually selected rather spontaneously and typically disband following a given contest. In sports, however, competing groups are generally selected with care and, once membership is established, maintain a stable social organization. Although individual persons may withdraw from such organizations after they are developed, their social positions are taken up by others, and the group endures.[15]

Another differentiating feature is that as a rule sports show a greater degree of role differentiation than games do. Although games often involve several contestants (e.g., poker), the contestants often perform identical activities and thus may be considered to have the same roles

---

15. Huizinga states that the existence of permanent teams is, in fact, the starting-point of modern sport (1955, p. 196).

and statuses. By contrast, in sports involving a similar number of participants (e.g., basketball), each individual or combination of just a few individuals performs specialized activities within the group and may be said to possess a distinct role. Moreover, to the extent that such specialized and differentiated activities can be ranked in terms of some criteria, they also possess different statuses.

IIA2. "Sponsorship." In addition to there being permanent social groups established for purposes of sport competition, there is usually found in the sport realm social groups which act as sponsoring bodies for sport teams. These sponsoring bodies may be characterized as being direct or indirect. Direct sponsoring groups include municipalities which sponsor Little League baseball teams, universities which support collegiate teams, and business corporations which sponsor AAU teams. Indirect sponsoring groups include sporting goods manufacturers, booster clubs, and sport magazines.

IIA3. "Government." While all types of games have at least a modicum of norms and sanctions associated with them, the various forms of sport are set apart from any games by the fact that they have more—and more formal and more institutionalized—sets of these cultural elements. In games rules are often passed down by oral tradition or spontaneously established for a given contest and forgotten afterwards; or, even where codified, they are often simple and few. In sports rules are usually many, and they are formally codified and typically enforced by a regulatory body. There are international organizations governing most sports, and in America there are relatively large social organizations governing both amateur and professional sports. For example, amateur sports in America are controlled by such groups as the NCAA, AAU, and NAIA; and the major professional sports have national commissioners with enforcing officials to police competition.

IIB. "Technological sphere." In a sport, technology denotes the material equipment, physical skills, and body of knowledge which are necessary for the conduct of competition and potentially available for technical improvements in competition. While all types of games require a minimum of knowledge and often a minimum of physical skill and material equipment, the various sports are set apart from many games by the fact that they typically require greater knowledge and involve higher levels of physical skill and necessitate more material equipment. The technological aspects of a sport may be dichotomized into those which are intrinsic and those which are extrinsic. Intrinsic technological aspects of a sport consist of the physical skills, knowledge, and equipment which are required for the conduct of a given contest *per se*. For example, the intrinsic technology of football includes: (a) the equipment necessary for the game—field, ball, uniform, etc.; (b) the repertoire of physical skills necesary for the game—running, passing, kicking, blocking, tackling, etc.; and (c) the knowledge necessary for the game —rules, strategy, etc. Examples of extrinsic technological elements associated with football include: (a) physical equipment such as stadium, press facilities, dressing rooms, etc.; (b) physical skills such as possessed by coaches, cheer leaders, and ground crews; and (c) knowledge such as possessed by coaches, team physicians, and spectators.

IIC. "Symbolic sphere." The symbolic dimension of a sport includes elements of secrecy, display, and ritual. Huizinga contends that play "promotes the formation of social groupings which tend to surround themselves with secrecy and to stress their difference from the common world by disguise or other means" (1955, p. 13). Caillois criticizes his contention and states to the contrary that "play tends to remove the very nature of the mysterious." He further observes that "when the secret, the mask or the costume fulfills a sacramental function one can be sure that not play, but an institution is involved" (1961, p. 4).

Somewhat ambivalently we agree with both writers. On the one hand, to the extent that Huizinga means by "secrecy" the act of making distinctions between "play life" and "ordinary life," we accept his proposition that groups engaged in playful competition surround themselves with secrecy. On the other hand, to the extent that he means by "secrecy" something hidden from others, we accept Caillois's edict that an institution and not play is involved.

IIC1. The latter type of secrecy might well be called "sanctioned secrecy" in sports, for there is associated with many forms of sport competition rather clear norms regarding approved clandestine behavior. For example, football teams are permitted to set up enclosed practice fields, send out scouts to spy on opposing teams, and exchange a limited number of game films revealing the strategies of future opponents. Other kinds of clandestine action such as slush funds established for coaches and gambling on games by players are not always looked upon with such favor.[16]

IIC2. A thorough reading of Huizinga leads one to conclude that what he means by secrecy is best discussed in terms of display and ritual. He points out, for example, that "the 'differentness' and secrecy of play are most vividly expressed in 'dressing up'" and states that the higher forms of play are "a contest *for* something or a representation *of* something"—adding that "representation means display" (1955, p. 13). The "dressing-up" element of play noted by Huizinga is certainly characteristic of most sports. Perhaps it is carried to its greatest height in

16. Our discussion of "sanctioned secrecy" closely parallels Johnson's discussion of "official secrecy" in bureaucracies (1960, pp. 295-296).

bullfighting, but it is not absent in some of the less overt forms of sport. Veblen writes:

> It is noticeable, for instance, that even very mild-mannered and matter-of-fact men who go out shooting are apt to carry an excess of arms and accoutrements in order to impress upon their own imagination the seriousness of their undertaking. These huntsmen are also prone to a histrionic, prancing gait and to an elaborate exaggeration of the motions, whether of stealth or of onslaught, involved in their deeds of exploit (1934, p. 256).

A more recent account of "dressing-up" and display in sports has been given by Stone (1955), who treats display as spectacle and as a counterforce to play. Stone asserts that the tension between the forces of play and display constitute an essential component of sport. The following quotation gives the essence of his account:

> Play and dis-play are precariously balanced in sport, and, once that balance is upset, the whole character of sport in society may be affected. Furthermore, the spectacular element of sport, may, as in the case of American professional wrestling, destroy the game. The rules cease to apply, and the "cheat" and the "spoilsport" replace the players.
>
> The point may be made in another way. The spectacle is predictable and certain; the game, unpredictable and uncertain. Thus spectacular display may be reckoned from the outset of the performance. It is announced by the appearance of the performers—their physiques, costumes, and gestures. On the other hand, the spectacular play is solely a function of the uncertainty of the game (pp. 261-62 in Larrabee and Meyershon). (Stone, 1955, p. 98).

In a somewhat different manner another sociologist, Erving Goffman, has analyzed the factors of the uncertainty of a game and display. Concerning the basis of "fun in games" he states that "mere uncertainty of outcome is not enough to engross the players" (1961, p. 68) and suggests that a successful game must combine "sanctioned display" with problematic outcome. By display Goffman means that "games give the players an opportunity to exhibit attributes valued in the wider social world, such as dexterity, strength, knowledge, intelligence, courage, and self-control" (*Ibid.*). Thus for Goffman display represents spectacular play involving externally relevant attributes, while for Stone display signifies spectacular exhibition involving externally non-relevant attributes with respect to the game situation.

IIC3. Another concept related to display and spectacle and relevant to sports is that of ritual. According to Leach, "ritual denotes those aspects of prescribed formal behavior which have no direct technological consequences" (1964, p. 607). Ritual may be distinguished from spectacle by the fact that it generally has a greater element of drama and is less ostentatious and more serious. "Ritual actions are 'symbolic' in that they assert something about the state of affairs, but they are not necessarily purposive: i.e., the performer of ritual does not necessarily seek to alter the state of affairs" (*Ibid.*). Empirically ritual can be distinguished from spectacle by the fact that those engaged in ritual express an attitude of solemnity toward it, an attitude which they do not direct toward spectacle.

Examples of rituals in sport are the shaking of hands between team captains before a game, the shaking of hands between coaches after a game, the singing of the national anthem before a game, and the singing of the school song at the conclusion of a game.[17]

IID. "Educational sphere." The educational sphere focuses on those activities related to the transmission of skills and knowledge to those who lack them. Many if not most people learn to play the majority of socially preferred games in an informal manner. That is, they acquire the required skills and knowledge associated with a given game through the casual instruction of friends or associates. On the other hand, in sports, skills and knowledge are often obtained by means of formal instruction. In short, the educational sphere of sports is institutionalized, whereas in most games it is not. One reason for this situation is the fact that sports require highly developed physical skills which games often do not; to achieve proficiency requires long hours of practice and qualified instruction, i.e., systematized training. Finally, it should be pointed out that associated with the instructional personnel of sport programs are a number of auxiliary personnel such as managers, physicians, and trainers—a situation not commonly found in games.

III. SPORT AS A SOCIAL INSTITUTION

Extending our notion of sport as an institutional pattern still further, we note that in its broadest sense, the term sport supposes a social institution. Schneider writes that the term institution:

> . . . denotes an aspect of social life in which distinctive value-orientations and interests, centering upon large and important social concern . . . generate or are accompanied by distinctive modes of social interaction. Its use emphasizes "important" social phenomena; relationships of "strategic structural significance" (1964, p. 338).

17. For an early sociological treatment of sport, spectacle, exhibition, and drama, see Sumner (1960, pp. 467-501). We note in passing that some writers consider the totality of sport as a ritual; see especially Fromm (1955, p. 132) and Beisser (1967, pp. 148-151 and pp. 214-225).

We argue that the magnitude of sport in the Western world justifies its consideration as a social institution. As Boyle succinctly states:

> Sport permeates any number of levels of contemporary society, and it touches upon and deeply influences such disparate elements as status, race relations, business life, automotive design, clothing styles, the concept of the hero, language, and ethical values. For better or worse it gives form and substance to much in American life (1963, pp. 3-4).

When speaking of sport as a social institution, we refer to the sport order. The sport order is composed of all organizations in society which organize, facilitate, and regulate human action in sport situations. Hence, such organizations as sporting goods manufacturers, sport clubs, athletic teams, national governing bodies for amateur and professional sports, publishers of sport magazines, etc., are part of the sport order. For analytical purposes four levels of social organization within the sport order may be distinguished: namely, the primary, technical, managerial, and corporate levels.[18] Organizations at the primary level permit face-to-face relationships among all members and are characterized by the fact that administrative leadership is not formally delegated to one or more persons or positions. An example of a social organization associated with sport at the primary level is an informally organized team in a sandlot baseball game.

Organizations at the technical level are too large to permit simultaneous face-to-face relationships among their members but small enough so that every member knows of every other member. Moreover, unlike organizations at the primary level, organizations at the technical level officially designate administrative leadership positions and allocate individuals to them. Most scholastic and collegiate athletic teams, for example, would be classified as technical organizations with coaches and athletic directors functioning as administrative leaders.

At the managerial level organizations are too large for every member to know every other member but small enough so that all members know one or more of the administrative leaders of the organization. Some of the large professional ball clubs represent social organizations related to sport at the managerial level.

Organizations at the corporate level are characterized by bureaucracy: they have centralized authority, a hierarchy of personnel, and protocol and procedural emphases; and they stress the rationalization of operations and impersonal relationships. A number of the major gov-

---

18. Our discussion of these four levels is similar to Caplow's treatment of small, medium, large, and giant organizations (Caplow, 1964, pp. 26-27).

erning bodies of amateur and professional sport at the national and international levels illustrate sport organizations of the corporate type.

In summary, the sport order is composed of the congeries of primary, technical, managerial, and corporate social organizations which arrange, facilitate, and regulate human action in sport situations. The value of the concept lies in its use in macro-analyses of the social significance of sport. We can make reference to the sport order in a historical and/or comparative perspective. For example, we can speak of the sport order of nineteenth-century America or contrast the sport order of Russia with that of England.

IV. SPORT AS A SOCIAL SITUATION

As was just noted, the sport order is composed of all social organizations which organize, facilitate, and regulate human action in sport situations. Human "action consists of the structures and processes by which human beings form meaningful intentions and, more or less successfully, implement them in concrete situations" (Parsons, 1966, p. 5). A sport situation consists of any social context wherein individuals are involved with sport. And the term situation denotes "the total set of objects, whether persons, collectivities, culture objects, or himself to which an actor responds" (Friedsam, 1964, p. 667). The set of objects related to a specific sport situation may be quite diverse, ranging from the elements of the social and physical environments of a football game to those associated with two sportniks[19] in a neighborhood bar arguing the pros and cons of the manager of their local baseball team.

Although there are many kinds of sport situations, most if not all may be conceptualized as social systems. A social system may be simply defined as "a set of persons with an identifying characteristic plus a set of relationships established among these persons by interaction" (Caplow, 1964, p. 1). Thus the situation represented by two teams contesting within the confines of a football field, the situation presented by father and son fishing from a boat, and the situation created by a golf pro giving a lesson to a novice each constitutes a social system.

Social systems of prime concern to the sport sociologist are those which directly or indirectly relate to a game occurrence. That is to say, a sport sociologist is often concerned with why man gets involved in sport and what effect his involvement has on other aspects of his social environment. Involvement in a social system related to a game occurence can be analyzed in terms of degree and kind of involvement.

19. The term sportnik refers to an avid fan or sport addict.

Degree of involvement can be assessed in terms of frequency, duration, and intensity of involvement. The combination of frequency and duration of involvement may be taken as an index of an individual's "investment" in a sport situation, while intensity of involvement may be considered an index of an individual's "personal commitment" to a given sport situation.[20]

Kind of involvement can be assessed in terms of an individual's relationship to the "means of production" of a game. Those having direct or indirect access to the means of production are considered "actually involved" and are categorized as "producers." Those lacking access to the means of production are considered "vicariously involved" and are categorized as "consumers." We have tentatively identified three categories of producers and three classes of consumers.

Producers may be characterized as being primary, secondary, or tertiary with respect to the production of a game. "Primary producers" are the contestants who play the primary roles in the production of a game, not unlike the roles of actors in the production of a play. "Secondary producers" consist of those individuals, who while not actually competing in a sport contest, perform tasks which have direct technological consequences for the outcome of a game. Secondary producers include club owners, coaches, officials, trainers, and the like. It may be possible to categorize secondary producers as entrepreneurs, managers, and technicians. "Tertiary producers" consist of those who are actively involved in a sport situation but whose activities have no direct technological consequences for the outcome of a game. Examples of tertiary producers are cheerleaders, band members, and concession workers. Tertiary producers may be classified as service personnel.

Consumers, like producers, are designated as being primary, secondary, or tertiary. "Primary consumers" are those individuals who become vicariously involved in a sport through "live" attendance at a sport competition. Primary consumers may be thought of as "active spectators." "Secondary consumers" consist of those who vicariously involve themselves in a sport as spectators via some form of the mass media, such as radio or television. Secondary consumers may be thought of as "passive spectators." "Tertiary consumers" are those who become vicariously involved with sport other than as spectators. Thus an individual who engages in conversation related to sport or a person who reads the sport section of the newspaper would be classified as a tertiary consumer.

In concluding our discussion of the nature of sport we note that a special type of consumer is the *fan.* A fan is defined as an individual

20. Cf. McCall and Simmons (1966, pp. 171-172).

who has both a high personal investment in and a high personal commitment to a given sport.

REFERENCES

Berne, Eric. *Games People Play*. New York: Grove Press, 1964.

Beisser, Arnold R. *The Madness in Sports*. New York: Appleton-Century-Crofts, 1967.

Boyle, Robert H. *Sport—Mirror of American Life*. Boston: Little, Brown, 1963.

Caillois, Roger. *Man, Play and Games*, tr. Meyer Barash. New York: Free Press, 1961.

Caplow, Theodore. *Principles of Organization*. New York: Harcourt, Brace and World, 1964.

Friedsam. H. J. "Social Situation." in *A Dictionary of the Social Sciences*, edited by Julius Gould and William L. Kolb, p. 667. New York: Free Press. 1964.

Fromm, Eric. *The Sane Society*. New York: Fawcett, 1955.

Goffman, Erving. *Encounters*. Indianapolis: Bobbs-Merrill, 1961.

Huizinga, Johan. *Homo Ludens—A Study of the Play-Element in Culture*. Boston: Beacon Press, 1955.

Johnson, Harry M. *Sociology: A Systematic Introduction*. New York: Harcourt, Brace, 1960.

Kahn, Roger. "Money, Muscles—and Myths," *Nation*, CLXXXV (July 6, 1957), 9-11.

Leach, E. R. "Ritual," in *A Dictionary of the Social Sciences*, ed. Julius Gould and William L. Kolb. New York: Free Press, 1964.

Lüschen, Günther. "The Interdependence of Sport and Culture." Paper presented at the National Convention of the American Association for Health, Physical Education and Recreation, Las Vegas, 1967.

McCall, George J., and J. L. Simmons, *Identities and Interactions*. New York: Free Press, 1966.

McIntosh, Peter C. *Sports in Society*. London: C. A. Watts, 1963.

Piaget, Jean. *Play, Dreams and Imitation in Childhood*, tr. C. Gattegno and F. M. Hodgson. New York: W. W. Norton, 1951.

Riezler, Kurt. "Play and Seriousness," *The Journal of Philosophy*, XXXVIII (1941), 505-517.

Roberts, John M., and others. "Games in Culture," *American Anthropologist*, LXI (1959), 597-605.

———, and Brian Sutton-Smith. "Child Training and Game Involvement," *Ethnology*, I (1962), 166-185.

Sapora, Allen V., and Elmer D. Mitchell. *The Theory of Play and Recreation*. New York: Ronald Press, 1961.

Schiffer, Donald. "Sports," *Colliers Encyclopedia* 21 (1965): 449-460.

Schneider, Louis. "Institution," in *A Dictionary of the Social Sciences*, ed. Julius Gould and William L. Kolb. New York: Free Press, 1964.

Smelser, Neil J. *The Sociology of Economic Life*. Englewood Cliffs, N. J.: Prentice-Hall, 1963.

Stone, Gregory P. "American Sports: Play and Display," *Chicago Review*, IX (Fall 1955), 83-100.

Sumner, William Graham. *Folkways.* New York: Mentor, 1960.

Torkildsen, George E. "Sport and Culture." M. S. thesis, University of Wisconsin, 1957.

Veblen, Thorstein. *The Theory of the Leisure Class.* New York: Modern Library, 1934.

Weiss, Paul. "Sport: A Philosophical Study." Unpublished manuscript, 1967.

SPORT STYLE AND SOCIAL MODES

Jan Felshin

The themes of sport are obvious and appreciable. As an ordered domain of emphasis on contesting and performing excellence, sport is understandable as a symbolic form of human culture. The actions and interactions of sport translate ambiguous aspirations into clear frameworks for achievement. The structure of each sport serves as both symbol and summary for some dimension of human motivation to affirm ability and document striving. The sum of all sport is represented by an attractive and endlessly available equation of means and ends.

The endurance of sport rests on the integrity of the reductive equation that defines the ends and specifies the means and the psychodramatic human elaboration of the relationship between the rules and outcomes. Logic might prompt the deployment of armored tanks to carry a football over the goal line or the scheduling of a pitching machine in the rotation order, but the rationality of sport depends on different sources.

Sport has symbolic power because essential testing and refinement of skill and mastery are clarified as human challenges. Sport has aesthetic and thematic compulsion because expressive modes of performing and contesting are significant and valued.

The symbolic summaries of sports represent and emphasize what being a tennis player or golfer or a gymnast means. Each structure, as a set of rules, impels an attitude toward task and self and others within the limits that pertain and in relation to the evaluative criterion of completion. There is a well-worn script for every contest and memories of those who have played the roles before, but the compelling fascination of sport lies

From *JOPER* (March 1975):31-34.

in the immediacy of each experiential reenactment of the psychodrama. As theater, sport relies on characterization for the infusion of excitement into a plot of human desire and struggle. Sport translates simple themes into complex dimensions of style and, in so doing, provides dramatic satisfaction. Style may also suggest meanings beyond the scope of sport, and when it does, the complexity of social themes is added to the drama of sport.

It is tempting to believe that there was a bygone time when sport was "pure" and that only contemporary social malaise has yielded corruption. In truth, the elemental nature of sport is rooted in social modification and interpretation. The persistence of sport as an expression of human style may be testimony to the strength of the dramatic form; the ubiquitousness of the social phenomenon raises the suspicion that sport functions to represent stylized modes of human meaning and fulfillment.

STYLIZATION

In *Against Interpretation,* Susan Sontag identified the distinctive feature of art as "something like an excitation, a phenomenon of commitment, judgment in a state of thralldom or captivation," and suggested that this yields knowledge as "an experience of the form or style of knowing something."[1] In sport, because the focus is on action rather than perception, the experience of style refers to the experience of *being* something.

The sport equation presents the elements of encounter; experience intensifies and lends luminosity to the visions of human capacity formulated within each encounter. Every choice to enter the *participational* domain of sport is impelled by the magical possibility of actualizing dreams of glory. Sport enhances experience by requiring and rewarding stylistic decisions about how to be and how best to triumph. An ambivalent style does not serve themes of prowess and excellence; the athlete must perceive the cruciality of action and exhibit strategic sensibility. Style is manifest in the expressive decisions of sport: the long pass or short yardage? sacrifice or hit away? the five iron or the nine? the short serve or the long? the baseline or the net? Glory resides within the risk: the interception, the fake, the smash, the shot for goal. Sport fosters style in a crucible of heightened self-awareness.

The pervasive model of sport is part of a highly organized and *presentational* context. Both individual players and specific contests bear the weight of institutional perspectives. Every run batted in is, finally, less

1. Sontag, Susan, *Against Interpretation* (New York: Dell Publishing Co., Inc., 1969), p. 30.

meaningful as part of the outcome of a game than it is as part of a cosmic schema that includes the World Series and the recorded history of baseball, as well as one's statistical lifetime.

The psychodramatic equation of sport is mitigated by the sociocultural hypothesis of commercial technological, and communicationally mediated contests. As Gary Giddens says, "Every society has its cultural as well as political elite, based not on power or wealth but on excellence. It is the vulgarization of elite achievements which makes up most of pop culture."[2] The social presentation of sport depends upon stylization and hence becomes "pop" in the sense that the media as well as the host of nonplaying, nonproductive personnel involved in sport all direct their efforts toward enhancing the attraction of certain rituals and symbols of sport.

Sport is vulgarized because the most clearly communicative symbols are emphasized in the process of popularization, and their essential relevance to sport is not the criterion for selecting them. In this way, associations are made between excellent and highly paid athletes, between performance in a game and cumulative statistical records, between the significance of contesting and the paid attendance or the television coverage or progress on a path toward playoffs. The variables of the sociocultural hypothesis as it affects football, for instance, foster allusions to the Super Bowl during the exhibition season and encourage the choosing of teams for the various college bowls long before the season has ended.

To the extent that sport can be understood only when it is stylized, popularized, and packaged to appeal to a range of realities of human nature, it serves social ends. In his analysis of desire, William N. Gass comments, "The trick, and it is a trick, a process of covering up, of masking of the original desire without retaining its identity . . . the original end, the culminating act of what has become a rather lengthy activity, may be pushed out altogether, the initial purpose forgotten entirely, and the whole form emptied of significance." He concludes, "Finally, I should say that while every ethic involves and specifies a style, stylization alone makes nothing moral."[3]

In sport, stylization displaces the human equation; the morality of the sensibility of experience gives way to the amorality of external measures of outcome or success. Contract signing and player drafts and trades are given the same stylization credence as performance. Athletic style falters in relation to a business ethic wherein a field goal kicker is embarrassed

2. Giddins, Gary, "On Elitest Culture," *The Village Voice*, October 24, 1974, p. 77.
3. Gass, William H., "The Stylization of Desire," *The New York Review of Books,* February 25, 1971, pp. 36, 37.

by winning a game for a team because the victory represents the more serious loss of a first draft choice. Stylization confuses personal style through a juxtaposition of goals of sport, identity, and social image. When sport encounters become ritualized interactions, the images created by them are affected by socialized agreements.

Style remains the expressive mode in sport, but the self-awareness of identity becomes a self-conscious process of evaluating images and assuming stereotypic characteristics. The psychodrama of sport can be a melodrama of forces that have more to do with social values than contesting themes. Stylization, of course, is never complete, and Joe Namath did triumph over John Unitas in a faded Super Bowl, and, so far, neither computers nor sportscasters predict outcomes with accuracy.

SOCIALIZATION

Sport, unlike many symbolic forms, tends to be stable and functions in societal life as an important aspect of human community and a feedback system for both commitment and consciousness. The characteristics of durability, clarity, and intensity that attend sport render it particularly attractive as a model for socialization.

Socialization themes, as norms and values, may be inherent in sport or promoted by and through sport. They may emanate from participational or presentational contexts of sport, and they may emphasize psycho or sociodramatic elements of experience. The sport/society relationship is multidimensional and dissonant. Sport must, in some way, be held separate, for the bounded order of time and space is an essential characteristic of the phenomenon itself. At the same time, it is clear that sport is, indeed, a "mirror" for social life and values. The logical dissonance of a socialized attitude like racism influencing choices in the ordered meritocracy of sport is thus made possible, and it is possible for baseball to accommodate the antithetical assumptions of a players' strike for better contracts and the major leagues exemption from anti-trust laws.

Sport also functions as a repository for some idealized values of the society, and George Steinbrenner, the principal owner of the New York Yankees, was suspended from any connection with the club for two years because of illegal contributions to a political campaign by Bowie Kuhn, a commissioner of baseball, whose powers are appropriately symbolic ones. This event is consonant with a vision of sport that permitted another commissioner, Pete Rozelle, to threaten the Jets' quarterback with suspension unless he sold his interest in a nightclub and encouraged a nation to applaud when Muhammed Ali was stripped of a heavyweight boxing title without a punch being thrown.

Somehow, the many facets of the sport/society relationship foster the confusion of values about each; sport socializes and sport is socialized. The stylization and socialization of sport interact at the juncture of values that are common to them both. The social potency of sport is manifest in the modes of style and meaning that are affirmed.

SOCIAL MODES

The dramatic equation of sports yields a stylistic and social formula for manhood. In social terms, athletic and masculine models are interchangeable. Successful athletes can identify with cologne and deodorant and appear on television in pantyhose in a society where the serious suggestion is offered that if boys learn cooking in school they will become homosexuals. Sport confirms the social assumption that doing and being, asserting and overcoming, striving and fulfilling aspirations are the appropriate modes and motivations of men.

Furthermore, the affirmations that sport offers are visible and significant; the social feedback of sport is invested with the connotations of what ought to be as well as what is. At the same time, sport is emphasized in terms of the importance of the feedback it provides. A recent series of advertisements by the Wilson Sporting Goods Company focuses on fathers and sons and sport, and includes the statement, "I'm not talking about the game, son, I'm talking about life. But it's life that the game is all about." In another, where a father is identified as teacher and idol, it is suggested, "And one of the ways this teacher and idol knows and also explores to help his son reach manhood and maturity simultaneously is sports."

The dual concept of sport as a representation of masculine assertion and the importance of the assertion of masculinity purveyed by sport expresses the socialized/socializing functions of sport. The rituals of sport are *rites* of manhood. As Eugene Bianchi says of big-time football, "Through these autumnal rites of passage, we avidly introduce our young to the saving knowledge of adult life: brutality, aggressive competition, profit-greed, male chauvinism, and the discipline of dull conformity to the status quo."[4] As rites, the modes of sport must be stylized to emphasize their relationship to manhood; the styles of sport express an ethic of competition, power, dominance, and male bonding. "Sports offer some insight regarding both power concepts and human relationships. Football and war as highly compatible activities is a timeless metaphor and a boring one."[5] Only the cluster of masculine values as the source for styli-

4. Bianchi, Eugene, "Pigskin Piety," *Christianity and Crisis,* February 21, 1972, p. 31.
5. Riley, Clayton, "Did O. J. Dance?" *Ms.*, March, 1974, p. 97.

zation explains how the inherent promise of the joy of the sport experience is translated into demands for the demonstration of militarism and power that characterize contemporary sport.

Harry Edwards suggests that "the conditions of American sport constitute a fundamental obstacle to the achievement of women's equality in American society."[6] Writing in *The Gay Alternative*, Jeffrey Escoffier says:

> A major obstacle to men's liberation (and therefore to women's and gay liberation) is that masculinism is afraid of and destructive of the feminine in other men and in oneself. Team sports are not inherently oppressive, but as long as they are important institutions in the socialization of "butch" men, they remain as obstacles to human liberation. The masculinism and exploitive commercialism of sports are supported by an economic system which requires competitive, aggressive, and objectifying men.[7]

Clayton Riley comments, "The thought of being a woman so terrifies most American males, athletes and nonathletes alike, that any other condition seems preferable—even death, which can at least be considered an 'honorable' state." He also identifies the Lombardian ethic as an important element in the conceptualization of the uses of power by the male, and comments, "Winning is part of an equation that is only completed by concomitant defeat. Winning a woman, by any other name, for example, is about defeating women."[8]

Contemporary sport stylizes social modes and reflects conceptions of social roles. "It is the male in our society, not the female, who expects Olympic performances of himself as a sexual partner."[9] "The male athlete, be he hetero- or homo-sexual, thinks of himself as the least feminized being in the universe."[10] Both men and women, socialized to believe in sport as a masculine domain, conspire to maintain the mythology. Jill Johnston, writing of a visit to a college campus, says,

> . . . the girls are girls and the boys are boys. The boys are jocks and the girls who play hockey or major in physical education which is the big thing there are trying to look like girls. The boys keep them in line by calling them jocks if they don't. The girls keep each other in line by voting for their home-coming queen along with the jocks.[11]

6. Edwards, Harry, "Desegregating Sexist Sport," *Intellectual Digest, November,* 1972, p. 82.
7. Escoffier, Jeffrey, "Sports and Sexuality," *The Gay Alternative,* Summer, 1974, p. 27.
8. Riley, *op. cit.,* p. 97.
9. Shephard, Martin, "Memoirs of an Ex-Sex Therapist," *The Village Voice,* October 31, 1974, p. 39.
10. Riley, *op. cit.,* p. 98.
11. Johnston, Jill, "Before the Jocks The Dykes—Before the Rains The Birds," *The Village Voice,* October 24, 1974, p. 49.

Doubtless there is no dearth of young women as would-be cheerleaders on the campus either. Elizabeth Janeway says of woman's subordination to man, "We can tell that it is important for her to *choose* submission. . . . What she is offered is the knowledge that by her submission she does what the man cannot do alone; she bestows on him his full status."[12]

It is apparent that women must serve as co-conspirators, for masculinity derives conceptual strength from opposing definitions of femininity. The superiority of modes of masculine assertion derives sustenance from the supportive activities and admiration of women.

In New Jersey, before Williamsport gave in, the bumper strips read, "Save Little League," and it was clear that more was at stake than the accommodation of a few ten-year-old girls who wanted to pitch or play the outfield. The symbolic rites of Little League were more threatened by the encroachment of women than they were by the victories of Taiwan, but only the "foreigners" were successfully excluded in the power plays to sustain a satisfying ethos for socializing chauvinist piglets.

The only human rite reserved by gender is that of giving birth, and it serves as initiation only to motherhood. Women's rights depend upon the annihilation of men's rites, for sexism endures in direct proportion to the strength of the assumptions of power and importance as qualities inherent in male activities. Because those assumptions accrue from the notion of "male activities," they obtain only as long as women are successfully excluded or kept in subsidiary, separate, and subordinate roles. Women's participation itself serves as a liberating statement. Every woman who wants to do something, who seeks access and involvement in an active mode, is a feminist—and becomes a humanist, too, in creating a less restrictive consciousness of the meanings of activities.

Sport, as we know it, is indeed in jeopardy. The version of sport stylized to represent proof and power of manhood cannot endure the simple truth of Cyndi Meserve's presence on the Pratt Institute's NCAA sanctioned basketball team. The rites of spring, 1975, are unalterably changed for all the boys and girls who do or do not answer the call for Little League tryouts.

Two days after Independence Day, on July 6, 1974, the National Federation of State High School Associations presented the following among its resolutions:

> NOW, THEREFORE, BE IT RESOLVED, that the National Council reaffirm its statement of philosophy advocating interscholastic athletic com-

12. Janeway, Elizabeth, *Man's World, Women's Place: A Study in Social Mythology* (New York: Dell Publishing Co., Inc., 1971), p. 48.

petition for girls be limited to girls' teams competing against girls' teams in programs which have been feminized in order to encourage girls to develop their leadership abilities.

Obviously, there is widespread resolve to maintain a sexist status quo for sport, but it is already too late. In Pennsylvania, for instance, new state regulations, effective July 1, 1975, state that, "No rules may be imposed that exclude girls from trying out for, practicing with, and competing on boys' interscholastic teams." The same regulations order "separate but equal" sports programs for girls and specify equality in relation to facilities, coaching and instruction, scheduling, numbers of activities, equipment, supplies and services, and funding appropriate to sport.

Women, less socialized to power than men, seek equal rights, but are drawn to the experiential style of sport. Speaking for blacks, Clayton Riley speaks for women, too:

> . . . for blacks, the movement, the act, the *fact* of living whole can be contained in an instant like that. It's about going where you are supposed to remain, about leaving your place, compelling your body to take you there, up high, outside or way past.
> Understand it as power, personally designed and executed, the ability to assert one's will to make something physically beautiful happen. A resonant, nearly cosmic encounter with action. To those denied other accesses to power, here is life.[13]

Men and women and their sport, style, and social modes are all vulnerable to contemporary changes in consciousness. Without an all-male cast, the themes of sport promise a more creative and humane psychodrama.

13. Riley, *op. cit.*, p. 96.

SYMBOLIC FORMS OF MOVEMENT:
THE OLYMPIC GAMES

ELEANOR METHENY

Today it is commonly conceded that men interpret their perceptions of reality in three ways. They may attempt to describe a perceivable form in terms of the composition of its substantial elements. They may recognize it as a representative of a general category of forms, as denoted by the name commonly assigned to it. And they may interpret it as a symbol or symbolic form that represents some meaningful conception of human interaction with the universe, other than that denoted by the common name of the form. The present analysis of sports competition is patterned along these lines.

For the purposes of this analysis, *human behavior* is construed in terms of interaction between a person and the universe. The term *personal behavior* is reserved for those forms of interaction that occur when a person knowingly makes an attempt to organize his own behavior in some self-chosen way. The concept denoted by the term *sports competition* is largely defined as participation in the Olympic Games.

I—THE CHARACTERISTICS OF SPORT COMPETITION

In general terms, the characteristics common to all forms of *sports competition* may be described with reference to four principles: a per-

From *Connotations of Movement in Sport and Dance* (Dubuque, Iowa: Wm. C. Brown Company Publishers, 1965), pp. 35-42. Reprinted by permission. Adapted from a paper presented at the Fourth Session of the International Olympic Academy, Olympia, Greece, August, 1964. Original text published in *Report of The Fourth Summer Session of The International Olympic Academy*, Athens, Greece, 1964.

sonal attempt to overcome inertia, finite limits, nonconsequential effect, and human control.

The Principle of Overcoming Inertia: All forms of sports competition are structured by a personal attempt to overcome the inertia of some specific organization of mass. The human objective is stated in terms of causing the mass to move through space and time in some way determined by the person. Within this general structure, the contest may be organized in three different ways:

1. *The person attempts to overcome the inertia of his own body mass.*

In all forms of foot-racing, broad jumping, swimming, platform diving, and free exercise, the contestant organizes his personal forces into an attempt to move his own body about within his milieu. In the hurdle races, high jump, and gymnastic events, he introduces certain man-made obstacles into the situation. In the pole vault, he erects a man-made barrier, and then increases his own mechanical advantage by applying his personal forces through a man-made device. Similarly, in springboard diving, skiing, ice skating, cycling, canoeing and sculling, he utilizes man-made devices to support his body and to amplify his own propelling powers. The team forms of this type of contest are represented by the relays and the two-or-more-man aquatic events. In all of these events, however, the outcome of the contest is measured in units that describe the displacement of his own body in space and time.

2. *The person attempts to overcome the inertia of some external unit of mass.*

In the shot put, the discuss throw, javelin throw, hammer throw, and weight-lifting, the person attempts to overcome the inertia of some external form of mass by direct application of force with his own body. In golf and bowling, which are not included in the Olympic list of events, the application of force is effected through a man-made implement. In the shooting events, including archery, the effective forces inhere in the man-made device, and the contest is structured as an attempt to utilize these man-made organizations of energy to overcome the inertia of another object. The team forms of this type of contest are represented by golf and bowling, in which teams of two or more persons make sequential attempts to achieve the objective, with each man performing individually within the sequence. However, in all of these events the outcome of the contest is measured in units that describe the displacement of the specified mass in space and time.

The equestrian events employ a nonhuman form of life as the inertial object, the outcome of the contest being determined by the extent to which the horse is induced to move in accordance with the rider's intent.

3. *Two persons, or two teams, designated as opponents, attempt to overcome the inertia in some external form of mass while opposing the efforts of the other.*

In wrestling, boxing, and judo, the specified mass is the body of the opponent, and the outcome is determined by the relative displacement of his body in space. In fencing, the specified mass is still the body of the opponent, but a spatial barrier is maintained between the opponents; an arm-extending device is used to bridge this barrier; and the outcome is determined by a physically inconsequential touch on some presumably vulnerable spot on the opponent's body. There are no team forms of these events in which the objective is to physically or symbolically subdue the opponent.

In handball, squash, badminton, and tennis, which are not included in the Olympic list, the inertial mass is a small object. The spatial barrier between the opponents is extended, and neither person intentionally touches the other's body or weapon. In handball, force is applied through the person's hand; in squash, badminton, and tennis, the force is applied through a light implement; and in badminton and tennis, the spatial barrier is maintained by a restraining net that serves to divide the playing area into two equal parts. The team forms of these events are organized as doubles, with the partners cooperating in the attempt to cause the inertial object to move through space in some specified way.

No new principles are introduced in the team sports, but the conception of cooperative effort is extended to teams of five or more persons. In all of these sports the team attempts to direct the movement of some relatively small and light object in space, either by applying force to it with some part of the player's body—as in basketball, soccer, water polo, and volleyball—or with the aid of a man-man device, as in field hockey and ice hockey. In all of these games, intentional body contact between players is prohibited by the rules. In volleyball, such contact is prevented by a restraining net. In American football, both body contact and an attempt to subdue the opponent physically are permitted and encouraged by the rules.

The Principle of Finite Limits: Within the infinite reaches of the universe, sports competition is intentionally confined to a small segment of reality, the limits of which are defined in finite terms, as follows:

Time: The circumstances which will determine the beginning and end of the sports competition, as such, are specified.

Space: The spatial boundaries of the area within which the sports competition, as such, may occur are clearly established, and other persons are excluded from this space during the appointed time.

Mass: The dimensions and substantial characteristics of all material objects utilized in the competition are specified.

Objective: The objective of the competition is defined in terms of the displacement of finite units of mass within the limits of time and space.

Outcome: Some way of quantifying relative degrees of achievement of this objective is designated.

The Principle of Nonconsequential Effect: When the sports competition is terminated by the finite limitations imposed on time, space, and mass, the contest area and all material objects in it are immediately restored to their precompetition state. The competitors leave the area. The contested inertial objects and all man-made devices used in the competition are taken away to be stored or discarded. The area is then made available for use by other persons. Thus, except for incidental deformation of the masses involved, no tangible evidence of the competitive effort remains, and the contest has no substantial continuing effect on the competitors, the spectators, or their environmental milieu.

The Principle of Human Control: The man-made rules that establish the finite limits of time, space, mass, objective, and outcome also impose certain limitations on the personal conduct of the competitors. Within the Olympic Games, the conditions imposed by these rules include:

Public Statement of Intent: Each competitor must publicly identify his personal intention to enter the sports competition. Additionally he must testify that he has systematically prepared himself by practice, that he is entering the contest voluntarily and without coercion from other persons, and that he has no expectation of receiving any material reward for his efforts within the competition.

Personal Behavior within the Competition: Forms of personal conduct deemed appropriate within the limits of the competition are defined, and penalties for inappropriate behavior are designated.

Personification of Authority: Authority to enforce the man-made rules, to judge the appropriateness of personal behavior, and to penalize or punish personal transgression is vested in some person not involved in the contest, as such.

II—SPORTS COMPETITION AS A SYMBOLIC FORM

The category of personal behavior called *sports competition* has been characterized as an intentional personal effort to overcome the inertia of mass, conducted under man-made rules that serve to govern personal behavior within a finite segment of reality. This elaborately constructed form of personal interaction with the forces of the universe is essentially futile, in that no tangible or seemingly consequential effect is produced by it. Nonetheless, men attach great value to this seemingly futile effort. It would seem, therefore, that this behavioral form must symbolize some more significant conception of man's interaction with the universe of his existence.

One symbolic interpretation is suggested by the central theme of a contest between man and inertia. In its larger outlines, this contest must be waged continuously by all living organisms within the infinite dimensions of the universe.

Living organisms are brought into being by the action of universal forces. In order to survive within this life-giving universe, the organism must continuously organize its own lesser forces into an attempt to overcome the inertia of the organism's own body masses and the inertia of other forms of mass in its immediate milieu. The penalty for failure to overcome these forms of inertia is death. Thus, life may be construed as a contest between the forces *of* or *in* the living organism and the forces that act *on* it. Human life, as distinguished from animal life, is characterized by full awareness of the inevitability of eventually being destroyed by the forces that brought it into being. Thus the human question is: Why was I born? What is the significance of my life as a man? What consequential effect does my life have on the continuing structure of the universe?

In sports competition, men seem to be answering that question by staging a dramatic demonstration of the effect they *can* have on the universe, as denoted by their ability to overcome the inertial forces of its masses in accord with some human plan. This demonstration is planned on a stage set apart for this purpose, and the finite limits imposed on this time-space area clearly set it apart from the limitless reaches of space and time within which men must attempt to accomplish their significant human purposes. Every act performed within this finite area is ritualized by the imposition of man-made rules. The events enacted in this ritualistic situation resemble the actions men perform within their ongoing attempts to survive within the universe, but there is no expectation that the usual consequences will ensue from them.

It may be noted, however, that the performers are not play-acting. In drama, the performer assumes the role of a person other than himself, and hides his own identity within the illusion he is attempting to create. In sports, the performer calls attention to his own identity as a person as he, literally or figuratively, stands naked before his gods and other men to testify to the extent of his own personal powers. Then, within the ritualized context of the dramatic event, he makes a wholly realistic attempt to actually overcome the inertia of his own body and other real forms of mass.

All drama serves to call attention to some idea about the relationships between man and man within the context of their common relationship to the forces that structure the universe. In sports, this idea deals specifically with some conception of man's personal ability to "move the earth"—or, by extension, with some more comprehensive conception of the performer's power to cope with the physical forces that structure his own earthly existence, within the finite limits of his personal life.

This interpretation is suggested in Homer's description of the funeral games that were held to honor the fallen warrior Patroclus. His comrades had been wrestling with the Trojans for many years; they had thrown spears beyond counting and repeatedly performed every action represented by the games many times over. Nonetheless, in the truce that was called to honor Patroclus, they asked their gods to witness a demonstration of how the warrior had proved his manhood by mastering the forces of mass, space, and time during his all-too-brief life.

This interpretation is re-enforced by the parallels between a man's conception of "my work" and the sports forms he chooses. In Homeric Greece, no man was exempt from heavy manual labor. Even the master of many slaves worked the earth with his own muscular powers, and he used those powers directly in overcoming the forces in other men as he warred against them. These strength-oriented conceptions of human power are represented in all of the oldest events on the Olympic list: wrestling, boxing, the now-discarded pancratium, the foot races, the jumps, shot put, and the discus, javelin, and hammer throws. It may be noted, too, that the right to rule was centered in the strength of one powerful man—as suggested by the fact that none of the team sports were developed during this era.

The earliest forms of the team sports were developed by the peasants of feudal Europe, perhaps as an indication of some emerging sense of the power represented by a group of men, each of whom might be individually at the mercy of a strong ruler. These early team forms involved the inertia of large and heavy objects, and intentional body contact used to physically subdue the opponent. But as the concept of the team was adapted to suit the needs of the emerging class called gentlemen, the fact that these priviliged persons did not labor with their strong muscles is suggested by their preference for smaller and lighter objects that might be manipulated with skillfully-designed implements. Thus, the elements of brute force and bodily contact with the opponent were eliminated from the gentlemanly team sports, and the objective of the contest was focussed on moving symbolic objects with skill rather than with strength.

Similarly, games like tennis, badminton, handball, and squash were developed by gentlemen who prided themselves on their intellectual powers rather than on their muscular strength. This sense of class distinction is associated with these sports as they are played today.

Turning now to the significance attached to the code of personal conduct, as prescribed by man-made rules and judged, rewarded, or punished by some personification of authority. Perhaps the earliest formulation of this code is represented by Hesiod's concept of "the good strife," in which men strive together in mutual respect as they attempt to improve their common human situation. In contrast, Hesiod identified "the bad strife" in which men strike against each other, attempting to establish mastery over the lives of other men even as they might establish personal mastery over the life of an animal. Thus, in "the good strife" men treat each other as partners in a common enterprise; in "the bad strife" they treat each other as animals or things.

The concept of "the good strife" is implicit in the word *competition,* as derived from *cum* and *petere*—literally, *to strive with* rather than *against.* The word *contest* has similar implications, being derived from *con* and *testare*—*to testify with another* rather than *against* him. The concept of "the bad strife" is implicit in the idea of "beating the opponent" as distinguished from "winning the contest."

In the larger context of Greek thought, the code that governs "the good strife" is denoted in the concept of *aidos.* In the English language, it is represented by the term *sportsmanship* or *sportsmanlike behavior.*

These interpretations suggest that sports competition may well symbolize some conception of a self-imposed code of behavior that marks the distinction between men and animals. It seems significant, too, that the earthly power to judge and punish men who violate that code is not vested in the gods, but in man, himself. Thus, men seem to be identifying their own sense of kinship with the gods, who have the ultimate power to judge, reward, and punish men and animals for their earthly behavior.

The concept of the athlete as a god-like being is well represented in the sculptured marble forms that have come down to us from ancient

Greece. It is also expressed in the poetry of the period, as in Pindar's ode to the winner of a boys' wrestling match: "Thing of a day! such is man; a shadow in a dream. Yet when god-given splendor visits him, a bright radiance plays over him, and how sweet is life." The modern athlete's sense of kinship with his gods may be less explicit, but he may still be accorded well-nigh worshipful adoration as an exemplar of superhuman or extraordinary powers.

Thus it would seem that the forms of sports competition embodied in the modern Olympic Games may well symbolize man's conception of himself as a consequential force within the grand design of the universe, as well as each man's conception of his own ability to perform those functions that identify him as a man among men.

BIBLIOGRAPHY

Section A. Theories and Definitions

Avedon, Eliot and Sutton-Smith, Brian. *The Study of Games.* New York: John C. Wiley, 1971.

Caillois, Roger. *Man, Play and Games.* New York: The Free Press of Glencoe, 1961.

Ellis, M. J. *Why People Play.* Englewood Cliffs, N. J.: Prentice-Hall, Inc., 1972.

———. "Play and Its Themes Re-examined," *Parks and Recreation.* vol. VI, no. 8, August 1971.

Erbach, Gunther. "Enlargement of the Sphere of Social Influence of Physical Culture," *International Review of Sport Sociology* 1 (1966):59-73.

Felshin, J. "Sport and Modes of Meaning," *Journal of Health, Physical Education and Recreation,* May 1969.

Gerber, Ellen. *Sport and the Body.* Philadelphia: Lea & Febiger, 1972.

Huizinga, Johan. *Homo Ludens: A Study of the Play Element in Culture.* Boston: Beacon Press, 1950.

Kando, Thomas. *Leisure and Popular Culture in Transition.* St. Louis, Missouri: C. V. Mosby, 1975.

Kane, J. E. and Murray, C. "Suggestions for the Sociological Study of Sports," in *Readings in Physical Education.* London: Physical Education Association, 1966, pp. 111-27.

Kenyon, Gerald S., ed. *Aspects of Contemporary Sport Sociology.* Chicago: The Athletic Institute, 1968.

Kretchman, R. and Harper, W. "Why Does Man Play?" *Journal of Health, Physical Education and Recreation,* March, 1969.

Metheny, Eleanor. *Connotations of Movement in Sport and Dance.* Dubuque, Iowa: Wm. C. Brown Company Publishers, 1965.

———. *Movement and Meaning.* New York: McGraw-Hill Book Co., 1968.

Natan, A., ed. *Sport and Society.* London: Bowes and Bowes, 1958.

Osterhoudt, Robert, ed. *The Philosophy of Sport: A Collection of Original Essays.* Springfield, Ill.: Charles C. Thomas, Publisher, 1973.

Sapora, A. V. and Mitchell, E. *The Theory of Play and Recreation,* 3rd ed. New York: The Ronald Press Company, 1961.

Slovenko, Ralph and Knight, J. A., ed. *Motivations in Play, Games, and Sports.* Springfield, Ill.: Charles C. Thomas, Publisher, 1967.

Slusher, Howard. *Man, Sport and Existence: A Critical Analysis.* Philadelphia: Lea & Febiger, 1967.

Ulrich, C. and Nixon, J. E. *Tones of Theory.* AAHPER, 1972.

Vanderzwaag, H. J. "Sports Concepts," *Journal of Health, Physical Education and Recreation,* March 1970, pp. 35-36.

———. *Toward a Philosophy of Sport.* Boston: Addison-Wesley, 1972.

Weiss, Paul. *Sport: A Philosophical Inquiry.* Carbondale, Ill.: Southern Illinois University Press, 1969.

SECTION B

B

CULTURAL PERSPECTIVES

After arriving at some workable definitions of play, game, and sport the next logical step is to place these three phenomena into the cultural setting. The authors in this section present several ideas and theories as to the functions of and interaction between sport and the larger cultural environment.

In the first article, Marshall McLuhan considers games as information and communication media that are extensions "not of our private but of our social selves." He concludes that "games are situations contrived to permit simultaneous participation of many people in some significant pattern of their own corporate lives."

Lüschen, in the second article, helps the reader to make a transition from Huizinga's more sweeping descriptions of play, sport, and culture (Section A) to specific examples and discussions of the interdependence of these phenomena. Lüschen first asks the question, "What factors make for the appearance of sport? Or more specifically, what are the underlying cultural values?" In considering this question, his discussion of cultural values in relation to technology, Protestantism, and achievement orientation create a framework within which a clearer, more systematic understanding of sport can be developed. The second question asked is: "How does sport influence the sociocultural system at large?" Because sport has often been considered apart from culture or specifically apart from "higher" culture, Lüschen's second question takes on importance for the study of sport and cultural process.

Much of our knowledge of technology as related to sport has been from a normative position. We have accepted both technology and sport as having positive value, with only the benefits of each presented and without an analysis of all the consequences. Lüschen suggests the necessity of researching this relationship. Technology is such a pervasive determinent of the Western European and American environment that it must be included in one's thinking as background for the consideration of contemporary sport.

Profound changes have occurred in the technology of the media. These changes have come about so rapidly that it has been impossible to assess the effect on the behavior and belief system of society. Does the media report sports news in a direct and straightforward manner or does the reporting reflect the views and philosophy of editors, sports club owners, nations, and other vested interest groups? McIntosh asks, "Are journalists accepting or rejecting responsibility for how they effect and influence sport?" He suggests that the methods of training those concerned with the mass media and sport be analyzed and improved. The two pervasive themes in McIntosh's article seem to be the social responsibility of mass media personnel and suggestions for analysis and research about the fundamental relationship between sport and the media.

The article by Harf, Coates, and Marsh is a careful analysis of the complex and extensive network of transsocietal associations. The linkages and interaction between cultures has developed rapidly in the past twenty-five years and the authors demonstrate this pattern clearly in their research. Two important and multifacted variables which have influenced the rapid development of these associations would be technology and the electric speed of communication now available.

GAMES:
THE EXTENSIONS OF MAN

MARSHALL McLUHAN

Alcohol and gambling have very different meanings in different cultures. In our intensely individualist and fragmented Western world, "booze" is a social bond and a means of festive involvement. By contrast, in closely knit tribal society, "booze" is destructive of all social pattern and is even used as a means to mystical experience.

In tribal societies, gambling, on the other hand, is a welcome avenue of entrepreneurial effort and individual initiative. Carried into an individualist society, the same gambling games and sweepstakes seem to threaten the whole social order. Gambling pushes individual initiative to the point of mocking the individualist social structure. The tribal virtue is the capitalist vice.

When the boys came home from the mud and blood baths of the Western Front in 1918 and 1919, they encountered the Volstead Prohibition Act. It was the social and political recognition that the war had fraternalized and tribalized us to the point where alcohol was a threat to an individualist society. When we too are prepared to legalize gambling, we shall, like the English, announce to the world the end of individualist society and the trek back to tribal ways.

We think of humor as a mark of sanity for a good reason: in fun and play we recover the integral person, who in the workaday world or in professional life can use only a small sector of his being. Philip Deane, in *Captive in Korea*, tells a story about games in the midst of successive brainwashing that is to the point.

There came a time when I had to stop reading those books, to stop practising Russian because with the study of language the absurd and constant assertion began to leave its mark, began to find an echo, and I felt my thinking processes getting tangled, my critical faculties getting blunted. . . . Then they made a mistake. They gave us Robert Louis Stevenson's *Treasure Island* in English. . . . I could read Marx again, and question myself honestly without fear. Robert Louis Stevenson made us lighthearted, so we started dancing lessons.

Games are popular art, collective, social *reactions* to the main drive or action of any culture. Games, like institutions, are extensions of social man and of the body politic, as technologies are extensions of the animal organism. Both games and technologies are counter-irritants or ways of adjusting to the stress of the specialized actions that occur in any social group. As extensions of the popular response to the workaday stress, games become faithful models of a culture. They incorporate both the action and the reaction of whose populations in a single dynamic image.

A Reuters dispatch for December 13, 1962, reported from Tokyo:

BUSINESS IS A BATTLEFIELD

Latest fashion among Japanese businessmen is the study of classical military strategy and tactics in order to apply them to business operations. . . . It has been reported that one of the largest advertising companies in Japan has even made these books compulsory reading for all its employees.

Long centuries of tight tribal organization now stand the Japanese in very good stead in the trade and commerce of the electric age. A few decades ago they underwent enough literacy and industrial fragmentation to release aggressive individual energies. The close teamwork and tribal loyalty now demanded by electrical intercom again puts the Japanese in positive relation to their ancient traditions. Our own tribal ways are much too remote to be of any social avail. We have begun retribalizing with the same painful groping with which a preliterate society begins to read and write, and to organize its life visually in three-dimensional space.

The search for Michael Rockefeller brought the life of a New Guinea tribe into prominent attention in *Life* a year ago. The editors explained the war games of these people:

The traditional enemies of the Willigiman-Wallalua are the Wittaia, a people exactly like themselves in language, dress and custom. . . . Every week or two the Willigiman-Wallalua and their enemies arrange a formal battle at one of the traditional fighting grounds. In comparison with the catastrophic conflicts of "civilized" nations, these frays seem more like a dangerous field sport than true war. Each battle lasts but a single day, always stops before nightfall (because of the danger of ghosts) or if it begins to rain (no one wants to get his hair or ornaments wet). The men are very accurate with their weapons—they have all played war games since they were small boys—but they are equally adept at dodging, hence are rarely hit by anything.

The truly lethal part of this primitive warfare is not the formal battle but the sneak raid or stealthy ambush in which not only men but women and children are mercilessly slaughtered. . . .

This perpetual bloodshed is carried on for none of the usual reasons for waging war. No territory is won or lost; no goods or prisoners seized. . . . They fight because they enthusiastically enjoy it, because it is to them a vital function of the complete man, and because they feel they must satisfy the ghosts of slain companions.

These people, in short, detect in these games a kind of model of the universe, in whose deadly gavotte they can participate through the ritual of war games.

Games are dramatic models of our psychological lives providing release of particular tensions. They are collective and popular art forms with strict conventions. Ancient and nonliterate societies naturally regarded games as live dramatic models of the universe or of the outer cosmic drama. The Olympic games were direct enactments of the *agon*, or struggle of the Sun god. The runners moved around a track adorned with the zodiacal signs in imitation of the daily circuit of the sun chariot. With games and plays that were dramatic enactments of a cosmic struggle, the spectator role was plainly religious. The participation in these rituals kept the cosmos on the right track, as well as providing a booster shot for the tribe. The tribe or the city was a dim replica of that cosmos, as much as were the games, the dances, and the icons. How art became a sort of civilized substitute for magical games and rituals is the story of the detribalization which came with literacy. Art, like games, became a mimetic echo of, and relief from, the old magic of total involvement. As the audience for the magic games and plays became more individualistic, the role of art and ritual shifted from the cosmic to the humanly psychological, as in Greek drama. Even the ritual became more verbal and less mimetic or dancelike. Finally, the verbal narrative from Homer and Ovid became a romantic literary substitute for the corporate liturgy and group participation. Much of the scholarly effort of the past century in many fields has been devoted to a minute reconstruction of the conditions of primitive art and ritual, for it has been felt that this course offers the key to understanding the mind of primitive man. The key to this understanding, however, is also available in our new electric technology that is so swiftly and profoundly

re-creating the conditions and attitudes of primitive tribal man in ourselves.

The wide appeal of the games of recent times—the popular sports of
baseball and football and ice hockey—seen as outer models of inner
psychological life, become understandable. As models, they are collective rather than private dramatizations of inner life. Like our vernacular
tongues, all games are media of interpersonal communication, and they
could have neither existence nor meaning except as extensions of our
immediate inner lives. If we take a tennis racket in hand, or thirteen
playing cards, we consent to being a part of a dynamic mechanism in an
artificially contrived situation. Is this not the reason we enjoy those
games most that mimic other situations in our work and social lives?
Do not our favorite games provide a release from the monopolistic
tyranny of the social machine? In a word, does not Aristotle's idea of
drama as a mimetic reenactment and relief from our besetting pressures
apply perfectly to all kinds of games and dance and fun? For fun or
games to be welcome, they must convey an echo of workaday life. On
the other hand, a man or society without games is one sunk in the zom-
bie trance of the automation. Art and games enable us to stand aside
from the material pressures of routine and convention, observing and
questioning. Games as popular art forms offer to all an immediate means
of participation in the full life of a society, such as no single role or
job can offer to any man. Hence the contradiction in "professional"
sport. When the games door opening into the free life leads into a
merely specialist job, everybody senses an incongruity.

The games of a people reveal a great deal about them. Games are
a sort of artificial paradise like Disneyland, or some Utopian vision by
which we interpret and complete the meaning of our daily lives. In
games we devise means of nonspecialized participation in the larger
drama of our time. But for civilized man the idea of participation is
strictly limited. Not for him the depth participation that erases the
boundaries of individual awareness as in the Indian cult of *darshan,*
the mystic experience of the physical presence of vast numbers of people.

A game is a machine that can get into action only if the players
consent to become puppets for a time. For individualist Western man,
much of his "adjustment" to society has the character of a personal surrender to the collective demands. Our games help both to teach us this
kind of adjustment and also to provide a release from it. The uncertainty
of the outcomes of our contests makes a rational excuse for the mechanical rigor of the rules and procedures of the game.

When the social rules change suddenly, then previously accepted
social manners and rituals may suddenly assume the stark outlines and

the arbitrary patterns of a game. The *Gamesmanship* of Stephen Potter speaks of a social revolution in England. The English are moving toward social equality and the intense personal competition that goes with equality. The older rituals of long-accepted class behavior now begin to appear comic and irrational, gimmicks in a game. Dale Carnegie's *How to Win Friends and Influence People* first appeared as a solemn manual of social wisdom, but it seemed quite ludicrous to sophisticates. What Carnegie offered as serious discoveries already seemed like a naïve mechanical ritual to those beginning to move in a milieu of Freudian awareness charged with the psychopathology of everyday life. Already the Freudian patterns of perception have become an outworn code that begins to provide the cathartic amusement of a game, rather than a guide to living.

The social practices of one generation tend to get codified into the "game" of the next. Finally, the game is passed on as a joke, like a skeleton stripped of its flesh. This is especially true of periods of suddenly altered attitudes, resulting from some radically new technology. It is the inclusive mesh of the TV image, in particular, that spells for a while, at least, the doom of baseball. For baseball is a game of one-thing-at-a-time, fixed positions and visibly delegated specialist jobs such as belonged to the now passing mechanical age, with its fragmented tasks and its staff and line in management organization. TV, as the very image of the new corporate and participant ways of electric living, fosters habits of unified awareness and social interdependence that alienate us from the peculiar style of baseball, with its specialist and positional stress. When cultures change, so do games. Baseball, that had become the elegant abstract image of an industrial society living by split-second timing, has in the new TV decade lost its psychic and social relevance for our new ways of life. The ball game has been dislodged from the social center and and been conveyed to the periphery of American life.

In contrast, American football is nonpositional, and any or all of the players can switch to any role during play. It is, therefore, a game that at the present is supplanting baseball in general acceptance. It agrees very well with the new needs of decentralized team play in the electric age. Offhand, it might be supposed that the tight tribal unity of football would make it a game that the Russians would cultivate. Their devotion to ice hockey and soccer, two very individualist forms of game, would seem little suited to the psychic needs of a collectivist society. But Russia is still in the main an oral, tribal world that is undergoing detribalization and just now discovering individualism as a novelty. Soccer and ice hockey have for them, therefore, an exotic and Utopian quality of promise that they do not convey to the West. This is the quality that we tend to call "snob value," and *we* might derive some similar "value" from owning race horses, polo ponies, or twelve-meter yachts.

Games, therefore, can provide many varieties of satisfaction. Here we are looking at their role as media of communication in society as a whole. Thus, poker is a game that has often been cited as the expression of all the complex attitudes and unspoken values of a competitive society. It calls for shrewdness, aggression, trickery, and unflattering appraisals of character. It is said women cannot play poker well because it stimulates their curiosity, and curiosity is fatal in poker. Poker is intensely individualist, allowing no place for kindness or consideration, but only for the greatest good of the greatest number—the number one. It is in this perspective that it is easy to see why war has been called the sport of kings. For kingdoms are to monarchs what patrimonies and private income are to the private citizen. Kings can play poker with kingdoms, as the generals of their armies do with troops. They can bluff and deceive the opponent about their resources and their intentions. What disqualifies war from being a true game is probably what also disqualifies the stock market and business—the rules are not fully known nor accepted by all the players. Furthermore, the audience is too fully participant in war and business, just as in a native society there is no true art because *everybody* is engaged in making art. Art and games need rules, conventions, and spectators. They must stand forth from the overall situation as models of it in order for the quality of play to persist. For "play," whether in life or in a wheel, implies *interplay*. There must be give and take, or dialogue, as between two or more persons and groups. This quality can, however, be diminished or lost in any kind of situation. Great teams often play practice games without any audience at all. This is not sport in our sense, because much of the quality of interplay, the very medium of interplay, as it were, is the feeling of the audience. Rocket Richard, the Canadian hockey player, used to comment on the poor acoustics of some arenas. He felt that the puck off his stick rode on the roar of the crowd. Sport, as a popular art form, is not just self-expression but is deeply and necessarily a means of interplay within an entire culture.

Art is not just play but an extension of human awareness in contrived and conventional patterns. Sport as popular art is a deep reaction to the typical action of the society. But high art, on the other hand, is not a reaction but a profound reappraisal of a complex cultural state. Jean Genet's *The Balcony* appeals to some people as a shatteringly logical appraisal of mankind's madness in its orgy of self-destruction. Genet offers a brothel enveloped by the holocaust of war and revolution as an inclusive image of human life. It would be easy to argue that Genet is hysterical, and that football offers a more serious criticism of life than he does. Seen as live models of complex social situations, games may lack moral earnestness, it has to be admitted. Perhaps there is, just for this reason, a desperate need for games in a highly specialized industrial culture, since they are the only form of art accessible to many minds. Real interplay is reduced to nothing in a specialist world of delegated tasks and fragmented jobs. Some backward or tribal societies suddenly translated into industrial and specialist forms of mechanization cannot easily devise the antidote of sports and games to create countervailing force. They bog down into grim earnest. Men without art, and men without the popular arts of games, tend toward automatism.

A comment on the different kinds of games played in the British Parliament and the French Chamber of Deputies will rally the political experience of many readers. The British had the luck to get the two-team pattern into the House benches, whereas the French, trying for centralism by seating the deputies in a semicircle facing the chair, got instead a multiplicity of teams playing a great variety of games. By trying for unity, the French got anarchy. The British, by setting up diversity, achieved, if anything, too much unity. The British representative, by playing his "side," is not tempted into private mental effort, nor does he have to follow the debates until the ball is passed to him. As one critic said, if the benches did not face each other the British could not tell truth from falsehood, nor wisdom from folly, unless they listened to it *all*. And since most of the debate must be nonsense, it would be stupid to listen to all.

The form of any game is of first importance. Game theory, like information theory, has ignored this aspect of game and information movement. Both theories have dealt with the information content of systems, and have observed the "noise" and "deception" factors that divert data. This is like approaching a painting or a musical composition from the point of view of its content. In other words, it is guaranteed to miss the central structural core of the experience. For as it is the *pattern* of a game that gives it relevance to our inner lives, and not who is playing nor the outcome of the game, so it is with information movement. The selection of our human senses employed makes all the difference say between photo and telegraph. In the arts the particular mix of our senses in the medium employed is all-important. The ostensible program content is a lulling distraction needed to enable the structural form to get through the barriers of conscious attention.

Any game, like any medium of information, is an extension of the individual or the group. Its effect on the group or individual is a reconfiguring of the parts of the group or individual that are *not* so extended. A work of art has no existence or function apart from its *effects* on human observers. And art, like games or popular arts, and like media of communication, has the power to impose its own assumptions by setting the human community into new relationships and postures.

Art, like games, is a translator of experience. What we have already felt or seen in one situation we are suddenly given in a new kind of material. Games, likewise, shift familiar experience into new forms, giving the bleak and the blear side of things sudden luminosity. The telephone companies make tapes of the blither of boors, who inundate defenseless telephone operators with various kinds of revolting expressions. When played back this becomes salutary fun and play, and helps the operators to maintain equilibrium.

The world of science has become quite self-conscious about the play element in its endless experiments with models of situations otherwise unobservable. Management training centers have long used games as a means of developing new business perception. John Kenneth Galbraith argues that business must now study art, for the artist makes models of problems and situations that have not yet emerged in the larger matrix of society, giving the artistically perceptive businessman a decade of leeway in his planning.

In the electric age, the closing of the gaps between art and business, or between campus and community, are part of the overall implosion that closes the ranks of specialists at all levels. Flaubert, the French novelist of the nineteenth century felt that the Franco-Prussian War could have been avoided if people had heeded his *Sentimental Education*. A similar feeling has since come to be widely held by artists. They know that they are engaged in making live models of situations that have not yet matured in the society at large. In their artistic play, they discovered what is actually happening, and thus they appear to be "ahead of their time." Non-artists always look at the present through the spectacles of the preceding age. General staffs are always magnificently prepared to fight the previous war.

Games, then, are contrived and controlled situations, extensions of group awareness that permit a respite from customary patterns. They are a kind of talking to itself on the part of society as a whole. And talking to oneself is a recognized form of play that is indispensable to any growth of self-confidence. The British and Americans have enjoyed during recent times an enormous self-confidence born of the playful spirit of fun and games. When they sense the absence of this spirit in their rivals, it causes embarrassment. To take mere worldly things in dead earnest betokens a defect of awareness that is pitiable. From the first days of Christianity there grew a habit, in some quarters, of spiritual clowning, of "playing the fool in Christ," as St. Paul put it. Paul also associated this sense of spiritual confidence and Christianity play with the games and sports of his time. Play goes with an awareness of huge disproportion between the ostensible situation and the real stakes. A similar sense hovers over the game situation, as such. Since the game, like any art form, is a mere tangible model of another situation that is less accessible, there is always a tingling sense of oddity and fun in play or games that renders the very earnest and very serious person or society laughable. When the Victorian Englishman began to lean toward the pole of seriousness, Oscar Wilde and Bernard Shaw and G. K. Chesterton moved in swiftly as countervailing force. Scholars have often pointed out that Plato conceived of play dedicated to the Deity, as the loftiest reach of man's religious impulse.

Bergson's famous treatise on laughter sets forth the idea of mechanism taking over life-values as the key to the ludricous. To see a man slip on a banana skin is to see a rationally structured system suddenly translated into a whirling machine. Since industrialism had created a similar situation in the society of his time, Bergson's idea was readily accepted. He seems not to have noticed that he had mechanically turned up a mechanical metaphor in a mechanical age in order to explain the very unmechanical thing, laughter, or "the mind sneezing," as Wyndham Lewis described it.

The game spirit suffered a defeat a few years ago over the rigged TV quiz shows. For one thing, the big prize seemed to make fun of money. Money as store of power and skill, and expediter of exchange, still has for many people the ability to induce a trance of great earnestness. Movies, in a sense, are also rigged shows. Any play or poem or novel is, also, rigged *to produce an effect.* So was the TV quiz show. But with the TV effect there is deep audience *participation.* Movie and drama do not permit as much participation as that afforded by the mosaic mesh of the TV image. So great was the audience participation in the quiz shows that the directors of the show were prosecuted as con men. Moreover press and radio and interests, bitter about the success of the new TV medium, were delighted to lacerate the flesh of their rivals. Of course, the riggers had been blithely unaware of the nature of their medium, and had given it the movie treatment of intense realism, instead of the softer mythic focus proper to TV. Charles Van Doren merely got clobbered as an innocent bystander, and the whole investigation elicited no insight into the nature or effects of the TV medium.

Regrettably, it simply provided a field day for the earnest moralizers. A moral point of view too often serves as a substitute for understanding in technological matters.

That games are extensions, not of our private but of our social selves, and that they are media of communication, should now be plain. If, finally, we ask, "Are games mass media?" the answer has to be "Yes." Games are situations contrived to permit simultaneous participation of many people in some significant pattern of their own corporate lives.

THE INTERDEPENDENCE OF SPORT
AND CULTURE

GÜNTHER LÜSCHEN

INTRODUCTION

Sport is a rational, playful activity in interaction, which is extrinsically rewarded. The more it is rewarded, the more it tends to be work; the less, the more it tends to be play. If we describe it in an action system frame of reference, this activity depends on the organic, personality, social, and cultural systems. By tradition, physical education has tried to explain this action system largely on the grounds of the organic system, and sometimes making reference to the personality system. Only on rare occasions has it been approached systematically from the social and cultural systems as well. Yet it seems obvious that any action going on in this system ought to be explained with reference to all of the subsystems of the action system.

Even such a simple motor activity as walking is more than a matter of organic processes initiated by the personality system. It is determined by the social and cultural systems as well, as is most evident in the way the Israelians from the Yemen walk. Since in their former society in the Yemen, the Jews were the outcasts, and every Yemenite could feel free to hit a Jew (whenever he could get hold of one), the Yemenitic Jew would always run in order to escape this oppression. This way of walking finally became an integrated pattern of his culture. And though the environment in Israel no longer is hostile to him, the Yemenitic Israelite still carries this pattern with him as part of his culture and walks in a shy and hasty way. This example shows in addition that the different subsystems of action are not independent from one another; they are

From *International Review of Sport Sociology* 2 (1967): 27-141. Reprinted by permission.

structurally related. Thus, in dealing with the cultural system of sport and its interdependence with general culture, we will not always be able to explain the culture of sport and that of its environment in terms of the cultural system, and therefore should refer as well to the social and personality system to describe and explain what we call culture. It was Radcliffe-Brown who stressed the point that culture should be explained through its social structure. Furthermore, one should discuss the function of a unit within general culture, as well as cultural process and change (1952).

CONCEPTS OF CULTURE AND REVIEW OF RESULTS

Culture as a concept does not refer to behavior itself. It deals with those patterns and abstractions that underlie behavior or are the result of it. Thus culture exists of cognitive elements which grow out of everyday or scientific experience. It consists of beliefs, values, norms, and of signs that include symbols of verbal as well as non-verbal communication (cf., Johnson, 1960).

Anthropologists have sometimes held a broader view of culture and given more attention to the material results of human behavior. Leslie White in a critique of the above-stated concept of culture has called for more attention to "acts, thoughts and things dependent upon symboling." These would include not only the study of the above-mentioned elements, but also those of art, tools, machines, fetishes, etc. (1959). As attractive as White's critique may be, especially for cultural anthropology as an independent science, this approach as related to the cultural study of sport has led more to mere curiosity about things than to theoretical insights. This methodological approach has also dealt more with the cultural diffusion of sport and games than with the social structure of which they are a part. For decades we have learned about all types of games in all types of societies (especially primitive ones), which may well lead to the conclusion that we know more about the games and sports displayed by some Polynesian tribe than those of our own children and ancestors. For an understanding of sport it is less important to find the same games in different cultures as Tylor did (1896). It is more important to analyze, for example, the different meaning of baseball in the United States and Lybia, which in the one culture has at least latent ritualistic functions, while it has also economic functions in the other (Gini, 1939).

Another concept of culture, mainly held in Central Europe, has almost led to the same results for sport. In this concept "higher" culture was separated from civilization and expressed itself significantly in the arts and sciences. On the basis of values attributed to sport *a priori*, it was related either to "Zivilisation" or to Kultur. Physical educationalists through Huizinga's theory on the origin of culture in play saw in the latter approach their main support (1955). Thus defining sport as a special form of play, physical educationalists felt safe in their implicit attempt to justify sport for educational purposes. Yet Huizinga's theory has not only been criticized on the basis of ethnological findings, (c.f., Jensen, 1942), but he himself was very critical about the play element in sport. Those that believed in the role of sport within higher culture were hardly able to prove their hypothesis. So, as recently as Rene Maheu (1962), they often expressed their hope that sport in the future would contribute to "Kultur."

One can hardly deny that sport has indeed some impact on "higher" culture, as may be shown by symbolic elements from sport to be found in script and language. In an analysis of the cultural meaning of the ballgame of the Aztecs and Maya, Krickeberg found that in their script there were elements related to this game. The symbol for movement, for example, was identical with the I-shape of the ball court (1948). "To get (take) a rain check" refers to baseball, but has now become in American English symbolic for any situation where you get another chance. "That's not cricket" refers to a dishonest procedure in everyday life. And though German is not as idiomatic as English, it contains elements which originated in sport and games as well. "Katzbalgerei," and the phrase "sich gegenseitig die Bälle zuspielen," refer to a game which today is still known in the Netherlands as "Kaatsen" and perhaps appears in the New York children's game of one-o-cat. As did football in Shakespeare's "King Lear," so appeared this game and its terminology in the 16th century poetry of J. G. Fischart.

How weak these relationships of sport indeed are to "higher" culture may be shown by the relatively unsuccessful attempts to establish through special contests in modern Olympics, a relationship between sport and the arts. Sport only rarely expresses itself in the material aspects of culture. It is what I would like to call a momentary activity. Just from a certain level on, an event may have its appearance on such a short range cultural element as the sports page of the next day's newspaper. This appearance of sport in the media of mass communication, in language, poetry, and the arts is significant for the overall meaning of sport within society, but these manifestations tell us little about sport itself and its interdependence with general culture as we define it.

It may also be interesting to discuss cognitive elements such as scientific insight coming out of sport. Also religious beliefs and ritual found in sport would be an interesting point of analysis. Yet after show-ing how sport is indeed bound to society and structured by general culture, we will mainly discuss our problem on the level of cultural values and their related social structure.

SPORT AS PART OF CULTURE AND SOCIETY

That sport is structurally related to culture and society has some-times been questioned. Yet it is quite easy to show how strong this relationship is. Sport is indeed an expression of that socio-cultural sys-tem in which it occurs. David Riesman and Reuel Denney describe how American football was changed through the American culture from rugby to a completely different game. It is now well integrated and quite obviously shows in its vigor, hard contact and a greater centrality on the individual the basic traits of the culture of American society (1954).

On the level of the so-called primitive societies we see the same dependence of sport and games on culture and its underlying social structure. The Hopi Indians had 16 different terms for foot races which nearly all referred to one aspect of the social organization of that tribe (Culin, 1907). A recent socio-historical study on three Illinois sub-cultures finds the same close relationship between socio-cultural system and sport (Hill, 1966). And Käte Hye-Kerkdal outlines the tight struc-tural relation between the log-races of the tribe of the Timbira in Brazil and their socio-cultural system. This ritualistic competition between two teams has symbolic meaning for nearly every aspect of the dual organiza-tion of this tribe. It refers to all kinds of religious and social polarities and is so strongly imbedded in this religious-dominated system that win-ning or losing does not have any effect on the status of the team or individual, nor are there any other extrinsic rewards. Yet these races are performed vigorously and with effort (1956).

Now that we have proven that there is a structural relationship between sport and culture, the first question is that of sport's depen-dency on culture. What factors make for the appearance of sport? Or more specifically, what are the underlying cultural values?

CULTURE VALUES AND SPORT

By values we mean those general orientations in a socio-cultural system that are not always obvious to its members, but are implicit in actual behavior. On the level of the personality system they are expressed partly in attitudes. Values should be separated from norms which are derived from values and are actual rules for behavior. For instance, health is a high value in the American culture, as it seems to be in all young cultures, while death is higher in the hierarchy of values in old cultures like India (Parsons, 1960). On this continuum we may explain why sport as an expression of the evaluation of health is more important in American than in Indian society. The whole emphasis on physical fitness in the United States may well be explained by this background, and the norm "run for your life" is directly related to it.

Sport, Industrialization and Technology

In comparing the uneven distribution and performance level of sport all over the world, one widely accepted hypothesis is that sport is an offspring of technology and industrialization. The strong emphasis on sport in industrialized societies seems to show that industrialization and technology are indeed a basis for sport. This would be a late confirmation of Ogburn's theory of social change, as well as of Marxian theory that society and its structure depend on its economic basis. However, there are quite a number of inconsistencies. Not all sport-oriented societies or societal subsystems show a relation to technology and industrialization, and historically games and sport have been shown to have existence prior to industrialization. Yet it can hardly be denied that certain conditions in the later process of industrialization have promoted sport, and technology has at least its parallels in modern sport. The above-stated hypothesis may, despite its obvious limitations, lead us to the independent variables.

Sport, A Protestant Subculture?

In an investigation that because of its methodological procedure turned out to be a profound critique of Marxian materialism, Max Weber studied the interrelationship of what he called "The Protestant Ethic and the Spirit of Capitalism." (1920). This investigation about the underlying values of capitalism in Western societies quoted data on the over-representation of Protestants in institutions of higher learning, their preference for industrial and commercial occupations and professions and the stronger trend towards capitalism in Protestant-dominated countries (most obvious in the United States). Weber found not the material basis but Protestant culture, with achievement of worldly success and asceticism held as the basic values, caused industrialization and capitalism. In accordance with the Calvinistic belief in predestination, the Protestant felt that he was blessed by God once he had achieved success. Thus, need for achievement became an integrated part of his personality and a basic value in Protestantism. Together with the value of asceticism this led to the accumulation of wealth and to Western capitalism. If we turn to sport, we find the same values of achievement and asceticism. Even the puritans, generally opposed to a leisurely life, could therefore justify sport as physical activity that contributed to health (cf., McIntosh, 1963). Today we find significance for this relationship in the YMCA, in a group like the American Fellowship of Christian Athletes, and also in the Protestant minister who in Helsinki became an Olympic medal winner in the pole vault. He showed the consistency between Protestantism and sport in his prayer right after his Olympic winning vault. Max Weber's findings about the relationship between the Protestant ethic and the spirit of capitalism may thus well be extended to the "spirit" of sport. Not only Weber was aware of this relationship, but also Thorstein Veblen who described the parallels in religious and sport ritual (1899).

The relationship between sport and Protestantism is not only to be observed in the emphasis on sport in the Scandinavian and other Protestant countries. A rough compilation of the probable religious preference of Olympic medal winners on the basis of the percentage of different religious groups in their countries also shows the dominance of Protestantism up to 1960. Protestantism accounted for more than 50 per cent of the medal winners, while its ratio among the world population is less than 8 per cent (Lüschen, 1962). Furthermore, in 1958 a survey of young athletes in West Germany by Lüschen showed the following distribution according to religious preference:

	Whole Population West Germany	Sport Club Members 15-25	Track Swimming	High Achievers Track/ Swimming
Protestants	52%	60%	67%	73%
Catholics	44%	37%	31%	26%
Others	4%	3%	2%	1%
n =	universe	1,880	366	111

These figures indicate the overrepresentation of Protestants in German sport. Moreover, they indicate a higher percentage in individual sports, and an even higher percentage of Protestants among those that have achieved a higher level of performance. Thus it may be concluded that there is a correlation between Protestantism and sport and the culture of both. This was obvious for individual sports, but less for team sports where in the German sample Catholics appeared quite often. Since in Catholicism collectivity is highly regarded, this inconsistency is to be explained by the value of collectivity in team sports. It is consistent with this hypothesis that Catholic Notre Dame University has been one of the innovators of football in America. At present, it is a leading institution in this discipline. And internationally Catholic-dominated South America is overall rather poor in individual sports, but outstanding in team sports like soccer and basketball.

This result on the overall, strong relationship between sport and Protestantism is, despite support by data, theoretically insufficient. As was the case with sport in its relationship to industrialization, there are many exceptions. The high achievement in sport of the Russians, the Poles, the Japanese, the Mandan Indians, the Sikhs in India, or the Watusi in Africa cannot be related to Protestantism though in Japanese Zen-Buddhism there are parallels.

The Centrality of the Achievement-Value

Since again Protestantism cannot be specifically identified as being the independent variable, we may hypothesize that there is a more general system of values as the basis for Protestantism, capitalism and sport. In his critique of Max Weber, McClelland has considered the ethic of Protestantism as a special case of the general achievement orientation of a system, this being the independent variable. Achievement orientation (or, as he puts it on the personality-system-level, need-achievement) precedes all periods of high cultural achievement in ancient Greece, in the Protestant Reformation, in modern industrialism and, as we may conclude, in modern sport. He referred in his analysis also to the related social structure of the achievement value (such as family organization), which should also be studied in relationship to sport.

If we turn again to the cross-cultural comparison of those systems that participate and perform strongly in sport, we find that in all of these societies achievement-orientation is basic. In Russia this value is expressed in the norm that social status should depend only on achievement. The Sikhs and the Watusi are both minority groups in their environment. In order to keep their position, they have to achieve more than the other members of the societies they live in. The Japanese (Bellah, 1957) and the Mandan Indians (McClelland, 1961) also place a heavy emphasis on achievement.

Similar results appear in cross-cultural investigations of different types of games as related to basic orientations in the process of socialization. Roberts and Sutton-Smith find in a secondary analysis of the Human Relation Area Files of G. P. Murdock that games of chance are related to societies that emphasize routine responsibility in the socialization process. Games of strategy are found in societies where obedience, games of physical skill in those where achievement is stressed (1963). Individual sports would mainly qualify as games of physical skill and again show achievement as their basic cultural value. Team sports as well are games of strategy. Their relation to training of obedience would support exactly what we called earlier the value of collectivity.

It remains an open question, for further research into the value structure of sport, as to which other values are related to this system. It is to be expected that the structure of values will be more complex than it appears on the basis of our limited insight now. Roberts and Sutton-Smith briefly remark that games of physical skill are related to occupational groups that exert power over others (1963). Thus, power orientation may be another value supporting sport. This would cross-culturally be consistent with power-oriented political systems that strongly emphasize sport. Here we could refer to countries like Russia or the United States, as well as to a tribe like the Mandan Indians.

The Culture of Societal Subsystems and Its Relation to Sport

Within a society we find subsystems that have their own subculture, which will be another condition for sport. The female role in modern societies still depends on a culture that stresses obedience as the main value-orientation, while the male culture is strongly oriented towards achievement. Thus we find a disproportionately high participation of men in sport which in most of the disciplines is a male culture. One of the most male-oriented sports, however, is pool, a game supported mainly by the subculture of the bachelor. This has, with the general change in the number of people marrying, lost its main supporting culture (Polsky, 1967).

Another subsystem which in its culture shows a strong relationship to sport is that of the adolescent age group (cf. Coleman, 1961). Sport is dependent more on the culture of the adolescent than on that of any other age group. Helanko raises the point, referring to his studies of boys' gangs in Turku, that sport has its origin in the gang-age and in boys' gangs. The fact that there are no rules for early sports to be found is seen as one of the supporting factors (1957). Generally speaking, achievement is again more central as a value in adolescence and early adulthood than later, where the main response to sport goes not so much towards achievement but towards values of health and fitness.

The different social classes have a culture of their own. The greatest emphasis on achievement, and thus the highest sport participation, is to be found in the upper-middle class. It is considerably less important in the lower class where routine responsibility is valued. The notion that there is no way to gain higher status accounts for the high regard for games of chance or those sports where one may just have a lucky punch, as in boxing (Weinberg and Arond, 1952). Loy has related the different types of games and the passive and active participation in sport to different modes of adaptation and to the members of social classes (1966). His theoretical analysis as to "innovation" found in the lower class, ritualism in the lower-middle class and conformity in the upper-middle class is supported by data (cf. Lüschen, 1963; Loy, 1969) that show the same ways of adaptation in sport. However, in responding to the social class system and its culture as related to sport one should have in mind that class determined behavior may not follow the traditional class lines in sport. Sport may indeed show or promote new orientations in the class system (Kunz and Lüschen, 1966).

Finally, sport is organized within, or relates to different associations whose cultures sometime have a profound influence on sport itself. This is especially true for physical education in schools where, with the same skills and rules, we may find a completely different culture as compared to sport in the military establishment. And while intercollegiate and interscholastic athletics are overall a surprisingly well integrated subculture within American schools and universities, the different values held by an educational (the school or university) and a solely success-oriented unit (the team) may well lead to strong value conflicts. This could result in a complete separation of school and athletics.

FUNCTIONS AND DYSFUNCTIONS

After we have found achievement, asceticism in individual sports, obedience (collectivity) in team sports, and exertion of power, the basic value orientations that give structure to this activity, we may then proceed to the second question: How does sport influence the socio-cultural system at large? Though we have little evidence through research, we may on the basis of structural-functional methodology be able to outline the basic functions of sport for pattern maintenance, integration, adaptation and goal attainment.

The Functions of Sport Within Culture and Society

As in the case of the Timbria, Hye-Kerkdal states that the basic values of that culture were learned through the log-race. Furthermore, the participants were functionally integrated into the social system (1956). Thus, we may hypothesize that the main functions of sport are pattern maintenance and integration.

Since sport implies (as we saw) basic cultural values, it has the potential to pass these values on to its participants. We know from studies of the process of socialization that the exposure of children to competitive sport will cause these children to become achievement-motivated; the earlier this exposure occurs, the more achievement-motivated they become (Winterbottom, 1953). And the child's moral judgment may, for instance, be influenced through games such as marbles. Again, according to Piaget, the child not only becomes socialized to the rules but at a later age he also gets an insight into the underlying structure and function of the rules of a game, and thus into the structure and function of social norms and values as such (1965). Overall, from the level of primitive societies to modern societies, sport not only socializes to the system of values and norms but in primitive societies it socializes towards adult and warfare skills as well.

Since we mentioned that sport is also structured along such societal subsystems as different classes, males, urban areas, schools and communities, we should say it functions for integration of these systems as well as for the society at large. This is most obvious in spectator sports where the whole country or community identifies with its representatives in a contest. Thus, sport functions as a means of integration, not only for the actual participants, but also for the represented members of such a system.

Sport in modern societies may function for goal-attainment on the national polity level. In primitive societies, sport functions for adaptation as well as goal-attainment since the sport skills of swimming, hunting and fishing are used to supply food and mere survival.

Possible Dysfunctions of Sport and Social Control

A question should be raised at this point asking whether sport is dysfunctional for culture and society as well. Th. W. Adorno called sport an area of unfreedom ("ein Bereich der Unfreiheit"), (1957) in which he obviously referred to the differentiated code of rules which earlier led Huizinga to his statement that excluded sport from play (1955). Both seem to overlook what Piaget called the reciprocity and mutual agreement on which such rules rest (1965). And they may also be considered as an expression of a highly structured system.

Another dysfunctional element for culture and for the sport system itself could be the centrality of achievement. It has such a high rank in the hierarchy of values of sport that, by definition, the actual objective performance of a member of this system will decide the status he gets. In the core of sport, in the contest on the sports field, there is only achieved status. It seems that there is no other system or any societal subsystem, with the exception of combat, where achievement ranks that high. It may create conflict once this value-orientation is imposed on the whole culture, and it may create conflict within the system of sport itself since its members bring other values into this system as well. M. Mead in an investigation of competition and cooperation (the first concept of which is related to achievement) of primitive peoples, however, finds that there seems to be no society where one of these principles existed alone (1946). And on the micro-sociological level, small groups seem to control this value by discriminating against those that deviate from the group norm of a fair performance (Roethlisberger and Dickson, 1939). Thus, one would notice some kind of a mechanism built into a social system like a group that keeps it in a state of balance. Exactly this seems to happen within sport where the sporting groups themselves and their differentiated organizational and institutional environment exert social control on those participants achieving beyond a certain level.

In a survey of sport club members in Germany, it was found that the norms expressed for an athlete's behavior referred surprisingly less to the achievement value but more often to a value of affiliation, which is to be defined as a positive orientation towards other group members or opponents. Fair play was the one mentioned most frequently. The value of affiliation expressed by the respondents was found more in normative statements the higher their level of performance. On the basis of the hypothesized mechanism of social control, they are under stronger pressure to affiliate with others (Lüschen, 1963). This may explain (on the basis of this structural relationship) why in the culture of sport we find not only the value of achievement but also that of fair play and other affiliative orientations.

However, achievement and affiliation may not necessarily be related. It depends on the amount of social control imposed on sport from the internal as well as external system, whether this relationship will be strong or weak. In professional boxing these controls are very weak; while in golf with the handicap rule, they seem to be comparatively strong (Lüschen, 1970).

How much this pattern would influence the culture as such is an open question. Yet it seems not so mis-oriented as often thought when Oetinger stated that sport would provide a good model for political partnership (1954). We may on the basis of our findings hypothesize that also on the political level the amount of social control will decide whether two or more systems will coexist or not.

Sport and Socio-Cultural Change

After we have discussed the culture and underlying social structure of sport and its function, we are left with Radcliffe-Brown's third programmatic point—that of social and cultural change. We know little about the role of sport in socio-cultural change, though we hypothesized earlier that it may have a function of innovation, or at least structural relationship to changes in the system of social classes. Sport has also functioned as an initiator for the diffusion of technical inventions, such as the bicycle or the automobile (Kroeber, 1963). The same holds true to a degree for conduct in regard to fashion and a healthy life. Typically, this question of change has been highly neglected so far.

Sport and Cultural Evolution

If we finally try to explain the different cross-cultural appearance of sport on the basis of an evolutionary theory, it is hard to justify on the basis of our present knowledge about the appearance of sport that there are such things as primitive and developed cultures of sport. The Mandan Indians had a highly developed sport culture, the Australian aboriginals, as perhaps the most primitive people known to us today, know quite a variety of recreational activities and physical skills, and the variety of competitive games in Europe and America in the past was perhaps richer than today.

An evolution can only be seen on a vertical level which on the one hand shows in a state of mechanic solidarity rather simple rules in sport and games, while in a state of organic solidarity, as in modern industrialized societies, the code of rules and the structure of games get more differentiated.

What we may furthermore state is that, on the level of primitive cultures, sport's function is universal, often religious, collectively oriented, and in the training of skills, representative and related to adult and warfare skills; while modern sport's function may be called specific for pattern maintenance and integration, is individual oriented and non-representative in the training of skills. The rewards are more intrinsic in primitive cultures, while they are more extrinsic in the sport of modern cultures. Thus, referring to our definition at the beginning, one may well differentiate between physical and recreational activities of primitive cultures and sport in modern cultures (c.f. Damm, 1960).

SUMMARY AND CONCLUSION

The interdependence of sport and culture, up to now mainly outlined on the basis of sport's contribution to higher culture (Kultur), was discussed on sport's relation to culture with the emphasis on values, sport's function for the socio-cultural system and its relation to change and evolution.

The system of sport, an integrated part of the socio-cultural system, seems to depend on the industrialized, technological or Protestant religious system. Yet cross-culturally it appears that these systems as intermediate variables are just special cases of a more general system. This is determined for sport by the achievement-value, a value of collectivity and supposedly power orientation. On the basis of these cultural value orientations one may explain the uneven distribution of sport as such, and of team sports versus individual sports in certain socio-cultural systems.

Sport's function for a socio-cultural system can mainly be seen for pattern maintenance and integration, in modern polity dominated societies as well for goal attainment. In primitive cultures it is universal and thus functions for adaptation as well.

Though a relation of sport to social change is obvious (sport fulfills a certain role for innovation), this neglected question of social change needs more careful investigation. Evolutionary theories applied to sport need more study as well; this might contribute to evolutionary theories as such. It appears that physical activity on the level of "primitive" cultures should be kept apart from sport in modern cultures since meaning and manifest functions are as universal on the one level as they are specific and segmentary on the other.

RELATED LITERATURE

Adorno, T. W. *Prismen*. Frankfurt, 1957.
Bellah, R. N. *Tokugawa Religion: The Values of Pre-Industrial Japan*. Glencoe, Ill., 1957.
Coleman, J. S. *The Adolescent Society*. Glencoe, Ill., 1961.
Culin, S. *Games of the North American Indians*. 24th Report, Bureau of American Ethnology, Washington, D. C., 1907.
Damm, H. "Vom Wesen sogenannter Leibesübungen bei Naturvölkern." *Studium Generale* 13 (1960): 3-10.
Gini, C. "Rural ritual games in Lybia." *Rural Sociology* 4 (1939): 283-299.
Helanko, R. "Sports and socialization." *Acta Sociologica* 2 (1957): 229-240.
Hill, P. J. A cultural history of frontier sport in Illinois 1673-1820. Unpub. Ph.D. Dissertation, University of Illinois, 1966.
Huizinga, J. *Homo Ludens*. Boston, 1955.
Hye-Kerkdal, K. Wettkampfspiel und Dualorganisation bei den Timbira Brasiliens. J. Haekel, ed. *Die Wiener Schule der Völkerkunde*. Wein, 1956: 504-533.
Jensen, A. E. "Spiel und Ergriffenheit." *Paideuma* 2 (1942): 124-139.
Krickeberg, W. "Das mittelamerikanische Ballspiel und seine teligiöse Symbolik." *Paideuma* 3 (1948): 118-190.
Kroeber, A. L. *Anthropology*. New York, 1963.
Kunz, G. and Lüschen, G. Leisure and social stratification. Paper at *International Congress for Sociology*. Evian, France, 1966.

Loy, J. W. Sport and social structure. Paper at the *AAHPER Convention.* Chicago, 1966.

Lüschen, G. "Der Leistungssport in seiner Abhangigkeit vom sozio-kulturellen System." *Zentralblatt für Arbeitswissenschaft* 16 (1962): 186-190.

———. "Soziale Schichtung und soziale Mobilität." *Kölner Zeitschrift für Soziologie und Sozialpsychologie* 15 (1963): 74-93.

———. Leistungsorientierung und ihr Finfluss auf das soziale und personale System. In Lüschen, G. ed., *Kleingruppenforschung und Gruppe im Sport.* Köln, 1966: 209-223.

———. "Cooperation, association and contest." *Journal of Conflict Resolution,* 14, 1970 (forthcoming).

Maheu, R. "Sport and culture." *International Journal of Adult and Youth Education* 14 (1962): 169-178.

McClelland, D. C. *The Achieving Society.* New York, 1961.

McIntosh, P. C. *Sport and Society.* London, 1963.

Mead, M. *Competition and Cooperation Among Primitive Peoples.* Berkeley, 1946.

Oetinger, F. *Partnerschaft.* Stuttgart, 1954.

Parsons, T. *Societies.* Englewood-Cliffs, N.Y., 1966.

———. "Toward a healthy maturity." *Journal of Health and Human Behavior* 1 (1960): 163-173.

Piaget, J. *The Moral Judgment of the Child.* New York, 1965.

Polsky, N. "Poolrooms and poolplayers." *Trans-action* 4 (1967): 32-40.

Radcliffe-Brown, A. R. *Structure and Function in Primitive Society.* Glencoe, Ill., 1952.

Riesman, D. and Denney, R. Football in America. Riesman, D., ed. *Individualism Reconsidered.* Glencoe, Ill., 1954: 242-251.

Roberts, J. M. and Sutton-Smith, B. "Child training and game involvement." *Ethnology* 1 (1962): 166-185.

Roethlisberger, F. J. and Dickson, W. J. *Management and the Worker.* Cambridge, Mass., 1939.

Stumpf, F. and Cozens, F. W. "Some aspects of the role of games, sports and recreational activities in the culture of primitive peoples." *Research Quarterly* 18 (1947): 198-218, and 20 (1949): 2-30.

Sutton-Smith, B. Roberts, J. M. and Kozelka, R. M. "Game involvement in adults." *Journal of Social Psychology* 60 (1963): 15-30.

Tylor, F. B. "On American lot-games." *Internationales Archiv für Ethnographie* 9 (1896 supplement): 55-67.

Veblen, T. *The Theory of the Leisure Class.* Chicago, 1899.

Weber, M. *Gesammelte Aufsätze zur Religionssoziologie.* Tübingen, 1920, I.

Weinberg, S. K. and Arond, R. "The occupational culture of the boxer." *American Journal of Sociology* 57 (1952): 460-463.

White, L. "The concept of culture." *American Anthropologist* 61 (1959): 227-251.

Winterbottom, M. R. The relation of childhood training in independence to achievement motivation. Unpub. Ph.D. Dissertation, Univ. of Michigan, 1953.

MASS MEDIA: FRIENDS OR FOES IN SPORT

PETER C. MCINTOSH

To demonstrate the involvement of UNESCO in sport, *Quest* departs from its usual format to present a topic in two sections.

To facilitate one of its primary objectives, the promotion of international understanding, in 1970 UNESCO requested the International Council of Sport and Physical Education to organize a seminar to discuss the promotion of international understanding through sport, with particular reference to the mass media. A seminar was held in Paris in June, 1971. Mr. McIntosh presented the first general introductory paper, which appears here as Part I.

Following the seminar, a working group was appointed to study the topic further. Under the sponsorship of UNESCO, the International Council of Sport and Physical Education, and the Sports Council of Great Britain, the group met in December, 1973, together with an observer from the International Olympic Committee. A statement was drafted and approved. It was decided to send the statement to as many international and national organizations of mass media and of sport as possible for their consideration. The statement—in English, French, German, and Spanish—was presented to the Conference of the International Association of the Sporting Press in Malaga, Spain, on March 25, 1974. It appears here as Part II.

Members of the working group which drew up the statement in London, 1973, include the following: P. McIntosh, Chairman, of Great Britain; D. Anthony, of UNESCO; H. R. Banks, of IOC; J. Borotra, of ICSPE; M. Boet, of University of Ottawa, Canada; Z. Chielewski, of Polskie Radio,

From *Quest*, Monograph XXII (June, 1974): 33-44.

Poland; M. J. Ferran, of Journal l'Equipe, France; W. Gitter, of DTSB, German Democratic Republic; W. Lyberg, Sveriges Riksidrottsforbund, Sweden; O. A. Milshstein, State Institute of Physical Culture, Minsk, USSR; B. Naidoo, of AIPS, Great Britain; P. Noel-Baker, of ICSPE, Great Britain; A. C. N. Preston, of European Union of Radio, Switzerland; H. Seifart, of NDR-Sport, Bundes Deutches Republic; O. State, General Assembly of International Sport Federations (GAIF), Great Britain; S. Skilton, formerly of *Christian Science Monitor*, United States of America; B. Tomaszewski, of Polskie Radio, Poland; E. Walter, of Radio Suisse, Switzerland; and Liliane Meunier, Secretary.

PART I

The purpose of this introductory paper is to set the scene for our discussions and to suggest some of the general problems which we may have to tackle. It is perhaps appropriate that this should be done by someone who, like myself, is not intimately connected with any of the mass media but looks at them from outside.

As far as sport is concerned it may be helpful to consider what the title of our seminar may include. The mass media as you see from our programme are grouped under three main headings, the written word, the spoken word and the visual image. The headings are not separate and distinct, for the written word may explain the visual image and the visual image today rarely appears without spoken commentary. Nevertheless these headings give us a rough framework for discussion of questions which concern particular media as well as mass communication in general.

Sport is notoriously difficult to define or delimit and I shall make no attempt to do so. We shall, for obvious reasons, be concerned principally with competitive sport but we shall be unwise to ignore the vast range and amount of non-competitive sport that now commands the attention of millions of people. The two most popular physical recreations in Britain for all ages and both sexes are swimming and dancing.

In other non-competitive sporting activities there have recently been two international or multinational ventures which have commanded widespread attention. One was a failure, the other a success. The recent attempt to climb Mount Everest by a new route failed for a number of reasons, but international tensions within the group were a potent factor. On the other and Thor Heyerdahl's multi-racial crew aboard the papyrus boat Ra appear to have worked together harmoniously and well in their isolation on the Atlantic Ocean. International understanding in non-competitive sport and recreation is a feature which we ought to study.

International understanding is a term which we must examine closely at the outset of our deliberations. Understanding sport in the sense of knowing more of the techniques and tactics, the rules and conventions of all manner of games and sports is something which has increased enormously as the result of objective presentation and didactic treatment by the mass media. The media have not only contributed to knowledge and inform public opinion, they have stimulated sensitivity and aesthetic appreciation. Indeed some of the great sports films have done more for the latter than they have for the former. All this information and treatment has increased international understanding of sport for spectators as well as for participants. A common interest and a common body of knowledge has been produced which is not unduly hampered by barriers of language, race or culture. This is not to say that mass media have ironed out national characteristics. The particular features of Russian girl gymnasts or Korean footballers remain, but they become subjects of worldwide knowledge and comment. International understanding of sport is thereby increased and sharpened.

But, of course, the term "international understanding" implies more than this. It implies friendship and good fellowship among individuals, teams, racial groups and nation states. The two uses of understanding are not necessarily closely connected. An increase in knowledge of an opponent does not necessarily lead to an increase of goodwill. Indeed it sometimes leads to the opposite. A few press references to recent sporting events show quite clearly a lack of goodwill in well popularised contests.

Evening Standard—14.5.71. Football:
"The dirtiest show in town."

Observer—28.2.71. Rugby:
"L'entente cordiale se termine à Twickenham."

ILEA P.E. Journal—Summer 71. Cricket:
"During a match against New South Wales . . . a section of the crowd rushed on to the field and assaulted the England captain."

Olympic Review Nr 33. Ski-ing:
"To promote international ill will . . . fights, cheating and chicanery have made a farce of the original purpose of the Olympic Games."

ILEA P.E. Journal—Summer 71. Football:
"Sadly this much vaunted cup tie . . . only served to prove George Orwell's point that sport is the unfailing cause of much ill will."

Of course there are many instances of the opposite situation, none more moving to my mind than the open farewell letter from Vera Nikolic of Yugoslavia to Lillian Board published in March 1971.

World Sport, March 1971: ". . . On and off the track you were my dear and wonderful friend and rival. I wish to express to you in my name and those of all the other runners of my country, our respect and devotion. Please accept our thanks for everything you gave to athletics and to us in this short time . . . Goodbye dear Lillian."

The first question which we have to consider at this seminar now becomes clear. The mass media incontrovertibly contribute to the understanding of sport across national frontiers. Does this increased understanding and knowledge increase goodwill or illwill? Both goodwill and illwill are apparent in contemporary sport. How is their balance affected by the mass media?

In answering this question it is necessary to distinguish between effects which mass media have which are almost inevitable and outside their control, and effects which may be the result of deliberate policy by those who control the media and those who operate them. The very existence of international sport and its world-wide coverage has brought it into the realm of political diplomacy. Its role in politics was clearly recognised by de Coubertin as long ago as 1894 and his vision is being fulfilled despite the ostrich-like behaviour of some of his successors. The cricket matches between England and Australia in 1932 should have alerted the English speaking world or at least the Commonwealth to the political significance of sport when "body-line bowling," a pejorative term invented by the Australian Press, was the subject of diplomatic exchanges between the two governments. Certainly the Olympic Games of 1936 should have made the whole world aware of the political importance of sport, for the festival was deliberately and ostentatiously used to further the political aims of the Third Reich.

There is no question but that the political importance of international sport is the result of its coverage by the mass media. Decisions about the admission of South Africa to the Olympic Games had to be taken in the full glare of world-wide publicity and could have been different had the coverage been less great. More recently in what has come to be known as "ping pong" diplomacy there would have been little political significance in the visits of table tennis teams from U.S. and U.K. to China without press coverage. Mass media therefore give to international sport a political significance which it would not otherwise possess. If, however, the coverage of sport is inevitable, it cannot be said that its treatment by editors, journalists and cameramen allows no variation of outlook and no slant of presentation. To what extent can the mass media affect chauvinism in sport? Can a chauvinistic attitude in the public mind be developed so that governments are forced, perhaps not unwillingly, to adopt chauvinistic policies to each other? Alternatively can reporters transcend their national allegiances to the extent that the ideals of sports override narrow national ambitions? There are deep psychological and sociological questions here which need some clarification and are as yet unanswered.

Sport is by nature aggressive and biologists are divided upon the nature of aggression. On the one hand are those who maintain that aggressive behaviour is produced by an environment and by frustration, and that such behaviour, far from being inevitable is capable of radical modification by training and education. Aggression whether in sport or in other spheres is certainly not inevitable. On the other side are those who claim that aggression, in common with other instinctive patterns of behaviour is spontaneous. Aggression is an internal drive which builds up until it must somehow find expression.

Whatever view biologists take of aggression and competitive sport the immediate problem for everyone is the control and presentation of a modern international phenomenon which is here to stay. In this situation I offer four points on which the mass media have most important decisions to make.

The first point is realism. It will do sport no good to expect the impossible. Table tennis can perhaps make a small contribution to international diplomacy, but to expect sport to make a serious impact upon the Vietnam War or upon the middle Eastern dispute between Israel and her neighbours, or to have solved the dispute between Biafrans and their fellow Nigerians is unrealistic. The Olympic Games have not prevented the outbreak of two world wars. But sport is not thereby condemned. It is only condemned if we are arrogant in our claims. An eloquent dominican Father Didon, remarked to someone who was bewailing the rise of democracy "When I come in I never complain about the weather outside, because it is not in my power to change it." Let us be humble in our approach and be content with what we find of good in sport and not blind to its shortcomings and deficiencies.

The second point is idealism. In an age of iconoclasm it is customary to sneer at the ideals of earlier generations. Baron de Coubertin was a great admirer of that concept known internationally as "fair play." We may feel that "fair play" admits of different interpretations in different cultures. We may think that such an universal concept cannot override completely local beliefs about honour and shame. For some it will be difficult to accept that there can be honour in defeat, yet that is implicit in fair play, as in chivalry to opponents. It will be the duty of sociologists and psychologists to reveal to us just how universal the concept of fair play can be in the world and how different are the interpretations of the term. Nevertheless the mass media must ask themselves whether they are to play an iconoclastic role and if they do, what will be left of international sport for them to work with. Co-operation of sports writers in awarding "fair play" trophies instituted by L'Association Internationale de la Presse Sportive (A.I.P.S.) and the International Council of Sport and Physical Education (ICSPE) suggests that idealism has not yet been thrown overboard.

Sport has been advanced as an activity which knows no boundaries of race or religion or politics. This is an idealistic view which has taken some hard knocks, yet there have been significant achievements. Some inroads have been made into racial discrimination in South Africa, not many but some. In 1967 a poll sponsored by Tass, picked the American girl swimmer Debbie Myers as sportswoman of the year. It is hard to imagine, writes Christopher Chataway, Tass declaring General Westmoreland as general of the year, indeed it is hard to imagine any other sphere in which Tass would have awarded such a distinction to an American. In the Olympic Movement, de Coubertin enunciated ideals which have often been called into question yet in a detailed analysis of twelve separate values in his Olympic idea, Hans Lenk has shown that the majority are being put into practice to a greater or lesser extent. Where then do the mass media stand? Are they on the side of the iconoclasts? If not, will they expose shortcomings from the ideal ruthlessly and fearlessly, in their own country as well as in other? Will they actively promote what de Coubertin called "Healthy democracy, wise and peaceful internationalism, preserving within the stadium the cult of honour and disinterestedness which will enable athletics to help in the tasks of moral education and social peace as well as of muscular development"?

The third feature of sport which concerns mass media is unreality. In sport the laws of ordinary life are superseded. In real life we do not throw things at others but in cricket and baseball we do. In real life we do not steal another's property with impunity, but in basketball and football the first objective is to gain possession of the ball. In real life we do not pin another man to the ground or strike him on the body, but in wrestling and fencing we do. Such conduct is permissible because and only because it is unreal. The rules and conventions of every game and sport are devised to emphasise and delimit the area of unreality. The results of sporting contests are utterly useless. This is not to say that they do not matter or are of no importance. They matter supremely and if they do not they will not satisfy man or nation, but victory in sport is never for all time nor is defeat irreparable. The individual, the team, the nation, even the ideological bloc lives to fight another day. This concept of unreality, even of fantasy, is as important for the spectators as for participants, perhaps more so. Mass media have a role here, sometimes a subtle one, in preserving the unreality of sport.

The final point to which I wish to draw attention is ritual. It is said that there is no great church without a ritual. So it is of sport. Indeed sport may be described as ritualized aggression. De Coubertin thought that it would be through ceremonies that the Olympiad would distinguish itself from a mere series of world championships. He was wrong. Many world championships, many international and many national sporting events now have their rituals. Even the informal procession of athletes of all nations mixed together on the closing day of the Olympic Games has become a ritual of international understanding.

Sport then is essentially different from other spheres of life. It is unreal and has its own peculiar rituals. The mass media cannot therefore treat it as they would the reality of politics or economics or war. The treatment of sport requires special knowledge and special techniques if it is to preserve its international unity. Of course sport cannot be divorced from the rest of life. Values and value systems in a community will almost certainly be reflected in sport. In a troubled world sport will be troubled. When new nations seek identity and status they will seek it in sport as in other spheres of life. International understanding is not a denial of change or even of revolution, but in sport international understanding means the rule of law with all its unreality and ritual, and the recognition that opponents are sportsmen whether victors or vanquished.

I must return to my opening theme. Mass media cannot and must not present a false picture of the world of sport. Misunderstanding and hostility must be revealed as well as understanding and goodwill. Perhaps the best known dictum on the press in Britain is that of C. P. Scott, the former editor of the Manchester Guardian: "Fact is sacred but comment is free." It is to discuss how to exercise this freedom that we have met in the UNESCO house to-day.

PART II

A statement for discussion by national and international organisations of mass media and sport, prepared by a working party set up jointly by UNESCO and the International Council for Sport and Physical Education, and meeting in London 13/14 December 1973. Facilities were provided by The Sports Council of Great Britain.

I. Preamble

Sport is a universal phenomenon of Modern Times and one of the most important "sub-systems" of our Societies.

This characteristic of universality is founded on a need for physical expression and relationship which is inherent in the modern man.

It influences, at the same time, numerous sections of human activity: such as education, leisure, labour, health, spectacle.

It also relates to four major themes which concern UNESCO and are included in its programmes:—

1. Respect of human rights.
2. Communications between nations.
3. Developing countries.
4. Balance and harmony of the human being.

This universality in terms of the phenomenon of sport implies the possibility of establishing exchanges, contacts and meetings. These latter have been encouraged all the more by the competitive aspect of sport, which not only assembles individuals and teams for competition but also attracts through its manifestations and international competitions a great part of the world.

Some nations and societies come to be known all over the world through the image of their sporting behaviour, so that it becomes possible to say that sport is inclined by its very nature to go beyond its own frontiers. Furthermore sport, being nonverbal, has become, as it were, a "lingua franca" between peoples.

This tendency to internationalisation and all that it means in the areas of information and propaganda, advertising, publicity and commerical exploitation cannot fail to have some influence over the relations between individuals, groups, or nations.

It sometimes tends to exacerbate nationalism, chauvinism, racism; it may even happen that it bursts into armed conflict, but it may also lead to fraternization and understanding between men so offering cultural enrichment and increasing the chances of peace.

The problem is *to determine the conditions that sport has to fulfil in order to contribute to the improvement of international understanding.* This question has to be approached without excessive optimism or unjustified prejudice.

From this point of view the importance of the role of the media is obvious—The Olympic Games and the World Football Cup are worldwide manifestations thanks to television. Thus the place given to sport by the written or spoken word, the film or the book enlarges the dimension and impact of sport in all its manifestations.

However, the way sport is presented by television and radio, and is analyzed and commented on by newspapers appears able to influence its very evolution, its integration into human life and its cultural and humanistic content. The mass media have a responsibility for the future and for the safeguarding of sport.

Are the journalists accepting or rejecting this responsibility? Is it possible to formulate a doctrine of the cultural and fraternal role of sport that would be accepted by all countries and all media?

Do the pressures either direct or hidden which are acting on the written, spoken or televised press as well as on sport itself help to give an illusionary character to this action?

What methods could improve the training, the competence and the sense of responsibility of those concerned with the mass media regarding the sporting phenomenon?

These appear to be the main questions this report will attempt to answer.

II. Differences between the Media

Differences between the media are such that the opportunities which are presented to them and the problems which they have to face are not uniform. Radio and television call for instant comment on an immediate sound or picture. On many occasions an instant selection of shot by cameraman and then by the controller must be made. The verbal comment is similarly instantaneous. The replay and the videotape provide only limited opportunities for second thoughts to be expressed and judgements to be revised. The written word provides opportunities for recollection, considered judgements and the editing of reports. The film affords the chance to achieve aesthetic, emotional or instructional effects by selecting and editing visual material and by matching sound to visual image. The different media are therefore faced with a number of common objectives but different tasks and problems.

III. The Informative and Instructional Role of the Media

The behaviour of the public, which can largely contribute to the rapprochement of nations, depends very often on an authentic and deep knowledge of the technical aspects of sport.

Spectators behave better when they know the rules of the game, the styles, the tactics, the training methods and above all the opponents.

It becomes, therefore, a duty for the media to give to the public information about all technical aspects of sport and the characteristics of the contestants.

This duty presupposes adequate professional training of sports reporters. This matter is referred to in section VIII of this statement.

The dissemination of technical information and the giving of instruction will often be the function of a specialised press, but in many parts of the world no such press exists at present and the press and the media in general must assume this function.

The exchange of written material, film and videotape between national organisations of the media can greatly help the dissemination of technical information and should be encouraged.

IV. The Social Responsibility of the Mass Media

Modern sport attracts a greater audience than any other comparable event. Everyone in any country can identify with popular athletes and sportsmen and sport cannot be separated from its social background.

Different social systems will be reflected by different motivations in sport so that regional and national sport will always be affected by the ideology prevailing in the region, nation or group concerned. Ideology can result in pressures on reporting. Such pressures, be they political, commercial or of some other kind, must be handled with discretion and kept relative. The international character of sport, mentioned in the preamble on the principles of UNESCO, demands that this be so. Mass media have an opportunity to work towards the socialisation of sport through the propagation of accepted values and standards of behaviour.

The attention given to "fair play" by the media is itself a contribution to international understanding.

Co-operation between sports organisations and mass media should help to develop a sense of self criticism in athletes. The athletes, for their part, should be ready for international co-operation, for co-education and for emancipation of all groups. One instance of progress which the media could foster would be the promotion of the position of women in international sports organisations such as the International Olympic Committee.

Mass media should make the social objectives of sport understandable to everybody regardless of the level of education of the individual or the group.

V. The Mass Media and the Personality of the Athlete

Everyone and thus every athlete has the right to have his personal prowess recognised in society and no society can exist without the recognition of excellence. The acceptance of sport as an important subsystem of society implies the acceptance of the athletic hero. In presenting an athletic hero the media have a decisive task. This is not to develop the cult of an individual but to help spectators and athlete alike to build a critical personal reflexion of the value of a sporting achievement. Mass media should therefore give, besides the sporting picture of an athlete, a clear human picture as well. Often they will enable a great athlete to transcend national frontiers and so to become a human object of international admiration and a focus for goodwill.

As an athlete approaches the end of his active career it is even more important that he should understand and cherish these positive qualities. When he finally retires he must then integrate in a changing social and professional life and may well need the help of social agencies as well as the media.

The awarding of prizes such as the Fair Play trophy or the Sievert prize for achievement in sport and then later in a profession or occupation is valuable. The presentation of the prizes can be used by the mass media to promote international understanding.

VI. Mass Media and Mass Sport

It is recognised that there are vastly differing systems of sports presentation and techniques in the publication of sport by the mass media in many countries. An international exchange of experiences could well benefit international sport.

The mass media, including technical magazines, should encourage people to go in for sports. Sport is taken to include all forms of sports activities and to use leisure time for useful physical recreation. The mass media should support the development of sport also by sponsoring and organizing leisure time activities that in any way help physical fitness. The merits of minor sports can be publicised and inactive people can be encouraged to participate.

The development of so-called "minority sports" at regional or local level should be given serious consideration. Public interest should not be focussed only on the spectacle event.

Just as the great national and international networks can help international understanding in their presentation of big events so local press and radio can do the same in the presentation of contests between clubs, schools, colleges and universities of different countries.

VII. Mass Media Rituals and Ceremonies

Rituals and ceremonies have developed as international sport has developed, and have always been an integral part of the Olympic Games as a result of de Coubertin's plans and intention to link ancient and modern games. These features of the Games are known to be popular. The indications are that the opening and closing ceremonies at the Munich Olympics attracted a larger number of viewers than any other events. In the German Federal Republic the figures supporting this statement have been reliably attested. Not all rituals are equally valuable in promoting international understanding and there is now considerable divergence of opinion on the relative value of different ceremonies.

There are those who feel that some ceremonies encourage chauvinism and others who believe that the same ceremonies produce international goodwill and mutual respect. Debate on these questions should and must continue. It is clear, however, that the treatment of rituals and ceremonies by the mass media is a most important element in the situation. Many reasons for or against rituals and ceremonies are advanced but their relevance to international understanding should be a matter of continuing concern and research by mass media.

VIII. Professional Training

The preceding paragraphs of this statement have suggested that the professional training of sports reporters in all media is of the greatest importance. At the present time it is often inadequate. It is difficult to see how the reporter can make a significant contribution to international understanding unless certain criteria have been observed.

First the sports reporter, because of his responsibilities, his need for linguistic ability and his judgements on events, must occupy a position within his journal or organisation which is in no way inferior to those of his colleagues. He must be recruited and trained on the basis of the quality which his position will demand.

Secondly the sports reporter needs a deep technical knowledge of the sports on which he has to comment. This knowledge, however, will not be productive unless it is part of a serious general culture and a highly developed art of language and communication.

Thirdly the continuous training of the sports reporter is essential and should enable him to acquire varied experience with a view to attaining competence wherever possible in all the related media of press, radio and television.

Fourthly the accepted ethical rules and code of practice must always be fully respected both by journalists within the profession and by those employed on a free lance basis. When athletes and past-champions are used as consultants they should work closely with experienced professional journalists.

The requirements of professional standards can be met only by the development of courses and seminars, the exchange of documents, meetings in foreign countries, and by recourse to universities and institutes capable of providing appropriate statistics and adequate documentation.

IX. Research

There is a dearth of scientific analysis about fundamental relationship between sport, mass media and international relationships.

It is therefore urgent that research be undertaken in this field, using, e.g., the methods of the psycho-social sciences and of the science of communications.

Among the many problems of interest, two are fundamental:—

(i) What are the "stereotypes" depicted in sports and the attitudes and opinions towards sports and sportsmen in various countries, as seen through the mass media?

(ii) From the point of view of international relations, and also that of the spectators and participants, what are the precise meanings and psychological effects of ceremonies, emblems, anthems, and, generally speaking, all the symbolic elements which accompany international sports events?

Such research should be conducted simultaneously and in a co-ordinated manner by researchers from different countries who will be using similar techniques.

The support of UNESCO, The International Council of Sport and Physical Education (ICSPE) and of the International Committee of Sports Sociology is essential.

From a philosophical point of view, it remains highly desirable that the Olympic conception of sport is specified, particularly vis-à-vis the potential contribution of sport to peaceful international relationships. This could lead to the idea of "Olympism" being more convincingly diffused through the mass media. Researchers should, of course, work in close collaboration with agencies already considering the topic (IOC, IOA and so on).

The role of the mass media in promoting international understanding through sport should be discussed at international conferences such as that of the International Association of Sports Writers in Malaga, Spain, 24-29 March 1974, and the Congress of Sports Sciences in Moscow in November 1974.

X. The Future

International sport is now firmly established as a most important part of the social life of all nations in the world. It will certainly continue to be so and will, in all probability, become more important with each year that goes by. International sport brings the great mass of people in different countries into contact with each other. The teams, the managers, the spectators, and the public come to share a common body of thought, knowledge and experience. There is no doubt that international contests in which mistakes and bad sportsmanship occur, create a temporary wave of ill feeling. Such contests, however, are rare exceptions among the many thousands of international sporting contests which happen every year, which are carried out in a spirit of friendship and which create strong bonds of international goodwill among nations in all continents. The mass media can if they will, help to produce conditions in which such contests flourish.

APPENDIX

At present no comprehensive statistical and descriptive analysis of the way sport is being treated by the mass media exists. A survey would allow a more extensive appreciation of the problems and their possible solutions. The plan for such an extensive and precise survey which would be handled by individual countries but might be co-ordinated by one of the national sports documentation centres at Graz, Liege, Waterloo (Canada) or Birmingham (G.B.) could include the following headings.

(I) *Specialised Newspapers*
  (a) Daily papers: number, issue, distribution, lay-out, publicity (advertising), exploitation, tendencies, distribution of the rubriques, illustration, place given to national and international sport.
  (Why some countries do not have daily sports newspapers?)
  (b) Publications (weekly, monthly) specialising in one sport.

(II) *Information papers*
  Consider the most important. Indicate the place given to sport in percentage, the number of editors (percentage, independence, tendencies, rubriques, place of international sport).

(III) *Radio*
  The place of sport
  The reporters

The form of the transmission
Imposition of advertising

(IV) *Television*
The time given to sports transmission
Form and content
Tendencies
Advertising—national and international sport

(V) *Films and Books*

TRANS-SOCIETAL SPORT ASSOCIATIONS: A DESCRIPTIVE ANALYSIS OF STRUCTURES AND LINKAGES

JAMES E. HARF, ROGER A. COATE, HENRY S. MARSH

The purpose of this article is to describe those formal trans-societal associations whose primary activities relate to sport and recreation. The fact that such associations are formed is taken for granted. Individuals from nearly every society are acquainted with the activities of the International Olympic Committee, for example. However, it is doubtful that the extent and complexity of the network of trans-societal sports associations are perceived by more than a handful of persons. These associations will be examined along several dimensions: these organizations themselves—the number and nature of specific sports types, their geographic breadth, the specificity of their functions; the network of formal inter-organizational links; the nature of each membership—the number and types of countries of membership origin, the transnational interlocking bonds suggested by common membership patterns, and the like; and the applicability to sports associations of some basic theories about the nature of membership in all types of trans-societal associations.

All data in this article are drawn from the *Yearbook of International Organizations,* 14th edition (1972-73), the definitive work for scholars of international political, social, and economic organizations. Published by the Union of International Associations in Brussels, the *Yearbook* enjoys universal reputation as the most comprehensive source of information about transnational associations. It should be emphasized, however, that all conclusions drawn in this article are subject to the limitations of the information collection and verification procedures of the *Yearbook.*

From *Quest,* Monograph XXII (June, 1974): 52-62.

TRANS-SOCIETAL ORGANIZATIONS

Since the advent of the nation-state 500 years ago, interaction among peoples of substantial geographic distance has usually occurred at the governmental level rather than at individual or group levels. To a great extent only national governments had the need, the resources, and the inclination to communicate with one another. However, the twentieth century, and particularly the post-World War II era, has seen the rapid development of non-governmental bodies whose community of activity minimizes the absoluteness of nation-state boundaries. These trans-societal groups—be they individuals such as an internationally popular recording group or a multi-national corporation such as I.T.T.—represent a phenomenon with far-reaching implications for the future international political, economic, and social system.

One prominent international actor is the trans-societal non-governmental association, an organization type whose principal activity focuses upon one of such diverse topics as religion, trade unions, the arts, social welfare, or sports and recreation. These trans-societal associations differ from other supranational bodies across several dimensions. First, unlike governmental organizations, a trans-societal non-governmental association (NGO) is not established by inter-governmental agreement; rather, *individuals and groups constitute its membership*. Second, unlike multinational corporations *no one national group usually controls the operation of the organization* (an American corporation with overseas operations, for example). Third, *the aims of the body must be truly trans-societal in character*, encompassing members which reside in at least three countries. And finally, there are a *number of less critical criteria* such as a formal structure, budget contributions from members within three different countries, officers from various nationalities, and evidence of activity during the past year.

CHARACTERISTICS OF SPORT NGO'S

According to the *Yearbook* there are 2470 associations that fulfill these criteria for trans-societal non-governmental status. Of this group 115 are categorized as sport and recreation associations. These are given in Appendix 1. This number has increased at a fairly consistent rate in this century, as Table 1 demonstrates. This list represents 45 different specific sports; foremost among these include football/soccer (7 associations), billiards (6), table tennis (6), chess (4), cycling (4), ice hockey (3), skiing (3), swimming (3), and weightlifting (3).

TABLE 1
Growth of Sports NGO'S

pre-1900	4
1900-1909	8
1910-1919	8
1920-1929	17
1930-1939	8
1940-1949	13
1950-1959	25
1960-1969	16
Total	99
No Date Given	16
Grand Total	115

Associations are not limited, of course, to specific sports. General purpose groups include 32 in number, either to meet the needs of a specific clientele (such as university student, worker, or disabled person) or to perform functions which are applicable across many sports (such as medical research). Among these topics represented by more than one association, seven are devoted specifically to health and physical education, four to sports for the handicapped, four to women's organizations, and two each to university and workers' groups.

Trans-societal sports associations may also be classified according to the breadth of their membership. One definition of breadth is *the extent to which an organization is global,* i.e., contains members from at least two of the five major geographic regions (Africa, America, Asia, Oceania, and Europe). Of the 115 organizations in the sample, 84 are global, with 54 of these represented by members from all five regions. By contrast, Asia and Latin America head the rest of the 31 remaining single-region organizations with seven each, followed by Europe with six members.

INTER-ORGANIZATIONAL LINKS

There are various formal links among trans-societal sports associations. Of the 115 associations, 73 were involved in the interlocking sports network. These bonds are, for the most part, centralized. For example, 53 NGO's (73%) were linked either directly or indirectly with the Interna-

FIGURE 1

International Olympic Committee Network

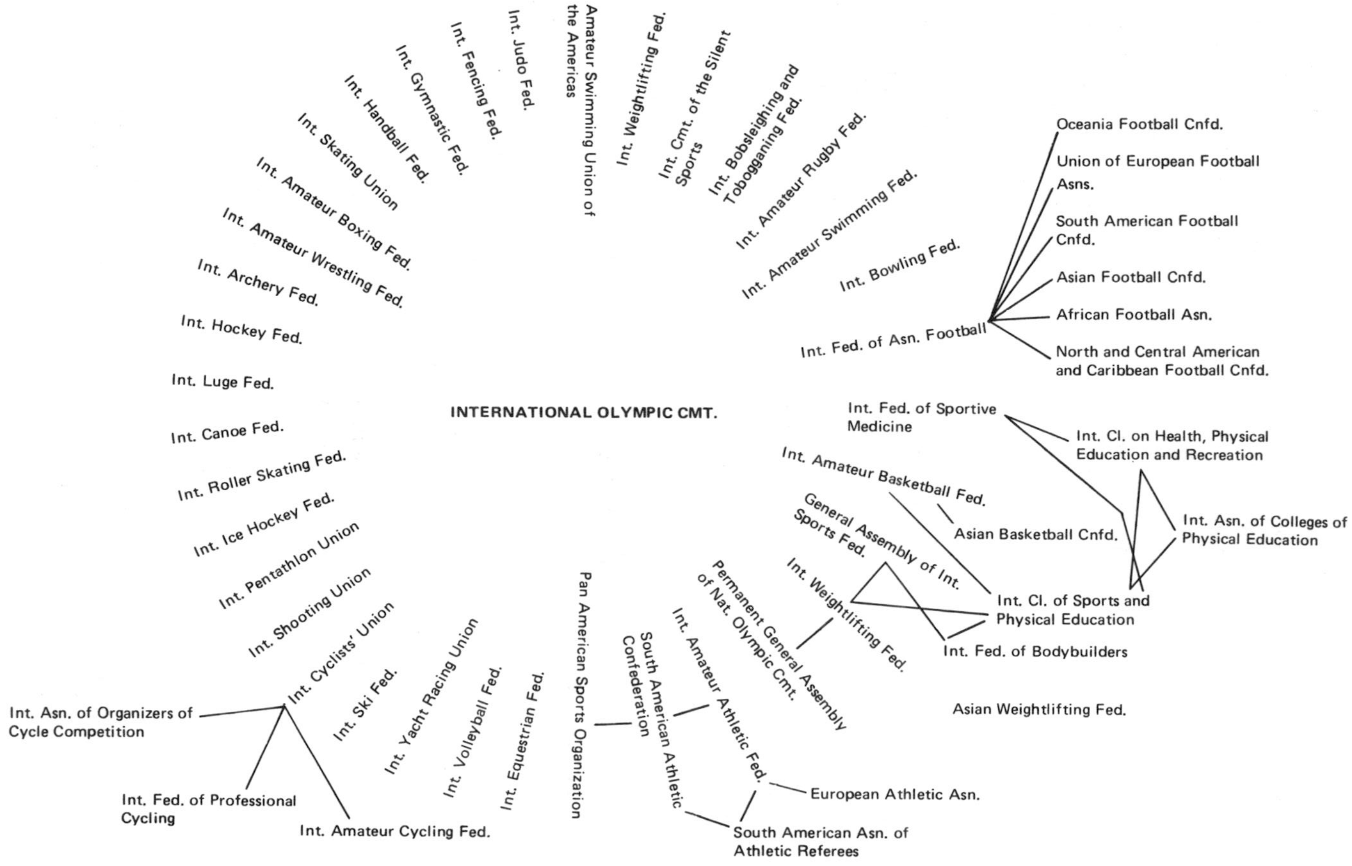

- Oceania Football Cnfd.
- Union of European Football Asns.
- South American Football Cnfd.
- Asian Football Cnfd.
- African Football Asn.
- North and Central American and Caribbean Football Cnfd.
- Int. Cl. on Health, Physical Education and Recreation
- Int. Asn. of Colleges of Physical Education
- Int. Cl. of Sports and Physical Education
- Int. Fed. of Bodybuilders
- Asian Weightlifting Fed.
- Int. Bowling Fed.
- Int. Fed. of Asn. Football
- Int. Amateur Swimming Fed.
- Int. Rugby Fed.
- Int. Bobsleighing and Tobogganing Fed.
- Int. Cmt. of the Silent Sports
- Int. Weightlifting Fed.
- Int. Fed. of Sportive Medicine
- Int. Amateur Basketball Fed.
- Asian Basketball Cnfd.
- General Assembly of Int. Sports Fed.
- Int. Weightlifting Fed.
- Permanent General Assembly of Nat. Olympic Cmt.
- European Athletic Asn.
- South American Asn. of Athletic Referees
- Int. Amateur Athletic Fed.
- South American Athletic Confederation
- Pan American Sports Organization
- Amateur Swimming Union of the Americas
- Int. Judo Fed.
- Int. Fencing Fed.
- Int. Gymnastic Fed.
- Int. Handball Fed.
- Int. Skating Union
- Int. Amateur Boxing Fed.
- Int. Amateur Wrestling Fed.
- Int. Archery Fed.
- Int. Hockey Fed.
- Int. Luge Fed.
- Int. Canoe Fed.
- Int. Roller Skating Fed.
- Int. Ice Hockey Fed.
- Int. Pentathlon Union
- Int. Shooting Union
- Int. Cyclists' Union
- Int. Ski Fed.
- Int. Yacht Racing Union
- Int. Volleyball Fed.
- Int. Equestrian Fed.
- Int. Amateur Cycling Fed.
- Int. Asn. of Organizers of Cycle Competition
- Int. Fed. of Professional Cycling

INTERNATIONAL OLYMPIC CMT.

tional Olympic Committee (I.O.C.). Figure 1 illustrates this formal relationship structure of the I.O.C.

Two additional organizations—International Table Tennis Federation and World Billiards Union—and their regional affiliates account for 13 of the remaining 19 links. Thus, three NGO's, through their direct and indirect networks, account for over 90% of the formal links within the sport and recreation network.

Although this network is relatively simple, there does exist substantial interaction. However, the pattern is different when the bonds between trans-societal sports/recreation associations and *other kinds* of international (governmental and non-governmental) organizations are examined. Only three of the sports NGO's—International Federation of Sportive Medicine, International Council of Sport and Physical Education, and International Recreation Association—have formal ties with non-sport intergovernmental organization. In each case, the sports NGO has consultative status with at least two organizations with the United Nations family. In addition, only three trans-societal sports associations—International Federation of Sportive Medicine, International Council Against Bullfighting, and International Motorcycle Federation—maintain formal relations with non-sport NGO's.

Thus, the emerging picture of the trans-societal sports network is one of internal centralization but external isolation.

CHARACTERISTICS OF THE MEMBERSHIP

The previous section focused on the formal linkage network of the sports and recreation NGO's. Now, in a discussion of the memberships within these organizations themselves, a caveat is in order. Although these associations are non-governmental in the sense that they are not established by inter-governmental agreement, most trans-societal sport and recreation organizations are composed of federations with national affiliations. Therefore, when "nations" are identified in this analysis, federations (and in some cases, individuals) which are located within these nations are in fact meant.

Table 2 rank orders the top 50 nations according to the number of organizational memberships. The intense membership patterns from the European region clearly stand out. France occupies first place by virtue of 73 memberships, followed by Belgium and West Germany with 71 each. It is interesting to note that the first 11 positions and 20 of the first 25 are occupied by European nations. The predominance of European representatives can also be seen by examining the average number of sports

TABLE 2

Rank Ordering of Countries of Origin of NGO Members

Rank	No. of I.O. Memberships	Country	Rank	No. of I.O. Memberships	Country
1	73	France	26	49	Ireland
2	71	Belgium	27	48	Mexico
2	71	F.R. Germany	27	48	D.R. Germany
4	69	Switzerland	27	48	Greece
5	68	United Kingdom	27	48	Luxembourg
6	67	Netherlands	31	47	U.S.S.R.
6	67	Italy	31	47	Chile
8	66	Spain	33	46	Turkey
9	65	Sweden	33	46	Israel
10	64	Austria	33	46	U.A.R.
11	62	Poland	36	45	Bulgaria
11	62	U.S.A.	37	44	Rumania
13	61	Canada	37	44	India
14	60	Denmark	39	43	Peru
15	59	Japan	40	41	Venezuela
15	59	Czechoslovakia	41	40	Colombia
15	59	Finland	42	39	Morocco
15	59	Norway	42	39	South Africa
19	58	Yugoslavia	42	39	Uruguay
20	55	Argentina	42	39	South Korea
20	55	Portugal	46	37	Cuba
22	54	Brazil	46	37	Philippines
23	53	Australia	48	36	Ecuador
24	50	New Zealand	49	35	Iran
24	50	Hungary	50	34	Pakistan

SOURCE: *Yearbook of International Organizations,* 1972-1973 (14th Edition).

organizations for each country within a region. The average European nation is represented in 47 organizations, more than double that of any other region (23 for the Americans, 19 for Asia, and 11 for both Africa and Oceania) and 10 more than the average for all nations (37).

More informative than the regional differences, perhaps, is the distinction between the so-called rich and the relatively poorer nations. When the European nations are joined with the United States, Canada, Japan, Australia, and New Zealand, their average number of memberships is over three times greater than the average for the poorer nations (48 vs. 15).

These findings do not provide a complete picture of the sports NGO membership patterns. Several of the relatively poorer countries are quite active in these associations. As Table 2 reveals, for example, several Latin American nations—Argentina, Brazil, Mexico, and Chile—are intensely involved in the trans-societal sports system.

The dominance of Europe remains, however, and can also be shown by the data relating to an organization's founding place and current headquarters. Of the 82 NGO's for which information exists, 66 were founded in Europe (19 in Paris and 11 in London alone). The headquarters or principal officer of 78 NGO's (from data available on 108 associations) are located there (with 22 in England, 16 in Belgium, 12 in Switzerland, and eight in France).

The dominance of Europe in international sport is even more evident when the linkages between nations, reflected in common membership pairs, are examined. Table 3 on page 132 lists *selected* ranked pairs of co-memberships. Two such sets, France-Belgium and France-West Germany, have the most common memberships (71). The first 65 pairs, in fact, are composed entirely of European nations. It is not until the 66th position that a non-European nation (the United States and Canada) is found.

We had also expected to find a distinctive pattern of co-memberships involving nations of the Soviet Union's political bloc. However, a contrary pattern emerged; each of the Eastern European countries (including the Soviet Union) had far more ties with the non-communist Western European nations than with each other.

TRANS-SOCIETAL ORGANIZATIONAL THEORY

Two basic theoretical frameworks will now be employed to study the implications of the expansion of trans-societal organizational activities. These two—feudality and entropy—are basically contradictory. Although they both focus on the relative equality of actors and the nature of the division of labor, each emphasizes polar extremes (Alger & Hoovler, 1974). The feudality model posits that the system consists of grossly unequal actors—Center and Periphery societies—involved in asymmetric relationships. The Center societies in such a system dominate the Periphery societies. The Periphery societies are thus isolated into vertical interactive networks (Galtung, 1971). The entropy model, on the other hand, suggests that a system which is characterized by high entropy consists of relatively equal actors involved in a symmetric and horizontal interaction network (Galtung, 1967).

TABLE 3

Rank Ordering of Co-Memberships of Countries
of Origin of NGO Members

Rank	Countries Linked		No. of Co-Memberships
1	France	Belgium	71
1	France	F.R. Germany	71
3	France	Switzerland	69
3	Belgium	F.R. Germany	69
5	France	Italy	67
5	Belgium	Switzerland	67
5	Switzerland	F.R. Germany	67
8	France	Spain	66
8	France	Netherlands	66
8	Italy	F.R. Germany	66
66	France	U.S.A.	57
66	Belgium	U.S.A.	57
66	Canada	U.S.A.	57
81	France	Canada	56
81	Belgium	Canada	56
81	F.R. Germany	U.S.A.	56
92	F.R. Germany	Canada	55
92	Belgium	Japan	55
92	France	Japan	55
155	Argentina	Brazil	51
155	Argentina	U.S.A.	51
309	Belgium	U.A.R.	44
309	France	U.A.R.	44
309	F.R. Germany	U.A.R.	44
309	France	Israel	44
309	F.R. Germany	Isreal	44
309	Switzerland	Isreal	44

SOURCE: *Yearbook of International Organizations,* 1972-1973 (14th Edition).

In this section the sports and recreation NGO interactive network will be examined with respect to these two conflicting models. According to Galtung (1971) there are four rules for defining a feudal system:

1. interaction between Center and Periphery is *vertical;*
2. interaction between Periphery and Periphery is *missing;*
3. multilateral interaction involving all three is *missing;*
4. interaction with the outside world is *monopolized* by the Center, with two implications:
   a. Periphery interaction with other Center nations is *missing;*
   b. Center as well as Periphery interaction with Periphery nations belonging to other Center nations is *missing.*

Figure 2 presents a diagram of the structure of a feudal interaction system.

To what extent does the trans-societal sports network conform to these four rules of feudal interaction? Three different units of analysis—national co-membership patterns, regional linkage patterns, inter-associational linkage patterns—will be employed in the examination. These findings can then be compared with the Alger and Hoovler (1974) analysis of the entire NGO membership system. This latter study examined the NGO membership systems of specified centers (Europe and North America) and peripheries (Africa, Asia, and Latin America).

In general, the Center-Periphery interaction pattern of sports NGO's is not characterized by a pattern of verticality. In fact, just the opposite

Figure 2

A Feudal Interaction System

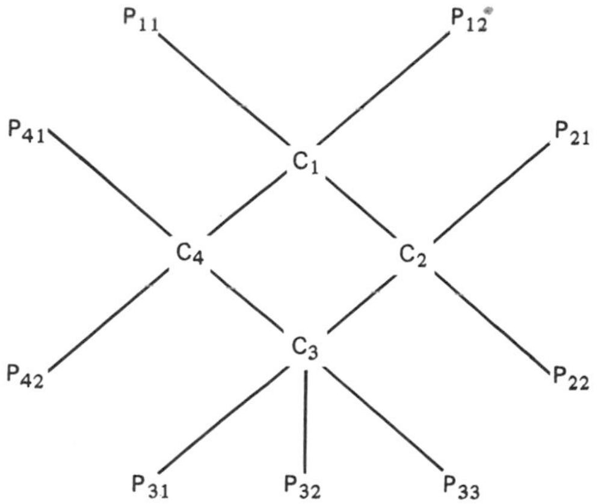

pattern emerges; the Center and Periphery areas, as specified, are involved in a large percentage of multilateral interactions. Table 4 indicates that 45.7% of all trans-societal sports associations are organized multilaterally to include members from each of the six areas specified. The percentage of organizations having maximum multilateral interactions jumps to over 50% when Oceania is omitted from consideration as a separate area (as in the Alger and Hoovler study). This figure (50%) is much

TABLE 4

The Number and Percentages of Various Regional Membership Compositions of NGO's, 1972*

Region						Number	% of Sports NGO's	% of All NGO's
Africa	L. America	N. America	Asia	Europe	Oceania	48	45.7	23.4
	L. America	N. America	Asia	Europe	Oceania	2	1.9	3.5
Africa		N. America	Asia	Europe	Oceania	3	2.86	2.1
Africa	L. America			Europe	Oceania	1	.95	0.0
Africa	L. America	N. America	Asia	Europe		6	5.7	5.9
		N. America	Asia	Europe	Oceania	1	.95	1.4
	L. America	N. America	Asia	Europe		1	.95	2.7
Africa			Asia	Europe	Oceania	1	.95	.2
Africa	L. America		Asia	Europe		2	1.9	1.3
			Asia	Europe		4	3.8	3.7
		N. America		Europe		1	.95	2.7
	L. America	N. America				4	3.8	1.6
Africa				Europe		4	3.8	.8
Africa			Asia			2	1.9	.2
					Oceania	1	.95	.1
				Europe		6	5.7	33.2
			Asia			7	6.7	.8
	L. America					7	6.7	2.2
Africa						3	2.86	.7
Other							0.0	13.5
N/A						10		

*Construction of regions with no links are not included in this table.
Errors result from rounding.

SOURCES: *Yearbook of International Organizations,* 1972-1973 (14th Edition). Alger and and Hoovler, 1974.

higher than the 29.3% reported for all NGO's in the Alger and Hoovler (1974) study. Not only do the data not support the rule of vertical interaction (what Alger and Hoovler term marginalization), they lend evidence to the position that the sports NGO system follows the entropy pattern. In short, a horizontal interaction network does appear to exist.

The only evidence which might question such a conclusion is the inter-associational linkage patterns. Such hesitancy grows out of the fact that the three major sports NGO's which have regional affiliates—International Federation of Association Football, World Billiards Union, and International Table Tennis Federation—are all located in Europe. Their affiliates comprise 17 of the 31 single region associations. However, the dominance of multilateral associational interaction remains fairly unobscured.

The data, however, support Galtung's second rule. For the most part, interaction between Periphery and Periphery is infrequent. Table 5 presents the intra-regional and bi-regional sports NGO membership patterns. The only exclusively bi-regional links between Periphery areas exist between Asia and Africa. It seems in error to label these links as bi-regional, however. Both of these links represent Arab regional organizations. Thus, the Periphery areas do not tend to link themselves in the absence of the specified Center nations. Too much emphasis should not be placed on such an observation, however, because the Centers themselves are exclusively linked by only a single association.

The third rule—multilateral interaction involving Center and Periphery, and Periphery and Periphery is missing—has been examined earlier. Thus, further discussion will be foregone here.

TABLE 5

Sport NGO Membership Patterns: Number of
Intra-Regional and Bi-Regional Links, 1972

	North America	Latin America	Europe	Africa	Asia
North America	0*				
Latin America	4	7			
Europe	1	0	6		
Africa	0	0	4	3	
Asia	0	0	4	2	7

*Since the customary definition of an international organization requires three nations as members, a region with only two nations (Canada and U.S.) cannot have regional organizations.

The extent to which the interactions of any of the specified Periphery areas are monopolized by its respective Center—Latin America by North America, and Asia and Africa by Europe—is minimal. For instance, the four countries in each Periphery area whose residents have the most links with non-region entities are almost equally linked with both Centers. Table 6 illustrates this fact. Clearly no one Center totally dominates any one Periphery. Similarly, the interactions between nations of one Periphery with nations of another Periphery are not missing. In fact, such interactions are only a little less frequent than the interaction between the Centers and their respective Peripheries. Although the nations illustrated in Table 6 might fall into the special category of "go-between" nations as defined by Galtung (1971), in general the other nations within the periphery areas demonstrate similar patterns.

The examination of the extent to which the sports NGO system follows either a feudalistic or an entropy pattern leads to the conclusion that

TABLE 6

Co-Membership Matrix of Selected Center and Periphery Countries, 1972*

	France	U.S.A.	Morocco	South Africa	Tunisia	U.A.R.	Argentina	Brazil	Chile	Mexico	Israel	South Korea	India
France													
U.S.A.	57												
Morocco	38	35											
South Africa	36	37	10										
Tunisia	32	30	30	18									
U.A.R.	44	42	33	29	30								
Argentina	49	51	33	31	29	39							
Brazil	48	49	36	30	30	41	51						
Chile	40	42	28	27	25	34	45	45					
Mexico	45	47	31	32	27	38	43	43	41				
Israel	44	39	30	25	26	34	37	39	36	36			
South Korea	36	36	30	25	24	31	31	33	27	30	30		
India	36	37	26	26	23	32	34	33	31	34	33	30	
Philippines	33	32	26	22	23	30	30	30	27	30	30	29	32

*The matrix represents the four most frequently occurring Periphery-Center co-membership dyads from each area.

the system is not feudalistic. The dominance of organizations with world-wide (i.e., at least one member from each region) membership enables the interactions to flow in a relatively symmetric and horizontal manner. Such a system of relatively high entropy is quite distinct from the general feudalistic NGO system as outlined by Alger and Hoovler.

CONCLUSION

This article has attempted to describe those trans-societal organizations which are involved in sport and recreation activities. Using the *Yearbook of International Organizations,* we have focused on structural characteristics of these associations, the formal network of organizational links, the nature of their membership, and the bonds among members of these associations. In addition, we have briefly examined the extent to which two competing theories of trans-societal organizational network bonds are applicable to sport and recreation associations. It is hoped that these brief surveys will provide insights into international sport.

REFERENCES

Alger, C. F., & Hoovler, D. The feudal structure of systems of international organizations. Paper presented at the meeting of the International Peace Research Association, Varanasi, India, January 1974.

Feld, W. J. *Nongovernmental forces and world politics: A study of business, labor, and political groups.* New York: Praeger Publishers, 1972.

Galtung, J. Entropy and the general theory of peace. Paper presented at the Second IPRA General Conference, Sweden, Summer 1967.

———. A structural theory of imperialism. *Journal of Peace Research,* 1971, 8, 81-117.

Tew, E. S., ed. *Yearbook of international organizations:* 1972-73 (14th ed.) Brussels: Union of International Associations, 1972.

APPENDIX 1

TRANS-SOCIETAL NGO SPORT AND RECREATION ASSOCIATIONS

African and Near East Billiards Cnfd.
African Football Cnfd.
African Table Tennis Cnfd.
Amateur Swimming Union of the
  Americas
Arab Table Tennis Fed.
Asian Amateur Athletic Asn.

Int. Fencing Fed.
Int. Gymnastic Fed.
Int. Handball Fed.
Int. Hockey Fed.
Int. Hockey Rules Board
Int. Hunting and Shooting Cl.
Int. Ice Hockey Fed.

Asian Badminton Cnfd.
Asian Basketball Cnfd.
Asian Billiards Cnfd.
Asian Football Cnfd.
Asian Weightlifting Fed.
Asn. of Track and Field Statisticians
British Commonwealth Games Fed.
British Commonwealth Weightlifting
    Fed.
Caribbean Table Tennis Fed.
European Athletic Asn.
European Billiards Cnfd.
European Bridge League
European Table Tennis Union
General Assembly of Int. Sports Feds.
Int. Amateur Athletic Fed.
Int. Amateur Basketball Fed.
Int. Amateur Boxing Asn.
Int. Amateur Cycling Fed.
Int. Amateur Rugby Fed.
Int. Amateur Swimming Fed.
Int. Amateur Wrestling Fed.
Int. Archery Fed.
Int. Asn. of Colleges of Physical
    Education
Int. Asn. of Organizers of Cycle
    Competitions
Int. Asn. of Physical Education and
    Sports for Girls and Women
Int. Asn. of Skal Clubs
Int. Asn. of Sport Research
Int. Badminton Fed.
Int. Bobsleighing and Tobogganing
    Fed.
Int. Bowling Board
Int. Bowling Fed.
Int. Braile Chess Asn.
Int. Bureau for Research on Leisure
Int. Canoe Fed.
Int. Cmt. of the Silent Sports
Int. Correspondence Chess Fed.
Int. Cl. Against Bullfighting
Int. Cl. of Sport and Physical
    Education
Int. Cl. on Health, Physical Education,
    and Recreation
Int. Cricket Cnfd.
Int. Cross-Country Union
Int. Cyclists' Union
Int. Equestrian Fed.
Int. Esperantist Chess League

Int. Judo Fed.
Int. Lawn Tennis Fed.
Int. Luge Fed.
Int. Military Sports Cl.
Int. Motorcycle Fed.
Int. Olympic Cmt.
Int. Pentathlon Union
Int. Playground Asn.
Int. Recreation Asn.
Int. Roller Skating Fed.
Int. Rowing Fed.
Int. Shooting Union
Int. Skating Union
Int. Ski Fed.
Int. Sporting Press Asn.
Int. Sports Organization for the
    Disabled
Int. Sports Union of Post, Telephone
    and Telecommunications Services
Int. Squash Rackets Fed.
Int. Stoke Mandeville Games Cmt.
Int. Table Tennis Fed.
Int. Technical and Scientific Org. for
    Soaring Flight
Int. Track and Field Coaches Asn.
Int. Union of Alpine Asns.
Int. University Sports Fed.
Int. Volleyball Fed.
Int. Weightlifting Fed.
Int. Women's Cricket Cl.
Int. Workers Sport Asn.
Int. Workers Swimming Cmsn.
Int. Yacht Racing Union
Maccabi World Union
North American Billiards Cnfd.
North and Central American and
    Caribbean Football Cnfd.
Oceania Football Cnfd.
Pan American Sports Org.
Permanent General Assembly of
    National Olympic Cmts.
South American Asn. of Athletic
    Referees
South American Athletic Cnfd.
South American Billiards Cnfd.
South American Football Cnfd.
South American Roller Skating Cnfd.
Supreme Cl. for Sport in Africa
Table Tennis Cnfd. of South America
Table Tennis Fed. of Asia
Union of European Football Asns.

Int. Fed. of Asn. Football
Int. Fed. of Body Builders
Int. Fed. of Orienteering
Int. Fed. of Physical Education
Int. Fed of Professional Cycling
Int. Fed of Sportive Medicine
Int. Fed. of Women's Hockey Asns.

Union of Int. Motorboating
Women's Int. Hockey Rules Board
World Billiards Union
World Bridge Fed.
World Chess Fed.
World Underwater Fed.

BIBLIOGRAPHY

Section B. Cultural Perspective—

Ball, Donald and Loy, John. *Sport and Social Order: Contributions to the Sociology of Sport.* Reading, Mass.: Addison-Wesley, 1975.

Daniels, A. S. "The Study of Sport as an Element of Culture," *International Review of Sport Sociology* 1 (1966):153-65.

Dunning, Eric. *Sport: Readings From a Sociological Perspective.* Toronto: University of Toronto Press, 1972.

———., ed. *The Sociology of Sport.* London: Frank Cass & Co., 1971.

Kenyon, Gerald S. and Loy, John W. "Toward a Sociology of Sport," *Journal of Health, Physical Education and Recreation* 36 (1965):24-5, 68-69.

———. *Sport, Culture and Society.* New York: The Macmillan Co., 1969.

Lüschen, Günther, ed. *The Cross-Cultural Analysis of Sport and Games.* Champaign, Ill.: Stipes Pub. Co., 1970.

Maheu, Rene. "Sport and Culture," *Journal of Health, Physical Education and Recreation* 34 (October 1963):30-32.

McIntosh, Peter. *Sport in Society.* London: C. A. Watts & Co., Ltd., 1963.

Talamini, J. T. and Page, C. H. *Sports and Society: An Anthology.* Boston: Little, Brown and Company, 1973.

Torkildsen, G. E. "Sport and Culture." Master's thesis, University of Wisconsin, 1967.

Wenkert, S. "The Meaning of Sports for Contemporary Man," *Journal of Existential Psychology* 3 (1963):397-404.

SPORT IN THE CONTEXT OF
AMERICAN CULTURE

This collection of articles is brought together to assist the reader in making a transition from definitions necessary to the study of sport in the larger Western cultural setting to sport in the context of American culture. The American sport scene is not only diverse but exceedingly complex. The life-styles and norms of culture set up the social environment in such a way as to shape the personal-social experience of people. Sport is no exception to that effect which is well illustrated by the writers represented in this section.

How to get a meaning is a complex task. Stone, in the lead article, pursues meaning by "exploring social relationships that are mobilized by sport and sport activities." He pursues the study of the social relationships in sport largely within the variables of sex and socioeconomic strata.

Friedenberg, in his two books, *The Vanishing Adolescent* and *Coming of Age in America,* takes a penetrating look at the youth of America. Athletic prowess, status, and experience are an integral part of his description of the life-style of those in high school. In the selection included here, his writing cuts deeply into some of the protected areas of sport. How revealing of a society is its choice of sport forms? Friedenberg states that "societies reveal much of themselves, and of their differences from other societies, in their preferences among sports. Basketball, for example, seems to me to provide an abstract parody of American middle-class life."

In considering competition as a primary value of Americans, Sadler suggests that competition in the society and in sport must be reassessed. He concludes that competition as a mode of experiencing sport is so over emphasized that concern for others and the spirit of play have been repressed. Competition is an element of sports, but Sadler insists that it must have well-defined limits so that it does not undermine other important values that are basic to human relationships.

Hart contends that the social situation of American sport and dance has functioned largely to reinforce male and female role expectations. The feminine-masculine game has distorted the range and diversity of experiences possible in sport and dance to such an extent that an individual may as easily achieve stigma as achieve prestige through these activities. This situation is most acute in the educational system where sport still functions largely to maintain tradition and therefore status quo. Not only is competition in the larger culture out-of-bounds, as discussed by Sadler, but also the macho male model as a norm in sport is out-of-bounds. Hart suggests that the male model for what is excellent in movement is only *one* criteria and should no longer be used exclusively for measuring excellence for either women or men. To do so is destructive of people and their experience in both recreational and performance levels of dance and sport.

The article by Riesman and Denney is a classic in the analysis of the relationship of sport to culture. These authors take football from its earliest stages in America (as a cultural inheritance from England) to modern-day football. The process of diffusion is clearly exemplified as the authors describe the make of American style football.

Lahr sees sport in America as the theatre of a highly industrialized state and further as a reaction to industry. He states, "But as the opportunity for physical prowess and uncomplicated, noble victory is denied mechanized man, the spectacle of sport has assumed a potency and ritual importance that most theatre has lost."

Lahr also takes a look at the "space game" in relation to sport. The connections are described in his statement, "Baseball and football make reality out of a game. The space race makes a game out of reality. Technology extends the demand, fed by sport, for continued, easy victory with no sacrifice from the community of observers."

It is impossible to separate into neat categories games, work, theatre, and technology when we consider them within the organically functioning and dynamically reacting force of human society. We have often studied these entities as if they operated in a laboratory situation. The extrinsic motivation for productivity in technology and sport, in the form of quotas, scores, and rewards, has caused us to lose sight of the personal process and the value of intrinsic motivation.

The last article is by Edwards, who sees American reporters as catering to public opinion in writing style and selection of content. He feels that the large majority of sports reporters (especially those who are white) have in no way demonstrated racial or social objectivity. There has been an effort on the part of the media to somewhat rectify this situation. However, there are still many changes necessary before the many ethnic groups, women, and a greater variety of sports get full and fair coverage. Sports with money-power still crowd the pages and the airways. The cultural emphasis on the spectator style of sport as the way of experiencing sport is reinforced by media programming and reporting. The question of the responsibility of the mass media surfaces again. What philosophy and cultural life-style does the media perpetuate?

SOME MEANINGS OF AMERICAN SPORT:
AN EXTENDED VIEW

Gregory P. Stone

What this paper represents is an extension of an earlier preliminary paper that I gave at Ohio State University a little more than a decade ago. At that time I had collected just under 200 interviews. The final sample consists of 566 interviews and for all intents and purposes that study is done.

First, a word about meaning—when I talk about meaning I use it in the sense of George Herbert Mead as the responses that are mobilized by a particular event. Consequently, the first matter of meaning has to do precisely with what kind of response people make when they are confronted with the symbol *sport*. It is this with which I am concerned and thus will get into it substantially.

To explore this problem I developed what probably is best called a proposive quota sample. I was interested not so much in making estimates of what's out there in the world or in the parameters of the problem if you like, as I was exploring social relationships that are mobilized by sport and sport activities. Consequently, I developed a box with three, six, twelve, with twenty-four cells. I was concerned in the first place with adults, married adults, with men and women, with older people and younger people, with urban and suburban residents and finally, with upper, middle, and lower socio-economic strata. Within each cell I selected relatively the same number of respondents, because I was concerned with getting at age, sex, residential and socio-economic differences. In selecting the urban sample I employed census tracts, and

From *Aspects of Contemporary Sport Sociology: Proceedings of C.I.C. Symposium on the Sociology of Sport*, edited by Gerald S. Kenyon, pp. 5-27. Chicago, Ill.: The Athletic Institute, 1969. Copyright © 1969 by The Athletic Institute.

using about seventeen different socio-economic variables, which I won't enumerate, picked out the top three tracts and told my students to go into those tracts, make a kind of reconnaissance and select only the best residences in their view within those tracts, for their sample. Then I took three tracts in the dead center of the distribution, again asking students to reconnoiter the tract areas in the city and try to reach some agreement among themselves on the model residents in those tracts. Next I took the three lowest ranking tracts and told the students to pick out the worst residences. So, I was trying to get socio-economic extremes, plus the dead center of the middle mass.

With suburbs it was more difficult because at that time, in terms of the tract data available, the suburban tracts were quite large and quite heterogeneous. So, I had to go pretty much on local reputation of the suburbs and thus we picked two of the high status suburbs, Edina and some parts of Minnetonka, two reputedly middle-class suburbs, and two working class suburbs, and then followed the same procedures in gathering interviews. One interesting point, I think, is that it was very difficult to find young, upper urban people who were married. The young upper-class seems to have abandoned the central city.

Now to begin with, all I did was ask these people what activities they thought of when they heard the word "sport." The number of activities that they reported are provided in Table 1.[1] Over 2,600 activities were mentioned so that each person on the average mentioned between four and five activities. There is a status relationship or socio-economic relationship between the number of activities that were reported or mentioned by these people. In general, the higher the status the greater the number of activities mentioned. This, I think, should be taken with a grain of salt because it may indicate merely a difference in verbalization among the strata and I may be reporting that rather than the fact that sport thas a greater saliency for upper status people than for lower status people. But the consistency between the middle and the lower socio-economic strata suggests that this may only be partially true, since there is no great difference between the middle strata and the lower strata. By the way, as is indicated in the footnote of the table, there are only 6 people of the 562 who answered the question who could not come up with any activities relating to sport, so certainly this underscores Dr. Lüschen's observations to the effect that sport has a profound saliency in our entire society.

1. For all tables only significant associations are presented. If age is not presented, there is no signficant association. I might say that because sport is still pretty much a male world, there are always significant sex differences, and thus I have only reported the ones that seem particularly interesting.

TABLE 1

Socio-Economic Differences in the Range of Activities
Interpreted as Sport by Metropolitan Residents

Number of Activities Interpreted as Sport	Socio-Economic Strata			Totals* (Per Cent)
	Upper (Per Cent)	Middle (Per Cent)	Lower (Per Cent)	
0-2‡	9.0	18.1	13.1	13.3
3	15.3	13.2	25.7	18.1
4	16.9	19.8	17.8	18.1
5	18.5	20.3	21.5	20.1
or more	40.2	28.6	22.0	30.2
Totals*	99.9 (n = 189)	100.0 (n = 182)	100.1 (n = 191)	99.8 (n = 562)

Chi square = 26.41 $.05 > p > .001$

*Four respondents, three in the upper stratum and one in the middle stratum, did not respond to the question.

‡Six respondents, two in the middle stratum and four in the lower stratum, mentioned no activities.

Some of the activities mentioned are quite interesting. Included as sport were such activities as relaxing, dancing, television, movies, woodworking and sex. Perhaps the inclusion of sex as sport is kind of apt testimony to the inappropriateness of the Freudian perspective for the interpretation of contemporary American sport David Riesman wrote about some time ago in a collection of very good essays on Freud. Freud viewed work as an inescapable and tragic necessity; and sex, too, was for Freud, a realm of necessity. He saw it not as presenting man with a problem to be solved nor with a game to be played nor coupled with love as a road to human closeness and intimacy, but rather as a teleological prime mover charged with the task of socializing and civilizing man and thus preserving the species. Sex could fulfill this task because of its ability to bribe with an elemental release. Work was then the means by which the species maintains itself while performing its endless procreative mission. Although, of course, in Freud's time sex was purchasable in the sporting houses of the day, the purchasers were probably not called athletes as some of them are called these days.

In spite of the mention of these rather unusual activities associated with the term sport, Table 2 indicates that the responses were, by and large, conventional. Spectator sports received the most frequent mention —football, baseball, and basketball; and that the mentioning of partici-

TABLE 2
The Differential Saliency of Various Sports
for Metropolitan Residents

Activities	Selected Social Characteristics*				Per Cent of Respondents Mentioning at Least One Sport (N = 556)
	Age	Sex	Residence	Socio-Economic Strata	
Football	———	———	———	———	72.7
Baseball	O-Y	M-F	———	L-M-U	66.9
Basketball	———	———	———	———	42.6
Hockey	———	M-F	———	———	21.0
Boxing	———	M-F	———	L-M-U	16.4
Wrestling	O-Y	———	———	L-U-M	10.2
Golf	———	———	———	U-M-L	35.2
Tennis	———	F-M	———	U-M-L	21.6
Bowling	———	———	———	L-M-U	19.4
Swimming	Y-O	F-M	———	U-M-L	30.6
Skiing	———	F-M	———	U-M-L	11.3
Fishing	———	M-F	———	———	29.0
Hunting	———	M-F	———	———	18.7

*Only significant associations as determined by the Chi-square Test are presented in the body of the table. The level of significance has been set at .05. Categories of informants making most mentions of any specified activity are listed first, those making fewest mentions are listed last, reading from left to right. In the age category, those less than forty years of age are designated "Y," those forty years of age or more are designated "O." In the sex category, men are designated "M" and women, "F." In the residence category, "U" designates respondents living in the Minneapolis city limits; "S," those living in the suburbs. In the socio-economic category, those in the highest category are designated "U," those in the middle, "M," and those in the lowest, "L."

pant sports is somewhat less. In short it seems that in the public mind, sport is still primarily a spectator or a spectatorial affair, a spectacle, if you like.

Again these are just words that people mentioned when they were presented with the symbol "sport" and I suppose that what is measured here is a kind of saliency of these different activities, but because the question is open-ended, again I would like to have you view these data with a kind of grain of salt. But saliency indicates what is salient. In other words I think we can say from these data that these particular sports are salient, are in the minds of people when we hear this term, but it doesn't indicate what is not salient. In other words, the fact that only 11 per cent of the people mentioned skiing does not indicate that skiing is not salient. The fact that 73 per cent mentioned football indicates that football is salient. Or that 10 per cent of the people mentioned wrestling does not indicate that wrestling is not salient as a sport in their minds. So some sports not mentioned or receiving very, very infrequent mentions may be much more salient than this table suggests. There may also be a seasonal kind of censure operating here. The fact that the interviews are taken in the fall may also affect these results. There certainly, I'm sure, is a status bias operating. I'm quite sure that people are loathe to confess to a higher status interviewer, a college student, that, in fact, wrestling is their bag.[2] So there are biases operating to distort those figures.

The two primary differentiating variables seems to be sex and status and some age differences which you would expect, particularly in the case of swimming. So that the sport audience, if you like, is "chopped up." As a sociologist might conceive it, it is differentiated. It is differentiated along the primary axes of sex and status.

The thing that I found also very interesting is the absence of any residential differences in these saliencies. I seriously had expected to see suburban-urban differences in conceptions of sport. Of course, there has been a vast literature on the leisure time of suburbia, but I uncovered no differences at all in terms of the saliency of these sports. This may indicate that, as another sociologist, Berger, has indicated, that of the sociological literature on suburbia is as biased as some of my own data

2. They are somewhat ashamed of being caught up in that marvelously curious spectacle which manages to outdraw professional basketball in Minneapolis. It will easily outdraw it. I'd say it gets about twice or three times the attendance of professional basketball, and that's only in the city and, of course, the wrestlers are working a circuit four or five nights a week. People probably don't know either that wrestling is probably the most lucrative professional sport. By and large, on the average, a third rate wrestler can count on about $18,000 a year.

are here, namely, dealing primarily with middle status suburban areas, not concerned with working class suburbs as I'm concerned with here or with high status suburbs.

I then asked people "what is your favorite sport?" Now, here we get into less difficulty in terms of saliencies and you can see that in terms of favorites, the people are about evenly divided between the selection of a spectator sport and a participant sport. The one point I think I'd like to make in terms of Table 3, is that we tend to think of spectatorship as being somehow low status or lower class in character.[3] So that we tend to look at spectatorship as being lower class. Now you will see a slight tendency—I don't think it's enough really to warrant a great deal of emphasis—for participation as a favorite sport to be somewhat greater in the lower strata than in the middle strata, which I think is rather interesting. There was one study done some time ago by Clarke on Leisure and Levels of Occupational Prestige in the *American Sociological Review*, in June of 1956, (Vol. 21, pp. 301-307) where he

TABLE 3

Socio-Economic Differences in the Designation of Spectator
or Participant Sports as Favorites by Metropolitan Residents

Favorite Sport	Socio-Economic Strata			Totals (Per Cent)
	Upper (Per Cent)	Middle (Per Cent)	Lower (Per Cent)	
Spectator	35.6	57.1	54.7	48.8
Participant	64.4	42.9	45.3	51.2
Totals	100.0 (N = 188)	100.0 (N = 175)	100.0 (N = 172)	100.0 (N = 535)

Chi square = 20.25   .05 > p > .001

3. I think sociologists themselves are pretty snobbish about sport. I think this is one reason that there has been so little done by sociologists in this country in sport. If you look at the two main journals, *The American Sociological Review* and *The American Journal of Sociology*, you will find that you can count the number of articles dealing with sport on one hand and on the fingers of one hand. I forget what the number actually is; I think it's only about four or five in the two journals. I have a friend who has been doing research on camping, for example. He sent his article first to the *American Sociological Review*, and received a letter back from the editor suggesting that he really should submit this article to Outdoor Life because it didn't belong in sociology. On the other hand, the editor seldom suggests that we submit articles on industrial sociology to Chamber of Commerce publications. However, through some mediation the paper was eventually published in the *American Journal of Sociology*.

did find in terms of leisure time activities a kind of U curve with more participation, more active forms of leisure occurring at the extremes of status rather than in the middle, and these data somewhat follow this. He was concerned with leisure activities; I'm concerned with sport, which is different, but there is a tendency to follow the U type of distribution which Clarke uncovered.

In Table 4 you will find the concrete activities designated as "favorites" and you will notice that there were some 26 respondents who

TABLE 4

Social Differences in Sports Designated as Favorites
by Metropolitan Residents

Favorite Sports	Selected Social Characteristics*				Per Cent of Respondents Selecting a Favorite Sport (N = 540)
	Age	Sex	Residence	Socio-Economic Strata	
Football	——	——	U-S	M-U-L	24.4
Baseball	——	M-F	——	L-M-U	15.4
Basketball	——	——	——	M-L-U	6.8
Boxing	——	M-F	——	L-M-U	3.3
Golf	——	——	——	U-M-L	11.3
Tennis	——	——	——	U-M-L	3.7
Bowling	——	F-M	——	L-M-U	6.3
Swimming	Y-O	F-M	U-S	M-U-L	7.6
Hunting	——	M-F	——	——	3.7
Fishing	——	M-F	——	——	9.6
Others too diverse to analyze	——	——	——	——	7.8

*Only significant associations as determined by the Chi-square Test are presented in the body of the table. The level of significance has been set at .05. Categories of informants making most mentions of any specified activity are listed first, those making fewest mentions are listed last, reading from left to right. In the age category, those less than forty years of age are designated "Y," those forty years of age or more are designated "O." In the sex category, men are designated "M" and women, "F." In the residence category, "U" designates respondents living in the Minneapolis city limits; "S" those living in the suburbs. In the socio economic category, those in the highest category are designated "U," those in the middle, "M," and those in the lowest, "L."

did not designate a favorite sport. Again you get the primary differentiation here of sex and status and although there are some differences
in the relationships reported in Table 4 as compared with Table 2, I
think that the relative presence of similarity in those two tables indicates something, some kind of argument for the validity of the data in
the second table.

I'm not primarily interested, of course, in what sports have saliency
in the population, because what a sociologist is concerned with is the
activities that are mobilized by sport itself and one very important activity is, of course, conversation. I mentioned earlier, for example, if a
man in our society does not have at least some conversational knowledge
of sport he's viewed as suspect, and I know of at least one psychiatrist,
who I mentioned in the earlier article, who used knowledge of sports as
a diagnostic device for recruits into the Army during World War II. If
the recruit didn't know, for example, who had won the last World Series
then perhaps it's better to give him a rather careful test in terms of his
maleness or homosexuality.

As to what is important in terms of conversation, it is that in the
presumed anonymity of the city a conversational knowledge of sports
gives strangers access to one another, so that if they meet in the bar or

TABLE 5
Sex Differences in Frequency of Sport Conversations
Carried on by Metropolitan Residents

Frequency of Sport Conversation	Sex		Totals* (Per Cent)
	Male (Per Cent)	Female (Per Cent)	
Rarely, Almost Never, or Never‡	10.6	28.5	19.8
Occasionally	25.9	32.0	29.0
Frequently	31.8	24.4	27.9
Very Frequently	31.8	15.1	23.2
Totals*	100.1 (n = 274)	100.0 (n = 291)	99.9 (n = 565)

Chi square = 44.45 $.05 > p > .001$

*One female respondent did not reply to the question.

‡Three males and seven females never discussed sports.

in other public places or on a plane or a train or a bus, one can immediately start up a conversation with a total stranger and gain access and penetrate the barriers or the insulations of anonymity that presumably we find in the city. So, Table 5 shows that in the first place it is a man's world; that the conversation about sports is quite frequent for men. About two-thirds of them say that they talk about sports frequently or very frequently, compared to somewhat more than a third of the women. Women, by the way, resent this, although I don't have time to go into it, but some of them are avid sports fans and they have a difficult time in finding anybody to talk about sport because the men refuse to discuss it with them. Imputing female interest in sports is probably somewhat on the order of an invasion of their world, and women then become indignant, and frequently you will find letters to the editors in the paper with women complaining that they are avid Twins fans, for example, but nobody will talk to them about sport. So, the fact that it is a man's world acts to seal off the sexual world, and particularly in the middle and lower strata, to set men and women a little bit further apart than perhaps they should be.

Table 6 shows the socio-economic differences and frequency of conversations. The most interesting datum is the polarization in the lower

TABLE 6

Socio-Economic Differences in Frequency of Sport Conversations
Carried on by Metropolitan Residents

Frequency of Sport Conversation	Socio-Economic Strata			Totals* (Per Cent)
	Upper (Per Cent)	Middle (Per Cent)	Lower (Per Cent)	
Rarely, Almost Never, or Never‡	10.4	17.5	31.6	19.8
Occasionally	33.3	32.8	21.1	29.0
Frequently	32.3	27.3	24.2	27.9
Very Frequently	24.0	22.4	23.2	23.2
Totals*	100.0 (n = 192)	100.0 (n = 183)	100.1 (n = 190)	99.9 (n = 565)

Chi square = 30.96   .05 > p > .001

*One lower stratum respondent did not reply to the question.

‡Two middle and eight lower stratum respondents never discussed sports.

strata between a third or almost a third who rarely or never talk about sports, and about a fourth of those who talk very frequently about sports. You will notice that in terms of frequent conversations the differences among the strata are so slight as to be negligible. I think what this means is that many lower strata people are left outside the world of sport. Based upon other data, I have found that there is a general alienation of the lower stratum when using such measures as integration with the neighborhood, and a sense of belonging to the larger city. There is a general alienation and perhaps this lack of involvement as measured by frequency of sport conversation on the part of the lower stratum indicates a larger alienation than being simply alienation from the sport world. But, once people in the lower stratum do get involved as are other people and the differences more or less disappear so that the association in Table 6 is primarily due to the relatively large number of lower strata people who simply are not involved in the sports world through their conversations.

Next, I asked in what situations did they discuss sport and here again we see the same shortcoming of open ended questions because the people answered this question spontaneously without being probed. Again, as shown in Table 7, you find it's a man's world, that most women

TABLE 7

Sex Differences in Situational Range of Sport Conversations
Carried on by Metropolitan Residents

Number of Situations Mentioned	Sex		Totals* (Per Cent)
	Male (Per Cent)	Female (Per Cent)	
0-1‡	18.5	32.1	25.5
2	30.7	29.3	30.0
3	30.4	23.4	27.0
4 or more	20.4	15.2	17.7
Totals*	100.0 (n = 270)	100.0 (n = 290)	100.2 (n = 560)
Chi square = 14.75 .05 $>$ p $>$ .01			

*Five respondents, three males and two females did not respond to the question. One male respondent gave a "Don't know" reply.

‡Fifteen respondents, four males and eleven females, did not converse about sports in any specific social situation.

talk about sports in relatively few situations. Most men identify a relatively large number of situations, three or more, so that sport, then, is
not only more salient to men and involves them more, but also carries
over into a larger number of the situations of their daily life. Table 8
shows largely the same status differences in terms of the situations as
is found in the frequency of the conversation.

TABLE 8

Socio-Economic Differences in Situational Range of Sport
Conversations Carried on by Metropolitan Residents

Number of Situations Mentioned	Socio-Economic Strata			Totals* (Per Cent)
	Upper (Per Cent)	Middle (Per Cent)	Lower (Per Cent)	
0-1‡	15.8	26.2	34.8	25.5
2	30.0	31.7	28.3	30.0
3	32.6	26.8	20.9	27.0
4 or more	21.6	15.3	16.0	17.7
Totals*	100.0 (n = 190)	100.0 (n = 183)	100.0 (n = 187)	100.2 (n = 560)

Chi square = 21.85   .05 > p > .01

*Five respondents, one upper and four lower stratum, did not respond to the question.
One upper stratum respondent gave a "Don't know" reply.

‡Fifteen respondents, one upper stratum, four middle, and ten lower stratum, did not
converse about sports in any specified social situation.

Turning to what situations are used for discussion in the mobiliza-
tion of involvement in sports, there are several comments I can make
about the data in Table 9. In the first place, there is the problem of the
open-ended question. Some people would say neighbors and some say
friends, and I was very literal in my code. Of course, I know not all
neighbors are friends. Anybody knows that who has a neighbor. But
some neighbors are friends and thus there is some overlap between these
categories. Nevertheless, there are some interesting differences here. In
terms of the family of procreation, that is, the immediate family, I did
get a residential difference which may testify somewhat to the sociological contention that familism is enhanced in the suburban environ-

TABLE 9

Social Differences in Situational Contexts of Sport
Conversation Carried on by Metropolitan Residents

Situational Contexts	Selected Social Characteristics*				Per Cent of Respondents Mentioning at Least One Situational Context (n = 945)
	Age	Sex	Residence	Socio-Economic Strata	
Family of Procreation	O-Y	F-M	S-U	U-M-L	63.4
Other Family	———	———	———	M-L-U	14.5
Neighbors	———	———	———	L-M-U	8.8
Friends	———	F-M	———	U-M-L	38.6
Parties and Other Social Gatherings	———	———	———	U-M-L	17.2
Work	———	M-F	———	L-M-U	40.3
Clubs and Voluntary Associations without Sports Facilities	———	———	———	———	6.4
Public Places (Bars, Taverns, Stores)	———	M-F	———	L-M-U	7.5
Sport Scene	———	———	———	U-M-L	22.2

*Only significant associations as determined by the Chi-square Test are presented in the body of the table. The level of significance has been set at .05. Categories of informants making most mentions of any specific activity are listed first, those making fewest mentions are listed last, reading from left to right. In the age category, those less than forty years of age are designated "Y," those forty years of age or more are designated "O." In the sex category, men are designated "M" and women, "F." In the residence category, "U" designates respondents living in the Minneapolis city limits; "S," those living in the suburbs. In the socioeconomic category, those in the highest category are designated "U," those in the middle, "M," and those in the lowest, "L."

ment as opposed to the environment of the central city. The interesting difference, I think, between the status differentiation of neighbors and friends may reflect the fact that in the lower strata there is a greater reliance upon neighboring as a source of friendship than is the case in the upper strata. I have some other materials on that. I would then point out that the prime situations then for the discussion of sports in the lower strata aside from neighbors, are at work. This is a very important activity at the work scene and in public places such as bars, taverns and the like. For the upper stratum it is in the family, with friends, on parties and on the sports scene itself. One of the consequences of this is that sport involvement may operate to increase family cohesion in the upper stratum. Although differences are not reported here, this may well be because membership in associations dealing with sport or peripheral to sport, like country clubs and so forth, are often family memberships in those strata; that sport may further set apart men and women in the lower strata; and in the middle strata simply from the data I have the same impression I had a number of years ago, that the middle class wife has possibly taken a course in famliy sociology where she has learned that it's important to have a companion in marriage, while the husband, who is a sports fan or sports follower anyway, then goes to the breakfast table, picks up the morning paper and begins reading the sports page. This is very threatening to the middle class wife who has had this course in family sociology because it's hardly companionable. I have the notion that she may be grasping at sport among several other straws as a way to build some companionship into the marriage, that it's a kind of frantic quest for companionship on her part as opposed to the upper class wife. In the lower stratum the sexual worlds are quite different and extend into leisure and work activities. For example, it would be unlikely, I think, in the middle strata of our society to follow a pattern that I've observed where the working class husband will take his wife to a dance hall and order her some beer, etc. and then leave here there to dance and go out with her friend's husband to some other bar to drink beer with a man and perhaps talk about sports with him. So that the insulation of the sexes is extensive in the lower stratum and perhaps sport functions to further insulate the sexes in that stratum. I, of course, have a number of other materials. The analysis is quite extensive but this is about all the time that I have to report today. Thank you.

FOREWORD TO MAN, SPORT AND EXISTENCE

Edgar Z. Friedenberg

Man, Sport and Existence is a unique work. So far as I know, it is the only book yet written that raises and explores serious philosophical questions about the role of conventional, organized sport in individual life experience of contemporary American participants, from surfers to football players. Countless authors have dealt with the social psychology of sport; and some, like Reuel Denney, have written perceptively about the involvement of spectators in terms that are philosophical as well as sociological. But only Professor Slusher has explored the state of being of the athlete in the course of his participation in American sport today, attending, with faint irony, to the continuous contrast between the sense of authenticity that athletic competence affords and the sense of instrumentality—of using oneself or being used as a thing—imposed on the player by the way sport is institutionalized in America and even by the rules and purpose of the game itself.

Philosophically, Slusher represents a pure existential position; he is nowhere concerned with establishing that athletics have a pragmatic function for the athlete, though he is, of course, interested in their value to the athlete as a form of self-realization. Nor is he interested in the social or psychological functions of athletics except insofar as these affect the athlete's sense of self. In fact, he does rather less with this aspect of the matter than might have been useful. So much of what a player experiences depends precisely on the way society uses sport and on the way players use it to establish or alter their position in society that even a strictly existential critique of sport requires a more concrete description of the athlete's life than Slusher gives. The book would be enriched by the kind of anecdotal detail found in such a work as George Plimpton's *The Paper Lion,* for example, which, at one level, depicts what it *is to be* a professional football player.

But experience of sporting life at the level described by Plimpton has been fully and vividly discussed by many other authors, while Slusher is the first to extend to the world of sport the kinds of questions about being and relationship that Buber, Heidegger, Kierkegaard and Sartre—to name only the most familiar of Slusher's rather technical array of sources—have raised. He extends these questions without being either pompous or patronizing about sport; he does not exaggerate the role of sport in the life of man in order to justify taking sport seriously; he does not deride sport in order to establish his philosophical gravity. He never sentimentalizes sport either through nostalgia for the lost Hellenic ideal of youthful physical perfection or, as has been more common since Victorian times, by attributing to it unusual power to build character or even sportsmanship. Sportsmanship is, no doubt, properly so called; but most sportsmen, as Slusher notes, play to win.

Since Slusher assumes, I think correctly, that existential philosophy deals with the key issues that affect central aspects of the athlete's experience, he has no occasion to be pretentious. The most important of these issues is *authenticity.* The terms, and even the idea, have become cliché, but few modern writers who have dealt with sport have considered how one's sense of one's own body contributes to one's sense of self, except in social-psychological terms, *e.g.,* whether one feels inadequate, or inferior, and compensates by psuedomasculine aggression, or whether athletes who are admired for their prowess tend to become alienated from their bodies and regard them as equipment that they own, polish, and display. Both these processes are common enough and, sometimes, important, but Slusher is more interested in how the athlete's sense of the peculiar grace that he brings to his life-space becomes a part of his consciousness and identity. In George Herbert Mead's terms, this book is almost totally concerned with how being an athlete affects the "I" rather than the "me."

Sport is a kind of applied art. Aesthetically, it resembles ballet in that the human body is the medium, but the limitations that the athlete must accept are more like those that are binding the sculptor whose work is to become part of a public building of traditional design. The expressive function of the athlete is subordinate to spectacle and profitability, while his performance must fit completely within a framework of rigid convention if it is to have any meaning at all. If the athlete insists on presenting a virtuoso performance without regard for its place in the total structure, he mars the whole work. Athletics, therefore, is among the most formal of the arts; and team-sports are more convention-bound than are athletic activities such as track-and-field or surfing in which the rules that govern what may be done, like those that govern classical ballet, grow out of the function of the human body in relation to the task rather than out of the need to create and regulate a contest. In German, track-meets are termed *Leichtathletik*, in the sense in which Mozart's music is light and easy.

Formality, however, does not make sport inexpressive; by limiting and channeling expression into previously established modes it makes expression more forceful. "Art is not a plaything, but a necessity," Rebecca West observed in *Black Lamb and Gray Falcon*, "and its essence, form, is not a decorative adjustment but a cup into which life can be poured, and lifted to the lips, and be tasted." Sport provides a rather shallow cup, but one which nevertheless tells us a great deal about the people who designed it and choose to drink from it. Societies reveal much of themselves, and of their differences from other societies, in their preferences among sports. Basketball, for example, seems to me to provide an abstract parody of American middle-class life. I have written elsewhere about what I think it reveals concerning the quality of adolescence itself, through its tempo and vividness; but it also mirrors the society we live in. How else could one dramatize so effectively our legalism and the intricate web of regulations among which we live and on which we climb? Who but contemporary Americans could have designed a sport in which status changes so swiftly that no lead can be considered commanding until the last few seconds of play, and in which the officials run back and forth like agitated ferrets looking for breaches of regulations? Basketball rules in fact affect the game quite differently from the way in which the rules of most other sports do. In football, for example, the actions defined as illegal, such as being offside or holding, generally either disrupt the game or are dangerous to the players, such as clipping or unnecessary roughness, and the penalities assessed are genuinely intended to discourage illegal play. But the basketball player—or, certainly, the coach—must respond to the rules of his game as a business executive does to the Internal Revenue and Fair Labor Practice codes. He wins, not by obeying them, but by cannily balancing the penalties risked by each violation against the strategic advantage that might be gained by, say, a back-court foul committed so as to interrupt a probable scoring drive by the team in possession, thus giving his opponents a chance to win one point instead of two, and gaining possession of the ball afterward on more favorable terms. Slusher quotes one of the early pioneers of basketball as having been dismayed that the present-day sport should have become the kind of game it has, with The Man blowing the whistle at every turn and the play so harrassed by interruption that it becomes all tactics and no strategy, as has become our life. A more leisurely sport would make us envious of the players and get on our nerves.

Perhaps the most peculiar thing about basketball is the way it reflects the anxiety about homosexuality that pervades our society. Is there any other sport in which bodily contact between opposing players is *itself* an offense? Certain kinds of body contact, which might be dangerous or which impede play, are forbidden in all sports in which such contact might occur. But to design a game in such a way that provides its "thinclads" with continuous occasion for physical encounter, but must be stopped the instant an encounter occurs, so that the boy judged more aggressive may be punished surely is a dramatic acting-out of a widespread anxiety in our society which could never, I think, accept high school or college wrestling as a genuinely popular sport. Among Americans, wrestlers must be ugly clowns who seek no real victory and yield no real submission.

Man, Sport and Existence has in it many valid and original observations about the silences—true moments of truth—in sports, and their relation to the players' occasional ecstasy. But it touches only by implication, and then gingerly, on the erotic function of athletics, which seems to me a regrettable omission from a book that includes a brilliant chapter on the related question of "Sport and the Religious." Athletic events occur, and always have occurred, in an atmosphere of erotic tension and excitement that enriches their contribution either to sacred or secular occasions. Our conception of physical beauty is still primarily that of the athlete, while the epithet "jock" applied to a young man expresses as much envy as scorn even now, in a bureaucratic, technically developed, utilitarian society in which physical prowess has little practical utility. Our religious tradition puts the athlete down; a beautiful body is regarded as either sinful in itself or a temptation to sin in others—to be valued only as evidenced of physical fitness. Still, there it is; the pupils dilate, along with certain of the smaller blood vessels, and the heart sings on beholding it—but not so loudly as it once did, for many young people have become aware that the heart of the athlete is less likely to sing back than is that of a wilder, hippier creature, who is less comely but more comforting, if you want somebody to love. So, the concept of beauty is changing its emphasis and becoming more various; Allen Ginsberg, people say, is a beautiful man—and it is true.

But the athlete is losing his status and part of his charisma in the course of the same reappraisal; much of this loss is attributable to the way sports have become institutionalized in this country. By experiencing himself as an athlete, a young man learns what it can mean to live fully in his body joyfully and exuberantly, though under self-imposed discipline. I cannot myself express how this feels nearly as well as a fifteen-year-old high-school athlete whom I interviewed a few years ago in the course of a research study:

> Well, I think there's no feeling quite like running down the track or something and winning. Or going out on the football field and suddenly deciding you liked this, and you do it and you feel kinda crazy. Like I was in a fall game last year that we lost by a very bad score but in the midst of it I was, seemed to be, having a fairly good day. And I just felt light-headed, and I just didn't play—I played for the heck of it, for the fun of it, because I just wanted to. And I was very, I mean, I'd be schmeared a couple of times—I'd get up and laugh my head off and I wouldn't know why I was laughing, and I certainly shouldn't have been laughing because I really got schmeared. And I'd go back to the huddle and I'd be dying laughing, and they'd think I was crazy, but I enjoyed it. And it was just, I couldn't stop it and I, I mean, after the game was over I felt terrible because we lost so bad. But during the game it was just this feeling of exuberance; I was having fun and nothing much could do anything about it, you know? And I was having fun because I was just—I was able to have fun; I was doing something that, at the time, I was doing reasonably well. And I just enjoyed it. During that time I was happy. But after the game I was not so happy, because we lost so badly. And that's the thing, I think that it's a temporary thing, when you're not realizing it, you're not really trying to think about it; you just know that you're enjoying what you're doing right now. . . . I just enjoyed it. And I don't see how, I mean we were getting schmeared all over the field. I was going out there; I was doing a fairly good job. It seems the fellow in front of me that was supposed to be first string wasn't doing so good; so I played. And I did a pretty good job; but I just enjoyed it, and I couldn't help it, and I'd get hit and bounced all over the ground and I'd get up laughing and the guys would think I was crazy . . . but I enjoyed it; it's a release. And you feel as if you don't have to worry about anything, it's too—I don't know, it's just exuberance. As if there's something that really can touch you. And you're running toward this . . . you're doing it because right then and there you're enjoying it. . . . You're not geting rid of anything, it's just *now*, and you're hoping that two seconds from now will be just like that. And that's the thing.

The inner glow from this experience is an important part of erotic attractiveness but to say this is to say little more than that being a good athlete contributes to animal, and therefore human, vitality. It is precisely this vitality, however, which the institutions that socialize youth are designed to stifle. Where, as in America, exuberant youth are regarded as a threat to good order and good adjustment, athletic activity will be channeled into organized sport; and organized sport will be dominated by authorities—usually school authorities—who will administer it in such a way as to deprive their students of the sense of themselves as beautifully coordinated aggressive young animals—the sense that they might otherwise have gained from participation.

The same thing happens outside of school also. In our society, it occurs wherever athletics are controlled by business-like—not necessarily puritanical—adults. Some of Slusher's most penetrating comments pertain to Little League sports, which he sees as frequently alienating the children who take part in them from any sporting sense they might develop: the children do not feel that they are doing their own *thing* and either go about the game as if driven or develop a slick professional approach inappropriate to their age and actual level of competence. Compared to the influence of the schools, however, Little League is peanuts.

Judging from the behavior of many high-school athletic coaches, and even the way the plant is designed, the characteristic attitude of physical education instruction toward the body, and the joy it may yield, is not merely repressive—it is truly counterphobic. It is the "phys ed" men, typically, who are the school disciplinarians—who snarl at "wise guys" and put down "troublemakers." It is they among teachers who show the most hostility to boys with long hair or odd, mod dress, and who encourage the members of their teams to harass these youths; if the "gung-ho" young athletes are provoked into assaulting the "long-hairs" verbally or physically, school authorities then use the incidents as a pretext for forbidding long hair or mod clothes on the basis that they are conducive to violence. School authorities, moreover, are increasingly recruited from former "phys ed" personnel; a large proportion of vice-principals and principals formerly were coaches. These men bring to school administration the spirit of the informal martinet, superficially jolly but intollerant of spirit in young people and of poetry in anything—especially in athletics itself. Generally speaking, sport as a social institution is hostile to precisely the existential values that Professor Slusher stresses in this book and that provide the occasion for writing it.

This is a paradox, for the athlete and the flower-children ought to be allies. It is only possible to be a first-rate athlete if you can allow yourself to feel sport in your blood and open up to what it means. As Slusher makes clear, you have to "dig" the experience. The best athletes, in short, are "hippy" about sport; they hang loose but tough—relax and let it "turn them on." This implies, perhaps, that athletics is to the world of organized sport what creative scholarship is to the university. Great universities need real scholars, and great teams need real athletes, but the universities' deans and coaches will never admit without regret that this is so; they will continue to try to use substitutes instead, thus permitting excellence to be more widely shared, and widely feared.

COMPETITION OUT OF BOUNDS:
SPORT IN AMERICAN LIFE

WILLIAM A. SADLER, JR.

When we examine the cultural scene in contemporary America we cannot help observing turbulence. Cultural cross-currents are countering each other to such an extent that major changes in American life appear to be inevitable. Revel (1971) might not be far from the truth in suggesting that a drastic cultural revolution is in process in America today. Unquestionably there are many people who hope that numerous freedom movements already in evidence will lead the way to a whole new order of civilization not only for America but for the world.

With the exception of the Black Power movement in athletics, it is safe to say that the world of sport is not part of the avant garde of the cultural revolution. It might even be suggested that the world of sport is part of what the counter culture is against. I have found no reference to sports or athletics in the counter culture literature; presumably it is assumed that the mere mention of sports is gauche.

In his book *Man, Sport and Existence,* Slusher (1967) has analyzed sport in terms of its great potential for existential meaning and value. Yet in the foreword to that book Edgar Friedenberg made the significant observation that "generally speaking, sport as a social institution is hostile to precisely the existential values that Professor Slusher stresses in this book [p. xiii]." Friedenberg noted that "Phys. Ed." people typically are opposed to longhairs and the culture they are assumed to represent. He suggested that athletes and flower-children ought to be allies; but in fact physical education as it is presently structured is repressive, especially of the freedom and the spirit in the new culture.

From *Quest,* Monograph XIX (January, 1973): 124-132.

Consider a purely imaginative and hypothetical comparison between the two ideal types: the coach and the longhair. To borrow a concept from Reich (1971), the coach is the embodiment of Consciousness II. He endorses a secularized version of the Protestant Ethic, emphasizing the necessity and virtue of hard work, sacrifice, and discipline to achieve mastery, domination, control, and eventually victory. One of his primary values is power. He often demands control over his organization and his athletes; and he hopes to exercise it over his opponents. The longhair represents a different mentality, that of Consciousness III. His motto is not "Give all to win!" but simply "Let it be." He is not interested in power and control, but in pleasure and freedom. The culture he seeks to fashion will not embody traits of an Americanized Protestant Ethic. If the revolution succeeds in America, then the coach will have to found a commune if he is to continue to do his own thing; and he will have to take with him incorrigible athletes who in the new social order will be regarded as deviants rather than as heroes. Apparently there is no promising future for organized sports in America if the counter culture becomes a dominant influence in our society.

If we recognize an incompatibility between the world of organized athletics and the counter culture, the question nags the mind as to why they are at odds. Those involved in the cultural revolution were not originally turned off sports by reading exposes of scandalous practices in organized athletics. Revelations of villainly, greed, violence, repression, deception, and hypocrisy may have reinforced individuals' judgments; but these in themselves are insufficient reasons to explain the divorce between sports and potential cultural reform. It is not sports as such so much as sport experienced as an institution integrally involved in an American cultural system, which offends many people. Sports are seen to embody values that run contrary to the primary values of the counter culture.

A primary value in today's version of the American Way of Life is competition. The counter cultures to be sure are extremely diversified, but there are a few convictions which individuals associated with them seem to hold in common. They generally are critical of much that is found in contemporary American society; and specifically they have singled out competition for attack. In his behavioristic Utopia, Skinner (1962) expresses criticism of competition through Frazier, the founder of the community:

> We are opposed to personal competition. We don't encourage competitive games, for example, with the exception of tennis and chess where the exercise of skill is as important as the outcome of the game; . . . A triumph over another man is never a laudable act [p. 169].

Many people in today's counter cultures would find Skinner's ideal community a science fiction nightmare; but they share that criticism of competition. One example is a sign on a communty bulletin board which reads in part: "Competition, an old pig tactic used to separate the people." Another is a statement attributed to Eldridge Cleaver: "Competition is the law of the jungle. Cooperation is the law of civilization [p. 76]." (Stickney, 1971)

Antipathy toward competition is not restricted to the counter cultures. There seems to be a growing suspicion throughout our society that competition may be getting out of hand. Many have suggested that competition is too much a part of our lifestyle, that it starts too early in life, becomes too intense, and leads to undesirable consequences in both personal and social life. It is my contention that the spirit of competition, which originally was an integral part of the political and economic structure of America, has overflowed into many other areas where it is not appropriate. It is competition beyond the boundaries of its traditional context that we must assess if we are to understand the significance which sports appear to have for many people who are critical of them.

It is commonly assumed that the competitive spirit is an inherent part of life. That assumption is in part a hangover of a faulty notion of survival. In contrast to the Darwinian emphasis upon survival of the fittest, biologists recently have stressed the more fundamental process of challenge and response along with the tendency toward equilibrium. Equally important in correcting a simplistic acceptance of competition is the perspective of history. It becomes clear that competition has not been a universal element in either simple or complex societies. Competition often has emerged after a people have sufficiently mastered the task of survival. When there has been opportunity to think about other things, then people sometimes have engaged in competitive activities such as war, games, and romance. Even Huizinga's notion (1960) that agonistic activity is the basis for the finest elements in Western Civilization, is highly questionable and should be recognized as provocative theory, and not accepted as an apodictic principle. A dominant concern in many cultures, particularly those that endured, had to do with stability and the preservation of traditions, which sometimes called for the suppression of competitiveness.

Unlike most societies, however, the spirit of competition has been uniquely located at the heart of our cultural heritage. The political solution of our Constitution employed the notion of competitive interests which supposedly are held in a balance of power. The competitive spirit also was expressed on the frontier, which Americans set out to win. During the nineteenth century the character of the frontier changed as it shifted from natural boundaries to the realm of industry. Here the competitive spirit thrived. There had been a competitive element in capitalistic industrialism since it began; but it was not until the 1870's, according to Dewey (1969), that competition received explicit, systematic attention in economic theory. Competition came to be recognized as a basic principle in sound economics and hence a part of the great American enterprise.

I suggest that during the latter part of the nineteenth century there was a subtle but significant change in the typical American attitude toward competition. As competitive economic activity became an American norm, competition itself was more deeply incorporated within American culture as a primary value. To some extent the celebration of competition was related to the success Americans experienced on the natural and economic frontiers as they overwhelmed people more committed to traditional ways of existence. However, it was the emergence of Social Darwinism in philosophy and science, at just the right moment in history, that provided a comfortable rationale for the American emphasis upon competition. In contrast to other cultures oriented toward values of being and becoming, the dominant American culture was oriented toward the value of doing; and by the end of the nineteenth century, the value of doing was interpreted within the framework of competition. In the American value hierarchy competition had climbed from an instrumental value, as seen in the arguments of the Federalist Papers, to a normative value. A means had become an end.

Ironically, by the end of the nineteenth century and increasingly during the next, the federal government has been obliged to restrain economic competition through regulations and controls. By the middle of this century Mills (1956) routinely observed that in the sphere of economics the language of competition and free enterprise is mere rhetoric. Champions of competition in other spheres should at least recognize that in the field of economics, where competition once seemed to be essential, there has been significant criticism of competitiveness. Galbraith (1968), for example, is notorious for his opposition to it; Clark (1961), Dewey (1969), and others who favor competition do so by advocating a modified form of it that is consistent with rational planning, control and fair practices. According to a substantial number of experts within the discipline, competition in economics, unless restrained, is self-defeating. Interestingly, business leaders today are beginning to emphasize cooperation and the need for careful planning to reduce risks. Their language scarcely is expressive of a spirit of unbridled competition.

In spite of these changes, competition has been thriving in other parts of institutionalized life. While it is in an uncertain state within industry, competitiveness still is emphasized in both military and political institutions. The goal in both activities usually is to win. American religion also is highly competitive. Unlike most other societies where there is an established religion, America is a denominational society, as Greeley (1972) has so well illustrated. Denominations have traditionally vied with each other for numbers, wealth, power, and status; and they increasingly are in competition with secular interest groups. In spite of ecumenical efforts, local denominations take pride in those things which set them apart from others. American preaching also is distinctive for its emphasis upon selling religion to vast numbers. Some preachers, such as Peal (1969), have even suggested that religion is a means of increasing one's chances to win in any number of endeavors. From this perspective, there apparently is more joy in heaven over one winner who succeeds than over the ninety-nine who have lost.

Another institution where competition has run strong is education. In elementary schools one lesson that many children learn effectively is to compete. They do so not merely to gain approbation of parents and teachers but to spare themselves the nightmare of failure. Children are urged to compete now so as to win more in later life. With greater pressure placed upon successful completion of high school and college, the competitive element in education has intensified. Entering college freshmen often display symptoms of academic weariness that some time ago were thought to be uniquely part of a graduate student syndrome. Competition has extended even into the academic profession itself. Teachers have even been known to engage in scholarship not for the sake of knowledge but for promotion and tenure.

Even more unsettling is the way the spirit of competition has invaded the realm of interpersonal relations. One of the institutionalized heroes of modern America, Dale Carnegie (1940), has counseled us on how to *win* friends. What he proposed is essentially a technique of how to con people. He has recommended his technique as the foundation for a new way of life. A major assumption is that the true spirit of a good life is competition. Though Carnegie wrote essentially for businessmen, his assumptions are to be found wherever people are overly concerned with winning popularity and manipulating people for their own success. The spirit of competition has even invaded the realm of sex. A male who has seduced a woman will proudly announce that he has "scored." It is no surprise that people raised on a system of competitive interpersonal relations now manifest a great need for intimacy and severe problems of loneliness. Sensitivity training and encounter groups in part represent countermeasures to the competitiveness in American life.

The spirit of competition also has helped shape our habits of consumption. Americans often are less concerned about what they actually experience than about the recognition they receive for having certain kinds of experiences. The American way of life has developed a style of competitive consumption to "keep up with the Joneses," and perhaps to outshine them.

Finally, the competitive spirit has begun to dominate the field of technology. It has become important for many Americans to be first in the world no matter what the consequences. One example is the rationale for the space race which seems to argue: win at all costs. Leaders of the space program have justified the enormous amounts of money, manpower, and energy expended on the principle that America must maintain its lead over Russia. In this instance the spirit of competition not only is out of bounds; it is literally taking us out of this world.

A survey of American institutions and their dynamics indicates that the spirit of competition has become an integral part of the American way of life. To compete is recognized as a very American activity; resistance to competition is viewed as suspiciously un-American. Over the span of our history, competition has come to occupy a primary place in our value orientation, largely through the agency of our economic development. However, as political and economic interests have forced us to repress the competitive spirit in the business world, that spirit was sublimated and re-expressed in other institutions.

In spite of a rationale for economic cooperation and fair practices, a typical American attitude has been strongly in favor of competition as an indispensable quality for wholesome and successful living. The value orientation which holds competition high is perpetuated as individuals participate in institutions which help to shape their perception of reality. There is, in other words, a convergence of social forces which fosters a common perception of the world so that it is viewed in competitive terms. Added to this institutional factor is the dissipation of forces that would inhibit competition. Customs and traditions within which competition made little sense increasingly have been swept away by rapid social changes. Enduring supportive networks of relationships which inhibited competitiveness have broken up with massive social and geographic mobility. There are few things left that Americans can rely upon to obtain acceptance and identity. One supposedly has to compete to win recognition and identity. From within this perspective Vince Lombardi was quite right: "Winning is the only thing."

Where do organized athletics fit into this picture of American life? Obviously sports have become a major social institution; accordingly they must be understood within the total context of the American social system. One reason why we have failed to interpret sports in their true context is because we often have assumed that they merely are forms of play and therefore divorced from the meanings of the everyday working world. However, we have recently become aware that sports acquire meaning from within the larger context in which they are played. In some cases political meaning becomes a dominant force within games, as in the Olympics where contests may become expressions of national interest. Sports in America also have patriotic undertones.

Another way that the larger context of a cultural system transforms the meaning of sports is when they are integrated into an economic system and commercialized. We are mistaken if we suppose that sports should be thought of simply as leisure time activities with their own inherent meanings. On the contrary, we should examine the close connection between the ethos of organized sports and the everyday world where a work ethic is predominant. Athletes often are well aware that what they do is not play. Their practice sessions are workouts; and to win the game they have to work harder. Sports are not experienced as activities outside the institutional pattern of the American way of life; they are integrally a part of it. That is, sports are so important to Americans not simply because of an increase in leisure but because they reinforce a competitive work ethic precisely at a time when it is being challenged and tamed in other spheres. Those who separate the meaning of sports from the workaday world fail to notice a distinctive quality about leisure in America. de Grazia (1964) has cogently argued that leisure in America exists on a continuum with the workaday world. Leisure is time-off from the job for the purpose of greater efficiency. Although sports may occur within leisure time, their meaning is directly related to values and expectations of the competitive world of work.

This point is important if we are to see the possible impact of sports upon the formation of American personalities. While experiments have failed to prove that organized sports develop specific personality traits, it has been discovered that they can affect a total personality system. The studies of Sutton-Smith, Roberts, and Kozelka (1969) indicate that games and sports provide achievement models which are important to developing personality structures. In other words the old cliché is true: "Sports prepare one for life." The question which must be raised is: "what kind of life?" The answer in an American context is that they prepare us for a life of competition. Sports contribute to the development of a lifestyle which is competitive in its total orientation as well as its means of expression. As Kenyon and Loy (1969) have observed, games and sports in the United States "permit youth to rehearse competitive roles without experiencing the adverse anxiety experienced by adults striving for success [p. 40]." For adults, games have the function of reinforcing a competitive perspective, providing an opportunity to support an orientation towards success without succumbing to pressures of its lifestyle. (Sutton-Smith, et al., 1969)

The kind of lifesyle endorsed by competitive sports in America is being called into question not only by the counter culture but by many sensitive adults who have begun to examine our modern way of life. Writing about growing up in middle America during the 1940's Schickel (1972) has recalled that all forms of entertainment for youth often were suspect except for sports. He writes:

> Aside from their obviously healthy aspects, they were widely believed to prepare boys for the wins and losses of life—especially the former. And in a way they did, for so many of us are little Nixons, secret sharers of the lunatic notion that life is a succession of game-plans and games, a thing that can ideally be quantified in a won-and-lost column. We are prisoners, I think, of middle America's only universal metaphor and we have tried, since the '40's, to cram everything into it—politics, wars, careers—and it has stunted me, stunted us all [p. 26].

Leaving aside his obvious political preferences, this statement suggests the highly competitive nature of an emergent average American perspective on life and the realization of some unfortunate consequences that issue from the perspective. Of course competitive sports have provided so-called healthy outlets for the release of energy and tension; but as socially approved activities they also have functioned within personality systems to contribute toward a point of view that provides a frame of reference for our most important ideas, concerns, and activities.

As an institution which reinforces and sanctions a primary value orientation, organized sports can be considered as closely related to organized religion. We are well aware today how religion can function toward the formation of a personal world. (cf. Sadler, 1970) Several factors from the sociology of religion are of particular relevance to this comparison. Religion as a cultural system relates persons to a dimension which is of ultimate concern; that is, it orients them toward a primary value. Fundamental beliefs express this value orientation; rituals provide opportunities wherein these beliefs are acted out and thereby reinforced. The group activity gives consensual validation to the emergent pattern of belief and practice. Though there are significant variables which can modify or offset this process, regular participation tends to incline a person toward the group value system.

As sport has become an institution which embodies an orientation toward a primary value, it has functioned as religious institutions have with respect to the shaping of our culture, life styles, and personality systems. Regular participation in organized sports helps to fashion a total life perspective (Weltanschauung) by establishing roles, expectations, and norms which apply to our everyday world. Concepts which apply to the ritual (games) filter through into everyday perception. A dominant social sentiment is revived by each game. Roles for everyday encounters are structured as competitive. Games are rehearsals for life. The rightness of competitive roles is reaffirmed in the cultic celebrations of organized sports. It may be an exaggeration to say that sport constitutes America's real religion; but in many parts of our society organized sports are functional equivalents of a religion in which salvation is interpreted within the framework of competitive success.

The institution of sport also is analogous to education. Education does more than impart knowledge. It also conditions a personal world by developing certain kinds of feelings, types of abilities and skills, and orientations toward goals which are socially acceptable. In this process, other types of feelings, abilities, and orientations are ignored or suppressed. Sports perform the same functions; when they are an integral part of an educational system they reinforce the developmental process of the schools. Equally significant, they can effect the entire nature of the educational enterprise as the competitive perspective of the game permeates the milieu of the classroom.

One of the tragedies of our era is that the spirit of competition, which has been a stimulating element in progress and individual development, has become so widespread and intense as to go out of control; many organized sports function to keep it out of control.

We are now confronted by a humorless irony. Competition now threatens to be destructive of our advanced level of civilization that it has helped to produce. The question to be asked of sports is similar to that which we must ask of our entire social system: Can we any longer tolerate so much competition? Can the world survive with it? Seen in terms of problems associated with industry and national rivalry, the answer seems to be that competition must be overcome in favor of harmony with nature and cooperation among men and nations. If we can agree that competition has become menacingly excessive, then what are we to do with sports in our society? Something has to be done to reduce the competitive element among Americans. In our concern for cultural reform we shall have to consider reforming the institution of sport along with other institutions that symbolize and sanction a highly competitive way of life.

One of the most urgent tasks in this regard is to re-examine competition itself and also some of its consequences. In his study of the crisis in modern education, Charles Silberman (1971) has argued that one of the primary sources of our difficulty is mindlessness. That charge is equally true of sports. We simply have not thought bravely and openly enough about what sport means in the full context of social and personal life. Some attention has been given to the consequences for those whose life stance is essentially competitive and whose pattern is failure. Arthur Miller's (1958) Willie Loman is a moving example of the tragic outcome of perpetual losers in our society; so important was it for Willie to win, that he madly sought to succeed through suicide where he had failed in life. Most of us know well the pathos of losing and being also runs in a society where only winners are recognized as full of grace. If winning is the only thing, what does life mean to the majority of us who must accept the role of losers? And what really are the benefits which come to those who consistently win? Are those who achieve success through tough competition really better for doing so? Our answer to that question will depend upon our existential values. Without plunging into that issue, we can at least recognize that our naive approach to competition which has assumed that winning is an unequivocal good is partly responsible for the shaping of massive policies that have brought upon us some of the most threatening problems in the modern world. We could do well to take a lesson from other cultures, especially that of the ancient Athenians, which would indicate how competition was restrained by other values considered to be more important, such as personal virtue, self-actualization, harmony, and justice.

An important step toward a reassessment of competition will require looking carefully at the intentional structure of competitive action. What is the nature of *care* in the experience of competition? Though there is not space to prosecute a phenomenological analysis here, I think such analysis would reveal the following essential traits. In competition one cares mostly about one's own existence; one's goal is to increase the worth of his existence, at the expense of someone else. In competition one's existence is put to the test; one's worth will be approved, if one wins, through the awarding of a prize. One's perspective is fixed on attaining a definite result. If this competitive posture were sustained, one's personality system would tend to become rigid. The care structure of competition thus hardly is compatible with the care underlying self-actualization, at least if an extrinsic goal such as a reward is decisive. Competitive concern tends to interfere with the realization of other values. For example, competition, though at first liberating, requires one to sacrifice his freedom in favor of discipline and a schedule of routines often determined by outside interests. Instead of expressing love for another person, competition involves an attempt to dominate the other. Though it may require the use of reason, the act of competition is not conducive to reasonableness that is open to questions about the meaning and value of one's own action. Though fair play has been an important part of sports, care about winning often precludes consideration of justice; and it often breeds contempt for those who do not, or cannot, or care not to win. As the Greeks well knew, the beauty of the human form in sports can match the beauties produced by an artist or by nature; but care about winning also can lead to the loss of form and expressions of the ugliest traits in human nature. Play can grace life with joy as well as fun; but hard-pressed care for winning can produce anxiety and disgust. Competition ultimately is inadequate as a life stance, interfering with communion between man and his world, and ill preparing persons for important existential moments such as marriage and friendship, sickness and death, ecstacy and grief.

While competition may be an element of sports, it must have well defined limits if it is not to undermine those values which make human life worthwhile. The care expressed in sports must be more complex than that which is defined by simple competition. An example from personal experience seems appropriate here. When I compete with a friend part of my care is competitive. I am interested in winning. But I also care about my friend, and what the game means to him or her; and I care about the quality of the play. I want it to be a good game. In fact, if it is really a good game, it does not matter who wins. The competitive element is tamed, because it is suffused with other cares which are equally important. The spirit of the game is not simply that of competition; it includes concern for others as a primary value.

If organized sports are to have a beneficial role in a future, more humane society, then those of us who are interested in both sports and human values will have to demonstrate meanings and values in sporting activity which transcend the level of competition. Many of us, not just those associated with the counter culture, care about integrating into the social order values such as personal growth, freedom, creativity, love, reason, happiness, beauty, and justice. We need to examine which forms of activity are most expressive of and conducive to those values and which forms are most obstructive. This will further require us to re-examine both our theoretical and our working definitions of sport; and it will lead us into a normative approach wherein we shall have to state what we think sports should mean in the life of individuals and in our own society. I believe the outcome will be to de-emphasize the competitive element in sports. That does not mean that we shall take all the excitement out of them. As Caillois (1961) and others have shown, there are numerous types of play and games which present challenge; we should not make the mistake of equating meeting a challenge with competition. There are many sports which can be exciting, can test the abilities and skills of individuals and groups, can bring harmony and happiness, can provide healthy exercise and an exhilarating change from the workaday world, can reunite persons with nature, can express and sanction of the highest human values, which do not require competition. I hope leaders in the American world of sports will have the vision and the courage to give such sports top priority over the highly competitive and much commercialized sports which now receive so much attention and support. The scientific and philosophic study of sports also has an important role to play, not only in exposing the artificial rhetoric surrounding sports but in demonstrating just what different types of sports can do to and for persons and groups.

Some of the most horrendous problems encountered not only in sports but throughout our society are in part due to the unprincipled expansion and virtual domination of our life styles by the spirit of competition. Competition has become a primary value which operates in many institutions and personalities as a driving force. I have not charged that sports have caused this condition; on the contrary, the institution of sport has become a victim of it. Like much organized religion, organized sports ironically and mindlessly express, endorse, and revitalize the spirit of competition which is becoming a significant factor in our undoing.

In his novel *Love in the Ruins*, Percy (1971) has made a frightening commentary on the narrow concern he finds in those who have become captivated by competition in the world of sports. The scene is the end of the world as we know it. There is a civil war; in addition noxious smoke from a sodium reaction begins to form clouds of lethal gas in the air above our country. The leaders of society who might yet act to save the lives of citizens are gathered on a golf course worrying not about the state of the world but about the outcome of a highly publicized tournament. In their care about the game and its prize, they refuse to listen to the one man who tries to call their attention to the evils that are about to destroy them. They will not be distracted. For them, winning has become more important than surviving, and losing is worse than dying.

To rescue sports from the madness of unbounded competition we can begin by recognizing the range, intensiveness, and consequences of competition in sports and in society. To be faithful to humanistic values within the world of sport will require taking a stand that will run counter to powerful forces in modern American life. Hopefully we shall find the courage not only to tell the truth but to do it. We might recover for sports the spirit of play which a serious competitive spirit has repressed. Since play can be an activity productive of freedom, creativity, and community (cf. Sadler, 1969) this could be a significant achievement. For all of us there remains the hard work of examining the values which are really expressed in our sports. Hopefuly we shall learn to play them not so that some may win while others lose, but so that man and the world may survive in peace and good spirit.

REFERENCES

Caillois, R. *Man, play, and games.* New York: The Free Press, 1961.

Carnegie, D. *How to win friends and influence people.* New York: Pocket Books, 1940.

Clark, J. M. *Competition as a dynamic process.* Washington, D.C.: Brookings Institute, 1961.

Dewey, D. *The theory of imperfect competition.* New York: Columbia University Press, 1969.

Galbraith, J. K. *The industrial state.* New York: New American Library, 1968.

de Grazia, S. *Of time, work, and leisure.* Garden City: Doubleday & Co., 1964.

Greeley, A. M. *The denominational society.* Chicago: Scott Foresman & Co., 1972.

Huizinga, J. *Homo ludens.* Boston: Beacon Press, 1950.

Kenyon, G. & Loy, J. Toward a sociology of sport. In *Sport, culture and society*, ed., J. Loy and G. Kenyon. New York: Macmillan, 1969.

Miller, A. *Death of a salesman.* New York: Viking Press, 1958.

Mills, C. W. *White collar.* New York: Oxford University Press, 1956.

Peale, N. V. *The power of positive thinking.* Greenwich: Fawcett Publications, 1969.

Percy, W. *Love in the ruins.* New York: Farrar, Straus, & Giroux, 1971.

Reich, C. A. *The greening of America.* New York: Bantam Books, 1971.

Revel, J. F. *Without Marx or Jesus.* Garden City: Doubleday & Co., 1971.

Sadler, W. A. *Existence and love.* New York: Scribner's, 1969.

———. Creative existence: Play as a pathway to personal freedom and community. *Humanitas*, 1969, 5(1), 57-79.

———. *Personality and religion.* New York: Harper and Row, 1970.

Schickel, R. Growing up in the forties. *New York Times Magazine.* Feb. 20, 1972.

Silberman, C. E. *Crisis in the classroom.* New York: Random House, 1971.

Skinner, B. F. *Walden two.* New York: Macmillan, 1962.

Slusher, H. S. *Man, sport and existence.* Philadelphia: Lea & Febiger, 1967.

Stickney, J. *Streets, actions, alternatives, raps.* New York: Putnam's, 1971.

Sutton-Smith, B., Roberts, J., and Kozelka, R. Game involvement in adults. In *Sport, culture and society*, ed., J. Loy and G. Kenyon. New York: Macmillan, 1969.

STIGMA OR PRESTIGE:
THE ALL-AMERICAN CHOICE

MARIE HART

Ignorance about, and lack of investigation concerning human social relationships in physical activity is due largely to preoccupation with numbers. Many students and faculty members have become increasingly disenchanted with the recitations of statistical measures as a means of understanding social behavior. It has become a professional and personal requirement in America to view life through numerical abstractions. The importance of facts as a basis for action, for knowledge about people in social relationships now and in the past, is undeniable. However, many researchers and scholars appear satisfied to stop when the statistics suggest that the hypothesis is, indeed, proven to be true.

However, we need to know more than correlations, standard deviations, insurance rate increases, and the statistics on incoming athletes. We need to know what social conditions, taboos, norms, superstitions, expected roles, and rewards make people behave as they do. In physical education, why do people group, regroup, divide, alienate, subdivide, collect and subcollect in such great diversity? The tension and conflict engendered by the archaic social rules and roles which govern sport and physical education are no longer tenable, and furthermore, they are the cause of the divisions within physical education and sport.

I propose that a social situation, heavy in prestige for some and laden with stigma for others, has been created and is perpetuated by the archaic male and female role expectations. Due to these role expectations, female athletes and male dancers live a stigmatized life much of the time. The male cultural environment of sport sets up this difficult social situation.

Beisser (1967) and Fiske (1972) have suggested that sport acts as a rite of passage into the male adult role in American society. The male is expected to be, or to act biologically superior, and sport is the major remaining testing ground. Sport gives the young male an opportunity to learn and practice the attributes still held and valued by his elders. Dance exposes the young female to accepted attributes of grace, poise, and beauty but dance is not nearly so pervasive and regulated as the sport system is for the male. Physical education is largely conducted according to male needs and expected role behavior, thereby creating the problems for female students and teachers.

Women's roles in society are in conflict with those perpetuated in physical education. In an investigation of women's roles, Griffin stated: "Being involved in sport and education, she combines the roles of women athlete and woman professor and accordingly, is perceived as possessing all the "unsavory" characteristics of the active and potent woman. She is seen as intelligent, competitive, aggressive, strong, and experimental. These characteristics, while desirable for success in realms of sport and academia, appear to be of much less value to a woman in the social world. Physical educators must be aware of the conflict of the traits expected of women in the social world and women in athletics and the professions" (1973, 98). These traits may not only be of less value in the social world, they may, indeed, bring stigma to and cause conflict for a woman.

Goffman's (1963) ideas on stigma and social identity may add insight to American social behavior in sport and dance. He defines stigma as "an attribute that is deeply discrediting, but it should be seen that a language of relationships, not attributes, is really needed. An attribute that stigmatizes one type of possessor can confirm the usualness of another, and therefore is neither creditable nor discreditable as a thing in itself" (p. 3). If this definition seems too harsh, he offers another: "the situation of the individual who is disqualified from full social acceptance" (preface). In Goffman's terms, attributes in certain situations and relationships create positive social identity (normalize an individual). Those same attributes in a different context may create negative social identity, and cause the individual to acquire stigma. In contrast with the stigmatized person, Goffman states: ". . . in an important sense there is only one complete unblushing male in America: a young, married, white, urban, northern, heterosexual Protestant father of college education, fully employed, of good complexion, weight, and height, and a recent record in sports."

(p. 128) It is suggested here that the only one complete unblushing American female is married to this unblushing male.

If this is the definition of the most normal and accepted people in America, what is the result for those individuals who do not measure up to this list of all-American attributes? They are "disqualified from full social acceptance." The female athlete and the male dancer, in particular, do not measure up to this unblushing individual.

The model which follows may help to illustrate the relationships between female and male roles, and the cultural forms of sport and dance. It is suggested that these relationships can result in negative social identity, and cause the formation of groups, based on stigma.

The acquisition of stigma appears to be the natural result, since women athletes are in male cultural territory and male dancers are in female cultural territory. Goffman (1963) suggests several behavior patterns engaged in by the stigmatized person. Three patterns seem especially appropriate to physical education and sex roles: 1) the stigmatized individual may use the disadvantage as a basis for organizing life; 2) a person may control carefully the stigmatizing information; and 3) may develop tension management activities.

Organizing life in terms of one's social disadvantage becomes apparent in the half-world of women's sport and dance, which largely take place in sexually segregated groups. Physical education and athletic organization for women are often organized around the recognition that women are not welcome in male sport groups. These groups were well established as all-male before women became involved in sport, and that tradition is often tenaciously maintained. Women are misrepresented, underrepresented, underbudgeted, and often not well trained as athletes because of the traditional male dominance of sport in American institutions. But organizing into a half-world is only a reaction; it does not answer the needs of the woman in sports.

Separatism in sport in contemporary American society is basically perpetuated by the middle class, which traditionally supports educational sport and dance. Such separatism does not provide for shared social experiences; it cannot form a basis for common interests, experiences, and conversation. Instead of providing a basis for interchange, sport tends to isolate and alienate people. In physical education male-designed architecture and separatist organizations contribute to isolation and alienation. Some sexual privacy may be necessary, but the present situation leads to exceedingly limited communication and little if any shared experience.

One important result of the stigmatizing process is how information is handled and controlled. When asked what he does, or what he teaches, a

I. *Through sport:*

A. The Male Achieves, Derives, Pursues and Accepts:

Prestige and Positive Social Identity

+

+   +

---

least (aesthetic and noncontact)   most (strength and contact)

B. The Female usually Acquires but can Avoid:

Stigma and Negative Social Identity

−

−   −

---

least (aesthetic and rhythmical)   most (strength and contact)

II. *Through dance:*

A. The Female Achieves, Derives, Pursues and Accepts:

Prestige and Positive Social Identity

B. The Male Acquires and rarely Avoids:

Stigma and Negative Social Identity

Figure 1. The American Sport Experience and Social Identity.

person may formulate the information carefully. Typical reactions from outsiders are often clumsy or, worse yet, insulting. Remarks like "I never would have guessed you were a dancer (to a male);" or "I wish there were more women athletes with your looks" are loaded with double meaning. Consequently, they set up tension within the recipient.

The media control information about women athletes in much the same way as individuals do. Either the media gives no information, or dresses up the message to be pretty, to be acceptable. Newspapers and magazines cover only selected sports for women, and most often show how attractive the woman is in her costume, rather than how skillful she is in action. *Women's Track and Field World Yearbook* (1968) is an extreme case in point. It emphasizes, through pictures and descriptions, the eyes, measurements, legs, and figures of the athletes as much as it does their athletic achievement. The captions read: "a woman athlete doesn't have to look like a horse to run like a thoroughbred;" "the lady with the alluring lips," "Diamond Lil is a darned attractive babe," and "the two sweetest dimples we've ever seen." The oversell of the femininity of these world class athletes is demeaning. They are presented as "super attractive" females as if they were competing in a beauty contest rather than competing in world class track and field. It is a way of protesting the masculine image and promoting the feminine one. There is never a need to sell male athletes in this way.

Finally, much effort is directed toward diminishing the tension created by the masculine attributes associated with women in sport, and the feminine attributes associated with male dancers. As meaningless, futile, and unnecessary as such behavior may seem to outsiders, it nevertheless continues endlessly. Women coaches often ask or require sports teams to wear dresses when travelling. Orientation meetings are held in many institutions, for the sole purpose of instructing women physical education majors in a special dress code. College women in history, drama, or sociology would not tolerate such humiliation. Men taking courses in dance may find wearing a leotard personally difficult, if not impossible. The stigma is heavy.

One woman college student illustrates the intensity of the conflict in the following statement: "The female athlete feels very unfeminine when she enters the male-dominated sports world. If she shows any athletic ability or correct technique, she is not praised because of ability or technique but because she can "move like a man." Our student then asks, "What does this do to the woman in sport? I can only answer that from my own feelings and those of my friends. It makes me question my own femininity—the very roots of my being. If I am a woman, why do I enjoy sport? Why do I participate?"

Women have not been publishing or writing about their sport experiences long enough for educators and the public to realize what meaning the experiences carry for the woman athlete. Current writing is often eloquent in its expression of the inner struggle for identity. There is also a drive to resolve the conflict, a drive reflected in a group of verses from the poem "First Peace," by Barbara Lamblin:

> i was the all american girl, the winner, the champion,
> the swell kid, good gal, national swimmer,
> model of the prize daughter bringing it home for dad
> i even got the father's trophy
> i was also a jock, dyke, stupid dumb blond
> frigid, castrating, domineering bitch,
> called all these names in silence,
> the double standard wearing me down
> inside
> on the victory stand winning my medals
> for father and coach

and perhaps a me deep down somewhere
who couldn't fail because of all the hours
and training and tears
wrapped into an identity of muscle and power
and physical strength
a champion,
not softness and grace
now at 31, still suffering from the overheard
locker room talk, from the bragging and swaggering
the stares past my tank suit
insults about my muscles
the fears, the nameless fears
about my undiscovered womanhood
disturbing unknown femininity,
femaleness
feminine power

The masculine-feminine game as now played needs careful and expert study. It also needs to be called off in departments of physical education and athletics.

In the preface to their book, *Masculine/Feminine: Readings in Sexual Mythology and the Liberation of Women* (1969), the Roszaks state with eloquence and force:

> He is playing the kind of man that he thinks the kind of woman she is playing ought to admire. She is playing the kind of woman that he thinks the kind of man he is playing ought to desire.
>
> If he were not playing masculine, he might well be more feminine than she is—except when she is playing very feminine, she might well be more masculine than he is—except when he is playing very masculine.
>
> So he plays harder. And she plays . . . softer.

But the female athlete does not always play softer. She does not always lose on purpose. She may not always see it as a compliment to have her athletic endeavors compared with male records and then disregarded. The final result of role playing is emphasized by the Roszaks when they state: "He is becoming less and less what he wants to be. She is becoming less and less what she wants to be. But now he is more manly than ever, and she is more womanly than ever." Examples of this phenomenon in sport and dance populate gymnasiums and dance studios in American schools. The inflated male athlete, girl cheer leaders, song leaders, "major and minor" sports, women in approved sports and dance acting superior to women in "masculine" sports are only a few examples of the roles played. The Roszaks draw a conclusion and make a final plea to a society caught up in these social roles: "She is stifling under the triviality of her femininity. The world is groaning beneath the terrors of his masculinity. He is playing masculine. She is playing feminine. How do we call off the game?"

REFERENCES

Beisser, Arnold. *The Madness of Sport.* New York: Appleton-Century-Crofts, 1967.

Cevasco, Rose. "Femininity and the Woman Athlete." Unpublished student paper. California State University, Hayward, 1972.

Fiske, Shirley. "Pigskin Review: An American Initiation." In *Sport in the Sociocultural Process,* edited by M. M. Hart. Dubuque, Iowa: Wm. C. Brown, 1972.

Goffman, Erving. *Stigma.* Englewood Cliffs, N. J.: Prentice-Hall, 1963.

Griffin, Patricia. "What's a Nice Girl Like You Doing in a Profession Like This?" *Quest* 14 (1973):96-101.

Lamblin, Barbara. "First Peace." Unpublished poem. Hayward, California, 1973.

Roszak, Betty, and Roszak, Theodore. *Masculine/Feminine: Readings in Sexual Mythology and the Liberation of Women.* New York: Harper Colophon, 1969.

Women's Track and Field World Yearbook. Claremont, Calif.: Women's Track and Field World, 1968.

FOOTBALL IN AMERICA:
A STUDY IN CULTURE DIFFUSION

DAVID RIESMAN AND REUEL DENNEY

1

On October 9, 1951, Assistant Attorney General Graham Morrison instituted an anti-trust action against a number of universities on account of their efforts to limit TV broadcasts of their games—efforts dictated by the terrible burdens of what we might speak of as "industrialized football." This action occurred only a few weeks after the scandal of the West Point student firings, which, along with the William and Mary palace revolution, indicated that football was indeed reaching another crisis in its adaptation to the ever-changing American environment. Small colleges such as Milligan—a church-supported school in the mountains of Eastern Tennessee—were discovering that football was now so mechanized that they could no longer afford the necessary entry fee for machinery and personnel. Last year, Milligan spent $17,000, or two-thirds of its whole athletic budget—and did not get it all back in the box-office net. Football had come to resemble other industries or mechanized farms, into which a new firm could not move by relying on an institutional lifetime of patient saving and plowing back of profits, but only by large corporate investment. The production of a team involves the heavy overhead and staff personnel characteristic of high-capital,

From *American Quarterly*, 3: 309-319. Reprinted by permission.

functionally rationalized industries, as the result of successive changes in the game since its post-Civil-War diffusion from England.[1]

It would be wrong, however, to assert that football has become an impersonal market phenomenon. Rather, its rationalization as a sport and as a spectacle has served to bring out more openly the part it plays in the ethnic, class, and characterological struggles of our time— meaning, by "characterological struggle," the conflict between different styles of life. The ethnic significance of football is immediately suggested by the shift in the typical origins of player-names on the All-American Football Teams since 1889. In 1889, all but one of the names (Heffelfinger) suggested Anglo-Saxon origins. The first name after that of Heffelfinger to suggest non-Anglo-Saxon recruitment was that of Murphy, at Yale, in 1895. After 1895, it was a rare All-American team that did not include at least one Irishman (Daly, Hogan, Rafferty, Shevlin); and the years before the turn of the century saw entrance of the Jew. On the 1904 team appeared Pierkarski, of Pennsylvania. By 1927, names like Casey, Kipke, Oosterbaan, Koppisch, Garbisch, and Friedman were appearing on the All-American lists with as much frequency as names like Channing, Adams, and Ames in the 1890's.

While such a tally does little more than document a shift that most observers have already recognized in American football, it raises questions that are probably not answerable merely in terms of ethnic origins of players. There is an element of class identification running through American football since its earliest days, and the ethnic origins of players contain ample invitations to the making of theory about the class dimensions of football. Most observers would be inclined to agree that the arrival of names like Kelley and Kipke on the annual All-American list was taken by the Flanagans and the Webers as the achievement of a lower-class aspiration to be among the best at an upper-class sport. The question remains: what did the achievement mean? What did it mean at different stages in the development of the game? Hasn't the meaning worn off in the fifty-odd years, the roughly two generations since Heffelfinger and Murphy made the grade?

1. The growing scale of college football is indicated by its dollar place in the American leisure economy. In 1929, out of $4.3 billion recreation expenditures by Americans, the college football gate accounted for $22 million. In 1950, out of $11.2 billion in such expenditures, it accounted for $103 million. While something less than 1% of the total United States recreation account, college football had ten times the gross income of professional football. The 1950 gate of $103 million suggests that a total capital of perhaps $250 million is invested in the college football industry. The revenue figures, above, of course, do not include the invisible subsidization of football, nor do they hint at the place that football pools occupy in the American betting economy.

There are many ways to begin an answer to such questions, and here we can open only a few lines of investigation. Our method is to study the interrelations between changes in the rules of the game (since the first intercollegiate contest: Rutgers, 6 goals—Princeton, 4 goals, in 1869) and to analyze the parallel changes in football strategy and ethos. All these developments are to be seen as part of a configuration that includes changes in coaching, in the training of players, and in the no less essential training of the mass audience.

Since football is a cultural inheritance from England, such an analysis may be made in the perspective of other studies in cultural diffusion and variation. Just as the French have transformed American telephone etiquette while retaining some of its recognizable physical features, so Americans have transformed the games of Europe even when, as in track or tennis, the formalities appear to be unaltered. Even within the Western industrial culture, there are great varieties on a class and national basis, in the games, rules, strategy, etiquette, and audience structures of sport. In the case of college football—we shall leave aside the symbolically less important professional game—the documentation of sportswriters (themselves a potent factor in change) allows us to trace the stages of development.

II

A study of Anatolian peasants now under way at the Bureau of Applied Social Research indicates that these highly tradition-bound people cannot grasp the abstractness of modern sports. They lack the enterprise, in their fatalistic village cultures, to see why people want to knock themselves out for sportsmanship's remote ideals; they cannot link such rituals, even by remote analogy, with their own. These peasants are similarly unable to be caught up in modern politics, or to find anything meaningful in the Voice of America. Nevertheless, football itself, like so many other games with balls and goals, originated in a peasant culture.

Football, in its earliest English form, was called the Dane's Head and it was played in the tenth and eleventh centuries as a contest in kicking a ball between towns. The legend is that the first ball was a skull, and only later a cow's bladder. In some cases, the goals were the towns themselves, so that a team entering a village might have pushed the ball several miles en route. King Henry II (1154-89) proscribed the game, on the ground that it interferred with archery practice. Played in Dublin even after the ban, football did not become respectable or legal until an edict of James I reinstated it. The reason was perhaps less ideological than practical: firearms had made the art of bowmanship obsolete.

During the following century, football as played by British school-boys became formalized, but did not change its fundamental pattern of forceful kicking. In 1823, Ellis of Rugby made the mistake of picking up the ball and running with it towards the goal. All concerned thought it a mistake: Ellis was sheepish, his captain apologetic. The mistake turned into innovation when it was decided that a running rule might make for an interesting game. The localism, pluralism, and studied casualness of English sports made it possible to try it out without secur-ing universal assent—three or four purely local variants of football, foot-ball-hazing and "wall games" are still played in various English schools. Rugby adopted "Rugby" in 1841, several years after Cambridge had helped to popularize it.[2]

This establishment of the running or Rugby game, as contrasted with the earlier, kicking game, had several important results. One was that the old-style players banded themselves together for the defense of their game, and formed the London Football Association (1863). This name, abbreviated to "Assoc," appears to have been the starting point for the neologism, "Soccer," the name that the kicking game now goes by in many parts of the English-speaking world. A second result was that the English, having found a new game, continued to play it without tight rules until the Rugby Union of 1871. As we shall see, this had its effects on the American game. The third and most important result of Ellis' "mistake," of course, was that he laid the foundations for everything fundamental about the American game between about 1869 and the introduction of the forward pass. (The forward pass is still illegal in Rugby and closely related football games.)

III

In the Colonial period and right down to the Civil War, Americans played variants on the kicking football game on their town greens and

2. A commemorative stone at Rubgy reads as follows:

THIS STONE
COMMEMORATES THE EXPLOIT OF
WILLIAM WEBB ELLIS
WHO WITH A FINE DISREGARD FOR THE RULES OF
FOOTBALL, AS PLAYED IN HIS TIME,
FIRST TOOK THE BALL IN HIS ARMS AND RAN WITH IT,
THUS ORIGINATING THE DISTINCTIVE FEATURE OF
THE RUGBY GAME
A. D. 1823

schoolyards. After the war, Yale and Harvard served as the culturally receptive importers of the English game. Harvard, meeting McGill in a game of Rugby football in 1874, brought the sport to the attention of collegiate circles and the press—two identifications important for the whole future development of the game. But if Harvard was an opinion leader, Yale was a technological one. A Yale student who had studied at Rugby was instrumental in persuading Yale men to play the Rugby game and was, therefore, responsible for some of Yale's early leadership in the sport.

It happened in the following way, according to Walter Camp and Lorin F. Deland.[3] The faculty in 1860, for reasons unknown, put a stop to interclass matches of the pre-Rugby variety. "During the following years, until 1870, football was practically dead at Yale. The class of '72, however, was very fond of athletic sports, and participated especially in long hare and hound runs. The revival of football was due in a large measure to Mr. D. S. Schaft, formerly of Rugby School, who entered the class of '73 and succeeded in making the sport popular among his classmates, and eventually formed an association which sent challenges to the other classes."

Soon after the period described by Camp, it became clear that American players, having tasted the "running" game, were willing to give up the soccer form. It became equally clear that they either did not want to, or could not, play Rugby according to the British rules. "The American players found in this code [English Rugby Rules] many uncertain and knotty points which caused much trouble in their game, especially as they had no traditions, or older and more experienced players, to whom they could turn for the necessary explanations," says Camp. An example of such a problem was English rule number nine:

"A touchdown is when a player, putting his hand on the ball in touch or in goal, stops it so that it remains dead, or fairly so."

The ambiguity of the phrase "fairly so" was increased by the statement in rule number eight that the ball is dead "when it rests absolutely motionless on the ground."

Camp's description of these early difficulties is intensely interesting to the student of cultural diffusion not only because of what Camp observed about the situation, but also because of what he neglected to observe. Consider the fact that the development of Rugby rules in England was accomplished by admitting into the rules something that we could call a legal fiction. While an offensive runner was permitted to carry the ball, the condition of his doing so was that he should *happen*

3. Walter Camp and Lorin F. Deland, *Football.*

to be standing behind the swaying "scrum" (the tangled players) at the moment the ball popped back out to him. An intentional "heel out" of the ball was not permitted; and the British rules of the mid-nineteenth century appear to take it for granted that the difference between an intentional and an unintentional heel-out would be clear to everyone. Ellis' mistake became institutionalized—but still as a mistake. This aspect of Rugby rule-making had important implications for the American game.

British players, according to tradition as well as according to rules, could be expected to tolerate such ambiguity as that of the heel-out rule just as they tolerated the ambiguity of the "dead" ball. They could be expected to tolerate it not only because of their personal part in developing new rules but also (a point we shall return to) because they had an audience with specific knowledge of the traditions to assist them. In America it was quite another matter to solve such problems. No Muzafer Sherif was present[4] to solidify the perceptions of "nearly so," and the emotional tone for resolving such questions without recurrent dispute could not be improvised. Rather, however, than dropping the Rugby game at that point, because of intolerance for the ambiguities involved, an effort was undertaken, at once systematic and gradual, to fill in by formal procedures the vacuum of etiquette and, in general, to adapt the game to its new cultural home.

The upshot of American procedure was to assign players to the legalized task of picking up and tossing back out of scrimmage. This in turn created the rôle of the center, and the centering operation. This in turn led to a variety of problems in defining the situation as one of "scrimmage" or "non-scrimmage," and the whole question of the legality of passing the ball back to intended runners. American football never really solved these problems until it turned its attention, in 1880, to a definition of the scrimmage itself. The unpredictable English "scrum" or scramble for a free ball was abandoned, and a crude line of scrimmage was constructed across the field. Play was set in motion by snapping the ball. Meanwhile Americans became impatient with long retention of the ball by one side. It was possible for a team that was ahead in score to adopt tactics that would insure its retention of the ball until the end of the period. By the introduction of a minimum yardage-gain rule in 1882, the rulemakers assured the frequent interchange of the ball between sides.

The effect of this change was to dramatize the offensive-defensive symmetry of the scrimmage line, to locate it sharply in time ("downs"),

4. Cf. his *An Outline of Social Psychology*, pp. 93-182.

and to focus attention not only on the snapping of the ball, but also on the problem of "offside" players. In the English game, with no spatially and temporally delimited "line of scrimmage," the offside player was penalized only by making him neutral in action until he could move to a position back of the position of the ball. In the American game, the new focus on centering, on a scrimmage line, and on yardage and downs, created the need for a better offside rule. From that need developed offside rules that even in the early years resembled the rules of today. American rulemakers were logically extending a native development when they decided to draw an imaginary line through the ball before it had been centered, to call this the "line of scrimmage," and to make this line, rather than the moving ball itself, the offside limit in the goalward motion of offensive players. At first, lined-up players of the two sides were allowed to stand and wrestle with each other while waiting for the ball to be centered; only later was a neutral zone introduced between the opposing lines.

Even with such a brief summary of the rule changes, we are in a position to see the operation of certain recurrent modes or patterns of adaptation. The adaptation begins with the acceptance of a single pivotal innovation (running with the ball). The problems of adaptation begin with the realization that this single innovation has been uprooted from a rich context of meaningful rules and traditions, and does not work well in their absence. Still more complex problems of adaptation develop when it is realized that the incompleteness of the adaptation will not be solved by a reference to the pristine rules. In the first place, the rules are not pristine (the English rules were in the process of development themselves). In the second place, the tradition of interpreting them is not present in experienced players. In the third place, even if it were, it might not be adaptable to the social character and mood of the adapters.

Let us put it this way. The Americans, in order to solve the heel-out problem, set in motion a redesign of the game that led ultimately to timed centering from a temporarily fixed line of scrimmage. Emphasis completely shifted from the kicking game; it also shifted away from the combined kicking and running possible under Rugby rules; it shifted almost entirely in the direction of an emphasis on ballcarrying. Meanwhile, to achieve this emphasis, the game made itself vulnerable to slowdowns caused by one team's retention of the ball. It not only lost the fluidity of the original game, but ran up against a pronounced American taste for action in sports, visible action. There is evidence that even if players had not objected to such slowdowns, the spectators would have raised a shout. The yardage rule was the way this crisis was met. This, in turn, led to an emphasis on mass play, and helped to create the early twentieth-century problems of football. But before we consider this step in the game's development we must turn to examine certain factors in the sport's audience reception.

IV

A problem posed for the student of cultural diffusion at this point can be stated as follows: What factor or factors appear to have been most influential in creating an American game possessing not only nationally distinct rules, but also rules having a specific flavor of intense legality about many a point of procedure left more or less up in the air by the British game?

We can now go beyond the rule-making aspect of the game and assert that the chief factor was the importance of the need to standardize rules to supply an ever-widening collegiate field of competition, along with the audience this implied. The English rulemakers, it appears, dealt with a situation in which amateur play was restricted to a fairly limited number of collegians and institutions. The power of localism was such that many an informality was tolerated, and intended to be tolerated, in the rules and their interpertation. American football appeared on the American campus at the beginning of a long period in which intercollegiate and interclass sportsmanship was a problem of ever-widening social participation and concern. Football etiquette itself was in the making. Thus, it appears that when early American teams met, differences of opinion could not be resolved between captains in rapid-fire agreement or penny-tossing as was the case in Britain. American teams did not delegate to their captains the rôle of powerful comrade-in-antagonism with opposing captains, or, if they did, they felt that such responsibilities were too grave.[5]

Into just such situations football players thrust all of the force of their democratic social ideologies, all their prejudice in favor of equalitarian and codified inter-player attitudes. Undoubtedly, similar considerations also influenced the audience. Mark Benney, a British sociologist who is familiar with the games played on both sides of the Atlantic, points out that, whereas the American game was developed in and for a student group, the English game was played before quite large crowds

---

5. "Fifty years ago arguments followed almost every decision the referee made. The whole team took part, so that half the time the officials scarcely knew who was captain. The player who was a good linguist was always a priceless asset." John W. Heisman, who played for both Brown and Penn in the 1890's, quoted in Frank G. Menke, *Encyclopedia of Sports*, p. 293.

who, from a class standpoint, were less homogeneous than the players themselves, though they were as well informed as the latter in the "law of the game. Rugby football was seldom played by the proletariat; it was simply enjoyed as a spectacle.

Held by the critical fascination the British upper strata had for the lower strata, the audience was often hardly more interested in the result of the game than in judging the players as "gentlemen in action." "The players," Mr. Benney writes, "had to demonstrate that they were sportsmen, that they could 'take it'; and above all they had to inculcate the (politically important) ideology that legality was more important than power." The audience was, then, analogous to the skilled English jury at law, ready to be impressed by obedience to traditional legal ritual and form, and intolerant of "bad form" in their "betters." The early Yale games, played before a tiny, nonpaying audience, lacked any equivalent incentive to agree on a class-based ritual of "good form," and when the audiences came later on, their attitude towards upper-class sportsmanship was much more ambivalent—they had played the game too, and they were unwilling to subordinate themselves to a collegiate aristocracy who would thereby have been held to norms of correctness. The apparent legalism of many American arguments over the rules would strike British observers as simply a verbal power-play.

Such differences in the relation of the game to the audience, on this side of the Atlantic, undoubtedly speeded the development of the specifically American variant. Native, too, are the visual and temporal properties of the game as it developed even before 1900: its choreography could be enjoyed, if not always understood, by nonexperts, and its atomistic pattern in time and space could seem natural to audiences accustomed to such patterns in other foci of the national life. The midfield dramatization of line against line, the recurrent starting and stopping of field action around the timed snapping of a ball, the trend to a formalized division of labor between backfield and line, above all, perhaps, the increasingly precise synchronization of men in motion—these developments make it seem plausible to suggest that the whole procedural rationalization of the game which we have described was not unwelcome to Americans, and that it fitted in with other aspects of their industrial folkways.

Spurred by interest in the analysis of the athletic motions of men and animals, Eadweard Muybridge was setting out his movie-like action shots of the body motion (more preoccupied even than Vesalius or da Vinci with the detailed anatomy of movement)[6] at about the same time

6. Sigfried Giedion, *Mechanization Takes Command*, pp. 21-27.

that Coach Woodruff at Pennsylvania (1894) was exploring the possibilities for momentum play: linemen swinging into motion before the
ball is snapped, with the offensive team, forming a wedge, charging
toward an opposition held waiting by the offside rule. In Philadelphia,
the painter Eakins, self-consciously following the tenets of Naturalism
and his own literal American tradition, was painting the oarsmen of the
Schuylkill. Nearby, at the Midvale plant of the American Steel Company,
efficiency expert Frederick Winslow Taylor was experimenting with
motion study and incentive pay geared to small measurable changes in
output—pay that would spur but never soften the workman.[7]

Since we do not believe in historical inevitability, nor in the necessary homogeneity of a culture, we do not suggest that the American
game of football developed as it did out of cultural compulsion and
could not have gone off in quite different directions. Indeed, the very
effectiveness of momentum play, as a mode of bulldozing the defense,
led eventually to the rule that the line must refrain from motion before the ball is snapped. For the bulldozing led, or was thought to lead,
to a great increase in injuries. And while these were first coped with
by Walter Camp's training table (his men had their choice of beefsteak
or mutton for dinner, to be washed down with milk, ale, or sherry), the
public outcry soon forced further rule changes designed to soften the
game. After a particular bloody battle between Pennsylvania and Swarthmore in 1905, President Roosevelt himself took a hand and insisted on
reform.[8]

Camp's colleague at Yale, William Graham Sumner, may well have
smiled wryly at this. Sumner was exhorting his students to "get capital,"

7. In view of the prejudice against "Taylorism" today, shared by men and management as well as the intellectuals, let us record our admiration for Taylor's achievement, our belief that he was less insensitive to psychological factors than is often
claimed, and more "humane" in many ways than his no less manipulative, self-
consciously psychological successors.

8. "In a 1905 game between Pennsylvania and Swarthmore, the Pennsy slogan was
'Stop Bob Maxwell,' one of the greatest linesmen of all time. He was a mighty man,
with the amazing ability to roll back enemy plunges. The Penn players, realizing
that Maxwell was a menace to their chances of victory, took 'dead aim' at him
throughout the furious play.

"Maxwell stuck it out, but when he tottered off the field, his face was a bloody
wreck. Some photographer snapped him, and the photo of the mangled Maxwell,
appearing in a newspaper, caught the attention of the then President Roosevelt. It
so angered him, that he issued an ultimatum that if rough play in football was
not immediately ruled out, he would abolish it by executive edict." Frank G.
Menke, *Encyclopedia of Sports*.

Notice here the influence of two historical factors on football development: one,
the occupancy of the White House in 1905 by the first President of the United
States who was a self-conscious patron of youth, sport, and the arts; two, the relative newness in 1905 of photographic sports coverage. Widespread increased photographic coverage of popular culture was the direct result of the newspaper policies
of William Randolph Hearst, beginning about 1895.

and cautioning them against the vices of sympathy and reformism—a theme which has given innumerable American academes a good living since—while Camp was exhorting his to harden themselves, to be stern and unafraid. In spite of them both, the reformers won out; but the end of momentum play was not the end of momentum. Rather, with an ingenuity that still dazzles, the game was gentled and at the same time speeded by a new rule favoring the forward pass. But before going on to see what changes this introduced, let us note the differences between the subjects of Sumner's and Camp's exhortations on the one hand, and Taylor's on the other.

Frederick Taylor, as his writings show, was already coming up against a work force increasingly drawn from non-Protestant lands, and seeking to engender in them a YMCA-morality, whereas Camp was inculcating the same morality into young men of undiluted Anglo-Saxon stock and middle- to upper-class origins. Not for another fifty years would the sons of Midvale prove harder, though fed on kale or spaghetti, and only intermittently, than the sons of Yale. Meanwhile, the sons of Yale had learned to spend summers as tracklayers or wheat harvesters in an effort to enlarge their stamina, moral toughness, and cross-class adventures.

Nevertheless, certain basic resemblances between the purposes of Taylor and those of Sumner and Camp are clearly present. In contrast with the British, the Americans demonstrated a high degree of interest in winning games and winning one's way to high production goals. The Americans, as in so many other matters, were clearly concerned with the competitive spirit that new rules might provoke and control. (British sports, like British industry, seemed to take it more for granted that competition will exist even if one does not set up an ideology for it.) Much of this seems to rest in the paradoxical belief of Americans that competition is natural—but only if it is constantly recreated by artificial systems of social rules that direct energies into it.

Back of the attitudes expressed in Taylor, Sumner, and Camp we can feel the pressure not only of a theory of competition, but also a theory of the emotional tones that ought to go along with competition. It is apparent from the brutality scandals of 1905 that President Roosevelt reacted against roughhouse not so much because it was physical violence, but for two related reasons. The first and openly implied reason was that it was connected with an unsportsmanlike attitude. The second, unacknowledged, reason was that Americans fear and enjoy their aggression at the same time, and thus have difficulty in pinning down the inner meanings of external violence. The game of Rugby as now played in England is probably as physically injurious as American football was at the turn of the century. By contrast, American attitudes toward football demonstrates a forceful need to define, limit, and conventionalize the symbolism of violence in sports.

If we look back now at England, we see a game in which shouted signals and silent counting of timed movements are unknown—a game that seems to Americans to wander in an amorphous and disorderly roughhouse. Rugby, in the very home of the industrial revolution, seems pre-industrial, seems like one of the many feudal survivals that urbanization and industrialization have altered but not destroyed. The English game, moreover, seems not to have developed anyone like Camp, the Judge Gary of football (as Rockne was to be its Henry Ford): Camp was a sparkplug in efforts to codify inter-collegiate rules; he was often the head of the important committees. His training table, furthermore, was one of the signs of the slow rise in "overhead" expense—a rise which, rather like the water in United States Steel Stock, assumed that abundance was forthcoming and bailing out probable, as against the British need for parsimony. But at the same time the rise in costs undoubtedly made American football more vulnerable than ever to public-relations considerations: the "gate" could not be damned.

V

This public relations issue in the game first appears in the actions of the rules committee of 1906—the introduction of the legalized forward pass in order to open up the game and reduce brutal power play. Between 1906 and 1913 the issue was generally treated as a problem centered about players and their coaches, and thus took the form of an appeal to principles rather than to audiences. However, the development of the high audience appeal that we shall show unfolding after 1913 was not autonomous and unheralded. If public relations became a dominant factor by 1915, when the University of Pittsburgh introduced numbers for players in order to spur the sale of programs, it had its roots in the 1905-13 period. The rules committee of 1906, by its defensive action on roughhouse rules had already implicitly acknowledged a broad public vested interest in the ethos of the game. Let us turn to look at the speed with which football was soon permeated by broad social meanings unanticipated by the founders of the sport.

By 1913, the eve of the First World War, innovation in American industry had ceased to be the prerogative of Baptist, Calvinist, and North of Ireland tycoons. Giannini was starting his Bank of America; the Jews were entering the movies and the garment hegemonies. Yet these were exceptions, and the second generation of immigrants, taught in America to be dissatisfied with the manual work their fathers did, were seldom finding the easy paths of ascent promised in success literature. Where, for one thing, were they to go to college? If they sought to enter the older eastern institutions, would they face a social struggle? Such anxieties probably contributed to the fact that the game of boyish and spirited brawn played at the eastern centers of intellect and cultivation was to be overthrown by the new game of craft and field maneuver that got its first rehearsal at the hands of two second-generation poor boys attending little-known Notre Dame.

The more significant of the two boys, Knute Rockne, was, to be sure, of Danish Protestant descent and only later became a Catholic.[9] During their summer vacation jobs as lifeguards on Lake Michigan, Rockne and Gus Dorais decided to work as a passing team. Playing West Point early in the season of 1913, they put on the first demonstration of the spiral pass that makes scientific use of the difference in shape between the round ball used in the kicking game and the oval that gradually replaced it when ball-carrying began. As the first players to exploit the legal pass, they rolled up a surprise victory over Army. One of the effects of the national change in rules was to bring the second-generation boys of the early twentieth century to the front, with a craft innovation that added new elements of surprise, "system" and skull-session to a game that had once revolved about an ethos of brawn plus character-building.

With the ethnic shift, appears to have come a shift in type of hero. The work-minded glamor of an all-'round craftsman like Jim Thorpe gave way to the people-minded glamor of backfield generals organizing deceptive forays into enemy territory—of course, the older martial virtues are not so much ruled out as partially incorporated in the new image. In saying this, it must not be forgotten, as sports columnist Red Smith has pointed out, that the fictional Yale hero, Dick Merriwell, is openly and shamelessly represented as a dirty player in the first chapters of his career. But the difference is that his deviation from standard sportsmanship consisted largely of slugging, not of premeditated wiliness. In fact, the Yale Era, even into Camp's reign, was characterized by a game played youthfully, with little attention to the players' prestige outside college circles. Again, the second-generationers mark a change. A variety of sources, including letters to the sports page, indicate that a Notre Dame victory became representational in a way a Yale or Harvard victory never was, and no Irish or Polish boy on the team could escape the symbolism. And by the self-confirming process, the Yale or

9. "After the church, football is the best thing we have," Rockne.

Harvard showing became symbolic in turn, and the game could never be returned, short of intramuralization, to the players themselves and their earlier age of innocent dirtiness.[10] The heterogeneity of America which had made it impossible to play the Rugby game at Yale had finally had its effect in transforming the meaning of the game to a point where Arnold of Rugby might have difficulty in drawing the right moral or any moral from it. Its "ideal types" had undergone a deep and widespread characterological change.

For the second-generation boy, with his father's muscles but not his father's motives, football soon became a means to career ascent. So was racketeering, but football gave acceptance, too—acceptance into the democratic fraternity of the entertainment world where performance counts and ethnic origin is hardly a handicap. Moreover, Americans as onlookers welcomed the anti-traditional innovations of a Rockne, and admired the trick that worked, whatever the opposing team and alumni may have thought about the effort involved. One wonders whether Rockne and Dorais may not have forgotten a particular pleasure from their craftiness by thinking of it as a counter-image to the stereotype of muscle-men applied to their fathers.

It was in 1915, at about the same time that the newcomers perfected their passing game, that the recruitment of players began in earnest. Without such recruitment, the game could not have served as a career route for many of the second generation who would not have had the cash or impetus to make the class jump that college involved.[11]

The development of the open and rationalized game has led step by step not only to the T formation, but also to the two-platoon system. These innovations call for a very different relationship among the players than was the case under the older star system. For the game is now a coöperative enterprise in which mistakes are too costly—to the head coach, the budget, even the college itself—to be left to individual initiative. At least at one institution, an anthropologist has been called in to

10. One of us, while a Harvard undergraduate, sought with several friends to heal the breach between Harvard and Princeton—a breach whose bitterness could hardly be credited today. The Harvards believed Princeton played dirty—it certainly won handily in those years of the 20s—while Princetonians believed themselves snubbed by Harvard as crude parvenus trying to make a trio out of the Harvard-Yale duo. The diplomatic problems involved in seeking to repair these status slights and scars were a microcosm of the Congress of Westphalia or Vienna—whether the Harvard or Princeton athletic directors should enter the room first was an issue. A leak to the Hearst press destroyed our efforts, as alumni pressure forced denials of any attempt to resume relations, but the compromise formulas worked out were eventually accepted, about the time that the University of Chicago "solved" the problem of the intellectual school by withdrawing from the game altogether.
11. See George Saxon, "Immigrant Culture in a Stratified Society," Modern Review, II, No. 2, February 1948.

study the morale problems of the home team, and to help in the scouting of opposing teams. To the learning of Taylor, there has been added
that of Mayo, and coaches are conscious of the need to be group-
dynamics leaders rather than old-line straw bosses.

Today, the semi-professionalized player, fully conscious of how many
people's living depends on him, cannot be exhorted by Frank Merriwell
appeals, but needs to be "handled." And the signals are no longer the
barks of the first Camp-trained quarterback—hardly more differentiated
than a folkdance caller's—but are cues of great subtlety and mathematical precision for situations planned in advance with camera shots and
character fill-ins of the opposing team. James Worthy and other advocates of a span of control beyond the usual half-dozen of the older
military and executive manuals might find support for their views in
the way an eleven is managed. Industrial, military, and football teamwork have all a common cultural frame.

Yet it would be too simple to say that football has ceased to be a
game for its players, and has become an industry, or a training for
industry. In the American culture as a whole, no sharp line exists between work and play, and in some respects the more work-like an
activtiy becomes, the more it can successfully conceal elements of playfulness.[12] Just because the sophisticated "amateur" of today does *not*
have his manhood at stake in the antique do-or-die fashion (though
his manhood may be involved, in very ambivalent ways, in his more
generalized rôle as athlete and teammate), there can be a relaxation
of certain older demands and a more detached enjoyment of perfection
of play irrespective of partisanship.

The rôle of football tutor to the audience has been pushed heavily
onto radio and TV announcers (some of whom will doubtless be mo-
bile into the higher-status rôle of commentators on politics or symphony
broadcasts). The managerial coalescence of local betting pools into
several big oceans has also contributed to the audience stake in the
game. Yet all that has so far been said does not wholly explain alumnus
and subway-alumnus loyalties. It may be that we have to read into this
interest of the older age groups a much more general aspect of American
behavior: the pious and near-compulsory devotion of the older folks to
whatever the younger folks are alleged to find important. The tension
between the generations doubtless contributes to the hysterical note of
solemnity in the efforts of some older age groups to control the ethics
of the game, partly perhaps as a displacement of their efforts to control
youthful sexuality.

12. Compare the discussion of Freud's playful work, pp. 331-333, below.

And this problem in turn leads to questions about the high percentage of women in the American football audience, compared with that of any other country, and the high salience of women in football as compared with baseball imagery (in recent American football films, girls have been singled out as the most influential section of the spectators). The presence of these women heightens the sexual impact of everything in and around the game, from shoulderpads to the star system, as the popular folklore of the game recognizes. Although women are not expected to attend baseball games, when they do attend they are expected to understand them and to acquire, if not a "male" attitude, at least something approaching companionship on a basis of equality with their male escorts.[13]

For all its involvement with such elemental themes in American life, it may be that football has reached the apex of its audience appeal. With bigness comes vulnerability: "inter-industry" competition is invited, and so are rising costs—the players, though not yet unionized, learn early in high school of their market value and, like Jim in Huckleberry Finn, take pride in it.[14] The educators' counter-reformation cannot be laughed off. With the lack of ethnic worlds to conquer, we may soon find the now-decorous Irish of the Midwest embarrassed by Notre Dame's unbroken victories. Perhaps the period of innovation which began in 1823 at Rugby has about come to an end in the United States, with large changes likely to result only if the game is used as a device for acculturation to America, not by the vanishing stream of immigrants to that country, but by the rest of the world that will seek the secret of American victories on the playing fields of South Bend.

13. Anthropologist Ray Birdwhistell convincingly argues that football players play with an eye to their prestige among teammates, other football players, and other men.

14. Their pride varies to some extent with their place on the team. Linemen, with the exception of ends, have lower status than backfield men. Many players believe that backfields are consciously and unconsciously recruited from higher social strata than linemen.

THE THEATRE OF SPORTS

John Lahr

*The human being is delivered helpless, in respect to life's most impor-
tant and trivial affairs, to a power (technology) which is in no sense
under his control. For there can be no question today of man's controlling the milk he drinks or the bread he eats, any more than of his controlling his government.*

—Jacques Ellul,
The Technological Society

Take me out to the ball game,
Take me out to the park.
Buy me some peanuts and Cracker Jack,
I don't care if I never get back . . .
　　　　　　　　　　—Old baseball song

Games are a means, through make-believe, of coping with the world.
So is theatre. But as the opportunity for physical prowess and uncomplicated, noble victory is denied mechanized man, the spectacle of sport
has assumed a potency and ritual importance in America that most
theatre has lost. Sports have become a twentieth-century obsession.
Sports are the nation's grand distraction, incorporating a tableau of
affluence once reserved for the Broadway musical into the larger ambitions of a highly industrial state. Formal, controlled, efficiently organized, the modern spectacles reflect the technological thrust of this
century. They offer not only escape but confirmation, adjusting the
public to the violence and inequities of the system. Theatre, emphasizing
immediacy, emotional depth, psychic and social change, is reminiscent

From *Evergreen Review* 13 (November, 1969): 39-76. Reprinted by permission.

of a humanity eroded by urban living. Spectacle is more comfortable and reassuring. It asks no questions of the viewer but provides the thrill of external action.

The sports spectacle has become America's right-wing theatre, affirming the status quo by making those processes which emasculate man palatable in "play." Spectacle is an important barometer of an age. Each type of spectacle has evolved with the demands of contemporary society, reflecting and influencing its view of the world.

I

Medieval pageants were a concrete expression of the living faith. They brought the teachings of the Church off the cathedral walls and into the town square. The floats which squeaked under the weight of peasant angels, devils, and biblical heroes were preceded at each station by the blare of trumpets and the hoots of an obstreperous crowd. The spectacles were an escape and an educational device, as well as a means of keeping the feudal population obedient to the Church. Spectacle was a local community activity. In the town of Wakefield, which produced the memorable cycle of mystery plays, records show that two hundred and forty parts were filled from a town of approximately five hundred and sixty people. The guilds competed in building floats. The actors, miming the drama of Heaven and Hell which surrounded their lives, often played roles parallel to their position in the town pecking order.

Although the pageants were referred to as "mystery" plays, there was no mystery for the medieval audience for whom the stories were a familiar affirmation of the Church's truth. With pulleys to suspend angels and trapdoors to dispatch devils, the medieval multiple set reinforced the hierarchical view of man's place in the Divine scheme. The process of man's life was not as important as the reassuring iconography which surrounded it. The groupings, gestures, symbols in spectacle had an orthodoxy that the words did not. The spectacle incarnated the medieval mentality, communicating in sculptural, vivid images to non-literate medieval minds. The simple images made profound sense of a confusing world. The people witnessing the spectacle were intimately involved with those performing it. They were seeing the Divine in themselves and themselves in the Divine. The effect was to create a political as well as spiritual unity. "The crowd assembled for the great festivals felt itself to be a living whole, and became the mystical body of Christ, its soul passing into his Soul."[1]

1. J. Huizinga. *The Waning of the Middle Ages* (New York: Doubleday and Company, 1934), p. 147.

While spoken sermons were few in the Middle Ages (a thirteenth-century papal decree commanded at least four a year), spectacle was used by radical priests like St. Francis of Assisi (who went among the people and made a "spectacle of himself") to dramatize the necessity of a saintly life and the onus of sin. St. Francis' attempt to embrace the mythic formula of spectacle for individual drama is described by Erich Auerbach in *Mimesis*:

> He forced his inner impulse into outer forms; his being and his life became public events; from the day when, to signify his relinquishment of things of the world, he gave back his clothes to his upbraiding father, down to the day when, dying, he had himself laid naked on the naked earth so that in his last hour, when the archfiend might still rage, he could fight naked with the naked enemy.[2]

St. Francis confronted his audience with immediate images. After a night of gluttony he had himself dragged through town with a rope around his neck while he confessed. The spectacle matched the pageants in clarity and scenic force. It demanded imitation and participation by the community. St. Francis used the contemporary sense of the world to captivate an audience.

In Elizabethan England spectacle was also a means of community control. The seasonal celebrations were organized anarchy intended to take the head off the frustration and violence of a stratified society. The Lord and Lady of Misrule mocked the Lords and Ladies of the Manor by mimicking and exaggerating their power. A Puritan observer described a typical May game:

> They have twenty or forty yolk of oxen, every ox having a sweet nose-gay of flowers on the tip of his horns, and these oxen draw home this Maypole which is covered all over with flowers and herbs, bound round about with strings, from the top to the bottom . . . with two or three hundred men, women and children following it with great devotion. And thus being reared up with handkerchiefs and flags . . . they strew the ground about, bind green boughs about it, set up summer halls, bowers and arbors hard by it. And then they fall to dance about it, like as the heathen people did at the dedication of Idols . . .[3]

Trespassing beyond the allotted festival period could bring severe penalties. But, once begun, the momentum of spectacle was sometimes hard to stop. In *Henry IV* (Part 1) Prince Hal criticizes Falstaff, the archetypal Lord of Misrule who forgets the boundaries of spectacle:

2. Erich Auerbach. *Mimesis* (New York: Doubleday Anchor Books, 1957), p. 141.
3. C. L. Barber, *Shakespeare's Festive Comedy* (Cleveland: Meridian Books, 1963), p. 21.

> If all the year were playing holidays
> To sport would be as tedious as work;
> But when they seldom come, they wished-for come . . .
>
> (1, ii, 228-230)

As C. L. Barber writes in *Shakespeare's Festive Comedy,* the anarchy allowed the mock lord to enjoy "building up his dignity, and also exploding it by exaggeration, while his followers both relish his bombast as a fleer at proper authority and also enjoy turning on him and insulting his majesty . . . the game at once appropriates and annihilates the mana of authority."[4] These popular spectacles fed theatre, especially Shakespeare's comedies. Shakespeare transported this "midsummer madness" to the stage, not merely by adopting its sights and sounds, but by applying the festival process of release and clarification through playing. In Shakespeare's comedies the characters move into a safe, festival world (Arden, Oberson's Wood, Olivia's house) where identities are tested and explored. Shakespeare's characters often *game* at the world in order to discover it, while remaining outside its passions. Viola says of Feste in *Twelfth Night:*

> This fellow is wise enough to play the fool
> And to do that craves a kind of wit.
> He must observe the mood on whom he jests
> The quality of persons and the time . . .
>
> (111, i, 66-70)

Festivals dramatized identity; people found out about the world by playing at it. In *As You Like It* Rosalynd escapes the chaos of the court, discovers the "liberty" of Arden, and finally returns to the real world. She is now socially and psychically whole. The play parallels the process of Elizabethan spectacle, a game which clarifies the actual experience.

Feste's final song in *Twelfth Night* emphasizes the illusion of spectacle: that man is not responsible for his actions. "The rain that raineth every day" is the stark reality which makes it necessary to play but also to realize the limitation of the spectacle. The paradox is built into the sadness of Feste's chronicle of his life:

> But when I came to man's estate,
>   With a hey, ho, the wind and the rain
> 'Gainst knaves and thieves men shut their gate,
>   For the rain it raineth every day . . .
>
> (V, i, 402-405)

Twelfth Night's popularity rests with Shakespeare's ability to harness the frenzy of folk spectacle to more responsible ends.

4. *Ibid.,* p. 9.

II

The pressure of technology molds the form of modern spectacle. Games admit a mechanized sense of time; they stress a system of rules and moves. The spectacle, before the development of technique, was eccentric. The modern spectacle has become national through the television set. In previous centuries a large portion of the society participated in the event, but the most popular modern spectator sports (baseball, football) are not the ones which Americans play most (golf, bowling). Football and baseball can be enjoyed in statistics as well as on the field. They have a fictional appeal in a society whose organization fractures work and puts a premium on efficiency rather than imagination. Sports recast man in an heroic mold. They are important for creating a sence of well-being in troubled times.

As the primal sources of man's identity are strangled by technology, as his primacy and his relation to the land are minimized, his fanaticism toward sports spectacle increases. Technology is both an oppressor and a reason for hope. The modern American games try to palliate this paradox. But the spectacles which set out to be diversion end up as cultural anesthesia. From childhood, the American male is stooped in the rules and lore of the games which imbue control, team play, and moral value. Life is equated with sport; the body (especially in football) aspires to become the machine which has replaced it in the real world. The spectacles institutionalize conformity and obedience, laying the groundwork for totalitarian response. The stress on toughness and violent victory ("slaughter," "kill," "pound," "ream," "cream," "mutilate") indicate a more primitive militarism:

> . . . . Technicized sport was first developed in the United States, the most conformist of all countries, and . . . it was then developed as a matter of course by the dictatorships. Fascist, Nazi, and Communist, to the point that it became an indispensable constituent element of totalitarian regimes.[5]

Sports spectacle also feeds a larger psychic yearning: the illusion of primitive power, now lost to the machine. As Lionel Tiger points out in *Men In Groups* (Random House, 1969) sports allow the spectator to rediscover his identity through "hunter-aggressive endeavors." The team names dramatize the spectators' wish-fulfillment; animals in the chase (Falcons, Tigers, Cubs, Bears, Hawks, Broncos) or mythic figures of power and bravery (Buffalo Bill, Giants, Vikings, Warriors, Braves).

Baseball is a spectacle of America's early industrialization. Football is the daydream of a passive, computerized society, melding violence

5. Jacques Ellul, *The Technological Society* (New York: Vintage Books, 1967), p. 383.

with elaborate efficiency. They are both epic struggles which have their real-life consummation in the astronauts, the game of the technological present. The space game takes its place as a popular spectacle, exhibiting the national fascination with teamwork and hardware which rationalizes and sublimates the social ulcer. With astronautics, the machine becomes the hero of the spectacle, assuming the mythic power once invested in man. The space program is named "Apollo"; the moonship has the imperial, predatory title of "Eagle"; and even the NASA satellites are called "Mariner," an image reminiscent of Viking journeys into uncharted waters, also a test of selfhood.

All these spectacles emphasize the American articles of faith: accomplishment, production, bravery, and goodness. In breaking in an audience to its technological environment, modern spectacle answers to the demands of the people. As individuality decreases in America, sports turn human beings into ritual objects, elevating the Mantles, Namaths, and Aldrins beyond public scrutiny. Spectacle becomes imaginative balm for new wounds.

III

Sport is tied to industry because it represents a reaction to industry.[6] Baseball became the nation's favorite game during violent, squalid industrialization. The game melded field with factory, incorporating the techniques of an emerging capitalism with a pastoral panorama. The sward of green turf still exists amidst the bleakness of surrounding industrial tenements it was meant to deny. The pace, now too slow for an electronic age, promised long outdoor hours as an antidote to the boredom of industry:

> He jeers the officials and indulges in hot arguments with his neighbors, stamping and ranting . . . All the time his vital organs are summoned into strenuous sympathy and he draws deep breaths of pure air. He may be weary when the game is over but for it he will eat and sleep better, his step will be more determined, his eyes will cease resembling those of a dead fish . . . He goes back to his desk or bench next day with a smiling face.[7]

Baseball was not only an escape; it reinforced capitalist values. The game treated people as property. "Trading" and "bonuses" were a means of improving efficiency and sharpening competition. Baseball also incorporated "stealing"— risk proportional to an individual's ability and his

6. *Ibid.*, p. 382.
7. Douglass Wallop, *Baseball: An Informal History* (New York: W. W. Norton & Company, 1969), p. 109.

luck. Industry increased production through standardization; so did baseball. Each player is a specialist; the team (with its "manager" and "front office") became a proto-corporation where the spectator could measure the output (of runs). Batting averages, earned-run averages were comfort percentiles: simple calculations in a world of outrageous figures and complicated equations. Medieval pageants attested to the Church's accuracy; baseball affirmed the new world of accounting and double-entry bookkeeping. "It is good to care in any dimension," William Saroyan said about the national pastime. "More Americans put their spare (and purest?) caring into baseball."[8] Seymour Siwoff, the accountant who keeps the statistics for the National League, has a sign above his door: ETERNAL VIGILANCE IS THE PRICE OF ACCURACY IN STATISTICS. If baseball reduces people to numbers the figures have, at least, a continuity and a relationship to the past. The faith in statistics prevents baseball from changing its rules because the hitting and pitching averages of the future would have no relationship to those of the past. The sentimental attachment to statistics is expressed by Siwoff in *Sports Illustrated* (August 18, 1969):

> What I enjoy most about statistics is the chance they give you to relive the past. When Ernie Banks gets seven RBIs in a game or when Reggie Jackson gets ten, it brings back memories of when Jim Bottomley drove in twelve or Tony Lazzeri drove in eleven. In looking up those things, I can see those guys as clearly as if they were playing again.

Invoking an uncomplicated past, statistics and the umpire's rule book bring the authority of "science" and "law" onto the field. The spectators and players respect both forces; they abide by a trained, "objective" decision. The game allows the illusion of freedom, but violent disagreement is not tolerated. Eccentricity, like Richie Allen's scribbling of words to the spectators in front of first base, is carefully patrolled. (The Commissioner of Baseball told Allen to stop writing "Boo," "No," "Why" in the dirt. No one balked when he wrote "Mom.") Allen is a renegade within a system that cannot tolerate friction. Baseball dramatizes acquiescence to system, law, and the mathematics of productivity.

IV

Technology creates its own demand. As America becomes increasingly systematized, unified, and efficient, the public wants more technique in its spectacles. Football offers a picture of the "gorgeousness"

---

8. A. Lawrence Holmes, *More Than a Game* (New York: The Macmillan Company, 1967), p. 11.

of enforced specialization of human effort. In the game, technique is concomitant with victory. Talking of coach Vince Lombardi, veteran guard Jerry Kramer stresses the importance of superhuman performance and accuracy:

> He makes us execute the same plays over and over, a hundred times, two hundred times, until we do every little thing right *automatically*. He works to make the kickoff return team perfect. He ignores nothing. Technique, technique, technique, over and over and over, until we feel like we're going crazy. But we win.[9]

The football player's ability to make a machine of his body sustains the spectator's faith in technology. The drama of football pits man-and-technique against man-and-technique. Films, training devices, medical equipment, special diets reflect the game's reliance on scientific discovery for *protection, defense,* and *victory*. When a Miami Dolphin end received a second concussion, a special helmet was devised to protect him. Joe Namath's million-dollar knees are guarded by a specially constructed brace. Scientific innovation is part of the team's efficiency.

Football's appeal rests with the intricacy of its system. The game emphasizes a mechanized, industrial sense of time. The players "watch the clock"; seconds become dramatic divisions. Even the vocabulary of play is in pseudo-mathematical language in which the offensive runner and his destination on the line of scrimmage are identified by number. Jerry Kramer mentions a "forty-nine sweep," which means that the number four back will take the ball into the "nine" hole, the area outside the right end.

Graceful, strong, fierce—the football player is an automation in the world of action. Jerry Kramer describes the fatigue of training:

> All I know is that when everyone else moves, I move, and when everyone files on the bus, I get on the bus . . . I really don't know what time it is, what day it is . . . I don't know anything at all.[10]

Joe Namath recounts the programming of new data ("automatics") on the line of scrimmage during the Super Bowl:

> When I change a play . . . they've got to drive the play they've been thinking about from their minds and they've got to replace it with a new one, and in a few seconds they've got to be ready for a different assignment, maybe on a different snap count, maybe in a whole different direction.[11]

9. Jerry Kramer, *Instant Replay* (New York: World Publishing Company, 1968), p. 41.
10. *Ibid.*, p. 35.
11. Joe Namath, "I Can't Wait Until Tomorrow . . . Cause I Get Better Looking Every Day," *True Magazine* (September, 1969), p. 54.

The implications of football are hidden by the excitement. The game confirms America's abiding faith in technology as a means of progress. Football is a spectacle of superhuman effort attesting to the value of research, training, discipline, and refinement. Although the players battle for money and publicize their off-season businesses, the contest on the field is beyond pecuniary consideration. There is a messianic atmosphere to football—the lockerroom talks, the bravado of the spectators which brings them to their feet or sends them out into the field after a game to rip down the goalposts. Football is a triumph of technique and community. The spectacle offers an image of athletic unity and creates an *emotional consensus*:

> Technique provides a justification to everybody and gives all men the conviction that their actions are just, good, and in the spirit of truth. The individual finds the same conviction in his fellow workers and feels himself strengthened.[12]

V

Baseball and football make reality out of a game. The space race makes a game out of reality. Technology extends the demand, fed by sport, for continued, easy victory with no sacrifice from the community of observers. The Apollo 11 was described in terms of a game. The familiar features of sport facilitate public acquiescence to the awesome specter of the machine being willed to power over man. The astronauts are the golddust twins of the galaxies; their training is an athlete's regimen of diet, study, and drills. Neil Armstrong's statement in *Life* (August 22, 1969) illustrates how the vocabulary becomes propaganda:

> This nation was depending on the NASA-industry *team* to do the job and that team was staking its reputation on Apollo 11. A lot of necks had been put voluntarily on the chopping block, and as more and more attention focussed on the flight it became evident that any failure would bring certain tarnish to the U. S. image.

The moonshot is an instant image of progress in a society where social reform is thought to involve sacrifice: "Landing men on the moon has proven easier than unraveling problems such as public welfare." (*Life*, August 22, 1969) Trained to witness gargantuan athletic feats, the American spectator accepts scientific hardware as matter-of-factly as a batting machine. The space program is its own justification:

> Modern men are so enthusiastic about technique, so assured of its superiority, so immersed in the technical milieu, that without exception they are oriented toward technical progress.[13]

12. Ellul, *op. cit.*, p. 369.
13. *Ibid.*, p. 431-32.

The moonshot is the triumph of system. Aficionados of the moon spectacle can only applaud and succumb. Yet a new world has been spawned
which will affect the way man works and how he relates to his environment. As a chauvinistic article in the July, 1969 *Fortune* testified:

> The really significant fallout from the strains, traumas, and endless experi-
> ment of Project Apollo has been . . . techniques for directing the massed
> endeavors of scores of thousands of minds in a close-knit mutually en-
> hancive combination of government, university, and private industry.

The space game makes man wetnurse to machinery. Armstrong,
Aldrin, and Collins manipulate dials. They were first on the moon, but
there are dozens waiting in the wings who can do the same thing as
efficiently. They do not fit the conventional heroic mold; their function
is not total. They are not free, lone men grappling with a recalcitrant
universe. Thousands of others, behind dials and levers, are keeping them
aloft. The hero is the machine, not man. As Michael Collins said, "The
computer, of course, had been telling me that everything was going
well. . . ." In the space game, as with all sports spectacles, man is the
master of external details which have no bearing on his inner life. The
technician's freedom is a slavery to machinery and the system that
organizes it. Human value is compromised, the inner life devalued in
the performance of tasks. Aldrin, discussing the content of his prayers
during the moon trip, told *Life*:

> I was not so selfish as to include my family in those prayers, nor so
> spacious as to include the fate of the world. *I was thinking of our par-
> ticular task* and the challenge and opportunity that had been given us.

The drama of teamwork, the tension of statistics and physical accuracy, are now firmly established in the real world as well as on the
playing field. Spectacle overwhelms the senses. The astronauts are
praised for characteristics which warp the human fiber. They represent
in life the process that Americans cheer in the stadium: "a new dis-
membering and a complete reconstruction of the human being so that
he can at last become the objective (and also total object) of technique.
He is also completely despoiled of everything that traditionally constitutes his essence. Man becomes pure appearance, a kaleidoscope of
external shapes, an abstraction in a milieu that is frighteningly concrete . . ."[14]

VI

Spectacle reinforces the illusion of objectivity. Events are paraded
before the eye and the spectator feels imaginatively in control of both
the game and its rules. Spectacle's clarity, its system, deny mystery:

14. *Ibid.*, p. 85.

> Technique worships nothing, respects nothing. It has a single role: to strip off externals, to bring everything to light, and by rational use to transform everything to means.[15]

The nonrational, the non-law-abiding, the emotionally unpalatable must be dismissed and ultimately eliminated.

Theatre cannot compete with the ritual experience of spectacle, but it can learn from it. As a handicraft industry in a technological age, theatre has lost its sense of ritual and forgotten how to deal with primal impulses. Too often our theatre is overly polite and self-conscious. It rarely understands the spectacle it offers and how to capitalize on the *forms* of pleasure which feed its audience's mythology. The fact of theatre being a game is often forgotten in the attempt to make a serious statement. Yet the process of "gaming" can have a more profound effect on an audience than a narrative plot. Theatre pieces like John Ford's Noonan's *The Year Boston Won the Pennant*, Peter Terson's *Zigger Zagger* (soccer), and Arthur Kopit's *Indians* have a radical stage potential because they invoke memories of comfortable spectacle and mythic appeal, only to work against those assumptions. The spectator subsequently becomes aware of his two faces: the dreamer and the diminished man.

By understanding the force of spectacle, American threatre can redefine itself more vigorously. It can forge an island of humanity and freedom in a sea of banal uniformity and data. The axioms of a technological society cannot be answered by an equally pat denial. But the forms which make them acceptable to the public can be imaginatively exploded. Technology and the forces which promote it are too large to be reversed, but a countervailing theatre may have an heroic destiny and a liberty the rest of America has lost.

15. *Ibid.*, p. 142.

SPORTS AND THE MASS MEDIA

HARRY EDWARDS

The mass media in America, particularly television, have done a great deal to bring about a greater awareness on the part of whites regarding the problems and life circumstances of Afro-Americans. There is little doubt but that the various desegregation drives in the South would have failed were it not for the fact that through television the grim realities of "southern hospitality" were brought into America's living rooms. It is also true that, through all forms of the mass media, many Americans have become for the first time aware of the depths of the frustrations and anxieties suffered by black people in white America. This is not to say, however, that the newspapers, television reporters, and radio announcers have been unfailingly fair to Afro-Americans. In fact, with fortunately many individual exceptions, the mass media has on frequent occasions been harsh, insensitive, and indifferent to the plight of black people. It has acted upon many occasions as an unofficial arm of the establishment in America—particularly with regard to the phrasing of new stories and the general slant of the coverage. Rather than assessing or clarifying public opinion, the press, television, and radio frequently have catered to public opinion in phrasing and presenting news reports. A network television program on urbanization fixes on ghetto "riots" as its main theme, for example. And in a white racist society this practice can be and has been extremely detrimental to the interests of black people. Most news reporters in America, however, are towers of morality, ethics, and truth when compared to this country's sports reporters.

THE WHITE SPORTS REPORTER

The large majority of white sports reporters in America have remained aloof from the problems of racial justice and injustice in the United States. As a group, they have seemingly been singularly unmoved by the frustrations and fate of black people, even of black athletes. With few exceptions—such as Howard Cosell and Jerry Eisenberg—many white sports reporters approved or stood mute as Muhammad Ali was immorally, unethically, and illegally stripped of his heavyweight boxing title. Not a single white sports reporter to my knowledge ever bothered to mention that John Wooten, in the incident mentioned in the last chapter, had been shunted aside.

The reasons behind this insensitivity on the part of white sports reporters are many. First of all, when a white American becomes a journalist, he does not all at once become a citadel of racial and social objectivity. A racist white man who becomes a journalist becomes nothing more than a racist white journalist, in much the same sense as a racist who becomes a cop becomes merely a racist cop. Reporters come from the same racially intolerant climate responsible for the denial of the American dream to black Americans for three hundred and fifty years, and in general their racial attitudes reflect that fact. These attitudes are inevitably reflected—either through omission or commission—in their work. I am not implying that all white sports reporters are dedicated racists. What I am saying is that many are simply insensitive to the magnitude and impact of the social problems that are festering beneath their very noses. In short, many are either racist or ignorant. Or worse, they are indifferent.

Another factor that determines the present state of sports reporting in America is that sports reporters must be responsive to the desires and needs of the sports industry. This is roughly analogous to a situation where the jury is chiefly responsive to the needs and desires of the criminal. Unfortunately, in sports reporting, considerations of social justice and moral responsibility often are of secondary consideration or fall by the wayside completely. This is essentially because athletics still are regarded by most people as primarily recreational—as all fun and games. And the sports establishment would love to keep it that way. But the very word "establishment" belies the claim. Sports in America is big business, and has a significant social, economic, and political impact on both the national and international levels. To many white sports reporters, it is unthinkable that anyone would want to upset the "happy, socially peaceful, and racially tranquil world of sports" by exposing some of the racial or social injustices, the recruiting and slush fund scandals, or the naked exploitation that tarnish the fanciful picture. Even if he were so inclined, the average sports reporter would probably be dissuaded in the end by the fact that he must have access to sports figures—including coaches, managers, and owners—if he is to present anything more than box scores under his by-line. These captains of the sports industry have demonstrated upon many occasions that they can make the life of an unpopular sports reporter miserable. This in turn could affect the reporter's livelihood, because a sports reporter with no access to sports figures is of little value to any newspaper or network.

Along similar lines, many reporters are responsible, again not to society or to justice, but to their sports editors. These men, like the mass media they serve, tend to be of a conservative bent in social and political matters. Many a significant and worthwhile sports story has been "deep-sixed" because the slant of the story clashed with the political and social attitudes of the sports editor. The dictum handed down from above runs "Your job is to report the sporting news, not to initiate a crusade." So usually, the only element that detracts from the fun-and-games syndrome in most sports reporting is the sad fact that for every winner, there has to be a loser.

Public opinion studies have shown time and time again that people will not buy or read anything with which they disagree. Americans are no exception. We tend to read only what reinforces our own attitudes. Newspaper reporters, editors, and publishers are keenly aware of this tendency. They have to be. For most newspapers operate to make money. Most do, however, try to strike a happy medium between service and profit. (The results of this, in the case of sports reporting, is that significant social injustices in the athletic arena are typically slanted to minimize embarrassment to the sports establishment, are mis-stated, or simply are ignored.) For no segment of the American mass media, basically a capitalistic enterprise, is going to risk financial disaster for the sake of principle—not even when that principle is the basic right of all United States citizens to social, political, and economic justice. And in this racist society where the vast majority of American citizens see sports as primarily a recreational activity, not too many sports reporters are willing to risk their personal futures in an effort to bring those instances of injustice based upon race to the attention of the public. Consequently, the sports world in America (on the basis of a few exploitative "breakthroughs" such as Jackie Robinson's entering white-dominated professional baseball) has been portrayed as a citadel of racial harmony and purity, and this distorted image has been fostered primarily by sports reporters and by persons who control the media through which sports news and activities are communicated to the public.

The simple truth of the matter is that the sports world is not a rose flourishing in the middle of a wasteland. It is part and parcel of that wasteland, reeking of the same racism that corrupts other areas of our society.

Not all of the guilt, however, should be thrust upon the white reporter and his white employers. Negro reporters and Negro-owned media too are responsible, for they have deluded many of their own followers with fanciful myths that belie the truth about the world of sports.

THE NEGRO SPORTS REPORTER

Negro sports reporters in many ways reflect the same orientation—and hence the same inadequacies—as most white reporters. Access to sports personalities, economic considerations, and lack of control over what they can and cannot write are sources of constant frustration for many. But many others destroy their effectiveness completely through crippling individual and personal tendencies. Many simply are "Uncle Toms" who have been crawling and shuffling for white people for so long that they have misplaced completely all sense of responsibility and loyalty. Such persons categorically denounce any reporting about black athletes that is "social" or "political." Their chief concerns are to keep everyone happy, though deluded. Most of the time they are too busy looking the other way, keeping the boat steady, to report objectively and with conviction. Baleful the day when they find themselves in a position of having to side with black people against a racist or patronizing white establishment.

A publication, of course, is no better than the people who write for it—black or white. Many high-circulation magazines that purport to speak for America's blacks actually are more concerned with maintaining a "respectable Negro image," meaning the image that portrays black people striving as hard as possible to be like white folks. At the very best, such publications take a middle-of-the-road position when it comes to approaching and handling critical racial questions. Invariably, in their worst guise they fill their pages with irrelevant, defensive drivel about the social life of the bourgeois Negro, the latest wig crazes, the experiences of the "only big-time Negro hunting master," the only Negro airline pilot, and so forth. But when it comes to socially, politically, and economically relevant issues, most of them play it right down the middle, or worse. For they have their white advertisers to consider, who buy pages of space to advertise bleaching creams, hair straighteners, wigs, and other kinds of racially degrading paraphernalia. In the area of sports, one generally encounters innocuous stories about Willie Mays' ability with a bat or the speed of halfbacks Walt Roberts and Nolan Smith, little men in a big man's game. But seldom, if ever, has the truth about the sports industry in America and the situation of black athletes found its way to the pages of these publications. There is, however, a rising new face on the sports reporting scene—the sensitive, socially conscious black sports reporter.

THE BLACK SPORTS REPORTER

Unlike Negro and white reporters, the black sports reporter possesses certain qualities that tend to place him outside of, and in many instances in opposition to, the sports establishment. He differs significantly from his white and Negro colleagues in his attitude, philosophy, and guts level. And neither the designation "black" nor the differentiating qualities are necessarily directly related to skin color or racial heritage. On the contemporary sports scene, the black sports reporter is typified by Sam Skinner of San Francisco's *Sun Reporter,* Dick Edwards of the *Amsterdam News,* Bob Lipsyte of *The New York Times,* Jerry Eisenberg of the Newhouse syndicate, Pete Axthelm of *Newsweek Magazine,* and Dave Wolfe of the Life-Time syndicate. The last-mentioned four just happen to be white.

The black sports reporter writes not only about developments on the field of play, but also of those influences that might effect athletes off the field. He does not pause to consider how the sports establishment will respond to his story. If his editor refuses to print it, he may soften it, but he always presses to maintain its central focus. The black reporter is undeterred by risks to his job or personal attacks against his reputation. For him such considerations are secondary to justice, fair play, and personal character and conscience. For the black reporter actually believes in all the principles and ethical considerations supposedly fostered by sports. His fight is against those who have violated these standards and sought to profit from their debasement. It will be men of dispositions and pursuasions such as these who will write the true history of American athletics.

PERPETUATING THE MYTH OF THE
BLACK ATHLETE

As we intimated above, many Negro and white sports reporters in America have contributed to the conditions in the athletic industry that have prompted the revolt of the black athlete. Much of their influence comes through their omission of relevant social, political, and economic conditions within sports, but they also have been active perpetrators of discrimination and unfairness. (Although Negro reporters are less guilty in this regard, many Negro reporters have succumbed to pressures from above to color and dilute their stories. In some instances they have actually authored reports more biased than those that a white reporter would write in order to show that they are "part of the team.") Many black athletes have felt at one time or another that they were discriminated against. Aside from the money, prestige is the greatest incentive to professional sports participation. In amateur athletics, it is the main incentive, along with love of the game. Prestige is typically accrued and measured by the frequency and general tone of publicity that an athlete receives in the various reporting media. Black athletes as a whole feel that many sports reporters have not always given credit where credit was due. In a pro grid game not too long ago, a black flanker had scored on an end-around play and caught passes from his quarterback and halfback for two more scores. Next day he was outraged to find out that the reporter covering the game had heaped praise on the white quarterback for his masterful game-calling while the flanker himself was barely mentioned in passing. Were this an isolated case, we could dismiss it as merely the complaint of a disgruntled glory seeker. But it is not an isolated case. It reflects a state of affairs that exists at the high-school level and extends on into professional sports. This type of reporting perpetuates the myth that black athletes are not capable of leading or inspiring a team to victory. In the minds of many spectators, particularly white spectators, black athletes are excellent performers—once they are told what to do. But for them to spark a team to victory or, through their own individual performances to raise the competitive morale of their teammates, is simply beyond them. There have been very few black quarterbacks; therefore, blacks are not intelligent enough to play quarterback, or to coach, or to manage an athletic team, so the thinking goes and the myths are continued.

BIBLIOGRAPHY

Section C. Sport in the Context of American Culture—

Beisser, Arnold. *The Madness in Sports.* New York: Appleton-Century-Crofts, 1967.

Betts, John. *America's Sporting Heritage: 1850-1950.* Reading, Mass.: Addison-Wesley Publishing Co., 1974.

Boyle, Robert. *Sport: Mirror of American Life.* Boston, Mass.: Little, Brown and Company, 1963.

Cozens, F. and Stumpf, F. *Sports in American Life.* Chicago: University of Chicago Press, 1953.

Dulles, F. R. *A History of Recreation: America Learns to Play.* 2d. ed. New York: Appleton-Century-Crofts, 1965.

Edwards, Harry. *Sociology of Sport.* Homewood, Ill.: The Dorsey Press, 1973.

Flath, Arnold. *Athletics in America.* Oregon State University Press, 1975.

Hoch, Paul. *Rip Off the Big Game.* New York: Doubleday Anchor Books, 1972.

Holtzman, Jerome. *No Cheering in the Press Box.* New York: Holt, Rinehart & Winston, 1974.

Izenberg, Jerry. *How Many Miles to Camelot? The All-American Sport Myth.* New York: Holt, Rinehart and Winston, 1972.

Lay, Marion. "A Content Value Analysis of Selected Newspapers Sports Columnist." Hayward, California: Master's thesis in Physical Education, 1972.

McGlynn, George. *Issues in Physical Education and Sports.* Palo Alto, Calif.: National Press Book, 1974.

Miller, Donna and Russell, Kathryn. *Sport: A Contemporary View.* Philadelphia: Lea & Febiger, 1971.

Rooney, J. F., Jr. *A Geography of American Sport.* Reading, Mass.: Addison-Wesley Publishing Company, 1974.

Sage, George H. *Sport and American Society: Selected Readings.* 2d ed. Reading, Mass.: Addison-Wesley Publishing Co., 1974.

Tunis, John. *The American Way in Sport.* New York: Duell, Sloan and Pearce, 1958.

Ulrich, Celeste. *The Social Matrix of Physical Education.* Englewood Cliffs, N.J.: Prentice-Hall, 1968.

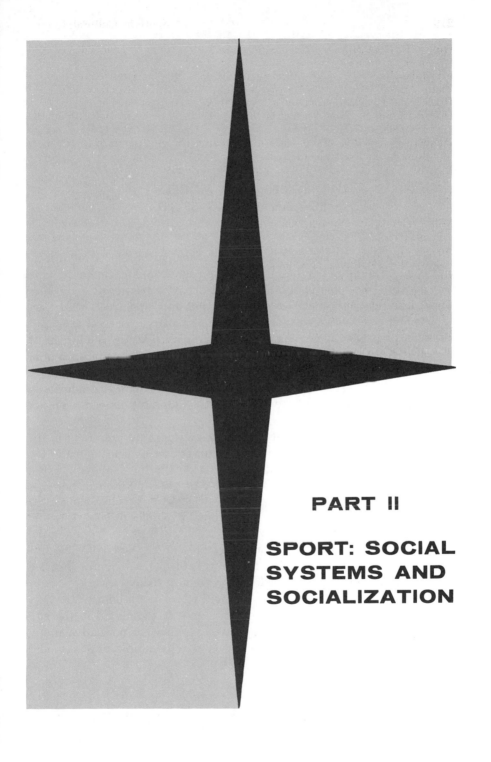

PART II

**SPORT: SOCIAL
SYSTEMS AND
SOCIALIZATION**

SECTION

A

THEORIES AND MODELS
FOR ANALYZING SPORT

The sociological analysis of sport behavior has become a significant part of physical education literature in the past ten years. However, until very recently the topic of sport as social behavior has received little or no attention from the fields of sociology and anthropology. The pattern is changing as attention to sport by serious scholars in several academic disciplines has been increasing. This encouraging sign was reinforced by the birth of a new organization, the Association for the Anthropological Study of Play. Even though research and knowledge pertaining to sport as a sociocultural phenomenon has been limited in the past the indications are that we have entered a new era of the study and understanding of sport.

Several theories and models for analyzing sport are presented in the following section. In the lead article, Seban addresses herself to the importance of the application of theoretical models to the analysis of sport. She summarizes some of the ideas presented in 1969 by Lüschen[1] but goes into more depth. Seban deals not only with sport as a subsystem of the larger social system but also with the internal dynamics of change within the sport system. How does a sport such as baseball evolve from a social club situation to the intricate structure of present-day baseball? The second half of Seban's article traces the process of internal change in baseball as it took on the characteristics we recognize today.

The authors Ingham and Loy "attempt to present a humanistic view of sport and contrast this view with sport as it it manifested in the empirical world." They state that they take a "somewhat normative premises; namely, that sport as institutionalized and reified forms of play should retain certain constituent elements of play."

1. Günther Lüschen, "Small Group Research and the Group in Sport," in *Aspects of Contemporary Sport Sociology,* ed. Gerald Kenyon (Chicago, Ill.: The Athletic Institute, 1969).

Oglesby presents two different theories pertaining to the coherence of social systems and continues by illustrating how they can be utilized in sport organization analysis. The first, a consensus theory, maintains that groups form and continue to exist because of a high degree of agreement as to pervasive values held by individuals within the group. The second theory "is built on the assumption that dissension and tension toward change are inherent in any social system." The author pursues the important concept of conflict control within the sport organization system. In a postscript to the article Oglesby suggests that it may be desirable to encourage social control mechanisms in sport that emphasize *voluntary* compliance by those who share in regulating the sport group. She concludes that sport governance cannot continue in its present form in which the governing bodies rule the lives of the athletes.

It is suggested by Tindall that both anthropologists and physical educators could benefit from the anthropological analysis of sport, provided they do so with mutual respect and trust. As an anthropologist in the Department of Physical Education at the University of California Berkeley, he adds special skill and insight to his suggestion. Tindall has conducted research including both Ute Indians and Anglo-Mormons of Utah in the sport setting of basketball. He presents research findings from various other cultural groups to illustrate the potential and value of such research.

It is amazing how ignorant one often is of the values and hidden understandings and practices of cultural groups other than one's own. In a tense high school racial situation a physical education department may insist that black male students play soccer and Latin students join heartily into basketball. With only a little information and limited anthropological knowledge such situations could be handled in a far more intelligent and sensitive manner.

A THEORETICAL CONSIDERATION OF THE INTERNAL DYNAMICS OF SPORT

MARTHA M. SEBAN

During the past decade increasing attention has been directed toward the theoretical study of sport. Historically sport has been studied in a descriptive manner. Chronologies of developments, changes in patterns of sport, specializations within sport, and the developments of administrative hierarchies have been recorded. Although descriptive studies have provided valuable information and insight into the growth and development of sport, it appears that emphasis has been, until recently, primarily directed toward identifying a variety of factors that have caused or contributed to developments and changes in sport (2, 3, 9, 12, 14, 18). Descriptive studies have continued to provide accounts of changes, growths and developments in the diverse realm of sport. However, emphasis on a theoretical approach to the study and explanation of various phenomena appears to have come into an area of its own within the past ten years. The study of sport within the field of the social sciences has lent itself to a more scientific and analytical concern for inquiry into the structure and function of the sport organization.

The theoretical study of sport is concerned with the application of theoretical models to given phenomena which occur or have occurred in sport. The purpose is to establish a scientific basis for explaining the "whys" and "hows" of the sport order. Rationale for theoretical analysis in the study of sport is based on concrete investigation, which is systematic, may provide explanations of the internal dynamics of sport. Dunning (1972) suggests the usefulness for the theoretical analysis of sport may result in explanations for changing patterns of sport. For example,

Printed with permission of the author.

how such changes related to social changes within the wider social structure; the function of recreational activities changed to accommodate the growing bureaucracy of professional and more highly organized forms of sport activities; how the function of sport changed as a result of its growing prominence as a social institution (10:xviii). These are a few possible areas which may invite further study. Inquiry into the function of sport as a cohesive agent in the national unification of peoples, and the function of sport as a means for social and political integration appears worthy of analysis. The effect that modern industrial society has had on the development of the "sport industry" is also of concern.

The productiveness that theories provide is found in a systematically organized body of knowledge which is applicable to a wide variety of situations and occurrences. Theory provides a basis for analyzing and predicting by providing the researcher with sets of guidelines. The purpose in the study of sport, as in any scientific study, is to question specific phenomena, formulate hypotheses, subject these ideas or notions to empirical testing, and ultimately formulate new theory. Dunning further suggests that "theories serve in the analysis and interpretation of known facts. They give them broader meaning by indicating ways in which they are related to different classes of facts, thus placing them within a wider framework of knowledge" (10:3).

The sociological orientation to the study of sport requires formulation of concepts and construction of theory. The analytical approach to the study of sport is in an early stage of development. Many studies have been done; however, research appears to have been limited to identifying trends in sport and offering explanations for individual behavior within the realm of sport (16, 10). The apparent lack of analytical study of the sport structure is noted by Lüschen in his theoretical analysis of the sport group (16). Lüschen is concerned with the structure and function of the sport group, in addition to the behavior and interactions of the individual within the group. The orientation of his research is towards the group as a social situation indicative of the larger society. Lüschen maintains it is this area of study where research is lacking. He views the sport group as having potential for the study and development of "theoretical propositions concerning the magnitude of social aggregates" (16:70).

Utilizing Parsons' theory of the social system as a theoretical framework, Lüschen directed his efforts toward identifying the structure of the sport group and its functional problems. Lüschen provided a theoretical and abstract explanation of social interaction within the sport group by identifying the structural levels of a sport group. Lüschen selected the

Parsonian theory on the basis that it is wide enough to apply to wider systems, such as society as a whole or to extremely small groups (16:73). He suggests that Parsons' theory

> "Provides a framework for systematically relating cultural, social system, and personality variables and even those of the behavioral organism" (16: 73).

The interrelationship among cultural, social, personality and behavioral organism systems is of primary importance in studying group interrelationships and interactions. These systems function to regulate the interaction and behavior within the group or wider system. By identifying the structural levels within the sport group, a better understanding of the function of the internal dynamics of the sport group might be achieved.

THE SPORT SYSTEM

The sport system viewed as a social system consists of four structural levels with each level functioning to meet the needs of the system. The first of these levels is the value structure. Sport as an institution possesses certain values which ultimately legitimize and justify its functioning as a subsystem of the wider social system. When identifying values of the sport system, those principles of sport representative of the "American Ideal" are generally considered—sportsmanship, fair play, achievement, and recreational activity (8:185; 14:215). In addition, engaging in sport for physical exercise and the development of a healthy body demonstrates the physical value found in sport. As illustrated in Chart I, these values of the sport system provide a motivational level which may be considered as a set of commitments to encourage participation in sporting activities. These commitments may take the forms of healthful living, exercise, social distinction or rewards granted for a successful performance (8:185). Values of the sport system also function to legitimize the actor's sport endeavors, to exercise, to seek achievement and recognition for his performance. Moreover, the values define the orientation of the system as a whole and legitimize the activity (8:36).

The second structural level of the sport system is the normative level. The normative order of the system, according to Parsons "is always relative to a given system of norms or elements whether ends, rules or other norms" (24:91). That is, certain laws or rules define behavior that "ought" or "ought not" be in everyday interest (24:75). In the case of sport, norms are those stipulations which define the player's behavior while participating in sporting activities. Norms include a set of expectations for the player's behavior on a scale of what is appropriate and correct (19:86).

CHART I
Sport System in the General Action System (16)

General Action System Subsystems of Human Action	Structural Levels of the Sport System	Functional Problems (Needs) of the Sport System
Cultural System Gives legitimization to normative order of sport	**Values** General principles of fair play, enjoyment, achievement; regulate attitudes towards participation	**Pattern Maintenance** Controlling patterns of system—maintaining values, attitudes toward sport
Social System **Sport System** Socialization system—becoming member of sporting activity—Interaction among members	**Norms** Laws, rules governing and regulating clubs, associations, leagues—specific to each group	**Integration** Internal integration of sport groups—provides harmony; agreement of baseball clubs on league rules
Personality System Learned behavior of participants in sport	**Collectivity** Given organized population—team, athletic club, spectators, group of players	**Goal Attainment** Attainment of cultural goals in relation to sport environment—i.e., need for outdoor sport, competition, livelihood
Behavioral Organism Genetic species type—human within physical world	**Role** Boundary structure of tasks performed by participant: captain, player, owner, member	**Adaptation** Adjustment to environmental conditions—situations resulting from rule changes, adapting to use of equipment

He must perform and play according to the rules of the game. The normative order of sport, for example, provides a criterion for winning a contest. Such means for determining the winner in sporting efforts include a series of contests, i.e., the best of five games, the most points scored in a given period of time, or the fastest time. Although one function the normative order provides is criteria for winning a sport contest, it must be noted that within this order each sporting activity has criteria for winning specific to that sport. For example, football rules define the winner of a game as the team which has earned the most points in four quarters of play. Horse racing defines the winner as the horse which has run a given distance in the fastest time. These norms are specific to each sport; they reflect the normative pattern of the wider sport system which requires criteria be established for determining the winner of a contest.

The behavior of the player must conform to the rules of the game. Although the rules of each game are specific to the game being played, there are certain norms which are generic to all games, such as rules regulating player behavior. From these general norms certain rules specific to each game ultimately develop. For example, the game of baseball, from the time of its inception, required that the player strike the ball with a bat and run to first base; in football the player must direct the ball towards the goal by either passing the ball or running with it. In racing the jockey rides his horse in a given direction toward the finish line.

Similarly there are sanctions specific to each sport; some are more stringent than others, depending on the nature of the game. Should a player demonstrate unsportsmanship like conduct, he must serve a penalty—often in the form of leaving the game. Should a player commit a foul, either he or his team, or both, acquire a penalty. Norms in this context function to protect the system from potential conflicts. For example, the player plays according to the rules; the referees sanction the rules; the spectators, governed by their own specific code, observe the game without becoming directly involved in the playing of the game. These normative patterns, as illustrated in Chart I function to integrate the sport system. They provide a commonality for participant behavior, winning, and playing the game fairly for all sporting endeavors.

Normative patterns cannot be effective unless they are "communicated, reinforced by appropriate sanctions and supported by appropriate symbols" (8:47). Rules of a game may be sanctioned by players who are willing to play according to them and referees who enforce those rules. The extent to which rules are enforced is dependent upon the degree of organization within the system, the attitude on the part of the participants, and the sincerity with which the contest is played. Generally speaking,

the more refined a game becomes and the greater the importance of rewards, both intrinsic and extrinsic, the more stringent the normative order.

In order for the normative level of the sport system to function to
meet the need of integration there must be an understanding and acceptance of the normative order by all actors within the system. Symbols
of the normative order, which serve to illustrate the meaning of this relatively abstract reference, include defined areas in which the contest takes
place, presence of officials to enforce game rules, costume, such as uni-
forms worn by players, and the use of equipment.

The third structural level of the sport system is the collectivity level.
This structural level is concerned with organized groups participating in
the various sporting activities, whether as players, owners, or spectators.
Clubs, teams, leagues, and associations are units concerned with a specific level of participation. The goal attainment the collectivity functions
to meet may be expressed in terms of the needs or goals that elicit
gratification for its members. Sport groups, such as clubs, leagues, and
associations must recognize and be impelled toward certain ends they
perceive as gratifications or felt needs (8:57). The coordination of sporting endeavors emphasized by groups and clubs allows the sport system
to advance towards the goals that it has established. Such goals might be
expressed as recreational enjoyment, physical exercise, competitive experience, or entertainment (9:120). Baseball clubs and gymnastic teams,
for example, provide a means for the sport system to meet the needs of
its members in these specific sporting endeavors.

The role level is the fourth structural level of the sport system. Roles,
the most fundamental unit of the system, are defined as expected patterns
of behavior which participants assume within a given sport activity. Within
the sport situation the participant is expected to interact with other members of the sport situation and ultimately the wider sport system. Roles
provide the guidelines and expectation for interaction. However, the
actors within each sport situation must be able to adapt and respond to
changing patterns between roles (19:85). For example, the player-coach
must be able to adapt to very different and clearly defined patterns of
behavior for the two respective roles. Each individual or actor, upon
assuming a specific role, functions within the sport situation. By adjusting or adapting himself to the complexity of the sport structure, the
participant makes himself fit into the situation (33:80).

On a broader level the role structure functions to meet the system's
need to adapt to environmental situations external to the system. If adaptation to given conditions is to succeed at the basic level of interaction,
the actor must yield somewhat to the current situation (33:80). The
player's role requires that he adapt to situations although a new environ-

ment may creat a situation which is unusual for him. For example, a player must adapt to conditions which are the result of technology—new playing surfaces, equipment, or coaching methods.

By identifying the four structural levels of the social system to the structural organization of sport, it may be concluded that sport at an organizational level is indeed a social system. The four structural levels of values, norms, collectivities and roles have been identified for sport. Further it has been illustrated that these four levels of the sport system function for the unit as a whole to maintain stability and equilibrium within the system.

Although Parsons' theory has obvious merits in supplying researchers of the social aspects of sport with a wide theoretical framework, it has often come under criticism. Charles Page has been critical of the use of Parsons' theory maintaining that it is too abstract, lacks concreteness, and probably benefits sociology rather than providing a clearer understanding of sport. The abstract nature and generality of Parsons' concept of the social system cannot be overlooked but neither can its applicability to the system of sport. There does seem to be a gap between the theory and reality. This problem is one that must be of concern to all researchers. Lüschen has suggested that the Parsonian system is the most conclusive theoretical system and points out that the problem with theory, not just Parsons' theory, is one of conflict

> "whether you want to explain certain problems in a particular frame of reference . . . or whether . . . you would just like to study the plain facts which, of course, would have meaning only if you apply certain models from the very beginning" (16:88).

Lüschen is suggesting that there is little chance of avoiding theoretical systems in conducting research. He does point out that easing the conflict between reality, the concrete, and theoretical orientation should be of primary concern.

Lüschen's application of Parsons' social system theory is one example of the theoretical study of sport. The focal point of Lüschen's study was the structure and function of the internal dynamics of the sport group. Social interaction within and among the structural levels were of concern. One of the criticisms of Lüschen's study was that the theory utilized did not allow for any analysis of change. Change within the sport group, as in any social group or system, is subject to change. The study of social change within the group is as important and beneficial as the inquiry into the group structure. Conceptualizing sport as a social system illustrates the feasibility of applying theoretical constructs to sport situations. Since sport may be viewed as constituting a social system further analysis may be directed toward examining the process of change within the sport system.

An example of the application of a theoretical model to change in a sport situation may be seen in the use of Smelser's structural differentiation model in providing an explanation for the development of professional baseball during the latter 1800's. Researchers and sport historians have frequently attributed the great expansion and development of sport during the latter nineteenth century to the effects of industrialization. When considering the growth and development of sport in American society, the general contention most often held is that industrialization and urbanization provided the major impetus to the change and development in sport. Other influences provided by social institutions, such as religion, education, politics, economics, and the family have also been underlined as having an important impact upon the development of sport. At the same time it would be difficult to deny that the innovation, both material and ideological, that was engulfing the American society at the end of the Civil War did not have an impact on the development of all social institutions.

Although descriptive studies have provided valuable information and insight into the growth and development of sport, inquiry into the process of change that occurred in the internal structure of sport has been negligible. Inquiry into the process of change, in the development of professional baseball may be investigated by applying Smelser's structural differentiation model. Identifying the sequence of events which occurred during the formation period of professional baseball provides an explanation of the change in baseball from a relatively leisure time sporting activity to a profitable business. In addition, studying the change which occurred in the baseball structure may illustrate the process of social change within the wider sport system.

THE MODEL OF STRUCTURAL DIFFERENTIATION

The structural differentiation model derived by Smelser explains long term change which is characteristic of growing and developing social systems. The model of structural differentiation may also be considered as a "general statement of social development applying to industrial systems and familial systems as well as many others" (27:164). Smelser elaborates on the generality and broad application of this model by maintaining that

in the development of the model there have been indications that its application is exceedingly wide, e.g., that fields as diverse as economic develop-

ment, small groups, and psychological processes of learning and socialization. To apply it vigorously to another empirical field, therefore provides
evidence as to the generality of this model (27:5).

It is the general nature of this model that provides the feasibility of
application to the empirical sport system.

The fundamental thesis of the differentiation models holds that a
breakdown occurs in the structural units of the system. The breakdown
is a result of some impinging force or crises at the goal attainment level
of the system. The outcome is a specialization of roles and collectives
which provides for greater efficiency in the functioning of the initial unit.
The emergent units, though an outgrowth of the original unit, are structurally distinct and functionally specialized. The new units continue to
function to attain the goals of the original unit. In other words, differentiation results in the emergence of the more distinct organizations to
fulfill more specialized functions and to provide greater efficiency in the
functioning of the system (27:2).

Prior to examining the process of differentiation, certain preliminaries
must be considered. First, the structure of the system, which according to
Parsons, consists of "sets of properties of its component parts and their
relations or combinations which for a particular set of analytical purposes,
can be treated as constant for particular types of systems" (19:84). The
development of professional baseball, and propositions about its development, may become empirical generalizations for the wider sport system.

Important to this discussion, is the distinction Parsons makes between
the concepts of structure and process and of stability and change. Parsons maintains that processes which act to initiate structural change are
different from those processes which operate to maintain stability and
equilibrium. The social system functions under conditions of equilibrium
and in any case of disturbance, such as differentiation, the system becomes
unstable and imbalanced. In order for the system to regain equilibrium
it is necessary for the system to change. A constantly changing equilibrium
is an example of the unstable condition of a growing and developing
social system which continually readjusts to the new structures which result from the process of change (19:87).

When considering the growth and development of the sport system,
one must also take into account the instability which results from differentiation and the adjustment of the system to unstable conditions. The concept of "process," as applicable to this discussion, implies an interchange
between the structure and the balance of the system. The alteration leads
to a new innovative state of the system, a state which must be identified
and evaluated in terms of change in its previous structure (19:85). When
the structures of the social system are altered, the system must be able

to adapt and adjust to the consequences of change if it is to regain its equilibrium and continue functioning. The ability of the social system to adapt to the results of structural differentiation allows it to move in a direction of development which provides for greater efficiency in the functioning of the system.

The initiation of change, according to Parsons, stems from pressure applied to "the definition of the situation for one or more classes of acting units within the system, and that has further repercussions which can put pressure for change on the normative institutional patterns" (19:89). The type of pressure visualized by Parsons results in the differentiation process.

Structural differentiation provides that there is a breakdown in the structure of the system which proceeds in a definite sequence and results in a greater specialization of roles when the original roles have become obsolete. Smelser (1959) has devised a seven step sequence of events which he maintains occurs in a temporal relationship to each other, resulting in the differentiation of a specific unit of the system. In other words, the process of differentiation occurs in a segmented order. Smelser has identified this sequence of social phenomena in the following seven steps (27:15-16)

1. The process of change begins with dissatisfaction of the goal achievements of the social system and an awareness that the system has the potential facilities to change.
2. Symptoms of disturbance, manifested by adverse emotional reaction, appear on the part of various members of the population.
3. A means of handling and controlling these tensions occurs and a movement toward realizing the implications of the existing value system takes place.
4. The "new ideas" are now encouraged but the responsibility for their implementation is not placed on any specific population.
5. Commitments are made toward positive attempts to attain a specification of the new ideas.
6. The innovations are carried out by persons or collectivities which are either rewarded or punished depending on how the innovations are evaluated in terms of the existing value system.
7. Should the implementation of Step 6 be received favorably, the new ideas are gradually routinized into customary patterns of performance.

In order for this process of change to take place a prerequisite must be present. As explained by Parsons, there must be "disengagement from the preceding pattern" on the part of the new unit. Some order of deprivation or inefficiency in the functioning of the system would result should the system adhere to "the old way" (17:76).

The idea of deprivation occurring within the system, if change fails to take place, reflects the concept that the social system will not function to its capacity if there is a "deficit of input at the goal attainment level of the social system" (19:89). Perceiving such a deficit from the point of view of the functioning of the system, it may be considered that the inability of the system's capacity to attain its goals occurs at the fundamental role level. This is the first step which initiates the differentiation process. Of utmost importance is the fact that "*whatever its source*," if a disturbance impinges on the goal-attaining subsystem of the social system, its effects will, in a first instance, be propagated in two directions (20:90). One of the directions concerns the problem of availability of facilities for performance of primary functions. The other direction concerns the required "integrative support which the unit receives within the system" (20:90). For differentiation to be legitimized it must no longer be thought or believed that only one specific unit within the system is capable of performing those functions for which the unit operated (19:90). The less differentiated unit which seemingly "lost functions" can still benefit the system while the new unit is functioning with more defined direction toward the goals previously sought by the more diffuse unit.

Differentiation in one sense frees a unit from previous functional responsibilities and in being so freed possesses the adaptive ability required for a higher level of functioning. "In differentiating . . . the unit gains certain degrees of freedom of choice and action which were not open to it before the process of differentiation had taken place" (19:90).

To summarize, differentiation is a process which is stimulated by a deficit in the goal attainment level of the social system. This sequence of social phenomena results in the formation of newly established units of the social system when an original unit becomes obsolete. The newly formed unit provides increased functioning of the original unit.

Parsons' concept of structural differentiation is based on the assumption that the value patterns of the social system remain unchanged even when new specialized units emerge. This assumption is based on the concept of systematic control of social systems. Specifically, the cultural system is viewed as controlling the social, personality, and human organism systems (19:96). This does not imply that changes fail to occur at the value level during the process itself. The new values of the differentiated unit become more extensive in the sense that they legitimize the functioning of the new unit more clearly. Further, they specify "the implications of the more generalized pattern of the more extensive system" (19: 97).

Differentiation does not occur without leaving certain consequences to bear on the system. Parsons maintains that consequences of differentiation include first, the opportunity factor, second, the way in which the new unit or classes of units are related to each other within the more general system, and third, the normative components that must be reorganized to apply not only to one unit but also to a number of collectivities. The opportunity factor refers to the necessity for some individual or group at the organizational level to assume responsibilities for both management and reorganization. The new units which are formed require the articulation of differentiated roles for the individual which will provide for a restructuring of the collectivities within the system (19:92). The third consequence which Parsons foresees is the higher order of generality of the norms governing the performance of the "functioning of the unit, including the relations of its performers to other units in the social structure" (19:96). These general norms define the standards which can no longer be performed by the original functioning unit.

STRUCTURAL DIFFERENTIATION OF BASEBALL

In order to discuss the process of differentiation as it occurred in baseball, it is first necessary to establish whether baseball may be considered as constituting a social system or subsystem of the wider sport system. It may be suggested that baseball's emergence into a concrete unit did not occur until 1858 when the National Association of Base Ball Players was established. Prior to that time, particularly between the period 1850 to 1858, baseball was still in a period of organization. At mid-century, although baseball clubs had been in existence for five years, baseball itself could not be considered a "structural system." There was little evidence of organized structure other than the administrative offices for each respective club. Further, there was limited uniformity in the manner in which baseball was played. Henry Chadwick recalls that in the days of its inception "the game was one merely for field recreation with a bat and ball, the rules being of the crudest kind" (6:420). The rules were not only ambiguous, but also, they were often not enforced. The ambiguity of the rules resulted in "no two localities interpreting them alike" (29:334). Each club had its own set of rules which ultimately led to the haphazard practice of using different rules in each community which played the game.

Further evidence of the lack of structural organization in baseball during the 1850's is found in the loosely defined role of the participants. For example, the player's position on the playing field and among his teammates was not specific. The opponents of the individual at bat were referred to as "adversaries," not as fielders or basemen. The player delivering the ball was the pitcher, but the area to which he was confined was noticeably ambiguous. The distance between home base and the pitcher was written as "not less than 15 paces" (25:347). The ambiguity in the rules and role expectations of the player remained until the rules were expressed more clearly.

The code of rules introduced with the establishment of the first baseball league, the National Association of Base Ball Players, is suggestive of a normative order specific to the baseball system. The rules and by-laws provided an integrating force by establishing a level of conformity to which the clubs adhered. Spalding (1911) points out that the new association

> . . . in 1858 therefore marked a new era in the history of the game, for it was then that there was put into operation for the first time a code of rules, framed by a special committee of the new association for that express purpose (28:70).

Originally the game was organized for the purpose of providing exercise, enjoyment and relaxation for individuals expressly interested in baseball. However, as the number of clubs increased, the National Association of Base Ball Players was established to control complications which became apparent when no two clubs interpreted the rules in the same manner (1:12). The need for standardization in the game's organization was apparent.

The game achieved an organizational status unknown to it prior to the establishment of the Association. The newly formed Association provided an integrating force which resulted in the uniformity of rules. The era in which clubs played according to their own rules was terminated. Although the rules of the Association were crude in comparison to those rules established in subsequent years, they did serve the purpose for which they were established. Chadwick (1901) has noted

> . . . The authorized code of playing rules of baseball was published in May 1858 and it was a very crude set of regulations, and admitted only of the playing of a very inferior kind of game; and it was sufficient for the character of the sport then in vogue (6:421).

By 1858, baseball had progressed to an organizational status which characterized the structural properties of a social system. It is proposed that examination of the internal changes in baseball is feasible beginning with the year 1858 since it may be postulated that at that time baseball constituted a system from the structural point of view.

The application of the structural differentiation model allows one to conceptualize the development of professional baseball as an outgrowth of the National Association of Base Ball Players. The initial purpose of the Association was to perpetuate "enjoyable field exercise" (25:500). However, clubs of the Association gradually adopted another purpose—to perpetuate baseball as a game of skill and perfect the quality of play (25: 510). In addition to the club's desire to perpetuate the game, the predilection of each club to possess superior players was being strengthened by the "spirit of local partisanship" on the part of the spectator. Spalding (1911) recalls that on September 10, 1858, in the final match of a series of games between Brooklyn and New York "the fight for supremacy . . . was very bitter. Both teams were on their mettle, every player feeling that the future welfare of that city represented by him depended on the result" (28:73).

The intense desire to win on the part of the club and its players was becoming an integral part of the game. John M. Ward recalled that at the time of its inception

> . . . Baseball was looked upon as merely pastime. Individuals of means and leisure organized clubs for pleasure, and were perfectly satisfied if at the close of the season the nine had won a fair majority of the games and receipts balanced expenditures (32:212).

Ward indicated the "necessity" to win in the period of the early fifties was a latent concern. However, with the increasing number of clubs, the instigation of admission fees, and the frequent gambling, pooling and throwing of games, the ability of baseball to function on an amateur level was undoubtedly questionable (28:75). The emphasis on winning, the desire of each club to possess the most highly skilled players and perfect the quality of the game may be postulated as crises initiating the process of differentiation.

THE PROCESS OF CHANGE

The process of structural differentiation, as developed by Smelser, requires that "certain social phenomena proceed in a definite sequence to produce specific types of structural change" (27:15). This sequence of social phenomena, as outlined above is summarized as follows: The initial stage of the differentiation process occurs with dissatisfaction at the goal attainment level of the social system. The process continues to develop with the demonstration of negative emotional reactions in response to the dissatisfaction in the goal attainment level and the attempt to control tensions within the system. Once the tensions have been controlled, the new ideas are openly encouraged which are then followed by a specification of the new ideas. The conclusion of this process of change is marked by the implementation of the new idea and finally the routinization and institutionalization of the innovation.

The *first stage* of the process of structural differentiation of baseball involved dissatisfaction at the goal attainment level. Dissatisfaction occurred as the result of players failing to find gratification in playing baseball for purely exercise and recreational purposes. New York gentlemen used to assemble to "engage in exercise for health, recreation and social enjoyment" (13:161). It may be noted that in the by-laws of the Knickerbocker Club, reference is made to "gathering for exercise" (25:341). There was no mention of gathering to "play a game of baseball." The groups of gentlemen found gratification in the exercise, the enjoyment, and the social distinction provided by their affiliation with a club.

The increased emphasis on the competitive aspect of the game resulted in the desire of each club to possess the most highly skilled players. The gratification of playing focused on the player seeking distinction as a skilled player, on reimbursement for his services, and on opportunity to engage in a more challenging game of baseball. The needs of distinction and success became of greater importance than exercise and enjoyment. The change in the purposes for which one participated in baseball was the source of dissatisfaction in the attainment of goal gratifications. Players began seeking satisfaction in the form of monetary reimbursement. However, the National Association did not function to provide for that specific goal and as a result dissatisfaction occurred.

Accompanying the dissatisfaction in the functioning of baseball to achieve goals and needs of the baseball system was the appearance of "symptoms of disturbance in the form of 'unjustified' negative emotional reactions and unrealistic aspirations on the part of various elements in the system" (27:15). The appearance of symptoms of disturbance is the *second stage* in the sequence of differentiation. They appear in the form of uncertain expectations about baseball. The possibility that baseball would be exploited, should the payment of players become an open practice, was a major concern. It was felt that the game would suffer should professionals be allowed to participate. "It meant the introduction of rowdies, drunkards, and deadbeats" (28:134). The occurrence of these emotional reactions can be correlated with the conditions that gave rise to it. Such conditions include the failure of the National Association to enforce the rules that forbade payment of players, and the desire for upgrading the caliber of the game. Spalding recalls that the "players were usually paid in part by promoters of the ball club and partly by the firms in whose employ the players were enrolled" (28:130). There was outspoken criticism by players and public about such practices. Negative emotional reaction was manifested in the form of

> Mutterings . . . showing that dissatisfaction was present in the minds of the press and public, were heard everywhere from those who had any interest in the welfare of Base Ball in America (28:133).

By the late 1860's players were being paid with semipro inducements (9:189). Some players were throwing games in return for bribes. Incidents such as these illustrate the negative reactions to the new idea of paying individuals for the playing of baseball.

If the new idea of playing baseball for monetary profit was to be institutionalized, the system had to control these disturbances. This need for control constituted the *third stage* in the sequence of differentiation. This stage appears in the form of a "covert handling of the tension" manifested in the second stage. The disturbances which accompanied the idea of playing baseball for money were not to be ignored. Motivational resources were mobilized in an attempt to realize the implications of the value system which governed the system and were reflected in the organization of baseball. Attempts were made to legitimize the new concept of professionalism within the framework of the value system of baseball.

The values of the baseball subsystem were characterized by those ideals of fair play, recreational activity, achievement, and entertainment (4:511). The perpetuation of the game as entertainment not only for the players but also for the public in general was of concern. This point of view illustrates a new attempt to realize the implications of the existing value system. The crises which disrupted the system were the desire to win and to make the game a means of livelihood. Players would devote themselves entirely to perfecting the quality of the game. As noted by Allen:

> . . . although baseball had begun as an amateur game that was civic in nature, the desire to win soon made it necessary to import players and pay them for their services (1:13-14).

The goal of the players to win began to outweigh the goal to engage in a pastime. By the mid 1860's, the new idea of professional players was thought to be a primary means of achieving that goal (1:15). Moreover, motivational resources were available to encourage the concept of advancement toward perfection of the game. One of the intentions was to provide increased entertainment for the public. Chadwick suggests that "development of the finer points of the game were retarded by the difficulty its amateur examplars experienced in finding time for the amount of practice and training so essential in bringing about the beauties of the game" (6:422). Control of tensions was maintained by both permissive and supportive attitudes which recognized the necessity to conduct baseball on a business level. The baseball system required businesslike administration if the quality of the game was to improve and its value as a form of entertainment was to be recognized. The value system was found to hold implications which were able to present a rational basis for legitimizing professional baseball. Professional baseball improved the quality of the game while maintaining the element of entertainment for the public (28:143). Supportive attitudes were adopted by the players, owners, managers, and the public although, initially, support was provided by a small percentage of these groups (28:145). When the tensions were controlled and motivational resources utilized, implications of the new idea of professional baseball were realized. The system proceeded to encourage the concept of players being paid for their services.

The encouragement of the new idea of professional baseball constitutes the *fourth stage* of the structural differentiation process. Encouragement of the new idea does not impose responsibility for implementation of this new concept on a specific group. Encouragement of professionalism in baseball was most noticeably manifested in 1869 when Henry Wright, manager of the Cincinnati Red Stockings announced that his baseball club would henceforth play as professionals (28:133). However, the Cincinnati Club was not held responsible for the implementation of professionalism in baseball. The idea was actually implemented before the Cincinnati Club openly endorsed professional baseball. There is little doubt that as early as the 1860's local pride had, in some instances, caused the offering of inducements to skilled players (11:6).

The Red Stockings proved the game could be played effectively and with superiority by winning all their games during an Eastern and Western tour in 1869 and 1870 (28:138-139). Spalding maintains that:

> Every game played was one presenting an important object lesson in professionalism for it demonstrated at once and for all the superiority of an organization of ball players chosen and trained and paid for the work they were engaged to do (28:137).

In addition, the new idea of professionalism in baseball was given encouragement by the public. Initially apprehensive about professional baseball, crowds watching the first professional games were undoubtedly demonstrating "popular endorsement of the innovation" (14:122). Civic leaders as well who realized that winning teams would bring notoriety to their cities also provided support for professional baseball. Turkin (1956) points out that

> Cincinnati had shown (civic leaders) how a successful baseball team can bring fame to a metropolis, and civic pride more than profit provided the impetus toward the formulation of baseball's first professional league (30: 7).

The success of the Red Stockings demonstrated that there was value in hiring highly skilled players. By 1871 there were already thirteen clubs who had changed their status from amateur to professional (28:160).

The increase in the number of professional clubs stimulated the establishment of the National Association of Professional Base Ball Players in 1871 (28:161). This organization was a direct attempt to formulate the new idea of professional baseball. The *fifth stage* of the sequence of the differentiation process requires that positive attempts be made to reach specification of new ideas which ultimately would become objects of commitments. Positive attempts were made to this new idea so that "the game would be presented in its highest state of perfection" (28: 160). This commitment demonstrated the new unit of professional baseball had separated from the older more diffuse unit. At the same time there was rapid administrative development demonstrated by the organization of the National Association of Professional Base Ball Players in 1871.

The formation of the National Association illustrated the organizational status of the new unit. The organization was predicated on conducting the game on a business basis and perfecting the game by developing its "scientific features" (6:421). The organizational bases of the Association also reinforced the commitment of the new unit to specification of the "new ideas." However, initially the organizational status of professional baseball was unstable. For example, there was no distinction between the management and player roles. The National Association of Professional Base Ball Players decided the organization would be guided by a player-president. In 1872, Robert Ferguson was elected President of the National Association of Professional Base Ball Players The new professional unit found that the player-president executive caused disruption in the effective functioning of the organization (1:27). Thus, the disruptions which had plagued the National Association in the late 1860's continued to disturb the newly founded professional association.

Gambling, throwing games, and players jumping contracts were problems which had to be overcome. These disruptions may be considered as temporary organizational failures. According to Smelser, such problems may occur if the new innovation (professional baseball) is not fully approved (27:42). At this point the new structured unit recognized its failure to function in its executive capacity.

Concern was then placed on a more positive and responsible implementation of professional baseball commitments. These commitments had been previously formulated in the fourth stage. If the newly formulated commitments were to become institutionalized, control over continued disruption was required. For example, clear distinction was made between management's role and player's role. This illustrates the occurrence of the *sixth stage* of the differentiation sequence. Direction was taken toward "responsible implementation of new ideas." Spalding noted that:

> It was apparent to some that the system in vogue for the business management of the sport was defective; that means ought to be adopted to

separate the control of the executive management from the playing of the game (28:193).

Specialization of the management and player roles was not only inevitable, but also necessary if professional baseball was to survive. Spalding provides evidence that the player must assume a player role and the manager a management role when he commented

> No man can do his best at ball playing unless his whole soul is in the effort. The man whose soul is absorbed in the business of playing ball has no soul left for the other business . . . of administering discipline, arranging schedules and finding the ways and means of financing a team (28:193-194).

The rationale supporting this distinction was that "a manager must be equipped to *manage* while the player must be qualified to *play* the game" (28:196).

Distinctions, such as those cited above, were made in order to perfect baseball and conduct it on a responsible business basis. As a result of these reforms, the National League was established in 1876 for the purpose of abolishing the unstable federation of players governing the National Association. This transition provided additional impetus to the responsible implementation of professional baseball. The National League illustrated confirmation of a means of achieving the promotion of the sport. The constitution of the National League stated the objectives of the new organization to be

> First—To *encourage, foster* and *elevate* the game of Baseball.
> Second—To enact and *enforce* proper rules for the exhibition and conduct of the game.
> Third—To make Baseball playing *respectable* and *honorable* (28:211).

These objectives may be viewed as the synthesis of responsible implementation of the new idea of professional baseball.

The *seventh and final stage* in the differentiation process demonstrates the routinization of professional baseball. The conditions by which players were hired and contracted to play baseball, which at one time was extraordinary, became a common occurrence. Gains achieved in the previous stages in the growth of professional baseball were accepted as part of the changing baseball system. Smelser maintains that as a result of standardization of new conditions the new unit continues to expand but not at the rapid rate as illustrated in the fifth and sixth stages (20:270). For example, Spalding notes that by 1877, "the game made slow progress, not many new clubs were organized, while financial failures attended most ventures in a professional way" (28:233).

Professional baseball associations and leagues continued to be established, generally the results of conflict and disruption among player contracts. The Brotherhood and Players Leagues were founded in an attempt to fight the reserve rule established in 1879 which was to be used initially as a means of "retaining the services of a player" (21:315). The conflict among the leagues stemmed from an interpretation of the rule which found clubs were using it as a means of selling players, not retaining them (31:318).

Disruption stemming from various interpretations of the reserve clause caused the stability of professional baseball ot be again threatened. From 1890 to 1894 Spalding recalls that baseball suffered a depression. The American Association of Base Ball Players in 1891 began to raid players from the National League. However, the National League "maneuvered a series of deals that brought over four of the best franchises from the American Association" (31:275). From 1892 to 1900, the National League remained the lone professional league with twelve clubs listed under its organization. The fluctuation in the number of leagues from the time the National Association of Professional Base Ball Players was established in 1871 until 1900 is indicative of what Smelser refers to as an occurrence of disequilibrium (27:41). Incidences of conflict within the baseball system illustrate the consequences of the process of change. Ultimately, stability and equilibrium of the system was regained through the standardization and the system's acceptance of the concept of professional baseball.

RESULTS OF DIFFERENTIATION

Professional baseball, in becoming institutionalized, reflected the normative order of the sport system. Although functioning more specifically to attain the goals which were initially a source of dissatisfaction at the first stage of the differentiation process, professional baseball maintained norms illustrating the normative order of the sport system. For example, the normative order of professional baseball provided the criteria for winning as the team which has earned the most points in nine innings of play. In addition, professional baseball players were to conduct themselves as gentlemen in a sportsmanlike manner as expressed in the Constitution of the National League (31:211). Such emphasis on behavior illustrates the normative order of the sport system which maintains that winning and sportsmanlike conduct be defined. Further, the normative order governing professional baseball sanctioned the league rules. Violations of contracts resulted in fines or expulsion of players from the League (31:211).

The structural differentiation model maintains that the new specialized unit must be fully integrated into the value structure of the system for the process to be complete. The values of the sport system became more specific to the new unit of professional baseball. For example, the values which supported the attitudes of fair play, sportsmanship, achievement, and entertainment were not discarded by the new unit but rather became more specific to the new unit. These values were maintained while at the same time role behavior was legitimized to seek both perfection of the game and payment of the individual for his performance.

An important aspect of the differentiation process is the fact that the old unit becomes obsolete in the achievement of the goals for which it was functioning. The original baseball unit became obsolete because of the inability of the National Association in 1858 to function to meet the needs of the baseball system at that time. The National Association in 1858 functioned primarily for the purpose of providing recreational pastime and enjoyment to those engaged in the sport. However, the increased emphasis on winning and various clubs attempting to secure highly skilled players resulted in the inability of the baseball unit of that time to achieve the goals desired by some clubs. The baseball clubs, dissatisfied with playing baseball for personal amusement, sought a higher caliber of play, and ultimately, monetary reimbursement for their skilled performances.

As the initial baseball system became differentiated, two distinct units emerged—the professional and the amateur (Chart II). Professional baseball had become independent of the widespread playing clubs which were initially unified for the purpose of enjoying baseball as an exercise. The new, strictly amateur unit functioned to attain the goals of relaxation and enjoyment for the sake of the sport itself while the professional unit functioned to play the game for profit and entertainment of the public (31:137). The values of fair play, achievement, and sportsmanship were maintained as criteria for defining the desirable behavior of both new units while each functioned to attain their own more specific goals.

The emergence of structurally distinct amateur and professional, as illustrated in Chart II, has provided the baseball system with more efficient means of functioning. This contention is based on the premise that new units will function effectively to meet the needs of the system. The initial baseball unit from which professional baseball emerged was the National Association of Base Ball Players. This unit functioned to attain such goals as entertainment for the public and perpetuation of the game. Chadwick has noted that prior to differentiation in baseball

> . . . Advancement toward perfection and development of the finer points of the game were retarded by the difficulty amateur examplars experienced in finding time for the amount of practice and training so essential in bringing about the beauties of the game—hence the introduction of professional baseball proved to be of great use in perfecting the game and in developing its scientific features (6:421).

CHART II

Differentiation of Baseball

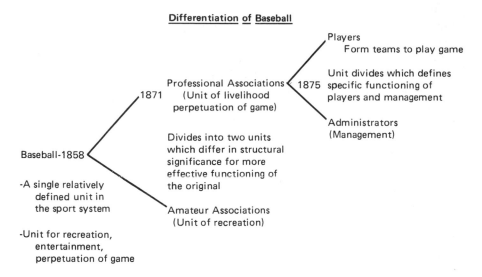

The process of differentiation resulted in the new structural units functioning more effectively in meeting the needs of both amateur and professional baseball. The baseball system functioned more efficiently by providing satisfaction for those who wished to pursue baseball as a livelihood and perfect the quality of the game.

SUMMARY

The growth and development of professional baseball has illustrated the change in the internal dynamics of a sport system. Smelser's structural differentiation model provides a theoretical framework by which the process of change may be analyzed. The "seven step process" of structural differentiation further serves as a mechanism for identifying the sequence of incidences and changes within the baseball system. These changes ultimately led to the development of professional baseball. The development of professional baseball was interpreted as a result of differentiation within the baseball system. Although the structural changes discussed apply specifically to baseball, an interpretation of change may be applied to the growth and development of the wider sport system, particularly during its rapid expansion during the latter nineteenth century.

The applications of the social system model to sport and the structural differentiation model to the growth and development of professional baseball provide the following considerations. First, there is sufficient rationale to legitimize the treatment of sport as a social system since the sport organization has been shown to constitute the structural and functional properties of a social system. Second, consideration of sport as a social system has demonstrated that the sport organization may be utilized to create a specific boundary maintaining unit which allows for analysis of change within the system. Third, the application of the structural differentiation model, as outlined by Smelser, provides a mechanism for analyzing and interpreting changes in the internal properties of baseball.

Additional inquiry and study in the area of growth and development of sport viewed as an outcome of the structural differentiation process is recommended. The primary intent has been to illustrate the feasibility of the theoretical study of sport through application of theoretical models to given phenomena which occur within the sport system.

REFERENCES

1. Allen, Lee. *100 Years of Baseball.* New York: Bartholomew House, Inc., 1950.
2. Betts, John R. *Organized Sport in Industrial America.* Ann Arbor, Mich.: University Microfilms, Inc., 1952.
3. Boyle, Charles. *Sport: Mirror of American Life.* Boston: Little Brown and Company, 1961.
4. Bryce, Lloyd S. "A Plea for Sport," *North American Review,* CXXVIII, no. 4, (1879), 511.
5. Chadwick, Henry. "New Playing Rules of Baseball," *Outing Magazine,* X, no. 1, (1887), 120.
6. ———. "Old Time Baseball," *Outing Magazine,* XXXVIII, no. 4, (1901), 420.
7. ———. "The Base Ball Season of 1886", *Outing Magazine,* X, no. 4, (1887), 120.
8. Devereux, Edward D. "Parsons' Sociological Theory," *The Sociological Theories of Talcott Parsons,* ed. Max Black. Englewood Cliffs, N. J.: Prentice-Hall, Inc., 1962.
9. Dulles, Foster R. *A History of Recreation.* New York: Appleton-Century-Crofts, 1965.
10. Dunning, Eric., ed. *Sport: Readings From a Sociological Perspective.* Toronto: University of Toronto Press, 1972.
11. Federal Writers Work Project Administration. *Baseball in Old Chicago.* Chicago: A. C. McClurg and Company, 1939.
12. Greene, Arnold W. *Recreation, Leisure and Politics.* New York: McGraw-Hill Company, 1964.
13. Henderson, Robert W. *Ball, Bat and Bishop.* New York: Rockport Press, Inc., 1947.
14. Krout, John Allen. *Annals of American Sport, The Pageant of America.* New Haven: Yale University Press, 1929. XV.

15. Loy, John W. "The Nature of Sport," *Sport, Culture and Society,* ed. Gerald Kenyon and John Loy. New York: Macmillan Company, 1968.
16. Lüschen, Günther. "Small Group Research and the Group in Sport," in *Aspects of Contemporary Sport Sociology,* ed. Gerald Kenyon, The Athletic Institute, Chicago, 1969.
17. McLeisch, J. *The Theory of Social Change.* New York: Schockem Books, 1969.
18. Nevins, Allen. *The Emergence of Modern America, 1865-1878, The Emergence of American Life.* New York: Macmillan Company, 1927, VIII.
19. Parsons, Talcott. "A Functional Theory of Change," *Social Change,* eds. Amitai Etziono and Eva Etzioni. New York: Basic Books, Inc., 1964.
20. Parsons, Talcott and Smelser, Niel J. *Economy and Society.* New York: The Free Press, 1969.
21. Parsons, Talcott. "A Pardigm for the Analysis of Social Systems and Change," *System, Change and Conflict,* eds. N. J. Demerath and Richard Peterson. New York: The Free Press, 1967.
22. ———. *The Social System.* New York: The Free Press of Glencoe, 1951.
23. Parsons, Talcott. *The Structure of Social Action.* New York: The Free Press, 1949.
24. Parsons, Talcott; Bales, Robert; and Shils, Edward A. *Working Papers in the Theory of Action.* New York: The Free Press, 1953.
25. Peverelly, Charles A. *Book of American Pastimes.* New York: Peverelly, 1866.
26. Smelser, Neil J., ed. *Sociology: An Introduction.* New York: John Wiley and Sons, Inc., 1967.
27. ———. *Social Change and the Industrial Revolution.* Chicago: University of Chicago Press, 1959.
28. Spalding, Albert G. *America's National Game.* New York: American Sports Publishing Company, 1911.
29. Steele, James L. "How the National Game Developed," *Outing Magazine,* XLIV, no. 3, (1904), 333.
30. Turkin, Hy and Tompson, S. C. *The Official Encyclopedia of Baseball.* New York: Barnes and Company, 1956.
31. Ward, John Montgomery. "Is the Base Ball Player a Chattel?," *Lippencotts Monthly Magazine, A Popular Journal of General Literature, Science and Politics,* XL, (July-December 1887), 444.
32. ———. "Notes of a Baseballist," *Lippincotts Monthly Magazine, A Popular Journal of General Literature, Science and Politics,* XL, (July-December, 1887), 212.
33. Weiss, Paul. *Sport: A Philosophic Inquiry.* Carbondale: Southern Illinois University Press, 1969.

THE SOCIAL SYSTEM OF SPORT:
A HUMANISTIC PERSPECTIVE

ALAN G. INGHAM and JOHN W. LOY, JR.

THE INSTITUTIONALIZATION AND REIFICATION OF SPORT

Sport is a social institution and, as such, is a part of the taken-for-granted sociocultural milieu. Like all social institutions, sport has legitimations which justify its existence, rules which guide the interactions of individuals holding positions within its structure, and prescriptions for the ways in which individuals' appearances are to be managed. That is, sport has a frame of values, defined forms, and prescribed fronts. As an institutionalized form of social behavior, sport can be transmitted from one generation of participants to the next. Therefore, sport may appear, as do other social institutions, to be external to and independent of the will of the individuals who are engaged in it.

This description of sport, although empirically plausible, affronts our humanism since it paints a picture of sport as a product divorced from its producers. This portrayal of alienated existence poses two questions for the humanistic sociologist: (1) How can the individual be brought back in as a constructor of social institutions? and, (2) How do the products of social construction become external to those engaged in their production?

The Objectivation and Legitimation of Sport

Elsewhere (Ingham and Loy, 1971),[1] we have presented the argument that the processes involved in the social construction of life-worlds

From *Quest,* Monograph XIX (January, 1973): 3-23.
1. This paper is a condensed and revised version of *The Structure of Ludic Action* (Ingham and Loy, 1971). The authors would like to acknowledge the helpful criticisms of R. J. Martin of the Department of Sociology, University of Massachusetts.

are also in evidence in the social construction of sport. In this earlier paper, we outlined the processes involved in the institutionalization of sport and suggested that sport should be traced to its origins in early sensori-motor schemes. That is, these rudimentary forms were viewed as the raw material out of which systematic game forms emerge.

In tracing the origins of sport to their genesis in sensori-motor schemes, we suggested that the transformation of rudimentary play forms into systematic game forms is illustrative of the institutionalization processes occurring in other domains of the social world. Through the processes of habitualization and regulation, *a* synthesis of rudimentary play forms becomes *the* systematic game form. A way of doing becomes *the* way of doing. Institutionalization, however, means more than an attachment to predictable synthesis of behavior. Institutionalization implies that these habitualized forms have been invested with a value system which legitimates the attachment of individuals to the form and justifies their adherence to the rules upon which the system is based. Habitualization and legitimation ensure that game forms take on a reality *sui generis*. The game participant accedes to structure and rules of form since they are a part of the legitimated socio-cultural milieu. It is in the creation of such legitimations that games become institutionalized as sport.

Rafky (1971) examines the levels of legitimation proposed by Berger and Luckmann (1966). The first level of legitimation is pretheoretical: A child in asking why the bases are placed in the shape of a diamond is told "because that is the way things are done!" Such legitimation invokes tradition. "The second level of legitimation contains theoretical propositions in a rudimentary form [Berger and Luckmann, 1966, p. 94]." The child in asking why he must play football is told that the game is necessary for his development into manhood. At the next level of legitimation, explanations are theoretical. For example, sport participation may be justified using socialization theory as a justification. Experiences in sport are claimed to be similar to those in life. Finally, "whole clusters of theories are synthesized and crystallized into a total world view [Rafky, 1971, p. 11]." At this level of legitimation, perspectives which legitimate sport are synthesized into the ideology of society. The legitimations of sport are incorporated into an ideology which legitimates the taken-for-granted social world. Accordingly, all the -*isms* (e.g., nationalism) are now legitimations for sport. Thus, only when habitualized forms of games are shrouded with taken-for-granted legitimations can sport be described as a social institution.

Sport as an institutionalized form of behavior requires that individuals accommodate their selves to predetermined roles. Predetermined roles are a product of reciprocal typification (cf. Berger and Luckmann, 1966, pp. 55-59). In short, individuals tend to attribute meanings to the behavior they observe. The more a person repeats a behavior in response to some goal, the more confident the observer becomes in attributing a meaning to that behavior. Performance, therefore, becomes relatively predictable. Knowledge of the goals permits the prediction of the behavioral means necessary for their attainment. Once the behavioral means become predictable they become taken-for-granted; knowing the goal, the means to the goal become expected. Thus, constitutive rules begin to be developed which give order to social interaction (cf. McHugh, 1968, p. 17). Role performance becomes bound by the situationally specific constitutive rules. In essence, a role becomes "a typified response to a typified expectation [Berger, 1963, p. 95]." For example, the behavior of the quarterback in a given field and down situation is predictable within a given range of options: There are only so many moves at a quarterback's disposal. This set of alternative actions is determined by the quarterback's ability to anticipate himself being anticipated. That is, the quarterback attributes meanings to his opponents' behaviors and at the same time recognizes that his opponents are attributing meanings to his actions. Typification is, therefore, reciprocal: while he is reading the defense, the defense is reading him. Play execution is also based on the attribution of meanings. Players on the same team cooperate much more efficiently after long hours of practice. A player knows what his teammates are going to do, having observed their style of play over and over again. Therefore, given certain cues certain behaviors become expected. In sum, team games operate on the attribution of meanings or upon reciprocal typification.

Since sport is a social institution with fairly rigidly defined prescriptions for role performance, it follows that role performance can be evaluated. Such evaluation is based upon a comparison between the actual performance and the expected performance or an idealized stereotype. Idealized stereotypes are often provided by "ghosts" who still occupy the position in the evaluator's mind (e.g., running backs might be evaluated by comparing their here-and-now performance to what Gale Sayers might have done given similar circumstances). Some idealized stereotypes are also provided by contemporaries who are presently undergoing ordination into "immortality" (e.g., Rod Laver or Jack Nicklaus). Evaluation is compounded by the fact that it is not restricted to the formal requirements of the sport, nor to the arena in which the formal role performance takes place, nor to the wise. Sport, being a public event, contains both play and display (cf. Stone, 1957, pp. 7-8). Hence, performers have to be concerned with their popular image. Performers are always on stage and must become adept at the techniques of impression management since they are required to present a front which does not affront popular conceptions. Thus, the athlete's performance on and off the field becomes typically stereotyped as the athlete's role performance must meet the expectations of both the wise and the unwise. As Charnofsky (1968) notes: ". . . the popular image suggests that baseball players love all children, gladly devote time and energy to signing autographs and making trips to hospitals, and are impervious to the ridicule but tolerant of the advice of adult fans, whom they also love [p. 51]." The expectations for the role have become rigidly defined—as the game becomes an institutionalized form, the roles contained within this form become institutionalized also.

In summary, a game develops form through synthesis and habitualization. The form is institutionalized through the creation of a frame of values which serves to legitimate the form so that it becomes a taken-for-granted part of the sociocultural milieu. Since, the form evolves from the problematical to the taken-for-granted through the process of typification, role performances required for identities within the form become somewhat taken-for-granted also. Fronts become established for the way in which the role performances are to be presented. Consequently sport attains reality, ". . . a quality appertaining to phenomena that we recognize as having a being independent of our volition (we cannot 'wish them away') . . . [Berger and Luckmann, 1966, p. 1]." Sport emerges as a social fact rather than a social process.

The Frames, Forms and Fronts of Sport

Neophytes entering the social institution of sport undergo socialization. Through socialization, sport as an entity imposes itself upon the individual, since in its transmission it assumes ontological status. The reality of sport appears immutable. Individuals learn and internalize the frame of values legitimating sport; they learn and internalize the constitutive rules which guide interaction and which give sport its form; and, they identify with idealized stereotypes exemplifying the necessary behavioral and attitudinal requirements for preferred role performance. From this over-socialized viewpoint, a person's assimilation of and accommodation to the social reality of sport helps to maintain the reality in the state it was transmitted. In short, socialization ensures that the individual learns to present a self which is form and frame maintaining.

The over-socialized conception of man is somewhat onesided. In its description of the interaction between the individual and social institutions, it leads to the conclusion that only the individual changes as a result of the interaction. Essentially, such a conception is deterministic. We would like to point out that in the preceding and subsequent discussion we attempt to avoid a deterministic conception of the interaction between the social institution of sport, and its constituent members.

Sport is both a social process and social entity: sport is socially constructed and yet once constructed attains reality, a reified form with reified roles. Sport is institutionalized and yet institutions are fragile, an institution is real only as long as the individuals who comprise it accept the consequences of that reality. Sport as an institutionalized form becomes vested with taken-for-granted meanings and yet individuals ask how such meanings are legitimated, and as a consequence contribute new meanings to sport. Sport has reified roles appearing to be independent of an athlete's volition and yet all athletes do not engage in bad-faith, many elect behaviors that reflect an honest sense of self rather than a slavish adherence to a rigid role (Berger, 1963, pp. 143-144).

In the discussion which follows, we shall attempt to present a humanistic view of sport and contrast this view with sport as it is manifested in the empirical world. Essentially, we shall contrast sport as an autonomous form of social behavior with sport rendered subservient to the concerns of everyday social life. Before we enter into this debate, we think it only fair to acknowledge our somewhat normative premises; namely, that sport as institutionalized and reified forms of play should retain certain constituent elements of play. That is, sport should be undertaken for its own sake, and those engaged in its production should present behaviors which increase the playfulness of sport. Sport from this perspective retains elements of voluntarism. Sport is an embodiment of human subjectivity, not an entity divorced from human intentionality. It follows from these premises that we would prefer to assume that role behavior in sport also retains elements of voluntarism. That is, the role should reflect an externalization of self and should not be a product of impression management or a reflection of internalized values and ego-identifications.

The three sections which follow describe in order the nature of the frames, forms and fronts of sport. Although the frame or ideational content of sport, the forms or structural components of sport, and the fronts or the behavioral expectations of sport statuses are irrevocably interrelated, we shall discuss each separately for analytical purposes. The basic thesis underlying our essay is that these three dimensions of the social institution of sport are not quite as taken-for-granted as they may appear, but are rather fragile reconciliatory products of the continual redefinitions which result from conflicting demands.

THE FRAME OF SPORT

Sport has become a serious enterprise affecting the lives of millions. Sport has, in fact, been put to serious use. As a result, sport has become increasingly rationalized and bureaucratized. The trend toward rationalization and bureaucratization, some would claim, has resulted in the atrophy of humanistic legitimations and humanistic concerns; the instrumental values of sport have negated the expressive. We would like to suggest that the tendency toward the instrumental, rather than negating the expressive, poses a fundamental dilemma for sport—how to reconcile instrumental and expressive concerns in a way that does not spoil sport (cf. Stone, 1957, p. 8). Too much emphasis upon the expressive might result in a reversion to an ". . . older amateuristic credo, that sport for its own sake should replace sport for the organization [Page, 1973]." Too much emphasis on the expressive may result in sport being reduced to playfulness and, as a consequence, constrict the mood of the game (cf. Stone, 1957, p. 8). Too much emphasis on the instrumental may result in a concern with extrinsic rather than intrinsic rewards and sport rendered servile to outside pressures.

In this section of the paper we would like to confront the paradox that sport while being autonomously real is subsumed by the paramount reality of the social world. Confronting this fundamental paradox facilitates the examination of the expressive versus the instrumental legitimations which justify sport as a firmly established part of the sociocultural milieu.

Maintaining Sport's Expressive Frame

The expressive legitimations for sport emphasize those values which are intrinsic rather than extrinsic to sport involvement. From this emphasis, sport needs no other justification than it provides a setting for sociability and fun. Therefore, to stress the expressive legitimations for sport essentially means that the ludic component of sport becomes of prime import. Sport, then, is undertaken for its own sake and those participating in it are expected to present behaviors which increase the playful nature of sport. The expressive frame of sport is maintained, therefore, if participants engage in sport out of expressive concerns and recognize that these concerns are dependent upon the diminution of the instrumental concerns characterizing everyday life.

An emphasis upon the expressivity of the ludic components of sport leads to the conclusion that sport should not be legitimated for its *func-*

tional significance in social life. Sport, like play becomes distinct from everyday life; and, "Once played, it endures as a new found creation of the mind, a treasure to be retained by memory [Huizinga, 1968, pp. 9-10]."

The values, goals, and purposes which constitute the expressive frame of sport contribute to its artificiality. By stressing the ludic components, the sport world, like the play world, is comprised of equals. Sport retains the "as if" quality of play which distinguishes it from ordinary life. This "as if" quality negates the intrusion of instrumental considerations and ego-demands.

Based upon the social contract perspective, Simmel (1950) formulates the principle of sociability ". . . as the axiom that each individual should offer the maximum sociable values . . . that is compatible with the maximum values he himself receives [p. 47]." That is to say, in sport as a ludic encounter the individual's pleasure or satisfaction is closely bound to the pleasure and satisfaction of those with whom he is interacting. The expressive frame can only be maintained when all participants are adhering to this principle. The probability that the expressive frame will not be maintained is increased when differences in participant input affect the ludic component of sport.

There is a minimum required input necessary if participants are to enter the expressive frame; and there is a point at which an over-emphasis upon expressive concerns can cause one to depart from the frame. For the expressive frame to be entered, and hence, for sport to be sociable, the instrumental concerns and ego-demands of the participants must be minimized, equalized, or ruled as irrelevant (cf. Goffman, 1961, p. 19). For sport to remain sociable, the intrinsic outcomes of the sport must be available to all.

Goffman (1961) has argued that fun is an intrinsic outcome of sociable games. Therefore, the expressive frame of sport is maintained if the encounter can "pay its way in immediate pleasure [p. 17]." A game which does not pay its way proportionately will result in the expressive frame being broken and in the indisposition of its participants toward further action. As Goffman (1967) expresses the matter:

> When an individual senses that he or other participants are failing to allocate their involvement according to standards that he approves, and in consequence that they are conveying an improper attitude toward the interaction and the participants, then his sentiments are likely to be aroused by the impropriety [p. 125].

There is nothing more likely to arouse ire and invoke rules of justice than a competitor who breaks the expressive frame of sport without breaking the form. The person who goes through the motions of the game but does not enter into its spirit is likely to be sanctioned for he destroys the euphoric mood of the encounter.

To cross the threshold into the expressive frame, the participant subordinates himself to and conforms to the approved, expressive reasons for participation. Fun in participation is dependent upon affable and equitable social interaction. Where marked individual differences in input exist, then, for mutual consummation of the approved expressive purpose of the game, systematic efforts must be made to counteract these differences. Informal compensations must be employed to offset the differences in participant input. This is particularly true where marked differences in skill exist. To retain the expressive frame participants are ". . . expected to go to certain lengths to save the feelings and face of others present, and they are expectd to do this willingly and spontaneously because of emotional identification with others and their feelings [Goffman, 1967, p. 10]." Therefore, to retain the expressive frame, the highly skilled are not expected to crush inferiors but to provide ". . . a means for common enjoyment or for achievement of common goals [Duncan, 1968, p. 57]." However, this informal compensation may cause a departure from the expressive frame. For example, in order to preserve the "as if all were equal" property of the expressive frame, the nice guy may make his informal compensations too apparent. The nice guy in his concern to preserve sociability and fun may play below par and in so doing remove the agonistic components of the game.

The Instrumental Frame of Sport

We have claimed that an analysis of sport should reflect sport's paradoxical nature. Sport as a social institution has a degree of autonomy, yet precisely because it is a social institution, sport is subsumed within the paramount reality of the social world. Sport can be simultaneously described as separate from the social world, and as a microcosm of the social world. It is precisely this paradoxical nature of sport which renders the expressive frame of sport highly permeable to instrumental concerns. Sport's autonomy is rather fragile.

Although we have stated that, from an expressive viewpoint, fun and sociability are sufficient justifications for sport, these legitimations have not been extensively used. Indeed, we might claim that the use of the ludic component of sport as its legitimation has been discouraged by the residues of Puritanism. We might even go so far as to claim that the growth of modern sport is not attributable to expressive legitimations but is, rather, the result of sport being justified for pragmatic and/or utilitarian reasons. Modern sport has been largely legitimated in terms of its servility to the concerns of everyday life. Sport, then, is a taken-for-granted part of the sociocultural milieu as a result of its functional import in character development, delinquency reduction, military preparedness, nationalism, strengthening of employer-employee relationships, improvement of race relations, etc. (cf. Berryman and Ingham, 1972). In short, the instrumental frame of sport in the last century has gained ascendent status over the expressive frame.

Sport which is legitimated on the basis of its instrumental value for the fighting of ideological wars presents us with a clear example of how sport has lost its autonomous nature. The participants involved in such representational sport become "the embodiment of their nation's strength and weakness [Goodhart and Chataway, 1968, p. 3]." From this instrumental viewpoint, the result of an international athletic event is not the consummation of the social euphoria of participation, but is the vindication of one nation's ideology over another. From this instrumental viewpoint the participant can be identified not by name but by country. Although somewhat extreme in position, Natan (1958) summarizes this instrumental position of sport as follows:

> Competition on the international level is a sop thrown to the warmonger in man. It has evolved into a ritualistic struggle of one national community against the other. Olympic athletes have become soldiers of sport who are indoctrinated with grotesque conceptions of national prestige. The ideals that sixty years ago moved Baron de Coubertin to give modern international sport new life have been debased by the hypocrisy and veiled political intentions of his successors to such an extent that its present adherents put one in mind of the loose women of Eastern temples who prostitute themselves in the shadow of sacred idols [p. 203].

A second, and most interesting example, of sports legitimation based on instrumental concerns is provided by the rationale that athletics are educational and an important mechanism of socialization. The experts in play (i.e., physical educators), when asked to justify physical activity in the curriculum, do not legitimate such activity with references to the expressive components but, generally, refer to the instrumental. As Veblen (1931) somewhat sardonically states:

> . . . those members of respectable society who advocate athletic games commonly justify their attitude on this head to themselves and to their neighbors on the ground that these games serve as valuable means of development. They do not only improve the contestant's physique, but it is commonly added that they also foster a manly spirit, both in the participants and the spectators. Football is the particular game which will probably first occur to anyone in this community when the question of

serviceability of athletic games is raised, as this form of athletic contest is uppermost in the mind of those who plead for or against games as a means of physical or moral salvation [pp. 260-261].

Instrumental legitimations negate the expressivity and autonomy of sport and seldom are subjected to validation. Physical educators have made few attempts to ascertain the nature of games, and have done little to confirm their assumption that participation in physical activity either directly or indirectly enhances socialization (cf. Loy and Ingham, 1972, p. 291). By using instrumental legitimations for sport's inclusion in the curriculum, the physical educator often ". . . fails to see play in its actual situation as a form of existential encounter, which is to say, a specific mode of freedom [Sadler, 1969, p. 213]."

Perhaps the tension between the expressive and the instrumental legitimations for sport is best exemplified in the conception of sport as entertainment. On the one hand, sport as entertainment can be legitimated on the basis of commercial enterprise. On the other hand, sport as entertainment allows the consummation of aesthetic form and can be so legitimated.

The expressive versus the instrumental nature of sport as entertainment might be seen in terms of a tension between play and display. As the instrumental concerns of business enterprise enter into sport, sport's expressive frame becomes somewhat warped. That is, sport as a spectacle begins to pander to the vicissitudes of the consumer. For sport to be profit making, its form must conform to consumer taste. As Goodhart and Chataway (1968) note: ". . . while Romans two thousand years ago no doubt felt themselves tingling pleasurably at the spectacle of lions eating Christians, modern housewives are content to watch professional wrestlers pretending to inflict agonies upon each other [p. 3]." Sport as a consumable product distorts the expressive frame and often distorts the intended form. As Stone (1957) notes: "In professional wrestling, for example, it is not only the rules that are flaunted in the display, but the keeper of the rule—the referee—is now a standard part of the performance [p. 8]."

Sport's paradoxical nature is also reflected at the level of the performer. Sport as an autonomous reality frees the participant from concerns of the life-world. Indeed, sport's autonomy is dependent upon the participant leaving concerns of the life-world behind when he enters into the sport-world. Sport as an autonomous reality is dependent, therefore, upon the diminution of ego-demands and instrumental concerns. Ego-demands and instrumental concerns must be subjected to rules of irrelevance and rules of transformation. Rules of irrelevance attempt to hold certain psychological states of the participants in check. Rules of transformation attempt to negate or equalize the social attributes of the participants so that the "as if all are equal" quality of sport is retained (cf. Goffman, 1961, pp. 19-34).

Sport possesses autonomy to the extent that ego-demands and instrumental concerns are minimized, equalized, or negated. However, as Goffman (1961) points out, rules of irrelevance and rules of transformation are not infallible. For example, one psychological state which does not appear to be held in check is that of prejudice. At the international level, apartheid as a policy of some nations has obliterated the expressive components and autonomy of sport. Nations adhering to such a policy are excluded from competing in the Olympic Games. At the personal level, individuals have refused to compete against athletes from such nations. For example, "At a time when he still could command attention as a possible opening bat for England the Reverend David Shepherd refused to play against a South African side [Goodhart and Chatway, 1968, p. 119]." Even within teams, rules of irrelvance do not always operate as is evidenced in the stacking of blacks at certain positions and their exclusion from decision-making roles (cf. Loy and McElvogue, 1969). The attribute of race is not subject, then, to rules of irrelevance and prejudice alters form.

We might claim, then, that instrumental concerns have distorted or negated the ludic components of sport. Consistent distortions, unfortunately, can be legitimated. If sport is competitive to the point of dehumanization, then, competition can be legitimated by suggesting that sport prepares for life. If sport is aggressive to the point of being bellicose, then, bellicosity can be legitimated as a healthy release of tension. Indeed, we might concur with Webb (1969) that the passage from play to sport is ". . . substantially influential in producing that final result, the urban-industrial man [p. 177]."

THE FORMS OF SPORT

We wish to suggest in the discussion which follows that the structural components of sport, in much the same way as the legitimations for sport, cannot be so easily taken-for-granted. Sport's form is not "once and for all" but somewhat fragile. At any given moment, sport's form is a precarious balance between the push for change and the pull for stability. Sport, then, reflects the human dilemma—whether to seek the psychic comfort of assimilating "things" given, or to seek the psychic stress of producing "things" new.

Maintaining the Forms of Sport

Elias and Dunning have observed that: "a fundamental characteristic . . . of practically all sport-games, is that they constitute a type of
group dynamic which is produced by controlled tension between at least
two subgroups [1966, p. 390]." Their observation suggests that the forms
of sport situations are sustained by what might be best termed "structural tension." A suitable state of tension is necessary within agonistic
activities to insure the fulfillment of the euphoric function of such encounters. As Elias and Dunning have further observed: ". . . it is one of
the characteristics of a game that the tension inherent in the configuration of players is neither too high nor too low . . . [1966, p. 397]."

In brief, two tension thresholds characterize every sport situation. A
lower or subliminal threshold which indicates the point up to which there
exists insufficient tension to make a gaming encounter possible. And an
upper threshhold which designates the point where the tension becomes
so great as to totally destroy the game form.

The fundamental problem of social order which concerns the forms
of sport is how to maintain structures that assure suitable states of tension between teams and among participants (both actual and vicarious).
Historical analyses of the rise and fall of games in general, and sports in
particular, reveal that the solution of this problem is not an easy one, and,
moreover, one which must be continually resolved. Constant attention is
required to keep the structural tension of agonistic activities from falling
below the lower threshold or rising above the upper threshold.

A major means of sustaining adequate structural tension in sport forms
is by ensuring that the outcomes of games and sports remain problematic.
For example, uneven competition greatly reduces the uncertainty of game
outcome, dulls the participant, and bores the spectator. Accordingly, the
structure and composition of sport-games generally assure a semblance of
equality.

> These efforts typically focus on the matters of size, skill and experience.
> Examples of attempts to establish equality based on size are the formation
> of athletic leagues and conferences composed of social organizations of
> similar size and the designation of weight classes for boxers and wrestlers.
> Illustrations of efforts to insure equality among contestants on the basis
> of skill and experience are the establishment of handicaps for bowlers and
> golfers, the designation of various levels of competition within a given or-
> ganization as evidenced by freshman, junior varsity and varsity teams in
> interscholastic athletics, and the drafting of players from established teams
> when adding a new team to a league as done in professional football and
> basketball [Loy, 1968, pp. 2-3].

As a qualifying note regarding equality and uncertain outcome, we acknowledge that upon occasion a mismatch of contestants is permitted; as the rare occurrence of such an event possesses its own excitement. For example, honor can be bestowed upon a great race horse who markedly overshadows his competition by giving him a "walkover" race. In a walkover race other horses are withdrawn as a tribute to the great horse, and the champion is permitted to walk over the distance of the course and collect the purse (Scott, 1968, pp. 20-21). Needless to say, the outcome of a walkover race is nonproblematic.

Another means of providing adequate tension levels within the sport context is in the creation of a balance between offensive and defensive actions. If agonistic contests are largely defensive in nature, then they typically lack the tension resulting from the anticipation of exciting offensive thrusts. Defensive games often imply a stalemate between antagonists as exemplified in the packed defense systems popular among some European soccer teams in the 1960's. "There can be 'drawn' games, but if they occur too often, one would suspect that something in the construction of the game was faulty [Elias and Dunning, 1966, p. 397]." It is interesting to note that most so-called spectator sports in American society have developed a diversity of ways for determining a clear-cut winner. Tiebreakers are the norm, rather than the exception in sport situations.

On the other hand, the structure and composition of sport-games must not grant predominant power to offensive patterns and processes. For a sport which permits an unlimited display of offensive skill and talent soon becomes a spectacle rather than an agonistic contest. Just as spectators and participants are soon staled by over-drawn defensive battles, they are similarly soon satiated by over-kill offensive pyrotechnics. Therefore, it is not surprising that the history of sport shows the development of alternating defensive and offensive innovations designed to retain a balance of power between the two poles of structural tension in sport settings.

Examples of efforts to minimize offensive power include the lowering of the pitcher's mound in professional baseball, the widening of the key in college basketball; and the outlawing of the flying-wedge in college football, the spitball in professional baseball, and the dunk shot in college basketball. Alternatively, efforts to afford offensive actions greater primacy include the development of two-platoon collegiate football, the enactment of the 24 second rule in professional basketball, the recent narrowing of the hash marks in professional football, and the creation of the tie-breaker in the scoring of professional tennis matches.

A third, and final, basic mechanism of assuring adequate tension levels within sport situations is the social conflict associated with the struggle for supremacy among contestants. Interaction between combatants greatly influences the eventual form a given sport will take. The positive values of social conflict for determining group structure and form are clearly indicated by the set of sixteen propositions drawn from several of Simmel's theories by Coser (1956).

In treating the unifying functions of social conflict, Coser (1956) describes:

> . . . three different ways in which conflict creates links between the contenders: (1) it creates and modifies common norms necessary for the readjustment of the relationship; (2) it leads each party to the conflict, given a certain equality of strength, to prefer that the other match the structure of his own organization so that fighting techniques are equalized; (3) it makes possible a reassessment of relative power and thus serves as a balancing mechanism which helps to maintain and consolidate [social systems] [p. 137].

Many illustrations of Coser's three points can be found in the world of sport. For example, Coser's claim that engagement in conflict creates and modifies norms is illustrated by the following extract from Danzig's (1971) description of the formative years of football:

> For some years Harvard and Yale had been trying in vain to get together on the football field, but were thwarted by the differences in their rules. Now finally, on October 16, 1975, their representatives met at Springfield, Massachusetts, and adopted what they called "Concessionary Rules," and on November 13, 1875, their teams met on the field in Hamilton Park in New Haven, Connecticut, and played a hybrid game that was part soccer and part rugby [p. xiv].

Coser's second point that conflict leads to some form of equalization and standardization is exemplified in the formation of athletic conferences which have schools of similar size agreeing to common patterns of recruitment, periods of training, scholarship standards, and, of course, adhering to common rules of form. Again drawing from Danzig's description of the development of intercollegiate football:

> At the 1875 game Princeton representatives had been observers, and they were so taken with rugby that they went back to Nassau and called a meeting. There was a near-riot when proposed that Princeton switch from soccer to rugby, so entrenched was the older game, but their powers of persuasion prevailed and Princeton went along. The Big Three stood together. After that, on Princeton's initiative, the Intercollegiate Football Association was formed on November 23, 1876 at Massasoit House in Springfield, with Columbia also represented . . . [pp. xiv-xv].

Coser's third point, that conflict serves as a power-balancing mechanism can be illustrated by the admission and exclusion of a particular college or university from a given conference because their athletic prowess either exceeds or fails to match their intended opponents (cf. Jackson, 1962).

Structural Change of Sport Forms

Forms surrounding sport situations are constantly being ruptured, repaired, modified, and at times destroyed. Several structural aspects of sport are subject to transformation. These structural dimensions include rules, roles, and relationships, as well as the technological props and mechanical supports associated with a given sphere of sport. As previously noted most structural modifications are made in order to maintain the euphoric function of an agonistic encounter. A successful game is a fun game. Goffman suggests that the two principal bases of fun in games are problematic outcome and sanctioned display (1961, p. 68). We have added the third principle of sociability. Thus a successful game consists of an encounter having an uncertain outcome, a relatively high degree of sociability, and permitting participants the maximum display of relevant skills and attributes.

It is virtually an impossible task to find or even design a sport form which satisfactorily combines the three main bases of fun. If emphasis is placed on a particular component then the other two are likely to suffer accordingly. For example, most games of chance reflect ideal forms as far as the principle of uncertain outcome is concerned. But few games of chance provide more than a modicum of sociability, and virtually none allow sanctioned display other than the manner in which dice are thrown.

Selected strategic rather than chance oriented board games come closer to achieving a satisfactory combination of the components of fun. Chess is an excellent example of an agonistic activity which ideally combines the principle of problematic outcome and sanctioned display. Unfortunately, however, the players in this form of agonistic combat are pieces rather than people engaged in moral and mortal struggle. The highly abstract nature of the game precludes sociability.

Team sports represent an effort to overcome the stated limitation of strategic board games such as chess, in that, they entail a satisfactory degree of sociability, are characterized by an uncertain outcome, and allow display by participants. However, the live nature of team sports makes it difficult to build-in the subtle complexity so characteristic of chess. Perhaps American football comes as close as any modern team sport to being like a "live" chess game, with its special playing field, strong strategic orientation, many players; and, different positions with relative power and various offensive and defensive responsibilities.

An historical analysis of the development and growth of American football reveals its structural complexity and shows how difficult it is to maintain a viable sport form. Perhaps a few examples drawn from such an historical analysis will suffice for present purposes to illustrate the transformation of sport forms in an effort to preserve a game and assure euphoria for both spectator and participants.

The first intercollegiate football game was played between Princeton and Rutgers on November 6, 1869. The style of play was similar to soccer as players were not allowed to hold the ball and run. However, players were permitted to run interference, catch the ball, and bat the ball with their hands. From this initial start the sport quickly evolved from a kicking game to a running game. Thus by 1876 Columbia, Harvard, Princeton and Yale were playing according to rugby rules. However, as Riesman and Denney (1951) have pointed out, American players had difficulty in accepting British rugby rules because of their ambiguous nature. For example, they had difficulty in accepting the legal fiction that a player could only take the heel out from the scrum "if he happens to be standing behind it." Thus the American game of football created the role of center to solve the heel out problem. But this solution led to other problems. With the concept of center the scrummage became a line of scrimmage with players lined up on both sides of the ball. The scrimmage sharpened the focus on offense and defense and placed added emphasis on ball carrying; which in turn resulted in stress on ball control. Again in turn, the emphasis on ball control resulted in the development of stall tactics in order that a team might keep possession of the ball for long periods of time. These stall tactics, of course, made for a boring game. Thus in 1882 a minimum yardage rule was adopted which required a team to advance at least five yards in three downs. The minimum yard rule resulted in mass play and led to the development of the flying wedge —an offensive bulldozing tactic for which the defense had no effective counterattack. This bulldozing technique resulted in a good deal of brutality as evidenced by the fact that eighteen players were killed in 1905. In an effort to reduce the violence of the sport and effect a more open style of play bulldozing was outlawed and the forward pass legalized in 1906. Thus within a quarter of a century the game went from a kicking game, to a running game, to a passing game. The evolution of American football outlined herein supports the observation of Elias and Dunning that:

> The whole development of most sport-games . . . centered to a very large extent on the solution of this problem: how was it possible to maintain within the set game-pattern a high level of group tension and the group dynamics resulting from it, while at the same time keeping recurrent physical injury to the players at the lowest possible level [1966, p. 395].

More importantly the above outline of the development of American football supports Elias and Dunning's pronouncement that: "the question was and still is . . . how to 'steer the ship,' as it were, between the Scylla of disorderliness and the Charybdis of boredom [p. 395]."

In our discussion of the forms of sport we have primarily emphasized the structure of the game patterns as such. Thus we have highlighted the institutional nature of sport and have ignored for the most part the role of individuals in the maintenance and transformation of sport forms. Thus by way of concluding our brief treatment of the forms of sport we wish to "bring men back in."

Notwithstanding the collective, bureaucratized, and institutionalized nature of sport, sport innovations are often, if not usually, developed and adopted by individuals as opposed to social groups. The archetypal account of Ellis of Rugby is a case in point. As well expressed by the wording of a commemorative stone at Rugby: "This stone commemorates the exploit of William Webb Ellis who with a fine disregard for the rules of football, as played in his time, first took the ball in his arms and ran with it, thus originating the distinctive feature of the rugby game—A.D. 1823 [as cited in Riesman and Denney, 1951]." It is, of course, an uncommon occurrence for an individual to be given full credit for the development of an entirely new sport form; however, there are examples of such occurrences in sport history. There is, for instance, the invention of the game of basketball in 1892 by Dr. James A. Naismith.

Most major individual creations of sport innovations are related to changes in patterns of offensive and defensive play. Thus one can think of many changes in play patterns developed by noted football coaches such as the single and double-wing formations, the split-T and wishbone-T formations, etc. Similarly, one can call to mind many offensive innovations developed by individual athletes which resulted in a restructuring of both the offensive and defensive patterns of play. For example, in the case of basketball we have seen the development of the one-hand set shot, the hook shot, and the two- and one-handed jump shot which did much to change the nature of the game at various points in time.

Although our treatment of sport forms in this section has focused on social change we wish to emphasize in conclusion that the sport order is essentially conservative in nature. The ancient Greeks, for example, confined their sport involvement to a limited range of athletic events for century after century. And in our modern age of athletics we find that most individual innovations in sport are largely a matter of style rather than structure. While individual athletes may develop unique ways of running, passing, dribbling, etc. these idiosyncratic displays of athletic ability do little to effect changes in a given sport's structural or regulatory form.

THE FRONTS OF SPORT

The final problem which we wish to confront in this paper concerns the relationship between *self* and sport *role*. Neophytes entering into the social institution of sport undergo a process of socialization. Through socialization we not only attempt to ensure a continuation of the institutionalized forms of behavior, but we also seek to instill into the neophyte that these are the correct forms of behavior. Through socialization then, we not only ask that the individual accept handed-down life-worlds divorced from their own intentionality, we also ask that the individual accept hand-down roles and allow them to mould their behaviors in the same deterministic way. As a consequence of socialization, not only do the structural components of a social institution appear immutable, but the prescriptions for role behavior also appear to share in this immutability. Individuals, therefore, are asked to accommodate their "selves" to the pre-established forms and pre-established roles. In short, the individual is asked to present a self which is form and frame maintaining. From this over-socialized and somewhat alienated conception of man, we might conclude that there is nothing more to self than a reflection of social structure and social norms, nothing more to self than internalized values and ego-identifications.

Humanistic sociologists cannot be satisfied with the over-socialized conception of man presented above. "Deeply concerned with the welfare of the individual, the humanistic sociologist must paint a picture in which man can avoid the alienated *de facto* conditions of human existence. Self must be reinstated or at least appeased [Ingham et al. 1972, p. 6]." Humanistic sociologists, then, must acknowledge that the self is derived from a continual conversation taking place between what Mead (1962) called the "I" (the spontaneous awareness of the externalization of subjectivity) and the "Me" (the self which is constituted through identification and internalization). Thus, the humanistic description of role behavior suggests that role playing is not divorced from intentionality but is a continuous reflexive act—the self flows between self as subject and self as object.

Role behavior in sport, then, reflects yet another paradox:

> on the one hand, the development of integrated belief and action clusters makes adaptive behavior more automatic and reduces the role of conscious deliberations; on the other hand, there appears to be emerging, inclusive cognition of self that allows greater awareness of the relatedness of acts to each other and to underlying dispositions [Jones and Gerard, 1967, pp. 182-183].

In C. W. Mills' (1959) terms, the individual can be simultaneously both a "Cheerful Robot" and a "Renaissance Man." The Cheerful Robot adheres to prescribed behavior patterns with the consequent diminution of self, whereas, the Renaissance Man is capable of role distance—the ability to step outside of the taken-for-granted routines of society (Berger, 1963, p. 136). Role performance for the Renaissance Man can be, therefore, a representation or misrepresentation of self, whereas, for the Cheerful Robot the role performance *is* a representation of an alienated self—the self becomes situated in the reified role. Thus, it follows that the sport role can be described as both an embodiment of human subjectivity or an institutionalized pattern of social action.

Sustaining the Fronts of Sport

To use a dramaturgical metaphor, the child through socialization, learns the script of the drama, his identity within that drama, and the approved ways in which to present this identity to an audience. In sport, this audience is composed of his playing peers, the non-playing persons having authority over him, and the vicarious participants of sport, the spectators. Since sport is an institutionalized and reified form of social behavior, we can claim that the approved ways in which an identity can be presented have become fairly circumscribed. Thus, the sport role leaves little room for redefinition by the here-and-now actor; the obligations of the role are predetermined. Indeed, the here-and-now actor, if he is to reap the rewards of sport, is constrained by these obligations. To reap the rewards of sport, the here-and-now actor learns to play-down personal volitions and play-up the obligations. That is, the actor learns to present a front which is form and frame maintaining; the actor engages in impression management.

If the frame is to be maintained, then, players entering the frame are by their entrance implicitly agreeing to subjection to constraints. They agree to abide by rules of irrelevance which deindividualize. They agree to the form of sociation. They agree to alternation. Assuming, alternation must indeed take place if one commutes between frames of reality, then, the maintenance of a frame is dependent upon the ability of the commuter to adapt to his new identity and present a front with sincerity. This front, or ". . . that part of the individual's performance which regularly functions in a general and fixed fashion to define the situation for those who observe the performance [Goffman, 1959, p. 22]," if sincerely acted out maintains the frame of the game. For example, to preserve the expressive frame of sport, impressions must be managed. One must give the appearance of being fair, a good sport, a gracious winner, a good loser. That is, one must preserve the decorum of the game by strict adherence to rules of etiquette, and by a liberal application of tact. According to Caillois (1959) the good sport, from this expressive viewpoint, is: "Someone who takes into account that he has no right to complain of bad luck, nor to grieve about misfortune, the possibility of which he had deliberately accepted if not courted [p. 159]."

Erving Goffman (1959) in his book, *The Presentation of Self in Everyday Life,* discusses the art of impression management in some depth. He identifies two major components of impression management; namely, "the setting" and "the front." He further dichotomizes the stimuli which comprise the front into "appearance" and "manner." Appearance refers to "those stimuli which function at the time to tell us of the performers' social statuses [p. 24]." Stimuli such as sex, age, size, and clothing are included in this concept. For instance, in the male chauvinist world of football, sex identifies who will play and who will cheer. Clothes function to identify status—a uniform conveys to others, the wearer's position. Stone (1970, p. 411) states that the uniform is part of the representation of self; it suggests a real identity. Moreover, the uniform specifies group affiliation (i.e., team colors). The act of donning a uniform, which Stone (1970) refers to as "dressing-in," carries with it the notion of responsibility—one is not only representing self but is a representative of an organization.

Although Stone primarily focused on the role of dress in the appearance of little children engaged in ludic activities, clothes as well enhance the credibility of an adult's performance in sport. For example, the professional football player's claim that he is engaged in an aggressive ludic activity is considerably bolstered by a padded body and helmeted head. Moreover, the insignia on his helmet and the colors of his uniform clearly denote what team he is a member of; and the numerals on his uniform reveal his playing position on the field; and finally, his identity is firmly established by the name labelled on the back of his jersey.

In addition to appropriate dress, physical props also enhance the presentation of a proper personal front. As Veblen observed in his *Theory of the Leisure Class* (1931): "It is noticeable, for instance, that even very mild-mannered and matter-of-fact men who go out shooting are apt to carry an excess of arms and accoutrements in order to impress upon their own imagination the seriousness of their undertaking [p. 256]." Today we have such modern physical props as golf and bowling gloves, fiberglass poles, steel and aluminum racquets, sweat bands, hair bands and sauna belts; not to mention exercycles, jogging shoes, sweatsuits, and heraldic insignia of the sport clubs to which one belongs.

Finally, an individual's own physical attributes such as height, weight, skin color, strength, endurance, etc. importantly influence the personal fronts he presents to others. These genetic props can aid or negate the credibility of one's performance in a front. Height thus enhances the stature of a male basketball player, but detracts from the form of a female figure skater; weight adds breadth to the wrestler, but does not provide substantial undergirding for the jockey; and whereas a bronze body highlights an athlete in many settings, a black body discolors the situation where "white is right" as in golf, tennis, and yachting.

Goffman has designated "manner" as the other major dimension of a front. Manner refers ". . . to those stimuli which function at the time to warn us of the interaction role the performer will expect to play in the oncoming situation [Goffman, 1959, p. 24]." A quarterback if he is to maintain his front must exude confidence and poise and express an air of authority if he is to have his front accepted in full by his teammates. Or to return again to Veblen (1931): ". . huntsmen are also prone to a histronic, prancing gait and to an elaborate exaggeration of the motions, whether of stealth or of onslaught, involved in their deeds of exploit [p. 256]."

To briefly summarize, a *front* is maintained by creating impressions through the artful management of physical and genetic props and by the display of an appropriate and stylish manner. One may think of the presentation of personal fronts in terms of two thresholds of credibility. The lower threshold falls at the dividing line between poor impression management and adequate impression management and can be readily discerned in the novice who has not had sufficient experience in putting forward a particular front. The upper threshold might be viewed as the point at which the individual is constantly obsessed by the feeling he is on stage. For example, the case might be cited of the weight lifter who cannot stop flexing his muscles. He loses sight of his "self" in the fronts he presents. The genetic props and physical props delude him as to who he really is. From this perspective, becoming involved in sport might be one way in which we lose our Renaissance consciousness: we fail to see ourselves as anything but a sport role exhibiting varying degrees of competence.

Adapting the Front to the Disposition

From a perspective free of over-socialized conceptions, we would make the claim that individuals do not always accept handed-down frames, forms, and fronts. Socialization as a process is not always effective in the production of the Cheerful Robot mentioned previously. Individuals are not quite capable of internalizing the frame without redefinition. They do not always internalize the norms undergirding the social structure and, therefore, do not always perform their roles according to institutionalized expectations. In short, the individual is capable of innovation, deviation, and in some circumstances, open rebellion. By way of terminating this paper, we would like to briefly present a typology of role adaptations which occur in response to the frames and forms of sport. That is, we would like to suggest that the Cheerful Ludic Robot is not the only front which occurs within the social institution of sport.

Borrowing from Merton's (1957) classic typology of individual modes of adaptation to cultural goals and structural means; and drawing from Harary's (1966) extension of Merton's paradigm, we have attempted to develop a typology of individual modes of adaptation to sport situations. We essentially consider specific fronts which individuals present in agonistic activities as a result of their particular perceptions of the frame and form of a given sport setting.

The paradigm presented in Figure 1 suggests that there are eight basic kinds of fronts which deviate in special ways from the nondeviant,

FIGURE 1

A Typology of Front Adaptations

		Frame Valences*		
		+	0	−
	+	Good-Sport	Game Addict	Hustler
Form Valences*	0	Gamesman	Agnostic Agonistic	Spoil-Sport
	−	Cheat	Wet-Blanket	Bad-Sport

*(+) = positive valence
(0) = indifference
(−) = negative valence

normatively approved front of the *Good-Sport* who behaves in a favorable manner toward and within the frame and form of sport. Let us briefly characterize each of these deviant types (eight-balls if you will).

1. *The Bad-Sport* is, of course, *diagonally* opposed to the Good-Sport. For he rejects both the frame and the form. If the Bad-Sport carries his rejection to the extreme he becoms the *non-sport* with his departure from the ludic arena.

2. *The Wet-Blanket* is similar to the bad-sport in that he also rejects the form of the sport. However, he merely remains indifferent to the frame. Whereas the bad-sport either destroys or departs from the encounter, the wet-blanket only puts a damper on the mood. Moreover, the wet-blanket it often passive in his deviancy and poses no problem if placed on the bench under cover.

3. *The Agnostic Agonistic* is also a passive deviant. He remains indifferent to the spirit of the game and sees nothing god-like in the rules of the game. The agnostic agonistic neither promotes nor demotes the values or modes which comprise the frames and the forms of ludic action.

4. *The Cheat*, of course, is familiar to all. He is the individual who pretends to play the game while covertly and illegitimately manipulating one or more structural aspects of its form. The cheat in essence accepts the frame of the encounter but destroys its form.

5. *The Hustler* is akin to the cheat, in that, he too pretends to be something he isn't. Whereas the cheat pretends to accept the form and ends up destroying it, the hustler pretends to accept the frame, but if his front is discredited the frame of the encounter is negated. In sum: "The hustler is a certain kind of con man. And conning, by definition, involves extraordinary manipulation of other people's impressions of reality and especially of one's self, creating 'false impressions' (Polsky, 1969, pp. 52-53)"

6. *The Spoil-Sport* like the hustler breaks the frame rather than the form, and is typically held in greater distaste than the cheat. As Huizinga has cogently observed:

> The player who trespasses against the rules or ignores them is a "spoil-sport." The spoil-sport is not the same as the false player, the cheat; for the latter pretends to be playing the game and, on the face of it, still acknowledges the magic circle. It is curious to note how much more lenient society is to the cheat than to the spoil-sport. This is because he shatters the play-world itself . . . He robs play of its illusion . . . [1968, p. 11].

7. *The Game Addict* is the compulsive ritualist of sport. The addict becomes obsessed with form and indifferent to frame. The means of play become the ends of play for the addict. In essence, the addict transforms

ludic reality into paramount reality; that is to say, for the addict the game has become a way of life.

8. *The Gamesman* may be characterized as the participant who has mastered the art of subversively winning games without actually cheating. The gamesman has perfected the art of impression management to a fine point. The classical treatise on the topic is Stephen Potter's elegant little volume entitled *The Theory and Practice of Gamesmanship* (1948). Potter describes in detail the subtle and not so subtle means of developing a front which in terms of appearance and manner will enhance the gamesman's achievement and insure his euphoria. Perhaps the following quotes from Potter's (1948) manual of gamesmanship will give the flavor of developing this deviant front:

a. *appearance*
   (i) *dress*—(clothesmanship)
"If you can't volley, wear velvet socks," we Old Gamesmen used to say. The Good-looking young athlete, perfectly dressed, is made to feel a fool if his bad shot is returned by a man who looks as if he has never been on a tennis court before. His good clothes become a handicap by virtue of their very suitability [p. 24].

   (ii) *physical props*—(ballmanship)
Odoreida, on his firs appearance at St. Ives brought with him a racket in which a stretch of piano wire, tuned to high C, was substituted for one of the ordinary strings. When "testing his racket" before play, he plucked the piano wire, adding smilingly: "I like something you can hit with [p. 49]."

   (iii) *genetic props*—(limpsmanship)
"I hope I shall be able to give you a game," says the middle-aged golfer to his young opponent, turning his head from side to side and hunching up his shoulders. "My back was a bit seized up yesterday . . . this wind [pp. 36-37]."

b. *manner* (sportsmanship play)
"In general, the rule holds—*Let your attiude be the anti-thesis of your opponent's;* and let your manner of emphasizing this different attitude put him in the wrong. For example, if your opponent is a great showman, assume (e.g., at snooker) an air of modest anonymity; be appreciative, even, of his antics; then quietly play your shot . . . [p. 31]."

Potter's ploys are not without practical consequence, and his irreverent view of the fronts presented in sport situations carries existential implications as:

> Things being seldom what they seem,
> Appearances are all that's deemed.
> Thus Potter's odd sorts,
> Are paraded as sports.
> Skim milk masquerading as cream.

REFERENCES

Berger, P. L. *Invitation to sociology: a humanistic perspective.* Garden City, New York: Anchor Doubleday, 1963.

Berger, P. L. & Luckmann, T. *The social construction of reality.* Garden City, New York: Anchor Doubleday, 1966.

Berger, P. L. & Pullberg, S. Reification and sociological critique of consciousness. *New Left Review,* 1966, 35, 56-71.

Berryman, J. W. & Ingham, A. G. The embourgeoisement of sport, 1860-1960. Paper presented at the American Sociological Association Annual Meetings, New Orleans, August, 1972.

Caillois, R. *Man and the sacred.* Glencoe, Illinois: The Free Press, 1959.

Charnofsky, H. The major league professional baseball player: self-conception versus the popular image. *International Review of Sport Sociology,* 1968, 3, 39-53.

Coser, L. A. *The functions of social conflict.* Glencoe, Illinois: The Free Press, 1956.

Danzig, A. *Oh, how they played the game.* New York: Macmillan, 1971.

Duncan, H. D. *Communication and social order.* New York: Oxford University Press, 1962.

Duncan, H. D. *Symbols in society.* New York: Oxford University Press, 1968.

Elias, N. and Dunning, E. Dynamics of group sports with special reference to football. *British Journal of Sociology,* 1966, 17, 388-402.

Friedenberg, E. Z. *The vanishing adolescent.* New York: Dell, 1959.

Goffman, E. *The presentation of self in everyday life.* Garden City, New York: Anchor Doubleday, 1959.

Goffman, E. *Encounters.* Indianapolis: Bobbs-Merrill, 1961.

———. *Interaction ritual: essays on face-to-face behavior.* Garden City, New York: Anchor Doubleday, 1967.

Goodhart, P. & Chataway, C. *War without weapons.* London: W. H. Allen, 1968.

Harary, F. Merton revisited: a new classification for deviant behavior. *American Sociological Review,* 1966, 31, 693-697.

Homans, G. C. *Social behavior: its elementary forms.* New York: Harcourt Brace and World, 1961.

Huizinga, J. *Homo ludens: a study of the play element in culture.* Boston: Beacon Press (7th Ed.), 1968.

Ingham, A. G. and Loy, J. W., Jr. The structure of ludic action. A paper presented at the 3rd International Symposium on Sociology of Sport, Waterloo, Ontario, August, 1971.

Ingham, A. G., Loy, J. W., Jr. & Berryman, J. W. Socialization, dialectics, and sport. A paper presented at Pennsylvania State University Conference on Women and Sport, University Park, August, 1972.

Jackson, M. College football has become a losing business. *Fortune,* 1962 (December), 119-121, ff.

Jones, E. E. & Gerard, H. B. *Foundations of social psychology.* New York: Wiley, 1967.

Loy, J. W., Jr. The nature of sport: a definitional effort. *Quest,* 1968, 10, 1-15.

Loy, J. W., Jr. & Ingham, A. G. Play, games, and sport in the psychosocial development of children and youth. In G. L. Rarick (Ed.), *Physical ac-*

tivity: human growth and development. New York: Academic Press, 1972 (in press).

Loy, J. W., Jr. and McElvogue, J. F. Racial segregation in American sport. A paper presented at the International Seminar on Sociology of Sport, Macolin, Switzerland, 1969.

McHugh, P. *Defining the situation: the organization of meaning in social interaction*. Indianapolis: Bobbs-Merrill, 1968.

Mead, G. H. *Mind, self, and society*. (C. H. Morris, Ed.), Chicago: University of Chicago Press, 1962.

Merton, R. K. *Social theory and social structure*. New York: The Free Press, 1957.

Mills, C. W. *The sociological imagination*. New York: Oxford University Press, 1959.

Natan, A. Sport and politics. In J. W. Loy, Jr. and G. S. Kenyon, eds. *Sport culture, and society*. Toronto: Macmillan, 1969.

Nisbet, R. A. *The social bond*. New York: Alfred A. Knopf, 1970.

Owen, L. Equality on the gridiron, opportunity on the court. *American Association of University Professors Bulletin*, 1971, 57, 8-9.

Page, C. H. World of sport and its study. In J. T. Talamini and C. H. Page, eds., *Sport and Society*. Boston: Little, Brown, 1973 (in press).

Polsky, N. *Hustlers, beats, and others*. Garden City, New York: Anchor Doubleday, 1967.

Potter, S. *The theory and practice of gamesmanship*. New York: Henry Holt, 1948.

Rafky, D. M. Phenomenology and socialization: some comments on the assumptions underlying socialization theory. *Sociological Analysis*, 1971, 32 (1), 7-20.

Riesman, D. and Denney, R. Football in America: a study of culture diffusion. *American Quarterly*, 1951, 3, 309-319.

Sadler, W. A., Jr. *Existence and love*. New York: Charles Scribner's, 1969.

Scott, M. B. *The racing game*. Chicago: Aldine, 1968.

Simmel, G. *The sociology of Georg Simmel* (trans. K. H. Wolff). New York: The Free Press, 1950.

Stone, G. P. Some meanings of American sport. *60th National College Physical Education Association for Men Convention Proceedings*. Columbus, Ohio, 1957, 6-29.

Stone, G. P. Sex and age as universes of appearance. In G. P. Stone and H. A. Faberman, eds., *Social psychology through symbolic interaction*. Waltham, Mass.: Ginn-Blaisdell (Xerox Co.), 1970.

Tenbruck, F. H. Formal sociology. In L. A. Coser, ed., *Georg Simmel*. Englewood Cliffs, N. J.: Prentice-Hall, 1965.

Veblen, T. *The theory of the leisure class*. New York: Viking Press, 1931.

Webb, H. Professionalization of attitudes toward play among adolescents. In G. S. Kenyon, ed., *Aspects of contemporary sports sociology*. Chicago: The Athletic Institute, 1969.

Wimsatt, W. K. How to compose chess problems and why. In J. Ehrmann, ed., *Games, play, literature*. Boston: Beacon Press, 1968.

SOCIAL CONFLICT THEORY AND SPORT ORGANIZATION SYSTEMS

Carole Oglesby

SOCIAL CONFLICT THEORY AND SPORT

The Nature of Social Conflict Theory

Two fundamentally different positions have been proposed pertaining to the coherence of social systems. The first, a consensus theory, posits that groups form and maintain themselves because of a high degree of consensus on pervasive patterns of values (Dahrendorf, 1959). Sport organizations, often described and explained on this basis, are perceived to form as communities of individuals like-minded in their interest in a particular sport, such as the United States Gymnastic Federation, or an event, such as the United States Olympic Committee.

A second theoretical position, exemplified by Dahrendorf's social conflict theory, is built on the assumption that dissension and tension toward change are inherent in any social system. Any position holder in a social system is a potential source of conflict vis-à-vis counter positions (other position holders). Coherence of systems through time is a function of social control mechanisms which regulate interaction among various position holders in the system.

Such mechanisms vary greatly in the degree to which regulatory control is distributed among the position holders. Parsons (1966) describes three modes of regulatory control: coerced compliance; compliance gained by advantaged position holders threatening others with loss of privileges; and voluntary compliance. It is assumed that in systems where regulatory control is *shared* by position holders, the occurrence of social control mechanisms based upon voluntary compliance will be maximized. Conversely, in systems where regulatory control is least distributed among

From *Quest*, Monograph XXII (June, 1974): 63-73.

position holders, mechanisms based upon coerced compliance will flourish. Thus, social control mechanisms vary in the degree to which position holders share in regulatory control.

The Limited Use of Social Conflict
Theory in Sport Organization Analysis

International and national sport organizations, with which this analysis will deal, are characterized by mechanisms which regulate interaction among members and with other organizations. These mechanisms are specifically designed to settle territorial disputes, resolve conflicts, and gain compliance. Journalists speak of power struggles and conflict resolution, within and between sport organizations, but sport administrators and researchers do not. The analysis of governance patterns in sport through the use of a conflict model has not been attempted. There are at least two reasons why such attempts have not been made.

First, there is a strong flavor of political maneuvering in mechanisms designed and utilized to regulate internal and external interactions. These machinations violate the mystique of apolitical sport. Maintenance of a stance that sport is beyond and apart from political considerations is a norm of sport organizations, particularly those with international membership. It is a violation of the norm, therefore, to demonstrate, formally and publicly, that such organizations inherently have political bases and are explicitly designed to regulate interactions and gain advantages in conflict resolution. Such a violation may be accompanied by negative consequences for the individual within, or related to, one of the large-scale sport organizations.

Second, sport organizations have treated conflict and its control as derivatives of "bad" or threatening organizations rather than as assumed expectancies in the organizational system. Reviewing the stated purposes and goals of many large-scale sport organizations reveals a mild paranoia, indicated by implicit references to possible diminution by other unnamed organizations' influence. To illustrate, the General Assembly of International Federations has five stated objectives, of which two deal with a protective issue:

1. To protect and maintain the authority and autonomy of the international (sport) federations;
4. To promote and protect the common interest of member federations.

Further, in their purposes, the National Collegiate Athletic Association, the Amateur Athletic Union, and the United States Olympic Committee all emphasize protecting their programs from professionalism. It appears that a perceived necessity for "protective reaction" has resulted from

simplistic attributions in which conflict is anticipated, arising from relations with threatening organizations, and control is viewed as necessary
protection until the threat is changed or neutralized. However, if it is
assumed that a social conflict model has applicability to the sport organization system, a different view emerges. Conflict and control become
reciprocal expectancies between position holders in the sport organization
system.

Toward an Analysis of Sport Organization Systems through a Social Conflict Model

In the analysis which follows, conflict and control mechanisms will
be treated as expectancies within the sport organization system. Any position holder group is a potential conflict group in relation to any other
(counter) position holder. Potential conflict groups (position holders)
together with their functions will be identified and the primary mechanism for conflict control within large-scale sport organization systems will
be examined. In addition to identifying position holder-conflict groups
and the primary control mechanism, the analysis will conclude with a
brief statement concerning one problem inherent in excluding some position holders from roles in regulatory control.

SPORT ORGANIZATION SYSTEM ANALYSIS

Identification of Potential Conflict Groups

Dahrendorf's essential thesis is that conflict in social groups arises between those position holders *exercising* authority and those position holders *excluded* from authority. (Authority is defined as the legitimate right
to acquire and use power [Parsons, 1966].) In the organization system
of large-scale, elite sport, it is hypothesized that conflict over authority
may occur between any of the position holders. The first step in an
analysis of the sport organization system through a social conflict model,
therefore, is to identify position holders and describe their functions. In
the diagram on p. 273, the position holders are schematically represented.
Arrows indicate systematic and formal linkages between position holders.

Position Holders and Their General Functions

International multi-sport governing organizations. This position, in the
large-scale, elite sport organization system, is filled by organizations re-

sponsible for premier athletic events encompassing many sports and many nations. The International Olympic Committee and the Federation Internationale du Sports Universitaire are examples of such organizations. Their general functions are listed below.

The *International Olympic Committee* has these general functions:

1. Stages the Olympic Games;
2. Identifies the site and recognizes the local organizing committee for the Olympic Games;
3. Assists regional components in staging regional games during each Olympiad (African Games, Asian Games, Mediterranean Games, Pan American Games, South Pacific Games);

Position Holders in a Sport Organization System

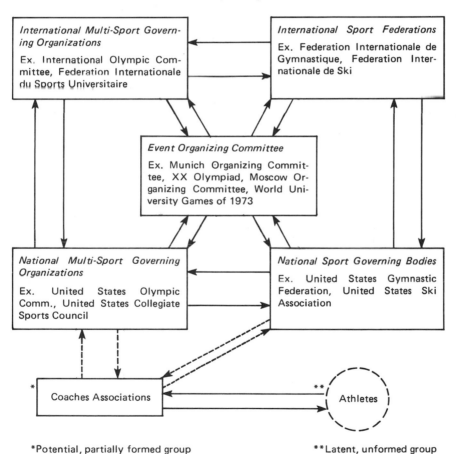

*Potential, partially formed group   **Latent, unformed group

4. Determines criteria for eligibility of members of the International Committee (a country must have sport organizations affiliated with at least five international sport federations before it can form a national Olympic Committee and petition to join the IOC);
5. Recognizes eligible organizations as national Olympic Committees (i.e., United States Olympic Committee);
6. Determines criteria for eligibility to compete in the Olympic Games;
7. Obtains the expertise and cooperation of the international sport federations in the technical aspects of the administration of the Olympic Games.

The *Federation Internationale du Sports Universitaire* has these general functions:

1. Stages the World University Games;
2. Identifies a site and local organizing committee for each Universiade;
3. Determines criteria for eligibility of members of FISU (i.e., organization must represent all the university sportswomen and sportsmen of the country);
4. Recognizes eligible organizations as national FISU representatives (i.e., United States Collegiate Sports Council);
5. Determines criteria for eligibility to compete in the World University Games.

National multi-sport governing organizations. This position is filled by organizations responsible for multi-sport, premier athletic events within a country. The United States Olympic Committee and the United States Collegiate Sports Council are examples of such organizations. Their general functions are listed below.

The *United States Olympic Committee* has these general functions:

1. Represents the country's sport organizations and athletes within the International Olympic Committee;
2. Provides funding for the team and staff traveling to the Olympic Games and appropriate regional games (i.e., Pan American Games);
3. Identifies Olympic Sport Committees, with representatives from the franchise-holding body and other appropriate national sport organizations, which propose team and staff selection procedures for the Olympic and regional games;
4. Coordinates and approves the proposals of the Olympic sport committees.

The *United States Collegiate Sports Council* has these general functions:

1. Represents the collegiate sport organizations of the country within the Federation Internationale du Sports Universitaire;
2. Provides funding for the teams and staff traveling to the World University Games;
3. Identifies sport committees which propose team and staff selection procedures for the World University Games;
4. Coordinates and approves the proposals of the sport committees.

International sport federations. These organizations are continually involved in the administration, improvement, and promotion of specific sports. Fifty-two federations have joined to form the General Assembly of International Federations (GAIF) in order to have a stronger voice in the sport organization system. The federation members·of GAIF may be of three types: those on the Olympic program; those not on the Olympic program; and those offering facilitative support, such as the Federation of Sport Medicine and the Federation for Sport Press. An example of an international sport federation and its general functions follows.

Federations in the Olympic program function in the following ways:

1. Hold world championships in the sport;
2. Determine criteria for eligibility of athletes to compete in the world championship and other federation-sanctioned events;
3. Determine rules governing play in federation-sanctioned events;
4. Determine criteria for eligbility of national organizations to be awarded the international franchise for the sport and recognize such organizations formally. (National sport governing bodies are those organizations recognized as international franchise holders.)

National sport governing bodies. Like other national sport organizations, these governing bodies are involved in the promotion and development of specific sports. As international franchise holders, however, they must fulfill two special functions: to approve all athletes for international competition where teams or individuals are to represent their country; and to assume primary responsibility for selection processes for national teams and coaches.

To further illustrate the relationship between international sport federations and national sport governing bodies, below are listed six United States sport organizations which have been designated international franchise holders by the appropriate international federation.

National sport governing body	*International federation*
Amateur Athletic Union	International Amateur Athletic Federation (I.A.A.F.—track and field)
Amateur Athletic Union	Federation Internationale de Natation Amateur (F.I.N.A.—swimming and diving)
Amateur Softball Association	Federation Internationale de Softball
United States Gymnastic Federation	Federation Internationale de Gymnastique
United States Ski Association	Federation Internationale de Ski
United States Volleyball Association	Federation Internationale de Volleyball

Event organizing committees. These committees usually are business-men and/or political figures prominent in the city or country where an event is held. Most recent examples would be the organizing committees of Munich, XX Olympiad, Montreal, XXI Olympiad, and Moscow, Uni-versiade '73. These committees have the following functions:

1. To stage the large-scale sport event through the provision of housing, facilities, food, medical services, publicity, and other services;
2. To finance the local arrangements for the event through gate receipts, live television and television rights receipts, movie receipts, and sub-sidiary tourist trade benefits.

An important requisite for fulfilling the second function above is the promotion of "name" athletes and "name" nations. As examples of the potential leverage available to such athletes or nations, one could cite the recent turnabout of the Federation Internationale de Gymnastique concerning certain combinations of Olga Korbut's routines and the ex-pelling of the Republic of China from the Asian Games in order to clear the way for participation by the People's Republic of China.

Coaches' associations. The coach's most direct function is the train-ing and development of athletes. Coaches are not formally organized at the international level. While there are national level coaching associ-ations in the United States, they usually exist within a sport governing body, i.e., Volleyball Coaches Association of the United States Volleyball Association. The coaches' input to authority and regulatory decision-making is primarily through appointment by the governing body to tech-nical sport committees.

Athletes. The most direct function of the athlete is to perform. Any systematic linkage to authority and the organization system is through the coach. Athletes are a latent (unformed) group or position holder. Until the present mood of reform following Munich, the efforts of Jack Scott and Harry Edwards to organize athletes were notable in their unique-ness if nothing else.

In summary, the first step of this analysis has been the identification of the major position holders and potential position holders within the large-scale sport organization system. The social conflict model suggests that, within an organization system, conflicts over authority will arise be-tween these position holders. The next step in this analysis will focus on the primary mechanism for conflict control in the sport organization system.

Conflict Control in Sport Organization Systems

The primary mechanism for conflict control within the sport organi-zation system is the differential distribution of authority based upon organizational stratification. This stratification, in its simplest terms, is based upon the *scope* and *"eliteness"* of the organization's program.

The stratification criterion of scope, that is the geographic area covered or number of sports offered in a program, may be objectively ascertained. The "eliteness" of an organization's program is less easy to assess. Dahrendorf's (1959) comments in *Class and Class Conflict in Industrial Society* provide insight when applied to this problem. In Marxian philosophy, control of the means of economic production is the crucial point around which social conflicts form. Dahrendorf went beyond this proposition in suggesting that having, or not having, authority is the focal point of social conflict and that control of economic production is but a special case of authority.

In the large-scale sport organization system, another special case of authority relations exists. Authority is exercised by an organization which controls the *production of elite athletes.* An organization which has the ability to produce many elite athletes is described as "powerful," and is accorded high prestige/status by other sports organizations and their members.

Producing elite athletes requires at least three conditions. First, expert personnel including trainers, officials, administrators, and coaches must be available. Second, the ability to produce revenue for organization programs is essential. Finally, systematic access to quality international experiences for athletes must be provided. A sport organization providing these conditions and producing many superb athletes would be assigned a high "eliteness" rating. If the organization also happened to serve a large geographical area, it would be high in stratification rankings and would be accorded a great deal of authority in regulatory control.

One of the clearest examples of the relationship between authority in the sport organization system and production of elite athletes is the case of the national organization which seeks an international franchise. Several years ago the Amateur Athletic Union was the franchise holder for gymnastics in the United States. The United States Gymnastic Federation made its case to the Federation Internationale de Gymnastique, proposing that its programs were the primary and foremost producers of elite gymnasts in the United States. The franchise was shifted to the USGF. In the following years, the authority of the United States Gymnastics Federation in gymnastic governance issues has risen tremendously when compared with other sport organizations dealing with gymnastics.

Based on the above discussion the stratification of selected position holders in the sport organization system is diagrammed on p. 278.

The organizations on the left are always ranked slightly higher than the analogous sport organizations on the right because the multi-sport or-

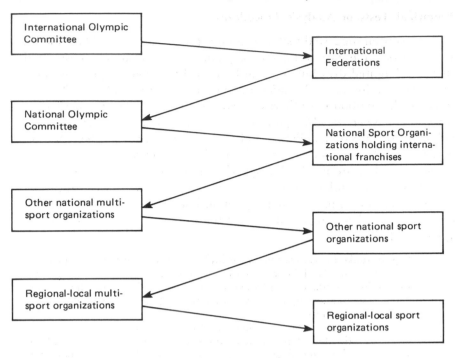

ganizations combine scope and "eliteness." The single-sport organizations have a higher involvement in the production of elite athletes *in the single sport* but have a narrow program. The bonding together of the 52 separate international federations into the General Assembly of International Federations would, in this hypothetical stratification diagram, greatly improve the position and authority claim of the international federations vis-à-vis the International Olympic Committee.

In summary, the position holders within the large-scale sport organization system have been identified. Within a social conflict model it has been theorized that any position holder is a potential source of conflict relative to counter position holders in the system. In examining the control of conflict within the system, a basic mechanism has been identified whereby authority is distributed differentially on the basis of an implicit process of organizational stratification. An organization's stratification level is determined by the scope of the organization's program and its ability to produce elite athletes. Organizations which have high ranking in the stratification system have high degrees of authority in regulatory control and vice-versa.

Empirical Tests of Analysis Procedures

It has been suggested that mechanisms for conflict control take modes varying from voluntary to forced compliance. It has also been postulated that a differential distribution of authority exists among large-scale sport organizations due to stratification rankings of the organizations. This differential distribution of authority, however, does not clarify whether interactions among specific sport organizations will be characterized by voluntary or forced compliance. Neither does it clarify whether the voluntary/forced compliance mode affects the perceptions of organization members as they are involved in specific conflict resolution processes.

However, the following relationships, based on the status (stratification ranking) of an organization (position holder), degree of regulatory control accorded the organization, and the modes of gaining compliance appear logical:

1. Highly ranked organizations have high degrees of authority/regulatory control. Conflicts of interest between high-status organizations are resolved by voluntary compliance actions preceded by bargaining and persuasion and accompanied by mutual perceptions of rationality among organization members.
2. Conflicts of interest between high- and low-status organizations are resolved by the low-status organizations' compliance, which would be accompanied by members' perceptions of threat because of potential sanctions which the high-status organization might invoke.
3. Conflicts of interest between high-status organizations and latent position holders (coaches and athletes) are resolved by latent group members' compliance accompanied by perceptions of systematic coercion.

Conflicts in which these relationships may be observed are numerous. Four examples are listed below:

1. Conflicts regarding organization membership: What countries shall be represented on the International Olympic Committee? What national organization shall be designated as franchise holder in a specific sport?
2. Conflicts regarding site selection for prestigious events: Shall the 1980 summer Olympic Games be held in Moscow or Los Angeles?
3. Conflicts regarding revenue distribution: How shall the television revenue for Olympic coverage be divided among the various international organizations and federations? How shall the revenue be utilized?
4. Conflicts regarding technical regulations: Who shall be eligible to participate in international events? What rules of play shall be utilized? Who shall select personnel for international events and by what procedures?

In each of the above conflict situations, resolutions occur on a regular basis. An analyst, attempting to utilize a social conflict model, could study each conflict resolution through the previously described analysis. The various position holders with a stake in the conflict would be identified. A stratification level would be assigned to each organization based on the criteria of scope and "eliteness." A direction of conflict resolution would be predicted and also the accompanying perceptions of voluntary compliance or coercion would be predicted. The *actual* results of conflict resolutions would be compared with the *predicted* results and meanings and implications derived. Continued monitoring of each situation could further clarify the effects of voluntary compliance and coercion on both the stability of the conflict resolution and the quality of the resultant interaction among sport organizations, sport administrators, and athletes.

POSTSCRIPT: AN OLYMPICS WITHOUT ATHLETES?

It has been postulated that social control mechanisms vary in the degree to which position holders share in regulatory control. The values of a democratic society support social control mechanisms of voluntary compliance based on rational thought and persuasive argument, rather than those of coerced compliance (Brown & Cassidy, 1963). In addition to the philosophical problem which coerced compliance poses in a democratic value system, Spady (1973) has indicated that coerced compliance often results in social settings which are unstable and marked with distrust. Thus, it seems desirable to encourage the development of social control mechanisms within the sport organization system, as in other aspects of society, which emphasize voluntary compliance by parties who share in regulatory control.

In the analysis presented, it is clear that two potential position holder groups are consistently found in coerced compliance settings. The functioning control mechanism (differential authority based on stratification criteria of program scope and "eliteness") is designed on an *organization system* base. Because coaches and athletes are latent conflict groups, they seldom, if ever, have direct and systematic *access* to regulatory control processes, much less *authority* in the processes. Coaches' organizations and athletes' organizations are legitimate position holders in the sport organization system and, on given issues, will have interests which diverge from those of the organizations presently designed to serve them.

Ingham and Loy (1973) have aptly described both the usual case of the athlete's role in sport regulatory control and what that role might be. They picture the Cheerful Robot athlete becoming whatever he/she must in order to meet the regulations of the institutionalized sport organization system. The present analysis further illustrates how the individual athlete and coach must comply with those sport organizations which are international federations or national governing bodies because of their role as gatekeepers for prized opportunities in elite sport.

Ingham and Loy also speak of the potential of a Renaissance Athlete, one who changes sport as well as being changed by it. The use of a social conflict model to analyze sport settings may indirectly enhance the occurrence of this potential. By viewing organizations, coaches, and athletes as position holders in the system and identifying their common and conflicting requirements, a pattern of mutual dependence and reciprocity becomes evident.

Three conclusions seem inescapable: (*a*) the athlete needs quality competition and coaching; (*b*) quality competition is not possible without technical organizations and business professionals with competence in marshalling necessary resources; and (*c*) there is no sport without the athlete. Each element—administrator, coach, and athlete—requires the other. Each has certain rights and responsibilities vis-à-vis the other. With this knowledge, each element should meet as equals to develop settings in which voluntary compliance based on rational persuasion is an actuality. Sport governance cannot continue in the present setting in which sport governing bodies rule the athletic lives of participants. Athletes are showing signs of a growing awareness of their potential power. What if they gave an "Olympics" and no one came?

The elite athlete needs:	*Franchised sport organization controls:*
1. To participate in systematic, high-quality competition	Access to 1
2. To have expert coaching	Indirect access to 2
3. To have the opportunity for high challenge/acclaim a. national title b. world games title c. Olympic title	Access to 3

The coach needs:	*Franchised sport organization controls:*
1. To attract quality athletes	Paths of access to top events
2. To be influential in the development of a "name" athlete sought for specific (or all) competitions	Selections of coaches and athletes for prestige tours and international competitions

The franchised sport organization
needs: *Coach/athlete controls:*

1. To demonstrate that the organi-   What sport events will be entered
   zation has a virtual monopoly on   (This control is limited, however, in
   the production of elite perform-   that refusal to enter an important
   ers and coaches   and/or qualifying meet will poten-
2. To stage events which showcase   tially harm the athlete and/or the
   the best talent available in the   coach as much as or more than the
   sport   organization.)

REFERENCES

Brown, C., and Cassidy, R. *Theory in physical education.* Philadelphia: Lea and
    Febiger, 1963.
Dahrendorf, R. *Class and class conflict in industrial society.* Palo Alto, Cali-
    fornia: Stanford University Press, 1959.
Ingham, A., and Loy, J. The social system of sport: A humanistic perspective.
    Quest, 1973, 19, 3-23.
Parsons, T. On the concept of political power. In R. Bendix and S. M. Lipset
    (Eds.), *Class, status, and power.* New York: The Free Press, 1966.
Spady, W. G. Authority, conflict, and teacher effectiveness. *Educational Re-
    searcher,* January 1973.

THE POTENTIAL VALUE IN THE
ANTHROPOLOGICAL ANALYSIS OF SPORT

B. Allan Tindall

INTRODUCTION

Anthropologists have not traditionally included an exhaustive analysis of sport in their studies of culture. The result is that the cultural descriptions we have are somewhat incomplete, and our ability to move toward a thorough and complete description of Man is somewhat impeded. On the other hand physical educators, in their preoccupation with exercise physiology, motor development and kinesiology, have not fully taken advantage of anthropology. The result is that physical education lacks a basis for understanding the universality of sport.

The anthropological analysis of sport has a potential value for both anthropologists and physical educators. Anthropologists will benefit from an understanding of the extent to which behavioral patterns are consistent in all spheres of culture. Physical educators will benefit through an understanding of the cultural complexity and diversity involved in the patterns of behavior we label sport.

Some research has been done which illuminates this value potential, but before proceeding to that research I shall briefly discuss a conceptual tool which distinguishes anthropology from other disciplines, and briefly discuss the focus of anthropological research.

THE DISTINCTION BETWEEN EMIC
AND ETIC DESCRIPTION

Cultural anthropologists seek to identify the core of behavioral phenomena which make us human, and about which there exists cultural

This article is a revised version of a paper presented at the Annual Convention of the National College Physical Education Association for Men, Phoenix, Arizona: January, 1975. Printed with permission of the author.

variation. Usually we begin with some very obvious biological or social phenomena and seek to describe the strategy used by cultural groups to deal with those immutable factors. For example the human phenomena of language has led linguists to a description of the essential parameters of human langauge, while also describing the type and extent of variation existing on those parameters.

Linguistic analysis is not of particular relevance to sport analysis, but the conceptual principle upon which linguists base their attempt to describe human language is of the utmost relevance so I shall pursue this example a bit further.

Over the course of many years the attempt to construct a description of human sound production led to the identification and solution of a crucial problem. The problem stems from the fact that each language system has meaning according to a different set of basic sounds. Although all humans can emit the same sounds, each language system makes differential use of a portion of this complete repertoire. A linguist is faced with two tasks: (1) the identification of the basic sounds which have meaning, the *phonemes* of a language, and (2) the comparison of the phonemic structure of one language to that of other languages.

But the two tasks appear to be mutually exclusive. If you are successful in describing the phonemic uniqueness of one language system and you attempt to describe a second language from that unique point of view, you will fail to capture the uniqueness of the second language.

The solution to the problem was the creation of a new language system especially designed to facilitate the comparison of different sound systems. The new language incorporates all of the basic sound units of all languages, but does not do so in their own terms. The use of the "meta language" to analyze the distinctive features of all languages is *phonetics*, while the study on one language is *phonemics*.

The principle which distinguishes anthropology from other disciplines has two components: (1) each culture must be described in terms of the phenomena seen by its members to be meaningful, but that (2) comparisons between cultures require another set of terms and symbols which include all of these independently meaningful phenomena. *Emic* analysis will provide a description of a culture in its own terms, while the application of an *etic* analysis will demonstrate the similarities and differences between cultures in a way which will lead us to the minimum number of concepts necessary to describe Man.[1]

1. The discussion of linguistics, and emic and etic analysis has been taken from Ward H. Goodenough, *Description and Comparison in Cultural Anthropology* (Chicago: Aldine Publishing Company, 1970), pp. 98-130.

The task of a cultural anthropologist thus becomes the production of emic descriptions which when analyzed along with other emic descriptions lead to a parsimonious etic description of the human group.

THE FOCUS OF ANTHROPOLOGICAL STUDY

In a fundamental sense cultural anthropologists are concerned with the human process of communication, and therefore provide emic descriptions of the structure and content of communication systems. This entails the careful identification of patterns of behavior, as these patterns are shared by varying numbers of people in varying situations.

The minimal interactive unit required for the analysis of any communicative behavior is a dyad, and the task is to describe those behaviors which have meaning to the participants in the dyad. Meaning is located in those behaviors which have an *observable* impact on the synchrony of interaction. Once a descriptive map of meaning can be produced for a pair of people, the task becomes the identification of meaningful patterns in other dyads, as the original pair of people interact with various others. As the communication system is described by patterns of meaningful behavior in a variety of situations those patterns of behavior which are shared by all of the members of a group can be identified, as well as those patterns shared by fewer numbers of people.[2]

The determination of the content of communication simultaneously depends upon time and level of analytic focus. By observing those behaviors which disrupt the synchrony of interaction, one can infer the "cause" of, and the "solution" for those disruptions. Thus over time patterns of syncrony disruption and restoration can lead to supportable emic descriptions of the essential content of dyadic communication.

I have argued elsewhere[3] that a Mormon physical education teacher's simple question: "Why aren't you dressed to play today?" dealt simultaneously with several levels of concern. When this question was asked of Ute Indian students it "caused" a change in the usual synchrony of dyadic interaction. At one level the question concerned the school rules regarding participation in physical education classes. But at a far more fundamental level the question dealt with disparate cultural premises

2. The discussion of dyadic analysis of behavior is taken from the work of the members of the Center for the Study of Cultural Transmission, State University of New York at Buffalo. The most recent report on this perspective can be found in Fred Gearing and Lucinda Sangree (Eds.) *A Cultural Theory of Education*, a volume in *World Anthropology* (The Hague: Mouton), in press.
3. B. Allan Tindall, "Ethnography and the Hidden Curricula in Sport," *Behavioral and Social Science Teacher*, II, 1975.

concerning relationships between man and man. For Anglo-Mormons life is conducted in a way which suggests the appropriateness of one man's control over another, while the Utes behave in ways which suggest the appropriateness of almost total independence. The teacher's question was simultaneously focused on a rather minor school rule and a fundamental difference in the way life is lived.

The event was no different than a hundred other events where the teacher asked Ute students questions, except that the pattern of verbal and non-verbal behavior was asynchronic as long as the topic concerned the right of individuals to be free to choose to play, or the right of the teacher to require the students to play. This behavioral asynchrony was inferred to be caused by the cultural premise nature of the question rather than the form of the question or its explicit content (the school rules). However, the inference is only supportable because it was based on observed patterns of dyadic communication over time. Thus this example suggests the importance of time and analytic focus for determining the content of a communicative sequence.

The structure and the content of communication must be studied carefully as varying numbers of people interact with one another over time. By identifying the structure of patterned synchronic and asynchronic behavior the content of communication systems can be determined. When we are able to identify the patterns of meaningful behavior used by members of a culture we will have an emic description of the structure and content of that culture.

THE POTENTIAL VALUE IN THE
ANTHROPOLOGICAL ANALYSIS OF SPORT

As anthropologists seek to describe human universals through the emic and etic analysis of communication they will be aided by the inclusion of sport, and their inclusion of sport will be of value to physical educators. Anthropologists cannot describe a single culture completely unless they include all of a people's behavior in all spheres of life: political, economic, religious, and "recreational." A complete etic description of humanity cannot be produced until we have complete emic descriptions.

As anthropologists include sport they will be providing descriptions which detail the complexity and diversity of the behaviors we call sport. These descriptions should be of value to physical educators as they are concerned about the universal nature of sport, and the educative potential of specific sports in a situation involving cultural diversity.

A few research projects illuminate the potential value of sport analysis for anthropology by demonstrating that the structure and content of behavioral patterns in sport are essentially the same as behavioral patterns in other spheres of cultural life. Research conducted by educational anthropologists at the University of Florida has demonstrated that "racial" integration in an urban southern city is patterned according to the task which must be accomplished. Black and White residents segregate themselves residentially and socially except when a common task brings them into contact. Integration occurs when people work, receive health care, use public transportation, or attend school. In school "racial" polarization occurs except when the students have a common task: to smoke (a smoking area exists on the school grounds), to relieve themselves, or to play football.

The football team reflects the overall community and school pattern of integration: segregation, by choice, except for common tasks. Thus before and after practice sessions or games the boys remain in their own groups, but for football they disregard ethnicity and associate according to "task and talent."[4]

Recently completed research in Appalachia will demonstrate that school basketball provides an opportunity for intricate patterns of kinship organization and political independence to be woven together to sustain a community's integrity. The forum provided by basketball is in structure and content analogous to other community activities.[5]

A research team in Montreal has demonstrated that the manipulation of professional wrestler's identities is organized to represent in structure and content the basis of prejudicial behavior in the involved communities. For example they cite an occurrence which took place at the Montreal Forum:

> First to enter the ring was Baron Fritz Von Erich who was introduced as a Nazi from Germany to a largely Jewish audience. Sporting a swastika on his arm and wearing high black boots the baron stomped around the ring screaming obscenities in German [and] raising his arm in Hitlerian fashion. Pointing to the skull-capped members of the audience, the baron promised

---

4. The report of this massive, long term research project was presented as a symposium at the Annual Meetings of the American Anthropological Association, New Orleans, Louisiana, November, 1973. The following authors are all members of the Department of Anthropology, University of Florida, Gainsville: Solon T. Kimball, "Parallel Racial Structure and School Integration;" Charles Wagly, "The Community as a Setting;" Reba Anderson, "Activities;" Edward D. McGough, "Planned Space Versus Social Space—Palmetto High School;" Murrel Rutledge, "Informal Structure Among Black High School Students;" Faye Harris, "The Marginals: Students on the Fringe of the School Environment;" Andrew Miracle, "Task and Talent—Football."
5. Walter Precourt, Department of Anthropology, State University of New York at Buffalo. Personal communication about recently completed research.

to send his opponent back to Auschwitz. Following the baron's dramatic five-minute prematch performance, his opponent, Rabbi Raphael Halpern ran into the arena with prayer book in hand, skull-cap on [his] head and wearing a blue and white costume covered with stars of David. The crowd roared its approval. Needless to say the forces of good prevailed and the Rabbi was victorious.[6]

These research examples illuminate the potential value of sport analysis for anthropology by demonstrating that behavior is similarily patterned across several, if not all, spheres of cultural life. While some of these research projects were not designed to be culturally comprehensive, they do suggest, in specific detail, that patterns of behavior associated with sport are the same as behavioral patterns in other spheres of life.

Many physical educators are concerned with the universality of sport, and while we are a long way from an etic formulation which will accurately describe the fundamental and unique elements of human play, games, sport, or exercise, we are on our way through a number of research projects which emically define the structure and content of behavior in sport.

My own research among Ute Indians and Anglo-Mormons in Utah demonstrates that the form and content of basketball behavior communicates dramatically different meanings for the two cultural groups. For the Anglo-Mormon community basketball is structured and played according to an apparent orientation toward mutality. Teamwork, individual sacrifice for the good of the team, group strategy, and group status are key principles adhered to in basketball. The Ute community, however, stresses individuality in team structure, in play, in skill acquisition, and in status. Basketball has no intrinsic meaning, but has at least several culturally specific meanings, expressed dozens of ways.[7]

In another research project Kendall Blanchard found that basketball structure and strategy differed between the Navajo and Mormons. This research, like my own, demonstrates that basketball has unique meaning for each group, and that those meanings stem from differences in cultural background.[8]

6. Allan Turowetz, Ron L. Fernandez, and Leon Jacobs, "Professional Sports and the Manipulation of Identity," research paper presented at the Northeastern Anthropological Association meetings, Burlington, Vermont, April, 1973.
7. B. Allan Tindall, *The Psycho-Cultural Orientations of Anglo and Ute Boys in an Integrated High School,* Unpublished doctoral dissertation, University of California, Berkeley, 1973.
8. Kendall Blanchard, "Basketball and the Culture Change Process: The Rimrock Navajo Case," *Council on Anthropology and Education Quarterly,* V (November, 1974), pp. 8-13.

Thomas Carroll[9] has argued a unique perspective on the cultural premises distinguishing "work" from "play" in an urban city in the United States. "Work" is defined, emically as it is an operating principle of the people he observed, to be the ". . . acquisition and the use of 'know-how,'" such "know-how" being required for the "discovery, creation and maintenance . . ." of the (proper cultural) ". . . order or pattern in the world that exists naturally and as a result of man's efforts."

The term "work" thus stands as a symbol or label for those activities which people engage in to sustain the order of the world, but the label also represents the fact that in order to maintain that order you must have "know-how." The label "work," in this example as it is used to symbolize people's activities, is not defined by the type of activity (washing clothes or building a house is equally work), the location of activity (home, office, playground, pool), or whether or not you are paid for your activity. "Work" is what people who have "know-how" do, to maintain (discover or create) the order of the world.

If you don't have "know-how" you cannot work, but you can help one who has "know-how" or you can learn. Thus Carroll found that children are being implicitly taught that some activities support the proper order of the world and that they must come to "know-how" to do those activities in order to be proper citizens. Other activities, they are implicitly taught, do not concern the proper order and therefore do not require "know-how" and can be defined as non-work.

According to this research game playing or other organized physical activities, which require "know-how" fall into the cultural premise category of "work" not play, even though the participants may be having fun, may describe their activities as recreation or leisure, or may not receive any pay for their participation. A problem occurs here as we try to exceed our language system (which contains words to distinguish work, play, leisure, and recreation) and try to exceed our folk logic which tells us that work is what you get paid for. To overcome this problem we must understand that culturally these urban people have two broad categories for activities: (1) activities which sustain the proper order of the world; and (2) activities which do not sustain the proper order of the world.

Physical education programs may in fact be part of the process of changing children, who don't have "know-how" and therefore cannot sustain the order of the world, into adults, as such programs take active

9. Thomas G. Carroll, "Transactions of Cognitive Equivalence in Hidden Curriculum Domains, 'Work' and 'Play,'" a research paper presented at the Annual Meetings of the American Anthropological Association, New Orleans, Louisiana, November, 1973.

participants in informal games and teach them *how to play* (i.e., give them "know-how"). I am wondering if physical education programs, in which we say we attempt to help people "play," are not really programs in which we are teaching people how to maintain the order of the world (i.e., work): the distinction being that the "play" of children cannot maintain the order of the world because it does not require "know-how," but the "play" of adults, as it requires one to "know-how" to follow cultural patterns of organizational structuring, interpersonal behavior, temporal and spatial orientations, is properly "work" because it contributes to the maintenance of the order of the world (i.e., how to organize and structure activities, engage in social interaction, observe time and space properly).

These research efforts describe sports as they are emically significant to cultural groups. Together with other similar descriptions they will lead to an etic description of the universality of certain patterns of human behavior, replete with the complexity and diversity of cultural life. Physical educators can use these and other works to examine their notions about the universal meaning, value, or significance of sport, and they can now get a feel for the tremendous variation in the educational potential for any number of sports; variations attributable to cultural differences. This, I should think, is of potential value to the profession of physical education.

CONCLUSION

As anthropologists increasingly provide emic descriptions of the structure and content of communication in sport we will be closer to our goal of providing a parsimonious etic description of humanity. As physical educators encourage, sustain, and integrate anthropological studies their search for an understanding of the universality of sport will be enhanced. The potential exists, if we can establish a common understanding and maintain respect and encouragement.

SECTION

B

SOCIAL SYSTEMS:
1. POLITICS

There can be no doubt even in the mind of a casual observer since the 1972 Olympics at Munich as to the importance of the relationship of sport to politics. Whether it be city, university, state, or nation the use of sport as a political tool seems everywhere apparent. It often appears to be the only socially shared experience either within a culture or cross-culturally.

During the baseball World Series of 1974, in Oakland, California, black and white people talked easily to each other on buses and in super-markets in their joint enthusiasm for the Oakland A's. The more common experience of social restraint and mistrust was lost momentarily in the shared experience of baseball.

The United States plays table tennis and competes in track with China while other cultural doors between the two countries remain closed. It is only natural that revolutionary political groups have seized on sport as the perfect social medium by which to gain an audience and thereby attempt to force social change.

Hitler was the most obvious and even flamboyant in his political presentation of the Olympics (1936). Olympics have served more and more as a showcase for the success of a nation's political belief system. Just the ability to host the Olympics may demonstrate and/or jeopardize the economic resources of a nation.

Some of the many other directions that sport can take because of political views and demands are discussed by Hanna in an article called "The Politics of Sport: Indonesia as Host to the Fourth Asian Games." (This article is not included in this collection but is well worth reading.) In the late summer of 1962 Indonesia was host to some 1,200 athletes from seventeen countries for the "Fourth Asian Games." Hanna relates:

> At the last moment, however, the Indonesian games committee and the Indonesian government deliberately excluded from the competition the

teams of two charter members of the Asian Games Federation whose governments are not recognized by Indonesia thus stirred up an international controversy which, after almost stalling the games themselves, led to the decision by international sports bodies that the events in Djakarta did not qualify as the Fourth Asian Games at all but must be regarded as merely another international competition, and climaxed in an Indonesian riot at the Indian Embassy in Djakarta.[1]

In light of the present Third World organizations and their demands, the outcomes of this upheaval seem especially pertinent. Hanna continues:

They have also taken up a suggestion which originated, it seems, with the Minister of Sports and past president of the Asia Games Federation, who has proposed the establishment of a new international games organization. The "emerging nations," the argument runs, should free themselves of the "domination" of Western "imperialists" sportsmen who "discriminate" against Afro-Asians. They should form a new sports association of Asian, African and Latin American nations which takes account of the "realities" of the present world political situation.[2]

McIntosh in the first article, takes the point of view that "very seldom has sport been free of politics." He looks into the effect of international politics on the Olympic Games, and also at the internal politics within one country, observing that sport can operate as a "cohesive agent" or as an agent of division when it it affected by the rivalry of governing bodies within the country.

There has been a great deal of opinion and uninformed assumption in the United States about sport practices and the organization of sport in both the Soviet Union and the People's Republic of China. Sport does maintain a prominent position within both societies, and Seban examines the reasons for such prominence. After traveling to both countries and reading available literature, Seban has made an effort to objectively present the systems of sport in both cultures to the American reader.

Kropke assesses his own article as "an attempt to whet the appetite of social science for international sport" as a worthy topic of research. He encourages a much closer examination of the phenomena of sport "within the context of global relations, peace research and the social sciences."

The longtime theme that sport could help solve problems of human understanding, even to the extent of supplanting war, is proposed again by Kropke. We still do not often heed the early warnings and questions raised by Huizinga[3] and later by Caillois.[4] How does a specific culture

1. W. R. Hanna, "The Politics of Sport," *Southeast Asia Series*. New York: American Universities Field Staff, (1962), p. 1.
2. Ibid., pp. 10-11.
3. Johan Huizinga, *Homo Ludens: A Study of the Play Element in Culture*. Boston, Mass.: Beacon Press, 1950.
4. Roger Caillois, *Man, Play and Games*. New York: The Free Press of Glencoe, 1961.

practice sport? Does the choice of sport and the way it is expressed reveal the health of a society?

Sport is not just a simple tennis or soccer game. Sport includes the belief system of a people and how they perceive their relationships with each other and to outsiders. Until we understand these perceptions and the interactions which occur, our progress in experiencing sport as a common human ceremonial for understanding will be exceedingly limited.

SPORT, POLITICS AND INTERNATIONALISM

Peter C. McIntosh

In 1956 the armed conflicts in Hungary and Suez caused six nations to withdraw from the Olympic Games which were to be held in Melbourne, Australia. Mr. Avery Brundage, President of the International Olympic Committe commented: "By their decisions these countries show that they are unaware of one of our most important principles, namely that sport is completely free of politics." A superficial glance into the past is enough to show that very seldom has sport been free of politics. Certainly Baron de Coubertin did not see sport completely free of politics when he founded the modern Olympic Games. On the contrary, he hoped that sporting activities might improve the political relationships between nations. He addressed a circular to the governing bodies of sport in January, 1894, expressing the hope that every four years the athletic representatives of the world might be brought together and that the spirit of international unity might be advanced by the celebration of their chivalrous and peaceful contests. If sport was to influence politics it was hardly conceivable that the interaction should be in one direction only and that politics should have no bearing at all upon sport. The naïveté of Mr. Brundage's statement, however, must not be allowed to obscure the relationship between sport and politics which is felt to exist by many people besides the members of the I.O.C.

The relationship may turn bad in at least two ways, by too much interaction and by the debasement of either one of the two agents. The injection of too much sport into politics might reduce the most serious of human activities to puerilism, while the seriousness of politics, if carried into sport in too great measure, could destroy its playfulness and so change its very nature. Again, corruption in sport might lead to corrupt pressure being brought to bear upon local or national politicians which could harmfully affect the life of the community. The greater danger, however, is from corruption acting in the opposite direction. If the political life of a community is corrupt or is organized for unworthy or inhumane ends then it will hardly be possible for sport to remain unaffected; it will be harnessed, however loosely, to the same unworthy ends. The ideals of sportsmen may for a while pull the polity back or slow down its regress but observation of Germany in the 1930s and of South Africa in the decades since World War II suggests that sportsmen share the corrupt political and social ideas of their community in about the same measure as other citizens. Even if they do not share those ideals they tolerate them and their application to sport in order to be able to continue to play. There is at least one noble exception to this generalization which ought not to pass unnoticed. When in 1848, the German State of Baden attempted to implement a liberal constitution, Prussia and the other big states at once invaded Baden. The provisional government appealed for help to oppose the aggressors. The *Hanau Turnverein* sent three hundred armed gymnasts, who increased their number to six hundred *en route*. For a time they held out against the best-trained army in Europe. The end was inevitable. Some escaped to Switzerland. The rest were killed in action or shot as rebels after capture. The collapse of the political movement for a united, free and democratic Germany caused many gymnasts to flee across the Atlantic. In America they reestablished their clubs. Their liberal ideals caused them to declare forcefully in favour of the abolition of slavery. They supported Abraham Lincoln politically and then enlisted in the armies of the North in considerable numbers.

Sport has certain characteristics which perhaps impel it more readily than other human activities towards an association with politics. Sport, especially competitive sport tends to identify the individual with some group and the individual welcomes this identity. Even the lone runner cannot escape his association with club or town, county or country. The member of a team inevitably sinks some of his individuality in the group. In the great age of sports development the extent to which the individual was submerged was an indication of merit in a game or sport. The young master in *Tom Brown's Schooldays* was made to say about cricket: "The discipline and reliance in one another which it teaches is so valuable, I think. It ought to be such an unselfish game. It merges the individual in the eleven; he doesn't play that he may win, but that his side may," to which Tom replies: "That's very true and that's why football and cricket, now one comes to think of it, are such much better games than fives or hare and hounds, or any others where the object is to come in first or to win for oneself and not that one's side may win."

The political significance of discipline, reliance on one another, and merging the individual in the group was not lost upon educators and statesmen in Victorian England. Furthermore, competitive sport fitted in well with the Victorian pattern of industrial and political rivalry. A belief in collisions, collisions of political parties, religious sects, industrial firms and teams of sportsmen was the light to illumine the broad road of social progress.

The merging of the individual in the group was not confined to the players themselves but to some extent was experienced by those who watched and those who shared a common club membership, a geographical location, or a racial affinity with the performers. In the later nineteenth century the growth of urban areas was so rapid and so amorphous as almost to smother the individual's sense of belonging to any group larger than the family, but on Saturday afternoons he could at least identify himself and his interest with those of eleven figures on the football field as he took his place on the terraces with thousands of others. Some transference of identity from local club to local government almost certainly helped the growth of civic sense and pride in cities such as Birmingham and Manchester. Local politicians who advocated measures to encourage or promote sport did so in the realization that they were helping the political development of their great towns.

In the United States the influence of sport on politics has been considerable. The line taken by German-American gymnasts has already been noted. In a broader sphere sport gave cohesion to a great variety of immigrants with different racial, religious and political backgrounds. It developed in America at about the same time as in Britain, in the latter part of the nineteenth century. Success quickly became an important matter of local prestige, and often the local representatives would be the high school or college; it thus united in rivalry different communities and townships. If the immigrants themselves retained some of their cultural isolation their sons found sport an easy avenue to the American way of life.

Success in sport was important to Americans and it is to their credit that in a community with a history of racial discrimination the racial complexion of the performer was not allowed to prevent his rise to the top in sport. He could represent his town, his state, his country if he were good enough. In boxing the negro Jack Johnson was heavyweight champion of the world from 1908 to 1915 at a time when the heroes of the American negro were almost all in sport because here could he meet and beat the white man on equal terms. Johnson himself in vaunting his superiority left a legacy of hatred. By 1937 the inarticulate and shy Joe Louis, the next negro heavyweight champion, was as beloved by white men as by negroes. In 1962 Floyd Patterson, the third of a great line, could write; "For myself I can truthfully say I feel no differently inside if I am fighting a white man or another negro." Later in that year he lost the world heavyweight title to the fourth negro to hold it, Liston.

In the Olympic Games many negroes have represented the United States with distinction. When in 1936 at the Olympic Games in Berlin Hitler refused to receive Jesse Owens because he was a negro after his great victories on the track, the action of the Führer was taken by Americans as an insult to them all.

North of the forty-ninth parallel the Canadians, with their federal constitution, provincial autonomy and large self-conscious minority population of French Canadians, have long experienced the lack of a sense of nationhood. In 1962 a government campaign for fitness and sport was launched by the Minister of National Health and Welfare who included this significant remark in his speech to Parliament: "Canadian participation in international competitive events is emerging as an important aspect of a growing spirit of nationhood."

Sport then has been found to be a cohesive agent and in countries where it is the policy of governments to keep a people divided as in South Africa or in Germany the community of interest in sport between different racial or political groups has been an embarrassment to the politicians.

In the planned societies of communist countries the interaction of sport and politics is deliberately carried a long way and the interaction is from politics to sport rather than in the opposite direction. At first, after the October revolution of 1917, the communist government in Russia took no official interest in sport. In 1925, however, sport was officially recognized and encouraged and in 1930-1 a number of tests in games and sports were instituted leading to the award of G.T.O. Badges ("Ready for Labour and Defence"). Sport was organized under an All Union Committee of Sport and Physical Culture, a government organ responsible to the Council of Ministers of the U.S.S.R. From then onwards there was no suggestion in communist countries that sport was or ought to be "free of politics." On the contrary, sport and training for sport were used extensively for political education so that it became impossible to train as a coach without instruction in Marxism-Leninism and it was impossible to compete in a stadium great or small without being bombarded with the political slogans and ideas of the government of the day. Many sports meetings were organized by political organizations for political purposes.

In countries where sport is organized piecemeal by voluntary bodies and is, to all appearances, independent of political organization and indoctrination, it cannot be inferred that interaction between sport and politics does not take place. The difference is rather in the pattern of organization rather than in the presence of absence of interaction. The pattern of sport in Eastern and Western Germany exemplifies extremes of political organization.

All the German sports organizations were dissolved by order of the Control Commission after the war ended in 1945. In East Germany the government party then decreed that anyone who wished to take part in sport must do so as a member either of the new political youth organization (F.J.D.) or of the workers organization (F.D.G.B.). In 1948 the *Deutscher Sportausschuss* was set up with an avowed political aim. This was followed in 1952 by a State Committee for Sport and Physical Culture.

By contrast, in the Western Zone the *Deutscher Sportsbund* was set up in 1950 with the stated object of solving its problems without reference to party political, religious, racial or military considerations. The establishment of the *Sportsbund* was the result of efforts to find an organization which would enable sportsmen to govern themselves and pursue their interests without control or interference from the government.

Whatever may have been the differing patterns of organization of sport the interest of government organs in West Germany has been no less than in the East. In 1960 the German Olympic Association published a *Memorandum on the "Golden Plan" for Health, Sport and Recreation.* The Golden Plan was based on nation-wide surveys of sports facilities and asked for expenditure of £568,900,000 (6,315,000,000 D.M.) over fifteen years. The first four years were to be used in building up a combined federal and provincial government expenditure of £28,000,000 in direct grants to local communities. By 1961 grant aid from government sources already totalled £13,500,000 (150,000,000 D.M.) or forty-eight per cent of the target for 1964.[1]

To a greater or lesser degree the governments of all western European countries and many others besides now finance sport for their people, all but three of the European countries drawing the revenue to do so from football pools. In Great Britain annual direct aid to sport from the government in 1962 still amounted to no more than £670,000 and that sum was reached only after the Chancellor of the Exchequer had announced an increase of £200,000 on the original sum budgeted. The Wolfenden Committee Report, comparable in some ways to the German Golden Plan but much more modest, had asked for £10,000,000.

Undoubtedly the parsimonious treatment of sport by the British Government has been largely the result of firmly held beliefs that financial aid would involve government interference and that interaction between politics and sport must stop well short of this point. The same beliefs caused the Wolfenden Committee to reject vigorously the suggestion that there should be established a new Department of State called the Ministry of Sport. Yet the Ministry of Education is already, within limitations, a Ministry of Sport. It accepts or rejects all plans for new schools and colleges and so determines the facilities which are provided there for sport in school and out. It provides some of the money for their construction; it sets limits on expenditure on sport by local authorities, it makes a small grant, already mentioned, to voluntary organizations. It helps to finance the coaching schemes of governing bodies of sport and it helps to maintain three national recreation centres. Where sport is educational, and, broadly speaking, is being taught or learned rather than played for its own sake the Ministry of Education already exercises the functions of a Ministry of Sport by permitting, assisting, controlling, inspecting and, some would say, by interfering. When sport is educational it is considered worthy of political direction and some measure of control, but when sport becomes an end in itself it has so far ceased, in Britain, to be an activity which is appropriate for political support.

There have been three occasions when the political disinterestedness of the British Government has been breached. In 1927 the Air Ministry entered an official team for the Schneider Trophy Air Race. It did so again in 1929 and 1931. The race was at this time an international sporting contest, nothing more, and the intervention of the British Government in a sporting event preceded similar intervention by any other government of whatever political complexion. In 1954 the British Government once again broke its principle of non-participation in the world of sport. Roger Bannister had just become the first man to run the mile in less than four minutes. The Foreign Office sent him on a "good will" visit to the United States in order to improve Anglo-American relations.

In January, 1963, the British Prime Minister, having rejected the recommendation of the Wolfenden Committee for a Sports Development Council with funds to allocate, assigned to Lord Hailsham the task of co-ordinating the aid given to sport and recreation by different Government departments, such as the Ministries of Education, Health, and Housing and Local Government. It looked as if Lord Hailsham was to be in fact but not in name a Minister of Sport. At almost the same time there appeared on the horizon a cloud no bigger than a man's hand in the form of a small sum in the estimates of the Commonwealth Relations Office, a government Ministry, to meet a deficit which had been incurred by the British Empire and Commonwealth Games organization in participating in the Games in Western Australia in November, 1962. Whether this was a precedent of political significance was not clear at the time.

It is in the international sphere that the modern development of sport has most significant political implications, for it is here that the hazard to the true nature of sport is most acute and it is here that sport may make its most significant contribution to human welfare and sanity. The rise of international sport has been meteoric. The America's Cup race instituted in 1857 for friendly competition by yachts of different countries was probably the first modern international sporting contest of any consequence. Before the end of the century other international events had appeared, but at the first modern Olympic Games in 1896 there was only thirteen competing nations. In 1960 the number was eighty-four and it has been during the first sixty years of the twentieth century that international sport has come into real prominence.

One of the most considerable achievements has been the setting up of International Federations for the organization and control of individual sports. In sports where times and distances can be measured it soon became necessary to have a body to ratify records so that the claimant to a record could enjoy world-wide acceptance and recognition. In all competitive sports, however, as competitors from one country met those from other countries it became necessary to agree upon the rules and the eligibility of competitors to ensure even competition. The desire for this international competition at all levels of ability became so strong and so widespread that differences of language, of local practice, of social and educational background and of political outlook were not allowed to stand in the way of agreement on an essential basis for competition. Federations were set up for athletics, football, swimming, lawn tennis and many other sports. From the start the decisions of these bodies enjoyed a remarkable acceptance and obedience from constituent bodies all over the world. Whatever defects there may be in international sport there have at least been forms of democratic world government which have had tolerable success within their own limited jurisdictions. Since 1960 there has also been an International Council of Sport and Physical Education under the aegis of UNESCO which was already in 1962 beginning to bring together the international federations and organizations of teachers, coaches and leaders in a further limited world organization.

The desire for international competition is not confined to the richer and more highly developed countries but is shared by these countries which might be thought to be preoccupied with the basic needs for survival. A complete analysis of participants in the Olympic Games of 1952 was carried out in Helsinki and showed that one hundred and sixty competitors came from countries so poor that the annual *per capita* income was less than $100. Rich countries with a *per capita* income of more than $750 sent one hundred and ninety-four competitors.[2]

The best performers anywhere want to test their skill against the best from elsewhere, but because at international level the best performer emerges some of his identity in the nation itself, whether he wants to do so or not, success in sport has political importance. This is true for the emergent nation as well as for the more highly developed countries. In February, 1959, the Indian Parliament debated a motion expressing concern at the deterioration of Indian sports, especially cricket. The motion was provoked by the previous failures of the Indian cricket team in the West Indies. One Member of Parliament suggested that no Indian team should be sent abroad for five years, to enable them to improve their standards. Canada, at the other end of the national income scale, launched a government campaign for fitness and amateur sport in 1962 in full recognition that "those who compete in the Olympic Games, the British Empire and Commonwealth Games, the Pan American Games and other international championship games are ambassadors of good will for Canada." The Prime Minister expressed the hope that the programme would add not only to the happiness and health of all people of Canada but to the international athletic prestige of Canada.

Direct intervention by a Head of State in sport because of its international and political significance took place in December, 1962. At that time in the United States disagreement between two rival governing bodies of sport, the Amateur Athletic Union and the National Collegiate Athletic Association, reached a climax. The Attorney-General failed to reconcile the two bodies. President Kennedy himself warned the American People in a Press conference on 12th December that the United States might not be represented at the next Olympic Games if the two factions refused arbitration. He said: "The governing bodies of these groups apparently put their own interests before the interests of our athletes, our traditions of sport and our country. The time has come for these groups to put the national interest first. Their continued bickering is grossly unfair. On behalf of the country and on behalf of sport I call on the organizations to submit their differences to an arbitration panel immediately." These were strong words, but the political importance of the statement lay not so much in the words used as in the fact that directions were given by the President of the United States to voluntary sports organizations which realized less clearly than he did their own inescapable political responsibilities.

Communist countries have long openly regarded their sporting representatives as political emissaries who can do more than diplomats to recommend the communist philosophy and way of life to those who have not adopted it. East and west sportsmen, whether they like it or not, are "ambassadors of good will" and are under pressure to vindicate not merely their own prowess but the ideology of their country. There are few governments in the world which do not now accept the political importance of success in international sport.

The desire to win is sometimes so strong that sport cannot contain it; when this natural human desire is reinforced with political pressures it is small wonder that on occasion the structure of the sporting event bursts assunder. It was argued in an earlier chapter that play is an essential element in all sport if it is to retain its intrinsic value, and that play implies a defined area of unreality in which the rules of ordinary life are superseded for the time being. It is possible for very great tension to be built up in a game or contest without the illusion of unreality being shattered. Often, however, it is shattered in international sports. A game of ice hockey may develop into an unregulated fist fight as it did in the Winter Olympic Games at Squaw Valley in 1960. A game of water polo may turn into a bloodbath as it did in the Olympic Games in Melbourne in 1956. Cricket or football matches may be destroyed as sporting events by bottles thrown by spectators. On these occasions the illusion is shattered and the contest has all the aggression, humiliation and bitterness of real life.

On the other side of the balance sheet there are many occasions when "strife without anger and art without malice" are maintained in the most intense competition. There have been numerous occasions at the Olympic Games when competitors from different ideologic blocks, even from countries in open hostility with each other have stood on the victor's rostrum, to receive their medals. Their nations' flags are flying, while the whole crowd stands to do honour to them. These moments and many honourable and friendly contests, unnoticed by the Press of the world, nevertheless enhance the dignity of man.

While competitors and spectators sometimes fail to sustain the unreality of sport, there are from time to time political forces which seek to destroy it. There is no reason in any sport why those who know and accept agreed rules and who have the necessary skill should not play together, yet in South Africa black and white races are not permitted to play together for fear of breaching the political doctrine of apartheid. In Europe, too, the political division of Berlin and the tension there in 1962 led to restrictions on movement between communist and non-communist countries which implied that no international sport would be possible between the two blocks.

In both these situations there was interaction from sport to politics as well as from politics to sport. The South African Olympic Committee was warned that it would be suspended by the International Olympic Committee if the South African government persisted with racial discrimination in sport. In the European situation the I.O.C. in March, 1962, stated that the Olympic Games would be held only in cities which would guarantee free access for all recognized teams. As no city in a country of the North Atlantic Treaty Organization would be permitted to admit East Germans, all these countries were debarred from holding the Olympic Games until they agreed to recognize the special and "unreal" nature of sport. The International Council for Sport and Physical Education urged UNESCO to try urgently to secure that the youth of the whole world and its officials might meet freely in sport. The Council cancelled its own general assembly which was to be held in Manila because the Government of the Philippines would not guarantee entry to delegates from communist countries.

The essential nature of sport is in danger internationally not only from restriction but also from domination by the two great power blocks, the U.S.A. and the U.S.S.R. It is inevitable in the present situation that they should be more than anxious for success and that this anxiety should be shared by their citizens and allies. In 1962 both global and local wars are likely to be suicidal ways of influencing people and winning support, and sport as a means of influence has assumed correspondingly greater political importance. The situation was analyzed in essence by Arnold Toynbee in 1948. In *Civilization on Trial* he wrote: "Communism is a competitor [with the West] for the allegiance of that great majority of mankind that is neither communist nor capitalist, neither Russian nor Western but is living at present in an uneasy no man's land between the opposing citadels of two rival ideologies. Both nondescripts and Westerners are in danger of turning communist today, as they were of turning Turk four hundred years ago, and, though communists are in similar danger of turning capitalist—as sensational instances have shown—the fact that one's rival witch doctor is as much afraid of one's own medicine as one is afraid oneself, of his, does not do anything to relieve the tension of the situation.

"Yet the fact that our adversary threatens us by showing up our defects, rather than by forcibly suppressing our virtues, is proof that the challenge he presents to us comes ultimately not from him, but from ourselves."

It may be that sport will provide opportunities for all people to meet this challenge but it may also happen that the Olympic Games and other top-level international competitions will change their character. There are indications that the U.S.S.R. will press for more and more sports to be included in the Olympic programme, for instance, parachuting, aerobatics and motor-racing, so that the Games become too vast for staging by any city other than one supported massively by a wealthy central government. The Russians may also press for the enlargement of the I.O.C. to such dimensions that it will be too unwieldy to exercise effective control and be a happy hunting ground for big powers. What could then happen is that the Olympic Games would be no more than a testing ground for two great political units. There would be no difficulty in training *élite* teams of participants whose efficiency and skill would be superb but who would cease to be sportsmen, just as the professional athletes of the Mediterranean arenas ceased to be sportsmen during the last five hundred years of the ancient Olympic Games. The competitions would be keenly contested but as predominantly political occasions they would cease to share with humbler events that playful unreality which is essential to sport. It remains to be seen whether the international bodies can so frame their regulations that a limit can be set to the political and financial exploitation of the best performers which will preserve their character as sportsmen. Most of these bodies have not so far shown signs of recognizing the problem and the International Olympic Committee, which has begun to see it, has not been markedly successful in finding a solution.

International sport is like an iceberg; a small part consisting of the Olympic Games and other world championships is seen, but most international contests go on unnoticed by Press or people. It is at this level that sport may have its greatest impact on world affairs. In his *Reith Lectures* in 1948 Bertrand Russell argued that the savage in each one of us must find some outlet not incompatible with civilized life and with the happiness of his equally savage neighbour. He suggested that sport might provide such outlets and that what was wrong with our civilization was that such forms of competition formed too small a part of the lives of ordinary men and women. Men must compete for superiority and it is best that they do so in contests which yield utterly useless results. This is not to say that the results do not matter. They matter supremely and if they do not they will not satisfy man or nation, but in sport victory is never for all time nor is defeat irreparable. The individual, the team, the nation, even the ideological block lives to fight another day.

The enormous growth of sport as a World-wide phenomenon may herald the birth of a new Olympic ideal and a new asceticism, an asceticism which looks to achievement and prowess in play as an end in itself. The final conclusion then is a paradox; sport, if it is pursued as an end in itself, may bring benefits to man which will elude his grasp if he treats it as little more than a clinical, a social or a political instrument to fashion those very benefits.

BIBLIOGRAPHY

1. MOLYNEUX, D. D., *Central Government Aid to Sport and Physical Recreation in Countries of Western Europe* (University of Birmingham, 1962).
2. JOKL, E. *et al.*, *Sports in the Cultural Pattern of the World* (Helsinki, 1956).
3. COZENS, F. W. and STUMPF, F., *Sports in American Life* (Chicago, 1953).

SEE ALSO

INTERNATIONAL OLYMPIC COMMITTEE, *Bullotino*.
RUSSELL, BERTRAND, *Authority and the Individual* (London, 1949).
TOYNBEE, A., *Civilization on Trial* (London, 1948).
UNESCO, *The Place of Sport in Education* (Paris, 1956).

POLITICAL IDEOLOGY AND SPORT IN THE
PEOPLE'S REPUBLIC OF CHINA AND THE SOVIET UNION

MARTHA M. SEBAN

> Just as the responsibility of struggling for the task of communism
> stands before them [young people]; so they must have strong and
> healthy bodies, must have a steel will and torso to meet this re-
> sponsibility.
>
> —V. Lenin

> We should move a step forward in developing physical culture and
> sports among the broad masses, effectively strengthen the peoples
> physical constitution and heighten our country's physical and
> sports level.
>
> —Chou En-lai

Sport and physical education in the People's Republic of China and
the Soviet Union maintain a significant position within their respective
societies. What are the reasons for such prominence? Are the reasons for
these programs clearly evident within the context of the cultural and political frameworks of the respective Communist Parties? Objective investigation and an understanding of physical education and sport in China
and the Soviet Union may be achieved only when these programs are considered within the value structure of the individual culture.

The value orientation within the political system of China places high
priority on the "collective good." Individual concern for social status receives low priority. According to Chairman Mao, "To serve the people
is the highest goal" (14:151). Honesty, hard work, frugality and sacri-
ficing for production is highly esteemed (14:151). Stress is also placed
on civic virtue, loyality, the Party, and the country. Kinship and clan ties

Printed by permission of the author.

which were held in high regard in pre-Communist China are deplored by the Communist Party.

> The Communists have engaged in carrying out a social revolution to bring into being eventually an ideal classless society in which there is no exploitation of one person by another and one in which the basic needs of all people are met (14:115).

Acceptance of the state value system by all Chinese is the goal of the Communist Party.

The multinational society of the Soviet Union contains a variety of traditionally held beliefs. Russian traditions are the most prominent in the Soviet Union. Russia, for centuries has dominated the Soviet Union "numerically, culturally and politically" (4:262). Characteristically, the Russian people have had a great emotional sense of "love of land" and a desire for unity. "The spirit of collectivity . . . became one of the values most emphatically preached by the Communist Party of the Soviet Union" (4:263). Hard work is also highly regarded but not as an end in itself. Labor is thought to be a major aspect of the continuous development of the socialist state. Individual endeavor for the good of the collective also brings high recognition. "Individuals are urged not to be selfish, but to consider other people, and to work for the good of all people" (4:269).

China and the Soviet Union are committed to political doctrines and ideologies predicated on the teaching of Marx and Lenin. Political commitments to socialism[1] as advocated by Marxist and Leninist theory are extended throughout all aspects of society—cultural, educational, economical, agricultural, and industrial. The political framework of the Chinese and Soviet Communist Parties provides the impetus for fostering and disseminating socialist ideology throughout all cultural activity. The Marxist-Leninist philosophy is inculcated in all citizens of the Soviet Union through all aspects of life. The intent is that every citizen achieve a "high sense of Soviet Patriotism and an attitude of sincere respect for the great Communist Party of the Soviet Union" (3:8). Similarly, in the People's Republic of China, "the whole range of human activities and thinking processes is defined, explained and rationalized in the language of Marxism-Leninism as interpreted by Mao and Mao Tse-Tung thought" (14:252). Although China and the Soviet Union subscribe to the same fundamental doctrine, ideology within these two systems differs accord-

1. The Soviet Union and People's Republic of China are referred to as "communist" by most Westerners. "*Socialism*, in their [Soviet, Chinese] terminology, is a transitional stage between capitalism and communism, during which all citizens are required to contribute to the building of Communism" (4:3).

ing to their interpretation. These interpretive differences have resulted in ideological conflict between the Chinese and the Soviets. Sino-Soviet disagreements which have gradually widened since approximately 1956 appear to be the result of dispute over ideology. The Chinese have responded to the Soviets "unorthodox" interpretation of Marxist-Leninist political, economic, and social doctrine as being *revisionist* or *counter-revolutionary* in nature (14:3-4). The flexibility in interpretation of political doctrine is noted here since it may account for contrasts to be noted later in Chinese and Soviet physical education and sport programs.

Justification for all sport programs stems from Marxist-Leninist philosophy. This philosophy holds physical education as an integral part of the socialist system. Marx maintained that["productive labor must be joined with education and physical education. [For] this is not only one means of increasing socialist production but it is the one and only means of bringing forth man's complete development"] (5:85). Physical education, according to Marxist philosophy, should receive the attention equal to intellectual education, productive labor and polytechnical education (5:85). Leninist philosophy also advocates physical education as an integral part of society.

Lenin suggested that:

> Just as the responsibility of completing the task of Communism stands before young people, just as the responsibility of struggling for the task of Communism stands before them; so they must have strong and healthy bodies, must have a steel will and torso to meet this responsibility (5:86).

The basic premise underlying sport and physical education philosophies is the firm belief that the people's health and fitness are directly related to increased industrial and agricultural production, as well as developing a people capable of defending the nation. S. Pavlov, Chairman of the Soviet Committee on Physical Culture and Sports, points out that:

> The principle aim and the major meaning of the development of physical culture and sports in our socialistic society lie in the active promotion of the comprehensive, harmonious development of the individual, in the preparation of every citizen of the U.S.S.R. for highly productive work and for the defense of socialism, and in the organization of a healthy way of life and recreation for the people (7:5-6).

The People's Republic of China also adheres to the Marxist-Leninist philosophy of physical education. This philosophy has been reinforced by political leaders, the most noted being Mao Tse-tung. In his speech "On the Correct Handling of Contradictions Among the People" Mao stated that: "Our educational policy must enable everyone who gets an education to develop morally, intellectually, and physically, and become a socialist-minded worker" (5:86-87). Additional supportive statements have been made periodically by China's leaders. The people have been called upon to "extend physical activity to serve production and national defense," "develop physical culture and sports, and strengthen health so as to serve socialist construction" (5:87). Essentially these directives support the Marxist-Leninist philosophy that sport and physical education contribute to the total well-being of the individual, and hence the society.

Implementation of these philosophies is under the jurisdiction of the respective Parties of these two nations. The nature of the Soviet system is such that no institution is exempt from Party control (4:4). Similarly in China the "infallibility of Party leadership" is another characteristic of Chinese Communist ideology. This concept of Party leadership

> has encouraged the notion that devout and unquestioning acceptance of Party authority and spontaneous participation in the Party movement would help to impel the people toward the height of communist virtue, that is, the selfless man motivated only by the desire to work for the good of the collectivity (14:253).

This feature of Communist ideology results in centralized state governing of all sport and physical education programs. This primarily includes strong administrative control at the national level. The Committee on Physical Culture and Sports is responsible for overseeing all aspects of sport and physical culture. This committee is part of the federal organization of the U.S.S.R. Council of Ministers. Through this organization and

> the constant attention and solicitude of the Party, the Soviet system of physical education and sports activities has achieved a level of development unprecedented in history and has demonstrated its strength and superiority (7:5).

Incorporating physical culture into the daily life of the people, strengthening Soviet athletes and advancing scientific methods in physical culture research are the primary areas of concern of the Committee.

The major body which provides for leadership and promotion of sport in the People's Republic of China is the Physical Culture and Sports Commission. The Chinese have established a governing body which functions, at the national level, in conjunction with the Chinese Communist Party. The Physical Culture and Sports Commission (PCSC) contains an encorporated body entitled the All China Athletic Federation (ACAF). The primary function of the PCSC is administrative while the ACAF appears to be concerned with the practical application and implementation of sport and physical education programs. The significance of the ACAF is found in the duplication of its organizational structure on the provincial and local level. This provides for regional as well as national promotion of sport and physical education activities. The ACAF has three main offices supervising numerous responsibilities of the Federation. These three divisions, which function at all levels of government include the Offices for Mass Sports, Competition and Training Organization (10). Duplication of the national model at the provincial, city and district level is based on the premise that implementation of programs is more efficient.

One of the major objectives of the Chinese and Soviet programs is to provide the masses with opportunities for improving their health and fitness level. The Soviets maintain that

> . . . the basis of our sports is their mass character, the accessibility of all forms of sports to the public at large. Since the aim of all sports activities is to improve public health, the Soviet state and trade unions allot large sums for building sports stadiums and sports centers, and training coaches for physical culture and sports (13:24).

Participation in sport is fostered through school physical education, mass exercise, fitness, and programs generally affiliated with the individual's place of employment. Competitive sport opportunities are also available to students at the school, city, district provincial (republic in U.S.S.R.), national and international levels.

Fitness programs of these two countries are probably one of the most important examples of the concern for the health of the people. Youths in the Soviet Union, throughout their school life, are tested to determine their capabilities in activities such as gymnastics, track and field events, swimming and paramilitary events. This category includes grenade throwing, rifle shooting, and parachute jumping. Various levels of achievement are determined through the GTO system. GTO is the abbreviation of the Russian words "Ready for Labor and Defense." This fitness program consists of three levels, the tasks becoming progressively more difficult at each stage (6:41). BGTO, "Getting Ready for Labor and Defense," is a preliminary level for school children approximately twelve to fifteen years of age. The first level GTO is for young men and women sixteen to eighteen. The second level is for men and women nineteen and older. The awards given for achieving national standards for each level are GTO badges. Those who attain these awards are highly commended, since achievement of these fitness standards indicate the individual's ability to defend the nation.

The Chinese also employ a national fitness program as a means of emphasizing the importance of exercise. Students are periodically tested in tasks which determine individual strength, agility, speed, endurance

and militarily associated tasks. Information on the specific activities performed and the frequency with which they are administered is not available. Awards are given usually in the form of a badge or pin and identification card. The standards which determine individual level of
achievement are also currently unavailable. Compared to the Soviet GTO
program, the Chinese system appears less specific in terms of publishing
criteria levels of performance. However, the intent is similar. Both nations
are striving to improve the health of their citizens. The capability of
each person to contribute to the defense of the country is also a concern.

Mass exercise programs are another means of emphasizing the need
for physical activity. The basic exercise plan takes approximately five to
ten minutes to perform. It is performed by school children, factory and
agricultural workers, small groups in a park, and families. Each radio
broadcast day, in both China and Russia, is begun with a recording of
the prescribed exercises. In China, broadcasts are frequently transmitted
over public address systems at approximately five thirty in the morning.
This type of public broadcasting is not employed in all cities but was
noted in Kwangchow and in Shichiachuang (10). The intent is to expose
to as many people as possible the importance of beginning each day
with physical activity. It is not uncommon to see groups of people, young
and old, gathered together in a park during the early morning hours faith-
fully exercising. It was also learned that students begin each school day
by performing routine calisthenics. For example, at the Ping Shan Road
Middle School in Tientsin regular morning exercises precede all academic classes. Workers in a cotton textile factory were also observed to
have two ten minute exercise breaks during their eight hour work shifts.
Those workers who hold sedentary positions are often given additional
periods of time for physical activity.

Two questions arise when discussing the fitness and mass exercise
programs of China. First, what is China's concept of physical fitness?
Second, how effective is the daily exercise plan in contributing to the
improvement of one's fitness level? One may only speculate in seeking
to provide answers to these questions. It may be surmised from discussions with some of China's sport leaders that fitness refers to one's general physical well-being. Fitness appears to be directly related to efficiency in contributing to the productivity of the nation. The Vice
Chairman of the Tientsin Branch of the All China Athletic Federation
pointed out that the Office of Mass Sport was responsible for "investigating the fitness level of the people and paying attention to their health"
(10). Fitness tests include a medical exam and a report on the overall
condition of the people. The tests also include push-ups, sit-ups, and
pull-ups. No other specific tasks were noted by the ACAF representative.

The frequency with which these tests are administered and the percentage of the total population tested are not known.

It must be noted that possibly the Chinese do not conceive of "fitness" in the same manner of speaking as do the Soviets or, for that manner, most Westerners. Fitness tests administered to school children which indicate the youths' levels of endurance, agility, strength and speed are probably most indicative of our concept of fitness.

The effectiveness of the mass exercise program in promoting physical fitness may not, at this point, be accurately determined. The intent of these exercise plans in factories and other places of employment appears to be directed at relieving tension and fatigue. The benefits of such exercise would seem to be temporary. One may surmise that the production rate of a factory or commune is a primary concern. One may further speculate that the Chinese view a direct correlation between work capacity and level of fitness.

Another related area of inquiry concerns the reasons why people engage in routine exercises. Are they genuinely concerned for their health or are the people responding to strong direction by the government? Again, one may speculate that encouragement by the state is probably the primary motivator. The Chinese have not convinced all people of the value of exercise. They have pointed out that there is some difficulty in persuading all people the importance of physical activity (10). For example, the representative of the All China Athletic Federation in Peking pointed out some of the shortcomings in the implementation of programs. He suggested that often people need to be better informed of the need for exercise. He said "youth rationalize they are fit and the old say they are too elderly to exercise" (10). Some factory cadres maintain that work is of primary concern, whereas some secondary school administrators favor study and work over physical education. These attitudes impede the progress of implementing sport programs. The ACAF representative further maintained that what is of greater concern is that those presenting opposition to programs are not adhering to Chairman Mao's idea to develop morally, intellectually and physically (10).

The need for an increased number of people to carry out the philosophy of sport for the masses is a constant concern. The Chinese have directed their efforts, particularly since the Cultural Revolution in 1949 and again during the Great Proletariate Cultural Revolution from 1966 to 1969, toward achieving this goal. The structural organization of China's sport hierarchy appears sound. However, disseminating the various aspects of sports programs according to socialist philosophy in such a relatively brief time to approximately 800 million people has been a monumental task. In contrast, the Soviet Union has been able to produce a more established sports program due to a smaller population of approximately 240 million and a longer time period. Consequently, rapid achievement of the goals calling for involvement of the masses in exercise and development of their health has been more difficult for the Chinese than the Soviets. The philosophies of the Chinese are sound, their efforts are sincere, and their determination strong—all reinforced by the will to succeed in their endeavors. Sport and physical culture programs seek to provide opportunities to develop the potentialities of all people, workers, laborers, cadres, peasants, students, and members of the People's Liberation Army. Chairman Mao declared in 1955:

> "The masses have boundless creative power. They can organize themselves and concentrate on places and branches of work where they can give full play to their energy; they can concentrate on production in breadth and depth and create more and more undertakings for their own well being."
> (Mao Tse-Tung, 1955, 8:118)

Sport programs of China are organized and directed toward achieving the goals of the state.

Fostering political thought, integrating the masses, and promoting nationalism are three political concerns which are also furthered through sport. The Soviets and the Chinese have viewed sport as a means of unifying the peoples of their respective nations. The Soviets have sought to achieve a type of class integration by providing a common experience through sport. This integration of the Soviet people provides a commonality of all peoples working towards increased productivity of the nation (2:140) Utilizing sport as a tool for bringing the people together is supported by the Chairman of the Soviet Committee on Physical Culture and Sport. He has suggested that "sports as spectator events broadcast by the mass media have a stimulating effect on a person's mood, arousing his energy, instilling optimism, and promoting his inculcation with the feeling of socialist patriotism" (7:6).

The People's Republic of China has also turned to sport as a medium for seeking commonality among the masses. Class struggle is a major part of revolution in overcoming elitism. One of the responsibilities of the party organizations outlined in Chapter IV of the Constitution of the Communist Party of China is to:

> Give constant education to the Party members and the broad revolutionary masses concerning class struggle between the two lines and lead them in fighting resolutely against the class enemy (11:257).

Kolatch has noted that in China "Physical culture serves not only the people's health, national defense and production, but also inspires the collective work spirit necessary for national unity which is a prerequisite to national construction" (5:94-95). Kolatch further suggests that participating in team sports teaches unity and cooperation while performing daily exercises with fellow workers provides a sense of togetherness in commitment (5:95).

Another concept held by the Chinese that lends itself to preventing elitism is that of "Friendship First, Competition Second" in all athletic contests. The Chinese have expressed the belief that friendship is eternal while winning and losing are temporary. Before the beginning of any contest, whether local or national, the teams acknowledge each other with the greeting "we learn from you" (10). Winning and losing create a separation between two groups by identifying one group superior to the other. In the interest of maintaining the socialist ideology of a classless society, the Chinese, until recently, were not concerned with identifying scores with outcomes of contests. Reports of contests, even at the National level, were made without mention of who won or lost. The Chinese identified the practice of reporting scores with "imperial chauvinism" (10). However, adherence to this aspect of the party value structure appears to have been relaxed. The party position now seems to recognize that games may be played with the intent of winning not only friends but the contest as well.

Integration of political ideology and doctrine is also sought through participation in sport. Carr (1) has expressed the idea that "the progressive development of socialism depends upon the socialist consciousness of each individual. Sport contributes to the development of political conviction because of the possibilities it provides for 'collective' training" (1:72). According to Stern, "it was thought that positive attitudes toward labor and hard work could be inculcating by having everybody, including school attenders participate in socially useful labor" (12:129). However, given the advanced industrial economy and accompanying distinction between labor and the elite, the Soviets have found this concept difficult to employ. As a result, all citizens have been given equal opportunity to participate in leisure time activities—sport, art, music, drama, etc. "Politics take command" has been the slogan of the Chinese and the Soviets since the take-over of the Communist governments. This aspect of the socialist system ultimately seeks to unify the people. Sport is a medium which assists in implementing the teachings of the Party line. In China, Jung Kao-t'ang, a member of the Chinese sport bureaucracy during the pre-cultural Revolution period, in an article entitled "Let Physical Culture Better Serve Socialist Construction" maintained that "dependence on the Party for leadership and adherence to the policy takes command" (5:90). This slogan, with reference to sport and physical education in

China, means "that political principles are to serve as the guideline for sports" (5:91). According to the Party line, sport has a distinct purpose. That purpose is to contribute to the goals of the government. The general aims of the state are to achieve socialism. According to this premise, the bourgeois concepts of 'sport for the sake of sport' and 'sport as an end in itself' bear no validity (5:91). The Soviet Union and the People's Republic of China utilized sport to meet political ends—a concept most Westerners feel uncomfortable in acknowledging.

To summarize, sport programs in China and the Soviet Union are directed by political control and guided by political ideology. The intent of this discussion has been to present explanations for the significance of sport and physical education programs in these two nations. The organizational structure of sport programs is directly related to the government at the national level. Programs are sanctioned according to Marxist-Leninist philosophies of education. Interpretation of these tenets appear to be based upon the political ideologies of the respective nations.

Encouragement of fitness and mass exercise programs illustrates the concern of government leaders for the physical well-being of the people. The primary purpose of these programs appears to be directed toward developing physically strong citizens who actively contribute to the productivity and defense of the nation. Sport functions not only to meet the needs of the people but also to fulfill the political objectives of the government. It serves to unify the masses and provide a medium for fostering political thought. The intensity which sport serves to fulfill these objectives differs within the Chinese and Soviet systems.

The organizational structure of sport programs in the People's Republic of China is patterned according to the Soviet prototype. China's programs in administration and implementation are not as advanced as those of the Soviet Union. However, the constant determination and confidence the Chinese have in their own self-reliance may ultimately contribute to extensive programs at all levels of involvement.

REFERENCES

1. Carr, G. A. "The Application of Marxist Leninist Philosophy to Physical Education in the German Democratic Republic," *Canadian Journal of History and Physical Education*, III. no. 2, (December, 1972), 62.
2. Jernigan, Sarah S. "A Composite of Olympic Sports Development," *The Physical Educator*, XXIII, no. 3 (October, 1966), 140.
3. Kalinin, Alexie. *The Soviet System of Public Education*. Moscow: Novosti Press Agency Publishing House, 1973.

4. Keefe, Eugene K. et al. *Area Handbook for the Soviet Union,* U.S. Government Printing Office, Washington, 1971.
5. Kolatch, Jonathan. *Sport, Politics and Ideology in China.* New York: Jonathan David Publishers, 1972.
6. Morton, Henry W. *Soviet Sport,* Collier Books, U.S.A., 1963.
7. Pavlov, S. "Organized Physical Education and Sports Popularized on the Mass Level," *Soviet Education,* XVI, no. 4, (February, 1974), p. 4.
8. ———. *Quotations From Chairman Mao Tse-Tung.* Peking: Foreign Languages, 1972.
9. Roberts, Glyn. "Physical Education in Russia," *Physical Education Around the World,* Phi Epsilon Kappa, Indianapolis, 1966.
10. Seban, Martha M. Interviews and Observations, Physical Education and Sport Study Tour, Peoples' Republic of China, April, 1974.
11. Snow, Edgar. *The Long Revolution.* New York: Vintage Books, 1972.
12. Stern, Robert. "Socialization and Political Integration Through Sports and Recreation," *Physical Educator,* (October, 1968), p. 129.
13. ———. "The Music Movement," *Soviet Youth: Life as They See It.* Moscow: Novasti Press Agency, 1973.
14. Whitaker, Donald P., and Shinn, Rin-Sup, et al. *Area Handbook for the Peoples' Republic of China,* U.S. Government Printing Office, Washington, 1972.

INTERNATIONAL SPORTS AND THE SOCIAL SCIENCES

Robert Kropke

No team or individual merely wins or loses an athletic competition any more. One is either toppled, eked out, rocked, trounced, routed, staggered, vanquished, or some timely combination thereof. But the violent intrusion of a Middle East war into the international sport arena vaporized an Olympics, as winning and losing were dramatically accentuated as little more than relative states in international relations. Myths of friendly competition were virtually extinguished. Millions of viewers were exposed to international athletics as significant social and political events of global import. Through the technological eavesdropping of global communications, the world citizenry has also witnessed individual demonstrations adumbrating domestic turmoil, such as black athletes manifesting their racial pride and discontent. Sporting events have frequently escalated from blasé festivity to hard-core international politics, with competitions employed as political tools, reflections of domestic schism, propaganda showcases, or economic lures and catalysts. National athletic heroes, a Nurmi, Keino, or Pelé, embody a nation's athletic prowess, and help secure sovereign recognition in the international political sphere. True, politicians have often thrown out the first ball, booted the initial goal, or dropped the first puck. But now millions see it, and not only a sports contest but an international political and social event is the occasion.

Such a significant transnational activity as international sport has been politely disregarded by the social sciences, particularly in the United States (US), as being a topic suitable only for a section in the newspapers.

From *Quest*, Monograph XXII (June, 1974): 25-32.

Political scientists and sociologists have regularly ignored such mundane nongovernmental activities as athletics, content to restrict what may be the globe's most ubiquitous behavior patterns to a few columns or box scores. Thus a tremendous sea of research potential has yet to be fished in, as social science continues to concentrate on more conventional, "scholarly" subjects.

This brief essay is an attempt to whet the appetite of social science for international sport as a topic of research worthy of more than the peripatetic glances and skeptical smiles it now receives. It is hoped that further ideas will mature into a greater realization of the social and political aspects of international sport, a transnational activity permeating world interaction patterns.

On the recent calendar there are more than enough stimulating international examples. Nigeria hosted the Pan-African Olympics in Lagos. The Associated Press dubbed a teenage Soviet gymnast as the woman athlete of the year. Colorado rejected the 1976 Winter Olympics. A black American tennis pro, once barred from competing in South Africa, was extended a tournament invitation. The Eastern European nations, particularly the USSR and the German Democratic Republic, continue to expand their presence and press their domination of international sport.

Headlines such as the above are not merely random events of momentary insignificance, but integral parts of more extensive international patterns of behavior which increase our overall awareness and understanding of global interactions. Granted, not all international sporting events are of equal social or political significance, but many possess such salience that they cannot be overlooked. The US men and women's basketball teams visited the Peoples' Republic of China (PRC) last year and played a series of exhibitions with the national teams of the PRC. To mark this historic encounter between the two teams and their representative nations, Chiang Ching personally received the American entourage, attired in a western dress and shoulder bag. In addition to being the wife of Chairman Mao Tse-Tung, Chiang Ching also functions as the cultural director of the PRC, a position of no small political significance. She had not worn a western dress for 27 years, nor is she known to sinologists as being particularly pro-Western, to say the least. Madame Chiang's appearance was another important symbolic indicator of the US-China rapprochement, a political event intertwined with international sports.

In recent years the German Democratic Republic has embarked on an extensive sports program, the results of which are just now coming to the international fore. Such a nationwide effort, a penetrating domestic commitment of both financial and human resources, rates the East German program as a vital component in that government's multilateral drive for international recognition and status.

There is little question but that national governments exhibit a serious concern for their international images. International athletic stature is an integral factor in these projections of nationalism. At times such anxieties have bordered on myopic obsessions, as in Mexico City, 1968. Student riots and demonstrations were brutally suppressed in harried efforts to restore some semblance of domestic order and stability before welcoming the Olympics.

The varied functions, thrills, and controversies that accompany international sport are not developments solely of this age. Surely the Olympic Games of the ancient world provided similar subjects for discourse and analysis. At the very least such athletic festivals were opportunities for reaffirming control and displaying the manifold greatness of the empire.

Previous writings on athletic encounters (Lüschen, 1970) have drawn our attention to the mutual consent of opponents, the similarity of beliefs and values, and rules of reciprocity. Athletics have been cited as possessing essential attributes for socialization, integration, and a general reinforcement of the social structure. Sports teams are points of identification with other social systems, such as nations. Rivalries emanating from external sources may be introduced into a sports contest, and lead to dissociation, and in extreme cases, to severe conflict. Friendly relations can experience strain following sports incidents, such as the endangered diplomatic relations between West Germany and Sweden following a 1962 soccer game. Such observations should set functionalists and neo-functionalists alike on a re-evaluation tour. The basic structure of a sport content often allows teams of conflicting systems to associate well; but one should rarely expect improvements in relations between these systems because of such contests. Athletic competition does not possess some innate force which guarantees that it is conducive to "good will and understanding."

There are active efforts toward a Sociology of Sports in Europe, with scholars examining the economic, political, and cultural aspects of international competition (Groll & Strohmeyer, 1970; Jokl, 1956). The comparative studies across nations, the case studies, the social psychology and group studies serve to heighten our awareness to the fact that international sports receive far more public coverage than academic outputs. The swelling international communications system possesses enormous potentials for influencing its viewers socially and politically. The fact that different social classes attend or follow different sports is an interesting subject in itself, even before pursuing such observations into measurements of the types and amount of leisure time available to various populations throughout the world. Why, for example, do the newly affluent of Nigeria now play golf? One proposition appears to be recurrent: the communist countries utilize sport as a social control, to channel activity to party goals, while the West, and especially the US, has a casual "athletic approach," a naive outlook toward the significance of East-West sport competitions and their political implications.

Authors such as Natan (1969) have indicted international athletics as solely propaganda weapons. Via the incitement of inherent nationalistic "instincts," such contests are viewed as encompassing new methods of psychological warfare. In the Cold War mold they have become a ritualistic struggle of one national community versus another. Olympic athletes are indoctrinated with grotesque conceptions of national prestige. International sport is castigated for its puerile ivory tower stance in a world of *realpolitik*. Fifty Hungarians seeking political asylum in the West during the Melbourne Olympics lends some credence to this paradigm.

As if it were a required quadrennial exercise for sports writers, the Olympics is lambasted as a testing ground for two separate political blocs. International sport transforms itself into an arena for ideologies, reflecting the identical tensions on the political plateau. It often appears that such confrontations serve only to incite latent chauvinistic impulses, as the individual performers are somehow enveloped by the event. The athlete is prostituted by the economics and politics of the actual competition. Victories are mystically trumpeted as evidence of "successful societies," symbols of national vitality and prestige, as sports are fully integrated into the global political system.

Looking beyond the baroque trappings of Olympic gatherings, the observer becomes aware of the less salient, but persistent transnational sport competitions. Such extensive activities are continually penetrating and transgressing national borders. Nation-states have appeared to acquiesce in this network involvement as a necessary fee for entrance into the global sports community. Successful international athletic participation is viewed as a requisite accoutrement for national sovereignty. The intensive hockey and soccer programs of the PRC are excellent examples of a people preparing to enter more fully into global athletic affairs by mastering the more universal sports.

It is difficult to avoid discussion of the Olympics, as these events have been *realpolitik* since their inception. The morbid gears of Hitler's propaganda machine exploited such an occasion to the hilt, both for national and international purposes, solidifying nationalism at home, and impressively packaging the proceedings for export (Mandell, 1971). Berlin was cherished as a great psychological victory for Hitler, Nazi superiority and self-confidence, while ironically scoring points for Germany in the "peaceful image" column. Berlin 1936 underlined the malleability of sports competitions as propaganda tools. Most unfortunate was the exploitation of the athlete as society's tool, cheered only as an impersonal unit of propaganda. The individual athlete was now more than ever a national asset of political importance, de-individualized in the face of drives for patriotic supremacy.

In various forms the Berlin precedent has been repeatedly utilized. In 1964 Sukarno organized the Asian Olympics, the Games for the New Emerging Forces (GANEFO), as a political thrust at the US and the International Olympic Committee (IOC) in retaliation for the exclusion of Indonesia from the 1964 Olympics (Pauker, 1965). Indonesia had excluded Israel and Taiwan from the 1963 Asian Games, and Sukarno expelled the Vice President of India, who had attempted to intercede on behalf of the rebuffed teams. The IOC then barred Indonesia from the Olympics, prompting Sukarno to stage his own anti-Olympic, anti-colonialist, anti-imperialist games.

GANEFO was also employed to divert attention from Indonesia's internal problems. Sukarno emphasized the united effort of the newly emerging Third World, stressing pride and prestige. With all the communist countries in attendance, Indonesia used this forum to project an image of strength and influence. It was a pure example of "people-to-people diplomacy," as all the athletics were given tours of the country, with extended doses of the indigenous culture and national image of friendliness. GANEFO served as China's debut in international competition, with the PRC sending the largest team, many cultural groups, and the funds to pay the total bill. Ironically, the sports complex which hosted the games was constructed with Soviet aid, while the highway linking the complex with Djakarta was US made.

Over 20 years ago Fuoss (1951) examined the Olympics from a functionalist perspective. He assumed that sports provide a common basis for international understanding, positive experiences for the individual competitors and international relations in general. The Olympics were found to be incapable of transcending nationalism and politics. The detrimental incidents were continually magnified out of proportion. National pride was a permeating factor in such contests. Through the decades, however, it appears that international sports has evidenced a resilience, an ability to recover from political abuses. This hypothesis alone opens wide fields for research concerning conflict behavior and peace.

It may well be the case that such extravaganzas are an opportunity for nation-states to display their colors other than through armed conflict. International athletic contests may be cathartic experiences, peaceful outlets for national pride and frustration.

Sport as a substitute religion is another interesting framework (von Kortzfleisch, 1970). Athletics do possess an ideology, classical Olympic-religious elements, and physical development ideals. The Olympics can be compared to a super-religion, expected to bring peace on earth, with the glorification of amateurism, equality, and the purity of morals, as embodied in the oath. "In reality the Olympics is a political-religious-secular syncretism for all to be happy in [p. 235]," a mythical buffet with something for everyone.

Pondering whether international sport is a national or international force for the advancement of civilization is akin to a lifelong search for the left arm of the *Victory of Samothrace*. Such ethereal thoughts of athletics as a teleological force or a moral contribution to mankind vaporize into irrelevance. Citing sports enthusiasm as indicative of a process of social, cultural and political maturation is following the time-worn path of comparing everyone else to those few affluent nation-states at the development peak. It is far more stimulating to ask, for instance, whether the lack of women in international sport, or more precisely, the lack of recognition of their athletic accomplishments, reflects their global social status.

Personal and social values (*Values in Sports,* 1963) appear to be inextricably linked with sports activities. American values, for example, have come under increasingly intense examination. Have the highly regarded sportsmanship concepts of the past lost their previous status and acceptance because of the introduction of mass audiences? What are the effects of the American high-powered promotion approach to sports? How prevalent is unethical conduct, or more significant, peoples' perceptions of such behavior?

The *Yearbook of International Organizations* (1972-73) lists over 120 organizations active in international sports. The work of organizations such as the International Society for Sports Psychology is rich and extensive, conveying the universality of this transnational activity. The organizations range from small regional federations to the global IOC. Almost every nation in the world partakes in transnational athletics. There are numerous organizations for coaches, referees, statisticians, doctors and educators, running the gamut to European workers and the disabled. An indepth mapping of this network and its overlaps with other organizational activities would afford us a clearer view of the international social system.

The International Olympic Academy meets annually in Greece to re-hash and reaffirm the ideals of fair play, good will, and understanding, continually attempting to keep the political, commercial, and racial issues from the Olympic ivory tower. The perennial concerns are for amateurism, rules, facilities, and the overall purity of the event. Little if any attention is devoted to the social and political ramifications of assembling thousands of people from a myriad of backgrounds. The human aspects of this global competition seem swallowed by the narrow concern for mechanics.

Perhaps in the near future the world will view the sports sovereignty of East Germany, those projected fruits of its annual $300 million pro-gram. Will the Organization of African Unity achieve the exclusion of white supremacist nations from world competition? Will Asians be al-lowed to compete for Kenya or Uganda in Montreal? Such developments will closely reflect the political and social policies, questions, and crises of the nations of the lower echelons attempting to cope with their posi-tions vis-à-vis the nations of the upper crust.

The lessons, tragedies, and nonlessons of Munich will be debated *ad nauseam*. Myths were crushed before one billion viewers. Nations ex-hibited a juvenile fear of political shame through athletic defeat. It is the winning, not the taking part, that clearly fuels the contest. Individual athletes have now been so sensitized by immersion into a state of political consciousness that they will scrutinize all aspects of their behavior to avoid political repercussions. Government control of national Olympic committees and other national sports bodies appears to be increasing. Many Latin American and East European nations already have ministers of sport or the equivalent, as such activities are an increasingly important element of international policy projections.

Newspaper sports commentary often resembles a ludicrous scene of nationalism, as the British castigate the "filthy" play of the English Rugby Team as a "national disgrace." Americans worry about their flag bearer of Czechoslovakian descent dipping the colors during an Olympic cere-mony particularly when she is a peace militant who petitions against the Vietnam War. It is a "national disgrace" when Team Canada woefully struggles against a Soviet team that it had previously tagged second-rate competition.

In recent years it has become all too clear that such athletic commit-tees as the IOC have been overtaken by the events of *realpolitik* (John-son, 1972). Such self-perpetuating groups have been out of step with reality, relegated to anachronistic pedestals by high-powered international relations. Yet even a de Coubertin idealist such as Avery Brundage real-izes that the Winter Olympics are little more than a showcase for winter sports equipment, since two-thirds of the world's population has rarely if ever even seen snow. International sport appears to be exploited by the institutionalization process. After a period of adolescent excitement, the sports are forgotten and the politics and economics of the events become the ultimate goals. Yet a nation will crown its victories with the superiority of liberal democracy and free enterprise, and cry foul and "injection of politics" when it loses. The winning nation is mystically claimed more virtuous than the loser.

The petty claims are frequently eclipsed, however, by sports competitions providing the catalyst for international violence. Israeli forces retaliated against Syria and Lebanon following Munich. A double Czech victory over the USSR in the Hockey World Championships in Sweden, 1969, set off anti-Soviet protest riots throughout Czechoslovakia, as the nation erupted in vindication for the 1968 invasion. A soccer game between Honduras and El Salvador fell victim to a perennial border conflict, culminating in the Soccer War.

At present the USSR is pushing political efforts to secure Moscow as the site of the 1980 Olympics. Following the recent incidents in Moscow involving the visiting Israeli and Chilean teams, UC and IOC machinations in the face of the Soviet campaign will provide an excellent opportunity for studying governmental-nongovernmental interactions directly concerning a transnational activity.

International sports are often the only sources of awareness of other nations and peoples to which the general public is exposed. Such events may also be the only international awareness sought by a major portion of the citizenry. Those who do not have strong opinions, nor even interest in international relations, might well know who is the world's strongest man or fastest human. How many more people are aware of Tanzania when one of its runers sets the 1500 meter world record? What is the impact of the World Weightlifting Championships upon a city such as Columbus, Ohio? How do such events affect our international perceptions? Do athletes at this level experience role conflicts? To what degree do the viewers and participants experience attitude changes toward other nations and peoples? Perhaps sports activities are reliable indications of the utilization of leisure time, the level of affluence of a geographic area, or social class differentiations. Future research may confirm that sports are useful predictors, indicators, and symptoms of global structures and events, another litmus for social science to employ to increase our knowledge and understanding of the world.

Examples of international sports activities appear to fall into these primary functional categories: (a) the political *tool,* as with ping pong diplomacy; (b) the social and political *mirror* reflecting domestic problems, as with US black athletes demonstrating during Olympic ceremonies; (c) *propaganda showcases,* such as GANEFO and the Pan American Games; (d) *national outlets,* as with anti-Soviet riots following a hockey series; and (e) *economic showcases,* including each Olympic site. These crude categories can be juggled and abstracted further to distinguish international sports competitions functioning as *diversions* from internal problems, *substitutes* for more intense international conflict, *prestige symbols, socialization* processes, or activities primarily increasing *functional ties.*

The entire entourage of sports, the waves of athletic, economic, political, and technical personnel require classification and analysis. With developing nations seeking to employ their outstanding sport as a ticket to the international arena, the need is immediate for a closer examination of this phenomena within the context of global relations, peace research, and social sciences. The potential rewards in increased awareness and understanding are totally worthy of such efforts.

REFERENCES

Fuoss, D. *The Olympic games, revival.* (M.A. thesis, University of Oregon) Eugene: Microcard, The Ohio State University Library, 1951.

Groll, H., and Strohmeyer, H., eds. *Jugend und sport.* Vienna: International Seminar on the Sociology of Sport, 1970.

Johnson, W. *All that glitters is not gold: The Olympic games.* New York: Putnam, 1972.

Jokl, E. *Sports in the cultural pattern of the world: A study of the 1952 Olympic games at Helsinki.* Helsinki: Institute of Occupational Health, 1956.

Lüschen, G. Cooperation, association and contest. *Journal of Conflict Resolution,* 1970, 14, 21-34.

Mandell, R. *The Nazi Olympics.* New York: Macmillan, 1971.

Natan, R. Sport and politics. In J. Loy and G. Kenyon, eds. *Sport, culture and society.* New York: Macmillan, 1969.

Pauker, E. GANEFO I: Sports and politics in Djakarta. *Asian Survey,* 1965, 4 (4), 171-185.

Union of International Associations. *Yearbook of international organizations.* (14th ed.) Brussels: Union of International Associations, 1972.

Values in sports. Washington, D. C.: American Association for Health, Physical Education, and Recreation, 1963.

von Kortzfleisch, S. Religious Olympism. *Social Research,* 1970, 37, pp. 231-236.

BIBLIOGRAPHY

Section A. Social Systems—
1. Politics—

Edwards, Harry. "Munich Now, Montreal Next," *Intellectual Digest,* Dec. 1972.

Ganefo, I. "Sports and Politics in Djakarta," *Asian Survey* 5 (1965):171-85.

Green, A. W. *Recreation, Leisure and Politics*. New York: McGraw-Hill Books, 1964.

Hanna, W. R. "The Politics of Sport," Southeast Asia Series. New York: American Universities Field Staff, 1962.

Heinilä, K. "Notes on Inter-Group Conflicts in International Sport," *International Review of Sport Sociology* 1 (1966):29-40.

Kotlatch, J. *Sport Politics and Ideology in China*. New York: Jonathan David Pub., 1972.

Lapchick, Richard E. *Politics of Race and International Sport: The Case of South Africa*. Westport, Conn.: Greenwood, 1975.

Mandell, Richard. *The Nazi Olympics*. New York: Macmillan, 1970.

Morton, Henry. *Soviet Sport: Mirror of Soviet Society*. New York: Collier Books, 1963.

Natan, Alex. "Sport and Politics," in *Sport and Society*. London: Bowes & Bowes, 1958.

Padwe, Sandy. "Sports and Politics Must Be Separate—At Least Some Politics, That Is." *The Philadelphia Inquirer*, Dec. 14, 1971.

"Politics and Sports: The Deadly Game Nations Play." *Senior Scholastic* 102: 14-15, February 26, 1973.

Stone, Gregory. *Games, Sport and Power*. New Brunswick, N. J.: E. P. Dutton, 1971.

Washburn, J. W. "Sport as a Soviet Tool," *Foreign Affairs* 34 (1956):490-99.

SECTION

B

SOCIAL SYSTEMS:
2. ECONOMICS

The close association between sport and business has grown out of the American value of productivity and commercial opportunism. If anything looks like a potential commodity it will soon be exploited to full commercial potential. It is a cultural must to maximize profits even if the usefulness and quality of the commodity is compromised in the process. This process has been applied to sport in an uneven fashion. Professional golfers took control of their situation early. Boxers were victims of this system for a long time by overexposure on T.V. for commercial purposes. Will we see professional baseball, football, and basketball players bid themselves beyond the spectators paying potential?

The sporting goods market, recreational sport, school athletics, and professional women athletes are all affected by the economic situation of the culture and by the growing emphasis on sport as a commodity. The articles in this section give some information and insight into the diversity of the economic situation in sport.

Houston's Astrodome, which cost over $45,000,000, was opened in 1965. There has been a mania to outdo that stadium and undue the taxpayers ever since. The story is aptly recorded by Burck in the first article of this section. The monuments of past cultures have been pyramids, cathedrals, museums, and palaces. It seems that the culture of the United States is destined to leave the sports stadium, both domed and undomed, as the monument to the cultural focus of its society. Only earlier Roman culture can compete on such a grand scale as no contemporary society matches the stadium building of the United States. The only possible modern-day sequel are the sites prepared every four years for the Olympic games.

Gooding presents some revealing economic facts about "the tennis industry." He estimates that well over $500 million a year is spent on tennis—and that the amount is increasing at a rapid pace.

The economics of the sporting goods market is not as widely publicized as other aspects of the business of sports. Richard Snyder, an
economist, analyzed the market for the National Sporting Goods Association for many years. He reports that thirty or forty years ago the sporting goods market as an economic phenomenon was "hardly anything but
a nothing" but now is "very much of a something." The sporting goods
market, according to Snyder, topped one billion dollars for the first time
in 1947. Twenty years later in 1967, it was over 3 billion dollars.[1]

Although not specifically presented by any of the authors, it might
be interesting to investigate who spends most in the sporting goods market.
Gilbert, in an article in *Sports Illustrated* in 1965, stated: "Industry buys
more sport gear than all U.S. schools and colleges put together—at least,
so say the representatives of sporting goods manufacturers, who are very,
very high on industrial recreation."[2] By all appearances the recreational
spending in industry has continued over the past ten years.

The sporting goods market reports done by Irwin Broh, associates
for the National Sporting Goods Association, are obtained by an extremely
different process than the reports compiled for years by Richard Snyder.[3]
Snyder analyzed the sales of goods on the market, whereas Broh Associates now base their predictions on a consumer survey. The 1974 survey
was of unique interest as it reflects the first big effort by the government
to force consumers to conserve gasoline.

Rosalie Wright, Editor of *womenSports Magazine* adds the "last word"
to this section by defining professional sport and its entertainment value.
She puts right some uninformed views on the drawing power of professional women athletes and their right to equal prize money.

1. Richard Snyder, *Trends in the Sporting Goods Market: 1947-65,* Chicago, Illinois:
National Sporting Goods Association, 1965.
2. Bill Gilbert, "Sis-Boom-Bah! For Amalgamated Sponge," *Sports Illustrated* 22
(January 25, 1965):54.
3. Snyder, *Trends in the Sporting Goods Market: 1947-65.*

IT'S PROMOTERS vs. TAXPAYERS IN
THE SUPERSTADIUM GAME

CHARLES G. BURCK

The ubiquitous monument of urban America in the Seventies is the sports stadium. Nearly a score of these imposing edifices have been completed in cities across the nation in the past decade, and another seven are under construction or on the planning boards. Stadium promoters perceive them not just as homes for football and baseball teams, but as cultural assets that can attract tourists, fill hotels, and spill money out into the community in a variety of ways. As monuments, they are hardly the aesthetic equals of medieval cathedrals or the railroad stations of the nineteenth century—nobody has yet built the Chartres or even the Grand Central Terminal of stadiums. Still, today's great structures, like their distinguished antecedents, seem peculiarly to express the spirit of a time. They have come to symbolize a city's willingness to undertake ambitious projects, and they provide highly visible evidence of "big-league" status.

Civic pride can carry a high price tag, however, when expressed in concrete and steel. A relatively modest stadium can cost upwards of $30 million—and then fail to make enough money to pay for itself. Most, therefore, are financed with bonds issued by state, county, or city governments that are supposed to be paid off by revenues derived from the project. But in practice these revenue bonds almost always turn out to load an open-ended general obligation upon the taxpayer.

The taxpayer rarely understands what he is in for when a stadium project is first announced. To drum up public support, the advocates of a stadium generally understate the probable costs, which invariably balloon as construction proceeds. They also overstate probable revenues by

From *Fortune*, LXXXVII, No. 3 (March, 1973): pp. 104-107, 178-182.

anticipating multiple uses for the structure—rock concerts, races, fireworks displays, and conventions—that in actuality dwindle to a few. The stadium's recurring deficits prove to be much higher than promised, and the taxpayer discovers that civic pride has been compromised by special interests, blind boosterism, and inept planning. Tainted with deception, the "can-do" spirit becomes vitiated by a lingering bitterness that can undercut a city's ability to finance other and perhaps more important projects.

Even a seemingly simple, utilitarian stadium can expose the public pocket to unexpected depredations. Stadium planners are seldom inclined to think small, and their simple structures tend to become palaces. The reasons go beyond the obvious fact that frills cost money. Enchanted by monumentality, stadium promoters tend to assume too much utility, and allow themselves to be caught up in a process of feverish rationization to prove the economic soundness of the stadium they dream of.

IDEALIZING THE ASTRODOME

Nothing has done more to inflate the ambitions of stadium planners than Houston's glittering Astrodome, which cost $45,350,000. Ever since it was opened in 1965, stadium advocates across the land have cited it as the great, all-purpose civic monument that can serve not only as a community entertainment center but as a magnet for lucrative convention business. Besides being profitable and wonderfully useful, they say, the Astrodome has brought scads of new business to Houston.

Unfortunately, what has actually happened with the Astrodome is not exactly what its boosters elsewhere imagine it to be. Most convention activities are held not in the stadium but in an adjoining specially built hall. The Astrodome proved unsuitable for small-field sports—basketball, hockey, and the like—and Houston is about to build a new arena to house them. Nor is the Astrodome profitable, even though it has been able to attract many events like rodeos and motorcycle races. Late last year, when Houston moved to impose an annual tax of $385,000 on the stadium's operator, Astrodomain, Inc., the company produced figures showing that the dome itself had lost $569,000 in 1971. Astrodomain had made money only on its related enterprises: the Astros baseball team and the Astrodomain amusement park, hotel, and convention-hall complex. Even the monument's impact on Houston is debatable. Says Jay Taylor, economic-development manager of the Houston Chamber of Commerce, "I know of almost no case in which the Astrodome was a factor in a business' moving to Houston."

In any case, the Astrodome has produced a sort of dome mystique among stadium planners that seems to preclude consideration of anything *but* a dome. The experiences of two cities, Seattle and New Orleans, that are now building domed stadiums provide some chastening lessons for other cities that might dream of building a monument to sport.

By comparison with the Astrodome, Seattle's King County Multipurpose Stadium is a modest effort. Costing an estimated $43 million, including $5 million for land and site preparation, it will seat 65,000 people for football or 60,000 for baseball in a spare-looking building that will have exposed ramps and columns. The stadium was planned and promoted by a commission of local politicians and businessmen appointed by Washington's Governor Dan W. Evans in 1967, after two earlier proposals for stadiums had been turned down by the voters. To broaden public support for their plan, the commission and an organization of civic boosters, Forward Thrust, joined forces with Seattle's two daily newspapers to promote the domed and, hence, multipurpose utility of the proposed stadium.

A PLACE TO SEE THE PRESIDENTS

The commission was armed with a feasibility study by Western Management Associates, a Phoenix-based firm of economic consultants. But the commissioners drew rather selectively from the material compiled by Western Management, as well as from studies by other consultants. For instance, Western Management made no mention of conventions and minimized the chances of holding nonsports events in the stadium. Nevertheless, a brochure issued by Forward Thrust just prior to the vote on the bond issue promised that the stadium would offer, besides baseball and football, the opportunity for Seattle to "be playing host to the nation's largest conventions." Forward Thrust asserted that the stadium would be a place to see and hear "the world's most famous entertainers . . . Presidents of the United States and the great religious leaders of our times . . ." These events would be witnessed, Forward Thrust prophesied, from "warm, dry, cushioned seats on the dampest of Puget Sound days" at a modest cost to the taxpayers—only $1.21 per year over a ten-year period for the owner of a home assessed at $20,000. To assure widespread support, the commission let it be known that sites throughout the metropolitan area were being considered.

The voters of King County approved the stadium bonds. But once the vote was in, it turned out that the commission and its allies had just one site in mind. They favored the Seattle Center, a cultural and exhibition complex in downtown Seattle that includes the Space Needle and other structures from the 1962 World's Fair. Notes Victor Steinbrueck, a stadium opponent who is a professor of architecture at the University of Washington,"No politician could afford to come out against a downtown site."

In considering sites, the commission ignored its consultants' finding that the three best sites were suburban. Any one of them would be cheaper than the Seattle Center site, said the consultants, and would better serve the needs of King County because all would be more convenient to the suburbs, where most potential sports fans live. This preference for the suburbs enraged supporters of a downtown site. The morning *Post-Intelligencer,* in a front-page editorial, demanded (vainly) that the commission dismiss all its consultants.

The downtown business community immediately set up an Ad Hoc Committee for the Seattle Center Stadium Site under the leadership of Edward E. Carlson, then president of Western International Hotels, and now the head of United Air Lines. This group put together a report defending the Seattle Center site, glossing over the considerable problems of traffic access and congestion that had weighed against the site in the consultants' report. Gratefully accepting the Ad Hoc Committee's report, the commission voted to go ahead with construction at the Seattle Center.

But the issue was not yet settled. Washington, like several other western states, provides for citizen-originated legislative initiatives. A coalition of opponents—businessmen, lawyers, and architects among them—amassed enough petition signatures to put the choice of site on a special ballot. Despite a chorus of cries from politicians and press that "the people" wanted the stadium at the Seattle Center, the commission's site was voted down.

The opponents had won the battle, but they lost the war. When the commission called its consultants back to restudy sites, it had a new proposal to make. The Burlington Northern was abandoning 37.5 acres of railroad yards at the south end of the downtown area, and would sell the land at a reasonable price. The consultants found the site generally adequate. The commission quickly bought it, though critics maintain that the traffic and crowds will overwhelm nearby Pioneer Square, with its handsome old buildings, and the International District, where most of the city's Chinese, Japanese, and Filipino residents live.

FANS AND THEIR AUTOMOBILES

Unresolved troubles shadow the future success of the stadium itself. Standard rules of thumb call for 10,000 or more parking spaces for a

65,000-seat stadium, but only 2,500 will be provided. Stadium officials count on existing downtown parking capacity to ease the demand. They also hope, even less realistically, that many fans will travel to the stadium by bus; other cities have found it next to impossible to separate sports fans from their automobiles.

And driving to the stadium could prove difficult. Somebody—the city's taxpayers, most likely—will have to pay for ramps from the nearby freeway, and for several other major highway improvements. Seattle's mayor estimated late last year that these highway projects could cost $6,500,000 or more. Another large headache involving access arises from the stadium's proximity to major rail lines. The Burlington Northern and the Union Pacific have pointed out that there will continue to be heavy rail traffic through the area, and all roads leading to the site are at grade level. One or more of the streets leading to the stadium will have to be elevated above the tracks, at a cost of some $2 million.

There are other threats to the basic economic structure of the stadium. One is that at this point Seattle has neither baseball nor football franchises; its stadium is tenantless. The city will probably have to offer generous terms to attract ball clubs—if, indeed, it can find any willing to move. Nor will there be any convention income. In the past year Seattle has come to accept what Western Management told it in 1968—i.e., that stadiums are unsuitable places for conventions because of the way seats, utilities, and floor space are laid out. If Seattle is to have conventions at the stadium, they will have to be held in an adjoining hall that would cost an estimated $10,500,000, and there is no money at present to build it. The management of Seattle Center has reason to hope it will never be built; it fears that its own convention hall, a medium-sized one, will lose business if the new hall goes up.

One promising aspect of the King County Stadium is that the cost and quality of construction are being tightly controlled by Gerald R. Schlatter, manager of the county architect's office. Nevertheless, Seattle's domed stadium will cost far more than an open-air one of the same capacity. Such a stadium was proposed after the bond issue was approved, but it was not seriously considered. County Executive John Spellman argued that any deviation from the domed plan would represent a "breach of faith with the voters." Yet the domed stadium rising today is a far, far cry from the proposal approved by the voters in 1968. Even the promised cushioned seats have vanished; 15,000 spectators will enjoy hard-bottomed plastic seats, and the rest will sit on metal benches. That owner of a house assessed at $20,000 can expect to pay an average of $1.38 a year for forty years toward the stadium's costs, instead of the promised $1.21 for only ten years.

Altogether, the voters' faith seems pretty well breached already. Jerome L. Hillis, a lawyer who headed a stadium study group appointed by the Seattle city council, considers the project generally worthwhile. But he thinks the tactics of its backers have alienated the public. "People have killed initiative after initiative," he says. "They're saying of any issue, 'If the Chamber of Commerce is for it, we're against it.'"

GOOD VIEWS FROM THE SQUIRCLE

In New Orleans, the planners' grandiose dreams have been reined in by few of the restraints imposed on the builders of the King County Stadium. The Superdome, rising from flatlands near the Mississippi and New Orleans' civic-center complex, comes closer to the idea of providing truly multipurpose use than any stadium yet built. But the price is enormous: at least $151 million.

The Superdome will have 72,104 permanent seats. A "squircle," or squared circle of movable seats, will provide generally good sight lines for both baseball and football—unlike some other convertible stadiums such as those in Atlanta and Oakland, where football fans sometimes think the worst seats in the house are those on the fifty-yard line, because they are so far from the playing field. In addition, a section of the Superdome's grandstand seats can be shoved halfway across the playing field for small-court games like basketball. The Superdome will have its own closed-circuit television coverage, with the plays, replays, scores, and—inevitably—commercials beamed to six twenty-two-by-twenty-six-foot TV screens on a centrally hung gondola that will be visible from everywhere in the stands. The stadium's lighting is described as "theatrical" in that it is concentrated on the playing field, leaving the stands in darkness. Some 39,500 seats will be upholstered; the balance will be molded plastic. Besides spectator amenities, Superdome will have four large meeting rooms behind the stands, each of which will theoretically be able to meet the needs of a convention attended by 3,000 people.

All of these amenities are not likely to mollify a public that was badly deceived about the nature of the stadium and its costs. The Superdome was launched early in 1966, when Governor John J. McKeithen announced, in the euphoria of a Louisiana State University victory in the Cotton Bowl that "Louisiana will build the best stadium in history." Later that year the state legislature proposed a constitutional amendment, the form in which many major pieces of Louisiana legislation are couched, authorizing the stadium. The voters approved it after being told that (1) the stadium would cost $35 million; (2) it would be self-supporting; (3) in the wording of newspaper advertisements put out by it promoters, "Neither the state nor the city backs the construction bonds."

THE PROHIBITION DOESN'T COUNT

There was no clear explanation of how the best stadium in history could be built for only $35 million. But a joker was buried in the amendment, in print so fine and language so obscure that few voters either noticed it or grasped its meaning. In essence, it authorized the Louisiana Stadium and Exposition District (L.S.E.D.), the entity that would build and operate the stadium, to issue bonds backed by state money for whatever amount it wanted. This provision, said the amendment, would supersede any prohibitions—even the one written into the amendment itself—against securing stadium bonds with the state's full faith and credit.

The import of this clause did not dawn on the public, or even fully on the state legislature, for more than two years. By that time the estimated costs of the stadium had almost tripled. The original stadium plan had been described vaguely as a sort of Astrodome with 55,000 seats. But to the stadium builder bigger means better, and L.S.E.D. had no restrictions on its ambitions. No matter that the costs of building a covered stadium rise exponentially after the number of seats passes 65,000 or so. L.S.E.D. decided that Superdome would have to be big enough to handle the crowds of 80,000 that pack New Orleans' old-fashioned Tulane Stadium for the annual Sugar Bowl. And anyway, went the reasoning, New Orleans really ought to have a larger stadium than Houston.

As Superdome's published price tag approached $100 million, a previously subdued opposition began fighting back in earnest. But there was little to be done. The device that gave the stadium builders their vast powers survived a court test engineered by the L.S.E.D. itself. There was a setback when an Orleans Parish Civil District Court judge, Oliver P. Carricre, found against the stadium authority. "The lease arrangement," he wrote, was a sham that did "not follow the clear mandate voted by the legislature and the people of Louisiana." But his decision was soon overturned by the state supreme court in a four-to-three decision. The majority held that the intention of the legislature was irrelevant and that of the voters impossible to ascertain; therefore, the case could be decided on the literal ground that the general purpose of the amendment was to issue bonds and pledge lease revenues.

A LOT DEPENDS ON IMAGINATION

According to an optimistic estimate prepared by the Stanford Research Institute, the Superdome will be making money after only a few years. But the Stanford report included the caveat that its projections "will depend on the imagination and showmanship of [the stadium's] operating management." Stanford projected 170 events of various types during the first year of operation, and 189 by the fifth year. Besides professional, college, and high-school sports, Stanford anticipated ten days of "closed-circuit television events"—i.e., boxing matches and races—with an average attendance of 20,000; a dozen musical and entertainment events drawing 25,000 each; and no fewer than sixteen conventions and trade shows.

The Stanford forecast is actually a table of maximum possible benefits. It includes a full professional baseball season and all of Tulane's football games. But New Orleans does not yet have a baseball franchise, and Tulane has no practical reason to abandon its own amortized and profitable stadium. The table of non-sports events is greatly out of line with any other stadium's experience and projections, even taking into account the splendiferousness of the Superdome. Seattle hopes for a total of 124 days of use annually; the Astrodome, whose promoters are probably the most skilled in the business, managed only 134 days of use last year.

Stanford's projections contrast sharply with those in a Booz Allen & Hamilton report submitted to the L.S.E.D. in 1968. Stanford's total revenue projections add up to $4,400,000 in the first year of operation, rising to $7,700,000 in 1988. Booz Allen presented three projections based on different assumptions: a conservative estimate of $843,000 a year, based on "events definitely committed," a "more probable set of events" that would bring the total up to some $1,700,000, and a third best-possible figure, adding some less probable events, of about $2,200,000. Booz Allen was to have undertaken two subsequent studies for L.S.E.D., but its contract was canceled after that first study failed to enhance the rosy glow surrounding the stadium proposals. "It's an excellent firm, and I wouldn't criticize it," says a stadium official. "But even a good restaurant can give you a bad meal once in a while."

L.S.E.D. argues that the Booz Allen report overlooked convention revenues of some $400,000 annually, and completely omitted income from "non-event" revenues generated by daily use of the stadium's 5,000 parking spaces. Stanford estimated that parking revenues would rise from $890,000 at the outset to $2,400,000 in ten years, which could narrow considerably the gap between its own report and Booz Allen's "best-possible" schedule. But Stanford was counting on the presence of a huge health and social-services complex that had been proposed for a nearby spot; it has since been canceled. The Stanford report has shown itself to be conservative in only one respect. It anticipated that revenues from a hotel-motel tax surcharge allocated to the stadium would reach $2,200,000 by 1974; that figure was approached last year.

"A REAL SHOT IN THE ARM"

The Superdome is also haunted by the faint but troubling specter of engineering problems. Late last year, the foundation pilings that were being driven began showing an unusually high failure rate. A number of pilings were replaced, and the engineers are satisfied that there is an ample margin of safety. But an advisory committee composed of architectural and engineering experts from Tulane and L.S.U. is still concerned that undetected piling flaws could eventually cause parts of the stadium to settle slightly.

Supporters of the Superdome insist that, above all, it will give New Orleans a new and better self-image. "It's good to see us get up and really fly," says one banker. Even some of those who are appalled by the cost take a booster's pride in the stadium's grandiose scale. Herman S. Kohlmeyer Sr., head of a brokerage firm that played an early role in putting the bond deal together, says that "what's been done here is the most extravagant thing I've seen in my life." But, he adds, "it's been a real shot in the arm for this community."

There are plenty of people in New Orleans who argue that the shot in the arm is really a kick in the stomach. Superdome, they fear, will place a continuing financial drain on the state treasury. And it has already deepened the cynicism that is to some degree endemic in the Louisiana voter. Stadium proponents see nothing terribly wrong with bypassing the public in order to build something like a Superdome. "The man who built the Taj Mahal didn't ask the permission of the people," says Kohlmeyer. "Ditto here."

Since 1969, Louisiana's voters have turned down virtually every constitutional amendment put before them. Critics say there is no question that the unprecedented wave of voter negativism is a direct product of the deceptive amendment. "The people here have come to accept rape as a matter of course," says Ben C. Toledano, a New Orleans lawyer, businessman, and lonely Republican leader. "But they don't enjoy it."

New Orleans and Seattle have suffered with their stadiums through more trials than generally accompany the building of a large public structure. The way to avoid their agonies for cities planning stadiums in the future would seem to be a closer examination of alternatives to the standard concepts of financing and construction.

One fundamental question that taxpayers should ask is whether the goal is a stadium or a palace. A covered stadium overcomes the vagaries of weather, which simplifies scheduling problems and boosts attendance. It also offers the sheer sensual appeal of a large enclosed space—a sense of grandness of scale that may be the main reason for its hold upon the imagination. But in most climates teams can play perfectly well while fans watch contentedly in well-planned open stadiums.

Careful scrutiny of costs and benefits is going to become even more important in the future. As more stadiums are built, particularly in cities hoping to attract big-league sports, planners are going to have to face another reality: the supply of teams to fill them is not infinite. Baseball's recent expansion is not likely to be duplicated; some sportscasters and fans claim attendance is suffering already because talent is stretched thin. Nor is there any prospect for new football franchises in the foreseeable future. As competition for existing teams heats up, the subsidies cities will have to offer to keep or attract a team will naturally rise.

An oversupply of stadiums is not inconceivable. In the New York metropolitan area, for example, plans are currently afoot for two new mammoth stadiums, one in New Jersey and another on Long Island. At the same time, New York City is undertaking a $23-million renovation of its venerable Yankee Stadium. If all of these plans come to fruition, somebody's stadium is almost certain to be empty much of the time.

DEALING IN THE VOTERS

Boosters of publicly financed stadiums argue that their palaces really earn their keep by creating a lot of economic activity. The construction itself will provide jobs, and the arena will draw tourists as well as fans who will spend money in the community on retail goods and services. The enthusiasts bolster their case by hiring economic consultants to dignify these assumptions with impressive tables and figures. As a practical matter, however, it is enormously difficult, if not impossible, to pinpoint the exact contributions to a city's economy of something like a stadium. The consultants are under considerable pressure to produce the best possible figures, and their findings often crumble under close scrutiny.

It is imperative, therefore, that a city weigh a stadium proposal mainly on its own merits. In so doing, officials must be more realistic about assessing the true cost, and less extravagant in claiming benefits that cannot be realized. Common sense, to say nothing of the niceties of democratic principle, also suggests that the voters be dealt more fully into the decision making. While it may be hard to make a persuasive case for a stadium based on its intangible benefits—and the intangible benefits can be very important—it seems pretty clear that the answer is not to over-inflate the tangible ones to the point of bursting. Civic pride can take a terrible battering when the voters feel they've been had.

THE TENNIS INDUSTRY

Judson Gooding[1]

Tennis, in its present form, is one hundred years old this year, and the country is observing the anniversary with an explosive expansion of interest in the game. Businessmen are planning their vacations around resorts that feature tennis. Their wives are getting slimmer because of strenuous hours on the courts, and mothers are leading their children to tennis classes almost as soon as they can walk. Courts—around, inside, and even on top of apartment projects—have become a significant factor in the real-estate business. The metropolitan landscape is spotted with bubbles housing indoor courts, and in the backyards of suburbia the tennis court is becoming a status symbol more coveted than the swimming pool. A homeowner in Brentwood, California, strapped for space but mad for tennis, recently spent $45,000 to build a court cantilevered over a hillside.

WHEN PROS WERE SHAMATEURS

Now that the boom is on, it somehow seems not so much surprising as overdue. At a time when people have more leisure and more money, and are concerned about physical fitness, tennis has a lot to recommend it. It is a stylish, fast-paced game, and few other sports can produce such a satisfactory state of exhaustion so quickly.

But the boom has been helped immeasurably by a few overdue changes in the game. Oddly enough, although tennis was invented and popularized by the British upper class, which is noted for fair play, competitive events were long run under a dubious code of ethics. Top tourna-

From *Fortune*, LXXXVII, No. 6 (June, 1973): 124-133.
1. Research associate: Libby Watterson.

ment players were prohibited from taking prize money and so took it under the table, a practice that came to be called "shamateurism." In 1968, when the major tournaments were at last opened to pros, the game's new era began, with its millionaire stars, its rich endorsement contracts and big purses.

In turn, television coverage of the big-money tournaments, and the emergence of attractive new stars such as Stan Smith and Chris Evert, have brought tennis the visibility it needed. As Smith, the thoughtful champion of Wimbledon, says, "The big purses made people watch who didn't know a lob from a volley, and suddenly a lot of people realized tennis was good for spectators, and good to play."

A $500-MILLION MARKET

Nobody has counted tennis players since A.C. Nielsen Co. found 10,665,000 of them in 1970. On some estimates they now outnumber the 12,750,000 golfers. According to the results of a study done by Alfred S. Alschuler Jr. of Tennis Planning Consultants, the once minuscule tennis market—the money spent for equipment, courts, resorts, lessons, clubs, and the like—now comes to some $500 million a year and is growing by 12 percent annually.

Some companies that are well established in the market can expect to do even better. Bancroft Sporting Goods, a privately owned company that is the oldest maker of rackets in the U.S., increased its sales by 44 percent last year and forecasts a 60 percent increase this year. Head Ski & Sports Wear, Inc., has doubled its sales of tennis clothing each year since entering the business in 1969. Sales are expected to top $3 million this year. "I just don't know where the saturation point might be," says Alex Schuster, president of the A.M.F. subsidiary.

New courts are being built at the rate of 5,000 a year, and big corporations like Borden, Chevron, and 3M are competing for the market in all-weather surfacing, which costs anywhere from $1,000 to $11,000 per court. Tennis magazines bulge with ads addressed to club managers for smaller items, like ball machines, nets, lines, fences, lights, lockers, and backboards, and to individual players for myriad accessories from rackets to elbow guards to sweatbands.

The most glamorous side of the tennis industry is the tournament business, and no one stands to profit more handsomely from the boom than the promoters who created a mass audience for the game. Now in its third season, World Championship Tennis, the touring tournament developed by oil millionaire Lamar Hunt, put on twenty-six events in the U.S. and overseas from January to May, drawing one million spectators and reaching a peak audience of 21 million more on television. Sixty-four players competed for prize money totaling $1 million. The counterpart tour for women, the Virginia Slims circuit, is putting on twenty-two matches worth $830,000 in prize money.

The managers of W.C.T. have developed the tournament concept along sound business lines. Local sponsors of the matches put up most of the purses and pay for the stadium, tickets, publicity, and other operating expenses. The players pay for their own travel and expenses. W.C.T. has only to assure that the promised playing conditions and purses are met, and that the players and W.C.T. staff members appear on time. It collects a share of any profits, and also collects the payments for television rights, a closely guarded figure that probably comes to something over $350,000 for the season. It's sort of like owning oil wells, except that there's no depletion allowance.

Tennis on television is good business for the networks, too. Since 1970, NBC, the leader in tennis broadcasting, has tripled the amount of time devoted to the game. All its scheduled broadcasts sell out to sponsors long before the matches. This year, NBC covered eight W.C.T. tournaments, paying $100,000 each time for rights and production costs, and selling $192,000 worth of commercial time at the rate of $12,000 a minute. Commercials for the W.C.T. finals in Dallas brought $19,000 a minute, and attracted sponsors like Lincoln-Mercury, Michelob beer, Sears, Roebuck, and Kemper Insurance.

Television has also been responsible for one of the most noticeable changes in the game: because brightly colored clothing shows up better on screens, "all whites" are no longer the universal standard, a development that saddens traditionalists but delights clothing designers and manufacturers.

And since television has turned tennis pros into celebrities, they have been able to cash in at a rate beyond the dreams of the old-time shamateurs.

LAVER'S LITTLE EMPIRE

For example, Rod Laver, who in 1972 became the first tennis player to rack up a lifetime total of more than $1 million in prize money, will collect royalties totaling $250,000 from twenty-nine companies this year. Laver pays about a quarter of his earnings to his deal maker, International Management Inc., a Cleveland company that handles 100 athletes and other stars. Laver lends, or rather rents, his name to various brands of balls, ball machines, shoes, socks, razor blades, tennis bags, gut, watches, sunglasses, suitcases, tennis gloves, gasoline, two kinds of sport clothes (in the US and Japan) and even a line of women's tennis clothes. He endorses three different makes of rackets in the U.S., Europe, and Australia. He has written a book, and this summer he and his doubles partner, Roy Emerson, will teach adults at various resorts. "Everyone works with kids," Laver says, "but a lot of those developing club players around the country want instruction, and in one week we can improve them out of sight."

THE CLINICIAN

Tennis instruction offers such enticing rewards that more than a dozen top pros have, like Laver and Emerson, set themselves up as teachers. Most of them have modeled their instruction programs on the concepts worked out by John Gardiner, who started the country's first tennis ranch in Carmel Valley, California, in 1957. During his thirty years as a teaching pro in California, Gardiner had become convinced that players would benefit from, and pay for, intensive stroke-by-stroke instruction in a resort setting.

He has expanded from the small Carmel ranch, which accommodates only twenty at a time, and now oversees instruction on fifty courts at six resort locations from Hawaii to Arizona. He is looking at other possible sites and is starting a twenty-four-hour-a-day tennis clinic in Las Vegas. Gardiner says interest in tennis has exploded because "suddenly the snobbishness is gone, and people are finding they can have fun even if they are hackers."

Gardiner's Tennis Ranch on Camelback Mountain in Scottsdale, Arizona, opened only two and one-half years ago and is already running at its capacity of 164 players. The forty-one condominium cottages were snapped up (at $57,500 each) by such affluent fanciers of the game as Charles Gates of Gates Rubber Co., John Murchison, the Dallas financier, Joseph Coors of Coors Brewery, and Robert Galvin, chairman of Motorola, Inc. (When the owners are not in residence, the cottages are rented to other customers.)

The ranch has its full share of hackers, some of whom turn out dressed like world champions although they can barely hit the ball. The heart of the program is individualized instruction on basic strokes and tactics. There are fourteen courts, and a staff of ten teaching pros, who make use of video tape, films, and sophisticated rapid-fire ball-throwing machines, as well as a lot of exhortation ("Come on, tigers—hit 'em!".) Gardiner charges his customers $375 for a five-day stay that includes seventeen and one-half hours of instruction, unlimited use of the courts, accommodations, meals, saunas, and massage—which often is sorely needed.

A NEW FOCUS FOR BUILDERS

Those who can't afford the time, the money, or the energy for the total-immersion tennis-clinic experience can buy or rent in a more modest condominium complex, one that is centered around tennis courts but does not offer the instruction and other services provided at Gardiner's Ranch. Such condominiums are springing up by the dozens, particularly in Florida, Texas, Arizona, New Mexico, California, and Hawaii.

World Championship Tennis has already signed up potential participants for a project to open soon near Austin, Texas. It will have 106 "tennis townhouses," each house overlooking one of the twenty-six courts. Sea Pines Co. of Hilton Head, South Carolina, has a tennis community at Hilton Head and is building the Monte Sol tennis village in Puerto Rico, where condominium owners will have forty courts at their disposal. James Luckman, the Los Angeles architect and developer who is chairman of Charles Luckman Associates (he is the son of the founder), is designing a tennis condominium to be built on Maui Island in Hawaii with thirteen courts. In Fort Lauderdale, the Tennis Club, less than three years old, already has nine buildings with 216 apartments clustered around thirteen courts. A few weeks ago the club bought another sixteen acres and plans to add twenty-one more courts, which will make it one of the largest tennis clubs in the world.

More practical for even more people than the condominiums are the hundreds of indoor tennis centers that are strategically sited in and around the northern belt of cities. There are now some 750 in operation, and hundreds more are planned. They typically have from four to eight courts, cost from $250,000 to $1,800,000, and are lighted for around-the-clock play. This full-time, all-season availability of tennis has contributed importantly to its growth.

Chicago has been swept by what may be the most severe case of tennis mania in the country. As recently as 1961, only one indoor tennis center was operating in the Chicago area, but there were twenty-three last year, there are forty-nine today, and next year twenty more will open.

One of the most profitable establishments around Chicago is the Northbrook Racquet Club, Inc., twenty miles from the Loop. It represents what the company's president, Maxwell Skenazy, calls the "second generation" of clubs, more elegant and comfortable than their relatively spartan predecessors. Four of its eight courts are air-conditioned, and it has indirect lighting, saunas and whirlpool baths, and a well-run nursery, important in attracting housewives during daytime hours.

Northbrook's two acres of land cost $125,000, and the steel-frame building, which has a fancy Tudor exterior, cost $650,000. With lighting and accessories, the total investment came to $1 million, of which $450,000 is covered by an 8.5 percent mortgage. Open from 9:00 A.M. to 11:00 P.M. every day from October to May, and part time during the summer, it has been running at 95 percent of capacity. Players pay small membership fees and $8 or $12 per hour for court time (the higher rate for evenings and weekends), usually booking the same hour for each week and paying $240 or $360 for the thirty-week season. Last year, after paying $38,400 in mortgage interest, a $24,000 electricity bill, and assorted payroll and maintenance costs, the eight owners divided $76,000 in profit. Skenazy is planning an even more luxurious eight-court establishment nearby. He says gloomily that it will cost $200,000 more than his present gold mine and that with the increased competition it won't be nearly as profitable. He is, nevertheless, going ahead.

The business of tennis is growing so rapidly in so many different directions, including equipment, instruction, condominiums, tournaments, and publications, that it even has its budding conglomerates. The prime example is Tennis America Inc., which is involved in every one of these profit-making aspects of the game. Billie Jean King, the women's champion, who won $236,000 in prize money in 1971 and 1972, is its president. Her husband, Larry King, a lawyer, is a vice president. The company manages tournaments, publishes *Lob,* the thick, slick-paper program for the women's pro matches, and owns eight tennis specialty shops. It runs tennis camps at fifteen locations across the country, and operates a tennis resort in Incline Village, Nevada. It also manages Tennis America University, a grandiosely titled program that provides pros with two weeks of instruction on how to teach tennis, install courts, and run clubs and tournaments. "In the past, no one taught a pro how to be a pro," Larry King says. "We're changing that." Tennis America's revenues have grown from $140,000 in 1970 to a projected $1,500,000 this year.

BALLS FOR ALL

While none of these tennis-based companies seems likely to make the FORTUNE 500, their owners see nothing but growth and handsome profits ahead. The equipment makers, repeatedly surprised by the size of the boom, worry more about supply problems than about stimulating sales. Now it can be reported, for example, that for a few perilous weeks last summer, the country teetered on the brink of a ball shortage. Only two companies, Spalding and Pennsylvania, manufacture balls in the U.S. (although the balls are sold under several labels). They were unable, despite their best efforts, to keep up with unprecedented demand. But

Britain's Dunlop has announced plans to begin making balls here, and fresh supplies are on the way from overseas. Hoarding will not be necessary. The hiss of opening ball cans, the bang of rebounds on backboards, and the thunk of hard-hit volleys will be heard in the land.

THE SPORTING GOODS MARKET—1974

Irwin Broh, Associates, Inc.

INTRODUCTION

This 1974 report on the size of the sporting goods market represents a sharp departure from previous reports in that the projections are based on a survey of 40,000 families. This representative sample of families was sent a list of 60 sporting goods items and asked to record their 1973 purchases of these items. Replies were received from 32,000 or 80% of this sample, and the data presented in this report is based on the 1973 purchases reported by these 32,000 families.

The reason for conducting a consumer survey to project sporting goods sales is that there is a lack of accurate information on the manufacturer level and in government statistics. *Because of the difference in sales projection techniques between this and previous reports, the 1973 and 1974 figures in this report cannot be compared to projections of earlier years shown in previous reports.* Future reports will be based on surveys of consumer purchases, thus permitting an analysis of trends.

Going to consumers for purchase data provided considerable advantages. It enabled us to study purchases of clothing and athletic footwear for the first time and allowed us to obtain average and median prices paid for sporting goods items. We were also able to break down sales by purchaser demographics including geographic region and annual family income, thus giving an additional insight into the market and providing a basis for preparing regional sales forecasts. In addition, this

346

report breaks down previously shown broad product categories into more meaningful product line components.

As a result of this consumer research effort, we have identified 1973 sports equipment purchasers, and interested firms may avail themselves of more comprehensive market data by re-surveying these purchasers with a detailed questionnaire. The cost of doing this, however, is substantial, as the list of names is not freely available but is maintained by National Family Opinion, Inc. Anyone interested in additional market research should contact either the National Sporting Goods Association or Irwin Broh & Associates.

Another *first* is a survey of team distributors which resulted in an estimate of athletic goods team sales. This is shown as a separate item, and the total is also broken down by geographic region to provide additional data for market analysis.

The following section of the report deals with the economic outlook. It should be noted that while some economists are predicting a recession during the remainder of this year, the forecast for sporting goods products remains optimistic.

The economic outlook section also presents the results of a consumer study among 60,000 families that was conducted during January, 1974, to measure the effect of the fuel shortage on participation in six selected leisure time activities.

ECONOMIC OUTLOOK

On April 18, the Commerce Department reported that *real* gross national product declined during the first quarter of this year at a seasonally adjusted annual rate of 5.8%. During the same quarter, the GNP price index rose to an annual rate of 10.8%.

The Commerce Department attributed the decline in economic activity to the cutback in automobile production and a slump in home building. While some economists are expecting a recession (defined as two consecutive quarters of actual decline in economic activity), the Administration economists are not, as they expect the second quarter to be relatively stable. There is little conviction on the part of either optimists or pessimists, as the data does not show a clear trend. The Commerce Department's composite list of sensitive indicators rose 1.7% in March following rises in both January and February. Inflation, however, may be warping the index.

At present, we are beset with both serious inflation and shortages of materials. This price rise of almost 11% during the first quarter was the highest since the Korean war. While no one expects inflation to continue at this rate, there is little reason to expect it to average under 8% this year.

The sales projections for sporting goods this year show increases of from 13% to 20% for most items, and in all instances, between a third and a half of the percentage increases are attributable to price increases.

On January 2, 1974, we sent a questionnaire to a representative sample of 60,000 U.S. families asking how the fuel shortage would affect their leisure activity plans in 1974.

Completed questionnaires were received from 48,000 of these families, representing an 80% response rate. All questionnaires were completed between January 4 and January 25, 1974.

The following question was asked about 6 leisure activities—camping, fishing, hunting, golf, tennis, and skiing.

> Check each activity that anyone in your family did in 1973. Then check whether they plan to do that activity More, the Same, or Less in 1974 as a result of the FUEL SHORTAGE.

LEISURE ACTIVITY PLANS FOR 1974 AMONG 1973 PARTICIPANTS
(Based on families who participated in each of the activities during 1973)

Plans for 1974 v. 1973 as a result of the fuel shortage

	Camping	Fishing	Hunting	Golf	Tennis	Skiing
More	26%	28%	22%	33%	44%	28%
Same	46	55	64	56	49	45
Less	28	17	14	11	7	27
Total	100%	100%	100%	100%	100%	100%

The results show the following:

Except for camping, the percentage of families that plan to increase their participation exceeds the percentage that plan a decrease.

Tennis should continue its strong growth and may be benefiting from the fuel shortage. Of those families that played tennis last year, 44% plan to play more this year, while only 7% say they will play less.

Golf shows the second best increase (after tennis) in planned participation.

Families with skiers plan about the same level of activity in 1974 as they did in 1973.

Of the families that camped last year, a slightly larger percentage plan to decrease their camping this year than plan to increase it.

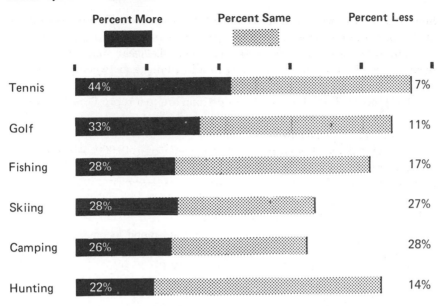

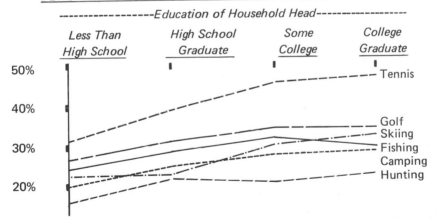

PERCENT OF FAMILIES PLANNING INCREASED PARTICIPATION

Considerable differences in planned participation are found in terms of the head of household's education. Families with better educated husbands plan more increased participation than families where the husband did not attend college.

The differences are particularly sharp for tennis and skiing, and least evident for hunting.

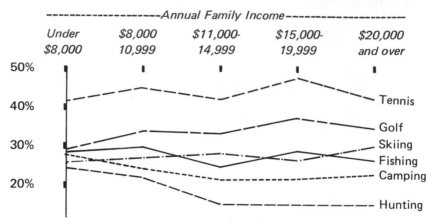

There were only slight differences among income groups as to the percentage of families that plan to do more or less of each of the activities this year.

For tennis, golf, and skiing, the percent of families planning increased participation is slightly greater among those with annual incomes of $15,000 or more. The reverse is true for camping and hunting, where plans for increased participation are greater among families with incomes of under $15,000.

LAST WORD

Rosalie Wright

It would seem that the question was not worth the asking. In fact, when posed to us the first few times, WOMENSPORTS was incredulous that the question was being asked at all. (And the only people who seem to ask it are male sportswriters who haven't done their homework, so they are at a loss to ask intelligent questions about the magazine.)

If women can't beat men in sports, why should they be entitled to equal prize money?

We were asked one time too many when a gossip columnist, whom nobody will remember when he goes on to that great scandal sheet in the sky, suggested that if Billie Jean were to gain equal prize money at Wimbledon this year under threat of boycott, then she should demand also to take on the male Wimbledon winner in order to justify the equal prize money.

Let's make it clear right here that we are now talking about professional sports in this column, since that's usually the arena in which equal prize money so often becomes an issue.

Our gossip columnist equates exercises in brute force with sport. We don't see it that way. We see professional sport, rather, as entertainment. And in show business the name of the game is *draw.*

Let's examine the difference between brute physical power and drawing power. If physical power were the criteria for entertainment, then the strong man at the circus should get big crowds and hence more money than, say, the lion tamer or a trapeze artist who depend more upon finesse for their acts. But we all know that the strong man is a sideshow—not the main event.

From *womenSports Magazine* (February, 1975):72.

So, you might say that the circus isn't sport. But it is entertainment. And so is almost every other event you pays yer money to see, from NFL football to a Helen Reddy concert. If Helen Reddy can draw larger crowds than, say, Andy Williams, she should get proportionately higher fees for her performances. And that's how show biz works—from rock concerts to stage plays, the performers' fees are computed on a base fee plus a certain percentage of the ticket take. What that percentage is depends upon the impresario's expectations of how many tickets he can sell to people wanting to hear that particular entertainer.

If Evonne Goolagong and Chris Evert can fill the stands at Forest Hills to overflowing (13,000); if the Virginia Slims Championship last fall boasted the largest tennis audience for *any* tennis event since 1961; if CBS has signed up to televise the women's tennis tour in 1975, then *somebody's* watching women's tennis and the women should be compensated for their ability to bring out the crowds.

At Forest Hills, the first day's matches are men's and the second day's matches are women's. For two years in a row, now, the women's matches have outdrawn the men in total number of spectators.

Now comes the clincher. Television moguls put their support where they think it will do the most good to hype their ratings. ABC recently passed up showing the February 2nd match between Rod Laver and Jimmy Connors because the contest, according to ABC, "lacked the dramatic potential of the King-Riggs match."

But ABC *did* sign on to carry again the Dinah Shore Winners Circle Golf Classic, and will again repeat a special like Colgate's "Women's Sports Special" which aired a year ago January. (That show, produced by Eleanor Riger, and the first women's sports show in prime time, drew 6.6 million 18-34-year-old women viewers, more than *any* 1974 sportscast, including the Super Bowl.) ABC will also carry the $100,000 L'eggs World Series of Tennis on April 19-20, and will carry it every year thereafter. And we all know that ABC carried the Women's Superstars, which this magazine helped produce. They'll also carry the U.S. Women's Open Golf event in July, and the World Invitational Tennis Classic, featuring the top four men and top four women players, May 4-July 13, as well as the Lady Borden golf event. Other networks are following suit, with NBC presenting the Family Circle Cup tennis playoffs in May.

Now you don't think these networks are supporting women's sports because they're wedded to the idea of women's sports, do you? It's just proven that women's sports events do draw audiences.

One factor not mentioned in this support (except for ABC's turning down the Laver-Connors match) is that the women tennis players have much more panache than the men, (outside of Ilie Nastase). A sassy Rosie

Casals, a thoughtful Chris Evert, a powerful Evonne Goolagong—these are the people who bring out the crowds, not to mention the ol' lady herself.

Take the Hilton Head tournament last fall. ABC, which televised it, was ecstatic when Billie Jean beat out Stan Smith. Stan who? You're right. He's a damned good tennis player, but he doesn't have nearly the draw that Billie Jean has.

It's show biz, folks, and if not more than a handful of women have achieved star status, it's because of the age-old attitudes like that of the gossip columnist above. It takes people of unusual fortitude and drive to attain the virtuosity of a Chris Evert, a Margaret Court (and just wait till she returns to tournaments this year—that'll be news copy for a week), a Sandra Haynie, a Kathy Whitworth or a Wyomia Tyus.

But as the younger women, just now recognizing that they might indeed be able to make a living in their sport, start to pursue their sport seriously, we'll have bucketsful of top-flight performers to draw crowds—and not only in tennis. Women's golf, basketball, volleyball and softball already have devotees, not to mention the fast-growing football phenomenon.

We see the benefits of professional sports in entertainment, and not in the contest between two people to see who can bludgeon a ball across the court or green the most powerfully. Let's face it, women in sport. If we can draw equal crowds, we deserve equal prizes.

BIBLIOGRAPHY

Section A. Social Systems—

2. Economics—

Demmert, H. G. *The Economics of Professional Team Sports.* Lexington, Mass.: Lexington Books, 1973.

Durso, Joseph. *The All-American Dollar.* Boston: Houghton Mifflin Co., 1971.

Gilbert, Bill, "Sis-Boom-Bah! for Amalgamated Sponge," *Sports Illustrated* 22 (January 25, 1965):54-65.

Lineberry, William, ed. *The Business of Sports.* New York: H. W. Wilson Co., 1973.

Jackson, Myles. "College Football Has Become a Losing Business," *Fortune* (Dec. 1962):119-21.

Mahoney, Stephen. "Pro Football's Profit Explosion," *Fortune* 70 (November, 1964):153-230.

Neale, W. C. "The Peculiar Economics of Professional Sports," *The Quarterly Journal of Economics* 78 (Feb. 1964):1-14.

Ryan, Pat. "A Grim Run to Fiscal Daylight," *Sports Illustrated* 34 (Feb. 1, 1971):18-23.

Snyder, Richard. *Trends in the Sporting Goods Market: 1947-65.* Chicago: National Sporting Goods Association, 1965.

SECTION

B

SOCIAL SYSTEMS:
3. EDUCATION

The topic of education and sport usually reflects research and commentary about interscholastic and intercollegiate athletics for male students. There is information on that aspect of sport in education in this book but it is so well covered in most all other sources that there is no effort at an extensive coverage here. Unfortunately, it is often presented as the only concern or major concern of education in regard to sport.

The effect of physical education programs on sociocultural change is examined by Tindall. He suggests "a process by which teachers can gather the type of information they need to understand their students and their students' perceptions of the meaning of physical activity." If people are introduced to alternatives through understanding their life-style then change can occur—as desired and understood by those individuals.

Clark presents the Olympic Movement as "an international movement of Olympism." He contends that the maze of conflict that surrounds the International Olympic Committee and the Games (only part of the Olympic Movement) obscures the educational goals, idealism, and commitment to amateurism that is the driving force of the Olympic Movement. Clark examines the concept that "Olympism is predicated upon the assumption that the perfection of mankind can be attained through the harmonious development of the physical and intellectual nature." The article by Clark helps in an understanding of the total system of the Olympic Movement and its educational ideals.

Though not included in this book, the direct confrontation of the educational system with the Olympic Movement was illustrated in an article by David Wolf.[1] The National Collegiate Athletic Association (representing a part of the United States educational system) and the Amateur

1. David Wolf, "The Growing Crisis in College Sport," *Sport* 49 (Part I, June 1970): 24-92 and 50 (Part II, July 1970):30-74.

Athletic Union (representing the Olympic Movement) are notorious for their inability to arrive at a truce. The struggle between these two associations for power and control over the performance and life of the athlete reveals a long and unchanging pattern. The effect of this continued battle on the life of college students is also described by Wolf.

The reaction in educational circles to Title IX of the Education Amendments is discussed in an open manner by Marjorie Blaufarb, editor of *Update*. She presents many of the questions asked at national meetings and conferences. Blaufarb contends that these questions "reveal unconscious prejudices and preconceptions" about the emerging issues of equal sports opportunities for female students.

ORGANIZING PHYSICAL EDUCATION FOR CHANGE:
AN ANTHROPOLOGICAL PERSPECTIVE

B. Allan Tindall

Physical education activity programs are, in large measure, dedicated to change, or at least to development. Activity programs are most obviously concerned with biological change; the attention given to physical fitness, and to psycho-motor change; in the attention given to skill development. In addition socio-cultural changes are sought through physical education activity programs. Many programs seek to instill concepts and behavioral patterns variously labeled the development of character traits, democratic practices, teamwork, or interactional skills.

To make changes, however, one needs to know the nature of the object to be changed, and the nature of the tool to be used to make those changes. This, I propose, is somewhat axiomatic and needs no more defense than to point out that you do not use a hand saw to cut linoleum or a linoleum knife to cut a 2 by 4.

In applying this axiom to the attempts of physical educators to provide an environment in which changes can be made at least two factors must be considered: (1) the possibility of cultural variation within the student population of a school; and (2) the possibility of variation in the students' perceptions of the meaning of a specific physical activity. These factors deal with understanding the people (i.e., the thing) you want to change, and understanding the tool (a physical activity) you have chosen to use. Regardless of the specific goals you have in mind, you must consider these two essential factors.

To explicate the importance of these two factors, I shall discuss some research which I conducted among Anglo-Mormon and Ute Indian stu-

Printed with permission of the author.

356

dents in a high school in Utah.[1] My intention is to demonstrate how cultural variability and idiosyncratic perceptions of the meaning of an activity can combine to thwart the efforts of a physical education teacher to make changes. After explaining the importance of these two factors I shall suggest a process by which teachers can gather the type of information they need to understand their students and their students' perceptions of the meaning of a physical activity.

I conducted my research in Roosevelt, Utah, a town of 2,006 people. Roosevelt is surrounded by the Uintah and Ouray Indian Reservation where the 1,600 members of the Ute Indian Tribe live. The high school is attended by both Ute and Anglo students, but the Ute students comprised only 20% of the student body.

Both community cultures use modern technological facilities, both have more than adequate economic support, and for cursory intents and purposes they are active participants in the social and economic fabric which constitutes Roosevelt, Utah. However, while they have much in common, the Ute people are fundamentally different from their Anglo neighbors. These differences are cultural differences and are carried into Union High School by the adolescent members of the two cultural groups.

The Anglo residents of the Roosevelt area are predominantly members of the Church of Jesus Christ of Latter-Day Saints (Mormon Church), which functions through mutual participation for the collective benefit of the membership. My data[2] indicate that these people are generally oriented toward group cooperation for the collective benefit of the membership. Individualism is recognized and encouraged, but it always takes a subordinate position to the interests of the group.

The Ute people can be distinguished on the basis of the primacy of their orientation toward individualism. Great pains are taken to avoid trespassing against someone else. Concerted actions are undertaken by groups of Utes, but always with an acknowledgment of the ultimate right of the individual.

These culturally based differences can be used to conceptually distinguish one group from the other, and are descriptions of different objects. We are concerned with understanding the people the physical education teacher wanted to change.

1. Tindall, B. Allan, *The Psycho-Cultural Orientations of Anglo and Ute Boys in an Integrated High School*, Unpublished Doctoral Dissertation, University of California, Berkeley, 1973.
2. Data derived largely from specially drawn projective plates depicting various basketball scenes. The inferences here are extensions from patterns, evident in the responses to those plates, to more pervasive patterns, supported by ethnographic data on the larger communities.

These cultural differences can be seen in the way basketball is played in the Anglo and Ute communities. Anglos play a controlled strategic game designed to exploit the strengths of their team and the weaknesses of their opponents' team. The emphasis is on teamwork and individual sacrifice for group success. The Utes, on the other hand, utilize a style of play which emphasizes individual skill and individual effort. Teamwork is not stressed, and group success is defined to be a function of individual success.[3]

These cultural differences are also expressed in the perceived benefit, to the individual, of group success. If an Anglo team wins each member is entitled to a measure of *individual* status. However, if a Ute team wins, the individual members of the team do not receive any *individual* status. The difference here is one of emphasis upon mutual as opposed to individual orientation. Anglos receive individual status from a collective effort, but Utes do not.

In physical education classes at Union High School, the teacher was faced with a group of students, but that group of students, those people he tried to change, was composed of two different cultural groups.

Now let me turn my attention to the selection of a "tool" or a medium through which physical educators often attempt change: basketball. I want to take the students' perspective and define the meaning of basketball as the students at Union defined it. But instead of being very particular about this meaning, I shall confine myself to a discussion of the extent to which similar meanings are shared by the students tested. The point to be made here is that any one game can have different meanings to different people once you get beyond the structural aspects of rulebook rules, playing area, and equipment.

One way to look at meaning is to look at the perceived values of basketball related behavior. Values are concerned with goals and therefore with motivations. By eliciting the goals perceived to be achievable through basketball, I was able to attend to some of the aspects of the meaning of that game for the students of Union High School.

For the purposes of my research I defined meaning to be stipulated in the arrangement of a specific activity which in turn would lead to a goal. Meanings were defined by statements of means-to-ends, or means-to-means. These statements were termed "value configurations," and each value configuration stipulated a distinct meaning of basketball. All told, the 38 boys who comprised the sample for my projective test identified 63 distinct value configurations related to basketball.

3. A more thorough description of these differences can be found in B. Allan Tindall, "Ethnography and the Hidden Curricula in Sport," *Behavioral and Social Science Teacher*, vol. 2, no. 2, 1975.

Let me digress for a moment and comment on this last fact. Basketball is not simply fun, or sport, or work, or any other single item. Basketball is at least 63 different things to the students sampled. Basketball is a very complex, very sophisticated, and a highly elaborated element in the combined minds of the 38 students tested.

To return to the point I was about to make concerning the differences in the perceived meanings of basketball; the extent to which the students tested *shared* the meanings of basketball. In order to determine the extent of sharing, I first calculated the number of students who shared each of the 63 value configurations. For instance 3 students (08%) perceived (shared the perception) playing pick-up basketball to be meaningful for physical development, 22 students (58%) perceived playing alone to be meaningful for developing skill, and 31 students (82%) perceived being skillful to be meaningful for making an organized team.

The next step was to group all those value configurations by the extent to which they were shared. In order to simplify this procedure, I grouped the percentages into tens (00-10%, 11-20%, 21-30%, . . . 91-100%). The total number of configurations perceived by less than 10% of the informants was calculated; the total number of value configurations perceived by more than 10% but 20% or less (11%-20%), etc. all the way up to calculating the total number of value configurations perceived by more than 90% of the students (91-100%).

The result of this was a table which demonstrates the number of value configurations, and the percentage of all of the value configurations (N=63), shared by certain percentages of the students tested. (See Table I)

You can see that 27 (43%) of the 63 value configurations were shared by 10% or less of the students tested; 15 (24%) were shared by between 11 and 20% of the students; and none of the value configurations were shared by more than 91% of the students.

These figures suggest a number of different things which are important for the purpose of understanding the variations in the students' meanings of basketball, as these meanings are important for understanding how and if basketball can be used as a change agent.

1. There is not one single perception which is shared by every student tested.
2. 43% of all of the value configurations were shared by 10% of the students or less.
3. 81% of all of the value configurations were shared by 30% of the students or less.

These data suggest that the meaning of basketball is highly idiosyncratic, and that great difficulty would be involved in using basketball in a standardized way because basketball has no standard meaning.

TABLE I

GROSS ESTIMATE OF THE EXTENT TO WHICH STUDENTS
SHARED THE MEANING OF BASKETBALL

Extent to Which Perceptions Are Shared	Value Configurations Perceived by the Students*	
	N	%
00-10%	27	43
11-20%	15	24
21-30%	9	14
31-40%	4	06
41-50%	2	03
51-60%	3	05
61-70%	1	02
71-80%	1	02
81-90%	1	02
91-100%	0	00

*The total number of value configurations perceived = 63.

Let me illustrate what happened when a teacher, faced with cultural diversity on the one hand and individual perceptual diversity on the other, tried to make changes through the use of basketball.

The physical education teacher at Union felt that basketball could provide an opportunity for his students to: (1) develop their skill, (2) get to know the other students by playing with them, (3) develop their physical fitness, and (4) help them prepare for outside of school play activities. But, when he conducted his basketball unit not all of his students participated.

Most of the Anglo boys participated, as a matter of course, because in their culture the teacher had the right to control them and to demand their participation. However, only half of the Ute boys participated, on an irregular basis, even though they all were skillful enough to play. For the Ute boys the decision to play was a personal decision, and could not be controlled by the teacher.[4]

The teacher's effort to use basketball to make changes was ineffective for those boys who chose not to be full participants in his instructional

4. Ibid., and B. Allan Tindall, "Exploration of a 'Troublesome Agenda' Based on the Non-Sharing of 'Property-Like' Information," a research paper presented at the Annual Meetings of the American Anthropological Association, New Orleans, Louisiana, November, 1973.

program. The program was of little consequence to the participants because they already possessed highly elaborated idiosyncratic perceptions
of basketball. His efforts to use basketball to make changes were problematic because of the student's preexisting beliefs about why one plays
basketball. In effect the teacher's efforts were thwarted because he understood neither the students he was teaching nor the tool he attempted to
use.

I have tried to point out that if you are going to have any impact
as change agents you must be cognizant of the population you want to
change, and be cognizant of the peoples' perceptions of the tool you are
going to use to make changes. Using my Utah research as an example,
I pointed out the cultural variations among the Ute and Anglo students,
and the fact that basketball, as defined by the students, is a highly differentiated complex of activities and goals. The consequence of the cultural and perceptual variability was problematic change.

But, the question remains, what can you do to understand the people
you are working with and how can you understand how they define the
activities you are planning to use to make changes?

A definitive or programmatic answer to the questions I have posed is
not possible for three reasons: (1) we do not have enough solid research
data to indicate the specific details of cultural variations among even the
most obvious cultural groups in this country, not to mention the less obvious cultural groups; (2) even if we did, those details might be mis-
leading as we attempted to apply them to any specific community culture; and (3) we have very little solid research data to indicate the
specific details of group, sub-group, or idiosyncratic perceptions of basketball, let alone any of the other activities commonly used in physical education programs. But, in-service teachers and prospective teachers need
not wait for researchers to begin to provide answers, you can do it yourself.

The first step is to set aside the assumption that you know the reason
for playing a game, or what that game means, and you must not presume
to know the nature of your students. If you set aside these preconceived
notions you will have to assess the meaning of every activity and the
cultural background of those with whom you are working. In order to
make this assessment you will have to engage in the process of inquiry
and set about to gather pertinent information.

The most accessible tool you have is your power of observation, which
can be used to gather reliable and accurate information about meanings
and cultural variations. A useful strategy for learning the process of systematic observation has been developed by the Project in Ethnography

in Education, Department of Anthropology, State University of New York at Buffalo.[5] You can also read written reports about patterns of behavior for almost any group in this country. This literature would be of general aid, but would not be predictive of specific behaviors. In addition to observing systematically, and reading, you can interview or talk in a controlled fashion to your students. This can be very useful, if you are careful not to judge them but to let them inform you.

The key to discovering the nature of your students, and the nature of your tools, physical activities, lies in the suspension of your belief that you know what your students are like, and that you know how to define the activities you want to use. If you are unable to understand the population you want to change, and the nature of your tools, your chances for positive change are very slim.

5. See Tindall, B. Allan, and Wayne D. Hughes (editors), *Improving Observational Skills for Better Understanding.* The Project in Ethnography in Education, Center for the Study of Cultural Transmission, Department of Anthropology, State University of New York at Buffalo, 1974. Also see "Ethnography and the Hidden Curricula . . ." op. cit.

AMATEURISM, OLYMPISM, AND PEDAGOGY

Stanley J. Clark

In recent years amateurism, the philosophical cornerstone of the Olympic Games, has come under increasing attack. The staunch support of this ideal by the International Olympic Committee has resulted in violent reactions from many quarters of the international sports community against what they view as unwarranted restraints imposed by an outmoded, antediluvian philosophy. As in most disputes of a philosophical nature the solutions to this conflict are not clearly apparent. Practically speaking, those opposed to the amateur regulations have a number of seemingly valid arguments. Critics state that the eligibility rules simply lead to hipocrisy. It is impossible to achieve the high level of performance required in world class competition and still adhere to the amateuristic goals espoused by the I.O.C. Cynics also point out the logical inconsistency of an Olympic motto which proclaims swifter, higher, stronger while placing restrictions on the training necessary to achieve those goals. The problem is difficult. The idealism of Pierre de Coubertin and Avery Brundage does not seem at all reconcilable with the pragmatism of a Suzy Chaffee and the World Sports Federation (5). The International Olympic Committee, the much maligned culprit in this conflict, is but a part of a larger movement seeking to spread the philosophy of Olympism throughout the world. The Olympic Movement, itself a quasi-religion, is concerned exclusively with the promulgation and dissemination of idealism and moral dogma. The Olympic Games and the I.O.C. are the implements through which the Movement hopes to gain worldwide acceptance of the doctrine of Olympism. If, in dealing with the maze of conflict that surrounds the I.O.C. and

Printed with permission of the author.

the Games, one simple idea can be kept in mind, the arguments and the apparent inconsistencies in statements and actions will be more readily understood. The Olympic Movement—of which the I.O.C. and the Games are but a part—is an international movement bent on spreading the educational goals of Olympism. It is concerned with world class athletic performances only in so far as they assist in the proliferation of the Olympic dogma.

To gain an appreciation of the amateur concept promulgated within the Olympic Movement it is necessary to make a clear distinction between the Olympic Games and the Olympic Movement. It is unarguable that the most dominating force within the structure of international sport today is the International Olympic Committee. This situation exists because the I.O.C. sponsors and controls all facets of the most prestigeous international sporting event, the Olympic Games. Although the National Olympic Committees and the International Sports Federations enforce the rules governing international sports, the I.O.C. dictates the general philosophy upon which these decisions are based. Since the I.O.C. controls the Games themselves it can, and does, exert considerable influence over the National Committees and the International Federations. Consequently, the I.O.C. controls the international sporting scene.

One of the fundamental tenets of the Olympic philosophy as presented by the I.O.C. is an overwhelming commitment to amateurism. From the foundation of the Games in 1896 by Baron Pierre de Coubertin through the presidency of Avery Brundage and up to the present day leadership the I.O.C. has staunchly advocated amateur athletics as an example of all that is good and pure within the realm of sport. Professionalism, on the other hand, was seen to represent the crass materialism that destroys the idealistic goals of international goodwill and brotherhood fostered by the Olympic Movement.

> The aims of the Olympic Movement are to promote the development of those fine physical and moral qualities which are the basis of amateur sport and to bring together the athletes of the world in a great quadrennial festival of sport thereby creating international respect and goodwill and thus helping to construct a better and more peaceful world (2:1).

These works of de Coubertin express the flavor of the philosophy of Olympism. It is a philosophy concerned with the development of physical and moral qualities quite similar to those promoted by the reforms of Arnold in the English Public Schools. In fact, de Coubertin visited England to view this pedagogical system and became enamoured with its results. "It was the atmosphere prevailing in the English Public Schools which made him realize that the antique idea could live again, in a practical and attainable form, on the eve of the twentieth century" (3.73). de Coubertin felt that the English games not only developed the individual physically, they also built a strong and upright character (25:50). Indeed, the youth of de Coubertin's native France seemingly lacked both of these qualities.

With the defeat of the French at the hands of the Germans in the Franco-Prussian War of 1870 the French government became increasingly concerned with the physical fitness of their youth. The poor physical condition of the young men of France, combined with governmental encouragement, comprised the original motivation for de Coubertin to seek out an alternative means of education that could increase the fitness level of the French. He viewed the English system as admirable, and noted the comradery and physical prowess inherent in athleticism. This experience added to the myth of the brotherhood that was supposedly encouraged by the ancient Olympic Games, and prompted de Coubertin to embark on a crusade to revive the Games as a ". . . four yearly festival of universal youth, of the 'human springtime,' the festival of passionate endeavors, of multiple ambitions of each generation appearing on the thresh-hold of life" (17:141). Thus from the very beginning both the Olympic Movement and the Olympic Games were cast in an educational mold. de Coubertin longed to give the youth of his native France the advantages he had witnessed across the channel.

The foundation of the Games was only the initial phase of de Coubertin's plan. They were intended ". . . to create sufficient interest to induce governments, educators and the general public to demand the establishment of physical education and amateur competitive sport" (16:59-60). A major assumption of the Olympic Movement has been, and continues to be, that massive sport and physical education program will counteract the adverse effects of industrialization and urban life, in particular the rampant materialism present in the modern world. It thus becomes evident that Olympism is concerned with far more than the staging of the Olympic Games. It is a philosophic movement geared toward ". . . motives that are purely educational and are based on the principle of pure amateurism, equality, and justice. It attempts to spread and foster the amateur spirit and to teach young people that participation in any sport whatsoever is first and foremost of benefit to themselves" (18:27).

Within this philosophy the Games become a means by which great athletes demonstrate their skills and present the youth of the world with ideal models to copy. It is assumed by the members of the Olympic Movement that a high level of performance in the Games will encourage the world's youth to emulate the competitors (17:119). Hence the Games themselves are the showcase of Olympism. In the eyes of the leaders of the Olympic Movement they are the means by which the few with exceptional talent draw the interest of the many toward sport and toward the goals and ideals espoused by the Movement. As such, the importance of the Olympic Games are clearly subservient to the aims of Olympism itself.

Olympism is predicated upon the assumption that the perfection of mankind can be attained through the harmonious development of the physical and intellectual nature. The Olympic ideal is a direct descendant of the classical concept of Mens Sana in Corpere Sano, a sound mind in a sound body. de Coubertin believed

> . . . that man did not consist of body and soul, but that man was one entity and that this entity was created by acquiring a strong and stable character. A strong character is not acquired by knowledge but by the cultivation of the body (18:24).

de Coubertin and leaders of the Olympic Movement saw three periods in history where the perfection of man was approached. Initially there was the Classical Greek period symbolized by the ancient Olympic Games where it was believed men competed only for the love of sport, the praise of their peers, and the symbolic award of a wild olive wreath. This era lasted some twelve centuries and prevailed through periods of peace and war. The Age of Chivalry followed some seven hundred years later and was said to have been characterized by the disinterested pursuit of honor, purity, and loyalty by noble knights. Finally, the third period of history in which mankind approached perfection was marked by the revival of the Olympic Games in 1896, whereby a system of sport was established to develop the physical aspect of human nature, build character, and generally provide the opportunity to cope with, and combat, the effects of industrialization and urbanization generated in the nineteenth century (24:139). These ideals were to be pursued through the medium of competitive sport.

> de Coubertin indicated that we must not forget that the objective of exercise was not solely that of creating a powerful body, but the creation of a person capable of responding to the demand of contemporary life, and he stressed that the development of all the capabilities of the individual was more important, and set as the principle and basic aim the need for the occupation of men at every age with competitions and sports (17:118).

It is evident that those involved with Olympism view it as a pedagogical movement aimed at assuming within itself ". . . a school of moral nobility and purity and a school of physical endurance" (16:57) geared toward the development of people who possess characters consistent with a classical ideal stressing the balance between the physical and the intellectual natures of the individual.

The goals pursued by the proponents of Olympism can be separated into two general concerns. First, the leaders of the Olympic Movement attempt to provide the means, in the form of competitive sport, by which an individual can develop the high sense of moral awareness that they judge essential to live a productive life in contemporary society. The second deals with international goodwill and understanding. The advocates of Olympism are convinced that through the meeting of athletes on the ostensibly friendly ground of the athletic field a step toward world peace and harmony will be taken. Thus of the two goals espoused by Olympism one is concerned with the individual as he relates to society as a whole and the other is concerned with the manner in which the nations of the world interact with one another.

Olympism, then, seeks to provide the means by which mankind can cope with the exigencies of contemporary society. Through the training and preparation for participation in sporting events the supporters of Olympism contend that an athlete will develop the qualities necessary to cope with the pressures that are brought on him by the quest for a satisfying life in a world oriented toward materialism. Members of the Olympic Movement constantly stress that,

> . . . the great benefit from the Games lies not in the victory, nor yet in participation, but in the honest, diligent and devoted preparation for participation in the Games, during which the whole of the high ideals of competitive rivalry are realized, that is regular and clean life, self-discipline, and devotion, to the moral principles of training, and the putting aside of human weakness and the improvement of the totality of the qualities of each man (17:124).

It is with particular regard to one glowing inconsistency that the emphasis on moral training through toil sheds a great deal of light.

One might think it rather curious that the Olympic Movement, which through its official governing body—the International Olympic Committee—seeks to impose limits upon the training of athletes,* would adopt a motto glorifying the pursuit of performances of ever-increasing magnitude. However, when one ponders the assumption that preparation for competition aids in the development of the character of the athletes, the use of the Olympic motto Citius-Altius-Fortius is readily understood. The essence of the contest, the truly educational facet of it, is the struggle. One cannot struggle meaningfully without a goal, and the more difficult the goal is to attain—the faster the time, the higher the leap, the longer

*See rule 26 of the Olympic Rules and Regulations.

the throw—the more intense the struggle becomes to achieve it. The greater the intensity of the struggle, the more valuable the experience. The crux of the entire philosophy rests on the belief that the lessons taught by the struggle on the sports field—perseverance, determination, magnanimity—carry over to every phase of life itself. de Coubertin states,

> Life is beautiful because the struggle is beautiful, not the sanguinary struggle, offspring of tyranny and bad passions, those which are born of ignorance and routine, but the struggle of souls searching for truth, for light and for justice (24:139).

Here the rationale behind the Olympic motto becomes clearly discernable. The pursuit of record performances as a motivating force in the athlete's training forces him to a greater degree of intensity. In this intensity he purges himself of the weakness and banality inherent in the human condition and elevates his character to the heights of physical excellence and moral purity. The athlete, in effect, educates himself through the agony of competition.

A final and undeniable tenet of Olympism is its religious character. In attributing to sport the moral qualities which proponents of Olympism do, and in attempting to use sport as a means for the establishment of world harmony and social peace, the leaders of the Olympic Movement have taken upon themselves an orientation strongly akin to the great religions of the world. Perhaps of greater significance is the belief also inculcated in Olympism that individuals can attain an inner peace comparable to a deeply mystical experience through sport. One of the first allusions to sport in the context of a personal, religious experience was made by Pierre de Coubertin himself.

> To know oneself, to regulate oneself, to conquer oneself; eternal beauty of sport, fundamental aspirations of the real sportsman, and the necessary conditions for success (24:140).

The knowledge of oneself gained from the sporting experience is quite analogous to religious involvement. To be in total control of one's body, one's existence, is perhaps the most fundamental kind of personal experience. Although it is devoid of a God-head in the traditional sense, the man himself becomes god-like and in a very real sense the object of his own adoration.

Sisto Favre, a member of the I.O.C. and active in the Olympic Movement, carries de Coubertin's statement one step further. He agrees with de Coubertin that through participation in sport man comes to reflect upon his inner being—he comes to know himself. In so doing, he comes to be aware of

> . . . the acquiring of light which, deep within is felt to be that of the Creator, the Supreme Being. The light may be unidentifiable, or it may be

defined according to capacity, and called Dvjious, Jahve, Zeus, Jove—or Deus, God (7:61).

Through the intensity of competition a person comes to know himself. By this recognition of his own being he comes to know the Power which created him.

The religious aspect of Olympism is really no different than the social or moral aspects of the philosophy. It is concerned primarily with two areas—the encouragement of world harmony and the development of an inner peace within the individual athlete. The vehicle of sport provides the perfect milieu in which the mettle of the athlete can be tested. In this testing process, including both the preparation for the contest and the contest itself, the opportunity is presented for each individual to attain an increased awareness and knowledge of himself and a higher level of social interaction.

The philosophy of Olympism is predicated on providing direction to individuals through sport, with the hope that it will result in the development of physically, intellectually and morally balanced human beings. Proponents of this philosophy insist that sport is a game, a learning tool, and not a means of pursuing material gains. When monetary concerns are introduced the educational goals and ideals promoted by the foundors of Olympism are stifled. Thus the proponent sof Olympism are adamant about the maintenance of the amateur code. In 1894 de Coubertin wrote:

> Above all it is necessary that we maintain in Sport all the characteristics of nobility and chivalry which have distinguished it in the past in such a way that they continue to form part of the education of the peoples of today just as they served so admirably in the times of ancient Greece. Humanity on the other hand has the tendency to transform the athlete into a paid gladiator. These two tendencies are incompatible (15:111).

Years later Avery Brundage would strongly support the position of de Coubertin. Brundage wrote:

> The first and most important of these rules, for good reasons, was that the games must be amateur. They are not commercial enterprise and no one, promoters, managers, coaches, participants, individuals or nations, is permitted to use them for profit (4:30).

> The amateur has an entirely different philosophy than the professional athlete, who does nothing unless he is paid. With a professional, sport is a vocation and his main objective is to win, because the more he wins th better he is paid. The amateur also wants to win, but it is the manner in which victory is won that is most important to him. He wants always to improve and he wants always to do his best in the circumstances that prevail but he does not wish to sacrifice his education or his vocation for hollow victory (4:36).

Finally, Otto Szymiczek provides a most explicit statement regarding de Coubertin's aversion to professionalism. "de Coubertin was afraid of professionalism because he attributed to it the decline of ancient athletics and because he believed that the professional outlook would neutralize the educational objectives of athletics" (18:29). In light of this then, the thrust of the amateur-professional controversy is concerned not so much with the boosting of amateurism, as with the subversion of professionalism. Paradoxically a group which de Coubertin preferred to have seen excluded from Olympic competition have had the greatest opportunity to realize the ideals and goals of Olympism. Women, who until recently have generated little interest on the international sports scene, were not the commercially marketable commodity that male athletes were. Because of this, material inducements were not offered and were not temptations to stray from the righteous path of Olympism. Now with the sudden upsurge in women's sport, the female athlete is fast becoming a very marketable commodity. Viewed from the standpoint of Olympism the unchallenged opportunity for the self realization of women through sport is fast on the wane. Unfortunately, in this area, she is rapidly achieving equality with her male counterpart. If, however, women can effectively reject the crass materialism of competitive sport they could very well come to represent the quintessence of Olympism and all that it symbolizes.

In view of these basic assumptions it should be clearly apparent that the Olympic Movement, the Olympic Games, and the International Olympic Committee are basically consanguineous. To promote the good life of sport, to spread those ideas throughout the world, to bring about international harmony, to foster moral uprightness, to provide opportunities for self-realization, and to enlighten individuals about these phenomena through the amateur Olympic ideal is the true work of the Olympic Movement. When viewed from this perspective the labyrinth of controversy surrounding the Olympics begins to unravel.

REFERENCES

1. *A Plan to Modernize the Olympic Rules by 1974.* New York: The World Sports Foundation, 1973.
2. Berlioux, Monique. *Olympism.* Lausanne, Switzerland: International Olympic Committee, 1972.
3. Brisson, Jean Francois. "How Did Pierre de Coubertin Conceive the Olympic Games? Is This Concept Adapted to the Imperatives of Modern Sport?," *Report of the Tenth Session of the International Olympic Academy, at Olympia.* Athens: The Hellenic Olympic Committee, 1970.
4. Brundage, Avery. "The Olympic Philosophy," *Report of the Third Session of the International Olympic Academy at Olympia.* Athens: The Hellenic Olympic Committee, 1963.

5. Chaffee, Suzy. *The Olympics—Tell It Like It Is or the Honor of Your Company is Kindly Requested at the Marriage of Mr. Citrus, Altius, Fortius to Ms. Mens Sana in Corpere Sano*, An Unpublished Poem, May 1, 1974.

6. Diem, Carl. "The Olympic Ideal and the Present-Day Reality," *Report of the Second Session of the International Olympic Academy at Olympia.* Athens: The Hellenic Olympic Committee, 1962.

7. Favre, Sisto. "The Philosophy of the Modern Olympic Movement," *Report of the Tenth Session of the International Olympic Academy at Olympia.* Athens: The Hellenic Committee, 1970.

8. Heatherington, Clark W. "The Foundation of Amateurism," *American Physical Education Review*, November, 1909.

9. Hughes, Thomas. *Tom Brown's Schooldays*, New York: Airmont Publishing Co., 1968.

10. Keating, James W. "The Heart of the Problem of Amateur Athletics," *The Journal of General Education*, vol. 16, no. 4, Jan., 1965.

11. Lammer, Manfred. "Amateurism and the Olympics," *The German Tribune Quarterly Review*, no. 20, November 16, 1972.

12. McIntosh, Peter C. *Physical Education in England Since 1800.* London: G. Bell and Sons Ltd., 1968.

13. *Olympic Rules and Regulations*, Lausanne, Switzerland: Comité Internationale Olympique, 1972.

14. Samaranch, Juan Antonio. "The Olympic Spirit in the Modern World," *Report of the Ninth Session of the International Olympic Academy at Olympia.* Athens: The Hellenic Olympic Committee, 1969.

15. Szymiczek, Otto. "Adhesion to the Principles of the Olympic Ideals," *Report of the Second Session of the International Olympic Academy at Olympia.* Athens: The Hellenic Olympic Committee, 1962.

16. Szymiczek, Otto. "The Fundamental Principles of the Olympic Ideology," *Report of the Tenth Session of the International Olympic Academy at Olympia.* Athens: The Hellenic Olympic Committee, 1970.

17. Szymiczek, Otto. "Materialism is the Enemy of the Olympic Ideology," *Report of the Third Session of the International Olympic Academy at Olympia.* Athens: The Hellenic Olympic Committee, 1963.

18. Szymiczek, Otto. "The Olympic Ideology," *Report of the Ninth Session of the International Olympic Academy at Olympia.* Athens: The Hellenic Olympic Committee, 1969.

19. Szymiczek, Otto. "The Olympic Ideology," *Report of the Eleventh Session of the International Olympic Academy at Olympia.* Athens: The Hellenic Olympic Committee, 1971.

20. Szymiczek, Otto. "The Olympic Ideology at the Sercie of Mankind," *Report of the Fifth Session of the International Olympic Academy at Olympia.* Athens: The Hellenic Olympic Committee, 1965.

21. Tzartzanos, Ath. A. "Amateurism," *Report of the Seventh Session of the International Olympic Academy at Olympia.* Athens: The Hellenic Olympic Committee, 1967.

22. Van Zijll, W. "Weakness and Strength of the Olympic Movement," *Report of the Fourth Session of the International Olympic Academy at Olympia.* Athens: The Hellenic Olympic Committee, 1964.

23. Vanderzwagg, Harold. *Toward a Philosophy of Sport.* Reading, Mass.: Addison-Wesley Publishing Co., 1972.

24. Vialar, Paul. "Monsieur de Coubertin and the Olympic Spirit," *Report of the Fourth Session of the International Olympic Academy at Olympia.* Athens: The Hellenic Olympic Committee, 1964.

25. Vialar, Paul. "Pierre de Coubertin," *Report of the Second Session of the International Olympic Academy at Olympia.* Athens: The Hellenic Olympic Committee, 1962.

RETROSPECT ON A YEAR OF
TITLE IX DISCUSSIONS

MARJORIE BLAUFARB

At the end of one year, during which it has been my duty and pleasure to participate in many meetings and conferences where a lot of time was taken up in discussion of Title IX of the Education Amendments of 1972 and other women's affairs, it seems appropriate to take a look at some of the concerns and trends revealed.

It is interesting to realize that although this legislation was signed by the President in June of 1972, it had little impact on the physical education and athletics establishment until November or December of 1973. And then the reaction was not to the law—not to its propriety or justice—but to what the HEW regulations might call for.

The law states that no person shall, on the basis of sex, be excluded from participation in, or be denied the benefits of, or be subjected to discrimination under any education program or activity receiving federal financial assistance. If one makes the effort, in good faith, toward including girls and women on a basis of equality in programs and employment opportunities, there should be no need to fear what regulations will say.

But for many, to do this requires the hardest change of all—a change of mindset—and the questions asked at meetings and conferences reveal unconscious prejudices and preconceptions.

For example, a favorite question when the subject of coeducational classes comes up is about liability. Tort liability for accidents occurring

From *Update* (February, 1975) AAHPER, 1201 Sixteenth Street, Washington, D.C. 20036.

during class is meant, of course. But how can teachers be more liable than they are now? If any accident occurs in the gymnasium or on the playing field, whether both girls and boys are involved or just children of the same sex, the supervising teacher is held to be liable if it can be proved that there was negligence. Unfortunately perhaps, liability is like pregnancy; you cannot be a little liable—you are or you are not.

Another question frequently brought up is about supervision of locker rooms in coeducational programs. Locker rooms will not be coeducational, of course. In many schools and communities there are already a number of coeducational classes and somehow or other locker rooms are receiving adequate supervision before and after these classes.

Where is the money for enlarged programs going to come from, is another often heard comment. This may be followed by a statement like, we cannot do what the girls want without damaging the boys program. These comments reveal exactly the kind of mindset that one hopes will be changed. It assumes that what is, i.e., a program offering much wider opportunities to boys, is what should be. However, just because something exists is no reason to continue it when it is demonstrably unjust. Ways will have to be found to reallocate available funds or raise new ones for the benefit of both sexes.

Frequently, pseudo-scientific arguments about anatomy and physiology are raised, but the sad truth is that until recently, objective research about women and physical activity has not been attempted. People have too often made assumptions based on popular misconceptions and then done research to validate the assumptions. Now that researchers are assuming that females are hardy and capable of greater physical efforts, research is beginning to validate that assumption also.

When the discussion group is mostly male, somebody almost always points out that whatever is being done is what the women wanted. There is some truth in this accusation, and it is also true that many women are still ambivalent about what they want and need. They sometimes tend to focus on side issues like which rules of games should be used, or which officiating rules, rather than on the main issue of how to provide equal opportunities without carrying along some of the admitted evils of big-time collegiate sports.

Many women involved in athletics continue to assume that they must accept the standards set by the men and that they have not the strength or backing to make reforms. Assuming that others will agree with the athletic establishment that might is right, they frequently advance their own valid point of view in a plaintive, despairing fashion which carries no conviction. But those who are determined and courageous find there is support for change and reformation.

Although the legislation does not touch on administration of departments, there is a tendency for men's and women's departments to be combined for many reasons, including those of economy. Many women are
apprehensive about coeducational physical education departments because they fear the men will have the leading positions and the women
will lose out all along the way. But this doesn't need to be so. Of course,
one cannot remain the most popular woman on the staff and also challenge the right of men to have all the administrative positions. One has
to accept the necessity for temporary unpopularity and the fact that being
an administrator is usually a lonely job.

Readers may challenge me, saying that I am a spectator so it is easy
for me to give advice. I acknowledge that, but the looker-on sees most of
the game, to quote the old cliché. It is hard to escape the feeling, as one
listens to the discussions and the questions, that those present (both men
and women) are focusing on minor issues—problems that are mostly administrative—because they don't want to face the basic dilemma or accept the fact that they have acquiesced in unjust situations for many years.

Women sometimes complain that they must accept inequality in pay,
conditions of service, and fringe benefits, because this is part of a ne-
gotiated contract on which they have no recourse. This is another in-
valid assumption. It is unlawful to make a discriminatory contract and
both parties to the contract, employer and negotiating agent, are equally
illegal when such contracts are agreed upon. This is part of the labor and
equal opportunity laws and has nothing to do with Title IX.

In many states it is not necessary to rely on federal legislation to right
inequities. There are state laws covering employment, equal opportunity,
and human rights. Sometimes it is more efficacious to use the state laws
than to rely on the federal agencies such as the Department of Health,
Education, and Welfare to follow through on complaints. Also all complaint procedures, however, are a necessarily long and slow process.

The National Association for Girls and Women in Sport has plans to
prepare a publication which would be a legislative follow-up to "Coping
With Controversy." A broad coverage of state and federal legislation is
intended which would answer the questions so often asked, including
those about complaint procedures.

During the past several months, many women AAHPER members
have told me that they find themselves doing some painful thinking about
stands previously taken. They have examined some of their preconceptions and realized they were based on assumptions unfair to themselves
and their female students. Such persons should be admired—it is hard to
admit that ideas one has cherished through the years were really prejudices and not golden rules.

One point seems clear. The reorganization of AAHPER occurred at the very time when the girls and women's sports profession had to face major upheavals because of societal changes. It has been accepted that they were outside politics, and suddenly it became necessary to know about politics and to take some stands. They had been against highly organized sports and yet became the sponsors of the association governing intercollegiate athletics for women. They had a reputation for being old-fashioned and slow to change and yet subjected themselves to a rigorous self-examination resulting in radical changes in their new structure.

The outlook is bright; it is not hard to be optimistic. There are many people of both sexes who have real sensitivity and good will and who are working on these problems constructively. Good models of what can be achieved are developing. Inertia and resistance to change exist in educational administrations at all levels, but changes will happen just as fast in our area of education as in others.

What one must say to those who are discouraged by the lack of action is, compare where we are now in all respects to where we were a few years ago. There have been positive changes, and there will be many more because of everybody's increased awareness.

Ruth Schellberg, president of the Minnesota Women's Equity Action League, and AAHPER Archivist, informs us of the following resolution passed at the WEAL National Conference, held in Washington, D.C. December 7 and 8, 1974:

WHEREAS educational institutions throughout the country are frequently merging their girls and women's physical education and athletic programs with their boys and men's programs under the guise of responding to the equal rights movement and

WHEREAS in reality many of these mergers are male take-overs of the women's physical education and athletic programs,

BE IT RESOLVED that where merger occurs, an affirmative action plan be written to insure that women employees are not demoted or removed and that they retain decision making authority, and that opportunities for women and girls be strengthened.

BIBLIOGRAPHY

Section A. Social Systems—

3. Education—

Flath, Arnold, ed. *Athletics in America,* Proceeding of the Conference, February, 1972 at Orgon State University. Corvalis, Ore.: Oregon University Press, 1972.

Leonard, George. *The Ultimate Athlete: Re-visioning Sports, Physical Education and the Body.* New York: Viking Press, 1975.

Padwe, Sandy. "Big-Time College Football Is on the Skids," *Look,* (Sept. 22, 1970):66-69.

Pullias, E. V. "The Role of Sport in Higher Education." D.G.W.S. National Conference on Sports Education for College Women, Estes Park, Colorado. (June 1969).

Saasta, Tom. "Athletics: A Question of Values." University of Southern California *Daily Trojan*, Sept. 27, 1971, p. 4.

Sage, George H. *Sport and American Society*, 2d ed. Reading, Mass.: Addison-Wesley, 1974.

Scott, Jack. *The Athletic Revolution*. New York: The Free Press, 1971.

Sievert, William. "Cost Burdens, Waning Student Interests Hit Intercollegiate Sports." *The Chronicle of Higher Education* (January 25, '71).

Welch, J. E. "A Challenge Answered," *The Physical Educator* (Dec. 1969): 155.

SECTION

B

SOCIAL SYSTEMS:
4. RELIGION

The connection between sport and religion has long intrigued philosophers and theologians. The sport experience as one that assists the participant in transcending the ordinary and thereby immortalizing the self via extraordinary feats of skill, strength, and discipline is often described as spiritual or religious in nature. The examination of sport as a religious experience is the task of the philosopher. Both Slusher and Weiss attempt to present the sport experience in the light of its religious components.

In the first article, Slusher takes a broad perspective of "sport and the religious." He draws parallels between sport and religion as systems that employ many of the same avenues to achieve the end experience (i.e., ritual, justice). Both systems also endeavor to create order and both function in maintaining tradition. Slusher suggests that there are at least three major categories of doubt a person must be concerned with if one is to enter into meaningful thought about one's sport involvement: namely, scientific doubt, pragmatic doubt, and existential doubt. The major emphasis of Slusher's article falls into this last category. The existential question of "Who am I when I perform?" is carefully and thoughtfully considered.

Weiss seems to concentrate more on the experience of the male athlete. As a man, the athlete is "like all other men obligated to do the best he can in every case." He then sets out to describe the ways the athlete is unlike other men. The athlete dedicates himself, prevents his body from acting on impulse and for a time puts aside the everyday world. Within the athletic endeavor Weiss sees the athlete as a man of action who "uniquely unites matter and meaning."

In the publication *Social Research* another facet of Olympism is explored by von Kortzfleisch.[1] He contends that "popular sports are repre-

1. S. von Kortzfleisch, "Religious Olympism," *Social Research* 37, no. 2 (Summer 1970):231-36.

sentative of the religious phenomenon of the present time." The author likens the Olympic Movement to a twentieth-century religion and suggests that it can be described as a substitute religion.

If the reader is interested in the relationship between sport and organized religion (i.e., the church) both Lüschen (Part I, Section B) and McIntosh[2] discuss that relationship.

2. Peter McIntosh, *Sport in Society* (London: C. A. Watts and Co., Ltd., 1963).

SPORT AND THE RELIGIOUS

Howard Slusher

At first impression it would normally be assumed there is little, if any, relationship between sport and religion. Sport is a competitive, dynamic, and, to a great degree, individualistic activity. Religion is a noncompetitive process founded upon deliberation and commonality of social organization.

Upon further investigation and analysis it can be realized both are areas of human activity expressing a strong desire to formulate a value structure in keeping with the "common good." Both sport and religion employ intricate rituals which attempt to place events in traditional and orderly view. Although both are rather emphatic about the demanded intellectual involvement, one cannot help but wonder if this trait has not been greatly exaggerated. One has to doubt whether intellect is not overshadowed by what the religionist calls "belief" and the athlete calls spirit. To put it another way, is there a great deal of difference between the *mystical* elements in sport and religion? Both realms weave extensive laws and rules around the activities and participants. Although often given logical explanations, relative to this form of externalized regulation, more often than not the basis is in traditional truths which may or may not have modern reasons for support of the order.

Another interesting parallel between sport and religion is in the area of *justice*. In religion God is *just;* while in sport the credo is "may the best man win." Somewhere, in both sport and religion, there is realization of the unjust or the unfortunate, but likewise, theoretically, it is ignored. God *is* just. And the best man *will* win.

From *Man, Sport and Existence: A Critical Analysis,* pp. 121-38 (Philadelphia: Lea & Febiger, 1967). Reprinted by permission.

Although both sport and religion are concerned with *justice*, it might be in error to assume both realms of human activity draw upon *truth* as the foundation for *rightness*. However, it is equally erroneous to assume truth is not a segment of both sport and religion. Although truth is dealt with in other sections of this work, it is important to look at this concern in relation to sport and religion. This is necessitated by the frequent observation that religious truth is fundamentally different from other categorizations of truth. This analysis will demonstrate the existence of areas of equivalence.

Literature is filled with the truths of statements. Scientists know well that they need be *amoral*. They might well formulate and *test* a hypothesis; however, to attempt to prove it to be true is simply not to be a scientist. The scientist must remain objective and "above" morality. Thus, truth is an impartial outcome. On the other hand, religious truth is a product of personalization. It is derived frequently from a system of beliefs, a process of extended morality with extreme personalized concerns.

I contend that religious truth is one often used in sport. While it may be clever logic to state that propositions in sport, as in religion, demand careful scrutiny because of the complexity of the task (truth *is* more than victory), it simply is not "the way the game is played." Evidence is for gotten, facts are reduced, tentative conclusions are founded upon the present and most often the expedient. Sandy Koufax, in a recent article, hinted at this type of truth as one when the *given* does not work: "truth" becomes anything as long as it spells victory. "When you have your stuff, you *should* win . . . when you can end up winning not on . . . your arm, which is, after all, a gift, but on the strength of your brains and your experience and your knowledge, it is a victory that you feel *belongs peculiarly to yourself* [*italics mine*]" (Koufax, 1966, p. 91). On the surface, one could say this is most unlike religious truth. Certainly, religious truth is beyond mere "I pray to gain" philosophy. However, in reality Koufax is indicating something much beyond *the pragmatic*. Is he, by saying "it is a victory that you feel belongs peculiarly to yourself," indicating a personalization of *true* religious involvement? This is not *just* a God-given victory. This is truly a religious experience of personhood.

The apparent non-religious perceptions of the truth of and/or sport are derived from the mistaken attempt to relate religious truth with either the natural or humanistic concerns. In reality the athlete needs to sponsor a personal search. Truth becomes a religious commitment. A type of personal "sentence" to locate truth through a process that Tillich might call doubt and faith.

Doubt, Faith and Concern. To locate the truth of a situation the man of sport must *free* himself to question, to inquire, to doubt. Doubting, as a process, is what makes man really human. It is in a sense, his mechanism to reach and fulfill human dignity. The sport situation not only provides this opportunity for the performer, it demands it. Each movement is subject to personal doubt. Is this one most efficient? Do I act now? How might I increase performance? It would indeed be rare for an athlete not to question his own worth and value each and every time he enters the sport situation.

At first glance the opportunity to doubt might well appear to be a great temptation. Given this freedom that is provided in sport, will man not doubt to excess? And secondly, will not the process of doubting bring about increased anxiety? The answer to both questions is unequivocally negative.

First, doubting must be recognized as a process of externalizing that which is already internal. Man does not and cannot doubt something that he does not possess as a prior awareness. That is to say, the sportsman cannot doubt if his act of hunting is really a desire for "game" as opposed to a desire to kill, unless he already has this question *within* his self. A doubt is simply not manufactured. It is an expression of uncertainty due to a prior condition. Therefore, if a doubt is present it must be responded to. There is no question of excess since the doubt represents an area of human dilemma requiring additional information and communication.

The question of increasing anxiety is still with us. It is almost as if man were completely Zen. Do we really believe that when man is thinking he is showing signs of illness? I think not. Anxiety is increased, not when the doubt is considered, but when the doubt is not dispelled. Bury a doubt, stop a doubt, hide it, refuse to seek the truth and one might reach short term "peace" but not a deeper peace that only the truth can achieve. Indoctrination and external censureship is something that man is constantly facing. To be stopped from the outside is bad enough, but to deceive the self by a type of self-indoctrination is still worse. Man must face his doubts. He must turn to them with an honest attempt to solve them. And to accomplish this he must employ real *concern*.

As the man of sport enters into meaningful thought about his activity, there are at least three major categories of doubt that must be answered by concern. First, he must encounter the *scientific* doubt. Will what I am doing "hold up" under the same conditions? Secondly, and usually a primary doubt for the sportsman, is the *pragmatic* doubt. Will what I am doing work? And finally we have the *existential* doubt. What is the meaning of this activity for me as an individual? Why do I participate? Who am I when I perform? It is this latter doubt that is basically the concern of this book. Namely, what is the role of sport in man's existence? The existential doubt can only be answered by deep concern of the individual. He cannot run away from the doubt. For if he does, the doubt will not disappear; rather it will increase the *felt* anxiety. The way to dissipate doubt is to demonstrate structured concern. Through the search, and perhaps the answer, man will achieve real life, a life that would be denied if man were to continue to live with the anxieties of doubt.

It has been my experience that sport has the potential to assist man in a demonstration of a meaningful concern relative to the existential doubt. In the awareness of human movement man could well come to develop a sensitivity of his own self that would be most rewarding. Perhaps some do. But in honesty most do not. In fact, sport is frequently *used* as a place to escape the existential doubt. "I will hit a little harder." "I will work a little more." "I will be a little tougher." "I will stay with it a little longer." In the fierceness of sport man tends to lose any form of existential concern. It is rare indeed when man enters sport with the desire to explore the self rather than defeat the other. Parenthetically, I might add that at times sport works in spite of the individual, and awareness is brought home without an extended concern.

Perhaps this is one of the most important dimensions of sport. In this *special* media of time of space, unlike the real world, man can use *concern* to arrive at a solution for his doubts. Certainly, he learns the realistic limits of his physical capacity. More frequently than not he comes to realize how much preparation he needs for a given event in life. And about this there can be little negative comment. But does he come to know himself? Does he learn the *real* lessons in life, and not the typical naive concept of "getting off the ground"? The application of concern takes time, real time. It requires man to analyze his own worth, and to question his own dignity. At the minimum it asks man to be committed to the search for truth of the self. It is truly a moral and religious process that goes beyond cognition. Again, we must ask if man truly takes the time necessary in sport or does he take the expedient road and *involve* himself so deeply in the *activity* of sport that he "shuts out" the potential for concern and ultimately a meaningful existence.

To employ concern is more than taking the time for reflection. As has been indicated, it is the embellishment in a truly religious situation. Concern would be directionless if it did not incorporate an element of *faith,* a faith that is *more* than *belief.* In typical theology, belief is a statement of probability. That is, if one says, "I believe we will win the game," he is expressing a statement of probability. He is saying, "We probably will win." If the coach says, "I have faith we will win the game," he is expressing a statement quite *beyond* an expression of probability. He is not asking for blind acceptance. Rather the statement of faith is one of concern, deep concern. His *faith* is an indication he is not going to sit back and "let the chips fall where they may." But rather, through *faith,* his deep concern will cause him to work, study and re-evaluate. To answer the doubt which belief shuts the doors to further learning. Probability, by definition, indicates there is no real reason to do anything more in life. One must take his chances. Belief (probability) will cause man to accept the fortunes in answering his doubt, a most unsatisfactory method for locating authentic existence. Conversely, constant concern, causing increasing searching, brings man to a new and open *existenz.* He now is able to come closer to an authentic answer to the prevailing doubt. Now, through the use of doubt and concern, he comes to recognize the truth of sport as applicable to the person. He comes to know himself, not as a thing, but as a person operating in a realm of existence that provides him with some partial solutions to very basic elements of life.

He has recognized the doubt. He has opened his self to it. He has employed concern, via faith, to reduce anxiety and to arrive closer to the truth. He is closer to the authentic life through his perceptive involvement in sport. He is more than what he was. Because of this religious experience in sport, is man now a "happy" person?

This question cannot be answered in either the affirmative or negative. The employment of faith to answer one's doubts does not guarantee any form of "perfect happiness." And yet man is truly better if this sport participation includes spiritual awareness. Perhaps the answer to this problem is given best by Paul Tillich in his work, *The Courage to Be.*

The use of faith to attempt to resolve man's doubts takes a great deal of *courage.* It is in faith that man *risks* what he considers to be valuable and important to him. When the man of sport inquires, of himself, about the *true* reasons he hunts, he might very well find out he is not motivated by the altruistic desires he was allowing himself to believe. In risking to find the true answer, man might well lose what he desires most. This indeed takes *courage.* It is easier to live in ignorance. It is easier to dogmatically shout down the doubt prior to the use of faith. Certainly it is easier to fire the gun or hit the man next to you than to ask, "why"? Why do I do the things I do?

Of course the reward of faith—if there is one—is that it brings man closer to authenticity. It allows him to know what is truly so. He risks. He might lose. But he also might win. In fact he always wins, through faith. How can man be less than a victor when he relates his sport activity to the self in a manner that constitutes a reflection of authentic personal existence, an existence that is predicated not on tradition but on the situation as it now presents itself, free *from* an unaware life and free *for* existential completeness—a life of *meaning*.

The Religious Meaning of Sport. If conceptual work on sport is to be fruitful, somewhere it must concern itself with the meaning sport has for man. In this way the sport experience can be viewed as a potential for reality rather than an abstraction.

Sport is real. It is very real. Its systematic position, with its emphasis on the contribution of physical things in their existential structure, illuminates the extremes of reality. Its events and phenomena occur in life and give rise to the indispensable synthesis of *personal* existence. The gymnast must consider the objectivity of science, the quiet of the aesthetic, and the instance of emotion. All are meshed into the total product. The gymnast, *in* his movement, means *all* that he can realize. In the language of the religionist, he culminates his personal life with a transcendence that is more than *mere human.*

Athletes, in general (or at least those that are judged good beyond their mechanization), at some point in time, come to realize that there is something beyond *all* that is mortal, *all* that is comprehensible by the human mind. Within the movements of the athlete a wonderful mystery of life is present, a mystical experience that is too close to the religious to call it anything else. The meaning of life arrives in the culmination of the possibilities.

In this, experiencing of the mystical, the athlete becomes aware of that which is *beyond* reality. To *the* athlete this is a personal sensation. It is more than *fascination* or *interest*. It is a form of dynamic voluntarism that extends man *beyond* the powers of rational mind and physical body. It is truly a wonder that the gymnast feels—he knows, in fact he *more* than knows, that he can *truly* express his own "state" in motion. He transcends the actual, and as most mystics, he performs so that *he is* now *available to the performance* in a way that is not completely understood by performer *or* spectator.

Like religion, sport offers its "followers" a grouping of myths, symbols and rituals that facilitate the total experience. It must be understood that basically religion makes life easier. It places life into an orderly sphere. The spirit of man, in sport and religion, is an exercise of personal venture into the scientifically unknown. The arenas and coliseums are little more than shrines for *spiritual* activity. They allow man to escape the boredom of everyday life and reach out to a larger existence.

> Through bodily activities subjected to the control of the will, energy and courage are sustained, and the individual seeking contact with nature draws nearer to the elemental forces of the universe. (Jaspers, 1957, p. 68)

Man transcends the daily life and even the sport itself. He goes beyond reality, nature and even imagination to a location for the self. "The one who experiences it knows that it is important for him; it concerns the *meaning of his existence*" [italics mine] (Guardini, 1962, p. 90). Suddenly, the athlete, in his movement through space, senses a quality of *allness*, a form of complete unification.

The performer becomes sensitized to life. He becomes responsive to his alliance with *another*. He cannot reduce spirit to function—a constant demand of the "real" world of sport—but he can transform the functional to make it *more* than real. The gymnast uses *nature* to defy it. As he is suspended from his "rings," he experiences a sense of the *unusual*. His *real* existence is precarious. One slip, one miss, one moment of loss of concentration and *all* is defeated. In a *whole moment* he instantaneously and simultaneously concentrates on the action but at the same time *detaches* himself from the real. He is in this world and yet another.

Man's wholeness (spirit, mind and body) is integrated in sport. The mystical element of sport attempts to clarify certain aspects that are not, in other ways, understood; yet the paradox is also true; it makes sport more difficult to comprehend. Man becomes intimate with himself and is now ready and available to others. He comes to learn what it is to be an individual, but in a rather distinctive way he learns imminent responsibility for the collective. (This is especially valid in "team sports.") *Others* are allowed in; fellowman becomes one through the mystery of sport involvement.

Sport, like religion, assists the participant in developing an idea of his self. Through the dependence on authority (rules and officials) and at the expense of personal determinism, man attains personhood. Of course in giving up his freedom, a rather expensive price for one to pay, he receives a commodity in exchange; namely, the security of personhood. In the game he *knows* what he is to do. He is to *win*. Regardless of the level of the competition he knows he is to win. He is told to advance the ball, enjoy himself, etc. Whatever the "directive" he knows well the "name of the game." It is *win*. It is rare that man's goals in life are so clearly defined.

As in religion, the athlete must place great importance on the worth of his fellowman. He needs to *recognize* "him" not as an aid to his transcendence as much as an awareness of a *reason for being*. But this in itself might well be a contradiction since it has not been established that man does have a reason for anything, much less sport. This *compulsion* for purpose is best translated as leading a life in a meaningful direction. Thus, sport as religion *gives* man a reason for his *being* and thereby really discovers its own significance in man's existence.

In the new and freshly rediscovered cosmos of each sportsman lies a *personal* approach to transcendence. Just as no valid claim can be made for any specific religion to have the *only* path to a deity, similarly for a specific sport to assume it best contributes to man's existence is nothing but presumption.

Sport, as religion, is a form of *symbolic* representation of meaningful realities. To be religious is to provide spirit to the symbols of the mystical. In religion man admits his dependence on the *nonrational*. So it is in sport. Much time is spent scouting an opponent and scientifically devising game plans. This type of activity will no doubt continue as man attempts to reduce empirically his degree of error through scientific validation. But when it is all done, the reasons for victory are frequently explained in mystical terms. "They *wanted* the game more than we did." "They had heart." "They showed great spirit and desire." We continue to *try* but admit life is *really* impossible to plan. We accept the compromise that reality forces upon us, or at least reveals to us.

To understand personhood is to comprehend truth. To insist on a proof for the truth of religion is to mistake the absolute for the known. Sport provides the truth of performance. The fact that truth is personal and subject to the situation is to say no more than that it is not universal. There is no one way to play the game. The performer must select a personal pattern, suited to himself and/or the team. He attains his truth and worth through the limitations of these confines. Once he has made the original choice of participation, he is condemned to act in accordance with established patterns, or else the contest is absurd.

There is a purpose to religion and sport that is located in the minds of man. It is meaning. In both realms man determines the limitations as he adapts his own disposition to the realm of the *almost* impossible. To comply with the dream of betterment, the religious and sporting both turn to metaphysical realities in an attempt to locate the finite and real. It is not surprising therefore that sport, like religion, employs an extensive ritualistic dimension to its relative activities.

RITUAL

Religion has been a constant force in the history of man. For some religion has formed a path to absolute thought; while for others it has expressed relativity of expression. However, regardless of personalized expression, the tradition, ceremony and rituals of religious life have traditionally given *order* to man's existence. In truth, whatever else religion is—and it is many things to many people—it is a media affording persons relatively stable ways of attaining the security necessary to live in a dynamically accelerated and changing world. To be sure, to understand religious life is to go beyond the obvious organizational doctrines. One has to be sensitive to the internalized and subtle relationships found within all of living. One has to *feel* the mystic to *really* understand. Yet the rituals of religious life are not to be considered superficially.

A similar relationship exists in sport. In and by itself sport provides man with a range of personalized meaning. Like religion sport situations are filled with ritual. This is not to say that one can understand sport by simply relating to ritual. Just as in religion, full appreciation depends on an awareness of what is not always obvious. Yet one can hardly ignore the place of ritual in modern sport.

The evolution of man has demonstrated a constant and prevailing need for ritual. Modern man's *need* for ritual continues. But to a greater degree than ever before, religion, and the associated rituals, plays less of a role in man's life than perhaps at any other point in history. With the reduction of ritual in religion, it is not surprising man turns to other "rites" to again see some form of quasi-order to his life. For many, sport fulfills this function.

Example after example could be utilized to illustrate the parallel in ritual between sport and religion. Perhaps two will suffice. In religious life *morality* is the *summum bonum*. To live as one *should* is to be valued. If one cannot lead the perfect way (and few of us do), there are established rituals ranging from confession to renunciation. In sport man is to play according to the rules. When he does not, he too faces "rituals" ranging from warnings to removal from the activity. One has to wonder if there is any relationship between the confessional "box" in church and the "penalty" box in ice hockey.

Any football "widow" can tell you that one of the first events of any football game is the "traditional" flip of the coin, a ritual determining who will kick-off, who will receive and who will defend which goal. Not too long ago this act was the *real thing*. However, today's game of football requires such intricate planning that the "flip of the coin" is *really* performed much before game time. This of course enables both teams to make extensive strategic plans. But the *ritual* continues. Prior to each contest the "captains" (an interesting ritualistic word in itself) go through this bit of acting. All for the sake of keeping *order* in the life of the spectator—and the television camera!

This discussion is not intended to develop a negative concept of rituals. Often rituals bring about "higher" outcomes for people than perhaps were originally intended by the participants. The man of sport like the man of religion must always ask, "What does one desire when he enters into the sport situation?" Frequently, the conscious benefits of victory, acclaim and monetary factors are re-evaluated by true appreciation of the value inherent in the activity.

A concomitant outcome associated with ritual in sport, which is frequently taken for granted, relates to the rather strong allegiance achieved through the various and sundry rites. As in religion, sport has maintained the interest of the populace by observation of rituals ranging from ingestion of specific foods (peanuts and hot dogs are as much a part of baseball as is home plate) to the recognition of special events (doubleheaders are normally played on July Fourth and Labor Day).

The codes of the hunter and fisherman, specifically related to *means*, perhaps are what differentiate the sportsman from the killer. The rituals of limits, bait, and test of line are as much an attempt to preserve the ideal of the spirit of sport as they are a realistic precaution to preservation of wild life. The rituals afford the average sportsman a *reason* to participate, a reason more noble than "just catching something to eat." Soon he becomes extensively involved in the *sport* situation and achieves strength through the associated values.

Festivities related to sport events, from the All-Star baseball game to the friendly golf game at the local club, include rituals which deepen and strengthen the impressiveness of the activity. Can a baseball game *really* start if each man were to just take the field when he was ready? I think not. The team must be *led* by the captain on to the field. In golf the player with the lowest score on the previous hole has *honors* on the next hole. Thus, he hits first. Although this ritual often slows up the golf game, the custom continues (generally the person with the highest score would be the shortest hitter and therefore could tee-off when a strong driver would need to wait). Nevertheless, the rite continues—each man aware of the *honor* and tradition.

Examples are almost endless. The huddle with players and coach with interwoven hands and arms prior to taking the basketball court; the traditional handshake between rival football players after the contest; the touching of the gloves by boxers at the start of the match; the tossing out of the baseball for the first game by a dignitary; touching *each* base when the ball is hit *out* of the baseball park; the seventh inning stretch; the meeting of umpires and representatives of each baseball team prior to *each game*—all of this does something to enshrine devotion to "societal values." I think it is more than coincidence that baseball, perhaps more than any other sport, appears filled with ritual. Could this be what we mean when we say it is the "national pastime"?

From the fields and streams to the sandlots, rituals attempt to unite man to the activity. The ritual in the church and the ritual on the field are both remnants of the actual. To a degree they are symbols attempting to communicate meaning to man in his activity. For this, modern man has desperate need. To many, sport *becomes* what religion *was*—it serves as the prevailing attempt to keep order and loyalty.

This, of course, is not to say that the meaning in sport is the same as one received in religion. The *real* ideal is too far removed. However, the ritual is there for those who need and want the necessary symbolization.

Again it is the ritual in sport, just as it is in religion, that plays a part in the unification of the participants. Through systematized forms, rules, commands, and prohibitions man is united with his fellow man. It is of interest that baseball, again, often makes use of religious terms to express the giving up of oneself for the good of the whole. The "sacrifice" shows man is *really* one of a team or group. This is in keeping with the earliest of religious rites. Sacrifice is of great import to the sport scene and let no one be naive in believing it does not appeal to the "religious in man."

I think it is fair to generalize to the point of saying that ritual maintains both a real and important role in sport and religion. Although it often might be outdated, sublime and unpractical, the ritual remains. In sport there is great action. Frequently, the ritual turns man away from the inward self and brings pressure to accept externalized stimulations. This external nature of sport is the facet that makes many sensitive individuals deplore the role of sport in our culture. For in itself it threatens to take the *sporting* aspects out of sport; and to replace it with superficial pomp and rite. In a word, it threatens to make all sport a "spectacle" and vocational, if not professional. This is frequently difficult to see because the rituals *themselves*, for the most part, appear to be joyous and festive.

SPORT AS A RELIGIOUS SYMBOL

Sport as a symbol of human involvement reflects a sensitivity to spirit. Man's intensity of participation and his commitment to movement, as *more than he knows it to mean*, is descriptive of the type of subjective sensitivity, at times identified with a religious structure. Certainly, on the surface, it appears that man's *symbolic movement* and religious symbolism are polarities. Sport is obvious, distinct, goal oriented and almost crude. Religion is mystical, supple, process centered and almost elegantly pure. But for one who sees beyond the surface there is more. Sport is a religious symbol in the sense that it does not *really* relate to a cosmos of *things* and *objects* but an expression of a meaningful reality of man as an *inner whole*.

In this sense, sport is *more* than a symbolic "set" eventuating into a genetic theory. Sport is more than an avenue for release of aggression. Its form extends beyond a *mechanism* for socialization. If any *one* thing (and certainly sport is beyond a single entity), sport endorses Nietzsche's "will to power." But again the symbolic figuration of sport is more than the expression of the definite.

Sport, as religion and, for that matter, politics, evolves into a symbolically developed *ideology*. Sport becomes both what it is and a declaration of the culture. If one needs objective evidence, he need look no further than the Americanization of sport in keeping with the technological and materialistic values of our society. Fencing, once a sport of beauty and grace, is now "aided" by electrical "gadgetry," all done so that we can better *judge* man. Collegiate athletics, personified by "big time football" is an accepted prostitution of mankind. In institutions espousing all the high-sounding ethics of mankind, faculty and administration "look the other way" so the "mighty buck" continues to roll through the gates. Thus, the creed of *play* is replaced by a *work-out*. Contrast the western world of goals with the eastern emphasis on process in sport. Herrigel demonstrates clearly that archery is a *within*, and deeply religious experience. To a certain degree, one could say that the sport phenomenon possesses a potential for the *immediate* which is only actualized when a process of transcendence occurs within the participant. In reality, one must admit this is rarely achieved on the American sport scene. Again, the materialistic cult to which we pay honor places a competitive premium on sport. The soul of the culture and the soul of man is typified by the often referred to quotation, "nice guys finish last."

If we leave sport, as empirically determined in the modern western world, and turn our attention to its transcendent quality, then again it is possible to perceive the religious symbol. Sport, played as is, may still express a "soul" to man. It is possible to appreciate a basically religious symbol if man can *extend* to beyond the empirical nature of the symbol. Thus, sport can be viewed as a symbolic force of religious dimension.

To say sport is symbolically significant is not sufficient. The truth that symbols are empirically representative of the culture indicates, to a degree, the *problem* of the sport-religious position. That is to say, transcendence must go beyond the societal imagery. It is this dimension that makes *meaning* a possibility. However, none of this is possible unless there is recognition of the sport symbol as *valid* in its own right, in its *existence*. The specific phenomenon, be it an Olympic performance or part of a junior high school track meet, has a potential for being-in-itself. One need do no more than look into the soul of the performer to recognize the religious association, one of depth, sensitivity, faith and tenderness. Listen to the words of Buddy Edelen, one of the great marathon runners of the United States, when he was asked, due to his long training regimen, when he has time to go to church. "I was closer to God out there on those roads than most people get to Him in a lifetime." Probably only Mr. Edelen *really knows* what he *means.*

Perhaps, at this point in the discussion, it is necessary to differentiate between two different types of symbols analogous to both sport and religion. First, there is the empirical symbol, one which establishes validity of sport and religion. Second, the symbol of transcendence, which goes beyond the actual.

In the first category, religionists are apt to place symbols that relate to divine beings. Religious symbols are representative of the eventuation of the mystical process. Although many examples can be given on this level to parallel religion, it is important to recognize that the present concern is with sport as a religious symbol and *not* the symbols contributing to religious and sporting life. Thus, many sport experiences actually form religious symbolization in that they signify a God-like concept. For many the experience is *ultimate* and, at the same time, potentialized with religious qualities.

The transcendence symbol is one that goes beyond the present. It is a concept which incorporates all of *life.* To objectify the conceptualization might be to demonstrate reality, but in no way does it represent the true feeling of the act. The sport performer accepts the elements, even if not as a believer, and becomes *aware* of the world. Although his specific act, as a sport occurrence, might not be religiously intended, it maintains the *potential* for true awareness through the conscious. How true this act *really* is is a function of the *inner man.*

SPORT AND RELIGION—AS INSTITUTIONS

An initial inquiry into sport and religion indicates the institutionalization of both facets of human life. The splendor of institutional religious life by clergy, temples, laws, and literature is comparable to commissioners, stadiums and arenas, rules of the game and an extensive heritage of truth and folklore.

Modern day sport has become institutionalized at almost all levels. Few youngsters can enjoy the feeling of playing a "pick-up" game. Interests of socialization initially led to specified customs. The higher the level of organization, the greater the psychic and financial involvement demanded by the institutionalizer. All of this has made serious impressions upon the participant.

Firmly established as a secular activity, sport has become a function of communal involvement. One cheers for the Green Bay Packers, the Los Angeles Dodgers (one is still tempted to say Brooklyn Dodgers) or the American Olympic team. In truth these designations are most artificial. In recent years baseball teams have changed city allegiance and basketball teams are "gypsy" in the way they leave one city for another. Who could ever believe the Brooklyn "Bums" would move to "hip" Los Angeles? But it did happen. The institution is there in name but not in roots. Nevertheless man identifies with *his* representative.

The paradox of this activity, of appearing change, is relative to internal and external alteration. In religion, the church edifice might alter its appearance or even move to another locale; perhaps clergy will even be reassigned. But the structure always remains constant with the basic ideology and purposes of the institution. So it is in sport. Man and facilities are altered but the basic purpose remains constant. The sport participant comes to recognize the "character" of the institution and identifies with the *meaning* of the institution. The New York Yankees capitalized on the "what it means to be a Yankee" attitude for years. Players who were "washed-up" were traded into near greatness when they joined the Yankees (John Mize, John Sain, and John Hoppe were just a few who learned to play "like Yankees"). The cry to "break-up" the Yankees was indeed a cry to *de*institutionalize.

Similar to religious institutions, the world of sport is slow to make internal alterations. Major league baseball remained in two leagues with a total of sixteen teams for roughly half a century. Weight classifications in boxing have not been considerably altered in recent years, despite changing conditions directly related to increased size of the human. Rules, although they undergo minor alterations, really are quite static (tennis is still scored with the traditional love, deuce, etc.), which in truth makes little sense and leads to a great amount of confusion.

Attached to the image of institutions, especially true in religion, is the idea that they are so large, and thereby secure, that they tend to be moral. Yet ethical conduct, in truth, is the last consideration of most institutionalized sports. Witness, if you may, the example of recruiting collegiate athletes or the "baby-sitting" system established during the wars between the National Football League and the American Football League. All of this is supposedly forgotten now that they have met on the field with the traditional handshake. Much like the "purification ceremonies intended to remove the effects of broken taboo," the sport scene attempts to demonstrate its morality for the world (Coe, 1916, p. 114).

The image of sport that confronts the populace is one that reflects, not the institution, but the spirit and vitality of that which should be sport. Frequently, it is little more than a symbol. From this form new and live meanings are derived. Thus, like the bowing at public worship, man's standing for the seventh inning stretch becomes a part of the image.

This is not to assume that the derived meaning presently held from sport in some way reflects the heritage of the symbolic form. Sport is more flexible than most institutions. Since the ideal is not *really* idealized virtue, a type of pragmatic loyalty develops, a legion to the ego of the institutional directors.

It is of interest to view the rather dynamic change (comparatively) in institutionalized sport during the latter half of the twentieth century. Although private organizations, mainly out for the *goal* (whether it be a Stanley Cup or the Little League Championship), support the institutionalization of sport, there is growing evidence that humanistic concerns can emerge. One example is the Stokes Benefit Game. This annual affair sees some of the greatest basketball players of all time volunteer their services for a charitable cause. Perhaps the tasks of sport are not all impersonalized. But yet one wonders if this, like the Shriner's East-West Football Classic, is not an example of the "exception that proves the rule."

BIBLIOGRAPHY

Coe, G. A. *The Psychology of Religion.* Chicago, University of Chicago Press, 1916.

Guardini, R. "The Phenomenology of Religious Experience." *Philosophy Today,* 6, 90, 1962.

Jaspers, K. *Man in the Modern Age.* New York, Anchor Books, Doubleday, 1957.

Koufax, S. "The Customers Come to Watch Us Live a Part of Our Lives." *Look,* 30, pp. 90-92, 1966.

Tillich, P. *The Courage to Be.* New Haven, Yale University Press, 1952.

A METAPHYSICAL EXCURSUS

Paul Weiss

Most men live without vision or wisdom. The few who act as large-sized men, do so only part of the time. Rarely do any of us push ourselves to the sticking point. Even more rarely do we raise our heads above the multitude of tasks and details that besiege us daily. The athlete avoids this sad propect by temporarily accepting a life which makes it desirable for him to learn to control his body and the agencies by means of which that body will meet the challenges of other bodies and the world about. As a consequence, though he does not thereby acquire vision, he escapes for a time from some of the confusions characteristic of daily life; and though he does not thereby become wise, he does benefit from the wisdom inherent in a well-toned, skilled, effective body.

Like all other men, the athlete is obligated to do the best he can in every case. Unlike most other men, he dedicates himself. As a consequence he accepts an obligation and makes a strong effort to fulfill it. He therefore prevents his body from acting on impulse, to make it the servant for achieving excellence. For a short period he uses his native freedom with maximum effect, to place himself for a moment alongside artists, religious men, and inquirers of every stripe.

The athlete's world is set over against the everyday world. Economic demands and the satisfaction of appetites are for the moment put aside. This is also what is done by ethical men in their endeavors to realize ideal goals. Artists and historians similarly bracket off their distinctive, dynamic spatiotemporal worlds. They are matched by religious men who make both private and public efforts to achieve a closer contact with and to conform to the demands of their God. All turn from the world of common sense and its practical demands to try to come to grips with distinct finalities.

Nature, the ideal Good, and God are ultimate and everlasting. Each has its own characteristic particulars which depend on it for their being, just as it depends on them for articulation and effectiveness The scholar and the athlete, the one through study and knowledge, the other through action, are directly related to limited versions of these ultimate finalities, and directly related to the unlimited form of another finality, which I have elsewhere termed "Actuality."

The more a man cuts himself off from the world around him, in order to identify himself with what is ultimately real, the more he opens himself up to the presence of Actuality, and is able to make use of it as the common referent for the particular items that environ him. Whenever he says "it is true that . . ." or "it is the case that . . ." he refers to Actuality as that which sustains forever what it is that is true or is the case. By becoming one with his body, the athlete in an analogous way makes what he does be more clearly that which is in fact and forever the case.

All particulars are contingent; none remains in existence forever. They now are, because they *have* being, because they for the present share, in a limited and distinctive way, the being of a finality. In his acceptance of himself as a body, the athlete faces Actuality, the being which that body and related particulars equally participate in. He, therefore, can become aware of himself as one who, despite his prowess, successes, and awards, is on the same footing of reality with all other men, and eventually with all other space-time particulars.

As the Bhagavad-Gita long ago affirmed, the man of action, once he has detached himself from the pragmatic import of his efforts, achieves what the contemplative does, once he has turned his mind away from contingencies to dwell on that which is forever. By a distinct route the athlete, too, can arrive at the result the yogi seeks. The distinction that existentialists like to draw between men and all the other entities in this space-time world, he completely abrogates in a dynamic acknowledgment of an eternal reality which sustains all.

The athlete is a man of action who responsibly tries to bring about a public result. Because he separates his activity from its fruits he becomes a part of a distinct, bounded situation. The dynamism of that world he has pushed aside, enabling him to create another domain with its own beginning, ending, process, and laws. What he is and what he does is for the moment thereby severed from the rest of the world.

Like an artist, the athlete is occupied with producing something with which he can live for a while, and which, so far, enables him to be self-sufficient. He does not make and is not interested in making something that is beautiful, or in grasping the very being of space, time, or energy; instead he holds himself away from everything else to give himself wholly to a game. Since he is no longer subject to the daily conventionalities and practices which overlay and obscure what is taking place, he is in a fine position to heal the breach that daily separates him and the world beyond. To be sure, he lives inside other conventions, but these are not supposed by him to be the very structure of reality, and he is, therefore, more able than most to return to his daily tasks with some sense of what is stable and fundamental there, and what is not.

Occupied with the present, directed toward the future, the man of action as a rule spends little time in mastering what links him to the past. That is why history rarely reveals him to be doing much more than continuing the processes which had been begun earlier by predecessors. Had he undergone anything like the degree of training to which the athlete submits himself, he would be more judicious, and would be readier to act with greater freedom and a sense of what is the case. Because he not only plays in a game but participates in it, the athlete engages in acts which preserve the past of his sport. His acceptance of rules, which bind his opponents as well, helps make the game a new occurrence within a distinctive history.

Like every other man, an athlete is a distinct individual. He, too, lives out his life in ineluctable privacy. But because of his dedication and his willingness to subject himself to tests which probe to the depths of his preparation, character, and creativity, he is sharply outlined.

Like a religious man who turns from the world to open himself up to his God, the athlete places himself before whatever eternal and impersonal judge there is. He accepts as basic the position that he will be judged objectively, and irrevocably. The religious man is, to be sure, more actively occupied with his presumed judge than the athlete is. Through his faith he tries to come closer to his God, whose evaluations are of vital importance to him. The athlete, instead, is content to allow himself to be judged by men, and makes no effort to come in closer contact with whatever eternal judge there is. In compensation, he can often watch his judges in action, and is able to learn, as the religious man cannot, just how he compares with others.

Both in religion and in athletics men are welded together intimately. Neither result has much lasting power. If the religious man is right, he also makes it possible for his God to be at once immanent in that whole and a better focused object outside it. The athlete must instead be content with nothing more than the totality that he and his fellow players together constitute. He makes less of a claim than the religious man does, but for that reason he does not take account of realities that may have much to do with his present and eventual welfare.

By participating in a public game with others, the athlete makes an intimately related whole with them. The more the players act together, despite competition, to produce a common game, the closer is the bond uniting them all. Athletes make more vital that harmonization of men which religious men suppose God's presence in the world entails.

Like every other body, the athlete's decays and eventually passes away. But there is also a sense in which he nevertheless continues to be. Since he has abdicated from all other positions to make himself a man who is an effective, excellent body, he has defined himself to be an incarnation of those persistent laws which cover the operation of that body. He is one with those laws, their very embodiment, and is so far forever. As an individual he passes away, of course, but his individuality is irrelevant to the more basic fact that he has made himself into a place where those laws for the moment are. The bodies of other men also embody those very same laws. But those men have not altogether identified themselves with their bodies and so far, though instantiating the laws, are not eternalized as these.

All men illustrate cosmic truths. All are localizations and carriers of structures which last forever. So far as anyone embodies these he, in a way, forever abides. But only he who identifies himself with a reality which those laws govern can be said to be able to benefit from the eternality of those laws. Something similar to what the mathematician attains when he thinks, the athlete attains when he acts.

Today we are so aware of the press of time and the fact of mortality that any reference to immortality arouses distrust. And there is so much crassness exhibited by athletes as to make suspect any account that has them appear to be more than men who are able to use their bodies a little better than others can. But it is not to individuals in their individual distinctive private nature that these observations apply; it is to those individuals as caught up and almost swallowed in the role of ideal athlete.

All of us are acquainted with the eternal in many ways. The numbers we write down are but marks to enable us to understand better the eternal possibilities which mathematicians know. They are the chemicals that allow us to read the invisible writings of eternity. The ideals of truth, beauty, and goodness, which obligate us all, though realized in partial and distorted forms, are possibilities that remain forever, unaffected by their lack of realization or by any realization we can manage. More evident, perhaps, is the fact that the truths of logic are necessities forever outside the corrosive grip of time. But any truth is a truth forever. It is always true that I am sitting here before my typewriter on January 29, 1968, revising once again what I had written on January 22d, 1966.

Each one of us represents all of mankind. When we assert something to be the case we assert it not merely for ourselves, or as expressive of ourselves, but as something which any other could assert. When I say "This is a book" I am not saying "This is a book for me," "This looks like a book to me," "I think it is a book," but that it is a book in fact. Ignorance, errors of judgment, differences in vocabulary, and an incapacity to see what in fact I confront will prevent another from knowing whether what I say is true or no; but if it is true, it is true. It will remain true even if no one knows it or no matter who it is that knows it.

Our judgments and our evaluations purport to be formulations of what is objective, permanent, and true, not subject to the vicissitudes of our individual biases, likes, or careers. To know what is, is to escape the remorseless flux of time.

When we attend to any truth we remove ourselves from the transient world, becoming one with eternity. The athlete, in his commitment, vivifies this fact. He not only represents all mankind—as we all do—when he judges and knows; he represents it in his effort to achieve a maximal result in his sport. The world of sport intensifies the meanings which any man in the course of his life inevitably expresses in his judgments and decisions. The athelete is sport incarnated, sport instantiated, sport located for the moment, and by that fact is man himself, incarnated, instantiated, and located.

Each of us is a unity of "local matter" with the meaning of man. The unity has only a short life. But the matter and the meaning continue to be. The athlete unites his local matter with the meaning of mankind, enriched and mediated by the meaning of excellence which he seeks to embody. When he understands himself to encompass these two abiding components and to provide a unique mode of union for them, he is in principle one who is the copresence of two eternities. His recognition of other athletes, as men who uniquely unite matter and meaning, is a recognition of them as also exhibiting the copresence of those eternities. Serving as distinctive carriers of what he also carries, they become his copresent counterparts. This fact is shown in team play and the respect accorded them.

Where others structure situations according to their affections and whims, the athlete submits himself to stringent rules, and dedicates himself to a superb performance, to make himself one who loves too coldly, perhaps, but persistently and well. In his play he exhibits in a steady, impersonal form that love which some men on occasion extend toward a few.

BIBLIOGRAPHY

Section A. Social Systems
4. Religion

Bannister, R. *First Four Minutes.* New York, Dodd Mead, 1955.

Caillois, Roger. *Man, Play and Games.* New York: Free Press of Glencoe, 1961.

Coe, George Albert. "A Philosophy of Play," *Religious Education,* LI (May-June, 1956), pp. 220-22.

Fink, E. "The Ontology of Play." *Philosophy Today,* 4 (1960):95-110.

Gerber, Ellen W. "Identity, Relation and Sport," *Quest* VII (May, 1967), pp. 90-97.

Harper, William A. "Man Alone," *Quest* XII (May, 1969), pp. 57-60.

Herrigel, E. *Zen in the Art of Archery.* New York: Pantheon Books, 1953.

Huizinga, Johan. *Homo Ludens.* Boston: Beacon Press, 1950.

Jolivit, R. "Work, Play and Contemplation." *Philosophy Today,* 5 (1961):114-120.

Slusher, Howard. *Man, Sport and Existence.* Philadelphia: Lea & Febiger, 1967.

Umminger, W. *Superman, Heroes and Gods.* (J. Clark, Trans.) London: Thames & Hudson, 1963.

Weiss, Paul. *Sport: A Philosophic Inquiry.* Carbondale: Southern Illinois University Press, 1969.

SECTION

C

1. SOCIALIZATION: SEX ROLES

Although it is sometimes necessary to extract certain concepts or social behavior for closer scrutiny it does at the same time create serious fragmentation of knowledge. The dynamic and interrelated nature of society gets lost if that fragmenting type of analysis predominates. "Women in sport" should not be treated as a separate category but in relationship to the whole environment of sport. The purpose of this section is to gain a perspective of sport that illustrates the cultural situation rather than the current practice in textbooks of setting aside a separate but unequal section to women in sport.

All kinds of social taboos and myths operate and affect the social environment of sport as it functions in the socialization process of sex role definition. Granted, those roles are undergoing explosive change. Because of the diverse nature of American society the changes are uneven, and the changes take on a different character specific to each social group. Another factor that affects the rate and kind of change is the heavily institutionalized nature of sport within the schools and certain sports associations (i.e., Amateur Athletic Union and the National Collegiate Athletic Association).

In the first article, Beisser contends that though changes in technology and family have occurred, the cultural expectations of masculinity have remained fixed. He takes a different point of view from some authors by emphasizing in the comparison of male and female athletic performance the man as consistently superior. Beisser concludes that man "has learned that this is one area where there is no doubt about sexual differences and where his biology is not obsolete. Athletics help assure his difference from women in a world where his functions have come to resemble hers." We now seem to be in the midst of redefinition of cultural values and sexual roles in American society. How will this redefinition relate to or cause change in this traditional function of sport?

401

Beisser contends it may well reinforce them. Unless social expectations change significantly it seems his conclusions may hold.

Maleness and femaleness become important considerations for the maturing individual. Several of the authors in this section clearly formulate theories on sexual identification in sport, as well as the variation in sexual roles and expectations within different socioeconomic classes. Coming of age in American society many times occurs through sport, especially for the male child. Fiske considers the male adolescent and football in this light. In an anthropological study, she presents the criteria for rites of passage from adolescence to adulthood and looks at American college football in relation to these criteria. The aim of the study was "first to show that the formal outlines of American college football can be considered an initiation ceremony, occurring on the threshold of the status change from adolescence to adulthood; secondly, to see what might be addended to a theory of initiation upon consideration of the cultural data in our own culture." She proceeds to carefully outline the roles of the elders (coaches) and novices (players) and the basic format of the ceremony.

Felshin adds the crucial perspective of feminism in her presentation of three options for women in sport. A pursuit of logical argumentation as to the social position and personal experience of women in sport may bring about "the development of new and more human modes for social interaction, behavior, and motivation" in the cultural domain of sport. The possibility, suggests Felshin, is that by the twenty-first century women will have liberated sport as a male domain and from its contemporary models. In the process men will also be liberated from their own treadmill of inordinate demands for success.

In a more personal vein Hart asks, what is it like to be a female in American Sport? What kinds of situations, experiences, and conflicts accompany sport involvement for many girls and for them later as women? It is hoped that if these experiences, which have evolved from myths and defunct social roles, are recognized and discussed that positive change will be facilitated and negative experiences will be diminished. Again, there is good reason to believe that the experience of both the female and male athlete will be enhanced by current changes. Though often ignored in an achievement and performance oriented society it seems exceedingly likely that the nonathlete (i.e., nonperformer-entertainer) will benefit from the examination and reordering of priorities in American Sport.

THE AMERICAN SEASONAL
MASCULINITY RITES

Arnold R. Beisser

Not all of the characteristics which are attributed to being male or female are to the same degree biologically determined. Some, considered to be basic to masculinity or femininity, are determined by the culture in which one lives rather than by obvious physical differences. In our culture athletics are considered the most masculine of activities. Let us turn now to a consideration of what part sexual orientation plays in the intense interest in sports in America.

Before puberty, boys can be distinguished from girls mainly on the basis of primary sexual characteristics. When puberty is reached, biological distinctions become more apparent. At that time, with the differences in hormonal balance, the distinct secondary sexual characteristics begin to develop. Boys begin to have hair on their faces, and their bodies and become more muscular and angular. Girls become more curvaceous and develop breasts. Primary and secondary characteristics are predictable and universal: girls' hips broaden; boys' shoulders grow wider.

Beyond these physical characteristics are others which are largely, if not exclusively, determined by the society in which one lives. These can be termed tertiary characteristics and are transmitted from generation to generation by the examples of the men and women in the culture. To suggest, as Margaret Mead does, that the nature of maleness and femaleness, outside the physical characteristics, is culturally

From Arnold Beisser, *The Madness in Sports* (New York: Appleton-Century-Crofts, 1967), Chapter 16. Copyright © 1967 by the author. Reprinted by permission of the author.

determined, may be an extreme point of view. For differences must develop just from living in a male body which has greater physical strength compared to living in a female body which experiences menstruation and pregnancy. Nevertheless, it is true that many of the male or female characteristics which are taken for granted in our society are determined by social custom rather than genetics. For example, up to very recently in this country, boys wore short hair and girls wore long hair, but in other parts of the world the reverse is true.[1] Similarly, an American boy would hide in shame if he had to wear a skirt, but in Greece it is the attire worn by a particularly virile and courageous group of soldiers.

There is a story which, although of doubtful validity, nevertheless illustrates the importance of these tertiary sexual characteristics: "Two children were playing outside a nudist camp. One of them discovered a hole through which he could look in the wall surrounding the camp. While he peeked through the hole, the other child excitedly inquired, 'What do you see, are they men or women?' The peeper responded in dismay, 'I don't know, they don't have any clothes on'!"

Tertiary sexual characteristics, such as dominance, mannerisms, dress, and speech, are often considered unalterable, yet studies of different cultures reveal quite different ideas about what constitutes male and female behavior. Each culture assumes that it "knows" how a man or woman should act. The folklore is justified by a self-fulfilling prophecy, as parents transmit to children their cultural expectations.

To be considered feminine in Victorian society women had to be frail, passive, and the potential victims of aggressive, lecherous males. Yet, according to the stories of Greek mythology, women were as urgently sexed as men. In our own age primitive tribes differ grossly in what we consider basic masculinity and femininity. Among the Arapesh tribes of New Guinea, for example, studies in the early twentieth century found that men as well as women showed such characteristics as concern, giving, protectiveness, which we in America associate with mothering. Their neighbors, the Mundugumor, living only a short distance away, had quite opposite attitudes, with both men and women

---

1. Since the above comments were first written, a remarkable change has taken place in the dress and hair styles of American teenagers and young people. Boys often now wear long hair and bright attention-getting clothing making their dress more similar to the traditional feminine attire. Girls frequently wear trousers and male-style shirts. These changes are consistent with the reduction of difference between the sexes in our society as discussed in previous chapters. For the purposes of of this chapter it is sufficient to note that standards of dress can change depending on taste and are not inherently either male or female.

being strong, tough, and aggressive, like the idealized pioneer male in the United States.[2]

Another tribe in New Guinea, the Tchambuli, showed a reversal of conceptions about masculinity-femininity in another way. The male job was head-hunting, war making, and war preparation. To carry out their plans the men congregated daily in the "men's house." The women on the other hand were charged with all of the economic responsibilities in the village, such as fishing, food preparation, pottery, basket weaving. When the British banned head-hunting and imposed a peace upon these people, the men became essentially unemployed, while the women continued their traditional activities. These women were temperamentally stable, secure, and cooperative with others, but the men, having lost their important function, became insecure, capricious, and aesthetic. Although men could no longer make war, the preparation rituals were continued. Their interest in the cosmetic arts and in creating suitable costumes, previously an important part of war, was now used instead to make themselves sexually attractive in competing through charm for the favors of the "important sex," the women. The women were tolerant of their men whom they viewed as gossipy, self-centered playthings.

Among the Manus it is the father who is endowed with what in America are considered maternal characteristics. While the women are occupied with the economy and have little time for children, the father cares for and raises them. When Dr. Mead brought dolls to the children of the Manus, she found that it was the boys who eagerly played with them, while the girls were disinterested. The boys in their play were emulating their fathers' activities.

Largely, then, the tertiary sexual characteristics of people, the ones which are most visible and apparent, are socially determined and subject to considerable change from one generation to another and from one culture to another. Sometimes, however, the roles assigned to certain members of a society are intolerable, and in order for such a society to survive and maintain stability there have to be safety valves through which those who are placed in ambiguous or deprecated positions can gain some satisfaction or status.

The Iatmul are a tribe of New Guinea natives who had such a culture. The men despised women, considered them unimportant, worth-

2. The information in this paragraph and the following paragraphs about New Guinea is from Margaret Mead, *Sex and Temperament in Three Primitive Societies: Manus, Mundugumor, and Tchambuli* (New York: William Morrow & Co., Inc., 1939), 2, pp. 1-384, 3, pp. 164-244, 237-322; and from a lecture by the noted anthropologist, Weston LaBarre.

less, almost subhuman, allocating to them only the most menial and routine of tasks. Men, in contrast, were considered to be the "real human beings," strong, brave, and courageous; they, too, were head hunters. The men were expected to be proud, the women self-effacing. Everything in this culture was either all black or all white, all good or all bad. There were no shades of gray. To be a man was to approach perfection; women epitomized all that was to be avoided. If a man showed the slightest feminine interests or characteristics, he was considered to be sliding toward the subhuman. Such rigid standards of human behavior placed each man in constant jeopardy of losing his humanity. This dichotomy was hard on the women, but it was equally difficult for the men. Adjustment in the Iatmul society was precarious: men walked a tight rope and women were scorned.

A society like the Iatmul has doubtful durability, for the tensions and resentment engendered are at an explosive pitch. This tribe's "safety valve" was the ceremony of Naven,[3] an annual occasion in which bitterness and tensions were discharged in a convulsive reversal of the year's pressures. Naven was a ceremony of cultural transvestism, during which men and women exchanged not only their clothes but also their roles. Boys who had been rigorously taught the shamefulness of femininity were now contemptuously called "wife" by their maternal uncles. They were bullied in the same way that women had been bullied throughout the year. The women, during Naven, were given a vacation from their despised roles and identified themselves dramatically as men, wearing their clothes and assuming their actions, strutting and swaggering. They could enter the "men's house" and could even beat certain designated men. They could engage in a theatrical simulation of the war games that men played. The men, who had spent the year taking elaborate ritualized precautions to avoid anything feminine could relax during the ceremony. It was a great relief actually to assume, in deliberate fashion, the female role.

By the end of the ceremony the tensions and resentments accumulated during the year were dissipated. The women felt better about their position in the community and the men admired the women for having been able to assume the masculine position. For a short time the women had become human and the men could love them. Over the next year the tensions built up again and hatred pervaded community life until the next Naven.

3. Gregory Bateson, "The Naven Ceremony in New Guinea," *Primitive Heritage: An Anthropological Anthology,* eds. Margaret Mead and Nicholas Calas (New York: Random House, 1953), pp. 186-202.

The Naven ceremony of the Iatmul is not unique, for other cultures have similar festivals. Rome's ancient feast of Saturnalia served a related function in discharging the year's accumulated tensions between masters and slaves. In this ceremony, slaves were waited upon by their masters and enjoyed all the privileges which they were denied during the year. It is easy to understand the necessity for such rites and their vital function in preserving a culture. Beyond a certain point, tensions and resentment would destroy any community life.

The Iatmul looked forward throughout the year to their ceremony of Naven. The Romans, both slaves and masters, eagerly awaited the festival of Saturnalia. In fact, in these cultures and others with similar rites, the populace lived from festival to festival. These were the most important events in their lives. Similarly Americans, particularly many American males, mark time by their own seasonal rites: football season, basketball season, baseball season, and so on. Many men live from one sports season to the next, with sports representing the most vital part of their lives.

Iatmul men and women were in a precarious psychological position as a result of the extreme demands which their culture placed upon them. The Naven rite offered an opportunity for the expression of strong feelings which had to be disowned throughout the year preceding the ceremony. For the women it was denial of self-assertion and aggression; for the men it was denial of passivity, with no opportunities for relaxation of their facade of superstrength. Naven saved the Iatmul people from the otherwise impossible demands of their culture and thereby saved the culture from extinction.

American men, as we have seen, are also on shaky cultural ground. Their position is precarious as a result of the contradictions in their lives. To an ever-increasing degree, American male children early in their lives have close physical and emotional experiences with their fathers. Fathers share almost equally with mothers in the maternal activities: feeding, bathing, cuddling, and comforting, which were once the exclusive domain of the American female. American parents are apt to take turns in getting up with the baby when he cries at night. When either parent has a "night out" the other serves as baby sitter. If the egalitarianism is disrupted it is likely for bitterness to develop.

"Togetherness" has largely meant the diminution of the uniqueness of the female position as well as the male position in the family. Father is no longer the ultimate authority; he has become a "pal"; he is now not a teacher but a co-learner. He has an equal, but not a greater voice in the collective activities of the household than have the children and his wife. The wife, who may have a job outside the home and may make as much as or even more money than her husband, quite naturally expects him to share the housecleaning, dishwashing, and caring for the children. The roles are diffused and the differences between male and female, between adult and child are diminished.

Like the Tchambuli, American men have had a change in status. The Tchambuli men lost their principal function, head hunting; American men have had to share with their wives their economic productivity as bread winners. Tchambuli men became superfluous; the authority and uniqueness of the American man has diminished. Previously, the main way men were superior to women was in their physical strength. Now, development of machines has caused male strength to be less important, almost obsolete. Machines are stronger than men, and the sexes are equally competent in running most machines. Dexterity has become more important than power, and women are at least as competent as men in this respect. The serious consequence is, that in their work, the new breed of factory and office workers are essentially neuter in gender.

While these changes in technology and in the family have taken place, the cultural expectations of masculinity have remained fixed as they were in pioneer days. Physical strength and agility were the qualities by which a man was measured, for then only the strong were able to survive. Obviously, such values are more appropriate to the frontier than to the office. Now, in order to fit this already obsolete image, men and boys must engage in artificial, nonproductive displays of strength.

As the real demands for what was considered traditional male strength have decreased, the expectation of show of strength has grown. Parents have a special concern that their boys are not aggressively masculine enough. Mothers are more apt to be concerned about passive, compliant behavior in male children than about their destructiveness. Often they are even relieved by, and subtly encourage, overt displays of aggression, for in that way, they are reassured that their sons are not "sissies." This is quite different from the concept of several decades ago that the quiet child was the "good" child.

As fathers and sons have grown closer together, an obsessive cultural concern with homosexuality has grown. In a counter move to avoid such taint, as already noted, children are pushed earlier and earlier into heterosexual relationships. The tragedy of this parental encouragement is that it is self-defeating, since the child in latency has other more important business to learn than sex appeal. In addition, his premature explorations in heterosexuality promote a sense of inadequacy within him as he recognizes his inability to perform as expected. This inadequacy, in turn, is interpreted as the "taint" and the parental efforts and encouragement towards aggression and heterosexuality are re-doubled, the situation becoming a vicious circle.

Just as Naven helps to relieve the Iatmul tensions, American sports have a similar function. The first man outside the home that a boy encounters is usually a coach. In school he meets a series of female teachers who are the purveyors of morality, knowledge, and competence. The coach is not only a man among men but, more important, a man among women teachers. Boys try to model themselves after the coach and find security in imitating him. Their roles are clearer on the dia-mond than in the classroom, for it is on the athletic field in those sea-sonal masculinity rites that males become the kind of men their grand-fathers were and their mothers want them to be. Strength is king; men are separated from boys, and boys, in turn, from girls. In the best tradition of the frontier, an athlete overpowers his opponent, and the sexual roles are re-established to conform with the expectancies of the culture. Male and female are relieved of their discrepancy just as they are following the Naven ceremony. Fortunately, this can be accom-plished, not only by participation, but by observation as a spectator who identifies with the players. They can both then return to the office and the home with renewed respect for the uniqueness of the sexes and the re-establishment of their own identities, until the distinction gradually diminishes and another masculinity rite is necessary.

In a subtle way, these supermasculine "frontier rites" also allow for the expression of warmth and closeness among men which society compels them to disown. In sports, players huddle together; they caress, pat "fannies," shout affectionate phrases, and engage in activities which are scorned elsewhere but condoned in sports. In a recent heavyweight boxing match, the victor was embraced and kissed by his manager before several thousand fans in the sports arena and perhaps several million more on television. Such behavior anywhere but in the context of sports would be highly suspect. But here, with full cultural approval and without detracting from the supermasculine atmosphere, men can satisfy either physically or vicariously their needs for close male companionship like that which they experienced in childhood. In this context, physical contact, either aggressive or friendly, is applauded rather than con-demned, and in the frenzy of American sports, males are purged of their femininity, and at the same time provided with an outlet for close contact.

Among the Iatmul, Naven takes place annually, and a single festival appears to take care of a year's accumulated tensions between the sexes. Fifty years ago a single sports season, namely baseball, sufficed for Americans. Today each season of the year is occupied with a different sport. Sport seasons now fuse with one another into a continuous succession of ceremonial demonstrations. The fall rite, football, now overlaps with the spring rite of baseball and track. The vacant moments are filled with transitional rites: basketball, hockey, tennis, and golf, to mention a few.

Although the potential for wild celebration is always present, the pitch of these ceremonies is somewhat lower than the yearly Naven in New Guinea. This is consistent with the lower pitch of all activities in our sophisticated country. Very little can be termed a "special event," since we are bombarded daily with the spectacular and the overwhelming. Just as the differences between sexes have diminished, the difference between holiday and weekday has also. Activities converge into a more integrated (for the hopeful) or amorphous (for the pessimistic) mass of ongoing activities. The Fourth of July, once fraught with danger and excitement, is now closely controlled and tame. Similarly, other holidays such as Armistice Day, Flag Day, St. Patrick's Day have lost their appeal except to the most enthusiastic. Since the range of the pitch is lower, the exposure time must be increased. Thus, sports go on continuously from the beginning to the end of the year.

Among primitives, the transition from boyhood to manhood is accomplished in a single, brief ceremony—the puberty rite. A symbolic gesture, such as circumcision or knocking out a tooth, bears witness to the cliché, "Today I am a man." For American men the transition is quite different. Puberty, the time of traditional manhood when the secondary sexual characteristics appear, is now only the signal for the prolonged period of suspension between boyhood and manhood called adolescence. Biologically and sexually, manhood has been reached, but the technical complexity of our society requires an extension of many years of education and preparation before the productive work of life can begin. The preparation extends temporally toward mandatory early retirement, which advances from the other side, allowing only a relatively brief period for the adult work career.

The adolescent is thus in a state of moratorium, suspended in his choices of occupation and a wife, prohibited from sexual activity, prevented from making any firm commitment.[4] No true identity can be achieved in the face of such a moratorium. In the medical profession this problem is well exemplified. A boy who decides that he wants to be a doctor must make this decision at least a score of years before his goal is

---

4. In the past decade young people have revolted against this state of suspension. They have adopted new and more permissive sexual mores and have often shown an unwillingness to delay gratification. They often choose not to wait the required period of time to achieve an occupational identity or traditionally defined marriage.

achieved. If, for example, he wishes to be a surgeon he may not complete his training until he is past thirty. Failure at any stage of this process would force him to seek a new occupation and a new direction for his life. With the endless series of what can be likened to initiation rites— high school, college for four years, medical school for four years, residency—it is as senescence approaches that the moratorium is over and the man can say with some degree of finality, "I have an identity, I am a doctor."

Because of the nature of this moratorium, adolescence is a period of turmoil. Rebellion and confusion can be expected from the man who has not yet found a place for himself, who is suspended, seemingly for an infinite length of time, between his family of origin and his family of procreation.

But as we have seen, a culture with contradictions and ambiguities, if it is to survive, must have some way of relieving and integrating its tensions. Sports form an elongated bridge across childhood, adolescence, and adulthood for American males. Although the adolescent boy may have to suspend decision and commitment on most of his affairs until many years hence, he can enter athletics with full exuberance and play and work at sports with a dedication which satisfies his personality and his society.

Among my patients has been a successful attorney who came to treatment because his marriage was on the point of dissolution. The bone of contention between him and his wife was that in her eyes he was not "man enough." She was bitterly disappointed that he was not handy around the house, that he did not make the family decisions, and was not more assertive—all qualities she had admired in her father. Her husband's competence in a learned profession seemed unimportant, while her father's physical strength resulting from his being an unskilled laborer was important. She feared that their son would develop into a "passive man" like her husband. The husband, too, doubted his own masculinity, shared her fears, and so sought therapy in order to try to conform to her expectations of him. The bickering that went on between them always subsided when they engaged in sports or jointly watched sports events. This seemed to adjust the perspective and after such activity each respected the other for his or her distinctiveness.

This is not an unusual case. Wives are worried about their husbands not being aggressively masculine enough; mothers are worried about their sons being too passive; men fear that they will be dominated or thought to be effeminate.

In reality, men are larger and weigh more than women, they do have more powerful muscles, they do have bigger lung and heart capacities, and they do have a sexual organ which makes them different. They are built for physical combat, for hunting, as well as for a unique sexual role. In the work and social world, however, this combat strength is largely obsolete. A 200-pound man can easily lose a business encounter (symbolic combat) to a 130-pound man or to a 90-pound woman. Slender feminine fingers can push the buttons on a computer as well as can thick, strong, male fingers, perhaps better. Machines are stronger than either men or women, and to the machine it makes no difference if its buttons are pushed hard or lightly. Male strength has, at least in part, lost its function and its value in society.

In sports, male and female are placed in their historical biological roles. In sports, strength and speed do count, for they determine the winner. As in premechanized combat, women can never be more than second place to men in sports. They can cheer their men on, but a quick review of the record books comparing achievements in sports of men and women confirms the distinctness of the sexes here.

It is small wonder that the American male has a strong affinity for sports. He has learned that this is one area where there is no doubt about sexual differences and where his biology is not obsolete. Athletics help assure his difference from women in a world where his functions have come to resemble theirs.

PIGSKIN REVIEW: AN AMERICAN INITIATION

Shirley Fiske

INTRODUCTION

> We anthropologists treat a familiar culture as though it were a
> strange one . . . we consciously choose this approach so that we may
> view the culture from a new angle and throw into relief features obscured
> by other forms of study. (Nadel 1951:7)

This statement succinctly sums the prime impetus for writing this
paper: it is imperative to adopt the analytic framework of anthropology
in order to explain in proper perspective events which occur in our own
culture. Let us consider what we Americans think to be a harmless athletic contest: when closely inspected through the Truth-Lens of anthropology, it is actually a stealthy type of ritual behavior escaped from
"primitive" camps. American traditions are ethnologically cubby-holed
curiosities paralleling those found in pre-literate cultures throughout the
world. Basic cultural processes which produce behavioral similarities
across technological gulfs may manifest themselves in forms somewhat
sheltered from the awareness of the natives, but they do not cease to
operate.

Having direct contact with several football players and the coaches
of a well-known university, I observed many of their quaint customs
and beliefs; as the season progressed, my Anthropology-Eyes brightened,
for the various ritual behaviors closely resembled that which in other
cultures is labeled "puberty rites," or "initiation ceremonies." Further
investigation along these lines has supported my hypothesis—this study
is an effort to demonstrate that the actual nature of a football season

Printed with permission of the author.

is an initiation into adulthood. The format for the body of this paper is first, a brief review of the theoretical background of initiation ceremonies, the presentation of the data gathered, and the analysis and interpretation of it. Finally, perhaps some alteration may be made in the models as a result of studying the rite in our own culture.

Before embarking on the major discussion of this paper, it might be well to justify the relevance of *collegiate* football to initiation ceremonies, and also the choice of the University of Southern California as the subject of analysis. Football events range in ritual content on a continuum from the football of high school to that of college and then professional ball. A cross-cutting dimension is that of athletic entertainment, an economic criterion relating to the outside society. High school football and professional football are at the extremes of these axes: high school football does not have the elaborate ritual of collegiate football, and furthermore it is primarily an athletic contest, without important economic ramifications. Professional football is on the other end of the

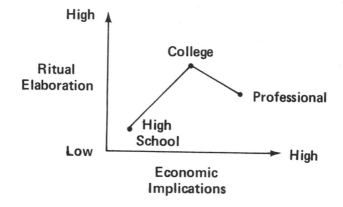

economic extreme—its very existence is determined by the economic conditions it creates. It rates lower on ritual concomitants than college, but higher than high school; it is not a a temporary status during one's lifetime, but is a mode of living for the players, so it has not the symbolic content of initiation ceremonies. Professional football is a specialized type of entertainment of a very different nature than collegiate football, where team members are competing among themselves for a livelihood.

The justification for the choice of schools from among many colleges is twofold: first, the proximity of location, and the accessibility of data; secondly, and more importantly, the University of Southern California is the epitome of a college enmeshed in football tradition. The fervor and pride generated by the football team are evident to an extreme degree. USC represents college life and the football centrifuge at its peak development, approximately as it was across the nation previous to the current trend to de-emphasize athletics in favor of intellectualism. *Middletown,* although published in 1929, illustrates the strength of the American pride even in the choice of a college: " 'My daughter plans to go to the University of ....,' said one mother, 'because, she says, 'Mother, I just *couldn't* go to a college whose athletics I couldn't be proud of' " (Lynd 1929:214). A successful football team brings honor and develops pride in the social, academic, and economic attitudes of individuals at SC; these attitudes represent the reverence and the un-questioning importance of the role of football in college life which was once the norm on all college campuses. This exposé, then, revolves around showing that American college football can be considered an initiation ceremony, occurring on the threshhold of the status change from adolescence to adulthood.

THEORETICAL BACKGROUND

The occurrence of ritual at puberty has posed a rather complex problem for anthropologists. It reflects both the physical aspect of reproductive maturity; as well, it is at this point that the individual has attained the socio-emotional responsibility of adulthood. In most socie-ties, there is some association in peoples' minds between the notion of sexual maturity and that of social maturity: for this reason, the puberty ritual is described by anthropologists as an "initiation ceremony," or "rite of passage" from one role to another. Puberty is a sign of the final and completed difference between the man's body and the woman's—a time when both sexes must assume their respective masculine and femi-nine roles.

The flexibility of these rites in marking both a cultural and physical change in the individual has shown amazing variability in the types of ritual of the event. The adaptability of the initiation ritual is one of its foremost features, for it is found in some form, however sublimated, in all societies. One group may stress the aspects of proper training for parenthood and emphasize appropriate role assumption. All primitive societies have some method of marking this dual change; the same pro-cess is at work in familiar institutions within our own society.

A consideration of initiation rites reveals many types, for each society marks the initiations of the individual throughout his life cycle without recognition of the modes of transition—e.g., baptism, confirmation, graduation, puberty, marriage. Most of these examples indicate a transition from one social role to another to be adopted. In our American society, a frequent, and one of the most obvious, types of initiation, is that into a closed group, club, or fraternity—often, interestingly, with a sex-linked membership requirement[1]—where there is some form of testing or hazing connected with entering the group. Naturally, sororities and fraternities stand as good examples of this type of initiation, as well as Shriners, Elks, and secret societies. These initiation ceremonies share much in common with the transition into adulthood, *viz.*, the individual is given new duties, rights, and responsibilities, and a new set of people with which to interact in a new role; nonetheless, they differ fundamentally from puberty rites, with which we are concerned, for they do not apply equally over the vast majority of men or women in that particular age-grade. The ceremony and the adoption of the new role has no wider significance than the small sub-group of the society to which it pertains, and would not be understood by the wider audience.

Hence the passage from one social situation to another is often accompanied by some form of *rite de passage*. However, the most important transition for any society is the transition from adolescence to adulthood, because it is here that the cognitive-emotional training for adult roles is condensed, and this is the most crucial period for transmission. The childhood bonds, especially with parents, are broken and adult values are instilled in both young men and young women. Each society must have a way of dramatizing the importance of adopting these values which will perpetuate the society; for if there were no importance attached to the way to become a proper adult person—if there were no values inculcated in growing citizens—then that society would function less than economically.[2]

Due to a desire for brevity, I will summarize only three of the authors who have written definitively on the anthropology of initiation into adulthood; Van Gennep (1909), Whiting (1958, 1960, 1964), and Young (1962, 1965).

Since the first major treatise elucidating the subject in 1909, Van Gennep's comprehensive *Les Rites de Passage,* no one has seriously shaken his basic postulates concerning the generic category of rites of passage. Throughout an initiation ceremony, Van Gennep emphasized

1. The sexes are also segregated in most preliterate societies' initiation ceremonies into adulthood.
2. Since values are usually (historically and in some contemporary societies) passed on from elders to younger generations with little or no questioning allowed, it will be interesting to see what comes out of the current situation where we are questioning the very validity of accepting without questioning the basic assumptions of our social systems that our elders hand down to us.

the importance of the transition from the profane world to that of the sacred. The person who enters a new status at variance with one formerly held becomes "sacred" to the others who remain in the "profane" world.

The rites have a common function, in easing the individual in transition from one social role to another, and they also have common stages. There is a separation or death from the old state of being, a transition between the two states, and an incorporation or rebirth into the new one. An important feature is often that of symbolic dramatization of the stages: separation or death is often symbolized in physical seclusion (a bush camp, or a separate building or corporal punishment (whipping, beating, etc.) of the initiates; "the purpose is to make the novice 'die,' to make him forget his former personality and his former world" (Van Gennep 1909:81, n. 2). The transition period allows the initiates to interact with the other members of the society, but often on a markedly different level—i.e., with special favors, compensations, etc., from others, for the novices are still in the "sacred" sphere relative to the rest of the society. Rebirth or incorporation is a phase which occurs variably in different societies. During this period, initiates may act as though they are newly born, and must relearn all the gestures of ordinary life. The individual is symbolically reintegrated into the ways of the society, only this time with a new social role—adulthood.[3]

While Van Gennep considers initiation to be a dramatization of role change through the opposition of profane and sacred worlds, the two authors who we will consider next felt that initiation emphasizes *sex* role adoption in adulthood. In three consecutive articles (Whiting, Kluckholn, and Anthony 1958, Burton and Whiting 1960, and Whiting 1964), Whiting, through thorough cross-cultural research, upheld what has become known as his "cross sex identity" hypothesis. This hypothesis maintains that in those societies where it is necessary to switch the child or adolescent abruptly from an identification with his mother to that of the father, then this will be marked by a severe initiation ritual. That is, where children grow up emotionally very close to their mothers, then,

---

3. Although the influence of Durkheim's previous work is evident in Van Gennep's theory (in the primacy of the social nature of phenomena, and the division of the world into sacred and profane spheres), Durkheim in his works subsequent to Van Gennep's perceived initiation ceremonies as essentially religious events. In his *Elementary Forms of Religious Life* he states that initiation ceremonies are, foremost, instruments which emphasize the "essential duality of the two kingdoms sacred and profane" (Durkheim 1913:39). It implies a "veritable metamorphosis" for Durkheim, who sees the ceremony as indicative of a transformation of the whole being. The individual leaves the purely profane world and enters the sacred world.
See also James Bossard and Eleanor Boll (1948), who analyzed the debutantes' presentation to society as a contemporary rite of passage using Van Gennep's criteria.

if they are a male, in order to insure proper adult behavior, the former bonds must be broken in favor of male role assumption.[4] The dimensions of a ceremony necessary to call that event an adolescent initiation are the presence of one of the following: (1) painful hazing by adult males; (2) genital operations; (3) seclusion from women; (4) tests of manliness (Whiting, Kluckhohn, and Anthony 1958:360).

Frank Young also looks at initiation ceremonies via cross-cultural methodology, and concludes somewhat similarly that initiation ceremonies serve to dramatize sex role recognition and reinforce social solidarity of adult males. Young removes the causation from the realm of infantile fixations and places it on a societal level.

Sex role dramatization is necessary where there is a high degree of male solidarity, defined as the consensus among the men regarding the purpose and activities of males (Young 1962:387).[5] Young notes that this situation usually occurs in societies where resources are exploited by cooperation, and where intergroup hostilities are conducive to male solidarity.

The social meaning of male solidarity must be dramatized in a memorable way; the candidate must participate intensely. Young offers a scale of degrees of dramatization of initiation rites, from the lowest step of customary minimal social recognition (gifts, party, change of names), to the next step, social seclusion (physical or social separation), then personal dramatization (initiate is ceremoniously dressed and/or gives a public performance), organized social response (group dresses ceremonially and/or performs), and finally the most dramatic step— emotionalized social response (beating or hazing) (Young 1962:385).

Whiting and Young led a spirited controversy over their respective interpretations of initiation ceremonies. Using the techniques available through their methodology, they come to a close agreement on the ultimate value of initiation as a technique of male sex identification: their main disagreement resides in the interpretation of systems of causation —Whiting emphasizes childhood patterns of behavior and emotions and the necessity of breaking them, and Young chooses to place causation on the societal level in the form of male solidarity.

---

4. Two conditions which might lead to this situation where there is maximum conflict in sexual identity—where a boy has initial exclusive sleeping arrangements with his mother, but where the domestic unit is patrilocal and controlled by men.

5. The degrees of male solidarity are indicated on the following scale from low to high: (1) informal solidarity that does not attain the behavioral expression; (2) exclusive male activity for adult males, protected by physical or normative perception barriers; (3) ritualization of male activity, at least in part; (4) definite ranking of men within the activity; (5) training for war a part of the activity (Young 1965:67).

CEREMONIAL DATA

I would like to demonstrate that the "athletic" phenomenon of American collegiate football may be considered an initiation ceremony celebrating the status change from adolescence to adulthood.

The data is of two kinds: first, the actual descriptions of the formal content of the ceremony itself. This data is derived from interviews with the players and coaches, and from my own observation. To clarify, the actual strategy employed in the defensive-offensive maneuvers on field during a game does not concern us except symbolically; the many plays and formations are relatively unimportant except inasfar as they demonstrate the elaborate and highly ritualized nature of the ceremony. I have interviewed four players, consulted manuals, and observed behavior. There is little or no disagreement among the sources about the formal characteristics of the program—these are explicit, clear-cut events.

The second type of data is what is generally referred to as the "native's viewpoint" of the reasons for and the effects of the ceremony. This aspect necessarily involves interpretation on the part of both informant and the anthropologist, so I spoke to many more individuals to get a representative view. As well as the four initiates, I spoke to three of their coaches, the head yell leader, and engaged innumerable individuals in informal discussion about the importance of the football festivals.

The duration of the ceremony is eight months, each year, with the activity concentrated in the first four months. During the four weeks of intense ritual activity, there are discrete weekly festivals. Membership in the novice group is a desirable goal for all young males, although only the most fit are allowed to participate. A boy may enter the activities for one year or up to four years, but not more; and once he has begun the yearly cycle, quitting it is accompanied by a heavy stigma both among the initiates and in the society at large.

The Setting: The sacred ground upon which the public part of the ceremony occurs (weekly for eleven weeks) is a rectangular field, 100 yds. long. The spectators gather on all sides to watch the ceremony. Public rites occur in this setting.

The Personnel: These people of the ceremony can be classified into the actual participant, the affiliates, and the spectators; each of these is removed one degree further from emotional identification with the novice group, respectively. The first group is the most important, obviously. It is composed of a set of seven directors (elders), one of which is the head co-ordinator who is oldest and who has accumulated vast wisdom. He is revered and respected. The other participants are the initiates themselves—usually about seventy—who are ranked internally according to ability to perform properly and according to senority. The hierarchy, from the top down, is composed of groups referred to as the "varsity," the "red shirts," and the "j.v.s."

The affiliated personnel travel with the novices when ceremonies occur at fields other than their own. They do not participate in the ceremony directly, nor are they admitted to the secret meetings or secluded areas. The affiliated personnel are of two kinds: there are specialized individuals hired to care for certain needs of the novices (team "trainers" and "managers"), and there are individuals whose goal is the interpretation of the novices' actions to the audience during public performances. These virginous dancers and their male counterparts ("yell leaders," and "song girls") lead organized chants and incite emotionalized responses from the crowd during the performance.

The last group is the audience, which is composed of multitudes of people, both kin and non-kin. They must remain off the sacred ground whenever the novices occupy it, but are encouraged to react vocally and with gestures to the movements of the novices on the field.

Various phases of the ceremony emerge from the data, and are given below along with a brief synopsis of their import.

Yearly Ceremonial Cycle
Phase I: "Double Days"

The official schedule starts in early September, for a period of two weeks before the first public ceremony. This period is termed "Double Days" (because the novices practice two times a day, and is designed to promote unity among the group through hard work, fatigue, and practice. There is a set number of gatherings which can occur, ruled by higher authorities in the nation. The novices are confined to a strict daily schedule. They are secluded from women, and their diet is controlled—the initiated eat all meals together in an institution known as "Training Table"—and certain foods with a high concentration of starch and carbohydrates are taboo. This period is characterized by the initiates as a very trying, tiring time, and very tense because all the novices are living in such close quarters. The daily schedule is reproduced below. There is a four-day break before the first public ceremony.

7:00 A.M.	Awakened
7:30	Eat first meal of the day together
9:00	On a secret field, dressed in costumes, participate in rigorous physical activity for two hours
11:00	Off field

12:00 P.M.	Eat second meal together
2:00	On field again, repeat same physical punishment as earlier
4:00	End punishment
5:30	Eat third meal together; the meals have been planned by the elders according to specific regulations
6:00	Meeting of all novices, presided over by elders, to discuss the inadequacies of the novices; psychologically harassed.
8:00	End of gathering; the novices are now free to mingle with each other, but they cannot leave the building.
10:30	Bed check by the elders to see if all novices are in bed.

Phase II: "The Season"

The cycle now enters a period lasting through December 7, characterized by weekly confrontations between the initiates of this group and those of the same age-group, but of a different locality. Traditionally, these are considered hostile encounters, varying in degree of hostility between the groups. Open hostility is precluded by the set ritual of the game in which the two groups engage.

This period, where the initiates are once again interacting with society, is still characterized by numerous taboos, such as sex on the nights preceding the contest, and on diet, and even implicitly on their personal appearance. There are secret meetings daily for two hours, during which time there is continued physical punishment. On the evenings and mornings before each public ceremony, the novices are secluded. In addition, they are also exempt from many of the requirements of their peers. Within their living groups (most noticeably, frats) they are excused from duties, both physical and mental. In interaction with their peers, they are given great deference and respect. Even in interaction with their superiors such as administrators of the educational institution and their instructors of formal education, they are excused from duties which others must execute, such as tests, papers, etc. On an even higher plane, the novices are exempt from induction (armed service) while they maintain their ability to participate (through mediation of the elders).

There are two variants of the weekly schedule; one is adapted for ceremonies which will occur on the sacred field of another institution, and the other is adapted for events which will occur on the home field. The major difference in the schedules is that the rally is usually moved up to Thursday, and the novices fly to the other field and back again. The generalized schedule is reproduced here:

Mon:	3:00	Meeting of all novices
	3:30	On field in secret session; wear "sweats"

	5:30	Off field
	6:00	Eat dinner together
Tues:	3:00	Meeting
	3:30	On field, with more elaborate dress than Mon., called "full dress"
	5:30	Watch films
Wed:		Same as Tues.
Thurs:	3:00	Meeting
	3:30	On field, work on entire ceremony together
	5:30	Off field
	6:00	Eat together
Fri:	3:00	Meeting
	3:30	Brief practice
	4:00	Off field—Nearing the culmination of the weekly routine, the peers of the initiates express their appreciation and devotion, loyalty and admiration, to the novices. The affiliates organize a crowd around the players as they exit from the secret practice and pass through their admirers, always showing extreme modesty, into another sacrosanct area called the "Locker Room." At this time, the elders take little part in the ceremony; they call upon the weekly leader ("team captain") of the novices, who speaks to the crowd. The crowd responds with traditional chants of encouragement to the novices, urging them to honorable victory in the forthcoming contest.
	6:00	Eat dinner together
	7:00	Seclusion (in the "Sheraton Wilshire Hotel")
	7:30	Entertainment (motion picture) viewed by the novices as a group, and apart from the rest of society. The lodging and entertainment are of the finest quality available.
	10:30	Elders "bed check" to make sure the novices are in bed
Sat:	8:00	Orange juice served in bed
	9:00	Last meal served before the contest: steak and eggs
	11:00	Meeting of the entire group; the *chief elder* (in a rare appearance) talks to the team
	12:00	Novices go to the sacred field, where they are dressed in colorful costumes and protective padding of debatable protectiveness. At this time the "trainer" lovingly massages, tapes, and wraps the bodies of the participants. The costumes are symbolic in that the whole team is identified by a particular color of the costumes, but each individual is given specific recognition by his identifying number.

1:00   The novices warm up, doing various gymnastics
1:30   The novices emerge as if by magic from the bowels of
        the stadium, and are greeted by the cheers of the crowd;
        there is much that is symbolic in the actual maneuvers,
        the setup of the players on the bench, the hierarchy of
        coaches, the acceptance of authority by the novices, the
        actions of the affiliates (especially the virgins and their
        male counterparts), and the reaction of the crowd, but
        space does not permit its analysis here.
4:00   End of contest—the novices are free.

Sun: 6:00   Novices assemble to watch "films," a magical method
        which can recreate the events of the last contest, and
        put the individuals' actions up for scrutiny and ridicule
        by the elders.

Ritual Elaboration: The novice group being victorious in all its confrontations, (USC was National Collegiate Champions in this year of 1967)
was invited to perform publicly in opposition to another champion group.
Since this is a *very* desirable goal (i.e., to play in a "Bowl" game), the
novices were further honored and lauded, and there was further ritual
elaboration of their initiation.

The daily schedule is the same as the one during "Double Days,"
and it continues for two weeks previous to the celebrated game. The
novices are again secluded in an all-male residence, they eat their meals
together, and are subjected to two brutal practices daily. During the
first week, they are free to leave the building in the evenings (until
10:00 P.M.); during the second week, they must remain with the elders
at all times.

The second week marks the highest degree of seclusion in the entire
ceremonial cycle: the novices change their residence from the first week
(dorms) and are secluded in the luxury accommodations formerly reserved for the night before the event. They are to speak only to their
elders or another novice, they may not receive messages, or send them,
or speak to anyone in the outside society.

The entertainment which is provided the novices is symbolically
important. Two events are of special interest, although others occurred;
there is no attempt to analyze them here. On the first Tuesday there is
held a gigantic feast, specifically for the novices, and hosted free by a
local merchant (Lawry's Prime Rib). The object of the feast is to con-
sume as much beef as possible; for there is a myth accompanying the
feast which states the prophecy that the group of novices which con-
sumes the greatest quantity of beef will triumph in the contest. The
feast is termed the "Beef Bowl," and the two groups of novices compete

on different nights. (USC consumed 349 lbs.: Indiana consumed 280 lbs.)

An evening festival (closed party) was hosted for the novices, with various performers entertaining them. The highlight of the evening was the presentation of gifts to the novices, from representative groups in the outside society. Each novice received a silver platter (Chrysler Corp.), a transistor radio (RCA), a watch (Jurgenson), a pair of binoculars.

Phase III: Latency

After the final public ceremony, the novices are released from their authoritarian submission, and re-enter the social network, ostensibly free from the restrictions once imposed. However, they are in effective communication with the elders at all times, and constantly under their surveillance. The coaches are omniscient: they know the families, the girls the players date, the brawls, and the problems of all the players.

The novices now enter a latency period, with no formal structure intervening between the novices and their directors; the taboos, though implicit, are no longer agents of direct punishment. There is still much contact between the novices and directors, but its nature has changed —the novices are now entrusted to help with jobs which the coaches would ordinarily do themselves (recruiting); and there are scheduled conferences between the novices and his coach every two weeks.

Phase IV: "Spring Ball"

This is the final phase of the yearly cycle, and involves an emphasis on the role played by the *individual* novice and his skills, in contrast to the unity emphasis during Double Days. There are few restrictions placed on him in the form of seclusion or taboos. The main object is the competition between individuals, to beat out the other person who is competing for the same position.

The two-week phase is culminated on May 5 by a public ceremony, which is intra-novice; the top-ranked novices are pitted against the second-ranked. There is little ritual elaboration associated with this ceremony. After this event the novices are freed of all formal restrictions, taboos, etc.; they are on their own to use their best judgment in all situations. The summer may be a period of trial of the effectiveness of the indoctrination and internalization of the precepts passed on by the elders.

INTERPRETATION AND CONCLUSIONS

Having presented the data on the formal mechanics of the ceremony, I would like to show that football, as expressed by USC, may be considered an initation ceremony, according to the criteria of Van Gennep, Whiting et al., and Young. Ultimately, all these analyses involve a re-identification with the adult role, so it is necessary first to show this transition.

The period of adolescence in the U.S. has long been known as a turbulent transition period. The teen-age period reaches a culmination toward the end, from ages seventeen to twenty, and a symbolic rite is necessary to focus attention of the adult dogma to be assimilated . . . this is the role of football.

Ralph Linton makes an important observation when he states that the puberty ceremony in the U. S. depends to a great extent on the social class of the individual. For the lower levels, the parents ask chil-dren to extend down the bottom level of adulthood and become wage-earners early. Conversely, professional groups and people who send their children to college treat adolescence as a continuum of childhood, with economic dependence on parents perpetuating the submissive role of childhood. "For males in the higher social levels, a similar transition comes when the individual leaves the sheltered environment of college and embarks in the cut-throat competition of modern business" (Linton 1942:602).

Or, as Talcott Parsons notes, values of the young male must change rather abruptly from the youth culture with its emphasis on fun to a "prosaic business executive or lawyer" (Parsons 1942:8). The young man is expected to assume the mundane responsibilities of adult status, and football prepares him for this.

In terms of Van Gennep's scheme, the three phases which occur in rites of passage are evident. During Double Days the novice is separated from his previous environment, in relation to which he is "lost from the world," according to Coach Marv Goux. The comments of the novices also emphasize the death state: "It kills you," "You have to eat, sleep, think football," i.e., the novice is dead to the rest of society (Oliver, McConnell). There is grueling physical and mental punishment. The object of this period is the separation (mentally and psysically) of the initiates from society, and to create among the novices a sense of work-ing as a *unit* for a desired goal. The behavior stressed during Double Days is opposed to the normal individually-oriented goal behavior, and hence symbolizes the death of the novice as an isolated individual, and entrance into a cooperative unit (*viz*. society).

The rites of transition are saliently marked by the increased inter-action of the novice in the society. No longer is he secluded, except for about three hours daily, and for the night before the public ceremony. The novices still eat together one meal daily, and the restrictions are more implicit than forced on them; the elders determine the right to dismiss any boy who by their judgment has not adhered to the taboos and whose behavior shows it. The transition period, then, swings from short periods of seclusion and ceremonial action to semi-normal inter-action within the society.

Rites of reintegration are accomplished during the third phase of the yearly cycle—Spring Ball. The reintegration does not utilize such drastic behavior as the novices pretending not to know how to walk, eat, etc. The rites are composed of the same elements of which the other phases are composed, but the emphasis is on the *individual*, and lends a contrasting atmosphere to that of Double Days of The Season. Spring Ball prepares the novice for action once again in the society, by con-centrating on the skills and performance of the individual player; com-petition within the group is high—this is a relearning process to prepare for reintegration within a competitive society.

Now let us turn to the dimensions of initiation as outlined by Whit-ing. Initiation is characterized by *one* or more of the following features according to Whiting's 1958 article: (1) painful hazing by adult males; (2) genital operations; (3) seclusion from women; (4) tests of endur-ance and manliness (Whiting, Kluckholn, and Anthony 1958:360). Foot-ball has all but the second element, and thus qualifies as an initiation ceremony.

Turning to Young's discussion of initiation ceremonies, we find that his solidarity hypothesis defines initiation ceremonies as dramatic forms of sex role recognition. On his scale of degree of dramatization of male initiation, football rates as one of the most dramatic of all possible rites. In addition, there are three criteria of the ceremonies: (1) it must be periodic in the same general form and supervised by adults. (2) it must apply to all adolescents of one sex only, and (3) of a series of initiation events only the most elaborate are to be considered. Football meets the demands of all three criteria, although the second deserves justification: the performance of football is a symbolic act of initiation for the entire male adolescent group. The college residence of each particular novice is conceived as his local tribal affiliation, although a pan-tribal identity with the age-grades of all adolescents exists above the provincial loyalty. The participation in the actual ceremony where the initiatory principles are displayed publically is limited to the few who are most capable and who represent most obviously the specifications of adult status. Although precipitation is limited to the fittest, the *principles* which are taught the novices apply to *all* adolescents of the tribe. And since the novices are objects of admiration and respect, the values which they represent are emulated by their male peers. The general precepts apply to all males;

football is a symbolic rite of transformation for the total adolescent group.

The previous analyses by Whiting, Van Gennep, and Young of the initiation event by a unidimensional model, i.e., in terms of the import on one conceptual level, bypasses much of the important ramifications of the ceremony. To understand the ceremony adequately it is necessary to view it through the cross-cutting levels of the individual, the peer age-grade, and the society. There is a different significance in the ritual for each subgroup of society, and it is inaccurate to interpret initiation as having an immutable or constant meaning for all members of the society. This tripartite view is more profitable to elucidate initiation, for it allows for the interplay of more variables in the explanation of it. The relation of the *individual* to the ceremony: The elders were much more adept and explicit in their answers to this question, having formulated the aims and hopes previously; the novices were more unsure about what it meant to participate in the event, and one novice refused to tell me, saying, "Do you think I'd tell *you?*" (McConnell). It emerged later that this was not a sexual taboo against telling me, but that the novice felt extremely moved by the ceremony and did not feel at ease in expressing his feelings.

There is, obviously, a physical aspect to the ceremony, and bodily fitness must be relevant to the novices. However, this element was rarely stressed when asked to relate their conceptions of the importance of football to their own lives. Instead, the importance of the ceremony to the novice is due to the development of personal qualities, all of which are deemed virtuous in adult society. The compiled list herein covers the most salient reasons why it is felt that the initiation cycle is significant in the lives of the novices.

1. Merlin Olsen, a celebrated post-novice, feels football allows men to concentrate on *work*, and develops a dedication which is carried on through one's life; he stresses that work is the greatest aid to creating *men*.

2. Closely related to this is the view that football forces an individual to become somewhat self-sacrificing for the good of a cooperative effort; it shows how to "sacrifice for the good of the whole organization and not just play for your own sake," as Coach Fertig puts it.

3. Within the general pattern of conformity, football teaches individuality (Kreuger). A player must conform to the training rules, and behavioral standards, but he is encouraged to express himself in

his playing formation. The second and third points together constitute a unitary quality: there is a contribution to the group effort wholeheartedly, and yet allowance for the development of individuality *within the norms.*

4. The football ceremonies develop the ability to think quickly and clearly under pressure; the novice must mobilize all his knowledge and physical resources in split-second decisions (Fertig).
5. Leadership is developed, e.g., each weekly team captain represents the group in all public appearances.
6. The equality of individuals is taught, for the novices are judged on ability and performance.[6]
7. Football allows individuals to focus their socially unacceptable drives into something worthwhile (Krueger).
8. The experience of traveling with the group, exposure to public performance, being on display, develops in the novices a sense of social competence. "They are able to meet people in any circle and can handle themselves socially" (Fertig).
9. Football heightens the competitive desire "to win."
10. Of course there are the obvious attributes which are implicitly inculcated and so explicitly demonstrated every Saturday afternoon: the sexual identification provided through the demonstration of manliness, aggressiveness, and prowess on the field. The traditional image of the "All-American male," and the "clean-cut football hero," is emphasized and re-emphasized as a model.

Ideally, then, football has the facility to turn out perfect ideal-types, according to the specifications of the older generation. The elders feel that an individual will become a different person through playing the game; the transformation will create adult members of a social organization. Phil Krueger cites the great number of football players who have achieved successful transformation and become leading businessmen. He emphasizes the point that football as a means to an end is all right; but if it represents the high point in a player's life, then he's in trouble. In effect, football should represent a transition phase through which one develops the qualities necessary for successful adult orientation. "You put yourself in a dangerous, yet controlled situation; and you become a better man for having faced the danger" (Krueger).

---

6. Perhaps football teaches as well the racial hypocrisy which often permeates the white world—although the black players are treated with all the respect due a white player, and are accepted as equals among the white players, the elders segregate along racial lines during the periods of seclusion: rarely does a white player room with a black player.

Relation of the *peer age-group* to the ceremony: Being a symbolic ceremony, the relationships between the novices and their peers is a unique one, a dimension not yet explored in initiation ceremonies. Yet the relation is obvious, and is consonant with the expectations: the behavior and values of the novices serve as a model for males to emulate; they are desirable sexual objects for females, and this fact reinforces the behavior of the age-group in adopting the values.

Interestingly, part of the male image (which the peers also identify with) is the cultivating of the ability "to get away with" as much as possible without being caught. It is considered manly to flaunt authority, but only *up to a point*; and the novices know exactly where that threshold is which will invoke supernatural punishment—expulsion from ceremonial participation.

The relation of the society to the ceremony: One aspect is particularly outstanding when the ceremony is analyzed on this plane—the economic benefits circulated by the occurrence of the event. The ceremonies act as an attraction for financial backing of the university, as well as supporting activities from the profits gained from admission, concessions, etc. The money made in net profit alone from the football season at USC supports all the other athletic programs in the university (Krueger). The economic ramifications of the football season is amazingly intricate, affecting the welfare of the players (through the sale of their tickets), producers of sports equipment, contractors, and even the city council of Pasadena.

People like to identify with a group which shows successful application of the discipline and qualities admired by them; the alumni will support the institution if it can be proud of its accomplishments, and they judge the quality of its accomplishments through the performance of its football team. The primary importance of the ceremony differs for each group—for the individual, it is foremost a program of personal development; for the peer age-grade, it is a model to emulate; for the society, the economic factor looms most important.

The foremost task faced by each society is to perpetuate its ethnocentricity—its values and traditions. It must fashion a sense of *identity* for each adult which will incorporate those elements that must be passed to future generations.

In a culture as heterogeneous as America, this task is not easily accomplished. The diversity of role choice open to the adolescent necessites a centripetal force, to focus on a coherent and perceivable bundle of adult values with which to identify. Initiation, in the football ceremony, is a symbolic process whereby a confluence of the desired roles

of adult life is achieved; and it is expedient to unify the diverse models
of identification in order that transformation occur *effectively*.

REFERENCES

Bossard, James H. S. and Eleanor D. Boll. 1948. Rite of passage—a contem-
    porary study. *Social Forces* 26:247-255.
Burton, Roger V. and John M. Whiting. 1960. The absent father and cross-sex
    identity. *Merrill-Palmer Quarterly* 7:85-95.
Durkheim, Emile. 1913. *Les formes elementaires de le vide religieuse*. Paris,
    Alcan. Trans. by Joseph Swain. *Elementary forms of religious life*. Glen-
    coe, Ill.: The Free Press, 1947.
Fertig, Craig. 1968. Interview February 9, at USC; quarterback coach.
Goux, Marv. 1968. Interview Feb. 23, at USC; defensive linemen coach.
Krueger, Phil. 1968. Interview Feb. 9, at USC; coach of defensive ends and
    linebackers.
Linton, Ralph. 1942. Age and sex categories. *American Sociological Review*
    7:589-603.
Lynd, Robert S. and Helen Merrell Lynd. 1929. *Middletown*. New York: Har-
    court, Brace, and Co.
McConnell, Steve. 1968. Interview February 10, at USC; middle guard.
Nadel, S. F. 1951. Foundations of social anthropology. Quoted from Honig-
    mann, John J., *Theory of Ritual*, Chapel Hill, U. of N. Carolina.
Oliver, Ralph. 1968. Interview Feb. 10, at USC; middle guard.
Olsen, Merlin. 1968. Speech delivered to Sigma Chi fraternity at USC, Feb. 7.
Van Gennep, Arnold. 1909. *Rites de passage*. Paris. Emile Nourry. Trans. by
    Monika B. Vizedom and Gabrielle L. Caffee. *The Rites of Passage*. Rout-
    ledge & Kegan Paul, 1960.
Whiting, John M. and Richard Kluckholn and Albert Anthony. 1958. "The
    function of male initiation ceremonies at puberty," In *Readings in social
    psychology*. Eleanor E. Maccoby, Theodore M. Newcomb, and Eugene
    Hartley, eds. New York: Holt, Rinehart and Winston.
Whiting, John M. 1964. "Effects of climate on certain cultural practices," *In
    Explorations in cultural anthropology*. Ward H. Goodenough, ed. New
    York: McGraw-Hill.
Young, Frank W. 1962. "The function of male initiation ceremonies: a cross-
    cultural test of an alternative hypothesis." *The American Journal of Soci-
    ology* 67:379-91.
———. 1965. *Initiation ceremonies*. New York: Bobbs-Merrill Co., Inc.

THE TRIPLE OPTION
... FOR WOMEN IN SPORT

Jan Felshin

Our visions and images of women in sport are circumscribed by existing societal values and sanctions. The dimensions of the possible for the future depend upon contemporary social emphasis. At any particular time, a host of variables of belief, attitude, and action characterize social phenomena. The concept of "women in sport" represents a syndrome of theoretical stances toward both women and sport as well as their interactive relationship.

Beyond analyzing the contemporary status of the concept, the problem of predicting the route of "women in sport" depends upon the ways in which the present and the future are understood to relate. Dichotomous perspectives exist for the prediction of social change and each has differing inferences for the future of women in sport. For instance, if it is assumed that social data are linear and continuous, then the future is predicted to be the present followed to its logical conclusion. In this view, social resolutions and change occur within the framework of existing values and visions and in accord with the flexibility of the prevailing social frame. According to this perspective, social reality of "women in sport" may well change; however, operant notions of both "women" and "sport" will be accommodated. An alternative view suggests that social trends may be discontinuous from the past. Revolutionary modes assume organic social power and imply that newly discovered attitudes may serve as catalysts of sufficient cruciality to negate and/or replace strictures of the past.

The social hypotheses of the present and the possible relationships to change seem to provide a triple option for the future of women in sport.

From *Quest*, Monograph XXI (January, 1974): 36-40.

Because these positions contain the potential for ideological compulsion, it is important to clarify them.

THE APOLOGETIC

Although women participate in sport, the conventional wisdom surrounding their athletic efforts and achievements is an apologetic for reality. To the extent that masculinity represents a mode of assertion and aggression, and femininity, passivity and social desirability, women and sport can exist only in uneasy conceptual juxtaposition. Each woman in sport is a social anomaly when sport is seen as the idealized socialization of masculine traits and the ideals of femininity preclude these qualities. Because women cannot be excluded from sport and have chosen not to reject sport, apologetics develop to account for their sport involvement in the face of its social unacceptability.

Women Athletes are Feminine

The cognitive dissonance inherent in traditional conceptions of femininity and athleticism can be dissipated by denial. The women athlete must document the validity of her womanhood within the cultural connotations of femininity. To do this, she frequently denies the importance of her athletic endeavors and avows the importance of her appearance and the desire to be attractive and to marry and raise a family as the overriding motivations of her life.

Women in sport, both the athletes themselves and their sponsors, especially those responsible for school and collegiate programs, have devoted themselves tirelessly to demonstrating that female athletes are real women. The apologetic has been served in countless ways from an insistence on "heels and hose" as an appropriate off-the-court costume to the sacrifice and exile of some women athletes whose non-conforming attitudes or appearance threatened the desired image of femininity. At the least, this point of view accounts for the inordinate attention to how female athletes look and the illogical commentaries on their social and sexual lifestyles.

Women's Sport is Feminine

Personal apologetics are less necessary as social views accommodate a wider range of appropriate role behaviors for women. Insofar as the assumptions that define femininity also imply male superiority, however, this apologetic for women in sport provides a rationale for limited patterns of participation by women. It presumes that women will stay in "their place" in sport; for to be "feminine" means to be less serious and less important, and to recognize men's activities as the consequential ones. Women's sport, then, develops forms unlike the male versions, and emphasizes the so-called "feminine" sport patterns.

Many women have avoided confrontations with their male counterparts in sport by developing programs that emphasize divergent rationales and administrative arrangements that deny any aspirations toward serious athletic endeavor. It is no accident that much of the women's "philosophy" of sport participation implies restriction and control.

THE FORENSIC

It is, of course, the changing sociolegal structures that suggest the possibility of discontinuity in the future roles of women in sport. The contemporary equality revolutions clarify the inequitable and illegal dimensions inherent in many social practices. The frameworks for change fostered by feminist ideology imply certain logical imperatives for sport.

Women are Equal to Men

The demands for equality for women in sport are predicated upon the inequities of the conventional social wisdom. Sex stereotyping is clearly responsible for differences in self-perception, aspiration, and ability between boys and girls, men and women. Logic demands that once the pernicious effects of stereotypic standards on women are recognized, there must be aggressive efforts to overcome them. The corollary assumption is that in a sexist society, all action is necessarily political.

The feminist point of view emphasizes the assertion of women's rights, and sport is an important focal point because of its significance in society and the fact that the premise of the separation of the sexes in sport is the lesser ability of women. Sport in both school and society is eloquent testimony to the importance of boys and men and the neglect of girls and women. The forensic position demands women's rights to equal protection under the law; to be treated as individuals, not as a group according to commonly held stereotypes. This legal principle is manifest in the diverse challenges that include the right of girls to play on boys' teams in both contact and non-contact sports; the right of women to the enabling licenses to be jockeys, motorcycle racers, wrestlers, boxers, and anything else they wish; the right to equal pay and equal prize monies, to equitable funding and use of public facilities, and to positions, whether as umpires, coaches, sports information directors, or whatever within the sports context.

There is no "Women's" Sport

Generally, feminist ideology has documented the fact that many of the alleged differences between men and women result from social bias. Even experimental findings in psychology and physiology have been demonstrated to reflect male assumptions of women's lesser abilities. It seems logical within this position, therefore, to conclude that the potential of women is unknown and untapped, and that sport particularly should provide opportunities for unhampered aspirations to be manifest.

Equity for women is translated into demands for the privilege and practices attendant to the male competitive model. Once the principle of discrimination as difference was established, women were able to petition successfully for equal treatment in terms of scholarships, budgets, coaching, facilities, and other aspects of athletic opportunity. In some contemporary programs, it is apparent that women's sport is developing in a fashion parallel to men's sport. In addition, the range of sports available to women is increasing, and football, soccer, and ice hockey teams and leagues have expanded.

THE DIALECTIC

The dialectic of women and sport suggests that the concepts themselves and their interactive mutuality may yield unique configurations of social attitudes and sport forms. The position depends on a feminist-humanist assumption, and rejects the model of sport that depends upon a harsh competitive ethic.

Women can be Athletes

Because sport is an enduring human phenomenon, a symbolic domain wherein the interactions of striving, contesting, and excellence are affirmed, it is rooted in human sources. This position suggests that women, no less than men, refresh and refine abilities and sensibilities within sport and that gender is irrelevant to the realm of sport as experience.

The dialectic of women and sport assumes that sexism, like racism, is social and that the disease should not contaminate the relationship between ethical and actual structures of sport as these depend crucially upon commitment and performance. Women, therefore, must be protected from the slander and limitations that arise from sexual stereotyping; they should share equally in athletic opportunities and fully in the testing and stretching of their abilities.

Women can Define Sport

The forensic position does not distinguish between women's rights and goals in the sense that it petitions entry to existing structures, and liberates institutional contexts for women. The androgynous point of view denies any validity for differences between men and women, and its organizing principle is one of access. Carried to its logical conclusion, this view supports the *status quo* of sport except that it includes women.

The dialectic position hypothesizes alternative social definitions for sport. It affirms differences between men and women without assuming genetic cause, and seeks changed visions for both sexes. The dialogue within the dialectic revolves around finding means to preserve the valuable qualities associated with women and actualizing these in human institutions. As the model of sport developed by men is found objectionable for all human persons, the possibilities for new conceptions of sport emerge as alternative options.

THE FUTURISTIC

Although the delineation of these perspectives implies a triple option, there is little doubt that the changing views and roles of women provide a significant element of social discontinuity that must affect sport. The last vestiges of the apologetic effects are presently apparent in the backlash efforts of some organizations to continue to restrict athletic opportunities for women in the face of sociolegal reality. The apologetic is manifest in such stances as the absolute opposition to girls playing on boys' teams, or to scholarships for women, or to women seeking roles as full-time coaches. It is obvious too in the failure of women leaders in sport to pursue the legal sanction for expanded opportunities for the girls and women in their charge, and their continued attitudes of "making do" with limited resources and facilities while their players clamor for expansion and their male counterparts enjoy every financial and actual privilege.

The liberation of women begins with a forensic view of human rights and affirmative action on behalf of self-worth. Only the powerless fear the repercussions of their demands for power, and the young women of the future will not be frightened by the logical conclusions of the apologetic to the effect that if women play on men's teams, there will be no teams for women, and if women insist on their rights, their few freedoms will be lost. It is beginning to be clear that the inflated price paid for sugar and spice is a function of a manipulated market of male superiority.

The immediate future for women's sport derives from the forensic position. Sport will be symbolic of women's rights and gains, and it will develop according to the principle that separate can never mean equal for the second class citizen. For a time, therefore, girls and women will seek access to existing teams in light of their established legal rights to do so. At the same time, the political view supports the idea that women deserve reparations for past inequities and affirmative action principles will be upheld as an antidote to a sexist society and the sport establishment it has created. Both women in sport and women's sport are entering an exciting era characterized by a heady sense of freedom to try anything. As women in sport test their own potential, their freedom to dare will free all sportspersons from the restrictive visions of the technological, predictable, exclusive character of the competitive establishment.

As the "men only" nature of sport is challenged successfully, and as budgets and facilities are shared by legal sanction, men and women will have to learn to co-exist in sport. The entry of women by itself will simply modify men's assumptions and programs. Budget will dictate more shared contests, greater flexibility of scheduling, co-sexual participation and consideration, and, at the same time, will provide a rationale for men to escape the treadmill of the demands for success that have transmuted dreams of glory into nightmares of failure. As women reject their "sex object" image, men may find that they don't have to be "success objects" either.

By the twenty-first century women will have liberated sport both as a male domain and from its contemporary models. Without the assumption of sport as a singular male preserve and the corollary of male superiority, new perspectives must emerge. In a sense, these will diminish the importance of particular contests and contexts, but in doing so they will suggest the attractiveness of the wonderful world of sport for more people in more varied patterns of participation. Because excellence and ability are essential components of the structure of sport, they will never be denied, but both men and women as high level performers will cease to serve as the viable model for all sport. Stadiums, like concert stages, contribute to our cultural life as the arenas for the few.

The shape of sport in the future is not easy to predict. Faith in the dialectic of women and sport implies the development of new and more humanistic modes for social interaction, behavior, and motivation. It also means that women must explore their options; they must be encouraged to try and to be whatever they are impelled to seek; for it is self that is sought, and no apology is required.

ON BEING A FEMALE IN SPORT

M. MARIE HART*

The topic of social and sexual roles in sport is a complicated one about which Americans seem particularly sensitive. The sexuality separated facilities and organizations that often accompany sport and physical education activities may be an extension of certain problems in this area. There is an urgent need to consider these problems if we are concerned about the quality of the experience for all those who engage in sport. Many times it seems that people find it difficult to consider such problems with any degree of objectivity. To remove the personal self from the social process being examined requires a thorough grounding in knowledge of self and a deep understanding of one's own personal sport involvement.

This article is particularly concerned with being a woman and being in sport. Although we have isolated and studied "Women in Sport," we have not so separated "Men in Sport" as a special topic. This is because the latter is the accepted, rather than the exception, in sport discussions. It seems well established that much of sport is male territory; therefore participation of female newcomers is studied as a peripheral, non-central aspect of sport. If one aspect of sport is social experience, it seems appropriate to study it in total context and to note the differences of role and reaction in the variety of people taking part. The separation and alienation of women in sport is not the healthiest of situations. It is only through interaction that we can gain awareness and acceptance of differences. Why is it that in most of the rest of the Western world women co-exist with men in sport with less stigma and with more acceptance as respected partners?

*An earlier version of this material appeared in *Psychology Today* Magazine, October, 1971. Copyright © Communication/Research/Machines, Inc.

Being female in this culture does not necessarily mean that one is perceived or accepted as "feminine." Each culture has its social norms and sex roles which one can recognize, but in the United States this definition seems especially rigid and narrow. For longer than one can remember, women in sport have known and experienced rejection due to their failure to live up to a particular concept of "feminine." It has been an unpleasant and painful memory for many.

Why has it been difficult for women to stay "woman" and be an athlete, especially in games emphasizing physical skill? Games of physical skill are associated with achievement and aggressiveness which seem to make them an expressive model for males rather than females. Women are more traditionally associated with high obedience training and routine responsibility training, and with games of strategy and games of chance which emphasize those qualities supposedly desirable in women (9) (11) (12). This all begins so early that the young girl in elementary school already begins feeling the pressure to select some games and avoid others if she is to be a "real" girl. If she is told often enough at eleven or twelve that sports are not ladylike, she may at that point make a choice between being a lady and being an athlete. Having to make this choice has potential for setting up deep conflict in female children, which continues later into adulthood.

The concept of conflict-enculturation theory of games is developed in an essay by Sutton-Smith, Roberts and Kozelka. They maintain that "conflicts induced by social learning in childhood and later (such as those related to obedience, achievement, and responsibility) lead to involvement in expressive models, such as games . . " (12:15). This process can be applied also to the game involvement of adults. Cultural values and competencies are acquired in games. It would appear that games operate on various levels as expressive models to ease conflict, with the exception of the case of the woman athlete. As girls become more and more proficient in sport, the level of personal investment increases which may, due to the long hours of practice and limited associations, isolate her socially. Personal conflict and stress increase as it becomes necessary for her to assure others of her sexual identity, sometimes requiring evidence. This level of tension and conflict may increase dramatically if a girl makes the choice to be intensely involved in a sport which is thought of as male territory.

In an interview Chi Cheng, who holds several world track records, was quoted as saying, "The public sees women competing and immediately thinks that they must be manly—but at night, we're just like other women" (14:15). Why does a woman (whether American or otherwise) often need to comment about herself in this way and how does this awareness of stigma affect her daily life? Chi goes on to say: "I'm gone so much of the day and on weekends. I give a lot of public appearances—where I can show off my femininity" (14:16).

Numerous occasions have occurred in college discussion groups over the past few years that convince one that we have imposed a great burden on women who are committed to performing or teaching sport. As an example, several married women students majoring in physical education confided to a discussion group that they had wanted to cut their hair but felt they couldn't. Members of the group asked why this was so, if their husbands objected, if they would feel less feminine, if they were in doubt about their own femaleness. In very case they responded that they simply didn't want the usual stereotype image and comments from friends and family in their social lives. Even when hairstyles are short women in sport are judged by a standard other than fashion. If the married sportswoman experiences anxiety over such things, one can imagine the struggle of the single woman. Unfortunately, this often results in a defensive attitude developed as a shield against those who poke and probe.

When young women do enjoy sport, what activities are really open to them? A study done in 1963 (4) shows recommendations made about sports participation by 200 freshman and sophomore college women from four Southern California schools. Although their own background had been strong in the team sports of basketball, softball and volleyball they did not recommend that a girl, even thought highly skilled, pursue these activities at a professional level. They strongly discouraged participation in track and field activities. The sports they did recommend for a talented young woman were those that they had not necessarily experienced personally. They were ranked as follows: tennis, swimming, ice skating, diving, bowling, skiing and golf. All of these recommended sports are identified with aesthetic considerations, social implications, and fashions for women. Physical strength and skill may be important components of these activities but are not their primary identifications.

Some may argue that the past decade has seen great change in the acceptance of women in a larger variety of sports. That is no doubt true, at least to a degree, but some limited observation would indicate that there has been no radical change. In fact, the wave of enthusiasm for women in gymnastics only reinforces the traditional ideal of the striving for aesthetic form as "appropriate" for women in sport—an aesthetic that emphasizes poise, smooth and rhythmic movement. Form is the ultimate criteria, not strength and speed. Could this be indicative of the status quo?

In contrast to the findings of the 1963 (4) study is the situation of the black woman athlete. In the black community, the woman can be strong and achieving in sport and still not deny her womanness. She may actually gain respect and status as evidenced by the reception of women like Wilma Rudolph, Wyomia Tyus Simburg, and other great performers. The black woman seems also to have more freedom to mix her involvement in sport and dance without the conflict expressed by many white women athletes. This in itself would be a rich subject for research.

The limitations on sport choices for women have been instituted largely by social attitudes about women in sport as previously discussed. These attitudes have a long history which is revealed in the sport literature. Early sport magazines reinforced the idea of women being physically inferior to men in sport and furthermore inferred that their female emotionality rendered them incompetent. As an example, in response to a strong desire of women to be involved in the new and exciting sport of flying in 1912, the editor of *Outing Magazine* was outspoken in his bias:

> Other things being equal, the man who has had the most experience in outdoor sports should be the best aviator. By the same token, women should be barred. . . . Women have not the background of games of strength and skill that most men have. Their powers of correlation are correspondingly limited and their ability to cope with sudden emergencies inadequate. (10: 253)

The social process by which women had arrived at this mythic helpless state of being was never mentioned or discussed.

In 1936 the editor of *Sportsman,* a magazine for the wealthy, commented about the Olympic Games that he was ". . . fed up to the ears with women as track and field competitors." He continued, "her charms shrink to something less than zero" and urged the organizers to "keep them where they are competent. As swimmers and divers girls are beautiful and adroit as they are ineffective and unpleasing on the track" (13: 18).

More recent publications such as *Sports Illustrated* have not been openly negative, but the implication is sustained by the limitation in their coverage of women in sport. Content is small and consists mostly of a discussion of fashions and of women in traditionally approved activities such as swimming, diving, ice skating, tennis and golf. The emphasis in periodicals is still largely on women as attractive objects rather than as skilled and effective athletes.

The magazines *Sportswoman* and *womenSports* have been dedicated to presenting a full and fair coverage of women in sport. The efforts of the editors and writers are excellent even though one occasionally gets the impression that the message is "see we're just as good, skilled and tough as the men but still attractive."

Granted the image is somewhat exaggerated but again care must be taken not just to accept and act out the traditional model of sport developed by and for men. There may be more alternatives and dimensions to be explored which would benefit a greater variety of personalities and social groups.

Attitudes toward women in sport have been slow to change because of misunderstandings like the muscle myth. It has been difficult to allay the fear that sport activity will produce bulging muscles which imply masculinity. Young girls are frightened away from sport by "caring" adults who perpetuate this false idea. The fact, well documented by exercise physiologists, is that "excessive development (muscles) is not a concomitant of athletic competition" (6:130). Klafs and Arnheim further affirm this situation, reporting: "Contrary to lay opinion, participation in sports does not masculinize[1] women. Within a sex, the secretion of testosterone, androgen, and estrogen varies considerably, accounting for marked variation in terms of muscularity and general morphology among males and females" (6:128). Participation in sport cannot make changes in the potential of hereditary and structural factors of any individual.

Perhaps what occasionally gives observers the impression that the muscle myth is true is the reality that some girl athletes are indeed muscular. However, it may be due to their muscularity that they enter sport, rather than it being a result of their participation. This is further explained by Klafs and Arnheim:

> Girls whose physiques reflect considerable masculinity are stronger per unit of weight than girls who are low in masculinity and boys who display considerable femininity of build. Those who are of masculine type often do enter sports and are usually quite successful because of the mechanical advantages possessed by the masculine structure. However, such types are the exception, and by far the greater majority of participants possess a[2] feminine body build. (6:128)

It would seem more accurate and scientifically sound to describe this difference in terms of hormone level and individual potential. (RIGHT ON!)[3] This kind of value laden language is used repeatedly by researchers in the fields of sport and physical education.

---

1. Even in their effort to dismiss the myth, Klafs and Arnheim seem to buy the cultural myth implying that muscles are masculine. The literature on this topic is loaded with such cultural slips.
2. The cultural norm hits again.
3. Just couldn't edit out this comment by the manuscript typist—a former career woman turned housewife.

Some of the most important considerations about women in Western culture have been written by Simone de Beauvoir. In her book, *The Second Sex,* she also discusses sport as a way of experiencing oneself in the world and of asserting one's sovereignty. She says that outside of participation in sport, a girl must experience most of her physical self in a passive manner (2). De Beauvoir makes one point that is worth the serious consideration of all who are concerned about the dilemma of the woman athlete. She states:

> And in sports the end in view is not success independent of physical equipment; it is rather the attainment of perfection within the limitations of each physical type; the featherweight boxing champion is as much of a champion as is the heavyweight; the woman skiing champion is not the inferior of the faster male champion; they belong to two different classes: It is precisely the female athletes who, being positively interested in their own game, feel themselves least handicapped in comparison with the male. (2:311)

Americans seem not to be able to apply this view of "attainment of perfection with the limitations of each" to the woman in sport. Women have been continually compared to males and have had male performance and style set as model and goal for them. Repeatedly young girls and women athletes listen to, "Wow, what a beautiful throw. You've got an arm like a guy." "Look at that girl run, she could beat lots of boys." Father comments, "Yes, she loves sports. She's our little tomboy." It would seem strange to say of a young boy, "Oh, yes, he is our little marygirl." We have ways of getting messages to boys who don't fit the role, but we haven't integrated it into our language terminology so securely.

These kinds of comments carry with them the message of expected cultural behavior. When well learned it results in girls losing games to boys purposely, avoiding dates which show her sports talent or risking never dating the boy again if she performs better than he does.

The male performance standards and the attending social behavior have extended into even more serious problems. In the early international competitions of the 1920's, women were not subjected to medical examinations. After doubt arose over one or two competitors, each country was asked to conduct medical examinations to determine if indeed the performer was female. Countries did not trust the honesty of nonsupervised tests so additional tests began to be employed. In recent international events women have had to pass the "Barr Sex Test" perfected by a Canadian doctor. The test consists of scraping cells from the inside of the cheek and then analyzing them for "Barr bodies." The number fluctuates normally during a month but all women have a minimum percentage of Barr bodies all the time. In the test, if the percentage drops below the minimum for females then the femaleness of the performer is suspect and she is dropped from the competition.

In 1968, the "Barr Sex Test" was administered for the first time at an Olympic Game, causing quite a stir. The scene was described by Marion Lay, a Canadian swimmer performing in both the 1964 and 1968 Olympics. The line-up awaiting the test in Mexico erupted in reactions ranging from tension-releasing jokes to severe stress and upset. Some performers suggested that if the doctor were good looking enough, one might skip the test and prove their femaleness by seducing him. At the end of the test the women received a certificate verifying their femaleness and approving their participation in the Games. Many were quite baffled by the necessity of the test, feeling that their honesty as much as their sexual identity was in question. Most could not imagine anyone wanting to win so badly that they would create a disguise or knowingly take drugs that might jeopardize their health.

In addition to the concern over proof of sexual identity, there has been much discussion about the use of "steroid" drugs by some women performers, particularly those from Russia and Eastern bloc nations. These drugs are derived from male sex hormones and tend to increase muscle size. The subject of the use of these drugs by women has been somewhat muted with the result that there is not much literature describing the effects of this drug on women performers. There have been continued warnings against its use by men because of its unknown or dangerous side effects but there is still somewhat limited information published about the effects of the steroid drug. It is known to increase body size and also to produce secondary male characteristics in women such as increasing of facial hair and lowering of the voice (1:135).

Why would a woman take such a drug? Is it because the values are on male records and performance, and the national pressure to win may cause her to attempt to come as close to this kind of goal as possible? This kind of expectation in regards to performance and the attending social behavior have caused serious problems for women athletes. If the performance of women could be recognized on its own merit without comparison to male records and scores, many painful social and medical experiences for women would be avoided.

If women in sport feel outside of the mainstream of social life in this country, perhaps another question could be posed to representatives of the new movements. Where has the feminist platform been in relation to women athletes? When the role of women is no longer limited to mother, secretary, or Miss America, isn't it about time that women were given not only freedom to be but respect for being successful in sport? Granted the early 1970's has been a time of increased interest and recognition from women's organizations but more support, understanding and coverage is still needed.

It seems apparent that the female athlete in general has much, if not more, to contend with than any other women in the American way of life as to sex role taboos. To entertain doubts about one's sexual identity and role results in more than a little stress. An editorial in *Women: A Journal of Liberation* states: "In America, dance is a field for women and male homosexuals. There is the dancer's cult of starving and punishing one's body (15:65)." In contrast, one might think of sport as a field for men and female homosexuals, or so the social role of the female athlete seems often to be interpreted. The need to change the environment of sport and dance from symbolic cultural territory for the establishing of sexual identity and acceptance to an environment of valued personal experience and fulfillment is long past due.

The aforementioned editorial goes on to say: "My dream is that dance will not have to be an escape from America's sick sexuality but a celebration of all our bodies, dancing" (15:65). What else could one wish for both men and women in sport? Why could not sport be a celebration, both personal and mutual, of the body-self? A celebration—rather than a conflict over best scores and most points, over who is most male and who is least female—a celebration of one's body-self whoever she or he is. The jokes, stories and oppression are old and far too heavy to be carried along further. The present-day women athlete may soon demand her female space and identity in sport.

Today women *have* begun to enter sport with more social acceptance and individual pride. After World War II the increase in the number of women athletes and their success became more apparent and better received. In 1952 researchers from the Finnish Institute of Occupational Health conducted an intensive study of the athletes participating in the Olympics in Helsinki. Their findings were of major importance in the study of women athletes. After studying their athletic achievements, physiological and clinical data, age, fitness and social status, the researchers stated that "women are about to shake off civic disabilities which millennia of prejudice and ignorance have imposed upon them" (5:84). The researchers concluded that the participation of women was a significant indication of positive health and living standards of a country.

In addition to the physiological and clinical data, the researchers observed other factors apparent in the performance of women athletes. Criteria for describing the performances expanded to include aesthetic considerations because it "added itself" to the researchers data. They stated:

> A third criterion for the evaluation of women's athletics is an aesthetic one. Parallel with the growth of athletic performance standards there has taken

place during the past fifty years or so a display of new dynamic patterns of motion and form which contain elements of artistic value and of creative beauty. The great woman hurdlers and discus throwers, fencers, and divers, gymnasts and canoeists have introduced, unwittingly, of course, features of elegance and of power, of force and of competence such as had previously not been known. That sports and athletics should be able to elicit in women categorical values of this kind and that performance and beauty should thus be correlated is a surprising and highly relevant experience. (5:84-85)

In the same vein, Ogilvie, a professor of psychology, stated:

The review of the data upon San Jose State College women swimmers presents evidence that there has been no loss of the feminine traits most valued within our culture. There was strong evidence that at least this small sample of women had outstanding traits of personality in the presence of outstanding success as competitors. I must reject the prejudiced view that would deny women the joys and rewards of high level athletic competition. It appears to this investigator that you would have to search the whole world over before you could find twenty women who measure up to these in both personality and natural[4] physical beauty. (8:7)

Personal fulfillment as expressed by woman in sports and dance experiences must not be manipulated or denied to anyone in the name of archaic cultural roles. They have been binding, limiting and belittling. This is the age of woman in command of her own space and movement. Men will also gain freedom from their role restriction as the process of social change continues.

The argument that "a person is a person is a person" is one to be heeded—and one wishes practiced. However, it seems necessary in this transitional time to name, discuss and research what is practiced so that social roles and systems can be fully understood and exposed. Only when individuals and more generally the society, becomes conscious of behavior can that behavior be changed. Until then it's all just so much talk.

BIBLIOGRAPHY

1. Blythe, Myrna. "Girl Athletes: What Makes Them Skate, Fence, Swim, Jump, Run?" *Cosmopolitan,* (October, 1969), pp. 110-114.
2. de Beauvoir, Simone. *The Second Sex.* New York: Bantam Books, 1952.
3. Hambric, Lois. "To Ski." Unpublished paper. California State College at Hayward, June, 1971.

4. Again there is the cultural concern and bias toward "feminine" traits and beauty. Conversely, there is full cultural appreciation of excellent male athletes, be they handsome or ugly.

4. Hart, M. Marie. "Factors Influencing College Women's Attitudes Toward Sport and Dance," Master's Thesis, University of Southern California, 1963.
5. Jokl, Ernst. *Medical Sociology and Cultural Anthropology of Sport and Physical Education.* Springfield, Ill.: Charles C Thomas, Publishers, 1964, pp. 73-85.
6. Klafs, Carl E. and Arnheim, Daniel D. *Modern Principles of Athletic Training.* St. Louis, Mo.: C. V. Mosby Company, 1969, pp. 127-134.
7. Novich, Max M. and Taylor, Buddy. *Training and Conditioning of Athletes.* Philadelphia, Pa.: Lea and Febiger, 1970.
8. Ogilvie, Bruce. "The Unanswered Question: Competition, Its Effect Upon Feminity." Address given to the Olympic Development Committee, Santa Barbara, California, June 30, 1967.
9. Roberts, J. M. and Sutton-Smith, B. "Child-Training and Game Involvement," *Ethnology* 1 (1962): 66-185.
10. "Still They Fall," *Outing* 67 (November, 1912): 253.
11. Sutton-Smith, B., Rosenberg, B. G. and Morgan, E. F., Jr. "Development of Sex Differences in Play Choices During Preadolescence," *Child Development* 34 (1963):119-126.
12. Sutton-Smith, B., Roberts, J. M. and Kozelka, R. M. "Game Involvement in Adults," *The Journal of Social Psychology* 60 (1963):15-30.
13. "Things Seen and Heard." *Sportsman* 20 (October, 1936):17-20.
14. Winner, Karin. "At Night We're Just Like Other Women," *Amateur Athlete.* (April, 1971), pp. 15-17.
15. *Women: A Journal of Liberation* 2 (Fall, 1970):1+.

RELATED LITERATURE

Harres, Bea. "Attitudes of Students Toward Women's Athletic Competition," *Research Quarterly* 39 (May, 1968):278-284.

Higdon, Rose and Higdon, Hal. "What Sports for Girls?" *Today's Health* 45 (October, 1967):21-23, 74.

Krotz, L. E. "A Study of Sports and Implications for Women's Participation in Them in Modern Society," Ph.D. Dissertation, Ohio State University, 1958.

McGree, Rosemary. "Comparisons of Attitudes Toward Intensive Competition for High School Girls," *Research Quarterly* 27 (1956):60-73.

Metheny, Eleanor. "Symbolic Forms of Movement: The Feminine Image in Sport," *Connotations of Movement in Sport and Dance.* Dubuque, Iowa: Wm. C. Brown Company Publishers, 1965, pp. 43-56.

Trekell, M. "The Effect of Some Cultural Changes Upon the Sports and Physical Education Activities of American Women—1860-1960," Paper presented at the History and Philosophy Section of the National Convention of the American Association of Health, Physical Education and Recreation, Dallas, Texas, March 18, 1965.

Watts, D. P. "Changing Conceptions of Competitive Sports for Girls and Women in the United States from 1880 to 1960," Ed.D. Dissertation, University of California, Los Angeles, 1960.

BIBLIOGRAPHY

1. Section C. Socializations: Sex Roles

Bouton, Jim. *Ball Four*. New York: World Publishing Co., 1970.

Crew, Louie. "The Physical Miseducation of a Former Fat Boy," *Saturday Review* (of Education), Feb. 1973.

Drinkwater, B. "Aerobic Power in Females," *Journal of Physical Education and Recreation* 46 (January 1975):36-38.

Edwards, Harry. "Desegregating Sexist Sport," *Intellectual Digest*, (Nov. 1972): 82-83.

Gerber, Ellen; Felshin, Jan; Berlin, Pearl, and Wyrick, Waneen. *The American Woman in Sport*. Reading, Mass.: Addison-Wesley Publishers, 1974.

Gilbert, B. "The Second Sex Engages in a First," *Sports Illustrated* (May 21, 1973), 96-98.

———, and Williamson, N. "Women in Sport: Part 1, Sport Is Unfair to Women: Part 2, Are You Being Two-Faced?; Part 3, Programmed to be Losers," *Sports Illustrated* (May 28, June 4, June 11, 1973).

Griffin, P. S., "What's a Nice Girl Like You Doing in a Profession Like This?", *Quest* XIX (January, 1973), 96-101.

Harris, Dorothy, ed. *Women and Sport: Proceedings of the National Research Conference*. University Park, Penn.: Pennslyvania State University Press, 1972.

———. "Psychosocial Considerations," *Journal of Physical Education and Recreation* 46 (January 1975):32-36.

Klafs, C. E. and Lyon, M. J. *The Female Athlete*. St. Louis: C. V. Mosby, 1973.

Meggyesy, Dave. *Out of Their League*. New York: Ramparts Books, 1971.

Neal, Patsy. *Sport and Identity*. Philadelphia: Dorrance and Co., 1973.

Oliver, Chip. *High for the Game*. New York: William Morrow, 1971.

Parrish, Bernie. *They Call It a Game*. New York: Dial Press, 1971.

Ryan, A. J. "Gynecological Considerations," *Journal of Physical Education and Recreation* 46 (January 1975):10-44.

Schecter, Leonard. *The Jocks*. New York: Paperback Library, 1970.

Scott, Jack. *Athletics for Athletes*. Oakland, California: An Other Ways Book, 1969.

Wolf, David. *Foul!* Canada: Holt, Rinehart and Winston, 1972.

SECTION

C

2. SOCIALIZATION: ETHNIC GROUPS

The first author in this section gives the reader a quick and potent look into the "roots of the revolt of the black athlete." Edwards was involved in organizing the efforts and energy of the black athletes prior to the 1968 Olympics. In his article he suggests that the athlete's revolt relates to the black liberation movement and he makes the reader keenly aware that the protest of athletes is in reaction to the same iniquities that cause other protests and rebellions in the United States.

For greater exposure to this topic read the book, *The City Game.*[1] In it author Axthelm contends that "every American sport directs itself in a general way toward certain segments of American life." He continues, "basketball belongs to the cities" and especially to New York, the most "dedicated basketball city of all." In his writing, Axthelm catches the style, rhythm, and drama of the game. Most of all he describes school yard basketball in Harlem as a "rite of passage" and a way of transcending life in the ghetto. The sad ending for most of the brilliant young players is that they never pass into manhood but drift off into the drug scene or meet other tragic ends. Axthelm exposes the process that creates the final outcome.

The plight of the black athlete is exposed in the second article, "Racial Segregation in American Sport," by Loy and McElvogue. It is an analysis of segregation and discrimination in professional baseball and football. The researchers pursue the relationship between discrimination and centrality. Are blacks excluded from central positions on the teams and, if so, how does this reflect possibilities for advancement in the sports world?

In a study of ethnic soccer clubs in Milwaukee, Pooley analyzes the aspect of cultural assimilation. Do these clubs exist within ethnic sub-

1. Peter Axthelm, *The City Game.* New York: Simon and Schuster. Pocket Books, 1971.

cultures and thereby inhibit assimilation of the ethnic group into "the standard setting" core culture? Or, one might ask, is it a way of maintaining ethnic identity? Pooley looks at ten different soccer clubs and their activities during club meetings, playing soccer, and at social occasions, to discern answers to these questions.

Eaglesmith presents the rich tradition of games and sport as integral to the ways of life of early Native Americans. He has brought together a variety of anthropological studies on Indian games. With a heritage so rich, he asks, where is the Native American in American sport today?

Before reading the last article in the book it may be wise to reflect briefly on the complexity and diversity of American sport. In earlier articles Tindall (Part II, Introduction and Section A) examined the possibility of cultural variations and the possibility of variation in students' perceptions of meaning in a specific physical activity. It has been precisely these kinds of cultural variations that we have often ignored in offering sports programs to diverse ethnic groups, woman and other participant interests.

To understand the "hidden curricula"[2] of various groups one must observe and listen. Andrews' article gives each reader that opportunity. An opportunity to sit in another seat and listen to him talk about sport in another language. Keep an open mind as your head spins and your feelings are made vulnerable, that is, if you are white. Information and feelings have to flow both ways if understanding and change are to result.

In addition to giving specific attention to several ethnic groups in this last section, there has been an effort throughout the book to utilize information and articles about many ethnic groups. It seems appropriate that ultimately such material should be included in all considerations of American sport. More importantly, it is hoped that all people (i.e., age, sex, color) will be included in an ongoing assessment of sport in American society.

---

2. B. Allan Tindall, "Ethnography and the Hidden Curricula of Sport," *Behavioral and Social Science Teacher*, vol. 2, no. 2, 1975.

PREFACE TO THE REVOLT OF THE
BLACK ATHLETE

HARRY EDWARDS

It's beyond me why these people would allow themselves to be misled by fanatics like Harry Edwards and H. Rap Brown. These athletes are seen by millions of people on nation-wide and world wide television, they have first-string-starting assignments at white schools, and they are invited to all the big athletic events. Why our Niggers right here at the University have never had it so good.

This statement was made by the Director of Intercollegiate Athletics at one of America's major universities, later to be "white-listed" by the Olympic Committee for Human Rights during the Spring, 1968, track and field season. He was speaking to the sports editor of one of America's leading weekly news magazines. His remarks are typical of the sentiment of many of the athletic administrations that determine policy in the world of intercollegiate, amateur, and professional athletics in America. Equally typical was the response of the sports editor. He merely shook his head, indicating that he, too, could not understand such ingratitude, and then went on about the business of obtaining a *publishable* story for next week's issue. All too often too many of these self-proclaimed guardians of the morals and ethics of the sports world lend tacit approval to such racially corrupt and hypocritical attitudes, thus further degrading and violating the basic human dignity and intelligence of black athletes.

Recreation and athletics have traditionally been billed as essentially therapeutic measures—measures that cure faulty or deteriorating charc-

ter, that weaken prejudice, and that bind men of all races and nationalities closer together. The evidence does not support the theory. Athletic
and recreational centers set up in high-crime or delinquency areas have
become merely convenient meeting places for criminals and delinquents.[1]
Recreational and athletic activities, far from inhibiting crime, actually
have spawned it in both the amateur and professional areas. As for
eliminating prejudice, whites may grudgingly admit a black man's
prowess as an athlete, but will not acknowledge his equality as a human
being. [In athletics, where the stakes are position, prestige, and money,
where intense competition prevails and a loser is anathema, a white racist
does not change his attitude toward blacks; he merely alters his inclination to abuse him or discriminate against him overtly.]

Recreational patterns in America widen and perpetuate racial separation. Recreation is exclusive, compounded of all sorts of considerations, not the least of which are racial and economic. There is, therefore,
usually little opportunity for recreation to narrow the gap between white
and black Americans. Moreover, there is absolutely nothing inherent in
recreation that would change attitudes. Recreation simply refreshes the
mind and body and gives old attitudes a new start and a fresh impetus.

At an athletic event, by no means are all the bigots and racists sitting in the stands. They also are on the field of play.

The roots of the revolt of the black athlete spring from the same
seed that produced the sit-ins, the freedom rides, and the rebellions in
Watts, Detroit, and Newark. The athletic revolt springs from a disgust
and dissatisfaction with the same racist germ that infected the warped
minds responsible for the bomb murders of four black girls as they
prayed in a Birmingham, Alabama, church and that conceived and
carried out the murders of Malcolm X, Martin Luther King, and Medgar
Evers, among a multitude of others. The revolt of the black athlete arises
also from his new awarenes of his responsibilities in an increasingly more
desperate, violent, and unstable America. He is for the first time reacting
in a human and masculine fashion to the disparities between the heady
artificial world of newspaper clippings, photographers, and screaming
spectators and the real world of degradation, humiliation, and horror
that confronts the overwhelming majority of Afro-Americans. An even
more immediate call to arms for many black athletes has been their
realization that once their athletic abilities are impaired by age or injury,
only the ghetto beckons and they are doomed once again to that face-
less, hopeless, ignominious existence they had supposedly forever left

1. For a brief discussion of value, delinquency, and organized recreation and athletics, see A. W. Green, *Recreation, Leisure, and Politics,* McGraw-Hill Book Company, New York, pp. 98-105.

behind them. At the end of their athletic career, black athletes do not become congressmen, as did Bob Mathias, the white former Olympic decathlon champion, or Wilmer Mizell, ex-Pittsburgh Pirate pitcher. Neither does the black athlete cash in on the thousands of dollars to be had from endorsements, either during his professional career or after he retires. And all his clippings, records, and photographs will not qualify him for a good job, even in any of the industries that supposedly produce the breakfast foods that champions feed on. These are only the most obvious of the inequities faced by the black athlete. Others are less obvious but no less humiliating and they have no less a devastating effect on the black athlete's psyche. Like other blacks, black athletes find housing, recreational facilities, clubs, and off-season jobs closed to them (unless the coach passes the word to a prospective employer or renter that the candidate is a "good" Negro, the implication of course being that most black people are in some mysterious fashion not "good").

In essence then, the black revolution in America has not been carried into the locker room, as one sportswriter has stated. What has happened is that the black athlete has left the facade of locker room equality and justice to take his long vacant place as a primary participant in the black revolution. Underlining the importance and significance of the political and social status of this new generation of black athletes is the fact that candidates for political offices at the local and national levels in both major political parties worked vigorously in 1968 to secure the endorsements and active support of black athletes. Where the athletes' amateur status would have been jeopardized by such public commitment, statements were sought from them regarding their approval of some particular candidate's program (for instance, that of Hubert H. Humphrey) to establish equality in amateur athletics or to give the athlete more say in settling disputes between such competing athletic organizations as the National Collegiate Athletic Association and the Amateur Athletic Union. Robert Kennedy with Rosey Grier and Rafer Johnson, Hubert H. Humphrey with Ralph Metcalf, Richard Nixon with Wilt Chamberlain, and Nelson Rockefeller with Jackie Robinson attest that the stupid, plow-jack stereotype of the black athlete is no more. Whether they made a truly significant contribution to black progress or merely prostituted their athletic ability for the sake of other aims is a matter of keen debate among politically conscious blacks.

In this book we will analyze the newest phase of the black liberation movement in America. Within the context of that movement we will define the goals that underlie the athletes' protests and clarify what has been portrayed as the substantially elusive and irrational tactics and direction of their efforts. The statements we will make are not the rantings of some sideline journalist, but the documentary facts of the movement from the perspective of a man who himself was victimized by the American athletic structure, who helped plan, direct, and implement the revolt, and who intends to continue the fight until the goals of that revolt have been achieved.

The exploitation and suffering of the black athlete in America is no more a recent development than is the inhumanity and deprivation suffered by Afro-American non-athletes. Nor do these recent athletic protests mark the first instances of black athletes speaking out. The difference in this instance is that they are speaking out not only on their own behalf, but on behalf of their downtrodden race, and the world and the nation are listening. America's response to what the black athlete is saying and doing will undoubtedly not only determine the future course and direction of American athletics, but also will affect all racial and social relations between blacks and whites in this country.

Hopefully this book will be read and understood by many people, but particularly by those who control athletics and exert political and economic power in America. For it is the latter who have the power to correct the injustices that beset the American sports scene before they spawn conflict. And by some means, somewhere along the line, these injustices shall be corrected.

RACIAL SEGREGATION IN AMERICAN SPORT*

JOHN W. LOY, JR. AND JOSEPH F. McELVOGUE

INTRODUCTION

Numerous journalists have commented on the social functions which sport fulfills for minority groups in American society. Boyle, for example, forcefully writes:

> Sport has often served minority groups as the first rung on the social ladder. As such, it has helped further their assimilation into American life. It would not be too far-fetched to say that it has done more in this regard than any other agency, including church and school (1963, p. 100).

Recently, journalists have placed special emphasis on the many contributions sport has made for the Negro. As Olsen observes:

> Every morning the world of sport wakes up and congratulates itself on its contributions to race relations. The litany has been so often repeated that it is believed almost universally. It goes: "Look what sports has done for the Negro" (1968, p. 7).

In view of the many journalistic accounts of the contributions of sport to the social success of minority groups, it is somewhat surprising that sociologists and physical educators have largely ignored the issue of minority group integration in American sport. The purpose of this paper is to direct the attention of sport sociologists to the issue by presenting a theoretical and empirical examination of racial segregation in America's major professional baseball and football teams.

*Appreciation is accorded to Mr. Schroeder, director, and Mr. Dyer, assistant director of Helms Hall for assistance in the collection of data for this paper.
From the *International Review of Sport Sociology* 5 (1970) 5-23. Copyright © 1970 ARS Polona, Krakowskie Przedmiescie 7, Warsaw, Poland. Reprinted with permission.

THEORETICAL OVERVIEW

Theoretically considered, our examination largely draws upon Grusky's (1963) theory of formal structure of organizations and Blalock's (1962) set of theoretical propositions regarding occupational discrimination.

Grusky's Theory of Formal Structure

According to Grusky, "the formal structure of an organization consists of a set of norms which define the system's official objectives, its major offices or positions, and the primary responsibilities of the position occupants" (p. 345). The formal structure ". . . patterns the behavior of its constituent positions along three interdependent dimensions: (1) spatial location, (2) nature of task, and (3) frequency of interaction" (p. 345). The theoretical import of Grusky's model is contained in his statement that:

> All else being equal, the more central one's spatial location: (1) the greater likelihood dependent or coordinative tasks will be performed and (2) the greater the rate of interaction with the occupants of other positions. Also, the performance of dependent tasks is positively related to frequency of interaction (p. 346).

Combining these three criteria, Grusky distinguishes positions of high interaction potential and position of low interaction potential within the social structure of organizations. He defines the occupants of these two types of positions as high and low interactors, respectively.

For our purposes, we prefer to use the concept of "centrality" in dealing with Grusky's three interdependent dimensions of organizational positions. With an extension to permit us to embrace all three of Grusky's criteria, we accepted Hopkins' (1964) definition of this concept:

> Centrality designates how close a member is to the "center" of the group's interaction network and thus refers simultaneously to the frequency with which a member participates in interaction with other members and the number or range of other members with whom he interacts (p. 28) [and the degree to which he must coordinate his tasks and activities with other members].

Blalock's Theoretical Propositions

Several years ago, Blalock (1962) made a very astute analysis of why "professional baseball has provided Negroes with one of the relatively few avenues for escape from blue-collar occupations." From his analysis, Blalock developed thirteen theoretical propositions concerning occupational discrimination which can be empirically tested in other occupational settings. His analysis is an excellent example of how the critical examination of a sport situation can enhance the development of sociological theory in an area of central concern. Blalock was, however, perhaps naive in assuming that professional baseball is ". . . an occupation which is remarkably free of racial discrimination" (p. 242).

We sought to test Blalock's assumption that professional baseball is relatively free of racial discrimination by drawing upon three of his propositions to predict where racial segregation is most likely to occur on the baseball diamond. The three particular propositions which we considered were:

1. The lower the degree of purely social interaction on the job . . . ,the lower the degree of discrimination" (p. 246).
2. "To the extent that performance level is relatively independent of skill in interpersonal relations, the lower the degree of discrimination" (p. 246).
3. "To the extent that an individual's success depends primarily on his own performance, rather than on limiting or restricting the performance of specific other individuals, the lower the degree of discrimination by group members" (p. 245).

On the one hand, the consideration of proposition 1 in conjunction with proposition 2 suggested that discrimination is directly related to level and type of interaction. On the other hand, the combined consideration of propositions 2 and 3 suggested that there will be less discrimination where performance of independent tasks are largely involved; because such tasks do not have to be coordinated with the activities of other persons, and therefore do not hinder the performance of others, nor require a great deal of skill in interpersonal relations.

Since the dimensions of interaction and task dependency treated by Blalock are included in our concept of centrality, we subsumed his three propositions under a more general one, stating that: "discrimination is positively related to centrality."

STATEMENT OF THEORETICAL HYPOTHESIS

Broadly conceived, discrimination ". . . denotes the unfavourable treatment of categories of persons on arbitrary grounds" (Moore, 1964, p. 203). Discrimination takes many forms, but a major mode is that of segregation. Segregation denotes the exclusion of certain categories of persons from specific social organizations or particular positions within organizations on arbitrary grounds, i.e., grounds which have no objective relation to individual skill and talent.

Since we were chiefly concerned with the matter of racial segregation in professional sports, we took as our specific theoretical hypothesis the proposition that: *racial segregation in professional team sports is positively related to centrality.* In order to test this hypothesis, we empirically examined the extent of racial segregation within major league baseball and major league football.

THE CASE OF PROFESSIONAL BASEBALL

Baseball teams have a well defined social structure consisting of the repetitive and regulated interaction among a set of nine positions combined into three major substructures or interaction units: (1) the battery, consisting of pitcher and catcher; (2) the infield, consisting of first base, second base, shortstop and third base; and (3) the outfield, consisting of leftfield, centerfield and rightfield positions.

Empirical Hypothesis

As is evident from Figure 1, one can readily see that the outfield contains the most peripheral and socially isolated positions in the organizational structure of a baseball team. Therefore, on the basis of our theoretical hypothesis, we predicted that Negro players in comparison to white players on major league teams are more likely to occupy outfield positions and less likely to occupy infield positions.

Methods

Data. On the basis of the *1968 Baseball Register* all professional players in the American and National Leagues who played at least fifty games during the 1967 season were categorized according to race and playing position.[1]

---

1. The criterion of fifty games was established in order to eliminate the partial participant, such as the pinch hitter or runner, the player brought up from the minor leagues on a part-time basis, the occasional utility man, and the unestablished rookie trying to make the team at any position.

Players were ethnically classified as Caucasians, Negroes or Latin Americans. The latter group was excluded from most analyses, however, as it was impossible in terms of the sources available to determine which Latin American athletes were Negroes.

Players at all positions were considered except for pitchers. They were excluded for purposes of analysis because: (1) data comparable to that collected for other players was not available, (2) the high rate of interchangeability among pitchers precluded accurate recording of data, and (3) pitchers are in a sense only part-time players, in that they typically play in only one game out of four, or if relief pitchers, play only a few innings in any given game. In order that the reader may make certain comparisons later in the paper, we note at this point that "only 13 of 207 pitchers in 1968 major league rosters were Negroes" (Olsen, 1968, p. 170).

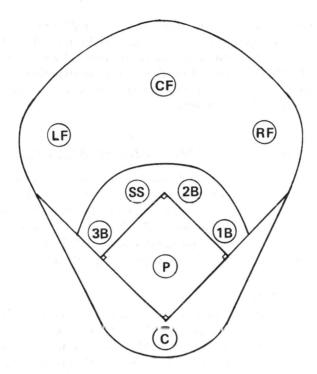

Treatment. The X^2 test for two independent samples was used to test the null hypothesis that there is no difference between white and black ballplayers in terms of the proportion who occupy infield and outfield positions. The .01 level of significance, using a one-tailed test, was selected as being sufficient to warrant the rejection of the null hypothesis.

Findings

Table 1 presents the number of white and black athletes occupying specific positions in the major leagues in 1967. It is clearly evident from the table that Negro players are predominantly found in the outfield. The highly significant X^2, resulting from the test of our null hypothesis, gives strong support to our empirical hypothesis and provides some confirmation of our theoretical hypothesis that racial segregation in professional sports is related to centrality. As a further test of our hypothesis we examined the extent of racial segregation in professional football.

THE CASE OF PROFESSIONAL FOOTBALL

Like baseball teams, football teams have well defined organizational structures. However, whereas the positions in baseball organization are

TABLE 1

**A Comparison of Race and Position Occupancy
in Major League Baseball in 1967**

Playing Position	American League		National League		Both Leagues	
	White	Black	White	Black	White	Black
Catcher	13	0	14	1	27	1
Shortstop	7	0	10	1	17	1
1st Base	11	2	7	5	18	7
2nd Base	10	3	6	1	16	4
3rd Base	9	2	7	4	16	6
Outfield	26	14	12	22	38	36
N =	76	21	56	34	132	55

Race

Position	White	Black	Total
Infield	94	19	113
Outfield	38	36	74
	132	55	187

$$X^2 = 20.32; \, p < .0005 \, (df = 1)$$

determined by defensive alignment, there exists both a distinctive offensive and a distinctive defensive team within modern professional football organization. Figure 2 shows the constituent positions of the offensive and defensive teams of any given professional football organization.

Empirical Hypothesis

It is clear from Figure 2 that the most central positions on the offensive team consist of center, right guard, left guard and quarterback; while the most central position on the defensive team are the three linebacker positions. Therefore, on the basis of our theoretical hypothesis, we predicted that Negro football players in comparison to white players are more likely to occupy non-central positions than central positions on both offensive and defensive teams.

Methods

Data. Using the *Official 1968 Autographed Yearbooks* of the American and National Football Leagues in conjunction with Zanger's *Pro Football 1968* we classified all starting offensive and defensive players according

to race (black or white) and playing position (central or non-central).[2]
Treatment. The X^2 test for two independent samples was used to test
the null hypothesis that there is no difference between white and black
occupancy of centrally located positions on either offensive or defensive
teams. The .01 level of significance, using a one-tailed test, was selected
as being sufficient to warrant the rejection of the null hypothesis.

2. The major difficulties we experienced in data collection were associated with the
problems of determining the race of the players and in determining who were the
first string or starting players. In the case of major league football, we used the
"official yearbooks" to ascertain the race of given players as these sources contained
photographs of the members of every team in a given league. Zanger's text was
used as a means of determining the first string or starting lineup for each team.
However, Zanger's lineups were preseason forecasts based upon the players' performance the previous season. A more accurate means of recording would have been
to determine the players having the most playing time at each position for every
team during the 1968 season.
An indication, however, that the data which we present in Tables 2 and 3 is reason-
ably accurate are the following facts cited from a study made independently of our
own:
"On on typical weekend in the 1967 NFL season, no Negro center started a game.
Of the 32 offensive guards in the starting lineups of NFL teams, 29 were white"
(Olsen, 1963, p. 171).
". . . (on that same typical weekend in the 1967 season, 48 linebackers lumbered
out on the field to start NFL games, and 45 of them, or 94 per cent, were white)"
(Olsen, 1968, p. 172).

Findings

Tables 2 and 3 present the number of white and black athletes occupying central and non-central offensive and defensive positions, respectively, in the major professional football leagues in 1968. It is evident from the tables that very few Negro players occupy central positions,

TABLE 2

A Comparison of Race and Position Occupancy within Offensive Teams in Major League Football in 1968

Playing Position	American League		National League		Both Leagues	
	White	Black	White	Black	White	Black
Center	10	0	16	0	26	0
Quarterback	9	1	16	0	25	1
Right Guard	9	1	15	1	24	2
Left Guard	10	0	15	1	25	1
Right Tackle	10	0	11	5	21	5
Left Tackle	8	2	11	5	19	7
Tight End	7	3	13	3	20	6
Split End	8	2	10	6	18	8
Fullback	4	6	11	5	15	11
Halfback	3	7	7	9	10	16
Flankerback	7	3	10	6	17	9
N =	85	25	135	41	220	66

Race

Position	White	Black	Total
Central	100	4	104
Noncentral	120	62	182
	220	66	286

$$X^2 = 32.37; p < .0005 \ (df = 1)$$

either defensively or offensively. The significant X^2 tests of our null hypothesis give strong support to our empirical hypothesis and provide further confirmation of our theoretical hypothesis.

DISCUSSION

The preceding findings leave little doubt that only a very small proportion of black athletes occupy central positions in America's professional baseball and football organizations. However, notwithstanding

TABLE 3
A Comparison of Race and Position Occupancy within Defensive Teams in Major League Football in 1968

Playing Position	American League		National League		Both Leagues	
	White	Black	White	Black	White	Black
Middle Linebacker	8	2	16	0	24	2
Right Linebacker	10	0	15	1	25	1
Left Linebacker	8	2	15	1	23	3
Right End	6	4	12	4	18	8
Right Tackle	7	3	13	3	20	6
Left Tackle	7	3	10	6	17	9
Left End	8	2	11	5	19	7
Right Safety	7	3	10	6	17	9
Left Safety	7	3	10	6	17	9
Right Cornerback	2	8	6	10	8	18
Left Cornerback	1	9	3	13	4	22
N =	71	39	121	55	192	94

Race

Position	White	Black	Total
Central	72	6	78
Noncentral	120	88	208
	192	94	286

$$X^2 = 29.26; p < .0005 \text{ (df = 1)}$$

our theoretical buttress, a number of telling questions can be raised regarding the revealed relationships between race and position occupancy. Three such questions are: (1) Does the discovered relationship between race and position occupancy indicate the actual presence of racial segregation? (2) If racial segregation is actually present, what are the "social mechanisms" linking it to centrality? (3) If racial segregation does exist in professional sports, what are its social consequences? Let us briefly consider each of these questions in turn.

DOES RACIAL SEGREGATION ACTUALLY
EXIST IN SPORT?

One can argue that showing that Negro athletes infrequently occupy central positions does not confirm that they are racially segregated. They may be excluded from central positions for objective rather than arbitrary reasons. On the one hand, Negroes may not have as great a talent or skill for certain tasks as white players, and are thus excluded from selected positions for that reason. On the other hand, Negroes may possess greater athletic ability than whites for certain activities, and are accordingly found proportionately more often in some positions than others. A third alternative, of course, is that Negro athletes exclude themselves from selected positions by personal preference.

Although we are not presently prepared to fully assess the validity of each of these three perspectives, we must frankly state we find them tenuous. For example, we have found no evidence which would lead us to believe that Negro athletes have inferior ability in comparison to white athletes for any role assignment in professional baseball or football. We observe that time and again in the world of sport athletic stereotypes of Negroes have been refuted. It will be recalled that, not too long ago, there existed the myth among track authorities that Negroes were racially suited for the sprints and perhaps the shorter distance races, but did not possess the capabilities for the endurance events. The success of black athletes in long distance running events, including the Olympic marathon, in recent years has dispelled the notion that Negro trackmen are speed merchants without stamina.

Similarly, we have discovered little support for the view that Negro athletes possess certain abilities in greater abundance than white athletes. We have, however, encountered some findings which indicate that a black athlete must be superior to his white counterpart before he is permitted to occupy a given position. For example, a recent study shows that the cumulative major league batting averages in 1968 were higher for Negroes at every position as follows: catcher-whites .238, blacks .279; first and third bases-whites .265, blacks .277; second and shortstop-whites .246, blacks .258; outfield-whites .253, blacks .266 (Los Angeles Time, May 15, 1969, part 3, p. 3).[3]

Finally, we find it difficult to believe that Negro athletes are largely selecting the positions which they occupy in baseball and football on the

3. For a more complete account of how Negro athletes must be superior to white athletes in professional baseball in order to maintain their positions, see Rosenblatt, 1967. Finally, we note that the three outfield positions were considered as a single category since data were not available for each of the three outfield positions taken separately.

basis of personal preference. What seems to be operating is a self-fulfilling belief. A black athlete assumes that he doesn't have much chance at being accepted at certain positions and thus tries out for other positions where his estimate of success is much higher. As Olsen succinctly states: "He *anticipates* the white man's categorization of him, and acts accordingly" (1968, p. 170). An interesting study, we suggest, would be to compare the playing positions of white and black athletes in professional football with those they filled in college football. Our prediction is that a greater proportion of black than white athletes will be discovered to have acquired new role assignments.

Some would perhaps contend that we are overstating our case regarding racial segregation in professional sports; because:

> The degree to which Negroes have moved into pro sports is astonishing. More than half the players in the National Basketball Association are Negroes—as were eight of the ten starters in the last NBA All-Star Game. A quarter of the players in the National Football League are Negroes, and the 1967 NFL team was 40 per cent black. Nearly 25 per cent of all players in major league baseball are American Negroes, and here too a disproportionate number of the stars are not white. For example, of the top ten hitters in the National League for the 1967 season, only one was a Caucasian (Olsen, 1968, p. 170).

Nevertheless, we point out that sport seems to mirror American life at large, in that, integration has been very slow, and where it has been rather fully achieved there remain many forms of discrimination other than that of segregation.

Professional baseball is a good example of how slowly the process of integration takes place. Many herald 1947 as the year "the color line was broken" with the entrance of Jackie Robinson into major league baseball. But, as illustrated in Table 4, ten years later there were only a dozen Negro players in the National League and as late as 1960 there were only a half dozen black athletes in the American League. Table 4 does reveal, however, that there has been a substantial increase in the number of Latin American players in recent years and indicates that there exists an intermediate "brown zone" between the "white and black belts" of major league baseball.[4]

---

4. It would be interesting to find out whether or not "darker" Latin American athletes are more often found in the outfield than the "lighter" Latin players. There are some small indications that "quota systems" are operating for American Negro players and Latin American players, in that, if members of one group are prominent occupants of a given field position within a league, then the members of the other group tend to be predominant at another playing position. For a discussion of the social relations between American Negro and Latin American players, see Boyle, 1963, pp. 108-113.

WHAT ARE THE SOCIAL MECHANISMS
OF SEGREGATION?

Assuming that there is racial segregation in professional baseball and football, one is led to inquire as to what are the underlying causes of this form of discrimination. We have argued that segregation is a function of centrality and its associated interdependent dimensions of spatial location, rate of interaction and task dependency. Sociologically viewed, our theoretical rationale is probably a fairly satisfactory one; but those of a more social psychological orientation would likely want to know what sort of personal qualities and behavioral dispositions are associated with centrality which influence segregation.

There are no doubt many kinds of normative beliefs and attitudes which act as antecedent and/or intervening variables in the relationship between segregation and centrality. We specifically speculate that there is a relationship between interaction and attitudes regarding persona intimacy; and a relationship between tasks dependency and beliefs concerning the qualities of judgment and decision-making ability.

A major generalization of discrimination research states that: "there is a range within discriminatory practice such that there is most discrimination and most prejudice as the practice comes closer to intimate personal contact" (Berelson and Steiner, 1964, p. 511). Thus, we reason that Negroes may be excluded from central positions because these positions involve high rates of interaction which lead to greater personal contact among players than do peripheral positions in an organization.

We conject, in passing, that there may even be normative beliefs regarding the interaction of Negro athletes among themselves. In the case of professional football, for instance, black athletes are most often found at the two cornerback positions. Similarly, in the case of professional baseball, we point out that in the infield Negroes are most often found at first and third bases. While the relationship may be a spurious one, it is interesting that Negroes are placed in the extreme corners of the field in both baseball and football. A related observation is that seldom does one find two Negroes playing side-by-side in either major league baseball or football.

In treating interaction, one should, of course, distinguish between task interaction and social interaction since there is probably only a moderate correlation between the two. Although we expect that there may be a substantial degree of prejudice regarding the intermixing of white and black players off the field, we are not sure that there is

TABLE 4
Distribution of White, Black and Latin American Players
by Position in Major League Baseball 1956-1967
National League

Year	Catcher	Short-stop	2nd Base	3rd Base	1st Base	Outfield	Total No.
1967	14	10	6	7	7	12	56
	1	1	1	4	5	22	34
	0	1	4	1	3	7	16
1966	13	9	8	8	5	15	58
	2	2	2	3	4	21	34
	0	2	4	2	3	8	19
1965	15	10	10	8	7	13	63
	1	1	1	3	5	19	30
	1	3	3	0	5	8	19
1964	13	8	11	8	8	18	66
	2	2	1	3	5	20	33
	0	3	2	2	2	8	16
1963	14	8	8	14	10	22	76
	1	2	2	2	4	18	29
	0	3	2	0	1	3	9
1962	Data not available						
1961	11	5	8	8	6	18	56
	1	2	2	2	2	11	20
	0	3	2	0	2	5	12
1960	12	6	7	9	9	21	64
	1	2	2	1	2	11	19
	0	1	2	0	2	4	9
1959	Data not available						
1958	12	7	8	9	10	18	64
	2	1	1	0	2	8	14
	2	1	1	0	1	2	5
1957	11	6	8	8	11	25	69
	1	2	1	2	1	5	12
	1	1	0	1	0	2	5
1956	11	9	8	9	9	20	66
	1	1	3	1	1	5	12
	0	0	2	0	0	2	2

TABLE 4 (cont.)

Distribution of White, Black and Latin American Players
by Position in Major League Baseball 1956-1967

American League

Ethnic Group	Catcher	Short-stop	2nd Base	3rd Base	1st Base	Outfield	Total No.
White	13	7	10	9	11	26	76
Black	0	0	3	2	2	14	21
Latin	2	4	1	1	1	6	15
White Black Latin				Data not available			
White	12	12	10	10	14	29	87
Black	2	0	1	1	1	12	17
Latin	1	3	2	2	1	6	13
White	12	9	13	10	12	29	85
Black	2	0	1	1	2	10	16
Latin	1	2	0	1	1	7	12
White	14	10	11	6	13	31	87
Black	2	0	2	1	1	7	13
Latin	2	2	0	1	1	5	1
White	13	11	11	9	11	34	85
Black	2	0	1	2	0	3	8
Latin	2	3	0	1	1	2	9
White	13	9	13	12	12	29	89
Black	2	1	1	1	0	9	14
Latin	1	3	0	0	1	3	8
White	10	6	9	11	11	27	74
Black	2	0	1	0	0	3	6
Latin	0	3	0	0	2	2	7
White	13	12	12	9	10	28	84
Black	0	0	0	0	2	3	5
Latin	0	2	0	1	2	2	7
White Black Latin				Data not available			
White Black Latin				Data not available			
White Black Latin				Data not available			

marked prejudice among players concerning racial interpersonal contact on the field.[5]

We speculate that segregation in professional sports is more a function of management than playing personnel. For example, there appears to be a myth among coaches that Negro players lack judgment and decision-making ability. This myth results in black athletes being excluded from positions requiring dependent or coordinative tasks as such activities generally require greater judgment than independent tasks. In short, the central positions in major league baseball and football are typically the most responsible or so-called "brains positions." The following quotations from Olsen with respect to central and peripheral defensive positions within football organization well illustrate the matter:

> "Most defensive football players have a single job to do, with little variation, but the linebacker has to exercise judgment" says a thoughtful NFL player. "He may wind up tackling the quarterback fifteen yards behind the line of scrimmage, and he may wind up knocking down a pass twenty-yards up the field. He has to be able to read plays-well, everybody knows all the things the linebacker has to do. It's one of the most responsible defensive positions. Therefore, he can't be a Negro" (p. 172).
>
> "Cornerback is not a brains position" says Bill Koman, retired St. Louis Cardinal linebacker. "You pick up the split end or the flanker and you stay with him all the way. That's it (p. 173).
>
> "Yassuh, white man, boss," says one NFL cornerback derisively when asked about the situation, "We ain't got the brains to play center, 'cause we can't count, but we can follow that flanker's ass all the way down the field, *yuck, yuck*" (p. 173).

In our discussion herein we have emphasized the interaction and task dependency dimensions of centrality; whereas in our empirical examination of racial segregation we stressed the dimension of spatial location. Additional limitations of our empirical analysis include the fact that our measure of spatial location was dichotomous rather than continuous in nature; and the fact that we only looked at major league baseball and football for specific one-year periods. In an effort to overcome these limitations, we extend our analysis of the racial composition of professional baseball to cover a twelve year period; and we developed

---

5. Charnofsky (1967), for example, presents evidence which suggests that while there exists a degree of racial prejudice among a number of players, the majority of athletes in professional baseball hold favorable attitudes toward minority group members on their teams. We note, however, that off the field the problem of discrimination may be a horse of a different color. For example, the 1969 season is the first where several teams have set forth explicit policies assuring the racial integration of teammates on the road via mixed room assignments.

an operational index of centrality which is continuous in nature and which reflects the interaction and task dependency dimensions of centrality.

Table 5 shows the approximate number of individual white and black athletes at each field position in the major leagues over a twelve year period.[6] The table also shows the rank order of playing positions in terms of the proportion of Negro players at each position. This rank order is nearly identical to that given in Table 1.

TABLE 5

Distribution of Individual White and Black Players
by Position in Major League Baseball 1956-1967.

Playing Position	White Players	Black Players	Total No. of Players	% of Black Players	Rank Order % White Players
Catcher	85	5	90	.0555	1
Shortstop	39	4	43	.0930	2
2nd Base	61	7	68	.1029	3
3rd Base	41	9	50	.1800	4
1st Base	54	13	67	.1940	5
Outfield	129	61	190	.3210	6
N =	409	99	508	.1948	

Having reaffirmed the relationship between segregation and spatial location, we turned our attention to the interaction and task dependency dimensions of centrality. We decided that the total number of "assists" made by occupants of given field positions during a season would serve as an adequate operational indicator of centrality.[7] On the one hand, assists are an indicator of the rate of interaction and the number and range of other group members with whom a position occupant interacts.

6. As is evident from Table 4, we were unable to obtain relevant data for a number of seasons for the two major leagues between 1956 and 1967. However, there does not appear to be much change in playing personnel from one year to the next. Moreover, our figures provide a conservative estimate of the racial composition of professional baseball, in that the missing data includes more white players. It was not difficult to keep track of a small number of players switching leagues over the period sampled, but a small number of players switching playing positions over the period covered did pose a bit of a problem. We arbitrarily assigned them the position where they had played the most games in their major league career.

7. An assist is the official credit awarded in the scoring of a game to a player who throws a ball in such a way that it results in a putout. Data regarding assists were obtained from the *American League Red Book* and the *National League Green Books*. These are annual publications of the two major leagues which report vital statistics about all players, teams and games each season.

On the other hand, assists are an index of the degree to which dependent tasks are associated with given positions.

We discovered that the rank order of field positions with respect to number of annual assists remained the same for both leagues for every year covered.[8] More strikingly, however, we found a perfect rank order correlation between our measures of segregation and centrality (see

TABLE 6

Ranks for Position Occupancy and Annual Assists in Professional Baseball

Field Position	Rank Order		d_i	d_i^2
	% of Whites*	Annual Assists**		
Catcher	1	1	0	0
Shortstop	2	2	0	0
2nd Base	3	3	0	0
3rd Base	4	4	0	0
1st Base	5	5	0	0
Outfield	0	0	0	0

$$r_s = 1 - \frac{6 \sum\limits_{i=1}^{n} d_i^2}{N^3 - N} = 1 - \frac{6(0)}{6(3)-6} \; ; \text{rho} = 1.00$$

*See Table 5.   **See Footnote 8.   (Siegel, 1956, pp. 202-213)

8. In the scoring of a game, the strikeouts made by the pitcher which are caught by the catcher are recorded as putouts for the catcher. For purposes of analysis we considered such putouts as assists. We reasoned that the catcher calls the pitch and assists in making the strikeouts by receiving the thrown ball from the pitcher. We note that a strikeout is recorded regardless of whether the ball is caught or not. An example of the consistency of the number of annual assists by position for both leagues is the following data for the 1963, 1964 and 1965 seasons:

Year	American League	Position	National League
1963	10,508	C	9,946
	4,724	SS	4,749
	4,427	2nd	4,253
	3,176	3rd	3,029
	1,119	1st	1,002
	325	Out	323
1964	10,713	C	10,112
	4,775	SS	4,939
	4,425	2nd	4,404
	3,225	3rd	3,096
	1,059	1st	1,018
	308	Out	322
1965	10,461	C	10,454
	4,696	SS	4,886
	4,274	2nd	4,831
	3,341	3rd	3,093
	1,050	1st	1,045
	274	Out	292

Table 6). Thus, we concluded that we had obtained substantial support for our theoretical hypothesis that racial segregation in professional team sports is positively related to centrality.

WHAT ARE THE SOCIAL CONSEQUENCES OF SEGREGATION?

It is exceedingly difficult to assess the social consequences of racial segregation in professional baseball and football because data is limited; and because the consequences are both manifest and latent, acute and chronic. It would appear, however, that one of the major disadvantageous consequences of segregation is the retardation of upward career mobility in professional sports. Grusky (1963) has shown that approximately three-fourths of all major league baseball managers are recruited from infield positions.[9] Therefore, to the degree that Negro athletes are denied access to central positions, they are also limited in obtaining positions of leadership in professional baseball.[10]

Grusky assumes that the position which an individual occupies influences his development of varying kinds of role skills; and further assumes that the occupancy of central positions enhances the obtainment of key role skills related to upward career mobility. These rather broad assumptions are likely related to Hopkins' (1964) set of fifteen theoretical propositions regarding small groups. For example, Hopkins states that: "For any member of a small group, the greater his centrality:

1. the greater his observability;
2. the greater his conformity;
3. the greater his influence; and,
4. the higher his rank" (1964, p. 51).

Another related proposition is that centrality is positively related to liking (Grusky, 1963, p. 347; Homans, 1950, p. 133).[11]

This latter proposition suggests that there may be a "vicious cycle" operating in professional sports. Negroes, because they are not liked by the white establishment, are placed in peripheral positions; and, as a result of this placement, do not have the opportunity of high rates of

9. In Grusky's study about twenty-five per cent of the managers were found to be ex-catchers. Recent investigations by Loy and Sage concerning collegiate baseball show that college coaches and college team captains are most often recruited from infield positions; especially that of catcher. Moreover, their findings indicate that, although there are relatively few Negroes playing college baseball, there are proportionately more Negroes in outfield than infield positions.

10. It is only recently that a token number of former Negro athletes have been hired as coaches in professional sports; and to date there are no Negro head coaches in major league football or Negro managers in major league baseball.

11. See Hopkins, 1964, pp. 112-117 for a critique of this proposition.

interaction with teammates, and do not receive the potential positive sentiment which might accrue from such interaction. In view of the nature of our problem, our discussion is likely too brief and superficial. However, we hope that we have been successful in directing the attention of sport sociologists to the matter of integration in American sport, and in providing stimulation for further theoretical and empirical analyses of the subject.[12]

REFERENCES CITED

American Football League Official Autographed Yearbook 1968. Dallas: Sports Underwriters, Inc., 1968.

American League Red Book. Boston: American League Publicity Department.

Baseball Register. St. Louis: Sporting News.

Berelson B. and Steiner G. A., *Human Behavior—an Inventory of Scientific Findings.* New York: Harcourt, Brace World, Inc., 1964.

Blalock H. M. Jr., "Occupational Discrimination: Some Theoretical Propositions," *Social Problems* 9 (1962): 240-247.

Boyle H. H., *Sport—Mirror of American Life.* Boston: Little, Brown Co., 1963.

Charnofsky H., "The Major League Professional Baseball Player: Self-Conception Versus The Popular Image," *International Review of Sport Sociology* 3 (1968): 39-55. Polish Scientific Publishers, Warsaw.

Grusky O., "The Effects of Formal Structure on Managerial Recruitment: A Study of Baseball Organization," *Sociometry* 26 (1963): 345-353.

Homans G. C., *The Human Group.* New York: Harcourt, Brace World, Inc., 1950.

Hopkins T. K., *The Exercise of Influence in Small Groups.* Totowa, N. J.: Bedminster Press, 1964.

Loy J. W. and Sage J. N., "The Effects of Formal Structure on Organizational Leadership: An Investigation of Interscholastic Baseball Teams." Paper presented at the second International Congress of Sport Psychology, November 1, 1968 in Washington, D. C.

Moore H. E., "Discrimination," pp. 203-204 in Julius Gould and William L. Kolb (eds.), *A Dictionary of the Social Sciences.* New York: The Free Press of Glencoe, 1964.

Olsen J., *The Black Athlete—a shameful story.* New York: Time, Inc., 1968.

National Football League Official Autographed Yearbook 1968. Dallas: Sports Underwriters, Inc., 1968.

National League Green Book. Cincinnati: National League Public Relations Department.

12. This article is based solely on an unrevised paper presented at the International Seminar on the Sociology of Sport, organized by the Research Institute of the Swiss Federal School of Gymnastics and Sports and the University of Bern on behalf of the International Committee for the Sociology of Sport, September 7-13, 1969 at Macolin, Switzerland. Since the presentation of this paper there has appeared two reports which treat the topic in much greater depth and which offer selected findings somewhat different from those given above; see: Anthony H. Pascal and Leonard A. Rapping, "Racial Discrimination in Organized Baseball," (Report for the RAND Corporation, Santa Monica, California, May 1969); and, Garry Smith and Carl F. Grindstaff, "Race and Sport in Canada," (University of Western Ontario, October 1970).

Rosenblatt A., "Negroes in Baseball: The Failure of Success," *Trans-Action* 4
    (September, 1967): 51-53, with a reply by Whitehead 4 (October,
    1967): 63-64.
Siegel S., *Nonparametrics Statistics*. New York: McGraw-Hill Book Co., Inc.,
    1956.
"Study Indicates Cracking Majors Harder for Blacks." Los Angeles: Times,
    May 15, 1969, Part III, p. 3.
Zanger J., *Pro Football 1968*. New York: Pocket Books, 1968.

ETHNIC SOCCER CLUBS IN MILWAUKEE: A STUDY IN ASSIMILATION*

John C. Pooley

INTRODUCTION

Sport has shown itself to be a factor in forming a point of contact between ethnic groups who find themselves living in close proximity. Expatriate groups in African countries, missionaries and traders in isolated communities and military forces representing different nations[1] are good examples of this. Immigrants who become lodged in already established "advanced" societies are equally affected. For example, West Indians who emigrate to Britain, Southern Europeans who emigrate to Australia and diverse ethnic groups immigrating to the United States would fall into this category. Whenever members of an ethnic group move to another society, some degree of assimilation occurs and their survival depends upon it.

The primary purpose of this study was to determine the role of sport in assimilation. More specifically, the study endeavored to deter-

*Part of this paper was read at the AAHPER Annual Convention, Boston, April 11, 1969. The author wishes to acknowledge the valuable assistance of Gerald S. Kenyon, University of Waterloo, who acted as advisor for the study which formed part of a Masters Degree at the University of Wisconsin, Madison, completed in 1968. Printed with permission of the author.

1. The point of contact made possible through sport, can lead to discord as Reid found. In his book which tells the story of an Allied prisoner of war camp in Germany, he relates how arguments developed as a result of a "wall game" competition *between* different nationalities, where as in games played by prisoners from within a single group (in this case Britain), arguments never occurred. P. R. Reid, *Escape from Colditz* (New York: Berkeley Publishing Corporation, 1952), p. 64.

mine the significance of the structure and function of ethnic soccer clubs in the assimilation of their members.

The terms used in this study are defined below:

Assimilation
> Assimilation is a process of interpenetration and fusion in which persons and groups acquire the memories, sentiments, and attitudes of other persons or groups, and, by sharing their experiences and history, are incorporated with them in a common cultural life.[2]

From the definition, it is clear that "acculturation" is included. As Gordon[3] has commented, the phrases "sharing their experiences" and "incorporating with them in a common cultural life" suggest the added criterion of social structure relationships.

Ethnic group. An ethnic group[4] is a group with a shared feeling of peoplehood.[5] According to Tumin,

> The term is most frequently applied to any group which differs in one or several aspects of its patterned, socially-transmitted way of life from other groups, or in the totality of that way of life or culture. Frequently, the group in question formerly enjoyed or still enjoys a separate political-national identity as well. Thus, various national-ethnic stocks in the United States would be considered as ethnic groups, e.g., Greeks, Poles, Hatians, Swedes, etc.[6]

Core Society. This term refers to "the dominant subsociety which provides the standard to which other groups adjust or measure their relative degree of adjustment."[7] According to Fishman,[8] the culture of this society is that "into which immigrants are assimilated, and it forms the one accepted set of standards, expectations, and aspirations, whether they pertain to clothing, household furnishings, personal beauty, entertainment or child rearing."

2. Robert E. Park and Ernest W. Burgess, *Introduction to the Science of Sociology* (Chicago: University of Chicago Press, 1921), p. 735.
3. Milton M. Gordon, *Assimilation in American Life* (New York: Oxford University Press, 1964), p. 62.
4. From the Greek word "ethnos" meaning "people" or "nation."
5. Gordon, *op. cit.*, p. 24.
6. Melvin M. Tumin, "Ethnic Group" in Julius Gould and William L. Kolb, *A Dictionary of the Social Sciences* (Free Press of Glencoe, 1965), p. 243.
7. Gordon, *op. cit.*, p. 72. Gordon prefers the term "core group," which used by A. B. Hollingshead to describe the old Yankee families of colonial, largely Anglo-Saxon ancestry who have traditionally dominated the power and status system of the community. See August B. Hollingshead, "Trends in Social Stratification: A Case Study," *American Sociological Review* 17 (December, 1952): p. 686.
8. Joshua A. Fishman, "Childhood Indoctrination for Minority-Group Membership," in "Ethnic Groups in American Life," *Daedalus: The Journal of the American Academy of Arts and Sciences* (Spring, 1961): 329.

SCOPE AND SIGNIFICANCE

In this study and attempt was made to assess the factors which accelerate or retard the rate of assimilation. Saxon[9] and Warner Srole[10] have recognized that the recreational habits of a group have considerable import in the degree to which such a group may identify themselves with, or be isolated from, the core society. This point has greater relevance in an age when increased leisure time is available to the majority of the population.[11]

The existence of a sport club provides varying degrees of social intercourse between active and non-active members of the same club and between different clubs. The amount and type of social interaction practiced depends upon the size of the club, makeup of its members, arrangement of social events, and type of club accommodation.

More specifically, this study was concerned with determining the factors which influence assimilation. Questions asked were as follows:

1. To what degree does participation in ethnic soccer influence assimilation?

   a. Positively
   b. Negatively

9. George Saxon, "Immigrant Culture in a Sratified Society," *Modern Review* 11 (February, 1948): 122.
10. W. Lloyd Warner and Leo Srole, *The Social Systems of American Ethnic Groups* (New Haven: Yale University Press, 1945), pp. 254-282.
11. This point is taken up by Martin when he says, "At present, we are participating in an extremely drastic and rapid cultural change, affecting our entire Western society. The rapid advance of technological science, spear-headed by automation, is causing a steady shrinkage of the workaday world. Plans now underfoot for a six-week vaction and a three-day weekend indicate that before long our work force will have 200 free days in the year." He goes on to qualify this as follows: "These changes do not apply, to the same extent, to professional executive and management groups. However, the fact remains that, coincidental with a rising standard of living, higher employment, and a steadily increasing national product, the American people are finding themselves with more and more time off the job. In other words, we have already acquired, in large measure, the latest and the greatest freedom of all —free time, unstructured time, discretionary time, time for leisure." (Alexander Reid Martin, "Man's Leisure and His Health," *Quest* 5 (December, 1965): 26.)
Three publications by Brightbill, Miller and Robinson, and Dumazedier, which discuss societal problems and current theories related to leisure, either directly or indirectly, point to the increase in leisure time during the current era. "It seems curious that at a time when many people have more leisure than ever before . . ." (Charles K. Brightbill, *Man and Leisure* (Englewood Cliffs, N. J.: Prentice-Hall, 1961), p. v. "The twentieth century finds man turning more and more to his increasing free time, to fulfill himself." (Norman P. Miller and Duane M. Robinson, *The Leisure Age* (Belmont, Calif.: Wadsworth Publishing Co., 1963), p. v. "Leisure today is a familiar reality in our advanced societies." (Joffre Dumazedier, *Toward a Society of Leisure* (New York: The Free Press, 1967), p. 1.)

2. What forces within ethnic soccer explain this influence?

    a. Structural factors

    b. Functional factors

While other studies have focused attention on the significance of religion,[12] color, [13] occupation,[14] and concentration,[15] on the acculturation or assimilation of ethnic groups, little has been written on the use of sport as a vehicle in this process. Participation in a single sport, albeit from a professional standpoint, as a means to assimilate, has been discussed by Andreano,[16] Handlin,[17] Saxon,[18] Boyle,[19] Shibutani,[20] and Weinberg.[21] These studies have been directed toward the individual's motives and attitude, whereas the present study was a departure from this approach in that it examined the role of the sport club as exemplified by the constitution of the club through the voice of the committee. Also, researchers have invariably confined themselves to a single ethnic

12. For example, Erich Rosenthal, "Acculturation without Assimilation: The Jewish Community of Chicago, Illinois," *American Journal of Sociology* 66 (1960): 275-288. Yaroslav Chyz and Read Lewis, "Agencies Organized by Nationality Groups in the United States," *The Annals of the American Academy of Political and Social Science* 262 (March, 1949). Harold L. Wilensky and Jack Ladinsky, "From Religious Community to Occupational Group: Structural Assimilation Among Professors, Lawyers and Engineers," *American Sociological Review* 32 (August, 1967): 541-542.

13. For example, Harry J. Walker, "Changes in the Structure of Race Relations in the South," *American Sociological Review* 14 (1949): 377-383. Clarence Senior, "Race Relations and Labor Supply in Great Britain," *Social Problems* 4 (1957): 302-312. Michael P. Banton, *White and Colored* (New Brunswick, N. J.: Rutgers University Press, 1960). J. A. Neprash, "Minority Group Contacts and Social Distance," *Phylon* 14, 19 (June, 1953), pp. 207-212. R. B. Davison, *Black British: Immigrants in Britain* (London: Oxford University Press, 1966), p. 170. Martin Luther King, Jr., *Where Do We Go From Here: Chaos or Community?* (New York: Harper and Row), p. 269.

14. For example, Raymond Breton and Maurice Pinard, "Group Formation among Immigrants: Criteria and Process," *Canadian Journal of Economics and Political Science* 26 (August, 1960): 465-477. Alexander S. Weinstock, "Role Elements: A Link Between Acculturation and Occupational Status," *British Journal of Sociology* 14 (1963): 144-149. Wilensky, *loc. cit.*

15. For example, Otis Dudley Duncan and Stanley Lieberson, "Ethnic Segregation and Assimilation," *American Journal of Sociology* 64 (January, 1959): 364-374. Stanley Lieberson, *Ethnic Patterns in American Cities* (New York: Free Press of Glencoe, 1963).

16. Ralph Andreano, *No Joy in Mudville* (Cambridge, Massachusetts: Schenkman Publishing Co., 1965), p. 133.

17. Oscar Handlin, "The Family in Old World and New," in *Social Perspectives on Behavior*, Herman D. Stein and Richard A. Cloward, p. 103. (New York: The Free Press, 1958).

18. Saxon, *loc. cit.*

19. Robert H. Boyle, *Sport-Mirror of American Life* (Boston: Little, Brown and Company, 1963), p. 97.

20. Tamotsu Shibutani and Kian M. Kwan, *Ethnic Stratification* (New York: The MacMillan Company, 1965), pp. 543-544.

21. S. Kirson Weinberg and Henry Arond, "The Occupational Culture of the Boxer," *American Journal of Sociology* 57 (1951): 462.

group[22] or they have analyzed the many factors which have contributed to the acculturation or assimilation process of an ethnic group or groups in a city or rural community.[23]

This study was concerned with the role of the sport club (soccer), in a culturally heterogeneous setting; it sought to uncover club policy rather than individual attitude; it incorporated six ethnic groups in a confined area.

Milwaukee was chosen as the location for the study. Soccer was introduced in the city in 1913; the Wisconsin State Football Association was organized in 1914, and the Wisconsin State Soccer Football League was initiated in 1924.[24] With a population of 1,149,977 in Milwaukee, 326,666, or 28.4 percent comprised the element of foreign stock.[25] It was they who originally were responsible for the introduction of soccer into the area.

The choice of soccer allowed the study to pay some attention to the "foreign game" element. Soccer is a world game, being played on all five continents.[26] Of the larger countries, it is probably played least in

---

22. For example, Pauline V. Young, *The Pilgrims of Russian Town* (Chicago: University of Chicago Press, 1932), Joseph S. Roucek, "The Yugoslav Immigrants in America," *American Journal of Sociology* 40 (March, 1935): 602-11; John S. Hawgood, *The Tragedy of German-America* (New York: G. P. Putnam's Sons, 1940); S. N. Eisenstadt, "The Place of Elites and Primary Groups in the Absorption of New Immigrants in Israel," *American Journal of Sociology* 57 (1951): 222-231; Alan Richardson, "The Assimilation of British Immigrants in Australia," *Human Relations* 10 (1957): 157-165; S. Alexander Weinstock, *The Acculturation of Hungarian Immigrants: A Social-Psychological Analysis.* Columbia University, Ph.D. (1962), *University of Microfilms, Inc.,* Ann Arbor, Michigan; R. Talf, "The Assimilation of Dutch Male Immigrants in a Western Australian Community," *Human Relations* 14 (1961): 265-281; Leonard Broom and E. Shevky, "Mexicans in the United States: A Problem in Social Differentiation," *Sociology and Social Research* 36 (1952): 150-158. In some instances, two ethnic groups have been studied allowing some comparative analysis. For example, Wilfred D. Borrie, *Italians and Germans in Australia: A Study of Assimilation* (Melbourns: Published for the Australian National University by F. W. Cheshire, 1954), pp. 217-231.

23. For example, Stanley Lieberson, *loc. cit.*

24. Wisconsin State Football Association, *Soccer Souvenir Book,* issued on the occasion of the United States Football Association Convention, June 30-July 1 (Milwaukee: Wisconsin State Football Association, 1928). Pages not numbered.

25. U. S. Bureau of the Census, *U. S. Census of Population:1960.* Vol. 1. Characteristics of the Population, Part 51: Wisconsin. (Washington, D. C.: U. S. Government Printing Office, 1963), p. 309.

26. "In May 1904 in Paris, five nations got together to found the F.I.F.A. (Federation Internationale de Football Association) . . . . Those five nations—France, Holland, Belgium, Switzerland, and Denmark . . . have increased and multiplied." There were eighty-one countries controlled by F.I.F.A. in 1954. Dengil Batchelor, *Soccer—A History of Association Football* (London: Batsford Ltd., 1954), p. 139. In 1963, there were ". . . 119 National Associations affiliated to it (F.I.F.A.) . . . ." A. G. Doggart (Chairman of the English Football Association), in *Fiftieth Anniversary Golden Jubilee Journal* (New York: 1963 U.S.S.F.A. Convention Committee, July, 1963). Hackensmith makes explicit reference to soccer on the five continents, C. W. Hackensmith, *History of Physical Education* (New York: Harper and Row, 1966), pp. 59, 89, 159, 233, 235, 258, 266, 280, 292, 303, 368.

America. By contrast, the countries of origin of the ethnic groups, represented by the sport clubs in Milwaukee, all have soccer as their major national outdoor game.

Since the sport of soccer is alien to the core society; and since soccer is the major national game of the countries of origin of the ethnic groups; and since members of the ethnic groups in question were involved in the activities of soccer clubs, either in the role of player, club official, manager, coach, spectator or social member; it is, therefore, hypothesized that ethnic soccer clubs in Milwaukee inhibit structural assimilation.

POPULATION

The population used for this investigation was the ten soccer clubs located within the City of Milwaukee. Some statistical information relating to the ten clubs is included in Tables I, II, and III. It will be seen from Table I that only three clubs were founded in the 1920's. Five clubs came into being within a span of seven years from 1947 to 1953 inclusive. The remaining two clubs, founded in 1961 and 1964, respectively, were formed from members of two existing clubs. Club I was

TABLE I
Dates of Foundation and Ethnic Orientation[a] of
the Soccer Clubs in Milwaukee

Club	Date When Founded	Ethnic Orientation
A	1922	Croatian
B	1926	Hungarian
C	1929	German
D	1947	German
E	1950	Polish
F	1950	Serbian
G	1952	Italian
H	1953	German
I	1961	German
J	1964	Serbian

[a]Demonstrated by ethnicity of committee members, players, ordinary members, original members, or a combination of these.

originally the second team Club C. When friction developed between the first and the second teams, three men contacted members of the second team and invited them to form a new club.[27]

Club J was founded as the result of a split in the Eastern Orthodox Church which served the Serbian community. Club F represented the original community; the splinter group formed Club J because a sufficient number of players wished to play soccer.[28] Therefore, the last occasion when an entirely new club was formed was in 1953.

The ethnic orientation of the soccer clubs is seen in Table I. Four ethnic groups are represented by one club as follows: Croatian, Hungarian, Polish and Italian. One ethnic group is represented by two clubs: Serbian. Another ethnic group is represented by four clubs: German. This does not mean that a club represented exclusively a single ethnic

TABLE II
Details of Club Membership[a]

Club	Total Membership	Membership According to Age				
		Under 18	18-25 Years	25-35 Years	35-45 Years	Over 45
A	84	14	10	10	10	40
B	71	16	0	40	15	0
C	540	150	100	100	100	90
D	300	50	60	50	40	100
E	160	50	20	45	35	10
F	410	100	30	120	60	100
G	135	25	30	35	30	15
H	240	40	45	75	60	20
I	25	0	12	12	1	0
J	200	20	50	50	40	40

[a]Membership figures are an approximation. Several clubs did not have membership lists.

27. Personal interview with the committee of Club I, April 11, 1967.
28. Personal interview with the committee of Club J. April 20, 1967.

group. It does mean that each club in question was predominantly represented by a single ethnic group, according to the criteria indicated in Table I.

Details of club membership are indicated in Table II. These figures are approximate only because it was difficult to obtain precise figures. Normally the payment of dues provides an exact indication of membership. However, in the case of some of the clubs, committee members indicated that dues were not demanded because clubs did not wish to restrict the use of the term "member" to those who had become paid members. In most instances, therefore, the figures were agreed upon following a consultation between the clubs' committee members. To be classed as a member, a person was required to demonstrate continuous interest in the club through support of club games or social functions, or through payment of dues.

A total of thirty-five teams were sponsored by the ten soccer clubs in 1967. These included eighteen adult teams and seventeen boys' teams. Details are indicated in Table III.

TABLE III
Details of the Number of Teams Sponsored by Each Club and the Leagues[a] in Which They Play

Club	Number of Teams Sponsored	Major Division	Major Reserve	First Division	Junior	Inter-mediate	Midget
A	3	1	1				1
B	3	1	1				1
C	5	1	1		1	1	1
D	5	1	1		1	1	1
E	4	1	1			1	1
F	4			1	1		2
G	3	1	1				1
H	5	1	1		1	1	1
I	1			1			
J	2			2			

[a]The most senior division is the Major Division. At the end of each season, the last placed club is relegated to the First Division. The team which wins the First Division is promoted to the Major Division. Each Major Division team is required to sponsor a reserve team.

NATURE OF THE BASIC VARIABLES

The nature of the dependent variable and the independent variable, and the procedures used for operationalizing them, are given below.

Dependent Variable: Structural Assimilation

The concept of "structural assimilation" was defined for this study as follows: entrance of an ethnic group into primary group relations with the core society.

In his model of the seven assimilation variables, Gordon demonstrates the key role of structural assimilation in the total process of assimilation.[29] He reiterates: "Once structural assimilation has occurred, . . . all of the other types of assimilation will follow."[30] The implication of this is that the price of such assimilation is the disappearance of the ethnic group as a separate entity and the evaporation of its distinctive values.[31]

The level of assimilation of club members was sought by directly questioning the club committees. The committees were asked to state whether the other six stages of assimilation has occurred. These variables, together with a brief definition of each, are listed below. They are taken from Gordon's model.[32]

Cultural assimilation (acculturation): Change of cultural pattern to those of the core society.

Marital assimilation (amalgamation): Large scale intermarriage between club members and members of the core society.

Identificational assimilation: Development of a sense of peoplehood based exclusively on the core society.

Attitude receptional assimilation: An absence of prejudice by the core society.

Behavior receptional assimilation: An absence of discrimination by the core society.

Civic assimilation: An absence of value and power conflict between club members and the core society.

Independent Variable: Club Policy

The concept of "club policy" was defined for this study as follows: Courses or actions of a club, either explicit or implicit, in matters per-

29. Milton M. Gordon, *Assimilation in American Life* (New York: Oxford University Press, 1964), p. 81.
30. *Ibid.*
31. *Ibid.*
32. See Table IV.

TABLE IV
The Assimilation Variables

Subprocess or Condition	Type or Stage of Assimilation	Special Term
Change of cultural patterns to those of host society	Cultural or behavioral	Acculturation
Large scale entrance into cliques, clubs, and institutions of host society, on primary group level.	Structural assimilation	None
Large scale intermarriage	Marital assimilation	Amalgamation
Development of sense of peoplehood based exclusively on host society	Identificational assimilation	None
Absence of prejudice	Attitude receptional assimilation	None
Absence of discrimination	Behavioral receptional assimilation	None
Absence of value and power conflict	Civic assimilation	None

taining to its organization and activities, demonstrated by the actions it has taken in the past and the opinions held by its present committee.

It was found desirable to divide the concept into two aspects. These were operationalized by utilizing a number of elements in each case, as follows:

A. Characteristics of and Policies Concerning Membership
  1. Membership characteristics
      a. Naturalization and generation
      b. Occupation
      c. Ability to speak English
  2. Choice of language, either English or ethnic, demonstrated on the following occasions:
      a. At club meetings
      b. When playing soccer
      c. On social occasions

3. Policy when accepting new members
4. Policies for the actions taken to attract new members from:
   a. Other ethnic groups
   b. Core society
B. Policies Pertaining to Structure and Maintenance of Club
   1. Need for existence
   2. Election of officers
   3. Changes in organization
   4. Degree to which club perceives itself either as:
      a. Soccer club
      b. Social club
   5. Degree of organized social contact between the club and:
      a. Other clubs
      b. Core society

THE INSTRUMENT

Data collected in this investigation consisted of responses to a structured interview which was employed between April 7-23, 1967. The structured interview schedule consisted of two parts. The question for Part One were sent to the President of each club at least seven days before the date of the interview. These questions related to the club's history, the number of teams being sponsored, the size of the club, the age, and other details concerning members.

The questions for Part Two were answered spontaneously because it was considered that prior knowledge of them might have adversely affected the answers. The questions were related to club policy concerning membership: questions directed toward the assimilation of members; constitutional procedures; and the language used at club meetings, on social occasions and in the dressing room before a game.

The questions used in both parts of the interview were designed by the investigator. The assimilation variables in Part Two were culled from Gordon's paradigm.[33] An average of four committee members were interviewed from each club.

TREATMENT AND ANALYSIS OF DATA

This study utilized the responses of the club committees to the structured interview. Primarily, questions devoted to club policy formed the basis of the analysis. The study examined the relationship between

33. *Ibid.*

TABLE V
Degree of Assimilation of Ethnic Soccer Clubs in Milwaukee Based Upon the Model by Gordon

Club and Main Ethnic Group Represented[a]	*Type of Assimilation*[b]						
	Cultural		Marital	Identifi- cational	Attitude Receptional	Behavior Receptional	Civic
	Intrinsic	Extrinsic					
"A" — Croatian	No	Partly	No	Partly	Yes	Mostly	Yes
"B" — Hungarian	No	Partly	No	No	Yes	Yes	Yes
"C" — German	No	Partly	Partly	Yes	Yes	Yes	Yes
"D" — German	Partly	Partly	No	No	Yes	Yes	Yes
"E" — Polish	Partly	Mostly	No	No	Yes	Yes	Yes
"F" — Serbian	No	Partly	No	No	Mostly	Yes	Mostly
"G" — Italian	No	Partly	Partly	No	Yes	Yes	Yes
"H" — German	Partly	Yes	Partly	Partly	Yes	Yes	Yes
"I" — German	Yes	Yes	Partly	Yes	Yes	Yes	Yes
"J" — Serbian	No	Partly	No	No	Mostly	Yes	Yes

[a] Clubs H and I were least representative of a single ethnic group. Club I was the smallest of the ten clubs by a substantial margin.

[b] Although Gordon identified seven types of assimilation, "structural assimilation" was omitted because it will be examined in the role of dependent variable.

the dependent and the independent variables and a logical analysis of that relationship.

The information accrued was analyzed in two stages: first, a measure of the level of assimilation already achieved by club members was determined by utilizing questions directly related to the six assimilation variables (excluding structural assimilation). Second, the effect of the policies of the clubs on structural assimilation was determined by utilizing the elements defined under the sub-heading "Independent Variable."

The hypothesis stated earlier, namely that ethnic soccer clubs in Milwaukee inhibit structural assimilation, was more specifically defined for this study as: club policy inhibits the structural assimilation of members.

The information was treated descriptively. In the first stage, the level of assimilation which had already occurred was analyzed deductively. In the second stage, each question was analyzed in terms of the independent variable. In conclusion, the relationship between certain

TABLE VI
Characteristics of Club Members:
Percentage Naturalized and by Generation

Club	Percent Naturalized	Percent by Generation[a]		
		First	Second	Third
A	90	50	15	5
B	75	90	10	0
C	90	60	20	20
D	75	80	19	1
E	75	75	20	5
F	50	80	15	5
G	70	65	25	10
H	75	90	7	3
I	98	99	1	0
J	65	90	10	0

[a]First generation, i.e., original adult immigrant.
Second generation, i.e., children of the original adult immigrant.
Third generation, i.e., children of the second generation.

elements of the independent variable and the dependent variable were deduced, and the hypothesis tested.

RESULTS

The hypothesis was tested by determining the degree of relationship between the dependent variable and the independent variable.

The results of this investigation showed that:

1. The perceived level of assimilation of soccer club members varied among clubs. (See Table V.) The two clubs whose members had

TABLE VII
Characteristics of Club Members:
Most Frequent Occupations[a]

Club	Most 1	2	3	Least 4
A	Unskilled Labor	Skilled Labor	Private Business	Professional
B	Skilled Labor	Unskilled Labor		
C	Skilled Labor	Private Business	Unskilled Labor	Professional
D	Skilled Labor	Private Business	Professional	Unskilled Labor
E	Skilled Labor	Unskilled Labor	Private Business	
F	Skilled Labor	Private Business	Unskilled Labor	Professional
G	Skilled Labor	Private Business	Unskilled Labor	Professional
H	Skilled Labor	Unskilled Labor	Private Business	Professional
I	Skilled Labor	Professional	Unskilled Labor	
J	Skilled Labor	Unskilled Labor	Private Business	Professional

[a]Homemakers and (high school) students not included.

assimilated most represented the German ethnic group, although they were less ethnic oriented than any of the clubs. The two clubs whose members had assimilated least represented the Serbian ethnic group.

2. In terms of three assimilation variables, namely civic, behavioral receptional and attitude receptional, the majority of club members were alleged to have assimilated in large measure. (See Table V.) In terms of three other assimilation variables, namely cultural, marital and identificational, the record of assimilation was poor. Of these, marital assimilation (amalgamation) had occurred least of all.

3. A review of the characteristics of soccer club members indicated that: (a) a large percentage were naturalized and first generation immi-

TABLE VIII
Characteristics of Club Members:
Ability to Speak English

Club	Very Good	Good	Fair	Poor	Very Poor
A	20%	20%	40%	10%	10%
B	10	60	20	10	——
C	40	50	10	——	——
D	15	40	40	5	——
E	50	10	35	4	1
F	25	25	25	20	5
G	30	30	20	10	10
H	30	40	20	10	——
I	100	——	——	— —	——
J	15	40	30	10	5

Mean Percentage:

	33.5	31.5	24.0	7.9	3.1

Mean Percentage without Club I:

	26.1	35.0	26.6	8.8	3.5

grants (see Table VI); (b) their most frequent occupation was in the area of "skilled labor" (see Table VII); (c) they spoke English only moderately well (see Table VIII); and (d) approximately one-third were playing members and two-thirds were social members (see Table IX).

TABLE IX
Characteristics of Club Members:
Percentage of Playing Members and Social Members

Club	Percentage Playing	Percentage Social
A	45	55
B	65	35
C	12	88
D	25	75
E	45	55
F	25	75
G	40	60
H	35	65
I	65	35
J	20	80
TOTALS	37.7	62.3

4. When accepting new members, approximately half of the clubs had developed a clear-cut, if not rigid, policy, whereas the other clubs had a very open policy.

5. Half of the clubs took no action to attract new members, either from other nationality groups, or the core society (see Table X). Three clubs took action to attract players to their clubs, but otherwise ignored other potential members. One club encouraged players but discouraged non-players. One club took positive action to attract new members, whether players or non-players.

6. Seven clubs were identified with a specific ethnic group by their choice of name. Three had neutral names.

7. The language used at club meetings, when playing soccer, and on social occasions varied according to the club (see Table XI). Only two clubs spoke English exclusively. Four clubs spoke their own ethnic language for the most part. The remaining four clubs spoke their own ethnic language and English.

TABLE X

Action Taken to Attract New Members to the Clubs from Other Ethnic Groups and the Core Society

Club	Other Ethnic Groups	Core Society
A	None	None
B	None	None
C	None (unless player)	None (unless player)
D	None	None
E	None (unless player)	None (unless player)
F	Players encouraged Non-players discouraged	Players encouraged Non-players discouraged[a]
G	None (unless player)	None (unless player)
H	None	None
I	Action taken to attract players and non-players, young and old.	Action taken to attract players and non-players, young and old.
J	None	None

[a]Unless parents of players.

8. There was little social contact between the clubs; with one exception, there was no contact between the clubs and the core society.

CONCLUSIONS

Within the limitations of this study, the following conclusions seem warranted:

With some exceptions, involvement in ethnic soccer is not conducive of furthering assimilation, and that more specifically, club policies of ethnic soccer clubs inhibit the structural assimilation of members.

TABLE XI

Language Used at Club Meetings, When Playing
Soccer and on Social Occasions

Club	Club Meetings	Playing Soccer	Social Occasions
A	Croatian	Croatian and Others[a]	Croatian and Others
B	English and Hungarian	Hungarian	Hungarian
C	English	English	English
D	English	German and English	German and English
E	Polish	Polish	Polish
F	English and Serbian	English and Serbian	English and Serbian
G	English and Italian	English	English
H	English	English	English and German
I	English	English	English
J	Serbian	Serbian	Serbian and English

[a]This expression was used by the committee of Club A, presumably because English and other languages were spoken according to the ethnicity of those present.

THE NATIVE AMERICAN BALL GAMES

Jerald C. Eaglesmith

For a subject so basically "American," the Native Americans remain the most misunderstood people of America. The common assumption that they were generally a savage race intoxicated with murder and plunder has been widely projected. The native games of North America are virtually ignored in most texts, while others only mention the games in general, as it appears that the numerous "Indian experts and scholars" evaluated the games as an insignificant aspect of ethnology. This attitude is understandable considering the basic nature of most traditional research, which tended to treat the Native American people as "objects" of study, not as fellow human beings. Furthermore, under this scholarly form of racism, the black man was classified as a slave or work animal, while the Indian was merely a wild animal, which supposedly legitimized their non-human treatment and slaughter. The classification as sub-human beings therefore may be recognized as affecting the non-consideration of the capacity to develop highly structured gaming activities. This viewpoint was of value only as a device to escape the guilt resulting from the treatment of "red brothers."

For centuries after the invasion of their land the Native Americans suffered a long death which systematically repressed and ultimately destroyed various native religious institutions, perhaps the most vital of which effected a divorce of the people from the land. The path of recent Native American history has been a "Trail of Tears" along which much of the religion and life style has been lost. It is an inspiring tribute to the spirit and courage of the people that any of the culture has survived the long history of genocide. The areas that have survived are

Printed with permission of the author.

493

music and dance, crafts, and language; as a result a small part of Native American life style and religion remains. Unfortunately many of the unique gaming activities have not survived. Who can remember when these people experienced leisure, let alone the enjoyment of their leisure? With the recent movements in Native American unity and awareness, it is also important now that the people realize one of their most outstanding and richest sources of pride, their inborn sporting spirit. Accordingly, it is important to realize that the Native Americans were far too individualistic to be assigned any single description, as they shared no common language and few customs, and yet even in those groups classified as "warlike" much of their leisure time included the universal amusement derived from games and competitive activities. It is important to realize that in early times war functioned as an honorable game in which the highest score or coup was counted by striking an opponent. Within this structure therefore coups (pronounced *küz*) were awarded for touching, not killing an opponent. In later times various Native American cultures revised their scoring qualifications in accordance with the unsportsman-like conduct of their sharp-shooting enemies.

In considering the native games of North America it is not appropriate to think of sharp, independent divisions of activity or behavior. It should be not only recognized, but emphasized that the Native American life style is a physical and spiritual blending of the people with the earth. Hence, all activity, including games, may be thought of as religious and therefore not divorced from the total meaning of things. In this general life style the Native Americans developed a variety of games ranging from the quiet fireside sitting games involving two individuals, to the vigorous field games of ball with over one-thousand participants. Native American games are truly both as enchanting and spectacular as any ever played on the North American continent.

The most comprehensive study in the description and classification of Native American games was published in 1907 as "Games Of The North American Indians" by Stewart Culin (5). While Culin's study was primarily descriptive in nature, a classification of games was included. The two primary classifications of one, games of dexterity and two, games of chance were supplemented by a third group entitled "minor amusements." The activities classified as minor amusements included: "shuttlecock, tipcat, quoits, stone-throwing, shuffleboard, jackstraws, swing, stilts, tops, bull-roarer, buzz, popgun, bean shooter and cat's cradle." Running races were included in an independent classification. Figure 1 is based upon Culin's classification system for the games of detexerity and chance.

D E X T E R I T Y		B A L L	– SHINNY – RACKET – DOUBLE – BALL – FOOTBALL – BALL – RACE – FOOT – CAST – BALL – HAND – FOOT – BALL – TOSSED BALL – HOT BALL – BALL JUGGLING
			– ARCHERY – HOOP&POLE – RING&PIN – SNOW – SNAKE
C H A N C E		G U E S S	– HAND GAME – MOCCASIN – STICK GAMES – 4 – STICKGAME
			– DICE GAMES

FIGURE 1

Even though Culin's study must be recognized as invaluable, it offers very little information or theory pertaining to the possible origin and distribution of games throughout the North American continent.

It appears that structured gaming activities evolved with the various native cultures and institutions independently because of the lack of extensive cultural sharing. However, there were similar forms of what appears to be the same games found throughout the North American continent. It is this similarity which suggests the possibility of the distribution of initial gaming concepts from nuclear regions. Furthermore, it is important here to note that an accurate description of the evolution, distribution, variety and socio-cultural significance of native North

American games may never be established; however, an attempt will be made to present a general theoretical explanation.

The original population of North America may be directly identified through regional associations with forms of various related games from coast to coast. Just as the United States is recognized as the geographic home of basketball, baseball and football, the variations of Native American ball games are geographically unique. It is the similarity of many of these games, most notably the ball play, which suggests that various gaming concepts may have radiated from a common nuclear region.

Native Americans were playing ball games long before the time of Jesus Christ. By approximately 1 A.D. the highly structured ball court cultures were well established in Meso-America. The development and distribution of corn in Meso-America may have functioned as the transporting vehicle which carried various additional cultural concepts to the north, such as religion, political institutions, architecture, art and games. While it has not been determined how far north the ancient Meso-American civilizations extended, the excavation of apparent Hohokam "ball courts" in the southwestern United States is evidence of the possible northern boundary of these highly structured ball court cultures (14, 28). Another outstanding observation which may be utilized to emphasize the possibility of the widespread distribution of Meso-American cultural institutions is in the comparison of many Southeastern Woodland mounds with the stone pyramids in Yucatan, Mexico (34). Although the materials used in their construction varied, the basic architectural designs exhibit remarkable similarities. Accordingly, ball play varied throughout the Americas, yet one of the outstanding common characteristics was that the ball was not touched with the hands. According to Stern's research (*The Rubber-Ball Games of the Americas*), the use of rubber balls was limited to the highly structured "ball court cultures" of Meso-America and South America (29). Stern's findings, however, do not eliminate the possibility of the radiation of the "concept" of ball play to North America. Furthermore, the absence of rubber-bearing flora in the north must have limited the acceptance of the classic Meso-American form of play.

It is also important to consider the possibility that the ball play "concept" radiated from a form of ball play which preceded the rubber-ball game in the north and south, all knowledge of which has been lost. In this discussion the most meaningful consideration is not when, but if, how and where, the initial ball play concept reached the inhabitants of North America. It has been previously mentioned that various religious and political institutions, and artistic and architectural similarities link early North American cultures with those of Meso-America. It is the religious comparisons which are most evident in ball play. Many of the religions across the continent are based on the realization of the Sun as the center of the universe, with spherical objects and patterns symbolically significant. Hence, the possibility of religious symbolism as favorably influencing the popularity of ball play, regardless of when the initial concept radiated north.

It is apparent that each socio-cultural group or tribe in North America utilized the ball play concept in producing its own unique form of play. In this dimension the ball game may be recognized as an expression of tribal religious, socio-cultural, and economic structure. Hence, ball play in North America must be qualified by tribal identification, both cultural and geographic. While there are various generalizations to

West Coast	Southwest	Great Plains	Northeastern Woodlands	Southeastern Woodlands	
X	X	X			SHINNY
X		X	X		RACKET (single)
				X	RACKET (double)
X	X	X	X		DOUBLE−BALL
X		X		X	FOOTBALL
X	X				BALL−RACE
X					FOOT−CAST−BALL
		X	X		HAND−FOOT−BALL
X	X	X	X	X	TOSSED BALL
X	X				HOT BALL
X	X	X			BALL JUGGLING

FIGURE 2

be recognized in the forms of ball play among tribes within common cultural and geographic areas, it must be additionally understood that intra-cultural variations also existed. That is to say, it is not correct to classify American football with the game the British call "football", even though both groups speak English.

Figure 2 exhibits the general regional or geographic appearance of the major ball games of native North America (1, 5, 11, 16, 27, 29).

The socio-cultural influence on the development of unique ball games by Native Americans is evident when the geographic appearance of gaming implements is established. The following map offers a general representation of the wide variation of ball playing sticks and rackets, as well as footballs.

Note the variety of gaming implements on the West Coast, while the Northeastern and Southeastern Woodlands lack in comparison. The game of "shinny" is represented by the hockey-type curved stick. "Double-ball" games utilized sticks in propelling the two balls or billets joined by a thong. The "football" used in the game of "ball-race" is represented by the soccer-type balls.

A close survey of the numerous forms of ball play in North America indicates that the games of "shinny" and "racket" appear to be the most popular and highly structured. At present it has not been determined which of these games has the greatest antiquity.

The game of "shinny" was played throughout the continent at one time or another; however, it appears to have developed in the western regions. Culin, Baldwin, (1) and Stern associate shinny with those people who relied upon gathering natural foods rather than those who developed agricultural practices. It appears that those groups with a history of agriculture developed semi-permanent villages and preferred the ball game with rackets. These people living west of the Rocky Mountains were labeled with the derogatory classification of "Digger Indians" (18) by the white man because they harvested the bulbous roots of the region with a digging stick. It is possible that the shinny stick evolved from the digging stick used by these people's ancestors. The close association between the appearance of the game of shinny and the utilization of digging sticks supports the possibility. It is also known that the ancestors of many western people used curved sticks to club rabbits and other small animals (28). The shinny stick possibly could have been born when a hunter's swing sent a rock flying.

In an attempt to recreate the possible evolution of pre-historic developments it is essential to maintain an open mind while taking all of the possible contributing factors into consideration. The Zuñi of the southwest claim that the game of shinny came from Mexico long ago (30). Hence, the game may have been adopted from an ancient Meso-American brand of shinny. The origin of the gaming stick is unknown and its development is uncertain, but shinny is an ancient game to be sure.

By the mid-nineteenth century shinny became widespread throughout the continent due to forced interaction between traditionally separated groups, as well as the increased range of trading capabilities resulting from the acquisition of the horse. When played in the west shinny was played by both men and women, but primarily men. When the eastern groups moving onto the Great Plains adopted the game it was primarily played as a women's field game. It is interesting to note that in most tribes women were not allowed to even touch the ball sticks and rackets (5, 6, 11, 12, 20, 26).

Shinny was played very much like contemporary women's field hockey. Each player was equipped with a single curved stick which was generally from 24 to 48 inches in length (5). The variation here was possibly due to the length of the players' limbs or individual preference. The buckskin ball was stuffed with deer hair or moss, and measured from 1 1/4 to 4 inches in diameter. The length of the playing field varied from 100 to 1,400 yards, depending on the number of participants (5). The goals consisted of either one post at either end of the field, or a pair at either end between which the ball was passed (1, 2, 5, 6, 20).

Unique variations in shinny play generally involved (1) sexual qualifications for participation, (2) the material used in the manufacture of sticks, and (3) the objectives of play. (The same factors identified variations in the game of rackets.) Shinny was played by men alone among the Assiniboin, Yankton, Mohave, and Walapai; by men and women alone among the Sauk and Foxes, Tewa, and Tigua; and by men against women among the Crows. Whereas a single stick or bat was the usual rule, the Makah (West Coast) used two, one for striking and the other for carrying the ball. In an unusual form of the game by the Miwok (West Coast) the objective was to pass the ball from station to station in relay fashion (5).

Shinny was a tremendously versatile athletic activity in that it could be played by two individuals or two hundred. It functioned both as an intra-village low keyed game, or as an inter-village or inter-tribal highly competitive and aggressive sport. When played among members of the same village or tribe it functioned as a supplemental activity in the celebration of a successful hunt, as with the Makah at the capture of a whale. (The Makah shinny ball was made from soft whale bone) (5). Another secondary function of inter-tribal shinny was the distribution of trade goods between the wagering parties. It should be noted here that heavy betting on the outcome of ball games was practiced extensively throughout the continent. Wagering may have been an expression of confidence rather than a careless obsession.

While shinny was played by both men and women, the game of "double-ball" was played exclusively by women. In fact, double-ball was generally known as the "women's ball game" (5). Double-ball appears to be closely related to shinny in both structure and objectives of play.

The ball games utilizing "rackets" were distinctly men's games. Hence, the pattern of sexual segregation in the ball games of shinny, double-ball and racket can be identified with the implements of each game. Accordingly, it may be concluded that the racket was definitely considered a masculine object. The segregation of the sexes in gaming activities therefore exhibited obvious correlations with the role of each sex in the given native culture. Among the Miwok (California) the women were identified strongly with their baskets, as baskets were used as seed beaters, storage containers, and as gambling trays. The basket became so basic in the role of the Miwok woman that it became part of their tribal costume as a hat, and hence, a true badge of womanhood. The appearance of the basket as a racket device was accordingly limited to the women's field game called "basket-ball" (2, 5). A survey of Culin's classification of ball games reveals that the Miwok game of basket-ball was also unique in that these women appear to have been the only group to have played the game as such in North America. In this game each woman was equipped with two large baskets, one being slightly larger than the other. The objective of the game was similar to that of both shinny and rackets. These baskets closely resembled the seed beating type and probably evolved from them. This would help explain the fact that the men were not associated with the game utilizing a clearly feminine implement (2, 5).

Racket ball play appears to have developed in the Eastern Woodlands and did not exhibit the wide distribution of shinny. In the Northeastern Woodlands the game was eventually to become known as "lacrosse," the national game of Canada. This form of ball play was engaged in at harvesting festivals, as well as political councils. The ball game was also prescribed by tribal shaman as a valuable means of combating sickness. The objective of racket play was to carry or hurl the ball through the opponent's goal using only the netted stick.

The most highly structured and popular form of ball play in North America was the double racket variety found only in the Southeastern Woodlands. Among the various confederacies of the region the ball game functioned as an inter-tribal activity symbolizing cultural and political unity. These games were played between "red" (war) and "white" (peace) towns. Hence, the ball game functioned additionally as a highly aggressive substitute for warfare. It is not surprising to discover that southeastern ball play was referred to as "the brother of war" (5, 19).

As an intra-tribal activity the double racket game was included in the annual harvest festival. During the spring festival the theme of annual renewing of the earth's productivity, as well as continued tribal harmony was celebrated. The climatic activity of the festival was the ball game.

An elaborate sequence of pre-game activities included: (1) the challenge; (2) purification through fasting and sexual abstinence; (3) erection of the goals; (4) the "ball play dance"; (5) wagering; and (6) the starting line-up (5, 21, 31, 32). Play was initiated with the center toss-up of the first ball by a noted member of the challenging town.

The sequence of a typical scoring play involved: (1) the toss-up; (2) the initial center scrimmage; (3) pass/carrying of the ball goal-ward;

and (4) the scoring drive through the goals (5). It is understandable that skilled players were those who possessed the combination of speed, strength, and jumping ability. The champion ball players must have been able to leap, catch, and whip-pass the ball away while still airborne. In this manner the ball could be quickly delivered to the players nearer the goals. The distance between the goals varied according to the number and ability of the participants.

Catlin's account of a Choctaw (Southeastern Woodlands) ball game is one of the most outstanding eye-witness accounts ever recorded. An estimated one-thousand young men competed ". . . with five or six times that number of spectators, of men, women, and children, surrounding the ground and looking on . . ." (5). Another eye-witness account by Capt. Basil Hall (Royal British Navy) while visiting the Creek (Southeastern Woodlands) noted that ". . . every one of them looked hard as iron and as agile as a puma" (13). Capt. Hall made these observations after being "treed" by the unpredictable flow of the scrimmage for the ball. While many historical accounts of ball play connote the wild free-for-all brawling image, it is important to note that although disputes did occur they were the exception rather than the rule. This general lack of bickering may have been due to the influence of the religious and legendary nature of respect for the rules of racket ball play. For example, the "no hands" rule apparently derived from the symbolic association of heavenly spherical bodies. This association is apparent in the following Native American explanation:

> The moon is a ball which was thrown up against the sky in a game long ago. Two towns were playing against each other, but one of them had the best runners and had almost won the game when the leader of the other side picked up the ball with his hand and tried to throw to the goal, but it struck against the solid sky vault and was fastened there, to remind players to never cheat. (5)

On June 4, 1763 an inter-tribal racket ball play was utilized as a stratagem of warfare. It was planned by the Chippewas and Sacs for a ball game to be played as a celebration for the birthday of King George III. As the racket game began and the players scrimmaged vigorously, the British soldiers came out of Fort Michilimackinac (Michigan). In their preoccupation with the game the soldiers left the gate of the fort open, and strangely enough the ball "accidentally" flew over the wall. Naturally the players rushed through the gate . . . in pursuit of the ball. Once inside the players became warriors, armed with war clubs and tomahawks which had been concealed under the blankets worn by the women spectators (27). The final score was indeed "hairraising!" Hence, in this dimension the ball game functioned as a Native American

"Trojan Horse" leading to an overwhelmng victory during the conflict known as Pontiac's War.

Even though the emphasis of contemporary American sporting activity does not outwardly reflect a Native American tradition, it is interesting to note that among the names of athletic teams are found the Chiefs, Braves, Redskins, Seminoles, Warriors, Blackhawks, Sun-devils, Indians, and many others. Hence, the Native American sporting spirit should be recognized as part of the rich sporting heritage of America. Native Americans have exhibited the ability to excel in the various gaming activities of contemporary America. The number of true "All-Americans," such as Olympic Gold Medal winners Jim Thorpe (Sauk-Fox) and Billy Mills (Sioux), has been limited.

If the Native Americans have not totally adopted the white man's games, perhaps it is because their sporting spirit is seeking identity. Accordingly, the exposure of the spectacular nature of Native American ball games emphasizes that the valleys, plains, mountains, and woodlands of this land were not lost in "savage" chaos before the arrival of the supposedly "civilized" invaders. Indeed this land has long echoed with the enthusiasm of the Native Americans at play.

Today in pow-wows across their land it appears that the Native American sporting spirit is experiencing a rejuvenation via the honorable competition of the "War Dance" contests. The nature of these contests rival the highest ideals of Olympic competition. Perhaps this atmosphere will render the possibility of additional rejuvenation in the area of Native American ball games, thus recalling a unique dimension to man's sporting capabilities.

BIBLIOGRAPHY

1. Baldwin, G. C. *Games of the American Indian.* New York: W. W. Norton & Company, Inc., 1969.
2. Barrett, S. A. *Miwok Material Culture.* Bulletin of Milwaukee Public Museum, Vol. 2, No. 4, March, 1933.
3. Catlin, G. *Episodes From Life Among the Indians, and Last Rambles.* Norman, Okla.: University of Oklahoma Press, 1959.
4. Culin, S. "American Indian Games." *The Journal of American Folk-Lore* 11 (October-December, 1898).
5. Culin, S. *Games of the North American Indians.* Twenty-Fourth Annual Report of the Bureau of American Ethnology. Washington, D. C.: Government Printing Office, 1907.
6. Grinnell, G. B. *The Cheyenne Indians: Their History and Ways of Life.* 2 vols. New York: Cooper Square Publishing Company, 1962.
7. Hassrick, R. B. *The Sioux: Life and Customs of a Warrior Society.* Norman, Okla.: University of Oklahoma Press, 1964.

8. Helm, J. C., and Lurie, N. O. *The Dogrib Hand Game.* Ottawa, Canada: R. Duhamel, 1966.
9. Hewitt, J. N. B. "Iroquois Game of Lacrosse." *American Anthropologist* 5 (April, 1892).
10. Hodge, F. W. "A Zuni Foot-Race." *American Anthropologist* 3 (July, 1890).
11. Hodge, F. W. *Handbook of American Indians.* Washington, D. C.: Bureau of American Ethnology, Bulletin 30, Part I, pp. 127, 483-486, 1907.
12. Hoffman, M. D. "Remarks On Ojibwa Ball Play." *American Anthropologist* 3 (April, 1890).
13. Hyrst, H. W. G. *Stories of Red Indian Adventure.* London: Seeley, Service & Co., 1921.
14. *Indians of the Americas.* Washington, D. C.: National Geographic Society, 1955.
15. Jones, W. *Ethnography of the Fox Indians.* Washington, D. C.: Bureau of American Ethnology, Bulletin 125, pp. 109-115, 1939.
16. Kroeber, A. L. "Games of the California Indians." *American Anthropologist* 22 (1920).
17. Kurz, R. F. *Journal of Rudolph Friederich Kurz.* Washington, D. C.: Bureau of American Ethnology, Bulletin 115, pp. 146-148, 1937.
18. LaFarge, O. *A Pictorial History of the American Indian.* New York: Crown Publishing Co., 1956.
19. *Life Magazine* 66 (April 18, 1969): 49-56.
20. Lowie, R. H. *Indians of the Plains.* New York: American Museum of Natural History, 1954.
21. Mooney, J. "The Cherokee Ball Play." *American Anthropologist* 2 (April, 1890).
22. Morgan, L. H. *League of the Ho-De-No-Sau-Nee or Iroquois.* Rochester, New York, 1851.
23. Parker, A. C. "Snow-Snake As Played By the Seneca-Iroquois." *American Anthropologist* 11 (1909).
24. Pennington, C. W. "La carrera de bola entre los tarahumaras de Mexico; Un problema de difusion." *America Indigena* 30 (1970): 15-40. Inter-American Indian Institute, Mexico, 1970.
25. Powers, W. K. *Indians of the Northern Plains.* New York: G. P. Putnam's Sons, 1969.
26. Reagan, A. B. "Some Games of the Bois Fort Ojibwa." *American Anthropologist* 21 (1919).
27. Schoolcraft, H. R. *The History, Condition and Prospects of the Indian Tribes of the United States.* Philadelphia, Penn.: Lippincott, Grambro & Co., 1854, Vol. II & VI.
28. Spencer, R. F., and J. D. Jennings, et al. *The Native Americans.* New York: Harper & Row, Publishers, 1965.
29. Stern, T. *The Rubber-Ball Games of the Americas.* New York: J. J. Augustin, Publisher, 1948.
30. Stevenson, M. C. "Zuni Games." *American Anthropologist* 5 (1903).
31. Swanton, J. R. *Source Material for the Social and Ceremonial Life of the Choctaw Indians.* Washington, D. C.: Bureau of American Ethnology, Bulletin 103, 1931.

32. Swanton, J. R. *The Indians of the Southeastern United States.* Washington, D. C.: Bureau of American Ethnology, Bulletin 137, 1946, pp. 674-686.
33. Underhill, R. *People of the Crimson Evening.* Lawrence, Kansas: United States Indian Service, No. 7, Haskel Institute, 1951.
34. Underhill, R. *Red Man's America.* Chicago, Ill.: University of Chicago Press, 1953, pp. 43.

PSYCHOBLACKOLOGY POETRY SUMMARY

Malachi Andrews

Tomorrow will be a Blacker day in sports, dance, drama, and all African expression in America.

The spirit of Blackness is creativity in motion. The purest and most healthy bodies are those who love movement the most.

> African Movement form is living form, going through
> rhythmic soul changes. The whole body is in tune with
> the rhythmic process, the characteristic unity of
> world Black life.
> That critical turn on the track, that bad move in
> basketball, or that movement in gymnastics and other
> sports that represents soul action, taking place in a
> sort of a trance where the Brother or Sister's S.S.P. guides
> their bodies to super marks and scores undreamed by
> mental principles. This summary of Blackness in
> kinesiology, sports, and physical education is the truth
> and nothing but the truth So help me God.

Since the major implications of psychoblackology in early African growth and development shows crumb crushers moving uncontrolled but turned on, high on the Thalamus, having fun, falling, crying cause it hurted a tiny bit, climbing, falling again still high, and goo-gobs mo, it is obvious that soul movement is continuous and soulfully endowed coming from the brain so cool where the roots of thought grow like grass ready for play, and they get high!

From *Psychoblackology: Science of Black Movement.* Oakland, California: Achebe Enterprises, Inc., 1974. Reprinted by permission of publisher and author.

Now how you be moving is a significant indicator of your ethnic origin and cultural patterns. Your motion may wobble and reveal mental deterioration or its opposite, anxiety, fear, hostility, insecurity, instability, or be so Black you can't never get back.

Psychoblackology is important man, cause it provides your head with some instinctive meaning, emotional release and catharsis, tripping, and gives all the people a multi-cultural opportunity in terms of energy and flow for styling sports action in human life.

African-American Kinesiology has a reality of its own which is more important than its physical existence. It is the embodiment of a system of thought in styling manifestations that makes moving an art where the move, the motion makes, is determined by artistic thinking rather than by a principle of scientific exemplar or sports arch type in the mind.

African tradition in dance reveals that African kinetics transforms from within. No matter what size, shape, or who you are, man, woman, all are of the community and caught up in the spirit of the activity. This "meaning" to Black people in America saved us from total acculturation. Ontogenetic and phylogenetic studies in Black history indicate that this movement phenomena of people of color was the most dominant reason we Africans were able to handle the dogmatic pressures laid on us for over 300 years by honkies talking about civilization. Our acting, singing, dancing, sports, are consistent in movement, and, now is the number one building tool in the liberation struggle.

So every Black action is a work of art in sports, and, if classified may be fundamentally (1) the visual-African Brother or sister jes standing there ready to play; and (2) psychoblackology kinesiology—the action.

If you hung up on structure we gots that too but we don't trip on it. Three major classifications of structure may be (1) soul tradition: where a dance or African movement is seen as a traditional dance or movement; (2) fluctuation between well-defined tradition and American whiteyfications; and (3) the creative, where a given sports move may be perceived as ambiguous to inventive and generally referred to as super bad. The athlete or dancer or actor can employ all of these classifications into the competition or performance.

But the clearest way, like i said before, for Americans to understand and appreciate African motion is through a knowledge of the cohesive and segregating forces of Black song, music, dance, art, poetry, life, and the spirits which determines the kinetics. These cohesive and segregating forces are produced by electro-chemical processes in the sector of the brain which deals with seeing. Then associations jam the T (Thalamus) blends with M (melanin) and then blow the rest of the brain to move the whole body and all that is within.

The expression, that is a result of those vibes thrives on human freedom. Freedom to get funky in the motion, set our own goals, to establish our own set of values to play the game, to experiment in the activity and try the unusual, and above all, freedom to fail without threat (if failure is possible).

African movement communicates world-wide, like talking drums if you reads me, our deepest instinctive human activity. Since world heritage is one of color it is no wonder that people who lack color is going crazy with money and psychology into lilly land, scared as hell.

During the 1972 Olympics in Munich, Germany, where color was overwhelming, I made some special efforts to observe and record the white controllers behavior, watch them getting freaky with the rules, and administering White Supremacy changes to hold back the color rush. Brundage and them other punks lied in the name of God, Bush, a track coach who thrives on Black talent failed in his support of a Black man who supported him to exhaustion, and many many other examples of White Supremacy and racism that are too long to write about in this book.

But it ain't gonna last cause color of the world been grazing in the grass ready to rise up and kick some ass. The description of this assertion in sports is Neuro-bio-chemical and will be achieved through world African idiosyncratic perception of brain sensory associations never before experienced. Brothers and sisters in sports will show this mental activity through our bodies starting in the 1976 Olympics. We of the world will be doing it cause the stimuli which is several got us so high we jes gotta be bad. Psychoblackology. Oh lord! I gots ma super bad body that you gave me, the glory of your creation, Black, ain't getting back, styling and leaning hea above all animals. And all my body parts? lord, ready to jam motion. Oh my body, bless my soul, like drums beating the earth and swooping or skying in sports. Or, whatever i do, beautiful strong limbs, moving, cause my brain is mellow with Melanin. Can you dig it oh lord, knowing my arteries are pouring with adrenalin, veins with rushing blood making me hard with kinetic joy? Oh lord, jes felt my brains again fraught with impulses mystifying my actions and my heart and lungs gushing mo blood and mo air giving me mo strength to my feelings and equilibrium to do it some mo, oh lord, some mo. Gotta stay in rhythm with you, nature, my Woman, other races of people, and with my own true self in sports and movement, and with my people. Amen, right on.

BIBLIOGRAPHY

Section C. Socialization

2. Ethnic Groups

Andrews, Malachi. *Psychoblackology: Science of Black Movement.* Oakland, Calif.: Achebe Enterprises, Inc., 1974.

Axthelem, Pete. *The City Game.* New York: Simon & Schuster Pocketbooks, 1971.

Bennett, Bruce. "Bibliography on the Negro in Sports." *Journal of Health, Physical Education and Recreation* 41 (Jan. 1970):77-78. Supplemental bibliography J.O.H.P.E.R. 41 (Sept., 1970):71.

Blalock, H. M., Jr. "Occupational Discrimination: Some Theoretical Propositions." *Social Problems* 9 (1962):240-247.

Cady, Susan. "Bibliography of the Negro in Sports." *Journal of Health, Physical Education and Recreation* 42 (Feb., 1971):70-71.

Edwards, Harry. "The Myth of the Racially Superior Athlete." *Intellectual Digest* (Mar., 1972).

———. *The Revolt of the Black Athlete.* New York: The Free Press, 1969.

Fox, J. R. "Pueblo Baseball: A New Use for Old Witchcraft." *Journal of American Folklore* 74 (1961):9-16.

Frederickson, F. S. "Sports and the Cultures of Man." In *Science and Medicine of Exercise and Sports.* (Ed.) Warren R. Johnson, pp. 633-646.

Henderson, E. B. *The Negro in Sports.* Washington, D.C.: Associated Publishers, 1969.

———, and the Editors of Sport, *The Black Athlete-Emergence and Arrival.* Washington, D. C.: Associated Publishers, 1969.

Izenberg, Jerry. "Pro Football's Lily White Position: The Conspiracy Against Black Quarterbacks." *True* (Feb., 1969):32-34, 78-79, 82.

Kane, Martin. "An Assessment of Black is Best." *Sports Illustrated* (Jan. 18, '71).

Olsen, Jack. *The Black Athlete—A Shameful Story.* New York: Time, Inc., 1968.

Pascal, A. H., and Rapping, L. A. *Racial Discrimination in Professional Baseball.* The Rand Corporation, 1970.

Peterson, Robert. *Only the Ball Was White.* Englewood Cliffs, N. J.: Prentice-Hall, 1970.

Ribalow, H. U. *The Jew in American Sports.* New York: Bloch Pub. Co., Inc., 1948.

Rosenblatt, Aaron. "Negroes in Baseball: The Failure of Success." *Trans-Action* 4 (Sept. 1967):51-53, with a reply by Whitehead, 4 (Oct. 1967):63-64.

Ruffer, W. A. "Symposium on the Problems of the Black Athlete." *Journal of Health, Physical Education and Recreation* 42 (Feb. 1971):11-15.

Russell, William. *Go Up for Glory.* New York: Coward-McCann, 1966.

———. "Success is a Journey." *Sports Illustrated* (July 8, 1970):81-93.

Thompson, Richard. *Race and Sport.* London: Oxford University Press, 1964.

Young, A. S. *Negro Firsts in Sports.* Chicago, Ill.: Johnson Pub. Co., 1963.